T0189921

Lecture Notes in Artificial Intelligence   13032

Subseries of Lecture Notes in Computer Science

Series Editors

Randy Goebel
University of Alberta, Edmonton, Canada
Yuzuru Tanaka
Hokkaido University, Sapporo, Japan
Wolfgang Wahlster
DFKI and Saarland University, Saarbrücken, Germany

Founding Editor

Jörg Siekmann
DFKI and Saarland University, Saarbrücken, Germany

More information about this subseries at http://www.springer.com/series/1244

Duc Nghia Pham · Thanaruk Theeramunkong ·
Guido Governatori · Fenrong Liu (Eds.)

PRICAI 2021: Trends in Artificial Intelligence

18th Pacific Rim
International Conference on Artificial Intelligence, PRICAI 2021
Hanoi, Vietnam, November 8–12, 2021
Proceedings, Part II

 Springer

Editors
Duc Nghia Pham
MIMOS Berhad
Kuala Lumpur, Malaysia

Guido Governatori ⓘ
Data61
CSIRO
Brisbane, QLD, Australia

Thanaruk Theeramunkong
Sirindhorn International Institute of Science
and Technology
Thammasat University
Mueang Pathum Thani, Thailand

Fenrong Liu ⓘ
Department of Philosophy
Tsinghua University
Beijing, China

ISSN 0302-9743 ISSN 1611-3349 (electronic)
Lecture Notes in Artificial Intelligence
ISBN 978-3-030-89362-0 ISBN 978-3-030-89363-7 (eBook)
https://doi.org/10.1007/978-3-030-89363-7

LNCS Sublibrary: SL7 – Artificial Intelligence

This Springer imprint is published by the registered company Springer Nature Switzerland AG
The registered company address is: Gewerbestrasse 11, 6330 Cham, Switzerland

Preface

These three-volume proceedings contain the papers presented at the 18th Pacific Rim International Conference on Artificial Intelligence (PRICAI 2021) held virtually during November 8–12, 2021, in Hanoi, Vietnam.

PRICAI, which was inaugurated in Tokyo in 1990, started out as a biennial international conference concentrating on artificial intelligence (AI) theories, technologies, and applications in the areas of social and economic importance for Pacific Rim countries. It provides a common forum for researchers and practitioners in various branches of AI to exchange new ideas and share experience and expertise. Since then, the conference has grown, both in participation and scope, to be a premier international AI event for all major Pacific Rim nations as well as countries from all around the world. In 2018, the PRICAI Steering Committee decided to hold PRICAI on an annual basis starting from 2019.

This year, we received an overwhelming number of 382 submissions to both the Main track (365 submissions) and the Industry special track (17 submissions). This number was impressive considering that for the first time PRICAI was being held virtually during a global pandemic situation. All submissions were reviewed and evaluated with the same highest quality standard through a double-blind review process. Each paper received at least two reviews, in most cases three, and in some cases up to four. During the review process, discussions among the Program Committee (PC) members in charge were carried out before recommendations were made, and when necessary, additional reviews were sourced. Finally, the conference and program co-chairs read the reviews and comments and made a final calibration for differences among individual reviewer scores in light of the overall decisions. The entire Program Committee (including PC members, external reviewers, and co-chairs) expended tremendous effort to ensure fairness and consistency in the paper selection process. Eventually, we accepted 92 regular papers and 28 short papers for oral presentation. This gives a regular paper acceptance rate of 24.08% and an overall acceptance rate of 31.41%.

The technical program consisted of three tutorials and the main conference program. The three tutorials covered hot topics in AI from "Collaborative Learning and Optimization" and "Mechanism Design Powered by Social Interactions" to "Towards Hyperdemocracy: AI-enabled Crowd Consensus Making and Its Real-World Societal Experiments". All regular and short papers were orally presented over four days in parallel and in topical program sessions. We were honored to have keynote presentations by four distinguished researchers in the field of AI whose contributions have crossed discipline boundaries: Mohammad Bennamoun (University of Western Australia, Australia), Johan van Benthem (University of Amsterdam, The Netherlands; Stanford University, USA; and Tsinghua University, China), Virginia Dignum (Umeå University, Sweden), and Yutaka Matsuo (University of Tokyo, Japan). We were grateful to them for sharing their insights on their latest research with us.

The success of PRICAI 2021 would not be possible without the effort and support of numerous people from all over the world. First, we would like to thank the authors, PC members, and external reviewers for their time and efforts spent in making PRICAI 2021 a successful and enjoyable conference. We are also thankful to various fellow members of the conference committee, without whose support and hard work PRICAI 2021 could not have been successful:

- Advisory Board: Hideyuki Nakashima, Abdul Sattar, and Dickson Lukose
- Industry Chair: Shiyou Qian
- Local/Virtual Organizing Chairs: Sankalp Khanna and Adila Alfa Krisnadhi
- Tutorial Chair: Guandong Xu
- Web and Publicity Chair: Md Khaled Ben Islam
- Workshop Chair: Dengji Zhao

We gratefully acknowledge the organizational support of several institutions including Data61/CSIRO (Australia), Tsinghua University (China), MIMOS Berhad (Malaysia), Thammasat University (Thailand), and Griffith University (Australia).

Finally, we thank Springer, Ronan Nugent (Editorial Director, Computer Science Proceedings), and Anna Kramer (Assistant Editor, Computer Science Proceedings) for their assistance in publishing the PRICAI 2021 proceedings as three volumes of its Lecture Notes in Artificial Intelligence series.

November 2021

Duc Nghia Pham
Thanaruk Theeramunkong
Guido Governatori
Fenrong Liu

Organization

PRICAI Steering Committee

Steering Committee

Quan Bai	University of Tasmania, Australia
Tru Hoang Cao	The University of Texas Health Science Center at Houston, USA
Xin Geng	Southeast University, China
Guido Governatori	Data61, CSIRO, Australia
Takayuki Ito	Nagoya Institute of Technology, Japan
Byeong-Ho Kang	University of Tasmania, Australia
M. G. M. Khan	University of the South Pacific, Fiji
Sankalp Khanna	Australian e-Health Research Centre, CSIRO, Australia
Dickson Lukose	Monash University, Australia
Hideyuki Nakashima	Sapporo City University, Japan
Abhaya Nayak	Macquarie University, Australia
Seong Bae Park	Kyung Hee University, South Korea
Duc Nghia Pham	MIMOS Berhad, Malaysia
Abdul Sattar	Griffith University, Australia
Alok Sharma	RIKEN, Japan, and University of the South Pacific, Fiji
Thanaruk Theeramunkong	Thammasat University, Thailand
Zhi-Hua Zhou	Nanjing University, China

Honorary Members

Randy Goebel	University of Alberta, Canada
Tu-Bao Ho	Japan Advanced Institute of Science and Technology, Japan
Mitsuru Ishizuka	University of Tokyo, Japan
Hiroshi Motoda	Osaka University, Japan
Geoff Webb	Monash University, Australia
Albert Yeap	Auckland University of Technology, New Zealand
Byoung-Tak Zhang	Seoul National University, South Korea
Chengqi Zhang	University of Technology Sydney, Australia

Conference Organizing Committee

General Chairs

Guido Governatori	Data61, CSIRO, Australia
Fenrong Liu	Tsinghua University, China

Program Chairs

Duc Nghia Pham	MIMOS Berhad, Malaysia
Thanaruk Theeramunkong	Thammasat University, Thailand

Local/Virtual Organizing Chairs

Sankalp Khanna	Australian e-Health Research Centre, CSIRO, Australia
Adila Alfa Krisnadhi	University of Indonesia, Indonesia

Workshop Chair

Dengji Zhao	ShanghaiTech University, China

Tutorial Chair

Guandong Xu	University of Technology Sydney, Australia

Industry Chair

Shiyou Qian	Shanghai Jiao Tong University, China

Web and Publicity Chair

Md Khaled Ben Islam	Griffith University, Australia

Advisory Board

Hideyuki Nakashima	Sapporo City University, Japan
Abdul Sattar	Griffith University, Australia
Dickson Lukose	Monash University, Australia

Program Committee

Eriko Aiba	The University of Electro-Communications, Japan
Patricia Anthony	Lincoln University, New Zealand
Chutiporn Anutariya	Asian Institute of Technology, Thailand
Mohammad Arshi Saloot	MIMOS Berhad, Malaysia
Yun Bai	University of Western Sydney, Australia
Chutima Beokhaimook	Rangsit University, Thailand
Ateet Bhalla	Independent Technology Consultant, India
Chih How Bong	Universiti Malaysia Sarawak, Malaysia
Poonpong Boonbrahm	Walailak University, Thailand
Aida Brankovic	Australian e-Health Research Centre, CSIRO, Australia
Xiongcai Cai	University of New South Wales, Australia
Tru Cao	University of Texas Health Science Center at Houston, USA
Hutchatai Chanlekha	Kasetsart University, Thailand
Sapa Chanyachatchawan	National Electronics and Computer Technology Center, Thailand
Siqi Chen	Tianjin University, China

Songcan Chen	Nanjing University of Aeronautics and Astronautics, China
Wu Chen	Southwest University, China
Yingke Chen	Sichuan University, China
Wai Khuen Cheng	Universiti Tunku Abdul Rahman, Malaysia
Boonthida Chiraratanasopha	Yala Rajabhat University, Thailand
Phatthanaphong Chomphuwiset	Mahasarakham University, Thailand
Dan Corbett	Optimodal Technologies, USA
Célia Da Costa Pereira	Université Côte d'Azur, France
Jirapun Daengdej	Assumption University, Thailand
Hoa Khanh Dam	University of Wollongong, Australia
Xuan-Hong Dang	IBM Watson Research, USA
Abdollah Dehzangi	Rutgers University, USA
Sang Dinh	Hanoi University of Science and Technology, Vietnam
Clare Dixon	University of Manchester, UK
Shyamala Doraisamy	University Putra Malaysia, Malaysia
Nuttanart Facundes	King Mongkut's University of Technology Thonburi, Thailand
Eduardo Fermé	Universidade da Madeira, Portugal
Somchart Fugkeaw	Thammasat University, Thailand
Katsuhide Fujita	Tokyo University of Agriculture and Technology, Japan
Naoki Fukuta	Shizuoka University, Japan
Marcus Gallagher	University of Queensland, Australia
Dragan Gamberger	Rudjer Boskovic Institute, Croatia
Wei Gao	Nanjing University, China
Xiaoying Gao	Victoria University of Wellington, New Zealand
Xin Geng	Southeast University, China
Manolis Gergatsoulis	Ionian University, Greece
Guido Governatori	Data61, CSIRO, Australia
Alban Grastien	Australian National University, Australia
Charles Gretton	Australian National University, Australia
Fikret Gurgen	Bogazici University, Turkey
Peter Haddawy	Mahidol University, Thailand
Choochart Haruechaiyasak	National Electronics and Computer Technology Center, Thailand
Hamed Hassanzadeh	Australian e-Health Research Centre, CSIRO, Australia
Tessai Hayama	Nagaoka University of Technology, Japan
Juhua Hu	University of Washington, USA
Xiaodi Huang	Charles Sturt University, Australia
Van Nam Huynh	Japan Advanced Institute of Science and Technology, Japan
Norisma Idris	University of Malaya, Malaysia
Mitsuru Ikeda	Japan Advanced Institute of Science and Technology, Japan

Hung Duy Nguyen	Thammasat University, Thailand
Phi Le Nguyen	Hanoi University of Science and Technology, Vietnam
Kouzou Ohara	Aoyama Gakuin University, Japan
Francesco Olivieri	Griffith University, Australia
Mehmet Orgun	Macquarie University, Australia
Noriko Otani	Tokyo City University, Japan
Maurice Pagnucco	University of New South Wales, Australia
Laurent Perrussel	IRIT - Universite de Toulouse, France
Bernhard Pfahringer	University of Waikato, New Zealand
Duc Nghia Pham	MIMOS Berhad, Malaysia
Jantima Polpinij	Mahasarakham University, Thailand
Thadpong Pongthawornkamol	Kasikorn Business-Technology Group, Thailand
Yuhua Qian	Shanxi University, China
Joel Quinqueton	LIRMM, France
Teeradaj Racharak	Japan Advanced Institute of Science and Technology, Japan
Fenghui Ren	University of Wollongong, Australia
Mark Reynolds	University of Western Australia, Australia
Jandson S. Ribeiro	University of Koblenz-Landau, Germany
Kazumi Saito	University of Shizuoka, Japan
Chiaki Sakama	Wakayama University, Japan
Ken Satoh	National Institute of Informatics and Sokendai, Japan
Abdul Sattar	Griffith University, Australia
Nicolas Schwind	National Institute of Advanced Industrial Science and Technology, Japan
Nazha Selmaoui-Folcher	University of New Caledonia, France
Lin Shang	Nanjing University, China
Alok Sharma	RIKEN, Japan
Chenwei Shi	Tsinghua University, China
Zhenwei Shi	Beihang University, China
Mikifumi Shikida	Kochi University of Technology, Japan
Soo-Yong Shin	Sungkyunkwan University, South Korea
Yanfeng Shu	CSIRO, Australia
Tony Smith	University of Waikato, New Zealand
Chattrakul Sombattheera	Mahasarakham University, Thailand
Insu Song	James Cook University, Australia
Safeeullah Soomro	Virginia State University, USA
Tasanawan Soonklang	Silpakorn University, Thailand
Markus Stumptner	University of South Australia, Australia
Merlin Teodosia Suarez	De La Salle University, Philippines
Xin Sun	Catholic University of Lublin, Poland
Boontawee Suntisrivaraporn	DTAC, Thailand
Thepchai Supnithi	National Electronics and Computer Technology Center, Thailand
David Taniar	Monash University, Australia

Thanaruk Theeramunkong	Thammasat University, Thailand
Michael Thielscher	University of New South Wales, Australia
Satoshi Tojo	Japan Advanced Institute of Science and Technology, Japan
Shikui Tu	Shanghai Jiao Tong University, China
Miroslav Velev	Aries Design Automation, USA
Muriel Visani	Hanoi University of Science and Technology, Vietnam and La Rochelle University, France
Toby Walsh	University of New South Wales, Australia
Xiao Wang	Beijing University of Posts and Telecommunications, China
Paul Weng	Shanghai Jiao Tong University, China
Peter Whigham	University of Otago, New Zealand
Wayne Wobcke	University of New South Wales, Australia
Sartra Wongthanavasu	Khon Kaen University, Thailand
Brendon J. Woodford	University of Otago, New Zealand
Kaibo Xie	University of Amsterdam, The Netherlands
Ming Xu	Xi'an Jiaotong-Liverpool University, China
Shuxiang Xu	University of Tasmania, Australia
Hui Xue	Southeast University, China
Ming Yang	Nanjing Normal University, China
Roland Yap	National University of Singapore, Singapore
Kenichi Yoshida	University of Tsukuba, Japan
Takaya Yuizono	Japan Advanced Institute of Science and Technology, Japan
Chengqi Zhang	University of Technology Sydney, Australia
Du Zhang	California State University, USA
Min-Ling Zhang	Southeast University, China
Shichao Zhang	Central South University, China
Wen Zhang	Beijing University of Technology, China
Yu Zhang	Southern University of Science and Technology, China
Zhao Zhang	Hefei University of Technology, China
Zili Zhang	Deakin University, Australia
Yanchang Zhao	Data61, CSIRO, Australia
Shuigeng Zhou	Fudan University, China
Xingquan Zhu	Florida Atlantic University, USA

Additional Reviewers

Aitchison, Matthew
Akhtar, Naveed
Algar, Shannon
Almeida, Yuri
Boudou, Joseph
Burie, Jean-Christophe
Chandra, Abel

Cheng, Charibeth
Damigos, Matthew
Dong, Huanfang
Du Preez-Wilkinson, Nathaniel
Effendy, Suhendry
Eng, Bah Tee
Feng, Xuening

Fu, Keren
Gao, Yi
Geng, Chuanxing
Habault, Guillaume
Hang, Jun-Yi
He, Zhengqi
Hoang, Anh
Huynh, Du
Inventado, Paul Salvador
Jan, Zohaib
Jannai, Tokotoko
Jia, Binbin
Jiang, Zhaohui
Kalogeros, Eleftherios
Karim, Abdul
Kumar, Shiu
Lai, Yong
Laosen, Kanjana
Lee, Nung Kion
Lee, Zhiyi
Li, Weikai
Liang, Yanyan
Liu, Jiexi
Liu, Xiaxue
Liu, Yanli
Luke, Jing Yuan
Mahdi, Ghulam
Mayer, Wolfgang
Mendonça, Fábio
Ming, Zuheng
Mittelmann, Munyque
Nguyen, Duy Hung
Nguyen, Hong-Huy
Nguyen, Mau Toan
Nguyen, Minh Hieu
Nguyen, Minh Le
Nguyen, Trung Thanh
Nikafshan Rad, Hima
Okubo, Yoshiaki
Ong, Ethel
Ostertag, Cécilia

Phiboonbanakit, Thananut
Phua, Yin Jun
Pongpinigpinyo, Sunee
Preto, Sandro
Qian, Junqi
Qiao, Yukai
Riahi, Vahid
Rodrigues, Pedro
Rosenberg, Manou
Sa-Ngamuang, Chaitawat
Scherrer, Romane
Selway, Matt
Sharma, Ronesh
Song, Ge
Su Yin, Myat
Subash, Aditya
Tan, Hongwei
Tang, Jiahua
Teh, Chee Siong
Tettamanzi, Andrea
Tian, Qing
Tran, Vu
Vo, Duc Vinh
Wang, Deng-Bao
Wang, Kaixiang
Wang, Shuwen
Wang, Yuchen
Wang, Yunyun
Wilhelm, Marco
Wu, Linze
Xiangru, Yu
Xing, Guanyu
Xue, Hao
Yan, Wenzhu
Yang, Wanqi
Yang, Yikun
Yi, Huang
Yin, Ze
Yu, Guanbao
Zhang, Jianyi
Zhang, Jiaqiang

Contents – Part II

Neural Networks and Deep Learning

Natural Language Processing

A Calibration Method for Sentiment Time Series by Deep Clustering

Jingyi Wu, Baopu Qiu, and Lin Shang[✉]

State Key Laboratory for Novel Software Technology,
Nanjing University, Nanjing 210023, China
{wujy,mf20330059}@smail.nju.edu.cn, shanglin@nju.edu.cn

Abstract. Sentiment time series is an effective tool to describe the trend of users' emotions towards specific topics over time. Most existing studies generate time series based on predicted results of the sentiment classifiers, which may not correspond to the actual values due to the lack of labeled data or the limited performance of the classifier. To alleviate this problem, we propose a calibrated-based method to generate time series composed of accurate sentiment scores. The texts are embedded into high dimensional representations with a feature extractor and then get fine-tuned and compressed into lower dimensional space with the unsupervised learning of an autoencoder. Then a deep clustering method is applied to partition the data into different clusters. A group of representative samples are selected according to their distance from the clustering centers. Finally combined the evaluation results on the sampled data and the predicted results, the calibrated sentiment score is obtained. We build a real-world dataset crawled from Sina Weibo and perform experiments on it. We compare the distance errors of predicted-based method with our calibrated-based method. The experimental results indicate that our method reduces the uncertainty raised by sampling as well as maintains excellent performance.

Keywords: Sentiment time series · Representative sampling · Deep clustering

1 Introduction

Nowadays people tend to share their emotions and attitudes towards specific topics online. Sentiment time series is an effective tool to analyze the change patterns of users' sentiment expressed in their posts over time. The posts are divided into different time slices according to their post time and then are aggregated to obtain the corresponding sentiment score. Sentiment time series is generated by connecting the sentiment scores in the time order. Figure 1 shows an example of the sentiment time series generation.[1]

The key problem of sentiment time series generation is to obtain an accurate sentiment score for each time point. Sentiment score is defined in many ways in

---

[1] https://www.weibo.com.

© Springer Nature Switzerland AG 2021
D. N. Pham et al. (Eds.): PRICAI 2021, LNAI 13032, pp. 3–16, 2021.
https://doi.org/10.1007/978-3-030-89363-7_1

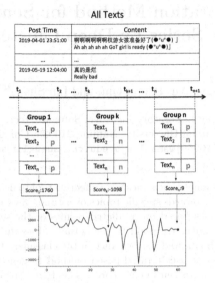

Fig. 1. An example of sentiment time series generation. The grouped texts belong to time slice t_1, t_k, t_n are aggregated to obtained the sentiment score of the time points colored in red. (Color figure online)

existing works to describe the overall sentiment of the grouped texts, including volume [8], percentage [1,6], velocity and acceleration [6], etc. No matter which definition is applied, the numbers of posts showing different sentiment orientations (e.g. positive or negative) are required to obtain the sentiment score. Most existing researches related to sentiment analysis aim to improve the classification accuracy of individual text, while few attempt to estimate the sentiment distribution in grouped texts.

We are motivated to make proportion estimation of the overall data based on the evaluation results on a sampling subset. In order to reduce the sampling error, we propose a sentiment calibration method based on representative sampling which could estimate the sentiment distribution in a stable way. Like other sentiment classification methods, the texts are passed through a classifier to obtain the predicted labels. Meanwhile, the high-dimensional embeddings of the texts are acquired from the output layer of the classification model, which are encoded with semantic features. Then the embeddings get fine-tuned and compressed under the unsupervised learning of an autoencoder. Based on the sentence embeddings we assign the data to different clusters by means of a deep clustering algorithm Deep k-Means (DKM) [14]. The k closest samples to the clustering centers are selected as representative samples by measuring the distance between the sample and its cluster centroid. Finally, we combine the predicted labels and the approximate evaluation results to obtain the corresponding sentiment score. The main contributions of our work can be summarized as the following:

- We propose a calibrated-based method to obtain accurate sentiment scores, which could estimate the sentiment distribution in a group of texts.
- Our proposed method requires only a small part of data to be labeled for distribution estimation, which reduces a lot of annotation work.
- With the use of encoded semantic representations and representative sampling strategy in the calibration process, the uncertainty caused by sampling is reduced while excellent performance is maintained.

2   Related Work

Sentiment time series has been widely used to describe the sentiment of users' online posts changing over time. It has been proved that sentiment time series analysis is effective in a variety of applications including politics, economics, public affairs and so on. Giachanou and Crestani [6] plot the sentiment time series of tweets and retweets containing the key word 'Michelle Obama', the sudden changes in which are found to have relations with Michelle Obama's political activities. Lansdall-Welfare et al. [12] generate time series of five affect components (positive, negative, anger, anxiety and sadness) of the public mood during the Brexit Referendum in UK. The change-points in the time series are identified to be corresponded with several real-life events. Daniel et al. [3] extract feelings implicit in tweets to detect and find the popularity of special events that may influence the financial market. An et al. [1] track public discussions on climate change to detect the connections between short-term fluctuations in sentiment and major climate events.

Based on sentimental classification results of individual texts, existing researches exploit various indicators to describe the sentiment trend. The most explicit way is to use the volume of tweets showing different sentiment orientations. The volume trend of tweets is helpful in analyzing the change patterns of users' attitudes [8]. The percentage of different sentiment polarities is another commonly-used indicator to measure the public mood. An et al. [1] have shown the significance of the sentiment polarity percentage in climate opinion studies by identifying sudden changes in the sentiment of twitters regarding climate change. In [6] the sentiment velocity and acceleration are proposed to represent the sentiment change rate. Plotting sentiment velocity and acceleration is useful not only to observe how a specific sentiment changes but also to detect if there is any emerging sentiment.

Most of the sentiment indicators are defined based on the predicted result of individual text, which is obtained by sentiment classifiers. A lot of classification models have been proposed to identify the sentiment polarity at a sentence level, including lexicon-based models [2,8], machine-learning methods [5,13,15,19] and deep-learning methods [9,10,16,18]. Most of the sentiment classification studies focus on correct classification of individual text, while few pay attention to the proportion estimation of different sentiment polarities. Even if a model shows excellent performance on sentiment classification for individual text, it could still lead to severe bias in sentiment proportion estimation. We propose a calibrated-based method to estimate the sentiment distribution for grouped texts based on evaluation results of representative samples, making the calibrated score closer to the ground-truth.

3   Methods

In this section, we introduce our proposed method for sentiment calibration in detail. On the first stage the texts are sent into a sentiment classifier to obtain the predicted labels as well as high-dimensional representations of the sentences. Secondly, the sentence embeddings are fed into an autoencoder and jointly trained with a deep clustering model. Based on clustering results, we select part of the samples from each cluster as representative samples. Finally, we combine the evaluation results on the representative samples and the predicted results to work out the calibrated sentiment score. The framework of our method is illustrated in Fig. 2.

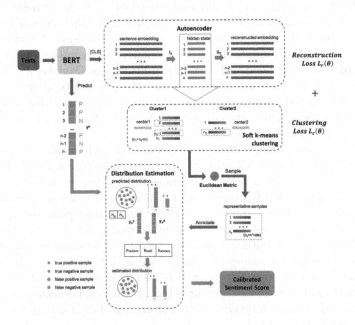

Fig. 2. Framework of our method for sentiment calibration.

3.1   Sentence Embedding

It is essential to obtain a sentence embedding suitable for clustering on the first stage. We expect an elaborate embedding which could extract the sentimental features and map the sentence to a high-dimensional space. We exploited the BERT [4] model as the feature extractor as well as the based sentiment classifier. BERT conducts pre-training tasks on top of the deep bidirectional Transformer and shows comparable performance on a variety of downstream tasks. A two-way classification layer is added to the pre-trained model to predict the sentiment labels of the sentences.

The hidden representation of the [CLS] token in BERT is utilized as the sentence embedding. During the training process of sentiment classification, the [CLS] token summarizes the information of contextual tokens via a self-attention mechanism, and thus it could capture sentence-level characteristics. Let $X = \{x_1, x_2, ..., x_n\}$ denote the dataset, $H = \{h_1, h_2, ..., h_n\} \in \mathbb{R}^{d \times n}$ denote the sentence embeddings, where d is the dimension of the hidden representation. Let $Y^p = \{y_1^p, y_2^p, ..., y_n^p\}$ denote the predicted labels of the data, $y_i^p \in \{0, 1\}$ for a binary classification problem. Given a sample x_i, the sentence embedding h_i and the predicted label y_i^p are generated as follows:

$$h_i = BERT(x_i)$$
$$y_i^p = \arg\max_C (W h_i + b) \tag{1}$$

where $W \in \mathbb{R}^{d \times 2}$, $b \in \mathbb{R}^2$, $C = \{0, 1\}$ is the set of the labels.

3.2 Representative Sampling

Representative sampling module aims to select representatives samples from a group of texts. Clustering is commonly used in representative sampling. With clustering the data can be partitioned into different groups according to their intrinsic features. We sample a fixed proportion r of data from the clusters to compose the representatives of the overall data.

The original sentence embeddings, however, are not reliable enough for clustering. The classifier has failed to distinguish between the texts with the same predicted label, and thus it is hard for a clustering model to separate samples with the same polarity. Besides, clustering algorithms based on distance metrics may no longer be effective in a high dimensional space. In order to obtain adapted embeddings for clustering, an unsupervised autoencoder structure is utilized to adjust and compress the embeddings. With autoencoder the predicted-based embeddings get fine-tuned for clustering as well as keep informative features from the classification task. Since it is hard for the original k-means algorithm to be implemented with the optimization of gradient descending, we follow the soft-k-means [14] method instead to perform the joint-training task of auto-encoder and k-means clustering. The loss of the problem is consisted of two parts: 1) a reconstruction loss of the auto-encoder; 2) a clustering loss of k-means objective function, combined with a parameter λ to trade-off between two parts.

$$\min_\theta L(\theta) = L_r(\theta) + \lambda L_c(\theta) \tag{2}$$

The reconstruction loss of autoencoder is depicted as:

$$L_r(\theta) = \min_\varphi \sum_i^n ||x_i - g_\varphi(f_\theta(x_i))||^2 \tag{3}$$

where f_θ and g_φ denote the encoder and decoder function respectively.

The formulation of the k-means loss is given by:

$$L_c(\theta) = \sum_i^n \sum_k^K ||f_\theta(x_i) - \mu_k||^2 G_{k,f}(f_\theta(x_i), \alpha; R) \qquad (4)$$

where μ_k is the center representation of the kth cluster, and $G_{k,f}$ takes the following form:

$$G_{k,f}(f_\theta(x_i), \alpha; R) = \frac{e^{-\alpha||f_\theta(x_i) - \mu_k||^2}}{\sum_{k'}^K e^{-\alpha||f_\theta(x_i) - \mu'_k||^2}} \qquad (5)$$

where $R = \{\mu_1, ..., \mu_K\}$ denotes the set of clustering centers.

Based on clustering results, the n_s closest samples to the clustering centroid are selected as the representatives of the individual cluster. The sampling size n_s is dependent on the sampling rate r. In our method we use euclidean distance to measure the distance between the embeddings and the clustering centroids.

3.3   Sentiment Score Calibration

Evaluation results on representative samples can be obtained with:

$$r_p = \frac{TP_s}{TP_s + FN_s} \qquad\qquad r_n = \frac{TN_s}{TN_s + FP_s} \qquad (6)$$

$$p_p = \frac{TP_s}{TP_s + FP_s} \qquad\qquad p_n = \frac{TN_s}{TN_s + FN_s} \qquad (7)$$

$$a = \frac{TP_s + FP_s}{TP_s + FP_s + TN_s + FN_s} \qquad (8)$$

where $\{r_p; r_n\}$, $\{p_p; p_n\}$, a denote the indicators of recall, precision and accuracy on the sampling dataset respectively. Based on the relationship between evaluation indicators and the predicted labels the sentiment score can be worked out. The sentiment score is simply defined as the difference between the numbers of positive and negative texts:

$$N_{pos} = \sum_i^n \mathbb{I}(y_i^g = 1) \qquad\qquad N_{neg} = \sum_i^n \mathbb{I}(y_i^g = 0) \qquad (9)$$

$$s_g = N_{pos} - N_{neg} \qquad (10)$$

where $y_i^g \in \{0, 1\}$ is the groundtruth label of the sample x_i. s_g is the groundtruth sentiment score of a group of texts with size n.

With sampling accuracy and recall the calibrated score can be formulated as:

$$s_c(r_p, a) = n_{pos} * \left(\frac{2a}{2r_p - 1} - 1\right) + n_{neg} * \left(\frac{2a - 2}{2r_p - 1} - 1\right) \tag{11}$$

or

$$s_c(r_n, a) = n_{pos} * \left(\frac{2 - 2a}{2r_n - 1} + 1\right) + n_{neg} * \left(\frac{-2a}{2r_n - 1} + 1\right) \tag{12}$$

With sampling accuracy and precision the calibrated score is given by:

$$s_c(p_p, a) = n_{pos} * (4p_p - 2a - 1) + n_{neg} * (1 - -2) \tag{13}$$

or

$$s_c(p_n, a) = n_{pos} * (2a - 1) + n_{neg} * (2a - 4p_n + 1) \tag{14}$$

where $n_{pos} = \sum_i^n \mathbb{I}(y_i^p = 1)$, $n_{neg} = \sum_i^n \mathbb{I}(y_i^p = 0)$ represent the numbers of positive and negative samples in predicted results respectively.

Proof. The relationship between evaluation indicators (i.e. TP, FP, TN, FN) and the numbers of texts can be depicted as following:

$$TP + FP = n_{pos} \qquad\qquad FN + TN = n_{neg} \tag{15}$$
$$TP + FN = N_{pos} \qquad\qquad FP + TN = N_{neg} \tag{16}$$

Combined with equations in (8), the solution of the equations gives (11)–(14).

The overall process of the sentiment calibration method is illustrated in Algorithm 1. For representative sampling we employ the joint training of the autoencoder and soft k-means model, the details of which is shown in Algorithm 2.

4   Experiment

In this section, we introduce the exprimental settings and results on our self-created dataset.

4.1   Dataset

We crawled 303,426 microblogs related to the topic 'Game of Thrones' from Weibo. The span of the post time varies from April 1st to May 31st in 2019. Preprocessing has been done on the raw data including redundant information removal and objective statements filtering. After preprocessing the texts showing obvious sentiment orientations are preserved. Details of the dataset are shown in Table 1.

In order to obtain the ground-truth score of a specific time point, we select several dates from the dataset and annotate all the texts belong to those dates, details of which are shown in Table 2.

Algorithm 1. Sentiment calibration algorithm

Input: Text set $X = \{x_1, x_2, ..., x_n\}$, sampling rate r, number of clusters n_c, trained model BERT
Output: Calibrated sentiment score
1: Initialize an empty sentence embedding set H;
2: **for all** x_i such that $x_i \in X$ **do**
3:     Compute h_i, y_i^p using (1)
4:     $H = H \cup h_i$
5: **end for**
6: $n_{pos} \leftarrow \sum_i^n \mathbb{I}(y_i^p = 1)$, $n_{neg} \leftarrow \sum_i^n \mathbb{I}(y_i^p = 0)$
7: Train the autoencoder parameters θ and cluster centers $\mathcal{R} = \{\mu_1, ..., \mu_{n_c}\}$ jointly by running Algorithm 2
8: **for** $i = 1$ to n_c **do**
9:     Initialize an empty cluster $cluster_i$
10: **end for**
11: **for** $i = 1$ to n **do**
12:     $e_i \leftarrow f_\theta(h_i)$
13:     $cluster_K = cluster_K \cup i$, with $K = argmin_k ||e_i - \mu_k||^2$
14: **end for**
15: Initialize an empty sample set $SAMPLE$
16: **for** $i = 1$ to n_c **do**
17:     $sz \leftarrow SIZEOF(cluster_i) \times r$
18:     **for** $j = 1$ to sz **do**
19:         $sample = \arg\min_k EuclideanDistance(e_k, \mu_i)$
20:         $cluster_i = \complement_{cluster_i}\{sample\}, SAMPLE = SAMPLE \cup sample$
21:     **end for**
22: **end for**
23: Initialize an empty predicted label set C and an empty groundtruth label set $\hat{C}$
24: **for all** i such that $i \in SAMPLE$ **do**
25:     $C = C \cup y_i^p$
26:     $\hat{C} = \hat{C} \cup Labeling(x_i)$
27: **end for**
28: Compute sampling indicators $p, r, a = Compare(C, \hat{C})$
29: Compute calibrated sentiment score based on (11) to (14)
    $Sentiment\_score = s_c(p, r, a, n_{pos}, n_{neg})$

4.2   Baselines

We compare the proposed method with the following baseline methods.

- **Bert-Predict-0.01** The BertForSequenceClassification model is utilized to obtain the predicted result, using bert-base-chinese [4] as pre-trained model and 0.01 data as training set.
- **Bert-Predict-0.05** A fine-tune model trained based on the same pre-trained model as **Bert-Predict-0.01**, whereas the training set contains more data up to 0.05.

Algorithm 2. Deep clustering algorithm

Input: Deep embedding set $H = \{h_1, h_2, ..., h_n\}$, balancing parameter λ, scheme for
  α, numbers of training epochs T, number of minibatches N, learning rate η
Output: autoencoder parameters θ, cluster representatives $\mathcal{R}$
1: **for** $t = 1$ to T **do**
2:   **for** $n = 1$ to N **do**
3:     Draw a minibatch $\mathcal{X}$
4:     Update parameter θ: $\theta \leftarrow \theta - \eta(\frac{1}{|\mathcal{X}|})\nabla_\theta L_r(\theta)$
5:   **end for**
6: **end for**
7: **for** $\alpha = m_\alpha$ to M_α **do**
8:   **for** $t = 1$ to T **do**
9:     **for** $n = 1$ to N **do**
10:       Draw a minibatch $\mathcal{X}$
11:       Update $(\theta, \mathcal{R})$:
            $(\theta, \mathcal{R}) \leftarrow (\theta, \mathcal{R}) - \eta(\frac{1}{|\mathcal{X}|})\nabla_{(\theta,\mathcal{R})}L(\theta, \mathcal{R})$
12:     **end for**
13:   **end for**
14: **end for**

Table 1. Game of Thrones dataset.

Number	Time Period	Time Slice
118,316	2019-04-01:2019-05-31	1 day

- **Proportion** A direct esimation method based on sampling result of sentiment category proportion $P(senti|all)$ to represent the proportion in total population.
- **Calibrate-Random** A calibration method similar to our proposed method, while using random sampling strategy instead. The distance result is an average value computed over 100,000 times repeated random sampling.

Table 2. Details of annotated corpora. Each row contains a time slice.

Date	Num	Ground-truth	Date	Num	Ground-truth	Date	Num	Ground-truth
04–01	2298	2162	04–02	2515	2155	04–11	689	521
04–21	3043	2313	05–19	1456	826	05–24	694	204

4.3 Experimental Settings

Based Classifier Description. The BERT model mentioned in 3.1 is utilized as our based classification model to obtain sentence embeddings and predicted labels. We select the 'bert-base-chinese'[2] version as the pre-trained model. The pre-trained model gets fine-tuned on a train set to adapt to sentiment classification task. The validation result of the classifier is given in Table 3. We exploit the model **Bert-Predict-0.01** as our based predicted model for calibration.

Autoencoder Description and Implementation Details. The autoencoder we used in the experiments is borrowed from previous deep clustering studies [7, 14,17]. The encoder is a fully-connected multilayer perceptron with dimensions d-500-500-2000-K, where d is the original data space dimension and K is the number of clusters to obtain. The decoder is a mirrored version of the encoder.

Follow the settings in [14], the number of ae-pretraining epochs is set to 50. The soft k-means model is fine-tuned by performing 100 epochs with a constant $\alpha = 1000$. Our training is based on the Adam optimizer [11] with standard learning rate $\eta = 0.001$ and momentum rates $\beta_1 = 0.9$ and $\beta_2 = 0.999$. The minibatch size is set to 256.

Hyperparameter Selection. The hyperparameter γ defined the trade-off between the reconstruction and the clustering loss is set to be 1.0. The number of clusters n_c is set to be 2. The sampling rate r is set to 0.04, which is only a small part of the overall data.

Table 3. Validation results of models on dataset Game of Thrones.

	Precision	Recall	F1
Bert-Predict-0.01	0.81356	0.96000	0.88073
Bert-Predict-0.05	0.86379	0.86667	0.86522

4.4 Evaluation Metrics

The evaluation metric is based on the distance between the groundtruth sentiment score and calibrated scores, which is defined as followed:

$$s_p = n_{pos} - n_{neg} \tag{17}$$

$$d_p = |s_p - s_g| \qquad\qquad d_c = |s_c - s_g| \tag{18}$$

where s_p is the predicted score defined in (17), s_g is the groundtruth score defined in (10), and s_c denotes the calibrated score obtained by our method which is defined in (11)–(14). d_p is utilized to measure the error of the predicted score obtained by predicted results. d_c is the error measurement of the calibrated score.

---

[2] https://huggingface.co/bert-base-chinese.

We use d_p and d_c for evaluation of predicted-based method and calibrated-based method respectively.

The experimental results are shown in Table 4. The result of our method is an average value computed over 10 runs. From the result we observe that the score distance d_c obtained by our method is smaller than other methods on all the dates except '05–19', which indicates the effectiveness of our method.

Table 4. Calibrated results of distance error on Game of Thrones.

Method	04–01	04–02	04–11	04–21	05–19	05–24
Ground-truth	2162	2155	521	2313	826	204
Bert-Predict-0.01	498	506	138	370	406	138
Bert-Predict-0.05	484	477	110	334	312	112
Proportion	276	279	73	203	226	71
Calibrate-Random	121	132	76	138	**121**	84
Calibrate-1 (Ours)[a]	84	**88**	59	108	136	**59**
Calibrate-2 (Ours)[b]	82	**88**	60	108	135	60

[a,b] **Calibrate-1** and **Calibrate-2** are calibrated results based on sampling indicators {**recall,accuracy**} and {**precision,accuracy**} respectively.

4.5 Analysis of the Parameter Cluster Number

In order to select an appropriate value for the hyperparameter cluster number, we perform a line search from 2 to 10 with increment of 1. Figure 3 describes the relationship between the distance d_c and the cluster numbers. From the figure we can conclude that the representative sampling result (i.e. the distance d_c) is insensitive to the choice of the cluster number.

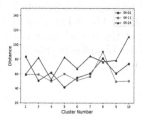 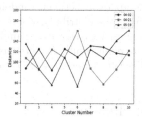

Fig. 3. Relation between the distance d_c and the parameter cluster number.

4.6   Compare with Random Sampling

It has been proved that random sampling is effective when one kind of sentiment dominates in the grouped data. However, random sampling suffers from the uncertainty especially when the sampling frequency is limited. Due to the lack of annotated data, the sampling process is performed only once for sentiment calibration. It is hard to ensure stable performance using random sampling. To be specific, even if random sampling shows excellent performance in most cases, it could still fall into bad cases with a small probability.

We conduct repeated random sampling to obtain the distribution of random sampling results and compare with the representative sampling result. Figure 4 depicts the experiment result. The repeat time is set as 100,000 in our experiment. The result shows that the representative sampling results outperform more than half of the cases of random sampling on all the dates except '05–19', which indicate the effectiveness of representative sampling in sentiment calibration.

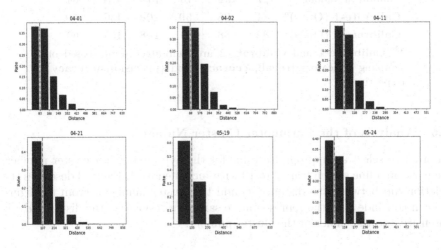

Fig. 4. Comparison between random sampling and representative sampling. The histogram shows the distribution of d_c in random sampling. The red vertical line denotes the d_c value of representative sampling. The value of the bar leftmost is the rate of random sampling results better than the representative sampling result. Thus smaller rate implies better performance of representative sampling.

5   Conclusion

In this paper, we propose a method to calibrate the sentiment score of grouped texts. The sentences are encoded into high-dimensional representations by feature extractors (i.e. the BERT model) at first. Then sentence embeddings are partitioned into different groups under the joint training of an antoencoder and a deep clustering model (i.e. the soft k-means model). From individual groups we select n_s closest samples to the clustering center as the representative samples based on the euclidean distance metric. Finally, the calibrated sentiment score is obtained based on evaluation results on the representative samples and the predicted labels. The encoded semantic representations and the representative sampling strategy reduce the uncertainty caused by sampling as well as maintain high accuracy. The experimental results on our self-created dataset demonstrate the effectiveness of our method.

Acknowledgments. This work is supported by the National Natural Science Foundation of China (No. 51975294).

References

1. An, X., Ganguly, A.R., Fang, Y., Scyphers, S.B., Hunter, A.M., Dy, J.G.: Tracking climate change opinions from twitter data. In: Workshop on Data Science for Social Good (2014)
2. Barbosa, L., Feng, J.: Robust sentiment detection on twitter from biased and noisy data. In: Proceedings of the 23rd International Conference on Computational Linguistics: Posters, pp. 36–44. COLING '10, Association for Computational Linguistics, USA (2010)
3. Daniel, M., Neves, R.F., Horta, N.: Company event popularity for financial markets using twitter and sentiment analysis. Expert Syst. Appl. **71**, 111–124 (2017). https://doi.org/10.1016/j.eswa.2016.11.022
4. Devlin, J., Chang, M.W., Lee, K., Toutanova, K.: BERT: pre-training of deep bidirectional transformers for language understanding. In: Proceedings of the 2019 Conference of the North American Chapter of the Association for Computational Linguistics: Human Language Technologies, Volume 1 (Long and Short Papers), pp. 4171–4186. Association for Computational Linguistics, Minneapolis, Minnesota (2019). https://doi.org/10.18653/v1/N19-1423
5. Ghiassi, M., Zimbra, D., Lee, S.: Targeted twitter sentiment analysis for brands using supervised feature engineering and the dynamic architecture for artificial neural networks. J. Manag. Inform. Syst. **33**, 1034–1058 (2016). https://doi.org/10.1080/07421222.2016.1267526
6. Giachanou, A., Crestani, F.: Tracking sentiment by time series analysis. In: Proceedings of the 39th International ACM SIGIR Conference on Research and Development in Information Retrieval, pp. 1037–1040. SIGIR '16, Association for Computing Machinery, New York, NY, USA (2016). https://doi.org/10.1145/2911451.2914702
7. Guo, X., Gao, L., Liu, X., Yin, J.: Improved deep embedded clustering with local structure preservation. In: Proceedings of the Twenty-Sixth International Joint Conference on Artificial Intelligence, IJCAI-17, pp. 1753–1759 (2017). https://doi.org/10.24963/ijcai.2017/243
8. Ibrahim, N.F., Wang, X.: Decoding the sentiment dynamics of online retailing customers: time series analysis of social media. Comput. Hum. Behav. **96**, 32–45 (2019). https://doi.org/10.1016/j.chb.2019.02.004
9. Kalchbrenner, N., Grefenstette, E., Blunsom, P.: A convolutional neural network for modelling sentences. In: 52nd Annual Meeting of the Association for Computational Linguistics, ACL 2014 - Proceedings of the Conference, vol. 1 (2014). https://doi.org/10.3115/v1/P14-1062

10. Kim, Y.: Convolutional neural networks for sentence classification. In: Proceedings of the 2014 Conference on Empirical Methods in Natural Language Processing (2014). https://doi.org/10.3115/v1/D14-1181
11. Kingma, D.P., Ba, J.: Adam: a method for stochastic optimization. In: Bengio, Y., LeCun, Y. (eds.) 3rd International Conference on Learning Representations, ICLR 2015, San Diego, CA, USA, May 7–9, 2015, Conference Track Proceedings (2015)
12. Lansdall-Welfare, T., Dzogang, F., Cristianini, N.: Change-point analysis of the public mood in uk twitter during the brexit referendum. In: 2016 IEEE 16th International Conference on Data Mining Workshops (ICDMW), pp. 434–439 (2016)
13. Li, L., Wu, Y., Zhang, Y., Zhao, T.: Time+user dual attention based sentiment prediction for multiple social network texts with time series. IEEE Access **7**, 17644–17653 (2019). https://doi.org/10.1109/ACCESS.2019.2895897
14. Moradi Fard, M., Thonet, T., Gaussier, E.: Deep k-means: jointly clustering with k-means and learning representations. Pattern Recogn. Lett. **138**, 185–192 (2020). https://doi.org/10.1016/j.patrec.2020.07.028
15. Pang, B., Lee, L., Vaithyanathan, S.: Thumbs up? sentiment classification using machine learning techniques. In: Proceedings of the ACL-02 Conference on Empirical Methods in Natural Language Processing, vol. 10, pp. 79–86. EMNLP '02, Association for Computational Linguistics, USA (2002). https://doi.org/10.3115/1118693.1118704
16. Wang, X., Liu, Y., Sun, C., Wang, B., Wang, X.: Predicting polarities of tweets by composing word embeddings with long short-term memory. In: Proceedings of the 53rd Annual Meeting of the Association for Computational Linguistics and the 7th International Joint Conference on Natural Language Processing (Volume 1: Long Papers), pp. 1343–1353. Association for Computational Linguistics, Beijing, China (2015). https://doi.org/10.3115/v1/P15-1130
17. Xie, J., Girshick, R., Farhadi, A.: Unsupervised deep embedding for clustering analysis. In: International Conference on Machine Learning, pp. 478–487. PMLR (2016)
18. Zhou, P., Qi, Z., Zheng, S., Xu, J., Bao, H., Xu, B.: Text classification improved by integrating bidirectional LSTM with two-dimensional max pooling. In: Proceedings of COLING 2016, the 26th International Conference on Computational Linguistics: Technical Papers, pp. 3485–3495. The COLING 2016 Organizing Committee, Osaka, Japan (2016)
19. Zou, H., Tang, X., Xie, B., Liu, B.: Sentiment classification using machine learning techniques with syntax features. In: Proceedings of the 2015 International Conference on Computational Science and Computational Intelligence (CSCI), pp. 175–179. CSCI '15, IEEE Computer Society, USA (2015). https://doi.org/10.1109/CSCI.2015.44

A Weak Supervision Approach with Adversarial Training for Named Entity Recognition

Jianxuan Shao[1,2], Chenyang Bu[1,2(✉)], Shengwei Ji[1,2], and Xindong Wu[1,2,3]

[1] Key Laboratory of Knowledge Engineering with Big Data (Hefei University of Technology), Ministry of Education, Hefei, China
{jxshao,swji}@mail.hfut.edu.cn, {chenyangbu,xwu}@hfut.edu.cn
[2] School of Computer Science and Information Engineering, Hefei University of Technology, Hefei, China
[3] Mininglamp Academy of Sciences, Mininglamp Technology, Beijing, China

Abstract. Named entity recognition (NER) is a basic task of natural language processing (NLP), whose purpose is to identify named entities such as the names of persons, places, and organizations in the corpus. Utilizing neural networks for feature extraction, followed by conditional random field (CRF) layer decoding, is effective for the NER task. However, achieving reliable results using neural networks generally requires a large amount of labeled data and the acquisition of high-quality labeled data is costly. To obtain a better NER effect without labeled data, we propose a weak supervision approach with adversarial training (WSAT). WSAT obtains supervised information and domain knowledge through labeling functions, including external knowledge bases, heuristic functions, and generic entity recognition tools. The labeled results are aggregated through the linked hidden Markov model (linked HMM), and adversarial training strategies are added when using the aggregated results for training. We evaluate WSAT on two real-world datasets. When compared to rival algorithms, the F1 values are improved by approximately 2% and 1% on the MSRA and Resume NER datasets, respectively.

Keywords: Named entity recognition · Weak supervision · Adversarial training

1 Introduction

Named entity recognition (NER) is a fundamental task in natural language processing (NLP). The task generally refers to recognizing entities with specific meanings in unstructured or semi-structured text. The recognized entities primarily include the names of people, places, organizations, and proper nouns. As the accuracy of NER determines the performance of downstream tasks, NER plays an important role in many NLP tasks, such as information extraction, question answering, and machine translation.

NER is often transformed into a sequence tagging problem. Utilizing neural networks for feature extraction, followed by CRF layer decoding, has been shown to be effective for the NER task [1, 2]. Based on the neural network feature extractor and CRF decoder, the representation of the input layer can be improved by adding additional information

© Springer Nature Switzerland AG 2021
D. N. Pham et al. (Eds.): PRICAI 2021, LNAI 13032, pp. 17–30, 2021.
https://doi.org/10.1007/978-3-030-89363-7_2

such as the token level, word level, and artificially defined features. Such improvements have been demonstrated to improve the effectiveness of NER. Improving and replacing the feature extractor can also improve the effectiveness of NER. Recently, using context-based language models, such as ELMo, BERT [3] and their related models, instead of recurrent neural networks for feature extraction has been shown to achieve state-of-the-art performance on NER tasks [4].

The abovementioned feature extractors, which are based on neural network structures, generally require a large amount of labeled data. Usually, 60%–80% of the data in a dataset will be used for training, and the remaining data will be used to verify and test the model's ability. These methods often fail to achieve good results when provided with no or very little labeled data.

Because the acquisition of high-quality labeled data is time-consuming, a few strategies that increase the effectiveness of NER in domains without access to hand-annotated data is proposed. A potential strategy for acquiring supervised data without hand annotation is distant supervision, which can automatically produce a large amount of labeled data. The concept of distant supervision was initially applied to the relational extraction task. In distant supervision relationship extraction, there is a knowledge base. In the knowledge base, if the relation between two entities $e1$ and $e2$ is r, then we apply this knowledge during the process of labeling data and assume that the relation between $e1$ and $e2$ in the sentence is r. In this way, a large amount of labeled data for the relation extraction task can be generated for model training. Similarly, in the NER task, we first obtain a dictionary containing a list of certain types of entities as a knowledge base. Then, large-scale labeled data are automatically produced by assuming that each entity that appeared in the sentence is an entity of the corresponding type in the knowledge base. However, the acquisition of high-quality entity list dictionaries is difficult, and entity list dictionaries often cannot cover all entity types in the data. Therefore, it is difficult to rely entirely on entity list dictionaries to obtain supervised data in a new domain.

In this paper, we propose a weak supervision approach with adversarial training (WSAT) for NER tasks. The WSAT does not require any hand-annotation for target data. It relies on multiple labeling functions. The functions can inject domain knowledge into the model and can be easily migrated between similar domains. The labeling results from multiple labeling functions are also aggregated using the linked hidden Markov model (linked HMM) model, and an adversarial training strategy is incorporated. It is demonstrated by the experiments described in this paper that the WSAT can improve the weak supervision NER effect.

The main contributions of this paper are as follows:

- For text data that has not been manually annotated, we introduce knowledge bases, heuristic functions, and generic entity recognition tools to label the data and aggregate the labeled data using the linked HMM.
- By incorporating an adversarial training method, the WSAT reduces the influence of noise in weak supervision data and improves the weak supervision NER effect on the MSRA and Resume NER datasets.
- The effect of WSAT is demonstrate by our experiment. When compared to rival algorithms, the F1 values improved by approximately 2% and 4% on the MSRA and Resume NER datasets, respectively.

The content of this paper is organized as follows: Sect. 2 focuses on the related work, and Sect. 3 describes the WSAT in detail. Experiments and results are shown in Sect. 4, and Sect. 5 presents our conclusions.

2   Related Work

Named Entity Recognition: The entity recognition problem is generally transformed into a sequence annotation problem. Using LSTM and CNNs as feature extractors and CRF as a decoder has been demonstrated to be the baseline structure for named entity recognition [5]. In addition, NER is usually enhanced by adding additional information and replacing the feature extractor [6]. By adding spelling features, text features, word vectors and gazetteer features to the model, it has been demonstrated that the accuracy of NER can be improved [7]. Reference [8] concatenates a 100-dimensional word vector with a 5-dimensional word shape feature vector to add additional information to the input, and these feature vectors help to improve the NER results. Reference [9] constructs word representations using word embeddings, token embeddings and word-related syntactic embeddings. These features introduce additional information to the model [10]. Reference [8] found that neural networks often discard most lexical features. Therefore, they propose a new lexical representation that can be trained offline and used in any neural network system. The lexical representation has a dimension of 120 for each word, and is obtained by computing the similarity of the word to the entity type. Changing the feature extractor can also improve the effectiveness of NER. Contextual acquisition of feature information through BERT and its siblings has also been demonstrated to significantly improve NER performance [3].

At the same time, some public tools can also be used to recognize general entities. The tools we used in our paper include Hanlp and FastHan. Hanlp is trained on the world's largest multilingual corpus, and it supports 10 joint tasks, including tokenization, lemmatization, part-of-speech tagging, token feature extraction, dependency parsing, constituency parsing, semantic role labeling, semantic dependency parsing, and abstract meaning representation (AMR) parsing. When writing the labeling functions, the lemmatization function is primarily used for nonentity labeling, and its named entity recognition function is utilized for entity labeling [11]. FastHan is a Chinese natural language processing tool based on fast NLP and PyTorch, and like spaCy, is user friendly. The kernel is a BERT-based federated model, which is trained on 13 corpora and can handle four tasks: Chinese word separation, lexical annotation, dependency analysis, and named entity recognition. FastHan has two versions, the base version and the large version; the base version is used in our experiments. When writing the labeling functions, the lemmatization function is mainly used for nonentity labeling, and its named entity recognition function is utilized for entity labeling [12].

Weak Supervision: The purpose of weak supervision is to reduce the amount of hand-annotated data. Generally, weak supervision acquires supervised information through distant supervision from external sources [13], active learning and heuristic rules [14]. Reference [15] uses deep active learning to efficiently select sample sets for annotation to reduce the annotation budget. Remote monitoring systems can also acquire weak supervision information using partially labeled data or external resources, such as web dictionaries, knowledge bases, and location tags, instead of using manually labeled data for training [16–19]. These approaches generally have certain requirements for the required external resources. Reference [20] designed a knowledge-enhanced language model for unsupervised neural network recognition. The model requires type-specific entity vocabularies to calculate the type and word probability of a given type and neural network recognition to determine whether a particular word is an entity. Reference [21] uses hidden Markov models to aggregate the results from multiple labeling functions to obtain supervision information. Reference [22] proposed a completely unsupervised entity recognition model for the NER task using only word embedding vectors without utilizing any external resources or annotation data.

The linked HMM which is used in our paper is proposed in reference [23]. The model is used to aggregate labeling functions such as labeling rules and linking rules. The main idea is to link the outputs of the labeling and linking rules, represent the sequence labels of the text as hidden variables, and generate a probabilistic generative model to generate the final labeling results. Our work not only uses heuristic and linking rules to obtain supervised information. More supervised information and adversarial training strategies are introduced to improve the overall effectiveness of the model. And the effect of WSAT is demonstrated by our experiments (detail in Sect. 4).

The input to the model is a text sequence $X = (x_1, x_2 \ldots \ldots x_i)$; for each x_i, there is a corresponding unknown label $y_i \in Y$ in the sequence, and Y is the set of labels. $L_1^{label}, L_2^{label} \ldots \ldots L_n^{label}$ are the given labeling functions. For each sequence, each label function L_j^{label} is able to generate a sequence of labels $\Lambda = (\lambda_1, \lambda_2 \ldots \ldots \lambda_i)$. The linked HMM then aggregates the results of the label sequences.

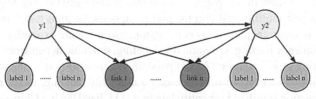

Fig. 1. Bayesian network representation of the linked HMM, with the first two true labels of the sequence illustrated. Label n is the labeled result obtained from the N-th labeling function. Link n is the labeled result obtained from the N-th linking function.

The linked HMM is defined as the joint distribution $p(Y, \Lambda^{tag}, \Lambda^{link})$ over the corresponding outputs generated by the sequence and label function. The distribution is defined by an initial distribution and a conditional distribution, as with other dynamic Bayesian networks and hidden Markov models, and is shown in Fig. 1. The initial distribution is defined as a Naive Bayesian distribution $p(y_1, \Lambda_{\cdot,1}^{tag})$ and

$$p\left(\Lambda_{\cdot,1}^{tag} | y_1\right) = \prod_{j=1}^{n} p(\lambda_{j,1}^{tag} | y_1).$$

The distribution is defined as $p\left(y_t, \Lambda_{\cdot,t}^{tag}, \Lambda_{\cdot,t}^{link} | y_{t-1}\right)$, which is the template for each linked HMM. First, the model allows the output of the labeling function to be independent, provided the true label y_t and

$$p\left(y_t, \Lambda_{\cdot,t}^{tag}, \Lambda_{\cdot,t}^{link} | y_{t-1}\right) = p\left(\Lambda_{\cdot,t}^{tag} | y_t\right) p(y_t, \Lambda_{\cdot,t}^{link} | y_{t-1})$$

Keeping $p\left(\Lambda_{\cdot,t}^{tag} | y_t\right)$ identical throughout the sequence, i.e., $p\left(\Lambda_{\cdot,t}^{tag} | y_t\right) = p\left(\Lambda_{\cdot,1}^{tag} | y_1\right)$ and then assuming that the different linking rules are conditionally independent, we produce the true labels of the two tokens:

$$p\left(y_t, \Lambda_{\cdot,t}^{link} | y_{t-1}\right) = p(y_t | y_{t-1}) \prod_{j=1}^{n} p(\lambda_{j,t}^{link} | y_t, y_{t-1})$$

The model uses maximum likelihood estimation to estimate the parameters of the linked HMM. We estimate all parameters of the linked HMM by maximizing the probability of the observed output:

$$\hat{\theta} = argmax \sum_Y P(Y, \Lambda^{tag}, \Lambda^{link})$$

Our work improves on the linked HMM model. Reference [23] only uses heuristic and linking rules to obtain supervised information. Our work introduces more supervised information and incorporates adversarial training strategies to improve the overall effectiveness of the model.

Adversarial Training: Adversarial training is a training method that introduces noise. By introducing noise, the parameters can be regularized, and the robustness and generalization ability of the model can be improved. The key to adversarial training is to construct adversarial samples. Generally, a certain perturbation is added to the original input to construct the adversarial sample. This enables the model to identify adversarial samples. The adversarial training problem can usually be defined as a min-max problem [24].

$$\min_{\theta} E(x, y) \sim D[\max_{r_{adv} \in S} L(\theta, x + r_{adv}, y)]$$

The equation can be divided into two parts: maximization of the internal loss function and minimization of the external risk. The purpose of maximizing the internal loss function is to find the amount of perturbation that allows the most judgment errors, i.e., to find the optimal attack parameters. The purpose of minimizing the external risk is to further optimize the model parameters for the abovementioned attacks so that the expectation is still minimized over the entire data distribution, i.e., to find the optimal defense parameters. In this paper, we mainly use two adversarial training strategies, Fast Gradient Method (FGM) and Projected Gradient Descent (PGD), to optimize the training process. FGM and PGD are two basic and widely used adversarial training methods. The two methods are used to prove the effectiveness of adversarial training in our work. These two adversarial training methods are briefly described below.

FGM: The FGM is scaled based on specific gradients to obtain a better antagonistic sample. The obtained perturbations are as follows [25]:

$$r_{adv} = \epsilon g / ||g||_2$$

$$g = \nabla_x L(\theta, x, y)$$

The additional adversarial samples are as follows:

$$x_{adv} = x + r_{adv}$$

The process of FGM during the training process is as follows: For each sample X, calculate the forward loss and backpropagation of X to obtain the gradient and calculate R based on the gradient of the embedding matrix and add it to the current embedding, which is equivalent to $X + R$; forward loss of $X + R$ and backpropagation is calculated to obtain the gradient of adversarial, and accumulate to the backpropagation of X.

PGD: Unlike FGM, which calculates the adversarial perturbation in one step, PGD tries to find the optimal perturbation by iterating several times [24]. The PGD perturbation gradually accumulates in the loop. It is important to note that the last update parameter uses only the gradient calculated from the last $X + R$.

Adversarial training method is added in the WSAT proposed in our paper. By adding the abovementioned adversarial training method to the training process, the WSAT improves the generalization ability of the model based on linked HMM and improves the problem of higher accuracy but lower recall when aggregating labeling functions. The experiments demonstrate that adding adversarial training is effective in improving the overall effect of the model. The experimental results detail is in Sect. 4.

3   Approach

In this paper, we aggregate the labeled results from multiple labeling functions and improve the generalization ability of the model using adversarial training. The aggregated multiple labeling functions include generic entity recognition tools, entity dictionary matching, heuristic rules, and linking rules. Compared with distant supervision, more supervision information can be obtained by introducing multiple labeling functions. In addition, all entity types in the data can be covered. The outputs from the labeling functions are aggregated by the linked HMM model, and the parameters of the model are estimated in an unsupervised manner. In general, the labeled data obtained from the labeling functions with heuristic rules or entity dictionary matching can only guarantee a high accuracy rate, while the recall rate is usually low. In application, the model has poor generalization ability. Therefore, in the WSAT, we add the adversarial training method, as adversarial training can regularize the parameters and improve the generalization ability of the model.

The overall structure of the WSAT is shown in Fig. 2. In this section, Sect. 3.1 briefly introduces the multiple labeling functions integrated into the WSAT, and Sect. 3.2 introduces the WSAT proposed in this paper.

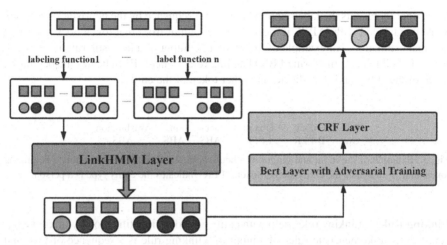

Fig. 2. Architecture of the weak supervision approach with adversarial training. The yellow rectangle represents the text, the circle represents the label corresponding to the text, and the different colors represent the different entity types. (Color figure online)

3.1 Labeling Functions

This section describes the four types of labeling functions used in the WSAT, including the generic entity recognition model, entity lexicon matching, heuristic rules and linking rules. In our application of the generic entity recognition model, two publicly available Chinese NLP tools are utilized. For entity lexicon matching, we construct a gazetteer to serve as external knowledge to match entities. The heuristic rules are written manually according to the features of the experimental dataset. To implement linking rules, language model similarity is used to link tokens in the text. The four types of labeling functions are described in more detail below.

Generic entity recognition tools: This type of labeling function uses trained and publicly available natural language processing toolkits to assist in labeling entities. The tools we used include Hanlp and FastHan.

Entity Lexicon Matching: As with distant supervision, we use a knowledge base to label toponymic entities. Specifically, we used a knowledge base comprised of geographical names, which includes all countries and regions in the world and some district-level geographical names in China. The place names in the database are matched with the text to perform toponymic entity labeling. In our experiments, we utilize only the geographical name knowledge base for the time being, and for other entities in the dataset, we can also utilize corresponding knowledge bases or large knowledge bases such as Wikipedia or DBPedia for matching to achieve better labeling results.

Heuristic Rules: We also inject domain knowledge into the model by writing heuristic rules. The heuristic rules are used to identify specific named entities, including entities related to nationality, ethnicity, position, profession, and education. Generally, the input to a heuristic rule is a sequence of text, and the output is a sequence of labels of the same length that represents the labels applied to the text sequence by the heuristic rule. When a token is labeled with 'ABS', it means that the output from that token does not affect the final estimation. An example of the input and output of a heuristic rule is shown in Fig. 3. Labeling takes the form of BIO labeling rules, where 'B' indicates the beginning token of the entity and 'I' indicates the other token of the entity.

In:	Barack	Obama	lives	in	Washington
Out:	B-PER	I-PER	ABS	ABS	ABS

Fig. 3. Example of the input and output of a heuristic rule. 'B' indicates the entity's beginning token, and 'I' indicates the entity's other token. 'PER' indicates the entity type is a person.

Linking Rules: Linking rules help with entity boundary identification by linking adjacent tokens. Like heuristic rules, the input to a linking rule is a sequence of text, and its output is a token that indicates whether the current token is of the same type as the previous token. A concrete example is shown in Fig. 4.

In:	Barack	Obama	lives	in	Washington
Out:		SAME	ABS	ABS	ABS

Fig. 4. Example of the input and output of a linking rule. SAME indicates that the current token has the same entity type as the preceding token. ABS indicates the token is independent.

As shown in the above example, SAME indicates that the current token has the same entity type as the preceding token, while ABS indicates that the current token is independent from the preceding token. These rules are responsible only for capturing the linking relationship between adjacent tokens. The linking rules do not care about the specific type of any token.

Other more common and valid linking rules are as follows:

Frequent N-Gram: If a sequence appears several times in a text, it can be concluded that the sequence may be a specific entity and that the tokens of the sequence can be considered for linking.

Language model similarity: Using context-based word embedding models such as ELMo and BERT, by obtaining the cosine similarity of embeddings between adjacent tokens and links adjacent tokens when that similarity is greater than a certain threshold value.

In the experiments of this paper, language model similarity is used as a linking rule to link the token in the text.

3.2 WSAT: Weak Supervision Approach with Adversarial Training

The WSAT is the approach proposed in this paper. For unlabeled text data, the WSAT uses multiple labeling functions to label the text data. Based on the weak supervision information provided by the multiple labeling functions, the WSAT aggregates the labeled results using the linked HMM model. When using the results of linked HMM for training, we incorporate adversarial training methods. The specific adversarial training methods used include Fast Gradient Method and Projected Gradient Descent.

In the WSAT, text data is labeled by the labeling functions introduced in Sect. 3.1. The weak supervision information provided by the multiple labeling functions is not fully effective, the linked HMM is widely used to aggregates the weak supervision information. Moreover, it can generate a probabilistic generative model by associating the outputs of the labeling functions to represent the sequential labels of the text as hidden variables to generate the final labeling results (detailed in Sect. 2). The labeled results aggregated by linked HMM are used to train the NER model after. However, the labeled results have the problem of higher accuracy but lower recall. In order to improve the generalization ability of the model, the strategy of adversarial training is introduced in the training process. Adversarial training is a training method that introduces noise. By introducing noise, the parameters can be regularized, and the robustness and generalization ability of the model can be improved.

In this paper, we mainly use two adversarial training strategies, FGM and PGD, to optimize the training process. The FGM is scaled based on specific gradients to obtain a better antagonistic sample. Unlike FGM, PGD calculates the adversarial perturbation in one step and tries to find the optimal perturbation by iterating several times. By adding the abovementioned adversarial training method to the training process, the WSAT improves the generalization ability of the model based on linked HMM and improves the problem of higher accuracy but lower recall when aggregating labeling functions.

The overall structure of the WSAT is shown in Fig. 2. We have tried two adversarial training strategies on the model, and the experiments demonstrate that adding adversarial training is effective in improving the overall effect of the model. The experimental results detail is in Sect. 4.

4 Experimental Results

Experiments are conducted on two real-world datasets to verify the effect of the WSAT. The WSAT is compared with the other two weak supervision models. The effect of the WSAT on the NER task was evaluated by incorporating different adversarial training methods. The experiments show that the WSAT can improve the effect of the weak supervision NER task.

4.1 Dataset

The WSAT is evaluated on two datasets: MSRA and Resume NER. The statistics for each of these datasets is shown in Table 1. The types 'Sentence' and 'Char' represent the number of sentences and characters in the dataset. 'Train' is the size of the training set, 'Dev' is the size of the development set and 'Test' is the size of the testing set.

- MSRA NER: The MSRA NER is from the newswire domain. The dataset consists of three main types of articles, including news, radio news, and blogs, and has three types of entities, including person (PER), locations (LOC), and organizations (ORG) [26].

- Resume NER: The Resume NER dataset contains the resumes of senior executives from listed firms in the Chinese stock exchange, and is taken from Sina Finance. The dataset has eight types of entities, including person name (NAME), nationality (CONT), race (RACE), title (TITLE), education (EDU), organizations (ORG), profession (PRO) and location (LOC) [27].

Table 1. Statistics of datasets.

Datasets	Type	Train	Dev	Test
MSRA [26]	Sentence	46.4k	–	4.4k
	Char	2169.9k	–	172.6k
Resume [27]	Sentence	3.8k	0.46k	0.48k
	Char	124.1k	13.9k	15.1k

4.2 Baselines

The WSAT was compared with the labeling results from the Snorkel and linked HMM models. The effectiveness of the WSAT in improving the generalization of the model in the weak supervision case is verified.

Snorkel [28]: Snorkel is a general framework for training discriminative classifiers from user-written heuristic rules, and by default uses a Naive Bayes generative model to denoise the rules. This model uses weak supervision data that has been labeled by various types of labeling functions to aggregate the labeling results.

Linked HMM Model [23]: The weak supervision data input into this model are the same as the weak supervision data input to Snorkel, with the exception of the data labeled using the linking rule. In our experiments, the linking rule only adopts the linguistic model of cosine similarity.

Bert-CRF: Utilizing context-based language models, such as BERT, for feature extraction followed by CRF layer decoding, has been shown to be effective for the NER task. The weak supervision data input into this model are the same as the weak supervision data input to Snorkel.

FLAT [29]: FLAT (Flat Lattice Transformer) is a model proposed for Chinese NER. FLAT designed a novel position code for lattice structure and use transformer to completely model the lattice input. It has achieved good results on Chinese NER. The weak supervision data input into this model are the same as the weak supervision data input to Snorkel.

4.3 Results and Discussion

The labeling results of labeling functions on train data and test data is given to illustrate the labeling effects of different labeling functions. For MSRA [26] dataset, organization (ORG) labeling function and person (PER) labeling function use generic entity recognition tools to identify organization entities and person entities. Location (LOC) labeling function combines entity lexicon matching and generic entity recognition tools to identify location entities. For Resume [27] dataset, organization and name (ORG&NAME) labeling function combines entity lexicon matching and general entity recognition tools to identify organization entities and person entities. Moreover, other labeling functions use heuristic rules to identify entities. The effect of the supervision signal provided by each labeling function is detailed in Table 2.

Table 2. Labeling functions results on data.

Datasets	Labeling functions	Precision	Recall	F1
MSRA [26] Train Data	ORG labeling function	0.9989	0.9053	0.9497
	PER labeling function	0.9982	0.8953	0.9440
	LOC labeling function	0.9910	0.8806	0.9325
	Overall	0.9983	0.8922	0.9422
MSRA [26] Test Data	ORG labeling function	0.9906	0.8080	0.8900
	PER labeling function	0.9900	0.9442	0.9713
	LOC labeling function	0.9695	0.7056	0.8168
	Overall	0.9959	0.8098	0.8933
Resume [27] Train Data	CONT labeling function	0.9872	0.9843	0.9857
	RACE labeling function	0.9914	0.9871	0.9892
	TITLE labeling function	0.9610	0.0674	0.1260
	EDU labeling function	0.8724	0.6224	0.7265
	PRO labeling function	0.7780	0.2911	0.4237
	ORG&NAME labeling function	0.8679	0.7660	0.8138
	LOC labeling function	0.9310	0.5696	0.7068
	Overall	0.8830	0.5421	0.6717
Resume [27] Test Data	CONT labeling function	0.9160	1.0	0.9561
	RACE labeling function	1.0	1.0	1.0
	TITLE labeling function	0.9438	0.0727	0.1350
	EDU labeling function	0.8433	0.6278	0.7208
	PRO labeling function	0.4259	0.3433	0.3802
	ORG&NAME labeling function	0.8670	0.7720	0.8170
	LOC labeling function	1.0	0.6060	0.7547
	Overall	0.8722	0.5428	0.6692

The WSAT is compared with the four baselines mentioned above, and the labeling functions are the same. The MSRA dataset utilize generic entity recognition models and entity lexicon matching. The BERT pretraining model is utilized for linking rules. The Resume dataset uses generic entity recognition models, entity lexicon matching and handwritten heuristic rules for entity labeling. After obtaining the labeling results, Snorkel, the linked HMM model, Bert-CRF, FLAT and WSAT are used to aggregate and train the labeling results, respectively, and the results are shown in Table 3.

The results of the experiments are shown in Table 3. The input of the models are all weakly supervised data from the labeling functions in Table 2. On the MSRA dataset, the WSAT's accuracy is almost indistinguishable from the effect of Snorkel and the linked HMM models, and the recall rate is improved. And the WSAT's accuracy and recall rate are both improved compared with the Bert-CRF. On the Resume dataset, the WSAT's accuracy is almost indistinguishable from the effect of Snorkel, linked HMM models and Bert-CRF, and the recall rate is improved.

For the MSRA dataset, the WSAT improves the recall by approximately 4% compared with Snorkel and the linked HMM models. For the Resume dataset, the WSAT improves the recall by approximately 2% compared with the Bert-CRF model. With guaranteed accuracy and improved recall, the F1 values improved by approximately 2% for the MSRA dataset and approximately 1% for the Resume dataset. The experiments demonstrate that when 1) there is no manually labeled data; 2) there is weakly supervised data obtained through labeling functions; 3) there are many false noise labels in the weakly supervised data, the WSAT achieves better effect than other models. The WSAT can improve the overall recall and enhance the generalization ability of the model in the case of weak supervision data.

Table 3. Results of experiments in the case of weak supervision.

Dataset	Approach	Precision	Recall	F1
MSRA [26]	Snorkel [28]	**0.9959**	0.8099	0.8933
	Linked HMM [23]	0.9946	0.8084	0.8919
	Bert-CRF[a]	0.9457	0.7384	0.8292
	FLAT [29]	0.7104	0.7339	0.7219
	WSAT without adversarial training	0.9926	0.8375	0.9085
	WSAT with FGM	0.9901	**0.8497**	**0.9145**
	WSAT with PGD	0.9900	0.8357	0.9063
Resume [27]	Snorkel [28]	0.8858	0.541	0.6717
	Linked HMM [23]	**0.8899**	0.5457	0.6765
	Bert-CRF[a]	0.8862	0.5829	0.7033
	FLAT [29]	0.8611	0.5753	0.6897
	WSAT without adversarial training	0.8856	0.5583	0.6848
	WSAT with FGM	0.8780	**0.6025**	0.7146
	WSAT with PGD	0.8837	0.6003	**0.7149**

[a] https://github.com/bojone/bert4keras

5   Conclusion

For the NER task, utilizing neural networks for feature extraction generally requires a large amount of labeled data. In this paper, a weak supervision approach with adversarial training (WSAT) was proposed. The WSAT acquires weak supervision data using various labeling functions. Based on the acquired weak supervision data, WSAT aggregates the labeling results using the linked HMM model and introduces the idea of adversarial training to reduce the influence of noise in weak supervision data. The proposed algorithm was verified on two datasets, and the experimental results showed that WSAT can effectively improve the recall rate and NER effectiveness. In the future, we plan to design methods that improve the model's effectiveness in cases where the labeled data have considerable noise, and we also expect to be able to automatically acquire labeling and linking rules to reduce manual involvement.

Acknowledgements. This work was supported by the National Key Research and Development Program of China (2016YFB1000901), the National Natural Science Foundation of China (61806065), and the Fundamental Research Funds for the Central Universities (JZ2020HGQA0186).

References

1. Lample, G., Ballesteros, M., Subramanian, S., et al.: Neural architectures for named entity recognition. arXiv preprint arXiv:1603.01360 (2016)
2. Maxwell, J.C.: A Treatise on Electricity and Magnetism, 3rd edn, vol. 2, pp. 68–73. Clarendon, Oxford (1892)
3. Devlin, J., Chang, M.W., Lee, K., et al.: Bert: pre-training of deep bidirectional transformers for language understanding. arXiv preprint arXiv:1810.04805 (2018)
4. Yan, H., Deng, B., Li, X., et al.: Tener: Adapting transformer encoder for named entity recognition. arXiv preprint arXiv:1911.04474 (2019)
5. Chiu, J.P.C., Nichols, E.: Named entity recognition with bidirectional LSTM-CNNs. Trans. Assoc. Comput. Linguist. **4**, 357–370 (2016)
6. Li, J., Sun, A., Han, J., et al.: A survey on deep learning for named entity recognition. IEEE Trans. Knowl. Data Eng. (2020)
7. Huang, Z., Xu, W., Yu, K.: Bidirectional LSTM-CRF models for sequence tagging. arXiv preprint arXiv:1508.01991 (2015)
8. Strubell, E., Verga, P., Belanger, D., et al.: Fast and accurate entity recognition with iterated dilated convolutions. arXiv preprint arXiv:1702.02098 (2017)
9. Lin, B.Y., Xu, F.F., Luo, Z., et al.: Multi-channel BiLSTM-CRF model for emerging named entity recognition in social media. In: Proceedings of the 3rd Workshop on Noisy User-generated Text, pp. 160–165 (2017)
10. Li, J., Bu, C., Li, P., et al.: A coarse-to-fine collective entity linking method for heterogeneous information networks. Knowl.-Based Syst. **228**(2), 107286 (2021)
11. The website of HanLP. https://hanlp.hankcs.com/docs/references.html. Accessed 21 May 2020
12. Geng, Z., Yan, H., Qiu, X., et al.: fastHan: A BERT-based Joint Many-Task Toolkit for Chinese NLP. arXiv preprint arXiv:2009.08633 (2020)

13. Mintz, M., Bills, S., Snow, R., et al.: Distant supervision for relation extraction without labeled data. In: Proceedings of the Joint Conference of the 47th Annual Meeting of the ACL and the 4th International Joint Conference on Natural Language Processing of the AFNLP, pp. 1003–1011 (2009)
14. Jiang, Y., Wu, G., Bu, C., et al.: Chinese entity relation extraction based on syntactic features. In: 2018 IEEE International Conference on Big Knowledge (ICBK). IEEE (2018)
15. Shen, Y., Yun, H., Lipton, Z.C., et al.: Deep active learning for named entity recognition. arXiv preprint arXiv:1707.05928 (2017)
16. Shang, J., Liu, L., Ren, X., et al.: Learning named entity tagger using domain-specific dictionary. arXiv preprint arXiv:1809.03599 (2018)
17. Fries, J., Wu, S., Ratner, A., et al.: Swellshark: A generative model for biomedical named entity recognition without labeled data. arXiv preprint arXiv:1704.06360 (2017)
18. Yang, Y., Chen, W., Li, Z., et al.: Distantly supervised NER with partial annotation learning and reinforcement learning. In: Proceedings of the 27th International Conference on Computational Linguistics, pp. 2159–2169 (2018)
19. Jie, Z., Xie, P., Lu, W., et al.: Better modeling of incomplete annotations for named entity recognition. In: Proceedings of the 2019 Conference of the North American Chapter of the Association for Computational Linguistics: Human Language Technologies, vol. 1 (Long and Short Papers), pp. 729–734 (2019)
20. Liu, A., Du, J., Stoyanov, V.: Knowledge-augmented language model and its application to unsupervised named-entity recognition. arXiv preprint arXiv:1904.04458 (2019)
21. Lison, P., Hubin, A., Barnes, J., et al.: Named entity recognition without labelled data: A weak supervision approach. arXiv preprint arXiv:2004.14723 (2020)
22. Luo, Y., Zhao, H., Zhan, J.: Named Entity Recognition Only from Word Embeddings. arXiv preprint arXiv:1909.00164 (2019)
23. Safranchik, E., Luo, S., Bach, S.: Weakly supervised sequence tagging from noisy rules. In: Proceedings of the AAAI Conference on Artificial Intelligence, vol. 34, no.04, pp. 5570–5578 (2020)
24. Madry, A., Makelov, A., Schmidt, L., et al.: Towards deep learning models resistant to adversarial attacks. arXiv preprint arXiv:1706.06083 (2017)
25. Miyato, T., Dai, A.M., Goodfellow, I.: Adversarial training methods for semi-supervised text classification. arXiv preprint arXiv:1605.07725 (2016)
26. Levow, G.A.: The third international Chinese language processing bakeoff: word segmentation and named entity recognition. In: Proceedings of the Fifth SIGHAN Workshop on Chinese Language Processing, pp. 108–117 (2006)
27. Zhang, Y., Yang, J.: Chinese NER using lattice LSTM. arXiv preprint arXiv:1805.02023 (2018)
28. Ratner, A., Bach, S.H., Ehrenberg, H., et al.: Snorkel: rapid training data creation with weak supervision. Proc. VLDB Endow. 11(3) (2017)
29. Li, X., Yan, H., Qiu, X., et al.: FLAT: Chinese NER using flat-lattice transformer. In: Proceedings of the 58th Annual Meeting of the Association for Computational Linguistics (2020)

An Attention-Based Approach to Accelerating Sequence Generative Adversarial Nets

Minglei Gao, Sai Zhang, Xiaowang Zhang$^{(\boxtimes)}$, and Zhiyong Feng

College of Intelligence and Computing, Tianjin University, Tianjin 300350, China
xiaowangzhang@tju.edu.cn

Abstract. Automatic text generation is widely used in dialogue systems, machine translation and other fields. Sequence Generative Adversarial Network (SeqGAN) has achieved good performance in text generation tasks. Due to the discriminator can only evaluate the finished text, and cannot provide other valid information to the generator. When evaluating a single word, the Monte Carlo algorithm is mainly used to generate a complete text. This process requires a huge computational cost. As the length of the text increases, the time to obtain rewards will increase significantly. For text, different words have different effects on semantics, and keywords determine the final expression of semantics. Evaluation of the importance of each word is particularly critical. In this paper, we propose a new framework called AttGAN. We allow the discriminator to provide more features to the generator. Specifically, we add an attention layer to the new discriminator. The attention score is used as the basic reward so that the discriminator can calculate the reward value of each word through only one evaluation without multiple sampling by the generator. And to meet the requirements of valid reward, we further process the attention score. Our large number of experiments on synthetic data and tests on dialogue systems show that AttGAN can minimize computational costs and generate high-quality text. Furthermore, it also has a good performance in the generation of lengthy text.

Keywords: Text generation · GAN · Attention

1 Introduction

Generating meaningful and coherent text is significant for machine translation [17], dialogue system [9], and so on. The essential problem of text generation is that in unsupervised learning, generating sequences that mimic the distribution of real data [19,20]. In the text generation task, the maximum likelihood estimation is used as the objective function. In the inference stage, there is a problem of exposure bias: predict the next token based on the previously predicted token, and generate the sequence in an iterative manner [12]. These tokens may not be existing in the training data [2]. As the Generative Adversarial Network was proposed for continuous data, it was later extended to discrete data,

© Springer Nature Switzerland AG 2021
D. N. Pham et al. (Eds.): PRICAI 2021, LNAI 13032, pp. 31–45, 2021.
https://doi.org/10.1007/978-3-030-89363-7_3

showing success results [19]. It contains a sequence generator and a discriminator. The discriminator guides the training of the generator through feedback rewards. Since the discriminator can only evaluate the completed sequence, a rollout policy is commonly used to evaluate a single token. When the rollout policy is applied, the model keeps sampling words from the generative model until a complete sequence is generated. The whole process is repeated N times, and the average value is taken as the reward for the current token. This process requires a huge computational cost. And as the amount of model parameters increases, the computational cost of this method will also increase. Li [9] attempts to judge the reward of incomplete sequence, but the accuracy has dropped. In addition, a major disadvantage is that the discriminator only provides the final classification result without any other information about the sequence. As we all know, the discriminator is a trained model, e.g., a Convolutional Neural Network (CNN) [8] or a Recurrent Neural Network (RNN) [4], rather than an unknown black box. LeakGAN [6] provides the generator with the feature information in the discriminator so that the generator can obtain more features about the sequence. However, the problem of a large amount of calculation in the training process still exists.

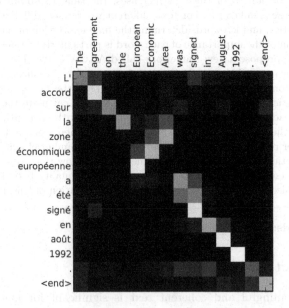

Fig. 1. An example of attention mechanism in machine translation [1].

Therefore, multiple repeated sampling calculations are costly during the training process. The key to the problem is that the discriminator cannot evaluate each token in the sequence through a single calculation. Solving this problem without reducing accuracy can make training faster, thereby significantly reducing training time.

It is well known that the importance of each word is highly context dependent [18]. The keywords determine the semantic result in real text. In other words, neutral words do not affect the results. The reward of each word is obtained by taking the average value after multiple sampling, which undoubtedly consumes a lot of calculation costs. Further, it is obvious that the attention mechanism can show the effect of different words on the final result. The attention mechanism plays an essential position in neural networks. And it was first used in Encoder-Decoder [3] translation tasks in NLP [1]. Figure 1 shows the application of the attention mechanism in machine translation, which can well capture the importance of different words. Zhou [21] propose Attention-Based BiLSTM [7] Networks (AttBiLSTM) to obtain the key information. This is consistent with the idea of our model. Yang [18] built a hierarchical attention network to serve as a document-level classification. The attention mechanism has a wide range of applications. The previous work using the attention mechanism can only acquire important characteristics. However, the attention mechanism has not been used as a way to reduce model training time. We combine the attention mechanism with the discriminator so that the discriminator can output the attention score of each word. By using the attention score as the basic reward, the process of repeated sampling is greatly reduced. There are two problems to be solved here. Firstly, the attention scores are normalized by softmax. As the length of the text increases, most of the attention scores will be very small, which can not be directly applied as a reward. Secondly, the attention scores only represent the importance of the words in the current text. It cannot represent the classification result of the discriminator. So it is an interesting challenge to apply the attention mechanism to the accelerated sequence adversarial generation networks.

In this paper, we propose a new sequence adversarial generation framework called AttGAN, which can greatly reduce training time without loss of accuracy. Our model has a generator and an attention-based discriminator. By combining the attention mechanism with the discriminator, the discriminator has the ability to evaluate each word, thereby guiding the training of the generator more quickly. To make the attention score can meet the requirements of the reward value, we adopt the scaling algorithm and the function mapping based on the classification result of the discriminator to process the attention scores. The generator can obtain more accurate reward information.

Experiments on synthetic data show that our model greatly reduces the time required for training, and as the length of the text increases, the time reduction becomes more obvious. In particular, it is not premised on the loss of accuracy. On the contrary, our model still has competitive performance. Tests on actual tasks show that our method requires almost one-tenth of the time needed by SeqGAN, and the evaluation indicators are all the best.

2   Related Work

GAN for Sequences Generation. Generative Adversarial Networks (GANs) [5] can learn complex distributions in unsupervised learning. It is also the generative model with the most development potential. Due to the discrete nature of natural language that makes it non-differentiable, GANs cannot be directly applied to text generation tasks. To solve this problem, SeqGAN [19] uses reinforcement learning combined with policy gradients [16] to deal with non-differentiable. Another issue here is that the discriminator can only evaluate the complete text and cannot evaluate the quality of a single token. The Monte Carlo search is used to complete the text. Zhang [20] applied this method to dialogue generation by building a Seq2Seq [15] model, using a hierarchical encoder as a discriminator, and achieved good results. Since the discriminator can only provide the results of two classes, this is far from enough for expressing diverse natural languages. RankGAN [11] learns the model through the ranking information between the model-generated sequence and the actual sequence. Similarly, LeakGAN [6] leaked the internal characteristics of the discriminator to the generator to better guide the generator. In the above work, when getting the reward of each token, the Monte Carlo search is used. This method requires a huge computational cost. Li [9] proposed to train a discriminator that can score partial sequences. The speed is indeed improved, but the accuracy is much lower than that of SeqGAN. Song [13] uses beam search instead of Monte Carlo search in the dialogue system but did not avoid repeated sampling. Our attention-based discriminator can feedback the reward value of each token through the attention mechanism without the need for repeated sampling. And it has success performance.

3   Our Approach

Our approach introduces the attention mechanism in the discriminator so that the discriminator can evaluate each token in the current sequence. As shown in Fig. 2, the attention mechanism can avoid using Monte Carlo search for repeated sampling, which greatly saves the time required for training. And the attention mechanism can point out the importance of each token, avoiding the error caused by random sampling of neutral words.

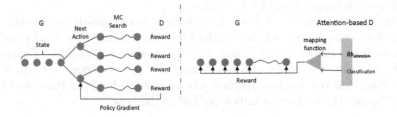

Fig. 2. Comparison of MC search and attention-based methods.

We denote the sequence generation task as: Given a dataset of real sequences, the generator G_θ is excepted to be able to generate a sequence $\hat{Seq}_{1:T} = \{token_1, token_2, \ldots, token_T\}$, to fit the distribution of real data. Where T is the timestep. Reinforcement learning is used to interpret this problem. The state s represents an incomplete sequence generated before timestep t, $s_{t-1} = \hat{Seq}_{1:t-1}$, $\hat{Seq}_{1:t-1} = \{token_1, token_2, \ldots, token_{t-1}\}$, and the action a is the next token $token_t$ to sample, $a = token_t$. We also train a attention-based discriminator $Att\_D_\phi(\hat{Seq}_{1:T})$ that can provide the reward value of each token in the sequence.

3.1   Attention-Based Discriminator

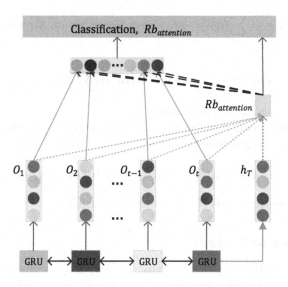

Fig. 3. The structure of discriminator.

The discriminator evaluates whether the current sequence is a real sequence or a sequence generated by the generator. We treat the real sequence as positive and the sequence from the generator as negative. Most discriminators only provide a reward value for the finished sequences. To evaluate each token, a common strategy is to use the Monte Carlo search. The generator remains to sample the next token until a complete sequence is generated. Repeat sampling several times and take the average value as the final reward. Each round of training has a huge computational cost. We introduce an attention mechanism in the discriminator to solve this problem. While CNN has problems learning remote semantic information, we choose RNN as our discriminator to better capture the attention relationship within the sequence.

The goal of our discriminator is not only to evaluate whether the current sequence is positive or negative but also to have the ability to point out the importance of each token. The structure of the attention-based discriminator is shown in Fig. 3. The discriminator mainly includes a two-layer bidirectional Gated Recurrent Unit(GRU) [3] and an attention module. Specifically, using the hidden state at the last moment, the output vector at each moment is used to calculate the attention, and the final classification result is made based on the result of the attention. The basic reward value comes from attention information.

$$O_T, h_T = BiGRU(\mathcal{E}_{1:T}) \tag{1}$$

where $\mathcal{E}_{1:T}$ is the embedding of the $\hat{Seq}_{1:T}$.

$$hidden = \sum_{i=1}^{M}(h_{Ti}) \quad M = num\_layers * num\_directions \tag{2}$$

$$Rb_{attention} = \{Rb_1, Rb_2, \ldots, Rb_T\} = softmax(\sum hidden \cdot (W_\alpha O_T + b)) \tag{3}$$

where $Rb_{attention}$ is the attention score.

The objective function of the discriminator Att_D_ϕ is to minimize the cross entropy. And the output from Att_D_ϕ is:

$$Classification, Rb_{attention} = Att\_D_\phi(\hat{Seq}_{1:T}) \tag{4}$$

where the $Classification$ is the result of the classification.

3.2   Attention to Rewards

We treat the attention score as the basic reward. The discriminator only needs one evaluation to reward each token. There are still two problems that need to be solved. One is that attention is calculated by softmax. As the length of the sequence increases, the attention score will decrease, which does not meet the requirements of the reward value. Therefore, we need to expand the attention score to an appropriate range without changing the size relationship. Another problem is that the attention score only represents the degree of attention, not the real output, so we need the result of classification to complete the reward together with the attention score.

For the first problem, We use mathematical scaling algorithms. The advantage of this algorithm is to scale the attention score to an appropriate range without changing the size relationship between the data. In this part, we are based on the assumption that the final output of the model is positive. By default, the current sequence is the real data.

$$Rb = \frac{Rb_{attention} - \min(Rb_{attention})}{\max(Rb_{attention}) - \min(Rb_{attention})} * \Delta + \mathbb{L} \tag{5}$$

where Δ is the size of the interval, and $\mathbb{L}$ is the lower bound of the interval.

For the second problem, we process the basic reward again. We keep the original data unchanged for the case where the classification result is positive; for the negative classification result, we let the data go through the mapping function $y = 1 - x$. The negative token could get a greater penalty. The reward value obtained after mapping the function is the real reward of each token in the current sequence. The goal of the generator is to get the greatest reward.

$$mask = \max(Classification).bool() \tag{6}$$

$$\mathcal{R}_{Att\_D_\phi}\left(\hat{Seq}_{1:t}\right) = mask * Rb + \neg mask * (1 - Rb) \tag{7}$$

where the type of mask is bool, and $\neg mask$ represents the inverse.

Each token can get the most realistic reward by effectively scaling the attention score and the final function mapping based on the classification result. The neutral tokens in the sequence will not be affected too much. The token that determines the actual semantics of the sequence can get the greatest encouragement or punishment. The generator can obtain more accurate information, making the training results more excellent.

3.3   Training of G

Maximizing the reward of the generated sequence is the training goal of the generator.

$$\mathcal{J}(\theta) = \sum_{t=1}^{T} G_\theta\left(token_t \mid \hat{Seq}_{1:t-1}\right) \cdot Q^{G_\theta}_{Att\_D_\phi}\left(token_t, \hat{Seq}_{1:t-1}\right) \tag{8}$$

where $G_\theta\left(token_t \mid \hat{Seq}_{1:t-1}\right)$ is the generator with the parameter θ, and the $Q^{G_\theta}_{Att\_D_\phi}(token_t, \hat{Seq}_{1:t-1})$ is the action-value function at timestep t. Firstly, we use a complete sequence $\hat{Seq}$. The discriminators evaluate $\hat{Seq}$ and return the corresponding attention score. After processing the attention score, it serves as the reward.

$$Q^{G_\theta}_{Att\_D_\phi}\left(a = token_t, s_{t-1} = \hat{Seq}_{1:t-1}\right) = \mathcal{R}_{Att\_D_\phi}\left(\hat{Seq}_{1:t}\right) \tag{9}$$

As mentioned above, we adopted the attention instead of the Monte Carlo search. So, with the attention, the gradient of the objective function $\mathcal{J}(\theta)$ can be derived as

$$\nabla_\theta \mathcal{J}(\theta) = \sum_{t=1}^{T} \left[\nabla_\theta \log G_\theta\left(token_t \mid \hat{Seq}_{1:t-1}\right) \cdot \mathcal{R}_{Att\_D_\phi}\left(\hat{Seq}_{1:t}\right)\right] \tag{10}$$

In summary, our overall framework is shown in Algorithm 1. First, we pretrain G_θ to use Maximum Likelihood Estimation (MLE). Negative samples are

---

Algorithm 1 Attention Generative Adversarial Nets

Require: generator G_θ, Attention-based Discriminator Att_D_ϕ, dataset S from
$Target$ Generator
 1: Initialize G_θ, Att_D_ϕ to the normal distribution N(-0.05, 0.05)
 2: Pretrain G_θ using MLE on S.
 3: Generate the negative samples from G_θ.
 4: Pretrain Att_D_ϕ on S and negative samples via minimizing the cross entropy.
 5: **for** each $epoch \in epochs$ **do**
 6:    **for** $it \in g - steps$ **do**
 7:       Generate $\hat{Seq}_{1:T}$.
 8:       Compute Q via attention.
 9:       Update the G_θ.
10:    **end for**
11:    **for** $it \in d - steps$ **do**
12:       Generate newly samples based on current G_θ.
13:       Train Discriminator Att_D_ϕ for k epochs.
14:    **end for**
15: **end for**
16: **return** AttGAN converges

---

generated according to the state of the current generator G_θ, and together with real samples are used as the training dataset of the discriminator. In the process of adversarial learning generation, the generator generates new samples, and the discriminator is responsible for providing rewards for each token based on the samples. Regularly update the parameters of the discriminator to ensure synchronization with the state of the generator. In the end, we get a better generative model.

4   Experiments

The experiment includes synthetic data experiments, tests in a dialogue system, and more internal analysis.

4.1   Training Settings

Synthetic Oracle. For the synthetic data experiments, similar to SeqGAN, we first initialize the $Target$ Generator (LSTM), and the parameters obey the normal distribution N(0, 1). Then generate 10,000 sequences and use them as real target dataset S. In particular, the length of these sequences is uniformly set to 20. To test the effect of generating long text, we add a set of experiments with 40.

GAN Setting. For the generator, similar to $Target$ Generator, the parameters of the generator are initialized to the normal distribution N(-0.05, 0.05). For the discriminator, we adopt the two-layer GRU with a hidden size 64. In addition, the vocabulary size is 5000. To avoid overfitting, we use dropout [14] with the keep rate of 0.75. As described in [19], different g-steps and d-steps will affect the final result. The best parameter of our model is when the text length is 20, the g-step adopted is 50, and when the text length is 40, the d-step is 10. And the d-steps is 4, and the k is 2.

4.2   Baselines

To evaluate the effectiveness, we compared our model with the following strong models:

SeqGAN. SeqGAN introduces the output of the discriminator into the training process of the generator through reinforcement learning. SeqGAN uses policy gradients to solve the problem that discrete data cannot be differentiated. Evaluate each token through the Monte Carlo search [19].

RankGAN. RankGAN learns the model through the ranking information between the model-generated sequence and the actual sequence [11].

LeakGAN. LeakGAN's generator can obtain the advanced features inside the discriminator to guide training [6]. Due to the generator of LeakGAN is different from the previous works, the focus of our comparison is SeqGAN and RankGAN.

4.3   Evaluation Metrics

Using such an oracle can provide the training data and accurately evaluate the quality of the generative model. The synthetic data experiment adopts the negative log-likelihood method (NLL.) to evaluate. Most importantly, we focus on the time consumption(T.) of different models. To compare the time consumption more accurately, we compare the time consumption of completing one epoch in Algorithm 1.

4.4   Synthetic Data Experiments

Experiments on synthetic data show that treating attention as the basic reward can effectively improve the training speed of the generator and make the generator have better performance.

We set the text length of the synthetic data experiments as 20 and 40. The training curves and the time consumption are displayed in Fig. 4. The time consumption and NLL performance are shown in Table 1. Since LeakGAN's generator is different from the other three, the focus of our comparison is SeqGAN and RankGAN. Firstly, Our generator obtains the best performance in the shortest time. We can see that training time is significantly reduced by using the attention mechanism, and the generator's parameters distribution is also closer to the target parameters. Secondly, we also compared the performance of the model when generating long texts. From the data listed in Table 1 that when the text length increases, the effect of each model decreases slightly, and the training time increases, but our approach can still obtain a better performance in the shortest time. In addition, although LeakGAN has a different generator, the effect achieved by our model is comparable to LeakGAN.

Table 1. The results of dialogue system.

Model	Text length 20		Text length 40	
	NLL.	T. (each epoch)	NLL.	T. (each epoch)
SeqGAN	8.683	167	10.310	303
RankGAN	8.149	84	9.958	152
LeakGAN[a]	7.038	260	7.191	613
AttGAN	**7.104**	**40**	**7.208**	**57**

[a] LeakGAN's generator is different from other models and is not the focus of comparison.

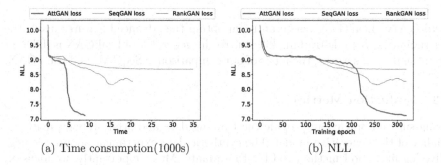

(a) Time consumption(1000s)   (b) NLL

Fig. 4. NLL and time consumption of different models.

In general, the experimental results show that the generator can obtain more accurate reward value information from the attention-based discriminator, and the model achieved excellent performance. It also shows that it is feasible to use attention feedback information.

4.5 Dialogue Generation: DailyDialog

By verifying real tasks, the use of the attention mechanism in the discriminator can provide more accurate rewards, and the time required for training is shortened dramatically. In real-world tasks, the generator generates higher-quality responses based on the guidance of the attention-based discriminator. The advantage of the attention mechanism is that neutral words will not get too much attention, avoiding errors caused by sampling.

Table 2. The results of dialogue system.

Model	ppl.	Loss.	Ave.	Grd.	Ext.	Dis-2.	T. (Total)
MC (SeqGAN)	257	5.930	0.739	0.496	0.883	0.0959	50345
AttGAN	**126**	**5.190**	**0.747**	**0.505**	**0.884**	**0.1001**	**4144**

We apply it to the dialogue model to test the real effect of using attention as the reward. We adopt a Seq2Seq [3] model as our generator. Through training, the generator is responsible for generating fluent sentences. And for the discriminator, we use the two-layer GRU with hidden size 300, and the structure is the same as AttGAN's. For the discriminator, the discriminator has the ability to classify and feedback rewards. Specifically, seq2seq generates an appropriate response from the above information of the dialogue, and the discriminator is responsible for efficiently scoring the generated replies. The discriminator provides real rewards for each word by judging the fluency and naturalness of the current response.

We choose the DailyDialog [10] Dataset. We use Perplexity (ppl.), the Cross-Entropy Loss (Loss.), Embedding Average (Ave.), Embedding Greedy (Grd.), Embedding Extrema (Ext.), distinct bigrams (Dis-2.), and the time (T.) consumption. Ave., Grd., and Ext. are based on word embeddings. We use Google-News 300D word vectors. Particularly, lower perplexity means better fluency. We mainly compare the use of Monte Carlo search and the use of attention information.

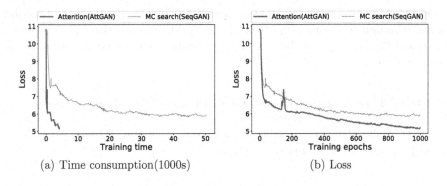

(a) Time consumption(1000s) (b) Loss

Fig. 5. The results of the Seq2Seq model.

Table 2 shows the result of the dialogue system. We can see that when using attention, all evaluation indicators are better than using Monte Carlo search. From Fig. 5, AttGAN's performance is better, although there is a small fluctuation in the middle. Since the training has just started, the discriminator is not stable yet. As the training progresses, our model performs better and better. Most importantly, the training time used by AttGAN is only one-tenth of the

Monte Carlo search. For the Monte Carlo search, although the evaluation of each token will be sampled multiple times and averaged, it is inevitable that the randomness in the sampling process will still affect the final result. The attention can be more precise to obtain which tokens have a more significant impact on the sequence, guiding the generator to achieve better results.

4.6   Internal Comparison Experiments

To further verify the details in AttGAN, we compared different attention mechanism, scaling algorithms and mapping functions.

For the attention mechanism, we use the concat attention:

$$Rb_{attention} = softmax(\sum W_\alpha[hidden; O_T]) \tag{11}$$

For scaling algorithms, we adopt the Sigmoid function:

$$S(x) = \frac{1}{1 + e^{-2x}} \tag{12}$$

This function can directly enlarge the attention to 0.5 to 1. It also means that the default sequence is positive. For the mapping functions, we use the following functions:

$$y = \frac{e^x - 1}{e - 1}(positive) \tag{13}$$

$$y = \frac{e^{-x+1} - 1}{e - 1}(negative) \tag{14}$$

For the selection of the mapping function, we require the mapping function to pass through two points $(0, 0)$ and $(1, 1)$ (positive), and through two points $(1, 0)$ and $(0, 1)$ (negative) because the reasonable range of reward value is the range of 0 to 1.

Table 3. The NLL performance of different attention processing methods.

Model	Only attention	Sig linear	Sig nonlinear	Nonlinear	(Linear) AttGAN
NLL.	9.007	12.647	11.258	8.85	**7.104**

The final results are provided in Fig. 6 and Table 3. Different forms of attention mechanisms have different effects, and general attention(AttGAN) is better. If only the original data of the attention is used, the generator does not obtain effective information. Because attention itself is not the final classification result, combining the classification results to be used as a reward is necessary. When using the Eq. (12) Sigmoid function, both models have very poor results because the Sigmoid function cannot effectively handle maximum values, making the reward or penalty too large, which leads to overtraining of the generator. Using

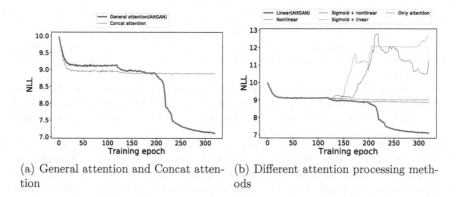

(a) General attention and Concat attention

(b) Different attention processing methods

Fig. 6. Different attention processing

Eq. (5) (AttGAN), the extreme value can be limited to a fixed range, which is more in line with the requirements of the real reward value. Equation (13) and Eq. (14) non-linear functions distort the relationship between the attention score so good results cannot be obtained.

By combining the attention with the scaling algorithm and the linear mapping function, the discriminator can provide more effective guidance to the generator to achieve the best result.

5   Conclusion and Future Work

In this paper, we proposed a new algorithm framework called AttGAN, which reduces the training time of the generative model and achieves better performance than similar algorithms. Attention mechanism could capture the importance of each token in the sequence more accurately, which can provide better guidance to the generator. In addition, the attention mechanism can also be used to accelerate other models, further shortening the training time. Although our model has indeed been improved following previous works, for future work, we will compare more variant models and more data sets to analyze the effectiveness of the attention mechanism in accelerating model training.

Acknowledgment. This work is supported by the National Natural Science Foundation of China (NSFC) (61972455), Key Research and Development Program of Hubei Province (No. 2020BAB026) and the Joint Project of Bayescom. Xiaowang Zhang is supported by the program of Peiyang Young Scholars in Tianjin University (2019XRX-0032).

References

1. Bahdanau, D., Cho, K., Bengio, Y.: Neural machine translation by jointly learning to align and translate. In: 3rd International Conference on Learning Representations, San Diego (2015)

2. Bengio, S., Vinyals, O., Jaitly, N., Shazeer, N.: Scheduled sampling for sequence prediction with recurrent neural networks. In: Advances in Neural Information Processing Systems 28: Annual Conference on Neural Information Processing Systems 2015, pp. 1171–1179. Neural Information Processing Systems, Montreal, Quebec, Canada (2015)
3. Cho, K., et al.: Learning phrase representations using RNN encoder-decoder for statistical machine translation. In: Proceedings of the 2014 Conference on Empirical Methods in Natural Language Processing, pp. 1724–1734. Association for Computational Linguistics, Doha (2014)
4. Elman, J.L.: Finding structure in time. Cogn. Sci. **14**(2), 179–211 (1990)
5. Goodfellow, I.J., et al.: Generative adversarial nets. In: Advances in Neural Information Processing Systems 27: Annual Conference on Neural Information Processing Systems 2014, pp. 2672–2680. Neural Information Processing Systems, Montreal (2014)
6. Guo, J., Lu, S., Cai, H., Zhang, W., Yu, Y., Wang, J.: Long text generation via adversarial training with leaked information. In: Proceedings of the Thirty-Second AAAI Conference on Artificial Intelligence, pp. 5141–5148. AAAI Press, New Orleans (2018)
7. Hochreiter, S., Schmidhuber, J.: Long short-term memory. Neural Comput. **9**(8), 1735–1780 (1997)
8. Kim, Y.: Convolutional neural networks for sentence classification. In: Proceedings of the 2014 Conference on Empirical Methods in Natural Language Processing, pp. 1746–1751. Association for Computational Linguistics, Doha (2014)
9. Li, J., Monroe, W., Shi, T., Jean, S., Ritter, A., Jurafsky, D.: Adversarial learning for neural dialogue generation. In: Proceedings of the 2017 Conference on Empirical Methods in Natural Language Processing, pp. 2157–2169. Association for Computational Linguistics, Copenhagen (2017)
10. Li, Y., Su, H., Shen, X., Li, W., Cao, Z., Niu, S.: DailyDialog: a manually labelled multi-turn dialogue dataset. In: Proceedings of the Eighth International Joint Conference on Natural Language Processing, pp. 986–995. Asian Federation of Natural Language Processing, Taipei (2017)
11. Lin, K., Li, D., He, X., Sun, M., Zhang, Z.: Adversarial ranking for language generation. In: Advances in Neural Information Processing Systems 30: Annual Conference on Neural Information Processing Systems 2017, pp. 3155–3165. Neural Information Processing Systems, CA, USA (2017)
12. Salakhutdinov, R.: Learning deep generative models. Annu. Rev. Stat. Appl. **2**, 361–385 (2015)
13. Song, H., Zhang, W., Hu, J., Liu, T.: Generating persona consistent dialogues by exploiting natural language inference. In: The Thirty-Fourth AAAI Conference on Artificial Intelligence, pp. 8878–8885. AAAI Press, New York (2020)
14. Srivastava, N., Hinton, G.E., Krizhevsky, A., Sutskever, I., Salakhutdinov, R.: Dropout: a simple way to prevent neural networks from overfitting. J. Mach. Learn. Res. **15**(1), 1929–1958 (2014)
15. Sutskever, I., Vinyals, O., Le, Q.V.: Sequence to sequence learning with neural networks. In: Advances in Neural Information Processing Systems 27: Annual Conference on Neural Information Processing Systems 2014, pp. 3104–3112. Neural Information Processing Systems, Montreal (2014)
16. Sutton, R.S., McAllester, D.A., Singh, S.P., Mansour, Y.: Policy gradient methods for reinforcement learning with function approximation. Advances in Neural Information Processing Systems, vol. 12, pp. 1057–1063. The MIT Press, Denver (1999)

17. Yang, Z., Chen, W., Wang, F., Xu, B.: Improving neural machine translation with conditional sequence generative adversarial nets. In: Proceedings of the 2018 Conference of the North American Chapter of the Association for Computational Linguistics: Human Language Technologies, pp. 1346–1355. Association for Computational Linguistics, New Orleans (2018)
18. Yang, Z., Yang, D., Dyer, C., He, X., Smola, A.J., Hovy, E.H.: Hierarchical attention networks for document classification. In: The 2016 Conference of the North American Chapter of the Association for Computational Linguistics: Human Language Technologies, pp. 1480–1489. Association for Computational Linguistics, San Diego (2016)
19. Yu, L., Zhang, W., Wang, J., Yu, Y.: SeqGAN: sequence generative adversarial nets with policy gradient. In: Proceedings of the Thirty-First AAAI Conference on Artificial Intelligence, pp. 2852–2858. AAAI Press, San Francisco (2017)
20. Zhang, Y., et al.: Adversarial feature matching for text generation. In: Proceedings of the 34th International Conference on Machine Learning, pp. 4006–4015. PMLR, Sydney (2017)
21. Zhou, P., et al.: Attention-based bidirectional long short-term memory networks for relation classification. In: Proceedings of the 54th Annual Meeting of the Association for Computational Linguistics, pp. 207–212. Association for Computer Linguistics, Berlin (2016)

Autoregressive Pre-training Model-Assisted Low-Resource Neural Machine Translation

Nier Wu, Hongxu Hou[✉], Yatu Ji, and Wei Zheng

College of Computer Science-College of Software,
Inner Mongolia University, Hohhot, China
cshhx@imu.edu.cn

Abstract. Pre-training methods have been proven to significantly improve language understanding ability of the model. However, when dealing with machine translation tasks involving two or more languages, the pre-training method can only handle a single language and prevent further improvement of machine translation performance. Therefore, there are two main methods to improve the quality of machine translation model by using the pre-training model. One is to use the word embedding generated by the pre-training model as the modeling unit. Second is to make the machine translation model learn the probability distribution of the pre-training model through the knowledge distillation method. In addition, the self-attention based pre-training model affects the effect of machine translation due to the "training-fine-tuning" difference and limited by the assumption of conditional independence. For this reason, we proposed a XLNet based pre-training method, that corrects the defects of the general self-encoding based pre-training model, and enhance NMT model for context feature extraction. We conducted experiments on the CCMT2019 Mongolian-Chinese (Mo-Zh), Uyghur-Chinese (Ug-Zh) and Tibetan-Chinese (Ti-Zh) tasks, our method significantly improves the quality compared to the baseline (Transformer), which fully verifies the effectiveness.

Keywords: Pre-training · XLNet · Low-resource · Machine translation

1 Introduction

General neural machine translation (NMT) [1,6,9,15] adopt attention mechanism to learn the alignment relationship between source language and target language on the basis of sequence-to-sequence framework. The model evaluates the cross-entropy between the generated token and the reference token through the maximum likelihood estimation method (MLE). The training goal is to minimize the cross-entropy to make the generated token more similar to the probability distribution of the reference token. In order to be able to achieve the bias-variance tradeoff in the training phase, the general approach is to improve the accuracy of the output probability and reduce the dispersion through Drop method,

© Springer Nature Switzerland AG 2021
D. N. Pham et al. (Eds.): PRICAI 2021, LNAI 13032, pp. 46–57, 2021.
https://doi.org/10.1007/978-3-030-89363-7_4

data augmentation, add constraints to the objective function, etc. Therefore, in addition to improving the network structure and training strategies, word embedding is the key to improve the quality of machine translation. One-hot word embedding can not learn semantic features due to the dimension disaster. Both Word2vec [3] and GloVe [10] belong to low-dimensional word embedding representation method, which maps the one-hot word embedding into the low-dimensional dense feature space. The feature extraction method is similar to N-gram language model [2], the cosine distance from the space origin to the word embedding position in the initial neighborhood is used as the measurement index. The closer the distance is, the greater the correlation is, and vice versa. However, the generated word embedding is fixed and cannot be dynamically optimized for specific tasks. At present, the pre-training method [5,11,12] has emerged in natural language process (NLP) tasks with excellent feature representation and extraction capabilities. However, NMT model combined with pre-training methods is less studied because of the particularity of NMT. [18] use the output layer of BERT as the word embedding representation of the NMT model, and add a new attention model to realize the interactive representation of the NMT model and the pre-training model. [16] proposed a hybrid strategy to make the NMT model fully learn the knowledge of the pre-training model. They graded the learned state representations according to correlation, and dynamically fused the representations with high correlation into the corresponding NMT model. In order to further learn the "dark knowledge" of the pre-training model, they used the knowledge distillation method to learn the output distribution of the pre-training model to improve the quality of the NMT model. [14] proposed masked sequence-to-sequence pre-training method (MASS), which predicts tokens by adding a certain proportion of masks to the encoder and decoder to learn language features. As we all know, the BERT model consists of masked language model (MLM) [13] and next sentence prediction model [8], the MLM model uses $Mask$ to randomly replace words in a sentence, and uses the context of the current $Mask$ to predict true value. However, $Mask$ is not used in the fine-tuning phase, resulting in "training-fine-tuning" inconsistent. In addition, due to the assumption of conditional independence, $Mask$ cannot use other $Mask$ as a condition for prediction. While the autoregressive XLNet [17] alleviates the "training-fine-tuning" difference and overcomes the context omission problem of traditional autoregressive models, thereby improving the quality of the NMT method combined with the pre-training model. Therefore, this paper is mainly divided into the following parts.

- We proposed a partial sampling method to obtain the partial factorization sequence of the sentence, and then use XLNet to encode the factorization sequence into the corresponding word embedding.
- We proposed an interactive attention mechanism to realize information transfer between NMT model and XLNet model, so that the NMT model can fully acquire the knowledge of the XLNet based pre-training model.
- The NMT model learns the output probability distribution of the pre-training model through knowledge distillation when the decoder predicts translation.

2   Background

NMT. NMT model can simulate the translation probability $P(y|x)$ from source language $x = \{x_1, ...x_n\}$ to target language $y = \{y_1, ...y_m\}$, as shown in Eq. 1.

$$P(y_i|y_{<i,x,\theta}) \propto exp\left\{f(y_{i-1}, s_i, c_i; \theta)\right\} \tag{1}$$

Where $y_{<i}$ indicates the translated tokens before the i-th decoding step, θ indicates the parameters of the NMT model. s_i indicates the i-th hidden state of the decoder, c_i indicates the corresponding context of the source language at time t, and $f(\cdot)$ indicates the nonlinear activation function in the current node of the decoder. Given N training sentence pairs $\{x^n, y^n\}_{n=1}^N$, the loss function is defined as Eq. 2.

$$L_{CrossEntropy} = \underset{\theta}{argmax} \sum_{n=1}^{N} logP(y^n|x^n; \theta) \tag{2}$$

Pre-training Model Assisted NMT Method. The pre-training method transfers knowledge from resource-rich tasks to low-resource downstream tasks. However, the NMT method takes the cross entropy between the two languages as the training goal to optimize the parameters, which is significantly different from the monolingual pre-training model.

Therefore, one approach is to use the resource-rich language pre-training model, and then put source language and the target language into the pre-training model to obtain the corresponding word embedding, and use pre-trained word embedding training NMT model. Another approach is to design a new sequence-to-sequence pre-training task to directly realize bilingual mapping in machine translation. Among them, XLM [4], MASS [14] and BART [7] are both cross-lingual pre-training method based on sequence-to-sequence.

3   Method

This section mainly introduces the framework of the autoregressive pre-training assisted NMT model, which including the partial factorization process of the sequence, the NMT model integrating the XLNet pre-training method, and the knowledge distillation method.

3.1   Partial Factorization Sequence Acquisition

For a sentence with n tokens, including $n!$ corresponding factorization sequences. The number of factorization sequences will increase exponentially as the number of tokens increases. Generally, only a portion of the factorization sequence will be encoded. For a factorization sequence, the corresponding maximum likelihood probability $E_{z \sim Z_T}$ can be defined as Eq. 3.

$$\underset{\theta}{max} E_{z \sim Z_T} \left[\sum_{t=1}^{T} logp_\theta\left(x_{z_t}|x_{Z_{<t}}\right)\right] \tag{3}$$

Where x represents the token in the sequence, Z_T denotes all permutation of sequences with length T, and $z \sim Z_T$ represents one of the permutations.

We proposed a partial factorization sampling strategy to relieve computational pressure: for a sentence s, the word at the front of the sentence has fewer corresponding contexts, so there are many candidate sets in prediction. However, the words at the end of the sentence have more corresponding contexts, and there are fewer high-probability candidate sets in prediction, making it easier to predict accurate words.

Therefore, we set an anchor point c on the sentence s and divide a factorization sequence into two sub-factorization sequence y_1 and y_2, which are called non-target sequence and tar-get sequence respec-

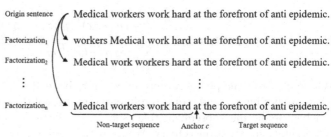

Fig. 1. Partial factorization sampling.

tively. We set a hyper-parameter K so that $\frac{1}{K}$ tokens in the sequence will be predicted. In this paper, K is set to 2. As shown in Eq. 4 (Fig. 1).

$$\frac{|s| - y_1}{|s|} = \frac{1}{K} \tag{4}$$

Through Eq. 4, it can be calculated that K is approximately equal to $\frac{|s|-c}{|s|}$, since we do not need to predict the first c tokens in the sequence, the consumption of computing resources is reduced.

3.2 NMT Model Integrated with Autoregressive Based XLNet

The essence of factorization sequence is to traverse the probability decomposition order of sentences instead of changing the word position order. However, according to the description of Eq. 5, the prediction probability of the target token will not change with the decomposition order.

$$p_\theta (X_i = x | x_{z_{<t}}) = p_\theta (X_j = x | x_{z_{<t}}) = \frac{exp \left(e(x)^T h(x_{z_{<t}}) \right)}{\sum_{x^j} exp \left(e(x')^T h(x_{z_{<t}}) \right)} \tag{5}$$

The representation of each word in Transformer is jointly predicted by word embedding and corresponding positions. However, context representation and current word position information need to be used when predicting the current word, and context representation and current word embedding and position need to be used when predicting subsequent words. The conflict can by solved by introducing two-stream self-attention. Similar to BERT, XLNet still uses $Mask$

to replace the target token, but the *Mask* will not be included in the calculation of the address vector K and the content vector V, the *Mask* only acts as the query vector Q, and the representation of all tokens will not get the information of the *Mask*, thus eliminating the difference between pre-training and fine-tuning caused by the introduction of the *Mask*. Therefore, it is common practice to construct new representation functions g_θ and introduce additional position information z_t to realize the content perception of the corresponding position, as shown in Eq. 6.

$$p_\theta \left(x_{z_t} | x_{z<t} \right) = \frac{exp \left(e\left(x \right)^T g_\theta \left(x_{z<t}, z_t \right) \right)}{\sum_{x'} exp \left(e\left(x' \right)^T g_\theta \left(x_{z<t}, z_t \right) \right)} \tag{6}$$

Where $g(\cdot)$ uses the position representation z_t instead of content representation when predicting x_{z_t}, and requires full representation of the current token (x_{z_t} and z_t when predicting subsequent tokens $x_{z(j,j>t)}$. Two-stream refers to the query representation attention (Query-Att) and the content representation attention (Content-Att), respectively.

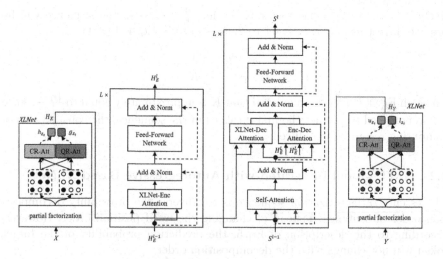

Fig. 2. The architecture of model. The dotted line indicates residual connections, H_X, H_Y and H_E^L denote the autoregressive based XLNet model corresponding to the source language and target language, and the output of the last layer of the NMT encoder.

– Query-Att: Predict the current token using only position information z_t, as shown in Eq. 7.

$$g_{z_t}^{(l)} \leftarrow Att \left(Q = g_{z_t}^{(l-1)}, KV = h_{z<t}^{(l-1)}; \theta \right) \tag{7}$$

– Content-Att: The current position information z_t and the content information $h_{z_t}^{(l-1)}$ are used to predict subsequent tokens, as shown in Eq. 8.

$$h_{z_t}^{(l)} \leftarrow Att\left(Q = h_{z_t}^{(l-1)}, KV = h_{z_{<t}}^{(l-1)}; \theta\right) \tag{8}$$

Where $g_{z_t}^{(l-1)}$ and $h_{z_t}^{(l-1)}$ represent the position and content of the $l-1$ layer to be queried respectively. Content-Att is consistent with the traditional self-attention method.

The two-stream self-attention mechanism can be abstracted as:

– Randomly initialize vector $g_i = w$ in the first layer of Query-Att.
– The Content-Att uses the word vector $h_i = e(x_i)$ and the network weights of the two-streams are shared. Query-Att is removed in the fine-tuning phase, and only the Content-Att is used.

The NMT model framework is shown in Fig. 2, where X and Y represent the domains of the source and target languages, respectively. For each sentence, $x \in X, y \in Y$. The outputs of the pre-trained XLNet-based autoregressive model are $H_X = XLNet(x)$ and $H_Y = XLNet(y)$. The i-th token in sentence x and y represented as $h_{X,i} \in H_X$ and $o_{Y,i} \in H_Y$. H_E^0 indicates word embedding, H_E^l indicates the l-th hidden layer representation. For any $i \in [l_x]$ and $l \in [L]$, the i-th element $\tilde{h}_i^l$ in H_E^l as shown in Eq. 9.

$$\tilde{h}_i^l = att_x(h_i^{l-1}, H_X, H_X), \forall i \in [l_x] \tag{9}$$

Where $att_x(\cdot)$ represents the attention module between the XLNet and NMT model. The output is encoded by the feedforward neural network FNN to obtain H_E^l. The specific calculation method is shown in Eq. 10.

$$H_E^l = (FNN(\tilde{h}_1^l), ..., FNN(\tilde{h}_{l_x}^l)) \tag{10}$$

Where $S_{<t}^l$ represents the hidden state of the i-th decoder layer, before the time step t, the decoder self-attention representation s_t^l can be expressed as Eq. 11.

$$\tilde{s}_t^l = attn_s(s_t^{l-1}, H_Y, H_Y) \tag{11}$$

Where $attn_s(\cdot)$ represents the self-attention model, which is used to learn the internal feature of sentence. In addition, external interaction representation can be divided into encoder-decoder interaction $attn_E$ and encoder/decoder-XLNet model interaction $attn_X$. The final interaction representation $\tilde{\tilde{s}}_t^l$ is obtained by combining these two external attention models. As shown in Eq. 12.

$$\tilde{s}_t^l = \frac{1}{2}(attn_X(\tilde{s}_t^l, H_X, H_X) + attn_E(\tilde{s}_t^l, H_E^L, H_E^L)), s_t^l = FFN(\tilde{s}_t^l) \tag{12}$$

s_t^L is finally obtained through iterative calculation, and then the t-th target word $\tilde{y}_t$ is predicted according to softmax function. We use the negative log-likelihood of the probabilities to generate reference tokens as the loss function L_{CE} for this model, as shown in Eq. 13.

$$L_{CE} = -\sum_{j=1}^{M} log(p(y_j|\hat{y}_{<j}))$$ (13)

Where $\hat{y}_{<j}$ denotes generated tokens, M indicate the length of the sequence. We also use drop-net trick to prevent over-fitting, we set the drop-net rate to 1.0 in this paper.

3.3 Knowledge Distillation Method

In order to learn the output probability distribution of the pre-training model, we also add the knowledge distillation method to jointly train the model. The training objectives include minimizing the cross-entropy between the output of the NMT model and the reference translation, and the relative-entropy between the NMT model and pre-training model. The common practice is to use the output of the pre-trained model as distillation data to optimize the parameters of the NMT model so that a more accurate and smooth translation can be output. The knowledge distillation method is similar to the general cross-entropy method. The difference is that the knowledge distillation method introduces an additional temperature hyper-parameter τ to dynamically adjust the output probability distribution, and appropriately increase the probability of some candidate sets to make the output distribution smoother. The output probability can be defined as Eq. 14.

$$p_{prt} = \frac{exp(z_{prt_i}/\tau)}{\sum_j exp(z_{prt_j}/\tau)}$$ (14)

Where z_{prt_i} represents hidden state representation, the equation also applies to the NMT model. By increasing τ we expose extra information to the NMT model. The calculation of KL divergence is shown in Eq. 15.

$$D_{KL}(p_{prt}||p_{nmt}) = \sum_{i=1}^{N} p_{prt}(i) \cdot log\frac{p_{prt}(i)}{p_{nmt}(j)}$$ (15)

Where p_{prt} and p_{nmt} represent the probabilities of the pre-training model and NMT model respectively, i represents the sentence number. Therefore, we define the KL divergence (relative entropy) loss between the output probability distribution of the pre-trained model and the NMT model, as shown in Eq. 16.

$$L_{RE} = \sum_{i=0}^{N} \tau^2 D_{KL}(p_{prt}||p_{nmt})$$ (16)

Training goal is to minimize the KL divergence loss of pre-training model and the NMT model. Therefore, the loss function of the model can be regarded as the weighted sum of cross-entropy loss (L_{CE}) and relative entropy loss (L_{RE}), as shown in Eq. 17.

$$L = \lambda L_{CE} + (1 - \lambda)L_{RE} \tag{17}$$

Where λ is hyper-parameter and empirically set to 0.5.

4 Experiments

Dataset and Configuration. Our low-resource corpus is all from the CCMT2019 data set, in which Mo-Zh corpus consists of 260 K sentence pairs training set, 1000 sentence pairs verification set and 1000 sentence pairs test set. Ug-Zh corpus consists of 300 K sentence pairs training set, 1000 sentence pairs verification set and 1000 sentence pairs test set. Ti-Zh corpus consists of 150K sentence pairs training set, 500 sentence pairs verification set and 500 sentence pairs test set. We use the directed graph method (DG)-conditional random field method (CRF) to identify and segment the agglutinated language into stem-affix to alleviate the problem of low-frequency words. In addition, we limit the vocabulary to 35K and limit the maximum sentence length to 50 words. We adopt BLEU scores[1] to evaluate the model. Parameters are set as follows: word embedding dimension = 30, number of hidden layer nodes = 512, number of layers = 4, number of heads = 6, dropout = 0.25, batch size = 128, and beam size = 5. The parameters are updated by Stochastic gradient descent algorithm (SGD) with learning rate controlled by Adam. All of the source language use XLNet method[2] to obtain vector representation. We employ single GTX 1080 to train model and obtained by averaging the last 5 checkpoints for task.

Baseline. Our baseline system includes the following:

- Transformer: An seq-to-seq framework based on self-attention, which has the best translation effect[3].
- XLM: A pre-training method based on cross-lingual supervised learning[4].
- MASS: A sequence-to-sequence pre-training method based on BERT[5].
- BART: A denoising sequence-to-sequence pre-training for machine translation[6].

---

[1] https://github.com/moses-smt/mosesdecoder/blob/master/scripts/generic/multi-bleu.perl.
[2] https://github.com/zihangdai/xlnet.
[3] https://github.com/tensorflow/tensor2tensor.
[4] https://github.com/facebookresearch/XLM.
[5] https://github.com/microsoft/MASS.
[6] https://github.com/pytorch/fairseq/tree/master/examples/bart.

4.1 Results and Analysis

As shown in Table 1, the performance of the pre-training model assisted NMT model is generally higher than that of the traditional Transformer model. This fully illustrates the advantages of the pre-training assisted NMT model. Among them, the XLM model iteratively replaces *mask* symbols with high-frequency symbol pairs, resulting in the model being insensitive to language types. MASS has used the

Table 1. Translation results in different languages.

Model	Mo-Zh	Ug-Zh	Ti-Zh
Transformer [15]	27.42	32.62	28.39
XLM [4]	29.53	34.59	29.96
MASS [14]	31.79	35.41	30.84
BART [7]	32.18	36.78	31.55
Ours	**34.98**	**38.02**	**33.46**

transpose mask mechanism to implement the sequence-to-sequence feature learning tasks, making the model have a certain generalization. BART is based on MASS and adds various noises to enrich the semantics. However, these three pre-training assisted NMT models are all based on self-encoding BERT methods. Due to inherent defects, the performance of the model cannot be significantly improved. While our method makes up for the defect, and encodes the source language and target language in an autoregressive mode to realize the translation between different languages. In three low-resource translation tasks, the BLEU scores increased by 7.56, 5.4 and 5.07, respectively.

4.2 Ablation Experiments

We conducted ablation experiments to observe the impact of various components on the performance of the model, including the use of pre-training model (XLNet), partial prediction methods (Partial), knowledge distillation (Knowledge), etc. In addition, in order to verify the impact of each granularity token on

Table 2. The Ablation experiment.

Model	Mo-Zh		Ug-Zh		Ti-Zh	
	Dev	Test	Dev	Test	Dev	Test
Morpheme	26.99	25.27	30.34	28.98	27.19	25.46
Stem-affixes	28.91	27.98	31.78	30.56	27.33	26.1
BPE	29.69	27.42	33.05	32.62	30.16	28.39
+XLNet	34.68	33.14	36.41	35.27	32.54	30.35
+Partial	37.35	34.64	38.39	37.94	34.93	32.76
+Knowledge	37.35	**34.98**	**38.58**	**38.02**	**35.07**	**33.46**

the model, we divided the modeling unit into three types: Morpheme, stem-affix and BPE. BLEU scores of NMT model are shown in Table 2. According to Table 2, although the number of low-frequency words is reduced when morpheme modeling is adopted, but local semantic and order adjustment information is also lost. The different between BPE and stem-affixes method is not obvious, BPE method divides high-frequency byte pairs by the frequency of continuous bytes. The stem-affixes method uses complex rules to extract word-building affixes and restore stem. Although it can obtain morphological feature, but consumes resources. Therefore, we mainly use BPE below.

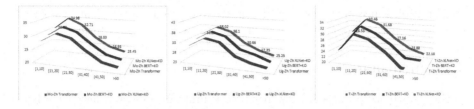

Fig. 3. The BLEU scores in different translation tasks.

When the pre-training model (XLNet) is added, the BLEU scores improved by 5.72, 2.65 and 1.96 respectively in the test sets of three low-resource tasks. The experimental results show that the pre-trained word embedding by XLNet has better representation and polysemous word recognition ability, it can update the word embedding matrix during the iterative training process. The partial prediction method (Partial) predicts part of the sequence token, which is more efficient in language modeling and feature extraction. In addition, the quality of the model after adding knowledge distillation is also significantly improved compared with other methods, it also shows that the NMT model can learn implicit knowledge representation from the pre-training model.

Source	ᠠᠶᠢᠯᠠᠳᠬᠠᠯ ᠨᠢ ᠭᠡᠯᠡᠬᠦᠶᠢᠨ᠂ ᠊ᠸ/ ᠊ᠸᠲᠪᠨ/ ᠠ ᠊ᠣᠳᠲᠠᠷᠬᠠᠢᠨᠸ/ ᠊᠊ᠲᠪᠨ/ᠿ ᠺᠣᠹᠬᠨ ᠁	قارا بۇگۇنمۇ نىستانسسى مىنبىورولوگىيە مامركزمى جقاردى ناگاھلاندۇرۇشى رەڭلىك سپرق يامغۇر.	ཁ་ལོ་བ་འདི་�་ཁ᠂ᡞᢝᢑᢍᢛᠣ᠂ᠬᢝᢛᢛᠴᠬᠣᢛᠯ᠂ᢛᢜᠣ᠂ᢘᢜᢛ ᢜ᠂ᢓ᠂ᢓᢛᢍᢛᢛᢐᢜ
Ref.	经过 多年，你 消除 你们 之 间的 分歧 谈何 容易 。	中央 气象 台 今天 继续 发布 暴雨 橙色 预 警。	这个 司机 是 个 不 遵守 速度 限制 的 人 。
XLM	多年，消除 你们 的 不何 说 来 容易 。	中央的 天气 观测台 持续 地 公布 暴风 雨 警。	车夫 是 这个 速度 限制 逃脱 人 的 。
MASS	多年 以后，你 考虑 到消灭 分裂 不容易 。	中央 天气 市局 监测 站 继续 布告 了 暴风 雨 红色 预警。	这个 车 老板 不 听命 速度 的 受限 。
BART	经过了 很多 年，你 消除 中 间的 分歧 说来 不容易 。	中央 天气 局联合 的 公布 了 暴雨 橙 警 告。	这 司机 不 遵循 超出 速度 人 。
Ours	经过 很多年，你 认为 消除 你们 的 分歧 谈何 容易。	中央 气象 台今日 不断地 发布 暴雨 橙色 预警。	这个 司机 是 不 需要 速度 限制 遵 从 的 人。

Fig. 4. Translation effects of different tasks.

4.3 Case Study

In case study, we mainly observe the BLEU scores of sentences with different lengths and analyze the translation quality of specific examples. As shown in Fig. 3, when the sentence length is between 11 and 20, the model has the best performance, and the BLEU scores in the three low-resource translation tasks are 34.98, 38.02 and 33.46, respectively. With the increase of sentence length, the BLEU scores decreases continuously, and reaches the lowest when it is longer than 50 tokens.

According to Fig. 4, our model significantly improves the translation fluency and faithfulness compared with the translation generated by the pre-training model based on BERT. It can be seen that our method pays more attention to semantic coherence in the process of context generation, and also alleviates the problem of missing translation by improving the length penalty term.

5 Conclusion

In this paper, we proposed a low resource neural machine translation method based on autoregressive pre-training model which combined partial sampling. Compared with various pre-training sequence-to-sequence models, our method improved the context semantic awareness and alleviates the mask independence assumption. The pre-trained word embedding method has better scalability for low-resource neural machine translation. In addition, the method of knowledge distillation provides help for NMT models to learn richer semantic knowledge. Therefore, in the future, we will research more neural machine translation models based on pre-training methods.

References

1. Bahdanau, D., Cho, K., Bengio, Y.: Neural machine translation by jointly learning to align and translate. In: 3rd International Conference on Learning Representations, ICLR 2015, San Diego, CA, USA, 7–9 May 2015, Conference Track Proceedings (2015). http://arxiv.org/abs/1409.0473
2. Chen, M., et al.: Federated learning of n-gram language models. In: Proceedings of the 23rd Conference on Computational Natural Language Learning, CoNLL 2019, Hong Kong, China, 3–4 November 2019. pp. 121–130 (2019). https://doi.org/10.18653/v1/K19-1012
3. Church, K.W.: Word2vec. Nat. Lang. Eng. **23**(1), 155–162 (2017)
4. Conneau, A., Lample, G.: Cross-lingual language model pretraining. In: Wallach, H.M., Larochelle, H., Beygelzimer, A., d'Alché-Buc, F., Fox, E.B., Garnett, R. (eds.) Advances in Neural Information Processing Systems 32: Annual Conference on Neural Information Processing Systems 2019, NeurIPS 2019, 8–14 December 2019, Vancouver, BC, Canada, pp. 7057–7067 (2019). https://proceedings.neurips.cc/paper/2019/hash/c04c19c2c2474dbf5f7ac4372c5b9af1-Abstract.html
5. Devlin, J., Chang, M., Lee, K., Toutanova, K.: BERT: pre-training of deep bidirectional transformers for language understanding. In: Proceedings of the 2019 Conference of the North American Chapter of the Association for Computational Linguistics: Human Language Technologies, NAACL-HLT 2019, Minneapolis, MN, USA, 2–7 June 2019, Volume 1 (Long and Short Papers), pp. 4171–4186 (2019). https://doi.org/10.18653/v1/n19-1423
6. Gehring, J., Auli, M., Grangier, D., Yarats, D., Dauphin, Y.N.: Convolutional sequence to sequence learning. In: Proceedings of the 34th International Conference on Machine Learning, ICML 2017, Sydney, NSW, Australia, 6–11 August 2017, pp. 1243–1252 (2017). http://proceedings.mlr.press/v70/gehring17a.html
7. Lewis, M., et al.: BART: denoising sequence-to-sequence pre-training for natural language generation, translation, and comprehension. In: Jurafsky, D., Chai, J., Schluter, N., Tetreault, J.R. (eds.) Proceedings of the 58th Annual Meeting of the Association for Computational Linguistics, ACL 2020, Online, 5–10 July 2020 pp. 7871–7880. Association for Computational Linguistics (2020). https://doi.org/10.18653/v1/2020.acl-main.703

8. Liu, J., Cheung, J.C.K., Louis, A.: What comes next? Extractive summarization by next-sentence prediction. CoRR abs/1901.03859 (2019), http://arxiv.org/abs/1901.03859
9. Luong, T., Pham, H., Manning, C.D.: Effective approaches to attention-based neural machine translation. In: Proceedings of the 2015 Conference on Empirical Methods in Natural Language Processing, EMNLP 2015, Lisbon, Portugal, 17–21 September 2015. pp. 1412–1421 (2015). https://doi.org/10.18653/v1/d15-1166
10. Pennington, J., Socher, R., Manning, C.D.: Glove: global vectors for word representation. In: Proceedings of the 2014 Conference on Empirical Methods in Natural Language Processing, EMNLP 2014, 25–29 October 2014, Doha, Qatar, A meeting of SIGDAT, a Special Interest Group of the ACL, pp. 1532–1543 (2014). https://doi.org/10.3115/v1/d14-1162
11. Peters, M.E., et al.: Deep contextualized word representations. In: Walker, M.A., Ji, H., Stent, A. (eds.) Proceedings of the 2018 Conference of the North American Chapter of the Association for Computational Linguistics: Human Language Technologies, NAACL-HLT 2018, New Orleans, Louisiana, USA, 1–6 June 2018, Volume 1 (Long Papers). pp. 2227–2237. Association for Computational Linguistics (2018). https://doi.org/10.18653/v1/n18-1202
12. Radford, A., Narasimhan, K., Salimans, T., Sutskever, I.: Improving language understanding by generative pre-training (2018)
13. Salazar, J., Liang, D., Nguyen, T.Q., Kirchhoff, K.: Masked language model scoring. In: Proceedings of the 58th Annual Meeting of the Association for Computational Linguistics, ACL 2020, Online, 5–10 July 2020, pp. 2699–2712 (2020). https://www.aclweb.org/anthology/2020.acl-main.240/
14. Song, K., Tan, X., Qin, T., Lu, J., Liu, T.: MASS: masked sequence to sequence pre-training for language generation. In: Chaudhuri, K., Salakhutdinov, R. (eds.) Proceedings of the 36th International Conference on Machine Learning, ICML 2019, 9–15 June 2019, Long Beach, California, USA. Proceedings of Machine Learning Research, vol. 97, pp. 5926–5936. PMLR (2019). http://proceedings.mlr.press/v97/song19d.html
15. Vaswani, A., et al.: Attention is all you need. In: Advances in Neural Information Processing Systems 30: Annual Conference on Neural Information Processing Systems 2017, 4–9 December 2017, Long Beach, CA, USA, pp. 5998–6008 (2017). http://papers.nips.cc/paper/7181-attention-is-all-you-need
16. Weng, R., Yu, H., Huang, S., Cheng, S., Luo, W.: Acquiring knowledge from pre-trained model to neural machine translation. In: The Thirty-Fourth AAAI Conference on Artificial Intelligence, AAAI 2020, The Thirty-Second Innovative Applications of Artificial Intelligence Conference, IAAI 2020, The Tenth AAAI Symposium on Educational Advances in Artificial Intelligence, EAAI 2020, New York, NY, USA, 7–12 February 2020, pp. 9266–9273. AAAI Press (2020). https://aaai.org/ojs/index.php/AAAI/article/view/6465
17. Yang, Z., Dai, Z., Yang, Y., Carbonell, J.G., Salakhutdinov, R., Le, Q.V.: XLNet: generalized autoregressive pretraining for language understanding. In: Advances in Neural Information Processing Systems 32: Annual Conference on Neural Information Processing Systems 2019, NeurIPS 2019, 8–14 December 2019, Vancouver, BC, Canada, pp. 5754–5764 (2019). http://papers.nips.cc/paper/8812-xlnet-generalized-autoregressive-pretraining-for-language-understanding
18. Zhu, J., et al.: Incorporating BERT into neural machine translation. In: 8th International Conference on Learning Representations, ICLR 2020, Addis Ababa, Ethiopia, 26–30 April 2020. OpenReview.net (2020). https://openreview.net/forum?id=Hyl7ygStwB

Combining Improvements for Exploiting Dependency Trees in Neural Semantic Parsing

Defeng Xie⬛, Jianmin Ji$^{(\boxtimes)}$⬛, Jiafei Xu⬛, and Ran Ji⬛

University of Science and Technology of China, Heifei, China
jianmin@ustc.edu.cn, {ustcxdf,xujiafei,jiran}@mail.ustc.edu.cn

Abstract. The dependency tree of a natural language sentence can capture the interactions between semantics and words. However, it is unclear whether those methods which exploit such dependency information for semantic parsing can be combined to achieve further improvement and the relationship of those methods when they combine. In this paper, we examine three methods to incorporate such dependency information in a Transformer based semantic parser and empirically study their combinations. We first replace standard self-attention heads in the encoder with parent-scaled self-attention (PASCAL) heads, i.e., the ones that can attend to the dependency parent of each token. Then we concatenate syntax-aware word representations (SAWRs), i.e., the intermediate hidden representations of a neural dependency parser, with ordinary word embedding to enhance the encoder. Later, we insert the constituent attention (CA) module to the encoder, which adds an extra constraint to attention heads that can better capture the inherent dependency structure of input sentences. Transductive ensemble learning (TEL) is used for model aggregation, and an ablation study is conducted to show the contribution of each method. Our experiments show that CA is complementary to PASCAL or SAWRs, and PASCAL + CA provides state-of-the-art performance among neural approaches on ATIS, GEO, and JOBS.

Keywords: Semantic parsing · PASCAL · SAWRs · CA

1 Introduction

Semantic parsing is the task of mapping natural language sentences into target formal representations, which is crucial for many natural language processing (NLP) applications. With the rapid development of deep learning, various neural semantic parsers [5,6,10,17,19] have been implemented based on sophisticated sequence-to-sequence (seq2seq) models [4] with Transformer [20]. Note that syntax information of natural language sentences can be used as clues and restrictions for semantic parsing. In this paper, we focus on incorporating syntax information from dependency trees of natural language sentences in neural semantic parsers.

© Springer Nature Switzerland AG 2021
D. N. Pham et al. (Eds.): PRICAI 2021, LNAI 13032, pp. 58–72, 2021.
https://doi.org/10.1007/978-3-030-89363-7_5

The dependency tree [15,16] of a natural language sentence shows which words depend on which other words in a tree structure that can capture the interactions between the semantics and natural language words. In specific, the dependency tree can be considered as the explicit structure prior to predicting corresponding semantic structures in semantic parsing. Then the encoder of a seq2seq based semantic parser can be enhanced by information from dependency trees. On the other hand, dependency trees can be efficiently generated by existing parsers, like Stanford Parser [14], with promising results. [24] encodes such dependency trees in a graph-based neural network for semantic parsing and achieves a great improvement in performance, which indicate potential advantages of incorporating dependency trees in semantic parsers.

It is unclear whether those methods which exploit such dependency information for semantic parsing can be combined for further improvement. In this paper, we examine three such methods for a Transformer encoder of a seq2seq based semantic parser and empirically study their combinations. In specific, we first follow the idea of parent-scaled self-attention (PASCAL) [2], which replaces standard self-attention heads in the encoder with ones that can attend to the dependency parent of each token. We also concatenate syntax-aware word representations (SAWRs) [27], i.e., the intermediate hidden representations of a neural dependency parser, with ordinary word embedding to enhance the Transformer encoder. At last, we insert constituent attention (CA) module [22] to the Transformer encoder, which adds an extra constraint to attention heads to follow tree structures that can better capture the inherent dependency structure of input sentences. We also aggregate multiple models of these methods for inference following transductive ensemble learning (TEL) [23].

We first implement a baseline semantic parser that is based on a simple seq2seq model consisting of a 2-layer Transformer encoder and a 3-layer Transformer decoder. Then we evaluate the performance of the above three methods and their combinations on ATIS, GEO, and JOBS datasets. We also evaluate aggregated versions of these methods by TEL. The experimental results show that the combination of PASCAL and CA provides state-of-the-art performance among neural approaches, which can also be easily implemented.

The main contributions of this paper are:

- We introduce three methods by applying PASCAL, SAWRs, or CA to incorporate dependency trees in the Transformer encoder of a seq2seq semantic parser. We show that all three methods can improve the performance.
- We evaluate the combinations of the three methods and show that they can be fruitfully combined with better performance. The result show that CA is complementary to PASCAL or SAWRs.
- We implement TEL for our models. We show that TEL is effective for these improvements on semantic parsing.
- We implement the combination of PASCAL and CA based on a simple seq2seq semantic parser. We show that this parser can be implemented easily and achieves state-of-the-art performance among neural approaches on ATIS, GEO, and JOBS datasets.

2   Related Work

Neural semantic parsing has achieved promising results in recent years, where various sophisticated seq2seq models have been applied. Many works focus on integrating the syntax formalism of target representation into the decoder of the seq2seq model. For instance, hierarchical tree decoders are applied in [5,18] to take into account the tree structure of the logical expression. Sequence-to-tree (seq2tree) model [5] updates the decoder by hierarchical tree-long short-term memory (Tree-LSTM), which helps the model to utilize the hierarchical structure of logical forms. [18,19,25] first map a natural language sentence into an abstract syntax tree (AST), then serve it as an intermediate meaning representation and incorporate it with grammar rules, finally parse the AST to the corresponding target logic form.

On the other hand, there are few works on incorporating syntax information of input natural language sentences to the encoder. Graph-to-sequence (graph2seq) model [24] constructs a graph encoder to exploiting rich syntactic information for semantic parsing.

It has shown that syntax information of input natural language sentences can be helpful for the encoder in neural machine translation (NMT) tasks [1]. In specific, [2] places parent-scaled self-attention (PASCAL) heads, which can attend to the dependency parent of each token, in the Transformer encoder to improve the accuracy of machine translation. [27] concatenates syntax-aware word representations (SAWRs), i.e., the intermediate hidden representations of a neural dependency parser, with ordinary word embedding to enhance the Transformer encoder. [22] introduces constituent attention (CA) module, which adds an extra constraint to attention heads to follow tree structures that can better capture the inherent dependency structure of input sentences. In this paper, we examine these ideas in semantic parsing and empirically study their combinations.

3   Three Improvements

In this section, we specify three improvements to incorporate dependency trees in the Transformer encoder of a seq2seq semantic parser.

As illustrated in Fig. 1, a dependency tree describes the structure of the sentence by relating words in binary relations, which can be efficiently generated by corresponding parsers, like Stanford Parser[1]. [15,16] have shown that dependency trees can be used to construct target logical forms for semantic parsing. In this paper, we focus on exploiting information from structures of these dependency trees to enhance the encoder of a neural semantic parser. Note that, we ignore the labels of corresponding dependency relations here, like 'obj', 'case', and 'conj' in the example.

---

[1] https://nlp.stanford.edu/software/stanford-dependencies.shtml.

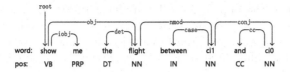

Fig. 1. A dependency tree

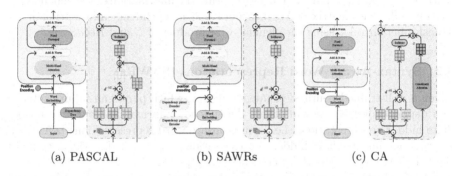

(a) PASCAL   (b) SAWRs   (c) CA

Fig. 2. Overviews of model structures for three improvements.

3.1 Parent-Scaled Self-attention (PASCAL)

Parent-scaled self-attention (PASCAL) is first introduced in [2] for NMT tasks. The main idea of PASCAl is to replace standard self-attention heads in the encoder with ones that can attend to the dependency parent of each token. Here we apply the idea in semantic parsing and evaluate its effectiveness.

In specific, the standard scaled dot-product attention mechanism in Transformer is defined as follows,

$$Attention(Q, K, V) = softmax(\frac{QK^\top}{\sqrt{d}})V, \tag{1}$$

where Q, K, V, d denote the query matrix, the key matrix, the value matrix, and the dimension of K respectively, as in [20]. We also denote $\frac{QK^\top}{\sqrt{d}}$ as *HeadScore*.

In PASCAL, *HeadScore* is replaced by its element-wise product with the distance matrix D, which is generated from each token's dependency parent in the dependency tree by utilizing a Gaussian distribution[2]. In particular, the attention mechanism used in PASCAL is defined as,

$$Attention(Q, K, V) = softmax(\frac{QK^\top}{\sqrt{d}} \odot D)V, \tag{2}$$

where $\odot$ denotes the element-wise product operation.

---

[2] The detailed procedure for computing D is specified in [2]. We omit the procedure due to the space limitation.

We implement the improvement by applying PASCAL in the Transformer encoder of a baseline seq2seq semantic parser, which consists of a 2-layer Transformer encoder and a 3-layer Transformer decoder. The model structure of the improved encoder is illustrated in Fig. 2(a), where the blue box on the right denotes the distance matrix D.

In this improvement, we first generate the dependency tree of an input sentence by a dependency parser. Then we capture the information of the dependency tree by its distance matrix D. We incorporate such dependency information in the Transformer encoder using the element-wise product of D and *HeadScore*.

3.2   Syntax-Aware Word Representations (SAWRs)

Given a well-trained neural dependency parser, which parses an input sentence to a dependency tree, we can obtain dependency information from its intermediate hidden representations, i.e., syntax-aware word representations (SAWRs). In [27], such intermediate hidden representations are specified as the outputs of the BiLSTM layer in the BiAffine dependency parser [7].

In this paper, we first train a neural dependency parser based on the model proposed in [8], which is simpler and performs better. We also specify SAWRs as the outputs of the BiLSTM layer in this dependency parser. Then we concatenate such SAWRs with ordinary word embedding to enhance the Transformer encoder for the semantic parser. In particular, the input of the Transformer encoder is improved from WE + PE to (SAWRs $\oplus$ WE) + PE, where $\oplus$ denotes the concatenate operation, WE and PE denote the word embedding and the position encoding, respectively.

The model structure of the improved encoder is illustrated in Fig. 2(b), where two yellow boxes on the left corner denote the pre-trained neural dependency parser. We will specify the training process for the dependency parser in Sect. 5.3.

In this improvement, we first train a neural dependency parser. Then we capture the information of the dependency tree by its intermediate hidden representations, i.e., SAWRs. We incorporate such dependency information in the Transformer encoder by concatenating SAWRs with WE.

3.3   Constituent Attention (CA)

[22] introduces Constituent Attention (CA) module, which adds an extra constraint to attention heads to follow tree structures, that can better capture the inherent dependency structure of input sentences. Here we apply the idea in semantic parsing and evaluate its effectiveness.

In specific, the attention mechanism in Transformer is improved to

$$Attention(Q, K, V) = \left(C \odot softmax(\frac{QK^\top}{\sqrt{d}}) \right) V, \tag{3}$$

where $\odot$ denotes the element-wise product operation, Q, K, V, d denote the same as above, and C denotes the constituent prior generated from CA module.

In particular, C is a symmetric matrix that describes the probabilities of whether two words belonging to the same constituent[3].

The model structure of the improved encoder is illustrated in Fig. 2(c), where the blue round frame and the blue box on the right denote CA module. We will specify the training process for the improved model in Sect. 5.

In this improvement, we add CA module to the Transformer encoder, which introduces the constituent prior C to attention heads. Such constraint encourages the attention heads to follow tree structures, which helps the encoder to capture the inherent dependency information of input sentences.

4   Combining Improvements

In this section, we consider all possible combinations of the three improvements and integrate the combinations into a single model. We also try to further improve the performance by using the ensemble learning method, i.e., TEL.

A combination $A + B$ denotes the seq2seq model that applies both improvements A and B in its encoder. In specific, both combinations PASCAL + SAWRs and SAWRs + CA can be directly implemented, as SAWRs does not affect the implementation of either PASCAL or CA. For combinations PASCAL + CA and PASCAL + SAWRs + CA, we need to improve the attention mechanism in Transformer to

$$Attention(Q, K, V) = \left(C \odot softmax(\frac{QK^\top}{\sqrt{d}} \odot D) \right) V. \tag{4}$$

Model structures of the improved encoders for all combinations are illustrated in Fig. 3.

In this paper, we use Transductive Ensemble Learning (TEL) [23] to aggregate multiple individual models for better performance. Note that, TEL is applied under the transductive setting, i.e., the model can observe the input sentences in the test set. TEL is first introduced for NMT tasks. Here we implement the idea in semantic parsing and evaluate its effectiveness.

In specific, following TEL, we first use all individual models to predict the input sentences from the validation and test sets, and construct a synthetic corpus by using these predicted results as corresponding labels. Then we select the model with the best performance on the validation set[4] and fine-tune this model on the generated synthetic corpus. At last, we use the fine-tuned model in the inference phase. Notice that, TEL is efficient and easy to be implemented, as only one model is selected for inference.

In the following, we use $A + TEL$ to denote the model that applies TEL for ensemble learning based on A.

---

[3] The detailed procedures for constructing CA module and computing C are specified in [22]. We omit the procedures due to the space limitation.

[4] The datasets of GEO and JOBS are small and do not contain validation sets. Then parameters and the selected model are cross-validated on their training sets.

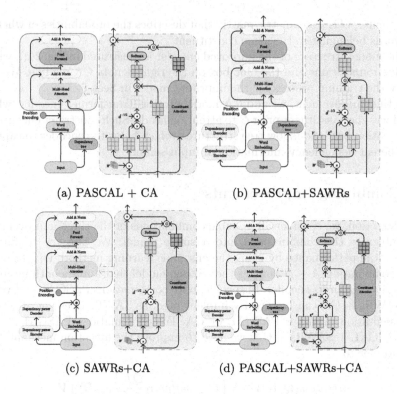

(a) PASCAL + CA   (b) PASCAL+SAWRs

(c) SAWRs+CA   (d) PASCAL+SAWRs+CA

Fig. 3. Overviews of model structures for combinations.

5   Experiments

5.1   Datasets

We evaluate the three improvements, their combinations, and TEL on three famous datasets for semantic parsing, i.e., ATIS, a set of 5,410 queries to a flight booking system, GEO, a set of 880 queries to a database of U.S. geography, and JOBS, a set of 640 queries to a database of job listings.

We follow the standard train-dev-test split of these datasets and use the preprocessed version as specified in [5]. We also adopt Stanford CoreNLP package [14] to do the tokenization. Then the target formal representations of these datasets are all λ-calculus expressions here.

5.2   Evaluation Metrics

We use Exact Match [17] and Tree Exact Match (Tree Match) [19] to evaluate the performance of different models. In particular, Exact Match computes the percentage of sentences whose predicted results are exactly the same as their labeled target logic forms, i.e., λ-calculus expressions. However, in some cases, the order of formulas can be equivalently changed in λ-calculus expressions. For instance, the order of two formulas in conjunction can be equivalently reversed. Then Tree Match is introduced to avoid these spurious errors by considering the tree structures of resulting logic forms. Note that, there is little previous work using Tree Match for JOBS. Then we only use Exact Match for JOBS.

5.3 Implementation Details

The baseline model for the semantic parser considered here is a seq2seq model consisting of a 2-layer Transformer encoder and a 3-layer Transformer decoder. We trained this model with the hyperparameters listed in Table 1, whose parameters were chosen based on the performance of the model on the validation set for ATIS and cross-validated on the training sets for GEO and JOBS.

Table 1. Hyperparameters for the baseline model.

Hyperparameter	Value
Word embedding dimension	512
Position encoding dimension	512
Transformer head number	8
Transformer attention dimension	512
Transformer feed forward dimension	2048
Transformer activation	ReLU
Dropout rate	0.1
Batch size	16
Learning rate	1e−4

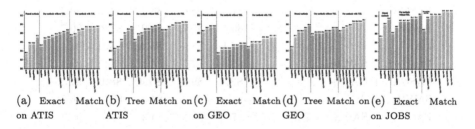

(a) Exact Match on ATIS (b) Tree Match on ATIS (c) Exact Match on GEO (d) Tree Match on GEO (e) Exact Match on JOBS

Fig. 4. Comparison of models on different datasets.

Notice that, the three improvements and their combinations do not affect these hyperparameters for the baseline model. Then all the models considered in our experiments were trained based on such hyperparameters for their baseline part.

Networks in our experiments are implemented in PyTorch and trained with the AdamW optimizer with its default parameters. We trained every model for 45 (resp. 250) epochs for ATIS (resp. GEO and JOBS) on two GPUs, i.e., Nvidia GeForce 2080Ti and Nvidia RTX 3090, which takes around 2 (resp. 3) hours for ATIS (resp. GEO and JOBS).

Table 2. Experimental results.

Model	ATIS		GEO		JOBS
Evaluation metric	Exact match	Tree match	Exact match	Tree match	Exact match
Pre-neural methods					
ZC07 [26]	84.6	–	86.1	–	79.3
FUBL [12]	82.8	–	88.6	–	–
DCS [13]	–	–	87.9	–	**90.7**
KCAZ13 [11]	–	–	89.0	–	–
WKZ14 [21]	**91.3**	–	**90.4**	–	–
TISP [29]	84.2	–	88.9	–	85.0
Neural methods					
Seq2Seq [5]	–	84.2	–	84.6	87.1
Seq2Tree [5]	–	84.6	–	87.1	90.0
JL16 [10]	83.3	–	89.3*	–	–
TranX [25]	–	86.2	–	88.2	–
Coarse2fine [6]	–	87.7	–	88.2	–
Seq2Act [3]	85.5	–	88.2*	–	–
Graph2Seq [24]	85.5	–	88.9	–	**91.2**
AdaNSP [28]	–	88.6	–	88.9	–
GNN [17]	**87.1**	–	**89.3**	–	–
TreeGen [19]	–	**89.1**	–	**89.6**	–
Our methods without TEL					
Baseline	85.0	86.2	83.2	87.5	87.9
PASCAL	87.5	88.6	85.0	88.2	90.7
SAWRs	86.6	87.7	85.0	87.9	90.7
CA	87.1	88.6	**85.4**	**88.9**	91.4
PASCAL + SAWRs	86.8	87.5	84.3	88.2	89.3
PASCAL + CA	**88.4**	89.1	**85.4**	**88.9**	92.1
SAWRs + CA	88.0	**89.5**	84.3	87.9	90.7
PASCAL + SAWRs + CA	87.7	89.3	84.3	87.9	91.4
Our methods with TEL					
Baseline + TEL	87.3	88.4	84.6	88.2	88.6
PASCAL + TEL	88.6	89.5	86.8	90.4	92.1
SAWRs + TEL	88.4	89.1	86.8	**90.7**	92.1
CA + TEL	89.1	90.0	**87.1**	90.4	**92.9**
PASCAL + SAWRs + TEL	87.5	88.4	85.7	89.3	91.4
PASCAL + CA + TEL	**89.2**	**90.2**	**87.1**	90.4	**92.9**
SAWRs + CA + TEL	89.1	**90.2**	85.7	88.9	**92.9**
PASCAL + SAWRs + CA + TEL	89.1	90.0	85.7	89.6	92.1

* Denotation Match [10] is used.

Table 3. Numbers of parameters and time costs per training epoch for our models.

Model	Number of parameters (M)	Time (s) ATIS	GEO	JOBS
Baseline	20.27	5.78	0.78	0.63
PASCAL	20.27	7.77	0.99	0.83
SAWRs	22.14	7.94	1.05	0.88
CA	20.42	7.89	1.07	0.87
PASCAL + SAWRs	22.14	9.69	1.19	1.03
PASCAL + CA	20.42	9.06	1.10	0.96
SAWRs + CA	22.29	9.49	1.26	1.06
PASCAL + SAWRs + CA	22.29	11.75	1.45	1.25

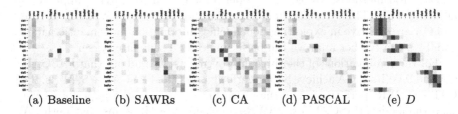

(a) Baseline   (b) SAWRs   (c) CA   (d) PASCAL   (e) D

Fig. 5. Heat maps of corresponding self-attention heads for each model and the distance matrix D.

In SAWRs, a neural dependency parser needs to be pre-trained to obtain its intermediate hidden representations. In this paper, we implement such a dependency parser based on the model in [8]. We first adopt Stanford CoreNLP package [14] to obtain the dependency trees and the corresponding part-of-speech tagging sequences. Then we use these dependency trees as labels for these sequences and train the dependency parser based on this synthetic dataset. it eliminates the need of manual work for labeling dependency data of ATIS,GEO or JOBS.

We use AdamW as the optimizer and set the learning rate as $1e-4$ for the training. We applied the ensemble learning method TEL to further improve the performance of models. We also tried the conventional ensemble method [9]. However, it did not perform well in our experiments.

5.4 Results

Table 2 summarizes the performance of our models in datasets, where 'Baseline' denotes the baseline model without any improvements, and 'PASCAL' (reps. 'SAWRs' and 'CA') denotes the model that applies the improvement PASCAL (resp. SAWRs and CA) on the baseline model. We also illustrate the results in Fig. 4.

The experimental results show that all three improvements can improve the performance of the baseline model. Although the baseline model is very simple,

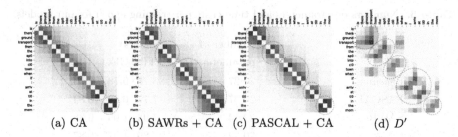

(a) CA	(b) SAWRs + CA	(c) PASCAL + CA	(d) D'

Fig. 6. Heat maps of corresponding constituent prior C for 'CA', SAWRs + CA, PAS-CAL + CA, and D'.

the models 'PASCAL', 'SAWRs', and 'CA' still achieve good performance among other neural methods. Moreover, the performance can be further improved by applying TEL. These results show that the improvements PASCAL, SAWRs, and CA are effective in exploiting dependency information for semantic parsing, and TEL can further improve the performance of a semantic parser.

For the combinations of the three improvements, we find out that PASCAL + CA and SAWRs + CA achieve better performance than PASCAL + SAWRs. PAS-CAL + SAWRs performs better than 'Baseline'. However, it even performs worse than the model 'PASCAL' or 'SAWRs' in some cases. It seems that both PAS-CAL and SAWRs obtain similar information from the dependency tree. Then the combination of both does not provide additional benefits. On the other hand, PAS-CAL + CA, SAWRs + CA, PASCAL + SAWRs + CA achieve good performance among all neural methods. This implies that the dependency information obtained from CA is complementary to the one from PASCAL or SAWRs. PASCAL + CA is much simpler than SAWRs + CA and PASCAL + SAWRs + CA. Then we suggests applying the combination of PASCAL and CA on the Transformer based seq2seq semantic parser. The performance of these combinations can also be further improved by applying TEL. These results show that CA is complementary to PASCAL and SAWRs, PASCAL + CA provides state-of-the-art performance among neural methods, and TEL can further improve the performance.

Notice that, our methods do not perform well for Exact Match on GEO. This is mainly due to the facts that the size of GEO is small and Exact Match causes spurious errors. We can observe that our methods perform well for Tree Match on GEO.

We also compare the training costs of the three improvements and their combinations. Table 3 summarizes numbers of parameters and time costs per training epoch on ATIS for our models. Note that, the size of 'PASCAL', 'CA', or PASCAL + CA is almost the same as 'Baseline'. 'SAWRs' and the combinations with it introduce a few additional parameters for 'Baseline'. The time cost per training epoch is slightly increased when an improvement is applied to 'Baseline' and a combination requires more time. Notice that, PASCAL + CA achieves state-of-the-art performance with the similar size of 'Baseline' and a slight increase in time cost.

5.5   Visual Analysis

In this section, we try to analyze what has been learned to help the baseline model by applying each improvement and what has been learned for CA and combinations with it.

We first visualize the heat map of the weights on V, i.e., the attention weights of tokens for the input sentence, which are obtained from the self-attention heads of the last layer in the encoder for each model. Figure 5 illustrates such heat maps for 'Baseline', 'SAWRs', 'CA', and 'PASCAL'. Figure 5(e) also illustrates the heat map of the distance matrix D obtained from the dependency tree of the sentence, as specified in Sect. 3.1. Notice that, the heat map for 'PASCAL' is similar to the one of D due to Eq. (2). We can also observe that, different from the heat map for 'Baseline', the ones for 'SAWRs' and 'CA' are more similar to the heat map for 'PASCAL'. This implies that both SAWRS and CA tend to encourage the self-attention heads to follow the structure of the dependency tree.

On the other hand, we also visualize the heat map of the constituent prior C used in CA. Figure 6 illustrates heat maps of corresponding constituent priors for 'CA', SWARs + CA, and PASCAL + CA. Notice that, C is a symmetrical matrix. Then we can generate a symmetrical matrix D' from the distance matrix D of the sentence by $D' = \frac{D+D^\top}{2}$. Figure 6(d) also illustrates the heat map of D'. We can observe that, the heat maps for PASCAL + CA and SWARs + CA are more and more similar to the one of D'. This implies that the combinations PASCAL + CA and SWARs + CA help the constituent prior C to capture information from the dependency tree of the sentence, and PASCAL + CA captures more information. This observation partially explains the reason why PASCAL + CA performs better.

6   Conclusion

In this paper, we implement three improvements, i.e., PASCAL, SAWRs, and CA, to incorporate the dependency information of input sentences in a Transformer encoder for a seq2seq semantic parser. We show that all three improvements are effective in exploiting such dependency information for semantic parsing with a slight increase in training cost. We also examine the combinations of these improvements. We observe that both PASCAL and SAWRs obtain similar information from the dependency tree, and the combination of both does not provide additional benefits. We find out that CA is complementary to PASCAL and SAWRs, and PASCAL + CA provides state-of-the-art performance among neural approaches on ATIS, GEO, and JOBS datasets. Moreover, PASCAL + CA can be implemented easily with a slight increase in training costs. We provide visual analysis that tries to explain why PASCAL + CA performs better among other improvements and combinations. We also implement TEL for the models and show that TEL is effective for these improvements on semantic parsing.

Acknowledgment. The work is partially supported by the National Key Research and Development Program of China (No. 2018AAA0100500), CAAI-Huawei MindSpore Open Fund, Anhui Provincial Development and Reform Commission 2020 New Energy Vehicle Industry Innovation Development Project "Key System Research and Vehicle Development for Mass Production Oriented Highly Autonomous Driving", and Key-Area Research and Development Program of Guangdong Province 2020B0909050001.

References

1. Bahdanau, D., Cho, K.H., Bengio, Y.: Neural machine translation by jointly learning to align and translate. In: Proceedings of the 3rd International Conference on Learning Representations (2015)
2. Bugliarello, E., Okazaki, N.: Enhancing machine translation with dependency-aware self-attention. In: Proceedings of the 58th Annual Meeting of the Association for Computational Linguistics, pp. 1618–1627. Association for Computational Linguistics (2020)
3. Chen, B., Sun, L., Han, X.: Sequence-to-action: end-to-end semantic graph generation for semantic parsing. In: Proceedings of the 56th Annual Meeting of the Association for Computational Linguistics, pp. 766–777. Association for Computational Linguistics (2018)
4. Cho, K., van Merrienboer, B., Gulcehre, C., Bougares, F., Schwenk, H., Bengio, Y.: Learning phrase representations using RNN encoder-decoder for statistical machine translation. In: Proceedings of the 2014 Conference on Empirical Methods in Natural Language Processing (2014)
5. Dong, L., Lapata, M.: Language to logical form with neural attention. In: Proceedings of the 54th Annual Meeting of the Association for Computational Linguistics, pp. 33–43. Association for Computational Linguistics (2016)
6. Dong, L., Lapata, M.: Coarse-to-fine decoding for neural semantic parsing. In: Proceedings of the 56th Annual Meeting of the Association for Computational Linguistics, pp. 731–742. Association for Computational Linguistics (2018)
7. Dozat, T., Manning, C.D.: Deep biaffine attention for neural dependency parsing. In: Proceedings of the 5th International Conference on Learning Representations (2017)
8. Dozat, T., Manning, C.D.: Simpler but more accurate semantic dependency parsing. In: Proceedings of the 56th Annual Meeting of the Association for Computational Linguistics, pp. 484–490. Association for Computational Linguistics (2018)
9. Hansen, L.K., Salamon, P.: Neural network ensembles. IEEE Trans. Pattern Anal. Mach. Intel. **12**(10), 993–1001 (1990)
10. Jia, R., Liang, P.: Data recombination for neural semantic parsing. In: Proceedings of the 54th Annual Meeting of the Association for Computational Linguistics, pp. 12–22. Association for Computational Linguistics (2016)
11. Kwiatkowski, T., Choi, E., Artzi, Y., Zettlemoyer, L.: Scaling semantic parsers with on-the-fly ontology matching. In: Proceedings of the 2013 Conference on Empirical Methods in Natural Language Processing, pp. 1545–1556 (2013)
12. Kwiatkowski, T., Zettlemoyer, L., Goldwater, S., Steedman, M.: Lexical generalization in CCG grammar induction for semantic parsing. In: Proceedings of the 2011 Conference on Empirical Methods in Natural Language Processing, pp. 1512–1523. Association for Computational Linguistics (2011)

13. Liang, P., Jordan, M.I., Klein, D.: Learning dependency-based compositional semantics. Comput. Linguist. **39**(2), 389–446 (2013)
14. Manning, C.D., Surdeanu, M., Bauer, J., Finkel, J.R., Bethard, S., McClosky, D.: The stanford CoreNLP natural language processing toolkit. In: Proceedings of 52nd Annual Meeting of the Association for Computational Linguistics: System Demonstrations, pp. 55–60. Association for Computational Linguistics (2014)
15. Reddy, S., et al.: Transforming dependency structures to logical forms for semantic parsing. Trans. Assoc. Comput. Linguist. **4**, 127–140 (2016)
16. Reddy, S., Täckström, O., Petrov, S., Steedman, M., Lapata, M.: Universal semantic parsing. In: Proceedings of the 2017 Conference on Empirical Methods in Natural Language Processing, pp. 89–101 (2017)
17. Shaw, P., Massey, P., Chen, A., Piccinno, F., Altun, Y.: Generating logical forms from graph representations of text and entities. In: Proceedings of the 57th Annual Meeting of the Association for Computational Linguistics, pp. 95–106. Association for Computational Linguistics (2019)
18. Sun, Z., Zhu, Q., Mou, L., Xiong, Y., Li, G., Zhang, L.: A grammar-based structural CNN decoder for code generation. In: Proceedings of the 33rd AAAI Conference on Artificial Intelligence, pp. 7055–7062 (2019)
19. Sun, Z., Zhu, Q., Xiong, Y., Sun, Y., Mou, L., Zhang, L.: TreeGen: a tree-based transformer architecture for code generation. In: Proceedings of the 34th AAAI Conference on Artificial Intelligence, pp. 8984–8991 (2020)
20. Vaswani, A., et al.: Attention is all you need. In: Advances in Neural Information Processing Systems, pp. 5998–6008. MIT Press (2017)
21. Wang, A., Kwiatkowski, T., Zettlemoyer, L.: Morpho-syntactic lexical generalization for CCG semantic parsing. In: Proceedings of the 2014 Conference on Empirical Methods in Natural Language Processing, pp. 1284–1295. Association for Computational Linguistics (2014)
22. Wang, Y.S., Lee, H.Y., Chen, Y.N.: Tree transformer: integrating tree structures into self-attention. In: Proceedings of the 2019 Conference on Empirical Methods in Natural Language Processing and the 9th International Joint Conference on Natural Language Processing, pp. 1061–1070 (2019)
23. Wang, Y., Wu, L., Xia, Y., Qin, T., Zhai, C., Liu, T.Y.: Transductive ensemble learning for neural machine translation. In: Proceedings of the 34th AAAI Conference on Artificial Intelligence, pp. 6291–6298 (2020)
24. Xu, K., Wu, L., Wang, Z., Yu, M., Chen, L., Sheinin, V.: Exploiting rich syntactic information for semantic parsing with graph-to-sequence model. In: Proceedings of the 2018 Conference on Empirical Methods in Natural Language Processing, pp. 918–924. Association for Computational Linguistics (2018)
25. Yin, P., Neubig, G.: TRANX: a transition-based neural abstract syntax parser for semantic parsing and code generation. In: Proceedings of the 2018 Conference on Empirical Methods in Natural Language Processing, pp. 7–12. Association for Computational Linguistics (2018)
26. Zettlemoyer, L.S., Collins, M.: Online learning of relaxed CCG grammars for parsing to logical form. In: Proceedings of the 2007 Joint Conference on Empirical Methods in Natural Language Processing and Computational Natural Language Learning, pp. 678–687 (2007)
27. Zhang, M., Li, Z., Fu, G., Zhang, M.: Syntax-enhanced neural machine translation with syntax-aware word representations. In: Proceedings of the 2019 Conference of the North American Chapter of the Association for Computational Linguistics: Human Language Technologies, pp. 1151–1161 (2019)

28. Zhang, X., He, S., Liu, K., Zhao, J.: AdaNSP: uncertainty-driven adaptive decoding in neural semantic parsing. In: Proceedings of the 57th Annual Meeting of the Association for Computational Linguistics, pp. 4265–4270. Association for Computational Linguistics (2019)
29. Zhao, K., Huang, L.: Type-driven incremental semantic parsing with polymorphism. In: Proceedings of the 2015 Conference of the North American Chapter of the Association for Computational Linguistics: Human Language Technologies, pp. 1416–1421 (2015)

Deep Semantic Fusion Representation Based on Special Mechanism of Information Transmission for Joint Entity-Relation Extraction

Wenqiang Xu$^{(\boxtimes)}$, Shiqun Yin$^{(\boxtimes)}$, Junfeng Zhao, and Ting Pu

Faculty of Computer and Information Science, Southwest University,
Chongqing 400715, China

Abstract. Joint entity and relation extraction is still a challenging problem in natural language processing, which goal is to extract all possible relational triplets from original texts. Nevertheless, previous work rarely considered the integration of relation information to capture fine-grained correlations over token and relation spaces before extracting the entity pair, resulting in the unreasonable matching of entities and relations. In this paper, we propose a deep semantics fusing representation method based on a special mechanism of information transmission for joint entity relation extraction (DSFR). Specially, we called this special information transmission mechanism with a gate structure as UMIT, and then fuse the fine-grained information of tokens and relations by stacking multiple layers of UMIT. Finally, we extract the head and tail entities of a sentence under a certain relation by sequence labeling. Experiments on two publicly available New York Times (NYT) and WebNLG corpus show that our proposed approaches can effectively extract overlapping triplets and achieve better performance.

Keywords: Joint entity relation extraction · Information transmission mechanism · Gate architecture · Overlapping triplet

1 Introduction

As a critical task in the area of natural language processing (NLP), entity and relation extraction has attracted increasingly more attention. Given a sentence, the task goal is to identify entity pairs from the original text and extract any number of semantic relations between entity pairs, resulting in a triple in the form of (*head-entity, relation, tail-entity*). The extracted triples are used widely in a great amount of downstream NLP tasks, such as large-scale knowledge graph construction [1] and question answering [2].

Early work [3–6] on relational triples extraction has achieved promising results. However, most of the existing methods ignore the scenario where a sentence contains a triplet of overlapping entities and multiple relations between

D. N. Pham et al. (Eds.): PRICAI 2021, LNAI 13032, pp. 73–85, 2021.
https://doi.org/10.1007/978-3-030-89363-7_6

74   W. Xu et al.

entity pairs. As shown in Fig. 1, the triples with different relationships between the same entity pair are called EntityPairOverlap (EPO), and the triples with the same entity between multiple entity pairs are called SingleEntityOverlap (SEO).

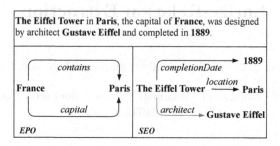

Fig. 1. Examples of EntityPairOverlap (EPO) and SingleEntityOverlap (SEO) overlapping triplets.

To address the overlapping issue, [7] proposed an end-to-end relation extraction model, which considers the interaction between named entities and relations through relation-weighted graph convolutional networks. [8] introduced a hierarchical reinforcement learning framework to enhance the interaction between entities and relations. The above works begins by recognizing head entities and then creating joint decoding strategies to extract the corresponding tail entities and relations.

We recognized that the meaning of the sentence, not the target entity, normally is determined by the relation. [9–11] proposed a relation-based joint extraction model, which takes relation classification as the first step of its joint extraction strategy. The relation information is introduced as prior knowledge to minimize the model's extraction of semantically unrelated entities, thereby reducing redundant operations. Therefore, how to effectively introduce relations information is crucial to the final performance. We realized that different words in a sentence should contribute differently to the representation of a certain type of relation. Similarly, if there are multiple relations in a sentence, different relations will also lead to different sentence representations. Therefore, the joint extraction of entity and relations will benefit from the close interaction between words and relations.

In this paper, we propose a special mechanism of information transmission (UMIT) to effectively interact relation and word information, thereby achieving mutual enhancement between word and relation representation. Afterward, through stacking multiple layers of UMIT, we perform a deep fusion of relations and words information and update their representation. After that, we use the method of sequence labeling to extract the entity pairs that exist in the sentence under a certain relation, which effectively solves the triple overlap problem. We further use a relation-level negative sampling strategy to avoid most of the redundant decoding processes during training. Eventually, we introduce focal loss [12] to pay greater attention to those harder training samples.

This work has the following main contributions:

- We propose a joint entity and relation extraction model called DSFR, which extracts fine-grained semantic features between relations and sentences to guide the entity recognition process.
- We design a special mechanism of information transmission that uses a gate mechanism to achieve multi-channel transmission of information to obtain enhanced representations of relations and tokens, and the stacking of this mechanism is used to update the representation of relations and tokens.
- We implement a negative relational sampling strategy to reduce redundant operations and use the focal loss to alleviate the out-off balance between positive and negative samples. Our model has proved its effectiveness on two public datasets.

2   Related Work

The traditional pipeline method is mainly based on the existing LSTM [13, 14], CNN [15,16], and GCN [17], and then improves the performance of the model by changing the network structure or input features of the model. To alleviate the error propagation problem in the pipeline method, subsequent works proposed joint learning of entities and relations, through the close interaction between entity recognition and relation classification, the performance is often better than the pipeline method. [4] used the attention mechanism together with Bi-LSTM for joint entity relation extraction for the first time. [5] proposed an entity relation extraction method based on a new tagging strategy, which completely turned the joint learning model of named entity recognition and relation classification into a sequence tagging problem.

However, most of the past methods cannot correctly handle the relational triplet scenes containing multiple overlapping entities in the sentence. Recently, some methods have been proposed specifically to overcome this problem. [9] proposed a Seq2Seq model with a copy mechanism for joint entity and relation extraction tasks, which sequentially extracts triples in sentences. [10] decomposed the joint entity relation extraction task into two interrelated subtasks, first extracts all head entities, and then identifies the tail entities and relations corresponding to each head entity. [18] proposed a novel cascading binary framework, which first obtains the subject entities in the sentence, and then identifies all possible relations and object entities corresponding to each subject entity. [11] proposed a relation-based attention network, which uses the attention mechanism of relation perception to construct a specific sentence representation for each relation, and then performs sequence annotation to extract its corresponding head and tail entities.

3   Task Definition and Tagging Scheme

Given a sentence as $S = \{w_1, w_2, ..., w_m\}$, where w_i is the i-th word, the goal of the relation extraction task is to identify all possible triples $\{\pi = (h, r, t)|h, t \in E, r \in R\}$ in the sentence, where (h, t) represents the mentioned entity pair, and r represents the relations between them, E and R are entity sets and predefined relation sets respectively.

In this paper, the predefined relations will be used as prior information for our method, and then the head and tail entities corresponding to a certain relationship in the sentence will be extracted. The data tagging scheme is similar to [11], as shown in Fig. 2. Combine the head and tail roles $\{H, T\}$ in the triple with the typical BIES signs (Begin, Inside, End, Single) as our entity tag. We only annotate the head and tail entities corresponding to the relation, and the remaining words are assigned the label O. If there are multiple relations in a sentence, separate corresponding tag sequences will be generated based on the different relations.

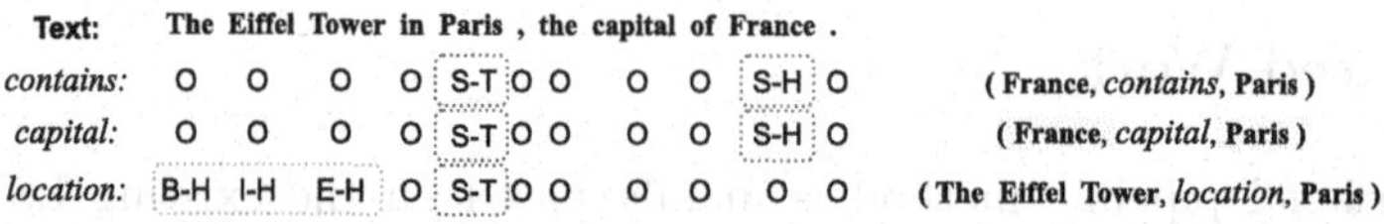

Text:	The Eiffel Tower in Paris , the capital of France .	
contains:	O O O O S-T O O O O S-H O	(France, *contains*, Paris)
capital:	O O O O S-T O O O O S-H O	(France, *capital*, Paris)
location:	B-H I-H E-H O S-T O O O O O O	(The Eiffel Tower, *location*, Paris)

Fig. 2. An example for tagging scheme. For different given relations, a corresponding tag sequence will be generated.

4   The Proposed Model

In this section, we will introduce the overall framework of DSFR in detail. Figure 3 shows an example overview of DSFR under a certain relation r_k, which consists mainly of three parts:

- **Representations of Token and Relation** Given a sentence and a predefined relation type, we encode the tokens and the relation as a vector, respectively.
- **Deep Semantics Fusion** Here, we stack multiple layers of UMIT for multi-channel transmission with gate structure to achieve further integration of tokens and relations representation.
- **Triple Extraction** The sentence representation will be directly combined with the current relation $\tilde{r}_k$, and then the head and tail entities will be directly extracted.

4.1   Representations of Token and Relation

Token Representations. Given a sentence containing m words, we need to map each word in the sentence to a real-valued embedding to express its semantic and syntactic meaning. In addition, we also used character embedding, which is generated by encoding using a Convolutional Neural Network (CNN). Then, the input representations of each token are a concatenation of character embeddings, part-of-speech (POS) embeddings, and glove embeddings [19]. In this way, the input vector $X \in \mathbb{R}^{m*d_s}$ of a sentence can be obtained, where $d_s = d_w + d_p + d_c$, and d_w, d_p, d_c represent the dimension of word embedding, POS embedding and character embedding respectively.

We utilize BiLSTM as the basic encoding component. Given a sequence of input vectors $X = [x_1, x_2, ..., x_m]$, BiLSTM can be used to output hidden representations $H \in \mathbb{R}^{m*d_h}$ as

$$H = BiLSTM(X) \tag{1}$$

Relation Representations. For each predefined relation label, we initialize it randomly, and represent it with a high-dimensional vector, then pass through a linear map layer to finally get the representation of each relation.

$$[\boldsymbol{r_1}, \boldsymbol{r_2}, ..., \boldsymbol{r_n}] = Linear([r_1, r_2, ..., r_n]) \tag{2}$$

where n is the number of predefined relations, r_i is random initialization vector of the i-th relation in the set of predefined relations, $\boldsymbol{r_i} \in R^{d_h}$ is obtained by mapping the vector r_i through $Linear$, $Linear$ is a linear mapping function.

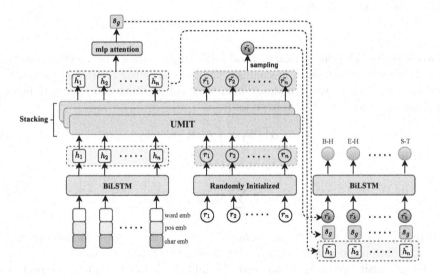

Fig. 3. The overall structure of our proposed DSFR for joint entity and relation extraction.

4.2 Deep Semantics Fusion

4.2.1 Special Mechanism of Information Transmission

We have constructed a special mechanism of information transmission (UMIT) based on a gate architecture to extract key semantic information. UMIT is composed of two $\mathcal{F}$ units and a gate structure. Through this architecture, we capture the semantic association between two types of nodes and then update their vector representations respectively. As shown in the left part of Fig. 4, given the semantic representation of two types of nodes: $\{u_i\}_{i=1}^m$ and $\{v_j\}_{j=1}^n$. The node u_i aggregates another type of node $\{v_j\}_{j=1}^n$ information through two $\mathcal{F}$ units, and then update the node u_i, so that the node representation incorporate more information and is more suitable for specific tasks. Following that, we elaborate on the two $\mathcal{F}$ units and the gate structure.

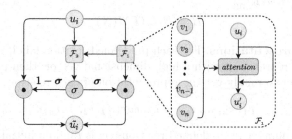

Fig. 4. The overall structure of UMIT. The left part is the overall architecture of UMIT, which includes two $\mathcal{F}$ units and a gate structure, and the right is the detailed internal structure of the $\mathcal{F}_1$ unit.

Two $\mathcal{F}$ units. The calculation method for $\mathcal{F}_1$ **unit** is shown in the right panel of Fig. 4. We use the attention mechanism [20] to achieve the preliminary semantic fusion of the two types of nodes. Then, to avoid gradient disappearing during training, we add a residual connection:

$$a_{ij} = \alpha^T[W_1 u_i + b_1; W_2 v_j + b_2] \tag{3}$$

$$\lambda_{ij} = softmax(a_{ij}) \tag{4}$$

$$u_i' = u_i + \sum_{j=1}^n \lambda_{ij}(W_3 v_j + b_3) \tag{5}$$

where $W_1, W_2, W_3 \in \mathbb{R}^{d_h * d_h}, b_1, b_2, b_3 \in \mathbb{R}^{d_h}, \alpha^T \in \mathbb{R}^{2*d_h}$ are trainable weights, λ_{ij} is the attention weight, $u_i, v_j \in \mathbb{R}^{d_h}$ means two types of nodes.

For $\mathcal{F}_2$ **unit**, we need to integrate the information of u_i' and u_i, we perform cascade operation after linear transformation of them. The calculation formula is as follows:

$$\beta_i = (W_4 u_i + b_4) \oplus (W_5 u_i' + b_5) \tag{6}$$

where $\oplus$ is concatenating operation, $W_4, W_5 \in \mathbb{R}^{d_h * d_h}, b_4, b_5 \in \mathbb{R}^{d_h}$ are trainable weights.

A Gate Mechanism. The above two $\mathcal{F}$ units preliminary finished the information fusion between two types of nodes. Now, we use a gate mechanism to allow information to be transmitted in multiple channels. At the same time, we added noise to the gate mechanism to enable it more robust.

$$\sigma = \sigma(\beta_i \odot (1 + \varepsilon)) \tag{7}$$

$$\tilde{u}_i = (1 - \sigma) \odot u_i + \sigma \odot u'_i \tag{8}$$

where σ indicates the element-wise sigmoid activation function, which returns values from 0 to 1, therefore the results σ can be viewed as percentage of information to keep. $\odot$ is element-wise production. ε represents a uniform random distribution of $[-0.1, 0.1]$.

4.2.2 Stacking Multiple Layers of UMIT

We briefly express the above general architecture (see Sect. 4.2.1) as follows: $\tilde{u}_i = UMIT(u_i, \{v_j\}_{j=1}^n)$. We perform deep semantics fusion by feeding token and relation features into a deep network that contains a carefully designed mechanism of information transmission. Given a sentence features $H = \{h_1, h_2, ..., h_m\}$ of length m, for a certain relation node r_i, then obtain relation node r_i's updated representation $\tilde{r}_i$ through UMIT. Similarly, the token node performs similar operations to obtain the updated node vector representation. A residual connection is also added here to avoid gradient disappearing during training.

$$r_i^1 = r_i^0 + UMIT(r_i^0, \{h_j^0\}_{j=1}^m) \tag{9}$$

$$h_j^1 = h_j^0 + UMIT(h_j^0, \{r_i^0\}_{i=1}^n) \tag{10}$$

When we get the representation of the new word node and the relation node through a layer of UMIT, we will further update these two nodes according to the new representation. The update process of layer $s(> 1)$ can express as:

$$r_i^s = r_i^{s-1} + UMIT(r_i^{s-1}, \{h_j^{s-1}\}_{j=1}^m) \tag{11}$$

$$h_j^s = h_j^{s-1} + UMIT(h_j^{s-1}, \{r_i^{s-1}\}_{i=1}^n) + UMIT(h_j^{s-1}, \{r_i^s\}_{i=1}^n) \tag{12}$$

where $r_i^s \in \mathbb{R}^{d_h}$ is the updated representation of the initial relation node $r_i^{s-1} \in \mathbb{R}^{d_h}$, $h_j^s \in \mathbb{R}^{d_h}$ is the updated representation of the initial token node $h_j^{s-1} \in \mathbb{R}^{d_h}$.

So far, we have obtained the sentence representation $S = \{h_1^s, h_2^s, ..., h_m^s\}$ that fused with the relational information and the relation nodes representation $R = \{r_1^s, r_2^s, ..., r_n^s\}$ that contains the word information.

4.3 Triple Extraction

To evaluate the importance of the tokens in each sentence, the more important tokens are assigned more attention weight. Here, we use MLP attention [21] to adjust sentence representation. Take the sentence S as an example.

$$\hbar_i = MLP_i(\tilde{h}_i) \tag{13}$$

$$\gamma_i = \frac{exp(\hbar_i)}{\sum_{j=1}^{m} exp(\hbar_j)} \tag{14}$$

$$s_g = \sum_{k=1}^{m} \gamma_k \tilde{h}_k \tag{15}$$

where $\hbar_i$ is a scalar, $i \in [1, m]$; γ_i is the attention weight of $\tilde{h}_i$, computed by Softmax function; s_g is the sentence global representation by matrix calculation on attention weights.

Note that the extracted entities will be directly combined with the current relation r_k, thus there are no extra relation classification operations in our model. $\tilde{r}_k$ is the reserved relational features of r_k^s. We concatenate $\tilde{h}_i$, $\tilde{r}_k$ and s_g to obtain the final representation of the i-th word.

$$s_g = tanh(W_s s_g + b_s) \tag{16}$$

$$\tilde{r}_k = W_k r_k^s + b_k \tag{17}$$

$$h_i^k = [\tilde{h}_i; \tilde{r}_k; s_g] \tag{18}$$

where $W_s, W_k \in \mathbb{R}^{d_h * d_h}, b_s, b_k \in \mathbb{R}^{d_h}$ are trainable weights, [;] is concatenating operation. Consequently, sentence S under a certain relation r_k is thus represented as $S^k = \{h_1^k, h_2^k, ..., h_n^k\}$ and will be used for the entity extraction process.

Here we run another BiLSTM network on the word sequence S^k, and map each of the words to the relation space, finally perform sequence labelling to extract its corresponding entities:

$$o_i^k = BiLSTM(W_h h_i^k + b_h) \tag{19}$$

$$p(y_i^k) = Softmax(W_o \cdot o_i^k + b_o) \tag{20}$$

where $i \in [1, m]$. $W_h \in \mathbb{R}^{3d_h * d_h}$, $b_h \in \mathbb{R}^{d_h}$, $b_o \in \mathbb{R}^{n_l}$ are trainable weights. Here $W_o \in \mathbb{R}^{2d_h * n_l}$ and d_h indicates the dimension of the BiLSTM hidden state, n_l indicates the number of entity labels. $p(y_i^k)$ indicates the probability of i-th word's predicted label under relation r_k.

4.4   Training

We adopt a relational negation sampling strategy, which is to randomly select n_{neg} relations from the negation set of the current sentence, where n_{neg} is a hyperparameter. Therefore, for a sentence S with n_{pos} positive relations, the model will generate a total of $n_s = n_{pos} + n_{neg}$ tag sequence when decoding.

However, we discovered that while the negative relation sampling strategy will help to mitigate the issue of a positive and negative sample ratio imbalance to some degree, there will still be situations where the loss is hard to converge. Therefore, we use the focal loss to not only adjust the weight of positive and negative samples but also control the weight of samples that are difficult to classify.

$$\mathcal{FL} = -\frac{1}{n_s * m} \sum_{k=1}^{n_s} \sum_{i=1}^{m} \delta(1 - p(y_i^k))^\gamma log(p(y_i^k)) \tag{21}$$

where the values of γ and δ are 2 and 1 respectively. δ is used to control the weight of positive and negative samples. By setting the hyperparameter γ, the weight of easy-to-classify samples is reduced, so that the model can focus more on difficult-to-classify samples during training.

5   Experiments

5.1   Dataset and Experimental Settings

We evaluate the model on two public datasets, New York Times(NYT) and WebNLG. Statistics of the two datasets are shown in Table 1. We set the dimension of word embedding $d_w = 300$, POS embedding $d_{pos} = 30$, character embedding $d_c = 50$, and relation embedding $d_r = 300$. All of these embeddings are initialized randomly, except that the word embedding uses a 300-dimensional glove vector. The window size of CNN for the character-based word feature vector is set to 3, the maximum of words is set to 10, and the number of filters is 50. Hidden State of the encoder BiLSTM, attention, gate and the decoder BiLSTM are all set to 300 dimensions. The sentence-level relational negative sampled number n_{neg} is set to 4. We use the Adam optimizer to optimize our model. The training batch size is 16, and the learning rate is 0.0001. We apply a dropout mechanism to the embedding layer with a rate of 0.3 to avoid overfitting, and UMIT's stacking layer number s is set to 2.

Table 1. Statistics about the datasets.

DataSet	NYT		WebNLG	
	Train	Test	Train	Test
Normal	37013	3266	1596	246
EPO	9782	978	227	26
SEO	14735	1297	3406	457
ALL	56195	5000	5019	703
Relation	24		246	

5.2   Baselines and Evaluation Metrics

We compare our model with several strong state-of-the-art model: **NovelTagging** [5], **CopyRE** [9], **GraphRel** [7], **ETL-Span** [10], **CasRel** [18], **RSAN** [11]. We report the standard micro Precision (Prec.), Recall (Rec.), and F1-score as in line with baselines. The predicted triplet is deemed right if and only if the relation and the two corresponding entities are correct.

5.3   Experimental Results

As shown in Table 2, experimental results demonstrates that our model's comprehensive performance F1 value is higher than that of all baseline models, positive to [11] 1.2% on NYT and 2.4% on WebNLG respectively. For Precision on the WebNLG dataset, ours' precision is only 1.8% lower than the highest [10], but ours' recall is 3.3% higher than it. Compared with the other baseline models, ours' precision, recall and F1 are superior. Therefore, it is proved that our work is effective and the comprehensive performance of our proposed model is outstanding.

Table 2. Results of different methods on NYT and WebNLG datasets.

Method	NYT			WebNLG		
	Prec.	Rec.	F1	Prec.	Rec.	F1
$NovelTagging$	0.624	0.371	0.42	0.525	0.193	0.283
$CopyRE$	0.61	0.566	0.587	0.377	0.364	0.371
$GraphRel$	0.639	0.6	0.619	0.447	0.411	0.429
HRL	0.781	0.771	0.776	–	–	–
ETL-$Span$	0.855	0.717	0.78	0.843	0.82	0.831
$CasRel_{LSTM}$	0.842	0.83	0.836	**0.869**	0.806	0.837
$RSAN$	0.857	0.836	0.846	0.805	0.838	0.821
DSFR	**0.869**	**0.847**	**0.858**	0.851	**0.839**	**0.845**

6   Analysis

6.1   Ablation Study

To demonstrate the effectiveness of each component, we remove one particular component at a time to understand its impact on the performance, using the best performing model on the NYT dataset. Concretely, we investigated character embedding, POS embedding, the gate mechanism (replaced with the tanh activation function), token node update and relation node update representation respectively. Table 3 shows the results. We find that the character-level representations are helpful to capture the morphological and dealing with OOV words. When we remove POS embedding, the score drops by 0.11, which indicates POS embeddings in the input layer effectively provides the sentence with additional syntactic detail. The value of F1 drops to 85% when the word node update is removed, demonstrating the importance of fusing relation and word representations.

6.2   Parameter Analysis

We determine the size of the negative sampling strategy n_{neg}. Experiments have found that when n_{neg} is greater than 4, the positive and negative samples will be seriously unbalanced, which will make the model more difficult to converge. So we set $n_{neg} = 4$. At the same time, we found that after replacing NLL loss with focal loss, the model convergence speed will be about 30% faster. To determine the number of layers of the UMIT stack, we studied the results of using different layers of UMIT on the NYT validation set. All models are trained for 50 epochs. Table 4 shows the results of different layers. If $s = 0$, which means to replace UMIT with a simple attention mechanism. We can observe that the result of $s = 3$ is the best, but it will take up more memory, so we set $s = 2$.

Table 3. Ablation tests on the NYT dataset.

Model	Precision	Recall	F1
DSFR	**0.869**	**0.847**	**0.858**
-Character embedding	0.862	0.845	0.853
-POS embedding	0.86	0.841	0.85
-Gate mechanism	0.844	0.841	0.842
-Word node update	0.850	0.843	0.846
-Relation node update	0.848	0.839	0.843
-focal loss	0.857	0.839	0.848

Table 4. The F1-score (%) corresponding to the number of layers of UMIT.

Number	F1-score
$s = 0$(attention)	82.8
$s = 1$	83.6
$s = 2$	84.5
$s = 3$	84.8

6.3 Analysis on Different Sentence Types

We follow [9] and perform further experiments on the NYT dataset to check our DSFR's ability to handle multiple triplets. Normal, SingleEntityOverlap (SEO), and EntityPairOverlap (EPO) are the three types of test sentences based on different overlapping instances. The detailed results on three different overlapping patterns are presented in Fig. 5. In contrast, the proposed DSFR model has achieved some performance improvements on all three overlapping modes. We attribute the improvement to the following fact: the deep integration of token and relation representation will mine some semantic information. At the same time, the focal loss will pay more attention to those harder training samples. Another observation is that [10] still performs best in Normal class, but our

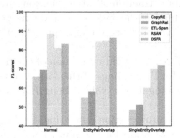

Fig. 5. F1-score of extracting triples from sentences with different overlapping pattern.

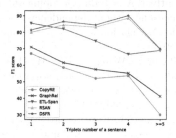

Fig. 6. F1-score of extracting triples from sentences with different number of triples.

DSFR has improved some effects compared to [11], enhancing the ability to extract Normal class.

We also compare how well the models extract multiple triplets from a sentence. The sentences in the NYT test set are divided into five sub-categories, each with a different number of triplets: 1, 2, 3, 4 and $\geq$5. Figure 6 shows that DSFR outperforms the baseline in terms of the total number of triplets in the sentence. When there are multiple triples in a sentence, DSFR is still better than [11].

7   Conclusion

This paper proposed a deep semantic fusion method for joint entity and relation extraction tasks and proves the effectiveness of the method in experiments. We used a special transmission mechanism of information(UMIT), which can effectively realize the interaction of relation and token information, and then perform deep semantic fusion to achieve the purpose of mutual enhancement between token and relation representation. Experiments are conducted on the NYT and WebNLG corpus show that our proposed model DSFR has achieved great improvements.

Acknowledgment. This work is supported by the Science & Technology project (41008114, 41011215, and 41014117).

References

1. Luan, Y., He, L., Ostendorf, M., Hajishirzi, H.: Multi-task identification of entities, relations, and coreference for scientific knowledge graph construction. In: Proceedings of the 2018 Conference on Empirical Methods in Natural Language Processing, pp. 3219–3232 (2018)
2. Yang, W., et al.: End-to-end open-domain question answering with bertserini. In: Proceedings of the 2019 Conference of the North American Chapter of the Association for Computational Linguistics (Demonstrations), pp. 72–77 (2019)
3. Goyal, A., Gupta, V., Kumar, M.: Recent named entity recognition and classification techniques: a systematic review. Comput. Sci. Rev. **29**, 21–43 (2018)
4. Katiyar, A., Cardie, C.: Going out on a limb: joint extraction of entity mentions and relations without dependency trees. In: Proceedings of the 55th Annual Meeting of the Association for Computational Linguistics (vol. 1: Long Papers), pp. 917–928 (2017)
5. Zheng, S., Wang, F., Bao, H., Hao, Y., Zhou, P., Xu, B.: Joint extraction of entities and relations based on a novel tagging scheme. In: Proceedings of the 55th Annual Meeting of the Association for Computational Linguistics (vol. 1: Long Papers), pp. 1227–1236 (2017)
6. Li, X., et al.: Entity-relation extraction as multi-turn question answering. In: Proceedings of the 57th Annual Meeting of the Association for Computational Linguistics, pp. 1340–1350 (2019)

7. Fu, T.J., Li, P.H., Ma, W.Y.: Graphrel: modeling text as relational graphs for joint entity and relation extraction. In: Proceedings of the 57th Annual Meeting of the Association for Computational Linguistics, pp. 1409–1418 (2019)
8. Takanobu, R., Zhang, T., Liu, J., Huang, M.: A hierarchical framework for relation extraction with reinforcement learning. In: Proceedings of the AAAI Conference on Artificial Intelligence, vol. 33, pp. 7072–7079 (2019)
9. Zeng, X., Zeng, D., He, S., Liu, K., Zhao, J.: Extracting relational facts by an end-to-end neural model with copy mechanism. In: Proceedings of the 56th Annual Meeting of the Association for Computational Linguistics (vol. 1: Long Papers), pp. 506–514 (2018)
10. Yu, B., et al.: Joint extraction of entities and relations based on a novel decomposition strategy. ECAI (2020)
11. Yuan, Y., Zhou, X., Pan, S., Zhu, Q., Song, Z., Guo, L.: A relation-specific attention network for joint entity and relation extraction. In: International Joint Conference on Artificial Intelligence 2020, pp. 4054–4060. Association for the Advancement of Artificial Intelligence (AAAI) (2020)
12. Lin, T.Y., Goyal, P., Girshick, R., He, K., Dollár, P.: Focal loss for dense object detection. In: Proceedings of the IEEE International Conference on Computer Vision, pp. 2980–2988 (2017)
13. Socher, R., Huval, B., Manning, C.D., Ng, A.Y.: Semantic compositionality through recursive matrix-vector spaces. In: Proceedings of the 2012 Joint Conference on Empirical Methods in Natural Language Processing and Computational Natural Language Learning, pp. 1201–1211 (2012)
14. Zhang, S., Zheng, D., Hu, X., Yang, M.: Bidirectional long short-term memory networks for relation classification. In: Proceedings of the 29th Pacific Asia conference on Language, Information and Computation, pp. 73–78 (2015)
15. Zeng, D., Liu, K., Lai, S., Zhou, G., Zhao, J.: Relation classification via convolutional deep neural network. In: Proceedings of COLING 2014, the 25th International Conference on Computational Linguistics: Technical Papers, pp. 2335–2344 (2014)
16. Zhu, J., Qiao, J., Dai, X., Cheng, X.: Relation classification via target-concentrated attention CNNs. In: Liu, D., Xie, S., Li, Y., Zhao, D., El-Alfy, E.S. (eds.) International Conference on Neural Information Processing. LNCS, vol. 10635, pp. 137–146. Springer, Cham (2017). https://doi.org/10.1007/978-3-319-70096-0_15
17. Guo, Z., Zhang, Y., Teng, Z., Lu, W.: Densely connected graph convolutional networks for graph-to-sequence learning. Trans. Assoc. Comput. Linguist. **7**, 297–312 (2019)
18. Wei, Z., Su, J., Wang, Y., Tian, Y., Chang, Y.: A novel cascade binary tagging framework for relational triple extraction. In: Proceedings of the 58th Annual Meeting of the Association for Computational Linguistics, pp. 1476–1488 (2020)
19. Pennington, J., Socher, R., Manning, C.D.: Glove: global vectors for word representation. In: Proceedings of the 2014 Conference on Empirical Methods in Natural Language Processing (EMNLP), pp. 1532–1543 (2014)
20. Bahdanau, D., Cho, K., Bengio, Y.: Neural machine translation by jointly learning to align and translate. arXiv preprint arXiv:1409.0473 (2014)
21. Dixit, K., Al-Onaizan, Y.: Span-level model for relation extraction. In: Proceedings of the 57th Annual Meeting of the Association for Computational Linguistics, pp. 5308–5314 (2019)

Exploiting News Article Structure
for Automatic Corpus Generation
of Entailment Datasets

Jan Christian Blaise Cruz[1], Jose Kristian Resabal[2], James Lin[1],
Dan John Velasco[1], and Charibeth Cheng[1(✉)]

[1] De La Salle University Manila, Taft Avenue, Malate, 1004 Manila, Philippines
{jan_christian_cruz,james_lin,dan_velasco,charibeth.cheng}@dlsu.edu.ph
[2] University of the Philippines Diliman, Quezon Hall, 1101 Quezon City, Philippines
jkresabal@up.edu.ph

Abstract. Transformers represent the state-of-the-art in Natural Language Processing (NLP) in recent years, proving effective even in tasks done in low-resource languages. While pretrained transformers for these languages can be made, it is challenging to measure their true performance and capacity due to the lack of hard benchmark datasets, as well as the difficulty and cost of producing them. In this paper, we present three contributions: First, we propose a methodology for automatically producing Natural Language Inference (NLI) benchmark datasets for low-resource languages using published news articles. Through this, we create and release NewsPH-NLI, the first sentence entailment benchmark dataset in the low-resource Filipino language. Second, we produce new pretrained transformers based on the ELECTRA technique to further alleviate the resource scarcity in Filipino, benchmarking them on our dataset against other commonly-used transfer learning techniques. Lastly, we perform analyses on transfer learning techniques to shed light on their true performance when operating in low-data domains through the use of degradation tests.

Keywords: Low-resource languages · Automatic corpus creation ·
Transformer neural networks

1 Introduction

In recent years, Transformers [25] have begun to represent the state-of-the-art not only in common NLP tasks where they have cemented their reputation, but also in the context of tasks within low-resource languages. Using Transformers, advancements have been done in various low-resource tasks, including low-resource translation [8,20], classification [7,21], summarization [14], and many more.

Transformers and transfer learning techniques in general owe their wide adaptation in low-resource language tasks to the existence of abundant unlabeled

D. N. Pham et al. (Eds.): PRICAI 2021, LNAI 13032, pp. 86–99, 2021.
https://doi.org/10.1007/978-3-030-89363-7_7

corpora available. While labeled datasets may be scarce to perform tasks in these languages, unlabeled text is usually freely available and can be scraped from various sources such as Wikipedia, news sites, book repositories, and many more. Pretraining allows transfer learning techniques to leverage learned priors from this unlabeled text to robustly perform downstream tasks even when there is little task-specific data to learn from [5,13].

However, while it is possible to produce large pretrained models for transfer learning in low-resource languages, there is a challenge in properly gauging their performance in low-resource tasks. Most, if not all Transformers that are pretrained and released open-source are evaluated with large, commonly-used datasets. In low-resource languages, these datasets may not exist. Due to this, it is often hard to properly benchmark a model's true performance when operating in low-data domains.

While it is possible to remedy this by constructing hard datasets in these languages, added concerns have to be addressed.

Dataset construction is slow and cost-prohibitive. For hard tasks such as various natural language inference and understanding tasks, datasets are usually sized around 500,000 samples and more [1,4,27]. This would entail a large enough budget to hire annotators to write text samples, and a different set of annotators to write labels. This process is also slow and may take months to finish. In that span of time, stronger techniques may have been created that require more difficult datasets to accurately assess them. In addition, once the dataset has been solved, harder datasets are needed to properly gauge further, succeeding methods.

This creates a need for a method to produce benchmark datasets for low-resource languages that is quick and cost effective, while still capable of generating tasks that are challenging for high-capacity models such as Transformers.

In this paper, we present the following contributions:

- We propose an automatic method to generate Natural Language Inference (NLI) benchmark datasets from a corpus of news articles.
- We release **NewsPH-NLI**, the first sentence entailment benchmark dataset in the low-resource Filipino language, created using the method we propose.
- We produce pretrained Transformers based on the ELECTRA pretraining scheme to further alleviate resource scarcity in Filipino.
- We perform benchmarks and analyses on commonly-used transfer learning techniques to properly and accurately gauge their true performance in low-data domains.

Our method has a number of advantages. First, since our method is automatic, it evades the issue of time and cost. This also allows datasets created this way to be updated regularly as news is released everyday. Second, given that news is freely available and published online even in low-resource languages, text data for producing benchmark datasets will be easy to source. Lastly, given that we generate sentence entailment tasks within the domain of news, our method will produce sufficiently challenging datasets to properly gauge the performance of large Transformers.

2   Methodology

In this section, we outline our experimental setups and methodology. First, we describe our proposed methodology for producing benchmark NLI datasets in any language, using our NewsPH-NLI dataset as an example. Second, we outline the creation of ELECTRA models in Filipino. Lastly, we outline our methodology for analysis using degradation tests.

2.1   NLI Datasets from News Articles

The creation of large datasets for NLI is often difficult, time-consuming, and cost-prohibitive. It may also be not be feasible in low-data and low-resource domains due to the lack of pre-encoded text data that can immediately be annotated.

We propose the use of news articles for automatically creating benchmark datasets for NLI because of two reasons. First, news articles commonly use single-sentence paragraphing, meaning every paragraph in a news article is limited to a single sentence [10,11]. Second, straight news articles follow the "inverted pyramid" structure, where every succeeding paragraph builds upon the premise of those that came before it, with the most important information on top and the least important towards the end [2,16,23]. A figure illustrating the inverted pyramid can be found in Fig. 1.

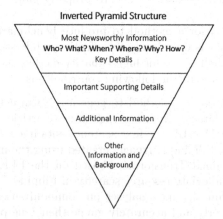

Fig. 1. Inverted pyramid structure of straight news articles. The most important facts are at the top with succeeding paragraphs containing facts of less and less importance. The structure of news articles makes succeeding paragraphs build up on the information of prior paragraphs. Figure taken from [22]

Due to the inverted pyramid structure, we can assume that every succeeding paragraph (our "hypothesis") entails the paragraph preceding it (our "premise"). This can be exploited to produce multiple samples of entailments from a single news article. This way, using a corpus of straight news articles, we can produce a large number of samples of entailments to make up an NLI corpus.

Contradictions, on the other hand, are more difficult to produce. To automatically make contradiction samples, we first randomly sample two news articles from the pool of collected news articles, then randomly sample one paragraph from each article to serve as our premise-hypothesis pair. To ensure that the produced pair is a contradiction, we must first make sure that the two randomly-sampled articles have two different topics. To do this, we train a Doc2Vec [17] model on all of the collected news articles. Afterwards, we then cluster the most similar articles. When sampling articles for contradictions, we sample from two different clusters to ensure that the topics are different.

One limitation of our proposed methodology is that it can only generate entailments and contradictions, as "neutral" premise-hypothesis pairs can only be obtained through manual annotation by humans. This lack of a third label makes the generated datasets easier as compared to standard NLI datasets with three labels. While a 2-label classification task is easier than a 3-label classification task, the generated dataset will still be harder than a standard single-sentence classification problem (like sentiment classification) as the model will have to be able to encode inter-dependent information between the sentence pairs.

In addition, there is a chance that an auto-generated dataset will have errors that can only be identified when checked and studied by human annotators. As the goal of the research is to produce a dataset with little-to-no human supervision nor annotation, this human-based check is not done. Correctness is instead ensured by thorough testing of the topic clustering model.

2.2 NewsPH-NLI

Using our proposed methodology, we automatically generate an NLI benchmark dataset in Filipino we call the NewsPH-NLI dataset.

To create the dataset, we scrape news articles from all major Philippine news sites online. We collect a total of 229,571 straight news articles, which we then lightly preprocess to remove extraneous unicode characters and correct minimal misspellings. No further preprocessing is done to preserve information in the data.

We then use our proposed methodology. First, we create a Doc2Vec model (via the Gensim[1] package) on our collected news corpus, using Annoy[2] as an indexer. We remove Tagalog stopwords and use TF-IDF to filter the functions words (e.g. "ng" and "nang") as these create noise. In testing, without the use of stopword removal and TF-IDF filtering, clustering was difficult as most articles were embedded closely due to their common usage of stopwords and function words. After producing the Doc2Vec embeddings, we then cluster, comparing two articles via the cosine similarity of the mean of their projected vectors. We consider two articles to be dissimilar if their cosine similarity is less than 0.65.

---

[1] https://radimrehurek.com/gensim/.
[2] https://github.com/spotify/annoy.

After clustering, we then take entailments by running through each article iteratively, and produce contradictions by sampling from two randomly chosen clusters. We shuffle the final set and randomly sample 600,000 premise-hypothesis pairs to be part of the final dataset. We set this size for our dataset in order to follow the size of the widely-used SNLI dataset [1].

From the full generated dataset, 420,000 of which form the training set, while the remaining 80,000 are split evenly to produce the validation and test sets. To generate the splits, we first sample 300,000 of both entailments and contradictions using our methodology, shuffle the set, then split them accordingly into training, validation, and testing sets.

2.3   ELECTRA Pretraining

We alleviate the resource scarcity of the Filipino language by producing pretrained transformers. We chose the ELECTRA [3] pretraining method because of the data efficiency of its pretraining task. While a large corpus of unlabeled text is available in Filipino, this consolidated corpus is still far smaller than the ones commonly used to pretrain English models. ELECTRA poses an advantage over the widely-used BERT [9] in its ability to use pretraining data more efficiently, as BERT only uses 15% of the training data for masked language modeling per epoch, leading to data inefficiency. We surmise that this increased data efficiency will provide improvements for tasks in low-resource languages.

We produce four ELECTRA models: a cased and uncased model in the base size (12 layers, 768 hidden units, 12 attention heads), and a cased and uncased model in the small size (12 layers, 256 hidden units, 4 attention heads). All our models accept a maximum sequence length of 512.

Our models are pretrained using the WikiText-TL-39 dataset [5], producing a SentencePiece[3] vocabulary of 320,000 subwords. We train the small models with a learning rate of 5e-4, batch size of 128, and a generator hidden size 25% of the discriminator hidden size. For the base models, we train with a learning rate of 2e-4, batch size of 256, and a generator hidden size 33% of the discriminator hidden size. Models are pretrained using the Adam [15] optimizer. We pretrain for a total of 1 million steps for the base models and 766,000 steps for the small models, using the first 10% of the total steps for linear learning rate warmup.

Pretraining was done using Tensor Processing Unit (TPU) v3 machines on Google Cloud Platform, with small models finishing in four days and base variants finishing in nine days.

2.4   Benchmarking

We then finetune to set initial benchmarks on the NewsPH-NLI using our ELECTRA models, comparing their performance against another Transformer-based finetuning technique (BERT) and an RNN-based finetuning technique (ULM-FiT). For Filipino versions of the aforementioned benchmark models, we use Tagalog-BERT [6,7] and Tagalog-ULMFiT [26].

---

[3] https://github.com/google/sentencepiece.

For finetuning, small variants of ELECTRA use a learning rate of 2e-4. Base variants of both ELECTRA and BERT use a learning rate of 5e-5. All transformers were finetuned on the dataset for a total of 3 epochs using the Adam optimizer, using the first 10% of the total steps for linear learning rate warmup. For transformers, the standard separator token [SEP] was used to convert sentence pairs into one single sequence.

ULMFiT follows a different finetuning protocol compared to the transformer models. We first preprocess the data using the FastAI [12] tokenization scheme. Sentence-pairs are turned into one sequence by using a special xxsep token introduced in finetuning.

Finetuning was done in two stages: language model finetuning, and classifier finetuning. For language model finetuning, we first finetune the last layer for 1 epoch, leaving all other layers frozen, before unfreezing all layers and finetuning for two epochs. We use a learning rate of 5e-2. For classifier finetuning, we perform 5 epochs of finetuning, performing gradual unfreezing [13] while reducing the learning rate from 1e-2 per epoch by a factor of 2. All experiments with ULMFiT also used discriminative learning rates [13] and cyclic learning rate schedules [24].

Finetuning, testing, and all other experiments were done on machines with NVIDIA Tesla P100 GPUs. For small ELECTRA models, finetuning on the full dataset takes three hours to finish. For base ELECTRA and BERT variants, full finetuning finishes in five hours. For ULMFiT, it takes two hours.

2.5   Degradation Tests

To further investigate the capacity and performance of these models especially when operating in low-data environments, we run a number of degradation tests [6].

Simply put, we reduce the amount of training data to a certain **data percentage** (p%) of the full dataset while keeping the validation and testing data sizes constant, then proceed to finetune a model. For each model, we perform degradation tests at four different data percentages: 50%, 30%, 10%, and 1%.

For each degradation test, we log the test loss and test accuracy. In addition, we take the **accuracy degradation**, which is described as:

$$AD_{p\%} = Acc_{100\%} - Acc_{p\%}$$

where $Acc_{100\%}$ refers to the accuracy of the model when finetuned on the full dataset, and $Acc_{p\%}$ refers to the accuracy of the model when finetuned on $p\%$ of the dataset. We also take the **degradation percentage**, which is described as:

$$DP_{p\%} = AD_{p\%}/Acc_{100\%} \times 100$$

where $AD_{p\%}$ is the accuracy degradation of the model when finetuned at $p\%$ data percentage. The degradation percentage measures how much of the full performance of a model is lost when trained with less data, at a certain data percentage $p\%$.

To compare which models are more robust to performance degradation in low-data domains, we also measure **degradation speed**, which we define as the standard deviation between the degradation percentages of a model for the 50%, 30%, 10%, and 1% setup. When the degradation percentages are more spread out, this indicates that the model degrades faster as the number of training data is reduced.

We perform degradation tests as a form of "stress test" to gauge the performance and effectiveness of models when forced to work in low-data domains. Most models in published literature show results as tested in environments with abundant data. While this is an effective way to compare performance against other models tested in a similar manner, it is not representative of a model's actual performance when adapting to low-data domains, especially with low-resource languages.

3   Results and Discussion

3.1   Finetuning Results

Finetuning results show that ELECTRA outperforms both the Transformer baseline (BERT) and the RNN baseline (ULMFiT). The best ELECTRA model (Small Uncased) outperforms the best BERT model (Base Cased) by +3.75% accuracy, and outperforms the ULMFiT model by +3.63%.

The ELECTRA models outperformed the BERT models on average by 3.01% accuracy (average ELECTRA performance being 92.17% while average BERT performance is only 89.16%). We hypothesize that the ELECTRA models perform better than the BERT, with the small variants performing better than their larger BERT counterparts despite the size and capacity difference, due to the pretraining scheme. ELECTRA leverages pretraining data in a more data efficient way, using all of the training data per batch to train the model. This is opposed to BERT's (particularly masked language modeling's) inefficient use of pretraining data, using only 15% of each batch to train the model. Since our pretraining dataset is considerably smaller than most common English pretraining datasets (39 million words in WikiText-TL-39 vs 2,500 million words in the Bookcorpus dataset), a pretraining scheme that uses data more efficiently will be able to learn more effectively.

Difference in performance among the ELECTRA variants is marginal at best, with the difference in accuracy between the best ELECTRA model (Small Uncased) and the weakest one (Base Cased) being only 1.22%. An interesting observation is that the small variants both outperform their base variants, albeit marginally. The small uncased model outperforms the base uncased model by 1.34%, while the small cased model outperforms the base cased model by 0.51%. We hypothesize that this is due to the small models being easier to train, given that there are less parameters to consider.

While the small variants outperform their base variants on the full dataset, we hypothesize that the base models have an advantage in settings where there is less data to learn from, since they have more effective capacity. We verify this through our use of degradation tests shown in the next subsection.

Table 1. Final Finetuning Results. The best ELECTRA model (Small Uncased) outperforms the best BERT model (Base Cased) by +3.75% and the ULMFiT model by +3.63%. An interesting observation is that the small ELECTRA models perform marginally better than their base counterparts. We also report the random seed used in our experiments for reproducibility with our released code.

Model	Val. Loss	Val. Acc.	Test Loss	Test Acc.	Seed
ELECTRA Tagalog Base Cased	0.2646	91.74%	0.2619	91.76%	4567
ELECTRA Tagalog Base Uncased	0.2502	91.98%	0.2581	91.66%	4567
ELECTRA Tagalog Small Cased	0.1931	92.58%	0.1959	92.27%	1439
ELECTRA Tagalog Small Uncased	0.1859	92.96%	0.1894	93.00%	45
BERT Tagalog Base Cased	0.3225	88.81%	0.3088	89.25%	1111
BERT Tagalog Base Uncased	0.3236	89.04%	0.3257	89.06%	6235
ULMFiT Tagalog	0.2685	89.11%	0.2589	89.37%	42

A table summarizing the finetuning results can be found in Table 1.

3.2   Degradation Tests

In total, we perform four degradation tests per model variant, for a total of 28 degradation tests. Each model is finetuned with a fraction of the entire NewsPH-NLI dataset (50%, 30%, 10%, and 1%), with the resulting performance compared against the performance of the same model when finetuned with the full dataset. A summary of all degradation tests can be found in Table 2.

As we start to reduce the training data to 50%, the ELECTRA models remain more resilient to performance degradation compared to the BERT models and ULMFiT. We hypothesize this to be due to the more effective means of imparting learned priors to the Transformer by its data-efficient pretraining scheme. At the 50% data percentage, ELECTRA has only degraded by 1.02% on average, while BERT and ULMFiT has degraded by 2.28% and 2.85% on average, respectively. This trend is still evident at the 30% data percentage mark, with ELECTRA degrading by 2.62% on average, while BERT and ULMFiT degrade by 3.38% and 5.57% on average, respectively.

The trend begins to shift as we approach settings with even less data. As the training data is reduced to 10% of the original (42,000 examples), we see that ELECTRA starts to begin degrading faster, while BERT degrades at about the same rate. ELECTRA has degraded by 5.11% on average. Meanwhile, BERT degrades by 5.89% on average, which is only minimally larger than ELECTRA's degradation. The same is true on the extremely-low data 1% data percentage mark, where ELECTRA has degraded by 15.04% on average, which is 6.2% higher than BERT's average degradation of 8.84%.

Table 2. Degradation Test Results. "Acc. Deg." refers to Accuracy Degradation, the difference between the performance of the model when trained with the full dataset and when trained with a smaller Data %. "Deg. %" refers to Degradation Percentage, the percentage of the performance of the model when trained with the full dataset that is lost when finetuned with a smaller Data %. Degradation speed is the standard deviation of a model's Degradation Percentages, lower is better.

Model	Data %	Test Loss	Test Acc	Acc. Deg.	Deg. %	Degradation Speed
ELECTRA Tagalog	100%	0.2619	91.76%			4.47
Base Cased	50%	0.3184	90.56%	−1.20	1.31%	
	30%	0.3769	88.85%	−2.91	3.17%	
	10%	0.4467	86.23%	−5.53	6.03%	
	1%	0.5046	79.78%	−11.98	13.06%	
ELECTRA Tagalog	100%	0.2581	91.66%			4.47
Base Uncased	50%	0.2920	90.85%	−0.81	0.88%	
	30%	0.3333	89.21%	−2.45	2.67%	
	10%	0.4041	87.20%	−4.46	4.87%	
	1%	0.5300	79.43%	−12.23	13.34%	
ELECTRA Tagalog	100%	0.1959	92.27%			5.69
Small Cased	50%	0.2260	91.56%	−0.71	0.77%	
	30%	0.2504	90.13%	−2.14	2.32%	
	10%	0.3075	87.66%	−4.61	5.00%	
	1%	0.4873	78.09%	−14.18	15.37%	
ELECTRA Tagalog	100%	0.1894	93.00%			6.92
Small Uncased	50%	0.2154	91.97%	−1.03	1.11%	
	30%	0.2439	90.86%	−2.14	2.30%	
	10%	0.2963	88.77%	−4.23	4.55%	
	1%	0.5303	75.91%	−17.09	18.38%	
BERT Tagalog	100%	0.3088	89.25%			2.49
Base Cased	50%	0.3800	87.09%	−2.16	2.42%	
	30%	0.4394	86.25%	−3.00	3.36%	
	10%	0.5046	84.15%	−5.10	5.71%	
	1%	0.5285	81.33%	−7.92	8.87%	
BERT Tagalog	100%	0.3257	89.06%			2.57
Base Uncased	50%	0.4126	87.15%	−1.91	2.14%	
	30%	0.4434	86.04%	−3.02	3.39%	
	10%	0.5232	83.65%	−5.41	6.07%	
	1%	0.5672	81.21%	−7.85	8.81%	
ULMFiT Tagalog	100%	0.2589	89.37%			8.33
	50%	0.3093	86.82%	−2.55	2.85%	
	30%	0.3699	84.39%	−4.98	5.57%	
	10%	0.4840	79.07%	−10.30	11.53%	
	1%	0.8140	67.50%	−21.87	24.47%	

In extremely low-data domains, we see that BERT is more resilient to performance degradation than ELECTRA is. ELECTRA is shown to degrade exponentially as the number of training examples is reduced. As shown in Fig. 2, while BERT's degradation on average remains relatively linear, ELECTRA starts degrading faster and faster as we approach the 1% (4,200 examples) data percentage mark. When looking at degradation speeds, it is also evident that ELECTRA degrades more (average degradation speed of 5.46) while BERT degrades less (average degradation speed of 2.53).

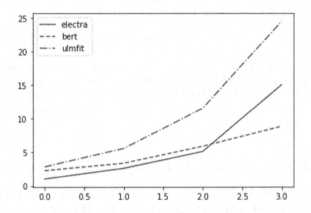

Fig. 2. Per-technique degradation curves, averaging the performance of all models belonging to one technique. ULMFiT still remains the easiest model to degrade as the number of training examples reduce. ELECTRA starts to degrade strongly after the 10% mark, while BERT remains to degrade slowly.

We hypothesize that this is a direct effect of their pretraining schemes. ELECTRA is trained without a specific downstream task in mind, while BERT is trained considering sentence-pair classification tasks, leading to its use of next sentence prediction as a secondary pretraining task. Since BERT's biases are more adjusted to sentence-pair classification, we can hypothesize that it should perform reliably well even when finetuned with little data, as it already has an "idea" of how to perform the task.

In terms of per-model degradation, while the small ELECTRA models outperformed their larger base counterparts in the full dataset, we show that the base models are more resilient to degradation. As shown in Fig. 3, this is more evident as we approach the 1% data percentage mark, with the small uncased model degrading 5.04% more than the base uncased model, and the small cased model degrading 2.31% more than its base cased counterpart. In terms of speed, we also see that the small models degrade more (average degradation speed of 6.31) than the base models (average degradation speed of 4.62).

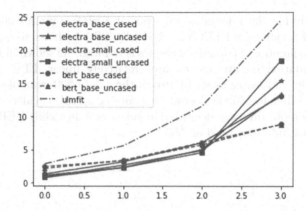

Fig. 3. Per-model degradation curves. ULMFiT degrades the fastest out of the three transfer learning techniques. ELECTRA begins to degrade at the 10% data percentage mark. Both ELECTRA and ULMFiT degrade exponentially, while BERT degrades nearly linearly, which is likely due to it's pretraining scheme designed for sentence-pair classification tasks.

3.3   Heuristics for Choosing Techniques for Low-Data Domains

Overall, the finetuning results and the degradation tests give us good heuristics for choosing which techniques are appropriate for different tasks when dealing with low-data domains.

ELECTRA is most effective in the general use-case. When there is a lot of task-specific data to finetune a model, we see that ELECTRA is more effective than the baselines BERT and ULMFiT. ELECTRA is also best to use when there is little pretraining data available, as is with the case of the low-resource language Filipino. Since there is less pretraining data, ELECTRA's more data-efficient pretraining scheme will impart more learned priors than BERT's masked language modeling objective will. From our results, we hypothesize that the same will be true when compared with other Transformer-based pretraining techniques that use the masked language modeling objective, such as RoBERTa [18].

However, while ELECTRA is effective in the general case, this does not mean that BERT will be deprecated anytime soon. BERT is very effective in the low-data case, especially in tasks that deal with sentence-pair classification such as natural language inference and sentence entailment. Since BERT's pretraining scheme is designed with sentence-pair classification tasks in mind, it will perform well for such tasks even with little finetuning data as it already has an idea how to perform these tasks due to its pretraining. As we show with empirical results, BERT also degrades slower than ELECTRA, and should be more robust for various tasks in low-data domains and low-resource languages.

While both Transformer-based finetuning techniques outperform ULMFiT in the degradation tests, this does not mean that RNN-based methods do not have a use in current research dealing with language inference tasks. On the full dataset, we see that ULMFiT performed with accuracy comparable to BERT,

albeit degrading the fastest on average on the degradation tests. ULMFiT's fast
degradation is likely due to it being RNN-based, which has significantly less
representational capacity than the larger Transformers that leverage attention
used in the study. While this is the case, in settings where there is enough data
to finetune, ULMFiT (and other RNN-based transfer learning techniques) will
perform comparably to the Transformer-based techniques when tuned properly.
ULMFiT's AWD-LSTM [19] backbone also enjoys the benefit of being cheaper
and faster to train. In cases where there is a lack of resources to use Transformers
effectively, RNN-based models will still suffice, assuming there is an abundance
of data.

4 Conclusion

In this paper, we proposed an automatic method for creating sentence entailment benchmark datasets using news articles. Through our method, datasets
can be generated quickly and cost-efficiently, while ensuring that they are challenging enough to accurately benchmark performance of high capacity models.
In addition, our method leverages the abundance of news articles online, which
allows datasets even in low-resource languages to be created.

Using our method, we produce the first sentence entailment benchmark
dataset in Filipino which we call NewsPH-NLI. We also produce pretrained
Transformers based on the ELECTRA pretraining scheme, which we benchmark
on our dataset against two widely-used techniques, BERT and ULMFiT.

We shed light on the true performance of transfer learning techniques when
operating in low-data domains to solve a hard task. We show the importance
of the choice of pretraining task to the effectiveness of a Transformer when
finetuned with little data. We also show that while newer techniques outperform
older established ones, they may still perform worse when dealing with low-
resource languages.

For future work, we recommend further studies on automatic corpus generation be done; particularly on correctness checking. The biggest disadvantage
that our method has is that to fully ensure correctness, humans will still have
to evaluate the resulting dataset. Should an automatic technique to verify correctness be made, our dataset generation method will be more robust, and can
then be adapted to generate other tasks that require more human supervision
in creating, such as summarization and translation.

References

1. Bowman, S.R., Angeli, G., Potts, C., Manning, C.D.: A large annotated corpus for learning natural language inference. arXiv preprint arXiv:1508.05326 (2015)
2. Canavilhas, J.: Web journalism: from the inverted pyramid to the tumbled pyramid. Biblioteca on-line de ciências da comunicação (2007)
3. Clark, K., Luong, M.T., Le, Q.V., Manning, C.D.: Electra: pre-training text encoders as discriminators rather than generators. arXiv preprint arXiv:2003.10555 (2020)

4. Conneau, A., et al.: XNLI: evaluating cross-lingual sentence representations. In: Proceedings of the 2018 Conference on Empirical Methods in Natural Language Processing. Association for Computational Linguistics (2018)

5. Cruz, J.C.B., Cheng, C.: Evaluating language model finetuning techniques for low-resource languages. arXiv preprint arXiv:1907.00409 (2019)

6. Cruz, J.C.B., Cheng, C.: Establishing baselines for text classification in low-resource languages. arXiv preprint arXiv:2005.02068 (2020)

7. Cruz, J.C.B., Tan, J.A., Cheng, C.: Localization of fake news detection via multi-task transfer learning. In: Proceedings of the 12th Language Resources and Evaluation Conference, pp. 2596–2604 (2020)

8. Currey, A., Heafield, K.: Incorporating source syntax into transformer-based neural machine translation. In: Proceedings of the Fourth Conference on Machine Translation (vol. 1: Research Papers), pp. 24–33 (2019)

9. Devlin, J., Chang, M.W., Lee, K., Toutanova, K.: Bert: pre-training of deep bidirectional transformers for language understanding. arXiv preprint arXiv:1810.04805 (2018)

10. Hinds, J.: Paragraph structure and pronominalization. Pap. Linguist. **10**(1–2), 77–99 (1977)

11. Hoey, M., O'Donnell, M.B.: The beginning of something important? corpus evidence on the text beginnings of hard news stories. In: Corpus Linguistics, Computer Tools and Applications: State of the Art. PALC 2007, pp. 189–212 (2008)

12. Howard, J., Gugger, S.: Fastai: a layered API for deep learning. Information **11**(2), 108 (2020)

13. Howard, J., Ruder, S.: Universal language model fine-tuning for text classification. arXiv preprint arXiv:1801.06146 (2018)

14. Khandelwal, U., Clark, K., Jurafsky, D., Kaiser, L.: Sample efficient text summarization using a single pre-trained transformer. arXiv preprint arXiv:1905.08836 (2019)

15. Kingma, D.P., Ba, J.: Adam: a method for stochastic optimization. arXiv preprint arXiv:1412.6980 (2014)

16. Lamble, S.: News as it Happens: An Introduction to Journalism. Oxford University Press, Oxford (2013)

17. Le, Q., Mikolov, T.: Distributed representations of sentences and documents. In: International Conference on Machine Learning, pp. 1188–1196 (2014)

18. Liu, Y., et al.: Roberta: a robustly optimized bert pretraining approach. arXiv preprint arXiv:1907.11692 (2019)

19. Merity, S., Keskar, N.S., Socher, R.: Regularizing and optimizing lstm language models. arXiv preprint arXiv:1708.02182 (2017)

20. Murray, K., Kinnison, J., Nguyen, T.Q., Scheirer, W., Chiang, D.: Auto-sizing the transformer network: improving speed, efficiency, and performance for low-resource machine translation. arXiv preprint arXiv:1910.06717 (2019)

21. Myagmar, B., Li, J., Kimura, S.: Cross-domain sentiment classification with bidirectional contextualized transformer language models. IEEE Access **7**, 163219–163230 (2019)

22. Norambuena, B.K., Horning, M., Mitra, T.: Evaluating the inverted pyramid structure through automatic 5w1h extraction and summarization. In: Proceedings of the 2020 Computation+ Journalism Symposium. Computation+ Journalism, pp. 1–7 (2020)

23. Pöttker, H.: News and its communicative quality: the inverted pyramid-when and why did it appear? Journal. Stud. **4**(4), 501–511 (2003)

24. Smith, L.N.: Cyclical learning rates for training neural networks. In: 2017 IEEE Winter Conference on Applications of Computer Vision (WACV), pp. 464–472. IEEE (2017)
25. Vaswani, A., et al.: Attention is all you need. In: Advances in Neural Information Processing Systems, pp. 5998–6008 (2017)
26. Velasco, D.J.: Pagsusuri ng RNN-based transfer learning technique sa low-resource language. arXiv preprint arXiv:2010.06447 (2020)
27. Williams, A., Nangia, N., Bowman, S.R.: A broad-coverage challenge corpus for sentence understanding through inference. arXiv preprint arXiv:1704.05426 (2017)

Fake News Detection Using Multiple-View Text Representation

Tuan Ha$^{(\boxtimes)}$ ⓘ and Xiaoying Gao$^{(\boxtimes)}$ ⓘ

Victoria University of Wellington, Wellington 6012, New Zealand
hatuan@myvuw.ac.nz, xiaoying.gao@ecs.vuw.ac.nz

Abstract. Fake news, or false information presented as news, is an increasing risk in today's society. The practice of automatically detecting fake news is by no means an easy task, since the authors of fake news intend to confuse the readers and make them vulnerable to false information. Traditional methods only consider a limited number of characteristics of fake news, and hence, they face many difficulties in predicting the credibility of the news. This paper proposes WES, an integrated stacking model where the multiple-view text representation from (i) Word-level features, (ii) Emotional features, and (iii) Sentence-level features are used to classify the news article. The proposed system is applied on a real-world dataset, FakeNewsNet, and the experimental results show that the proposed approach achieves significantly better performance than the current state-of-the-art fake news detection method.

Keywords: Fake news detection · Multiple-view text representation · Convolutional neural networks

1 Introduction

Recently there has been an increasing number of fake news on both traditional news media and social networks, which causes severe consequences on society. The typical examples are the false information about COVID-19 and the fake news during the U.S. 2020 presidential election. Not only is fake news written in a way to trigger extreme emotions of the readers, but it also misleads them to be more likely to accept false information in the future and hence reduces the ability of readers to distinguish between true and false information [13]. To make matters worse, the rapid development of social networks, such as Facebook, Twitter, enables fake news to be widely spread in a much easier way. As the negative impacts unfold, it becomes crucial to develop a robust system which can predict the credibility of a given news article. In order to solve the fake news detection problem, researchers have developed a variety of approaches, which can be categorised into two main categories based on the source of features used to predict fake news: *News Content* and *Social Context* approaches [13,18]. Our approach uses both and introduces a two-stage stacking model to integrate them.

Fake news detecting is a very challenging problem; existing approaches typically consider one particular representation of a document and may face many

D. N. Pham et al. (Eds.): PRICAI 2021, LNAI 13032, pp. 100–112, 2021.
https://doi.org/10.1007/978-3-030-89363-7_8

difficulties in fact-checking the news article. Text is information-rich, and hence, one representation might not be sufficient. One approach to address this limitation is to use *Multiple-view Text Representation* in which the features extracted are not limited to one type of text representation, but a combination of different types. However, there is not much research focusing on this new type of text representation. The proposed method is to use a system considering three views of representation (word, emotion, and sentence), and we expect it can outweigh the performance of existing methods. Our main contribution is the development of a novel Multiple-view Text Representation consisting of (i) Word-level features, (ii) Emotional features, and (iii) Sentence-level features to capture discriminative features from fake news.

The remainder of this paper is organised as follows. In Sect. 2, we will discuss the background and related work in the field of fake news detection. In Sect. 3, a proposed approach to overcome the limitations of current methods will be discussed. We then discuss the evaluation of the proposed method in Sect. 4. Finally, Sect. 5 contains the conclusion and future work.

2 Background and Related Work

2.1 Fake News Detection

The existing approaches of fake news detection can be categorised by the *source of features extracted* to predict the credibility of the news. The two main categories are News Content and Social Context. The former uses (i) fact-checking sources or (ii) linguistic-based features (title, body text of the news) and may combine with visual-based features (images and videos) [18], whereas the latter makes use of user profiles, posts and user networks which interact with the news article [17].

News Content models can be categorised into two sub-categories: Knowledge-based and Style-based approaches. Among the methods of fake news detection, *Knowledge-based* approaches can be considered as the most straightforward ones, which use external sources to predict the credibility of a news article. [3,15] make use of the factual information from Wikipedia to construct a knowledge graph; the credibility score of the claims in the news will be based on the path between the subject and object mentioned. [6] proposes a method which only pays attention to check-worthy claims by extracting information expressing key statements and viewpoints. *Style-based* approaches are based on the assumption that the publishers of fake news, whether intentionally or unintentionally, will use particular writing styles which are more deception-oriented and much less objectivity compared to true news. These writing styles' characteristics can be captured by analysing the text representation extracted from the news content. [13] uses *Unmasking* to detect *hyperpartisan* from the news. In [2], the authors propose a method which exploits the title of news to predict its veracity; their rationale behind is that news titles will summarise the main viewpoint the writers want to express.

On the other hand, *Social Context* models can be categorised into two sub-categories: Stance-based and Propagation-based approaches. *Stance-based* approaches refer to methods that use the stance of users who interact with a news article (whether they prefer fake news or not) to predict the credibility of the news. The stance of users toward fake news can be extracted either directly from their likes or indirectly via the sentiment in their posts [10,19]. *Propagation-based* methods use interrelations of relevant social media posts to predict the credibility of a news article. To put it another way, they assume that a news' veracity highly depends on the veracity of relevant social media posts, unlike their stance-based counterparts which focus on the users [7,8].

2.2   Text Representation

A classifier cannot use the text document directly as the input, and hence, it is necessary to use a specific method to map the text document into a suitable text representation. The most commonly-used text representations are *TF-IDF*, *Word Embeddings*, and *Sentence Embeddings*.

In TF-IDF representation, each document is represented as a very sparse vector $d \in \mathbb{R}^{N_t}$, where N_t is the number of terms in the *corpus*. Each component of d, which is the term weight of the term t_i, can be calculated as $TermWeight_i = TF_i \times IDF_i$. TF_i is the *Term Frequency* (the number of times the term t_i appears in a text document), and IDF_i is the *Inverse Document Frequency* whose main purpose is to penalize the terms appearing in many documents in the collection but are not useful for distinguishing between different documents.

In Word Embedding, each document is represented as an $m \times n$ matrix D; where m is the max sequence length, and n is the word embedding dimensions. Each row of this matrix is a dense vector $w_i \in \mathbb{R}^n$ which indicates the position of the word within the vector space, and it is called Word Embedding. Word Embeddings can be either trained using the input corpus or generated using pre-trained Word Embeddings such as GloVe and Word2Vec. Mathematically, by using Word Embeddings, the vector differences between $man - woman$ and $king - queen$ are roughly equal.

Sentence Embedding, as its name indicated, represents the sentence and its semantic information as a dense vector. The popular Sentence Embedding techniques include *BERT*, *InferSent*, and *Universal Sentence Encoder*. Among them, BERT (Bidirectional Encoder Representations from Transformers) [4] is a crucial breakthrough because not only does it achieve state-of-the-art results on a variety of NLP tasks, but it also inspires many recent NLP architectures and language models, e.g. TransformerXL, RoBERTa.

3   Proposed Method

As discussed in Sect. 2, most of the existing fake news detection approaches use either News Content or Social Context, and only a few of them make use of both sources [14, 16]. Typically for News Content models, only one text representation is used and this is not sufficient to capture useful information from the news article; as a consequence, the accuracy is not as high as expected. In order to resolve this issue, the proposed approach takes into account many aspects of news by utilising a variety of text representations. All text representations cannot be simply concatenated together, because there are many differences between them in terms of (i) shapes (vectors and matrices), (ii) density (sparse and dense vectors), and (iii) the number of dimensions as mentioned in Sect. 2. To overcome such limitations, this paper proposes a framework named **WES**. WES is an integrated stacking model, which utilises Multiple-view Text Representation consisting of (i) **W**ord-level features, (ii) **E**motional features, and (iii) **S**entence-level features from News Content and Social Context.

3.1 Multiple-View Text Representation

To capture the patterns at Word-level features of a document, we use *CNN (Convolutional Neural Network)* and *GloVe (Global Vectors for word representation)* [12] pre-trained Word Embeddings. CNN has been well-known for its robust performance in the field of Computer Vision because it can preserve 2D spatial orientation. Similar to images, texts also have an orientation. The main difference is that texts have 1D spatial orientation, where the sequence of words is essential. CNN has shown good performance in text classification [9]. Table 1a shows the parameter settings of the Word-level models.

Table 1. Parameter settings of Level 0 models.

(a) Word-level models

Parameter	Setting
Pre-trained word vectors	GloVe
Corpus	Twitter
# Dimensions	200
# Words in vocabulary	20,000
The max sequence length	500

(b) Emotional models

Parameter	Setting
Emotional word vectors	EmoLex
# Dimensions	10
# Words in vocabulary	20,000
The max sequence length	500

(c) Sentence-level models

Parameter	Setting
Pre-trained BERT model	BERT Large - Uncased - Whole Word Masking
# Sentences per news article	20
# Tweets per news	20
# Words per sentence or tweet	30
The chosen Encoder layer	The second to last Encoder

In addition to the Word-level features, the *Emotional features* of a document also play an important role in detecting the credibility of news. A recent study has shown that fake news is more likely to trigger extreme emotions of fear, disgust and surprise; on the other hand, real news tends to trigger joy, sadness, trust and anticipation from the readers [5,20]. For that reason, we believe that emotional text representation can increase the performance of fake news detection system significantly. In order to extract the emotions from the document, we use *NRC Word-Emotion Association Lexicon (EmoLex)* [11] to encode the document to *Emotional Embeddings*. In EmoLex, each word is associated with *eight* basic emotions (anger, fear, anticipation, trust, surprise, sadness, joy, and disgust) and *two* sentiments (negative and positive). Every word in a document is transformed into a vector $w_i \in \{0,1\}^{10}$ containing the emotional information, and as a result, we will have a matrix for each document (similar to Word Embeddings). The parameter settings of the Emotional models are shown as in Table 1b.

The last but not least information the system wants to extract from news is semantics. Nevertheless, we cannot use Word Embedding to capture the semantics of a document, since it has the *polysemy* issue. Word Embedding only gives each word one particular representation vector, for example, the "bank" words in "I need to go to the bank to withdraw my money". and "I want to see a river bank". will be vectorised into the same vector. To overcome this issue, we use *BERT-based Embeddings* [4] to capture the semantics of a document as *Sentence-level features*. BERT contains a number of *Encoders* based on its model; e.g. BERT Base has 12 Encoders, and BERT Large 24. The output of each Encoder can be used as a Sentence Embedding which captures the meaning of the input sentence. Table 1c shows the parameter settings of the Sentence-level models.

3.2 Integrated Stacking Model

In this section, an approach to combine the three aforementioned text representations to form the Multiple-view Text Representation will be discussed. The basic idea is to use an *integrated stacking model* with two levels to extract separate text representations from the document. Integrated stacking model is an ensemble method in which the model in higher level learns how to best combine the output of models from the previous level [21]. Figure 1 shows the overall architecture of the proposed framework to detect fake news. The integrated stacking model contains two main parts: (i) Level 0 models and (ii) Level 1 model. The former acts as feature extractors, while the latter a classifier.

Level 0 Models as Feature Extractors. The raw text inputs of Level 0 models are the News Content (the text body of the news article) and Social Context (the tweets posted sharing the news in Twitter). The raw text inputs are then vectorised into Word Embeddings, Emotional Embeddings, and Sentence Embeddings. Since we have two sources of input (News Content and Social

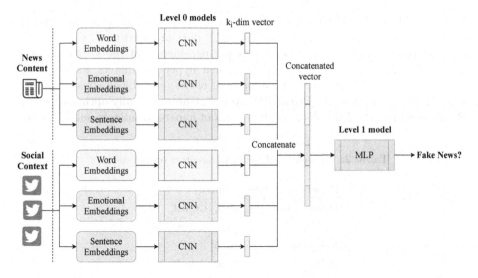

Fig. 1. The overall architecture of the proposed framework to detect fake news.

Context), and each has three types of text representation, the number of Level 0 models needed to process the embeddings are six models. Each text representation is fed into a Convolutional Neural Network i to output a vector $t_i \in \mathbb{R}^{k_i}$. For the fake news detection problem, this paper treats all types of text representation equally; therefore, all k_i values are set to 10. After that, the six output vectors are concatenated to form a single vector $\tau \in \mathbb{R}^{60}$. The concatenated vector τ, the expected result of the Level 0 models, is also the Multiple-view Text Representation that we want to extract from the News Content and Social Context.

Level 1 Model as a Classifier. The second part of the integrated stacking model is a Level 1 model whose primary purpose is to classify a news is fake or not. The learning algorithm used in this part is a Multilayer Perceptron (MLP). The aforementioned Multiple-view Text Representation τ is taken as an input to the MLP whose output layer uses a *sigmoid* function to predict the trustworthiness of the news (1: fake news, 0: real news).

Train the Integrated Stacking Model. Not only is the framework divided into two parts, but its training process also has two stages. The data are divided into five parts as follows: (1) the training set *train_0* for Level 0 models, (2) the validation set *val_0* for Level 0 models, (3) the training set *train_1* for Level 1 model, (4) the validation set *val_1* for Level 1 model, and (5) the test set *test* to evaluate the whole integrated stacking model.

Level 0 models and Level 1 model use different training datasets in order to prevent Level 1 model from being biased towards the best of Level 0 models.

Each Level 0 model is trained separately on the *train_0* data. They are trained on the fake news detection task, and the *val_0* data are used to (i) validate the training process and to (ii) learn the hyper-parameters of the CNNs. We do not fix the architecture of the CNNs, and their hyper-parameters, such as *drop out rate, the number of filters, the number of blocks* (each block consists of one *Conv1D* layer and one *MaxPooling1D* layer), are automatically optimised using Random Search [1]. Table 2 shows the ranges of hyper-parameters optimisation.

Table 2. The ranges of hyper-parameters optimisation.

Hyper-parameters	Ranges
Dropout rate	[0.2, 0.3, 0.4]
# Filters	[32, 64, 128, 256]
Kernel size	[3, 5]
# Blocks	From 1 to 3
Learning rate	[1e-2, 1e-3, 1e-4]

The trained Level 0 models are then integrated with the Level 1 model to form the integrated stacking model. In this second training stage, the output layers of Level 0 models are removed. As a result, instead of outputting the prediction about whether a news is fake or not, each Level 0 model i outputs a vector $t_i \in \mathbb{R}^{k_i}$ as shown in Fig. 1. The weights of the trained Level 0 models are set to untrainable, because the framework wants to train only the Level 1 model on the *train_1* data in this stage. In order to validate the training process of the Level 1 model (MLP), the *val_1* is used.

Finally, the whole fake news detection framework is tested on the *test* data to measure how well it performs on the unseen data. Our source code is made publicly available[1].

4   Evaluation

4.1   Metrics

Fake news detection is a binary classification problem, and hence, *Accuracy, Precision, Recall,* and *F1 Score* are the typical measures. This problem typically has a class-imbalanced dataset; therefore, Accuracy alone can not tell the full story about the effectiveness of the learned model. For that reason, other metrics such as Precision, Recall, and F1 Score are also used.

---

[1] https://github.com/TobiasTHa/WES_FakeNewsDetection.

4.2   The Compared Fake News Detection Methods

Our approach is compared with (i) three ensemble learning methods: AdaBoost, Bagging SVM (Support Vector Machine), and Random Forrest, (ii) Bi-LSTM (Bidirectional Long Short-Term Memory), and (iii) the current state-of-the-art fake news detection systems *dEFEND*. All compared methods make use of text representation from both News Content and Social Context. For the ensemble learning methods, their hyper-parameters are the default values of the *scikit-learn* Python package[2], and we utilise TF-IDF as the text representation. As regards Bi-LSTM, we use the standard implementation from *TensorFlow*[3], and GloVe is used as the word vectors. In 2019, Shu et al. proposed the *dEFEND* framework [16]. This framework makes use of a co-attention mechanism to capture the *explainability* of news sentences and user comments; it then selects top-k check-worthy sentences and user comments to predict the credibility of the news. The dEFEND framework has achieved significantly better results compared to the top existing approaches [16].

4.3   Dataset

The dataset used for evaluation is *FakeNewsNet* [17]. This dataset, which contains more than 20,000 fact-checked news articles, is commonly-used in fake news detection research. The dataset includes a variety of feature sources: (i) News Content, (ii) Social Context, and (iii) Spatiotemporal Information (how fake news spreads over time in different regions).

To make the comparison as fair as possible, we used the same split size of data and also the same number of candidate news from FakeNewsNet dataset that the authors of dEFEND [16] used in their paper. The statistics of the experimental dataset and its setting are shown in Table 3. The number of runs for each experiment is *five* times, which is the same as Shu et al. [16] used; the experimental results are the *average* values of those run.

Table 3. The statistics and settings of the experimental FakeNewsNet dataset.

	Value
Platform	GossipCop
# Candidate news	5,816
# True news	3,586
# Fake news	2,230
% Training set	0.75
% Test set	0.25

---

[2] https://scikit-learn.org.
[3] https://www.tensorflow.org/tutorials/text/text_classification_rnn.

4.4   Experimental Results

Results of the Whole Multiple-View Text Representation. The comparison results are shown in Table 4, and WES achieves the best results among the compared methods in all evaluation metrics, followed by Bi-LSTM and dEFEND. The accuracy and F1 Score of WES are higher than those of dEFEND by about *0.08* and *0.1* respectively. Due to the complexity of the fake news detection problem, the F1 Score of the compared ensemble approaches (AdaBoost, Bagging SVM, and Random Forrest) are not able to exceed the value of *0.75*. The observation, as a result, can confirm the effectiveness of WES in the fake news detection problem.

Table 4. The performance comparison for fake news detection.

	Accuracy	Precision	Recall	F1 Score
AdaBoost	0.774	0.702	0.719	0.710
Bagging SVM	0.811	0.813	0.663	0.730
Random Forrest	0.806	0.760	0.723	0.741
Bi-LSTM	0.823	0.769	0.774	0.771
dEFEND	0.808	0.729	0.782	0.755
WES	**0.892**	**0.869**	**0.856**	**0.863**

Results of the Single-View Text Representation. We further analyse the internal components of WES to investigate the contribution of each single-view text representation. There are three points that can be drawn from analysing the results in Table 5.

Firstly, using the whole Multiple-view Text Representation achieves significantly higher performance than using only one text representation. The only exception is the Precision metric, where the value of Sentence-level features of Social Context is higher than that of the whole Multiple-view Text Representation by 0.015. Secondly, the components using information from Social Context have considerably higher performance than their News Content counterparts. It shows that Social Context does play such an important role in predicting the credibility of news, and future research should pay more attention to Social Context when it comes to capturing the characteristics of fake news. Thirdly, for Social Context, Sentence-level features achieve the best results; however, regarding News Context, its performance is the worst. For this reason, by combining multiple types of text representation from different sources, these text representations can assist each other; therefore, the performance of the whole system can be improved.

Table 5. The performance comparison for each single-view text representation.

		Accuracy	Precision	Recall	F1 Score
News content	Word-level features	0.783	0.746	0.680	0.711
	Emotional features	0.775	0.754	0.634	0.688
	Sentence-level features	0.766	0.759	0.602	0.668
Social context	Word-level features	0.868	0.853	0.801	0.826
	Emotional features	0.864	0.842	0.800	0.820
	Sentence-level features	0.883	**0.884**	0.808	0.844
WES		**0.892**	0.869	**0.856**	**0.863**

Analysis of the Multiple-View Text Representation. We further investigate whether the Multiple-view Text Representation does extract useful information from fake news. The data used for this analysis are the Multiple-view Text Representations extracted from a subset of *300* fake news and *300* real news. As discussed in Sect. 3, this 60-dimensional Multiple-view Representation consists of the following three text representations: (i) 20 Word-level features, (ii) 20 Emotional features, and (iii) 20 Sentence-level features. We apply *PCA (Principal Component Analysis)* to project the feature vectors into *two* dimensions (number of chosen principal components = 2) for ease of interpretability.

Figure 2 demonstrates the projection of four different text representations. It is evident that the extracted Multiple-view Text Representation does capture useful information to separate between fake and real news. Compared to other text representations, using Multiple-view Text Representation as the input to the classifier can help decrease the complexity of the learned model and hence lead to better generalisation. The text representation which can achieve a result close to that of the Multiple-view Text Representation is Sentence-level features. However, it is worth noting that the transition region between false and real information in Multiple-view Text Representation is sparse, whereas that of Sentence-level features is very dense and overlapping. As a consequence, Sentence-level features may face difficulties in distinguishing between fake and real news in the transition region.

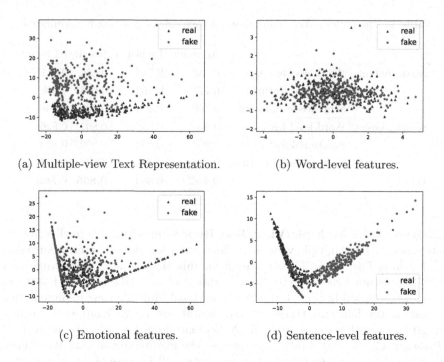

(a) Multiple-view Text Representation.   (b) Word-level features.

(c) Emotional features.   (d) Sentence-level features.

Fig. 2. Projection of text representations.

5   Conclusions and Future Work

This paper proposes the WES framework to detect fake news using Multiple-view Text Representation consisting of (i) **W**ord-level features, (ii) **E**motional features, and (iii) **S**entence-level features. To combine the features extracted from different sources, WES makes use of an integrated stacking model whose architecture is divided into two parts: Level 0 models and Level 1 model. The former acts as a feature extractor which contains six CNN models, each utilises a particular text representation from either News Content or Social Context of news. The latter serves the role of a classifier which contains an MLP model to predict the credibility of news. The experimental results using the FakeNews-Net dataset indicate that the WES system achieves significantly better results compared to the current state-of-the-art method.

We believe the proposed Multiple-view Text Representation can be applied on a broader range of domains rather than only fake news detection problem. By tuning parameters k_i (the number of dimensions of the feature vector for a text representation) to appropriate values, we can adjust the Multiple-view Text Representation so that it is suitable for a specific task. For example, Sentiment Analysis may need higher weights on the Emotional features. Our future research will investigate other domains and other tasks.

References

1. Bergstra, J., Bengio, Y.: Random search for hyper-parameter optimization. J. Mach. Learn. Res. **13**, 281–305 (2012)
2. Chen, Y., Conroy, N.J., Rubin, V.L.: Misleading online content: recognizing clickbait as "false news". In: Proceedings of the 2015 ACM on Workshop on Multimodal Deception Detection, pp. 15–19 (2015)
3. Ciampaglia, G.L., Shiralkar, P., Rocha, L.M., Bollen, J., Menczer, F., Flammini, A.: Computational fact checking from knowledge networks. PLoS ONE **10**(6), e0128193 (2015)
4. Devlin, J., Chang, M.W., Lee, K., Toutanova, K.: BERT: pre-training of deep bidirectional transformers for language understanding. In: Proceedings of the 2019 Conference of the North American Chapter of the Association for Computational Linguistics: Human Language Technologies, vol. 1 (Long and Short Papers), pp. 4171–4186 (2019)
5. Giachanou, A., Rosso, P., Crestani, F.: Leveraging emotional signals for credibility detection. In: Proceedings of the 42nd International ACM SIGIR Conference on Research and Development in Information Retrieval, pp. 877–880 (2019)
6. Hassan, N., Li, C., Tremayne, M.: Detecting check-worthy factual claims in presidential debates. In: Proceedings of the 24th ACM International on Conference on Information and Knowledge Management, pp. 1835–1838 (2015)
7. Jin, Z., Cao, J., Jiang, Y., Zhang, Y.: News credibility evaluation on microblog with a hierarchical propagation model. In: 2014 IEEE International Conference on Data Mining, pp. 230–239 (2014)
8. Jin, Z., Cao, J., Zhang, Y., Luo, J.: News verification by exploiting conflicting social viewpoints in microblogs. In: AAAI 2016 (2016)
9. Kim, Y.: Convolutional neural networks for sentence classification. In: Proceedings of the 2014 Conference on Empirical Methods in Natural Language Processing (EMNLP), pp. 1746–1751 (2014)
10. Mohammad, S.M., Sobhani, P., Kiritchenko, S.: Stance and sentiment in tweets. ACM Trans. Internet Technol. (TOIT) **17**(3), 1–23 (2017)
11. Mohammad, S.M., Turney, P.D.: Crowdsourcing a word-emotion association lexicon. Comput. Intell. **29**(3), 436–465 (2013)
12. Pennington, J., Socher, R., Manning, C.D.: Glove: global vectors for word representation. In: Empirical Methods in Natural Language Processing (EMNLP), pp. 1532–1543 (2014)
13. Potthast, M., Kiesel, J., Reinartz, K., Bevendorff, J., Stein, B.: A stylometric inquiry into hyperpartisan and fake news. In: Proceedings of the 56th Annual Meeting of the Association for Computational Linguistics (vol. 1: Long Papers), pp. 231–240 (2018)
14. Ruchansky, N., Seo, S., Liu, Y.: CSI: a hybrid deep model for fake news detection. In: Proceedings of the 2017 ACM on Conference on Information and Knowledge Management, pp. 797–806 (2017)
15. Shi, B., Weninger, T.: Fact checking in heterogeneous information networks. In: Proceedings of the 25th International Conference Companion on World Wide Web, pp. 101–102 (2016)
16. Shu, K., Cui, L., Wang, S., Lee, D., Liu, H.: Defend: explainable fake news detection. In: Proceedings of the 25th ACM SIGKDD International Conference on Knowledge Discovery and Data Mining, pp. 395–405 (2019)

17. Shu, K., Mahudeswaran, D., Wang, S., Lee, D., Liu, H.: Fakenewsnet: a data repository with news content, social context, and spatiotemporal information for studying fake news on social media. Big Data **8**(3), 171–188 (2020)
18. Shu, K., Sliva, A., Wang, S., Tang, J., Liu, H.: Fake news detection on social media: a data mining perspective. ACM SIGKDD Explor. Newsl. **19**(1), 22–36 (2017)
19. Tacchini, E., Ballarin, G., Vedova, M.L.D., Moret, S., de Alfaro, L.: Some like it hoax: automated fake news detection in social networks. CoRR abs/1704.07506 (2017)
20. Vosoughi, S., Roy, D., Aral, S.: The spread of true and false news online. Science **359**(6380), 1146–1151 (2018)
21. Wolpert, D.H.: Stacked generalization. Neural Netw. **5**(2), 241–259 (1992)

Generating Pseudo Connectives with MLMs for Implicit Discourse Relation Recognition

Congcong Jiang[1], Tieyun Qian[1(✉)], Zhuang Chen[1], Kejian Tang[2],
Shaohui Zhan[2], and Tao Zhan[2]

[1] School of Computer Science, Wuhan University, Wuhan, Hubei, China
{jiangcc,qty,zhchen18}@whu.edu.cn
[2] Jiangxi Branch, State Grid Corporation of China, Nanchang, Jiangxi, China
Jepctkj@sina.com.cn

Abstract. Due to the lack of connectives, the recognition of implicit discourse relations faces a big challenge. An early attempt overcomes this difficulty by predicting connectives with the use of the statistical language model. Recent years have witnessed the great success of masked language models (MLM). Then a new problem naturally arises, i.e., how can connectives benefit implicit discourse relation classification from such models? In this paper, we address this problem by developing a novel framework to generate the pseudo connectives using the pre-trained MLM. The key idea is to treat the absent connectives as missing words between two arguments and produce the pseudo connective from its contexts by fine-tuning MLM on the classification task. Moreover, we leverage the real connectives in explicit discourse relations to supervise the generation of pseudo connectives. Extensive experiments show that our model achieves the state-of-the-art performance on the PDTB benchmark.

Keywords: Implicit discourse relation · Connective · Masked language model

1 Introduction

Discourse relation analysis aims to recognize discourse relations that hold between two text spans (arguments) [22,28]. Discourse relation recognition is beneficial to many downstream applications including machine translation [21], question answering [14], text generation [3], and classification [12]. The task is defined as implicit or explicit discourse relation recognition (termed as IDRR and EDRR, respectively) depending on whether the discourse connectives like *but* and *before* exist in the texts.

Connectives provide strong linguistic cues to discourse relations. Indeed, general classifiers can yield a 93% accuracy on EDRR by using connectives alone for classification [33], whereas IDRR is still a challenging problem due to the absence of connectives [10,24].

© Springer Nature Switzerland AG 2021
D. N. Pham et al. (Eds.): PRICAI 2021, LNAI 13032, pp. 113–126, 2021.
https://doi.org/10.1007/978-3-030-89363-7_9

Several studies [1, 2, 29, 36, 44] exploit the manually annotated implicit connectives in the PDTB dataset under the framework of multi-task learning or multiple neural networks. However, annotated connectives may not exist in real text. As an early attempt, Zhou et al. [46] insert implicit connectives between arguments based on a language model trained on raw corpora without any hand-annotated data. While being in the right way, this method obtains the connectives using a statistical n-gram model. In recent years, pre-trained language models (PLMs), especially the masked language models (MLMs) like BERT and RoBERTa [7, 26], have shown significant improvements over statistic models in various natural language processing tasks. Consequently, a new question arises: how can connectives benefit implicit discourse relation classification from MLMs?

In this paper, we propose a novel framework to generate the pseudo connectives using the pre-trained MLM. Our basic idea is to treat the absent connectives as missing words between two arguments where each token is an embedding from a pre-trained MLM. We then produce the pseudo connective from its contexts by fine-tuning MLM on the target IDRR task. Moreover, we leverage the real connectives in explicit discourse relations as additional constraints to supervise the generation of pseudo connectives. The generated connectives are used to assist the prediction of discourse relations. Extensive experiments on various IDRR tasks show that our model achieves the state-of-the-art performance on the PDTB benchmark.

2   Related Work

After the release of PDTB 2.0 [34], the IDRR task has received much attention. A great deal of work has focused on direct classification based on the observed arguments, including feature engineering with linguistically-informed features [15, 20, 22, 32, 37]. With the development of deep learning, many researches encode arguments as dense and continuous representation based on various neural networks such as CNN, RNN, and other complex neural networks [24, 35, 42]. Further studies tend to discover more semantic interactions between two arguments from word-level [4, 19] or argument-level [9–11]. Recently, the pre-training methods have shown their powerfulness in learning general semantic representations. Shi and Demberg [40] find that the Next Sentence Prediction (NSP) pre-training task is beneficial to the IDR task. What's more, the encoder based on RoBERTa has achieved great improvement [23]. However, the lack of the effective cue of connectives makes learning purely contextual semantics challenging.

Previous work has also tried to take advantage of the labeled connectives in IDRR in the PDTB dataset as useful information. Zhou et al. [46] firstly uses the information of connectives in a pipeline way. Qin et al. [36] proposes an adversarial model in which an implicit relation network is driven to learn from another neural network. Other models [1, 2, 29] take the classification of connectives as an auxiliary task to help the main model in relation classification. Shi et al. [39] present a sequence-to-sequence model to generate a representation of the discourse relational arguments by predicting the relational arguments. The main drawback of this type of methods is that the connectives need to be labeled manually, which is impractical in real world scenario.

Explicit discourse relations have the exact connectives. Several previous models [18, 25, 41, 43] remove explicit discourse connectives and regard them as the "fake" implicit discourse relation data for IDR classification tasks. Dai and Huang [5, 6] classify the implicit and explicit data together in the paragraph level. Huang et al. [13] tackle this task as domain adaptation from explicit relations to implicit relations. Nie et al. [30] propose a post-training task which classifies the explicit connectives only based on the explicit arguments information before the IDR classification.

In summary, the connectives are extremely helpful for discourse relation recognition. While there are exact connectives in explicit discourse relations, it is laborious and impractical to get the connectives for implicit discourse relations. This drives us to generate the pseudo connectives for IDRR task and develop a multi-task learning framework for exploring the connectives in the EDRR task. Though an early attempt [46] also inserts the connectives, it is based on the statistic language model. Moreover, it does not exploit the connectives in explicit discourse relations.

3   Our Model

Given an argument pair $\mathbf{A} = \{w_1, w_2, ..., w_n\}$ and $\mathbf{A}' = \{w'_1, w'_2, ..., w'_m\}$, which does not have connectives, IDRR aims to predict the implicit discourse relation between them. In this study, we propose a **C**onnective **G**eneration and **S**upervision (**CGS**) framework which generates pseudo connectives for IDRR under the supervision of the real connectives in explicit discourse relations.

3.1   Model Overview

As shown in Fig. 1, CGS consists of three components: P_1 produces the connective embeddings, P_2 uses real connectives in explicit relations to supervise the generation of pseudo connectives, and P_3 predicts the discourse relation for IDRR and EDRR tasks.

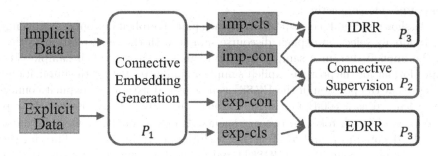

Fig. 1. An overview of our proposed CGS model.

3.2 Generating Connective Embeddings

MLMs have shown their powerful ability in learning contextual word embeddings. There are several special symbols in MLMs. [MASK] is used to replace the masked tokens in the input. [CLS] denotes the overall representation for the entire sentence which is added in front of each sample. [SEP] is used to separate sentences. MLMs can avoid training a new model from scratch. In light of this, we design a down-stream task to generate the pseudo connectives by fine-tuning MLM. Specifically, we treat the absent connective in IDRR as a missing word between two arguments and insert a [MASK] token at the beginning of *Arg2* which is the position of connectives in the arguments of PDTB, as shown in Fig. 2.

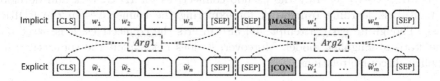

Fig. 2. The input format of implicit and explicit samples.

We then fine-tune MLMs on the discourse relation classification task. By doing this, we generate the pseudo connective from its contexts where its embedding is encoded in [MASK]. Besides, we get the corresponding representation of each token in two arguments **A** and **A**$'$ of the implicit discourse sample, denoted as h and h'.

3.3 Supervising the Generation of Connective

The [MASK] symbol in MLMs denotes a general representation for all masked tokens in the large corpus. Though we fine-tune it on our target task, the indication of [MASK] for pseudo connectives is not that strong due to the lack of labeled connectives. To address this problem, we propose to utilize the explicit discourse connectives in EDRR as the guidance to supervise the generation process of pseudo connectives.

As shown in Fig. 1, corresponding to each pair of implicit discourse arguments, we randomly select an explicit discourse sample with the same relation as that in the implicit discourse sample. We term this a positive explicit sample. The input format for the positive explicit sample is similar to that for the implicit one, except that the position of the [MASK] is now placed with a real explicit connective (denoted as a [CON] in Fig. 2). Through this way, we can also get the representation of each token in two arguments $\tilde{A}$ and $\tilde{A}'$ of the explicit discourse sample, denoted as $\tilde{h}$ and $\tilde{h}'$. Together with the pre-trained embeddings for the pseudo implicit connectives ([MASK]) and the real explicit connectives ([CON]), we now employ [CON] to guide the generation of [MASK] in our target discourse relation classification task. Given that the explicit relation is a positive sample, we assume that the relation prediction probability between implicit connective and its corresponding explicit connective is similar. Consequently, we introduce KL-divergence to measure the distance between two relation distributions as follow:

$$p^{mask} = softmax(\mathbf{W}_m \boldsymbol{h}'_{MASK} + \boldsymbol{b}_m), \tag{1}$$

$$\widetilde{\boldsymbol{p}}^{kc} = softmax(\mathbf{W}_m \widetilde{\boldsymbol{h}}'_{CON} + \boldsymbol{b}_m), \tag{2}$$

$$Loss_{KL} = D_{KL} (\boldsymbol{p}^{mask} \| \widetilde{\boldsymbol{p}}^{kc}), \tag{3}$$

where D_{KL} is the calculation function of the KL-divergence, $\mathbf{W}_m \in \mathcal{R}^{d_R \times d_c}$, $\boldsymbol{b}_m \in \mathcal{R}^{d_c}$ are the weights and bias, d_R denotes the word embedding dimension, and d_c is the number of relation classes. $\boldsymbol{p}^{mask}$ and $\widetilde{\boldsymbol{p}}^{kc}$ are the prediction probabilities of pseudo connectives and explicit connectives.

3.4 Relation Classification

At first, we simply leverage the explicit discourse samples by directly using their connectives as supervision for pseudo connectives. We then turn to a multi-task learning framework, i.e., one subtask for IDRR and the other for EDRR. The reasons are as follows. Firstly, the embeddings of real explicit connectives are also from the pre-trained MLMs, which may convey multiple meanings for different discourse relations. For example, "*since*" may denote a temporal relation in "*It's five years since I've seen her*" or a contingency relation in "*He is a changed man since he got that job*". It would be better to refine their representations using the relation labels in EDRR. Secondly, the connections between the explicit connectives and their contexts can be also strengthened during the learning process, which will improve both the representations of explicit connectives and those of contextual words. Below we detail the relation classification in IDRR and EDRR.

Since the final state of the symbol [CLS] denotes the representation of entire sentence, we use it for classification in IDRR.

$$p^{cls} = softmax(\mathbf{W}_i \boldsymbol{h}_{CLS} + \boldsymbol{b}_i), \tag{4}$$

where $\mathbf{W}_i \in \mathcal{R}^{d_R \times d_c}$ and $\boldsymbol{b}_i \in \mathcal{R}^{d_c}$ are the weight matrix and bias term of [CLS] for implicit discourse relation, respectively. Besides, the symbol [MASK] denotes pseudo connective and it contains rich relation information, we also employ it for classification. In summary, the optimization target for IDRR is to reduce the cross entropy loss between the predicted and true labels:

$$Loss_i = -\sum_{j=1}^{J} y_j * log(p_j^{cls}) - \sum_{j=1}^{J} y_j * log(p_j^{mask}), \tag{5}$$

where y_j is the ground-truth label, p_j^{cls} and p_j^{mask} are the labels predicted by [CLS] and [MASK] in IDRR, and J is the number of instances.

Similarly, we define the optimization target for EDRR based on the [CLS] and [CON] symbols. Note that if the explicit connectives correspond to multiple tokens, we take the mean value of their representations.

$$\widetilde{\boldsymbol{p}}^{cls} = softmax(\mathbf{W}_e \widetilde{\boldsymbol{h}}_{CLS} + \boldsymbol{b}_e), \tag{6}$$

$$\widetilde{p}^{con} = softmax(\mathbf{W}_c\widetilde{\boldsymbol{h}}'_{CON} + \boldsymbol{b}_c), \tag{7}$$

$$Loss_e = -\sum_{j=1}^{J} \widetilde{y}_j * log(\widetilde{p}_j^{cls}) - \sum_{j=1}^{J} \widetilde{y}_j * log(\widetilde{p}_j^{con}), \tag{8}$$

where $\widetilde{y}_j$ is the ground-truth label, $\widetilde{p}_j^{cls}$ and $\widetilde{p}_j^{con}$ are the labels predicted by [CLS] and [CON] in EDRR.

The overall loss in our CGS model consists of $Loss_i$ from IDRR, $Loss_e$ from EDRR, and $Loss_{KL}$ from KL-divergence. Moreover, we would like to balance IDRR and EDRR by introducing a hyper-parameter α $(0 < \alpha < 1)$ since IDRR is our major classification task while EDRR is an auxiliary one. The overall loss function is then defined as:

$$Loss = Loss_i + \alpha * Loss_e + Loss_{KL}. \tag{9}$$

We appropriately reduce the proportion of explicit data classification loss $Loss_e$ by α $(0 < \alpha < 1)$ [18]. During test, we employ the mean predicted probabilities of [CLS] embedding and [MASK] embedding for IDRR.

4   Experiments

4.1   Dataset and Settings

PDTB 2.0 [34] is an English corpus containing 2,312 Wall Street Journal articles. We report the training, development and test set sizes on 4-way classification using Ji split [15] for implicit and explicit data used in the paper (Table 1).

Table 1. Data statistics for implicit and explicit relations in PDTB 2.0.

Relation	Train	Dev	Test	Sum
Implicit relation	13902	1165	1188	16255
Explicit relation	14485	1321	1474	17280

We evaluate CGS on 4 top-level classification task using the Ji split [15], and on 11 s-level task [1] using Ji [15], Lin [22], and P&K [30] splits (Table 2).

Table 2. Data statistics for implicit and explicit relations in PDTB 2.0.

Split	Train	Dev	Test
Ji	Section 02-20	Section 00-01	Section 21-22
Lin	Section 02-21	Section 22	Section 23
P&K	Section 02-22	Section 00-01	Section 23-24

The neural parameters are trained up to 30 epochs using Adam [17] with an initial learning rate of 2×10^{-5} and a batch size of 16. The α in Eq. 9 is set to 0.4. The hyper-parameter settings of CGS (BERT) and CGS (RoBERTa) are the same. We use the base model of BERT and RoBERTa [7,26]. We add the trainable segment embeddings to RoBERTa as Liu et al. [23] do. Besides, we train models up to 30 epochs and take the best result on the test set, which strictly follows the previous studies [1,23]. All experiments are performed three times on three random seeds with 16 GB NVIDIA V100 GPUs to get the mean results. Our model and variants are all implemented by PyTorch.

4.2 Comparison Results

We choose three types of baselines: M1~M10 only use arguments, M11~M14 employ the labeled implicit connectives, and M15~M21 use explicit data. The comparison results on 4-way and binary classification and 11-way classification are shown in Table 3 and Table 4, respectively. Results for baselines are taken

Table 3. F1 and accuracy score (%) on 4-way classification and F1 score (%) on binary classification.

Model	F1	Acc	Comp.	Cont.	Exp.	Temp.
M2 [24]	46.29	57.17	36.70	54.48	70.43	38.84
M3 [19]	46.46	–	40.47	55.36	69.50	35.34
M4 [20]	47.15	–	43.24	57.82	72.88	29.10
M6 [9]	47.90	57.25	43.92	57.67	73.45	36.33
M7 [11]	51.24	59.94	47.98	55.62	69.37	38.94
M8 [23] (RoBERTa)	63.39	69.06	**59.44**	60.98	77.66	50.26
M9 [16] (BERT)	52.60	64.30	–	–	–	–
M9 [16] (XLNet)	56.00	66.30	–	–	–	–
M10 [46] (PLM)	51.34*	18.43*	24.55	16.26	60.70	14.75
M10 [46] (BERT)	58.05*	66.57*	–	–	–	–
M10 [46] (RoBERTa)	62.86*	69.98*	–	–	–	–
M12 [1]	51.06	–	47.85	54.47	70.60	36.87
M13 [39]	46.40	61.42	41.83	62.07	69.58	35.72
M14 [29]	53.00	–	48.44	56.84	73.66	38.60
M15 [25]	44.98	57.27	37.91	55.88	69.97	37.17
M16 [18] (Imp+Exp)	45.70	57.17	38.91	56.91	71.41	36.92
M17 [43]	44.48	60.63	–	–	–	–
M18 [5]	48.82	57.44	37.72	49.39	67.45	40.70
M19 [6]	52.89	59.66	45.34	51.80	68.50	45.93
M20 [41]	51.84	60.52	46.84	53.74	72.42	43.97
CGS (BERT)	58.30	67.15	51.01	56.30	76.05	50.25
CGS (RoBERTa)	**65.30**†	**71.48**†	58.09	**63.03**	**78.04**	**51.57**

Table 4. Results (Acc %) on 11-way classification.

Model	Lin	Ji	P&K
M1 [15]	–	44.59	–
M5 [40] (BERT)	54.82	53.23	–
M8 [23] (RoBERTa)	–	58.13	–
M9 [16] (BERT)	51.41	52.13	52.00
M9 [16] (XLNet)	55.82	54.73	54.71
M10 [46] (PLM)	19.32*	17.71*	19.70*
M10 [46] (BERT)	53.78*	53.67*	53.36*
M10 [46] (RoBERTa)	56.81*	58.67*	57.24*
M11 [36]	44.65	46.23	–
M12 [1]	45.73	48.22	–
M13 [39]	45.82	47.83	–
M14 [29]	46.48	49.95	–
M19 [6]	–	48.23	–
M21 [30] (BERT)	–	–	54.70
CGS (BERT)	55.09	54.02	53.93
CGS (RoBERTa)	**56.83**	**58.81‡**	**57.60‡**

from their original papers, except results with * which are replicated by ourselves. The best scores are in bold, and the second best ones are underlined.

It is clear that our CGS (RoBERTa) is the best on 4-way in Table 3, and it consistently outperforms all baselines on 11-way classification in all different splits in Table 4. As for the binary classification results, although our model performs slightly worse on **Comp.** than M8, it performs best on the other three classes. Results with † and ‡ are significantly better than M8(RoEBRTa) on 4-way classification and M9(RoBERTa) on 11-way classification ($p < 0.05$) based on one-tailed unpaired t-test, respectively. For t-test, we also rerun source codes of M8 and M9 three times.

M10 (BERT) and M10 (RoBERTa) are adapted from the method in [46] as follows: (1) Given the input "Arg1 + [MASK] + Arg2", we use RobertaForMaskedLM to get the mask's predicting probability for all words in vocabulary, and select the connective with the highest probability as the pseudo-connective. (2) We input the pseudo connectives and arguments into the PLM model and fine-tune them on the IDR task. (3) We use the final pseudo connectives and CLS to predict the sense. Note SLM doesn't include (2) and (3) and we add them for a fair comparison with our model. M10 (PLM) is the method which we discard them. As we can see, the results are extremely poor. This strongly demonstrate that simply replacing SLM with PLM may not bring about performance increase.

Among the baselines, M5, M8, M9, and M21 are based on PLMs (none of them involving pseudo connectives), and they far exceed other baselines. This demonstrates that PLMs (especially MLMs) have a positive impact on discourse relation classification. Moreover, our CGS (BERT) is slightly inferior to M8, M10 (RoBERTa) in Table 3, and slightly inferior to M8, M9 (XLNet), and M21 in Table 4. XLNet [45] is a generalized PLM which outperforms BERT on many tasks.

We make the following notes. (1) The choosing of PLM plays an important role in determining the performance. For example, M8 (RoBERTa), M9 (XLNet), and M10 (RoBERTa), outperform CGS (BERT), but are worse than our CGS (RoBERTa). The main reason is that RoBERTa is pre-trained with dynamic masking and a larger byte-level BPE [38]. (2) M21 is BERT based, but it benefits a lot from an extra huge dataset to post-train BERT and a fine-tuning on the target IDRR task.

Overall, the best performance of our CGS (RoBERTa) can be mainly due to the method itself. This can be concluded from the comparison among the RoBERTa based CGS, M8, and M10, and also from the comparison among the BERT based CGS, M5, M9, and M10.

4.3 Discussion

Ablation Study. We conduct the following ablation study and show the results in Table 5. (1) A0: We input the implicit argument pairs without [MASK] into the pre-trained base model, and use the final state of [CLS] for classification. (2) A1: We add the [MASK] symbol into the input sequence on the basis of A0, and employ its representation for classification besides the [CLS]. (3) A2: We add the explicit connectives in A1 to supervise the generation of pseudo connectives with KL-divergence loss $Loss_{KL}$. (4) A3: We add the loss $Loss_e$ for EDRR to A2. As we can see, adding the pseudo implicit connectives, the supervision of $Loss_{KL}$, and the supervision of $Loss_e$ gradually increase the model performance.

Table 5. Ablation results (%) on 4-way classification.

	Model	BERT		RoBERTa	
		F1	Acc	F1	Acc
A0	Base model	57.80	66.53	59.96	67.46
A1	A0 + Generation	58.17	66.57	64.25	70.55
A2	A1 + Supervision	57.56	67.11	64.81	71.54
A3	A2 + EDRR	58.30	67.15	65.30	71.48

Impact of Hyper-Parameter α. Impacts of the hyper-parameter α in Eq. 9 on CGS (BERT) and CGS (RoBERTa) are shown in Fig. 3.

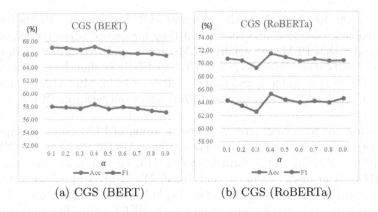

(a) CGS (BERT)   (b) CGS (RoBERTa)

Fig. 3. Impacts of the hyper-parameter α.

As we can see, both of them achieve the highest performance at 0.4. Remember that there are two subtasks in our model, where IDRR is our main task, and EDRR the auxiliary. The α controls the balance between IDRR and EDRR tasks. The smaller the α, the stronger the importance of the IDRR task. However, there is no guarantee of the quality of explicit connectives in EDRR, so the guidance from explicit connectives for IDRR is still limited. On the other hand, if the α is large, the classification quality of explicit connectives is guaranteed but the proportion of IDRR is reduced, and thus the performance on IDRR task is also affected. This shows that we need a hyper-parameter to constrain the balance between the importance of these two tasks. It can be obtained from experiments that this balance can be achieved when α is 0.4.

Impact of Special Token. We replace the [MASK] token with other special tokens in MLMs to prove the effectiveness of the [MASK]. The results are shown in Table 6. Experiments are done on the basis of removing explicit relation information. As we can see, [MASK] yields the best results among all tokens.

Table 6. Accuracy and F1 score (%) on 4-way classification with different special tokens.

Special Token	BERT		RoBERTa	
	F1	Acc	F1	Acc
[CLS]	58.14	66.73	63.34	70.04
[UNK]	57.99	**66.79**	63.55	70.49
Unused token	58.04	66.44	63.39	70.42
[MASK]	**58.17**	66.57	**64.25**	**70.55**

Visualization Analysis. We visualize the prediction probability vectors on 4-way classification task by using implicit connectives in PDTB[1] and those by using our pseudo connectives with the t-SNE method [27] in Fig. 4. Without model training, the prediction probability vectors of the implicit connectives and those of our generated ones are clearly separated (Fig. 4(a)). In contrast, as shown in Fig. 4(b), most of the probability vectors of these two types of connectives are mixed together or have small distance after training. This proves that our framework has successfully driven the pseudo connective embeddings close to the labeled ones.

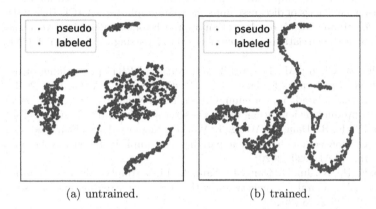

(a) untrained.   (b) trained.

Fig. 4. Visualization results.

5   Conclusion

We propose a novel method to generate the pseudo connectives by leveraging the MLMs and explicit discourse relation data for IDRR and prove its effectiveness by extensive experiments. Our study opens doors to more sophisticated methods in that (1) pseudo connectives generated from MLMs do offer a helping hand for IDRR, (2) a suitable MLM is more important than ever, and (3) the design of the model still takes the lead in yielding better performance.

Acknowledgements. This work has been supported in part by the NSFC Projects (61572376, U1811263, 62032016, 61972291). The work described in this paper was supported in part by a grant from the State Grid Technology Project (5700-202072180A-0-00-00). The numerical calculations in this paper have been done on the supercomputing system in the Supercomputing Center of Wuhan University.

---

[1] The implicit connectives are manually labeled and provided in PDTB, but we do not use them in our model since such connectives do not exist in real texts.

References

1. Bai, H., Zhao, H.: Deep enhanced representation for implicit discourse relation recognition. In: COLING 2018 (2018)
2. Bai, H., Zhao, H., Zhao, J.: Memorizing all for implicit discourse relation recognition. CoRR abs/1908.11317 (2019)
3. Bosselut, A., Çelikyilmaz, A., He, X., Gao, J., Huang, P., Choi, Y.: Discourse-aware neural rewards for coherent text generation. In: NAACL-HLT 2018 (2018)
4. Chen, J., Zhang, Q., Liu, P., Qiu, X., Huang, X.: Implicit discourse relation detection via a deep architecture with gated relevance network. In: ACL 2016 (2016)
5. Dai, Z., Huang, R.: Improving implicit discourse relation classification by modeling inter-dependencies of discourse units in a paragraph. In: NAACL-HLT 2018 (2018)
6. Dai, Z., Huang, R.: A regularization approach for incorporating event knowledge and coreference relations into neural discourse parsing. In: EMNLP-IJCNLP 2019 (2019)
7. Devlin, J., Chang, M., Lee, K., Toutanova, K.: BERT: pre-training of deep bidirectional transformers for language understanding. In: NAACL-HLT 2019 (2019)
8. Gerani, S., Mehdad, Y., Carenini, G., Ng, R.T., Nejat, B.: Abstractive summarization of product reviews using discourse structure. In: EMNLP 2014 (2014)
9. Guo, F., He, R., Dang, J., Wang, J.: Working memory-driven neural networks with a novel knowledge enhancement paradigm for implicit discourse relation recognition. In: AAAI 2020 (2020)
10. Guo, F., He, R., Jin, D., Dang, J., Wang, L., Li, X.: Implicit discourse relation recognition using neural tensor network with interactive attention and sparse learning. In: COLING 2018 (2018)
11. He, R., Wang, J., Guo, F., Han, Y.: Transs-driven joint learning architecture for implicit discourse relation recognition. In: ACL 2020 (2020)
12. He, G., Duan, Y., Li Y., Qian T., He, J., Jia, X.: Active learning for multivariate time series classification with positive unlabeled data. In: ICTAI 2015 (2015)
13. Huang, H., Li, J.J.: Unsupervised adversarial domain adaptation for implicit discourse relation classification. In: CoNLL 2019 (2019)
14. Jansen, P., Surdeanu, M., Clark, P.: Discourse complements lexical semantics for non-factoid answer reranking. In: ACL 2014 (2014)
15. Ji, Y., Eisenstein, J.: One vector is not enough: Entity-augmented distributed semantics for discourse relations. In: TACL 2015 (2015)
16. Kim, N., Feng, S., Gunasekara, R.C., Lastras, L.A.: Implicit discourse relation classification: we need to talk about evaluation. In: ACL 2020 (2020)
17. Kingma, D.P., Ba, J.: Adam: a method for stochastic optimization. In: ICLR 2015 (2015)
18. Lan, M., Wang, J., Wu, Y., Niu, Z., Wang, H.: Multi-task attention-based neural networks for implicit discourse relationship representation and identification. In: EMNLP 2017 (2017)
19. Lei, W., Wang, X., Liu, M., Ilievski, I., He, X., Kan, M.: SWIM: a simple word interaction model for implicit discourse relation recognition. In: IJCAI 2017 (2017)
20. Lei, W., Xiang, Y., Wang, Y., Zhong, Q., Liu, M., Kan, M.: Linguistic properties matter for implicit discourse relation recognition: combining semantic interaction, topic continuity and attribution. In: AAAI 2018 (2018)
21. Li, J.J., Carpuat, M., Nenkova, A.: Assessing the discourse factors that influence the quality of machine translation. In: ACL 2014 (2014)

22. Lin, Z., Kan, M., Ng, H.T.: Recognizing implicit discourse relations in the penn discourse treebank. In: EMNLP 2009 (2009)
23. Liu, X., Ou, J., Song, Y., Jiang, X.: On the importance of word and sentence representation learning in implicit discourse relation classification. In: IJCAI 2020 (2020)
24. Liu, Y., Li, S.: Recognizing implicit discourse relations via repeated reading: neural networks with multi-level attention. In: EMNLP 2016 (2016)
25. Liu, Y., Li, S., Zhang, X., Sui, Z.: Implicit discourse relation classification via multi-task neural networks. In: AAAI 2016 (2016)
26. Liu, Y., et al.: Roberta: a robustly optimized BERT pretraining approach. CoRR abs/1907.11692 (2019)
27. van der Maaten, L., Hinton, G.: Visualizing data using t-SNE. J. Mach. Learn. Res. 9(86) (2008)
28. Marcu, D., Echihabi, A.: An unsupervised approach to recognizing discourse relations. In: ACL 2002 (2002)
29. Nguyen, L.T., Linh, N.V., Than, K., Nguyen, T.H.: Employing the correspondence of relations and connectives to identify implicit discourse relations via label embeddings. In: ACL 2019 (2019)
30. Nie, A., Bennett, E., Goodman, N.D.: Dissent: learning sentence representations from explicit discourse relations. In: ACL 2019 (2019)
31. Peters, M.E., et al.: Deep contextualized word representations. In: NAACL-HLT 2018 (2018)
32. Pitler, E., Louis, A., Nenkova, A.: Automatic sense prediction for implicit discourse relations in text. In: ACL 2009 (2009)
33. Pitler, E., Nenkova, A.: Using syntax to disambiguate explicit discourse connectives in text. In: ACL 2009 (2009)
34. Prasad, R., et al.: The penn discourse treebank 2.0. In: LREC 2008 (2008)
35. Qin, L., Zhang, Z., Zhao, H.: A stacking gated neural architecture for implicit discourse relation classification. In: EMNLP 2016 (2016)
36. Qin, L., Zhang, Z., Zhao, H., Hu, Z., Xing, E.P.: Adversarial connective-exploiting networks for implicit discourse relation classification. In: ACL 2017 (2017)
37. Rutherford, A., Xue, N.: Discovering implicit discourse relations through brown cluster pair representation and coreference patterns. In: EACL 2014 (2014)
38. Sennrich, R., Haddow, B., Birch, A.: Neural machine translation of rare words with subword units. In: ACL 2016 (2016)
39. Shi, W., Demberg, V.: Learning to explicitate connectives with seq2seq network for implicit discourse relation classification. In: IWCS 2019 (2019)
40. Shi, W., Demberg, V.: Next sentence prediction helps implicit discourse relation classification within and across domains. In: EMNLP-IJCNLP 2019 (2019)
41. Varia, S., Hidey, C., Chakrabarty, T.: Discourse relation prediction: Revisiting word pairs with convolutional networks. In: SIGdial 2019 (2019)
42. Xu, S., Li, P., Kong, F., Zhu, Q., Zhou, G.: Topic tensor network for implicit discourse relation recognition in Chinese. In: ACL 2019 (2019)
43. Xu, Y., Hong, Y., Ruan, H., Yao, J., Zhang, M., Zhou, G.: Using active learning to expand training data for implicit discourse relation recognition. In: EMNLP 2018 (2018)
44. Xu, Y., Lan, M., Lu, Y., Niu, Z., Tan, C.L.: Connective prediction using machine learning for implicit discourse relation classification. In: IJCNN 2012 (2012)

126   C. Jiang et al.

45. Yang, Z., Dai, Z., Yang, Y., Carbonell, J.G., Salakhutdinov, R., Le, Q.V.: XLNet: generalized autoregressive pretraining for language understanding. In: NeurIPS 2019 (2019)
46. Zhou, Z., Xu, Y., Niu, Z., Lan, M., Su, J., Tan, C.L.: Predicting discourse connectives for implicit discourse relation recognition. In: COLING 2010 (2010)

Graph Convolutional Network Exploring Label Relations for Multi-label Text Classification

Ting Pu$^{(\boxtimes)}$, Shiqun Yin$^{(\boxtimes)}$, Wenwen Li, and Wenqiang Xu

Faculty of Computer and Information Science, Southwest University,
Chongqing, China

Abstract. Multi-label Text Classification (MLTC) aims to learn a classifier that is able to automatically annotate a data point with the most relevant subset of labels from an large number of labels. Label semantics and relationships are important information for multi-label text classification. Existing methods tend to ignore explore high-order dependencies among labels. In this paper, a model called HRGCN (Hop-Residual graph convolutional network) is proposed to capture label dependency and label structure. The hop-connected graph convolutional network can obtain the deep dependence between the labels through a label graph, where the label graph constructed by a correlation matrix and a feature matrix represents the co-occurrence of the labels. Meanwhile, the self-attention mechanism allows to assign different weights to the text features extracted by BiGRU. Fusion of text representation and label representation to form label-text awareness to achieve interaction and generate multi-label classifiers for end-to-end training. Experimental results demonstrate that the proposed model achieves better performance compared to baseline models on the dataset RCV1-V2 and AAPD.

Keywords: Multi-label text classification · Graph convolutional network · Self-attention

1 Introduction

Text classification is the most basic task in natural language processing. The amount of text information that people are exposed to shows an explosive growth trend, and the text appears to be multi-labeled. XMTC is the task of solving this problem, it assigns one or more labels for each given text. It has achieved great success in many important real-word applications, such as recommendation system [1], emotional analysis [2], suggesting keywords to advertisers on Amazon [3], information retrieval [4], and so on. Compared with multi-classification tasks, multi-label classification is more widespread and more difficult.

The research content of multi-label text classification mainly focuses on two points: 1) how to extract rich text features; 2) how to obtain label information including feature information and structure information and generate classifiers.

© Springer Nature Switzerland AG 2021
D. N. Pham et al. (Eds.): PRICAI 2021, LNAI 13032, pp. 127–139, 2021.
https://doi.org/10.1007/978-3-030-89363-7_10

A large number of studies have shown that these two parts are essential for multi-label text classification. Extreme multi-label classification methods include embedding-based method [5] and the tree-based method [6]. The embedding-based method maps data to a low-dimensional feature space, while the tree-based method constructs a hierarchical structure for the label semantics. With the development of deep learning, classical models have made remarkable achievements on this issue. However, most researches focus on the extraction of text features and label pair relationship, and rarely involve label structure and high-order relationships.

In this paper, we propose a model based on Graph Convolutional Network to solve the MLTC problem. Self-attention mechanism keeps a watchful eye on text feature information and enriches text representation by assigning different weights. The graph convolution neural network captures the label information using the label correlation matrix and the label feature matrix. The label representation is then combined with the text representation to obtain text-label awareness and sent to the multi-label classifier. Specifically, we accomplish this paper with the following contributions:

- We propose a model HRGCN, which leverages the hop residual graph convolutional neural network to find the semantic and structural information of labels and the high-order dependencies among labels.
- The label-text fusion method realizes the interaction between labels and text, portrays the association between the local semantic of text and high-order dependent labels for classification.
- Results on RCV1-V2 and AAPD benchmark datasets show that the proposed method outperforms the baseline multi-label text classification methods.

The rest of the paper is organized as follows. Section 2 introduces the related work. We describe our method in Sect. 3. In Sect. 4, we present the experiments and make analysis and discussions. Finally in Sect. 5 we conclude this paper.

2   Related Work

For a given dataset $\left\{(x^i, y^i)\right\}_{i=1}^{N}$, x^i represents the text, and $y^i \in \{0, 1\}^{d_l}$ is the d_l dimensional label vector corresponding to the text. MLTC can be expressed as a task for a text to find an optimal labels sequence $\hat{y}$ that maximize conditional probability $p(y|x)$, which is calculated as follows:

$$p(y \mid x) = \prod_{i=1}^{N} p\left(y^i \mid y^1, y^2, \ldots, y^{i-1}, x\right) \tag{1}$$

There are three types of methods to solve this task: embedding-based methods; tree-based methods; deep learning-based methods.

In the embedding-based method, each label vector can be projected into a lower dimensional compressed label space, which can be deemed as encoding. A regression is then learned for each compressed label. Finally, perform label decoding on the regression output of each test instance. The most representative embedding methods SLEEC [5] learns the low dimensional embedding matching scores between words and labels to construct an interaction matrix, and retains small scores to represent embeddings for more accurate classification.

Different texts in a dataset may have partially the same label. The tree-based method learns the label sharing relationship of texts by using tree structure, and introduces a label sharing relation on each non-leaf node to divide the text in a recursive manner to convert the original large-scale problem into a series of small-scale subproblems. AttentionXML [7] combines the ideas of k-means and decision tree, grouping all labels into a probabilistic label tree (PLT) [8], with each leaf node being a label group. PLT models that use shallow and broad top-down hierarchies can handle large datasets.

Deep learning emphasizes the depth of model structure and the importance of feature learning. Typical models include CNN, RNN, LSTM and GRU. Many CNN-based models have been proposed to solve multi-label classification, such as XML-CNN [9], TextCNN [10], DCNN [11]. XML-CNN is the first work of deep learning-based method, which uses CNN, dynamic maximum pool and bottleneck layer to build deep model. Another type of method, using the sequence-to-sequence model to transform the classification problem into a generation problem, has made a breakthrough in multi-label classification. It mainly uses RNN as encoder and decoder to predict and generate continuous labels. SGM [12] introduces global embedding in the decoding part, and Transform Gate controls the proportion of weighted average embedding. MDC [13] adopts LSTM as encoder and expands the receiving domain with empty convolution. However, these models assume that labels are ordered, which is obviously unreasonable.

Recently, graph neural network [14–16] has attracted widespread attention. The complex relational structure of graph neural network can save global information, which is effective in task processing. Graph-CNN [17] utilize the graph operations on the graph of words. MAGNET [18] uses graph attention mechanism to model label relationships. However, the structural information among labels is often ignored. To address the aforementioned problems, we use stacked graph convolutional network (GCN) [19] to capture essential features that determine the attributes of label nodes, and track the spatial structure of nodes by analyzing the relationship between adjacent nodes.

3   Proposed Method

In this part, we elaborate on our HRGCN model for multi-label text classification. We introduce some preliminary knowledge of GCN, and then explain the proposed HRGCN model in detail.

3.1   Graph Convolutional Network Recap

Most data in the real world is in non-Euclidean forms, such as social networks, protein interaction networks, transportation networks, etc. Graph Convolutional

Network was proposed on the basis of the inability of convolutional neural networks to handle non-Euclidean data. Compared with the complete connection of the traditional multi-layer perceptron (MLP) model, GCN reduces the computational cost by calculating a few parameters.

GCN uses a message passing mechanism to aggregate node information and update nodes. The adjacency matrix of the graph guides the aggregation of node information, and then the nonlinear function is used to update the node. The $(l + 1)$-th layer of GCN can be expressed as

$$h^{(l+1)} = f\left(\hat{A}h^{(l)}w^{(l)}\right) \tag{2}$$

where $\hat{A} \in R^{N \times N}$ is the normalized adjacency matrix that preserves the feature scale, $w^{(l)} \in R^{d \times d_l}$ is the weight parameter of layer l to be learned. And $f(\cdot)$ stands for the nonlinear function ReLU.

According to deep learning, the deeper the network is, the richer the features are obtained. In this paper, we propose to stack graph convolutional network to capture the high-order relationship of labels.

3.2 Hop-Residual Graph Convolutional Networks for Multi-Label Classification

In the following, we will introduce HRGCN model in detail from three parts: text representation, label representation and label-text awareness. Figure 1 shows the overall structure of the model.

Text Representation. The prerequisite for multi-label classification is to completely extract text features, which is the premise and focus for all related tasks. $x_i = \{w_1, w_2, \ldots, w_n\}$ represent the i-th text, $w_n \in R^d$ is a word vector in text whose length is n. In order to obtain contextual bidirectional information, we consider the model that introduce gate mechanism to solve the problem of long-distance dependence on text semantics. Specifically, we use BiGRU [20] to learn the past and future contextual information at each moment from the forward and reverse directions. To be specific, the computations is illustrated below:

$$\overrightarrow{h}_t = GRU\left(w_t, \overrightarrow{h}_{t-1}\right); \quad \overleftarrow{h}_t = GRU\left(w_t, \overleftarrow{h}_{t-1}\right)$$

$$\overrightarrow{h}_t = \left(\overrightarrow{h}_1, \overrightarrow{h}_2, \ldots, \overrightarrow{h}_n\right); \quad \overleftarrow{h}_t = \left(\overleftarrow{h}_1, \overleftarrow{h}_2, \ldots, \overleftarrow{h}_n\right)$$

$$H = [\overrightarrow{h}; \overleftarrow{h}] \tag{3}$$

where $\overrightarrow{h}_t \in R^d$ and $\overleftarrow{h}_t \in R^d$ are the forward and backward word context representations respectively, and $GRU(\cdot)$ function represents the nonlinear transformation of the word vector. The whole output of text is taken as a matrix $H \in R^{2d \times n}$.

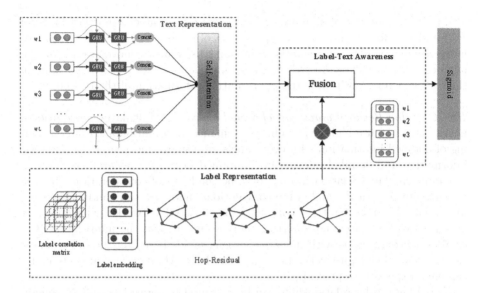

Fig. 1. The overall structure of the Hop-Residual graph convolutional network (HRGCN). Obtain the label representation from the label input and the text representation from the text input, combining the two parts of the label-text awareness for multi-label classification.

The self-attention mechanism [21] gives enough attention to the key information, highlights the local important information, and improves the quality of feature extraction. Text representation $S \in R^{k \times 2d}$ is calculated as follows:

$$S = \text{Softmax}\left(\frac{(HW_q)(HW_k)^T}{\sqrt{d_k}}(HW_v)\right) \tag{4}$$

where $W_q \in R^{n \times k}$, $W_k \in R^{n \times k}$, $W_v \in R^{n \times k}$ denotes the trainable parameters.

Label Representation. The label representation involve the label relationship extracted from the feature matrix and the relationship matrix by the label graph. The following describes the relationship matrix and the relationship extraction network. Each label $L_i \in R^d (i = 1, 2, \ldots, k)$ acquired from word2vec technique in the whole label set $L = (L_1, L_2, \ldots, L_k) \in R^{k \times d}$ represented by an r-dimensional dense vector.

Label Correlation Matrix. In order to capture label dependency better, adaptive attention weights are added to the feature matrix to perform graph convolution. We use the Pointwise Mutual Information frequency calculation technique to construct the label co-occurrence matrix as the attention weight. The pointwise mutual information can be obtained by

$$PMI(i;j) = \log\frac{P(i,j)}{P(i)P(j)} \tag{5}$$

$P(i, j)$ is the number of simultaneous appearances of label i and label j, and $P(i)$ and $P(i)$ are the number of appearances of i and j, respectively. When two labels are independent of each other, the pointwise mutual information is 0. The label correlation matrix $\widetilde{L} \in R^{k \times k}$ is a symmetric matrix, in which the value of the corresponding position is the point mutual information of the two labels.

HRGCN (Hop-Residual graph convolutional network). Multi-layer convolutional neural networks use high-level coding of semantic information and shallow coding of detailed information. However, labels are usually short, and the semantic information and detailed information contained in themselves are very limited. Encoding the label relationship has become the focus of consideration. But the relationship is intricate, and graph convolutional networks can handle this irregular relationship better than common convolutional networks. The one-layer graph network connects co-occurring pairwise labels, and the multi-layer GCN establishes connections with non-co-occurring labels based on the interconnection of nodes. The high-level connections established through intermediate nodes can enrich the label representation.

Label high-order relationships can be captured by multi-layer GCN domain extension. For example, an article belongs to both *computer vision* and *deep network*, and *deep network* and *machine learning* co-occur, then the two-layer GCN makes the representation of *computer vision* combines part of *deep network* and *machine learning* information. For articles to be classified, the possibility of being classified as *computer vision* and *machine learning* at the same time is increased, so that the classification results will be more reliable. However, the more GCN layers are, the more serious the over-smoothing phenomenon, and the smaller the difference between nodes. HRGCN takes the residual structure as a reference, and performs residuals in the aggregation phase rather than during update. This residual is a hop connection, with each layer of output retains part of the information from the input.

HRGCN has the same input as GCN and adds a hop connection from the initial input $h^{(0)}$ to the output of each layer. Formally, the $(l + 1)$-th layer $L^{(l+1)} \in R^{k \times d}$ is defined as

$$L^{(l+1)} = f\left(\left((1 - \theta)\widetilde{L}L^{(l)} + \theta L^{(0)} \right) w^{(l)} \right) \tag{6}$$

where $w^{(l)} \in R^{d \times d}$, and the parameter θ determines how many initial input features are retained by the hop connection. When it is equal to 0, it is GCN, when it is 1, it only changes the input, which does not meet our requirements. So $\theta \in (0, 1)$ and a smaller value is better. Because θ is introduced to alleviate over-smoothing, it will retain too much source information and reduce the aggregation of the graph network. In Sect. 4.4, we experiment to show the reasonable value.

Label-Text Awareness. Multi-label text can be annotated with more than one label, and each label has its most representative part of the text content. According to the association relationship between labels and the local semantics of text, we use the label-text fusion method to realize the interaction between labels and text. First, the text representation H extracted by the feature extraction network and the label representation $L^{(l+1)}$ extracted by the relationship extraction network are combined to generate a label-text representation, denoted by $C^{(lt)} \in R^{k \times 2d}$, where $w \in R^{n \times d}$ and "$\otimes$" stand for element-wise multiplication.

$$C^{(lt)} = L^{(l+1)} \otimes \tanh(Hw) \tag{7}$$

Both of the S and $C^{(lt)}$ will be input to the fusion part to get the label-text awareness. The former focus on text content, while the latter perfers to the label-text relations and label structure. Get weights $\lambda_1, \lambda_2 \in R^k$ through the fully connected layer with the parameters $w_t, w_{lt} \in R^{2d}$. The specific implementation process is as follows:

$$\lambda_1 = \sigma\left(w_t S\right); \quad \lambda_2 = \sigma\left(w_{lt} C^{(lt)}\right); \quad M = \lambda_1 \cdot S + \lambda_2 \cdot C^{(lt)} \tag{8}$$

where σ is sigmoid function to ensure the weights between 0 and 1, and label-text awareness matrix $M \in R^{k \times 2d}$.

Eventually the multi-label classifier is built of two fully connection layer. Mathematically, the predicted probability of each label for the coming text can be estimated via

$$\hat{y} = \sigma\left(w_2 f\left(w_1 M^T\right)\right) \tag{9}$$

where $w_1 \in R^{d \times 2d}$ and $w_2 \in R^{1 \times 2d}$ are trainable parameters, $f(\cdot)$ is denote nonlinear functions Relu and $\sigma(\cdot)$ is Sigmoid to make the output be a probability value.

3.3   Loss Function

We use binary cross-entropy as the loss function for multi-label classifier. Assuming that the ground truth label of a text is $y \in R^c$, where $\hat{y}^i = \{0, 1\}$ indicates whether label i appears in the given text.

$$L_{\text{loss}} = \sum_{c=1}^{c} y^c \log\left(\sigma\left(\hat{y}^c\right)\right) + (1 - y^c) \log\left(1 - \sigma\left(\hat{y}^c\right)\right) \tag{10}$$

where $\sigma(\cdot)$ is sigmoid activation function.

4   Experiments

In this section, we introduce three English datasets, evaluation metrics and our experiment settings as well as the baseline models that we compare with. Subsequently, we make a comparison of the proposed method with baselines and analyze the impact of two parameters.

4.1 Datasets

Arxiv Academic Paper Dataset (AAPD) [9] is an English dataset consists of 55,840 papers in computer science and related disciplines. A paper with a varying number of subjects and there are a total of 54 categories. The purpose is to predict the corresponding subjects of an academic paper based on the abstract content.

Reuters Corpus Volume I (RCV1-V2) [22] is an English dataset includes over 800,000 newswire stories hand-compiled by Reuters Ltd for scientific research, with a total of 103 topics assigned to each story.

Table 1. Details of the experimental datasets. N_{train} is the number of train instances, N_{test} is the number of test instances, D is the number of features, L is the total number of classes, $\overline{L}$ is the number of average labels per instance.

Datasets	N_{train}	N_{test}	D	L	$\overline{L}$
AAPD	54840	1000	69399	54	2.41
RCV1-V2	726554	77860	47236	103	3.24

4.2 Evaluation Metrics

We choose P@K [23] and nDCG@K [9] as evaluation metrics, which represent the Precision and Normalized Discounted Cumulative Gain at the highest K. We set $K = 1, 3, 5$. The calculation formula as shown in the following:

$$P(K) = \frac{1}{k} \sum_{n \in r_k(\hat{y})} y_n$$

$$\mathrm{DCG@K} = \sum_{n \in r_k(\hat{y})} \frac{y_n}{\log(n+1)} \tag{11}$$

$$\mathrm{nDCG@K} = \frac{\mathrm{DCG}\ @K}{\sum_{n=1}^{\min(k,\|y\|_0)} \frac{1}{\log(n+1)}}$$

Where y_n is the ground truth label vector and $\hat{y}$ is the prediction label vector output of the model. $r_k(\hat{y})$ is the label index ranking the top K in the current prediction result score. The correlation label $\|y\|_0$ of the ground truth vector y is introduced to normalize DCG@K. Calculate P@k and nDCG@K for each test data, and the average of all test data is the final result.

4.3 Baseline Methods and Setting Details

We compare the proposed HRGCN with four baseline methods, including the embedding-based methods SLEEC [5]; the tree-based methods AttentionXML [7]; and two deep learning methods XML-CNN [9] and LSAN [24].

Our model implemented and trained by Pytorch on an NVIDIA 1080Ti GPU. We obtained vocabularies from the training data. For both datasets, the size of the vocabulary is 30,000 and out-of-vocabulary (OOV) words are replaced with unk. Besides, we set the word embedding size to 300. And the batch size is set to 64 and the length of sentences is 500 words. To avoid overfitting, we use Adam optimizer to minimize the final objective function.

4.4   Analysis and Discussion

Table 2 shows the results of comparing our method with the baseline methods on P@K and nDCG@K ($K = 1, 3, 5$), respectively. According to Equation (11), we know that P@1 = nDCG@1, so nDCG@1 is not listed in the table.

Table 2. Comparison of our method and all baselines in terms of P@K and nDCG@K ($K = 1, 3, 5$) on benchmark datasets.

Datasets	Metrics	XML-CNN	SLEEC	AttentionXML	LSAN	HRGCN(ours)
AAPD	P@1	74.38	81.67	83.02	84.16	**85.19**
	P@3	53.84	56.60	58.72	60.91	**61.99**
	P@5	37.83	38.79	40.56	41.52	**42.10**
	nDCG@3	71.12	76.81	78.01	80.58	**81.27**
	nDCG@5	75.93	81.34	82.31	84.03	**84.94**
RCV1-V2	P@1	95.75	95.12	96.41	96.33	**96.87**
	P@3	78.63	79.47	80.91	81.54	**82.16**
	P@5	54.94	55.29	56.38	56.77	**57.03**
	nDCG@3	89.89	89.85	91.88	92.23	**92.86**
	nDCG@5	90.77	91.21	92.70	92.93	**93.25**

It is observed that HRGCN outperforms the other methods on AAPD and RCV1-V2 datasets. Since XML-CNN only considers text and ignores the importance of the relationships among labels. AttentionXML does not connect text and labels. When some labels have a few corresponding texts, it fails to adequately train the tail-labels, resulting in poor performance. The label structure is not considered by LSAN, leading to underutilized label information. Our method focuses on the text representation while considering the high-order relationship of labels, fully excavate the semantics and structure of labels, and further builds label-text perception to solve the problems in baseline methods. From the results, our model establishes a comprehensive graphical relationship among labels, which can effectively improve the performance of multi-label classification by improving the ability to capture label relationships.

Effect of the Number of GCN Layers. We conducted experiments on the effect of the number of GCN layers on the AAPD dataset. The deeper the GCN

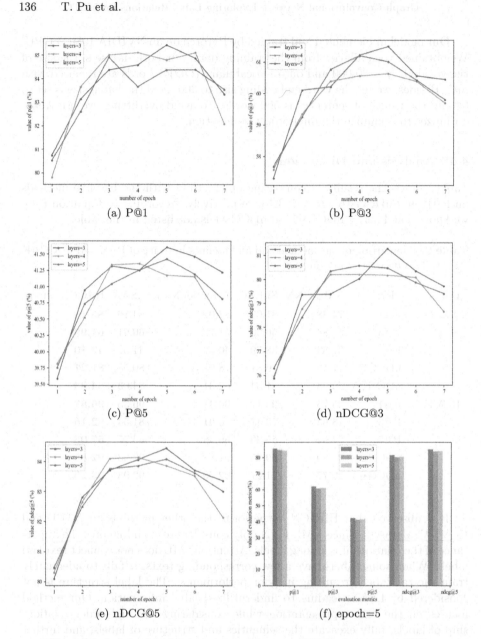

Fig. 2. Variation of evaluation metric values at different layers on AAPD.

layers are, the larger the receiving field is. To a certain extent, deeper layers of the network help to better aggregate neighbor information. A layer of GCN aggregates the first-order neighbors, while higher-order neighbor information requires multiple layer.

From Table 1, the average label number of samples in the AAPD is 2.41, we set the number of layers as 3, 4, and 5 respectively. When the number of layers is 2, it means the low-order co-occurrence relationship of label pair, which is not considered here. The corresponding results for each epoch are shown in Fig. 2. Wherein (a) to (e) represent the change of each evaluation metric value of different layers in the same epoch. It is observed that the performance is better when the number of layers is 3, and the best is obtained when the epoch is 5. In order to make a more intuitive comparison, we drew a histogram (f) of each result under different layers when the epoch is 5. For the GCN with various number of layers, the reason why their performances start decreasing in 5-th epoch may be due to the number of label categories in the AAPD dataset is small, so that a few rounds of training are sufficient. The average number of labels is rounded up to 3, which is why the optimal solution can be obtained when the number of layers is 3. It can maximize the inclusion of relevant label information without losing the co-occurrence relationship. Therefore, the number of GCN layers should be the rounded up value of the average number of labels in the dataset. Similarly, the average number of labels in RCV1-V2 is 3.24, so the number of layers is set to 4.

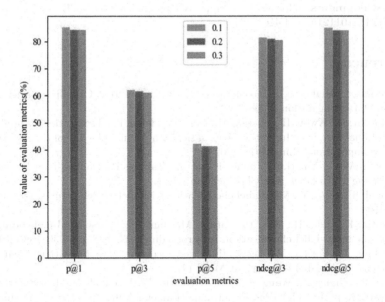

Fig. 3. When the number of layers is 3, parameter θ takes the result of 0.1, 0.2, 0.3.

Effect of Parameters θ. We conducted an experiment on the influence of parameter θ on the AAPD dataset. The parameter is to keep each GCN output retaining some of the label features from the original input. When the number of layers is 3, we select $\theta = 0.1, 0.2, 0.3$ for experimental comparison. As shown in

Fig. 3, the results of 0.1 are better than those of 0.2 and 0.3. The hop connection is added to alleviate the over-smoothness, but according to experimental results, retaining too much initial label information will reduce performance, because excessive emphasis on the node itself will weaken the GCN's function of aggregating the information of neighbor nodes. It is effective to properly keep the node itself when aggregating neighbors. We verify that the value of 0.1 is more reasonable.

5   Conclusion

In this paper, we propose a HRGCN model which employs graph convolutional networks to explore label relations for multi-label classification. Our proposed method outperforms the baseline methods by using hop residual graph convolution that capture high-order label semantic and structure, a feature extraction network composed of BiGRU and self-attention that differentially obtain text representations, a label-text interaction method that achieve deeper perception of labels and text. Numerical experimental results over two benchmark datasets verify the effectiveness of our proposed method.

Acknowledgments. This work is supported by the Science & Technology project (41008114, 41011215, and 41014117).

References

1. Katakis, I., Vlahavas, I., Tsoumakas, G.: Multilabel Text Classification for Automated Tag Suggestion (2008)
2. Gaonkar, R., Kwon, H., Bastan, M., et al.: Modeling label semantics for predicting emotional reactions. In: Proceedings of the 58th Annual Meeting of the Association for Computational Linguistics (2020)
3. Chang, W.C., Yu, H.F., Zhong, K., et al.: Taming Pretrained Transformers for Extreme Multi-label Text Classification (2019)
4. Gopal, S., Yang, Y.: Multilabel classification with meta-level features, pp. 315–322 (2010)
5. Bhatia, K., Jain, H., Kar, P., Varma, M., Jain, P.: Sparse local embeddings for extreme multi-label classification. In: Proceedings of NIPS, pp. 730–738 (2015)
6. Prabhu, Y., Varma, M.: FastXML: a fast, accurate and stable tree-classifier for extreme multi-label learning. ACM (2014)
7. You, R., Zhang, Z., Wang, Z., et al.: AttentionXML: Label Tree-based Attention-Aware Deep Model for High-Performance Extreme Multi-Label Text Classification (2018)
8. Jasinska, K., Dembczynski, K., Busa-Fekete, R., Pfannschmidt, K., Klerx, T., Hullermeier, E.: Extreme f-measure maximization using sparse probability estimates. In: ICML, pp. 1435–1444 (2016)
9. Liu, J., Chang, W.C., Wu, Y., et al.: Deep learning for extreme multi-label text classification. In: The 40th International ACM SIGIR Conference. ACM (2017)
10. Kim, Y.: Convolutional Neural Networks for Sentence Classification. Eprint Arxiv (2014)

11. Conneau, A., Schwenk, H., Barrault, L., et al.: Very deep convolutional networks for text classification. In: Proceedings of the 15th Conference of the European Chapter of the Association for Computational Linguistics: vol. 1, Long Papers (2017)
12. Yang, P., Xu, S., Wei, L., et al.: SGM: Sequence Generation Model for Multi-label Classification (2018)
13. Lin, J., Qi, S., Yang, P., et al.: Semantic-unit-based dilated convolution for multi-label text classification. In: Conference on Empirical Methods in Natural Language Processing (2018)
14. Cai, H., Zheng, V.W., Chang, C.C.: A comprehensive survey of graph embedding: problems, techniques and applications. IEEE Trans. Knowl. Data Eng. **30**(9), 1616–1637 (2017)
15. Yao, L., Mao, C., Luo, Y.: Graph Convolutional Networks for Text Classification (2018)
16. Hong, H., Guo, H., Lin, Y., et al.: An Attention-based Graph Neural Network for Heterogeneous Structural Learning (2019)
17. Hao, P., Li, J., Yu, H., et al.: Large-scale hierarchical text classification with recursively regularized deep graph-CNN. In: The 2018 World Wide Web Conference (2018)
18. Pal, A., Selvakumar, M., Sankarasubbu, M.: MAGNET: multi-label text classification using attention-based graph neural network. In: 12th International Conference on Agents and Artificial Intelligence arXiv (2020)
19. Kipf, T.N., Welling, M.: Semi-Supervised Classification with Graph Convolutional Networks (2016)
20. Dey, R., Salemt, F.M.: Gate-variants of gated recurrent unit (GRU) neural networks. In: IEEE International Midwest Symposium on Circuits & Systems, pp. 1597–1600. IEEE (2017)
21. Vaswani, A., Shazeer, N., Parmar, N., et al.: Attention is all you need. In: NIPS, pp. 5998–6008 (2017)
22. Cho, K., Merrienboer, B.V., Gulcehre, C., et al.: Learning phrase representations using RNN encoder-decoder for statistical machine translation. Computer Science (2014)
23. Jain, H., Prabhu, Y., Varma, M.: Extreme Multi-label Loss Functions for Recommendation, Tagging, Ranking & Other Missing Label Applications, pp. 935–944. ACM (2016)
24. Xiao, L., Huang, X., Chen, B., Jing, L.: Label-specific document representation for multi-label text classification. In: Proceedings of the 2019 Conference on Empirical Methods in Natural Language Processing and the 9th International Joint Conference on Natural Language Processing (EMNLP-IJCNLP) (2019)

Improving Long Content Question Generation with Multi-level Passage Encoding

Peide Zhu[✉]

Department of Software Technology, Delft University of Technology,
Delft, The Netherlands
p.zhu-1@tudelft.nl

Abstract. Generating questions that can be answered with word spans from passages is an important natural language task, which can be used for educational applications, question-answering systems, and conversational systems. Existing question generation models suffer from creating questions that are often unrelated to the context passage and answer span. In this paper, we first analyze questions generated by a common baseline model: we find over half of the generated questions that are rated as the lowest quality to be semantically unrelated to the context passage. We then investigate how humans ask factual questions and show that most often they are a reformulation of the target sentence and information from context passage. Based on these findings, we propose a multi-level encoding and gated attention fusion based neural network model for question generation (QG) which overcomes these shortcomings. Our experiments demonstrate that our model outperforms existing state-of-art seq2seq QG models.

1 Introduction

The ability to ask questions is essential for a wide range of applications, such as creating conversational systems like Google Assistant, Siri and Cortana or building education applications where questions are an essential tool for learners to aid their comprehension and memory [8]. As an important natural language processing task, question generation (QG) has received a lot of attention in recent years [3,4,7,8,10,11,22,25,29]. Based on the context information source(s), the QG task can be classified as QG from images, open-domain QG, table QG and text QG. Our work focuses on *text-based factual* question generation, which means that the answers are word spans from context passages. The early QG research works relied on rule-based or hand-crafted template-based methods [7,8, 16]. These methods faced scalability and generalization issues. More recently, QG research considers the QG task as a sequence-to-sequence (seq2seq) generation problem and tackles it with LSTM-based encoder-decoder models [4].

Despite the remarkable progress, it remains a challenge to generate high-quality questions from unstructured documents. Consider Fig. 1a for a concrete

D. N. Pham et al. (Eds.): PRICAI 2021, LNAI 13032, pp. 140–152, 2021.
https://doi.org/10.1007/978-3-030-89363-7_11

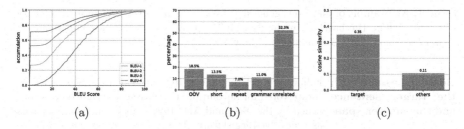

(a)   (b)   (c)

Fig. 1. Analysis of the QG baseline model [29] trained and evaluated on the SQuAD V1.1 dataset. **a**: Distribution of BLEU-4 scores. **b**: Generated questions with the lowest BLEU-4 scores were manually labeled according to their main issue. **c**: Cosine similarity between the TF-IDF encoded vector of the question (as provided in the SQuAD dataset) and the sentences within the context paragraph.

example: here we analyze the generated questions made by a recent baseline model [29] on the SQuAD V1.1 dataset [20]. Over 26.6%, 52.7% and 71.1% of the generated questions' sentence BLEU-2/3/4 scores respectively are under 1%, which means that they are of very poor quality as measured by BLEU [17]. Taking this a step further, we then sampled 200 generated questions with the lowest BLEU-4 scores and manually labeled them. Concretely, in line with [26], we employed five categories for labeling: out-of-vocabulary (OOV), too short or truncated questions (short), repeated phrases (repeat), grammar errors (grammar), and questions at least partly unrelated to the context passage (unrelated). As shown in Fig. 1b, more than 50% of the sampled generated questions are asking questions that are not related to the context passage; instead, they exhibit semantic drift [28]. Table 1 provides a typical example of a semantic drift error.

To further investigate the semantic drift issue, we conducted an analysis of *how humans ask factual questions* using the SQuAD V1.1 dataset which consists of 100k+ question-answer pairs posed by crowd workers on a set of Wikipedia articles, where the answer to each question is a segment of text from the corresponding context passage. We compute the cosine similarity between the question vector and each sentence in the context paragraph using TF-IDF word vectors. We refer to the particular sentence that contains the answer span as the target sentence. As shown in Fig. 1c, the cosine similarity between the question vector and its corresponding target sentence is 0.35, which is significantly higher than the question's similarity to the other sentences in the context. Based on this observation, we can conclude that often people ask questions that are to some extent a reformulation of the target sentence, i.e. the sentence which contains the answer spans.

Based on this insight, we argue that it is still necessary to investigate how to utilize multi-level context information for question generation. Thus, we propose a novel multi-level encoding and gated attention fusion-based neural network model for question generation and show that this model outperforms other seq2seq QG approaches. In addition, several recent QG works [1,28] optimize for the eventual evaluation metrics (which are not differentiable) using

Table 1. An example of questions generated by various models, and a case of semantic drift issue, where the baseline model S2S-MCP generates a question is not about the answer 'Scotland Act'. Our models are labels with ⋆.

Context passage with the target sentence and the answer span	Following a referendum in 1997, in which the Scottish electorate voted for devolution, the current Parliament was convened by the Scotland Act 1998, which sets out its powers as a devolved legislature. The Act delineates the legislative competence of the Parliament the areas in which it can make laws by explicitly specifying powers that are "reserved" to the Parliament of the United Kingdom. The Scottish Parliament has the power to legislate in all areas that are not explicitly reserved to Westminster. The British Parliament retains the ability to amend the terms of reference of the Scottish Parliament, and can extend or reduce the areas in which it can make laws. The first meeting of the new Parliament took place on 12 May 1999.
Gold standard	What act set out the Parliament 's powers as a devolved legislature?
S2S-MCP	where was the current parliament convened?
⋆RL-MT	what is the name of the act that sets the current parliament as a devolved legislature?
⋆ RL-MT without answer tag encoding	what act sets its powers as a devolved legislature?
⋆ RL-MT without attention fusion	what is the name of the act that sets the current parliament in 1997 ?

Reinforcement Learning (RL). We follow these existing approaches as well, and also show that we achieve significant performance improvement with automatic evaluation metrics as the reward.

2   Related Work

Past question generation research can be categorized as the rule-based and the neural network-based according to the generation approaches they employ. The rule-based approaches [7,8,10,14–16] rely on well-designed manually created templates and heuristic linguistic and semantic rules for question generation. Rule-based approaches are efficient and retains interpretability. They are especially effective for unsupervised question answering or generation applications [5]. However, template-based approaches have a lack of diversity, and usually create questions from sentence-level short texts. They cannot scale well on paragraph-level long content.

Inspired by the advances in machine translation, various neural network models have been proposed for question generation [1,4,11,12,22,23,25,27,29]. These models formulate the question generation task as a sequence-to-sequence neural learning problem with different types of encoders, decoders, and attention mechanisms. Despite all the achieved advances, these models only use either context or sentence for QG. As in the paragraph-level long context, there are usually several facts are related to the answer. Therefore, multiple questions are valid for the context and answer. However, on one hand, usually only one ground-truth is given in datasets for each context-answer pair; on the other hand, as we show in Fig. 1c, while further information from the whole paragraph is required for asking questions, human generally pays more attention to the target sentence which contains the answer. Thus, we argue that the multi-level information between the sentence and the whole paragraph requires further investigation for creating reliable and stable neural models for QG.

3   Architecture Overview

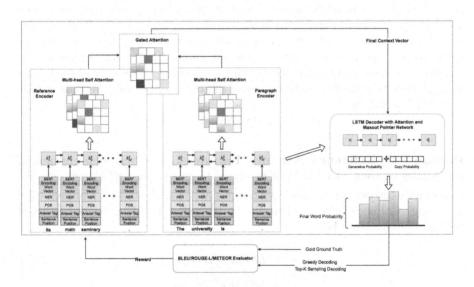

Fig. 2. Architecture of our proposed question generation model.

In this section, we now present and motivate our proposed neural architecture for question generation.

We use P, T, A to represent the passage, target sentence, and answer span respectively. The answer span is contained in the target sentence. We create a processed target sentence by replacing all words in the answer span with the special answer token <ans>. Let Q represent the generated question. Then, the question generation task can be formalized as:

$$\overline{Q} = \text{argmax}_Q Prob(Q|P, A, T)$$

where the passage is comprised of a sequence of words $P = \{x_i\}_{i=1}^{M}$ (with M being the size of the passage), similar to the reference sentence $T = \{x_i\}_{i=1}^{N}$ (with N being the size of the reference sentence) which contains the answer span. Figure 2 shows the end-to-end question generation model we propose in this work. We now explain its components in detail.

3.1 Encoder

Word Embedding. The encoder uses six different representations of each word x_i to form the final word embedding $\mathbf{e}_i$: word vector v_i, POS and NE, answer tag a_i, sentence position s_i and BERT encoding vector b_i. We encode the passage with BERT to obtain each word's context vector, as BERT provides deep bidirectional representations. For words out of BERT's vocabulary, we sum up the hidden states of all sub-tokens as their context vector. We use Glove [19] to obtain the word vector. We use Stanford's CoreNLP [13] package for labeling the named entities and determine the part-of-speech tags in each paragraph. The POS tags and named entity representation sizes are set as $\log_2 |POS| + 1$ and $\log_2 |NE| + 1$. The answer tag represents whether word x_i is part of the answer span. We use one float for sentence position embedding, which represents the sentence distance to the reference sentence containing the answer-span. In this way, we specify explicitly each sentence's importance. Overall, we thus encode each word as follows:

$$\mathbf{e}_i = [v_i; POS_i; NE_i; a_i; s_i; b_i]$$

Passage and Reference Sentence Encoders. The embedding output of the passage is then encoded by a two-layer bi-directional LSTM network. We concatenate the two direction's hidden states $\overrightarrow{h_i^p}, \overleftarrow{h_i^p}$ as the hidden representation h_i^p of any word at position i. Then, the bi-directional LSTM network is a list of hidden representation $\mathbf{H^P}$:

$$\begin{aligned}
\overrightarrow{h_i^p} &= \overrightarrow{LSTM}(\mathbf{e}_i^p, \overrightarrow{h_{i-1}^p}) \\
\overleftarrow{h_i^p} &= \overleftarrow{LSTM}(\mathbf{e}_i^p, \overleftarrow{h_{i+1}^p}) \\
h_i^p &= \left[\overrightarrow{h_i^p}; \overleftarrow{h_i^p}\right] \\
\mathbf{H^P} &= \left\{h_i^p\right\}_{i=1}^{M}
\end{aligned} \tag{1}$$

Analogously to the passage encoder, the embedding output of the reference sentence is also encoded by a two-layer bi-directional LSTM network. The bi-directional LSTM network output of the reference sentence is denoted as $\mathbf{H^q}$.

Multi-head Self-attention. Multi-head self-attention [24] allows the model to jointly attend to information from different representation subspaces at different

positions. We apply it here on the passage and reference sentence respectively
to embed their interdependency:

$$\text{M-attn}(Q, K, V) = \text{Concat}(hd_1, \ldots, hd_h)W^O$$
$$\text{where } hd_i = \text{Attn}(QW_i^Q, KW_i^K, VW_i^V) \qquad (2)$$
$$\textbf{Attn } = \textbf{softmax}(\frac{QK^T}{\sqrt{d_k}})V$$

Gated Attention at Passage and Reference Sentence Level. In our
model, we use gated attention between the self-attention output of the passage and reference sentence to aggregate information from both. Inspired by
[29] we conduct the following two steps: 1) we determine the matching between
the passage output $\mathbf{H}^p$ and the encoded reference sentence representation h_i^q to
compute a matching representation; 2) we combine the matching representation
with the passage encoding using a feature fusion gate [6]:

$$\mathbf{d^c}_i = softmax(\mathbf{H}^{p\mathbf{T}}\mathbf{W}^c\mathbf{h}_i^q)$$
$$\mathbf{g}_i = \mathbf{H}^{q\mathbf{T}} \cdot \mathbf{d^c}_i$$
$$\mathbf{f}_i = tanh(\mathbf{W}^f[\mathbf{h}_i^p, \mathbf{g}_i]) \qquad (3)$$
$$\mathbf{g}_i = sigmoid(\mathbf{W}^g[\mathbf{h}_i^p, \mathbf{s}_i])$$
$$\hat{\mathbf{h}}_i^\mathbf{p} = \mathbf{g}_i \odot \mathbf{s}_i + (1 - \mathbf{g}_i) \odot \mathbf{h}_i^p$$

Here, $\mathbf{W}$ refers to a trainable weight matrix.

3.2   Decoder

The decoder is a two-layer uni-directional LSTM network with attention mechanism and max-out copy mechanism. The decoder LSTM's hidden state is initial-
ized by concatenating the forward and backward encoder hidden states $[\overrightarrow{\mathbf{h}^p}; \overleftarrow{\mathbf{h}^p}]$.
At each decoding step t, the decoder calculates the current hidden state with
previous predicted word embedding w_{t-1} and previous attention context vector
c_{t-1}, and previous step hidden state $\mathbf{h}_{t-1}$:

$$h_t = \mathbf{LSTM}([w_{t-1}, c_{t-1}], \mathbf{h}_{t-1}),$$

where the context vector c_t is the calculated by concatenating the LSTM output
$\mathbf{h}_t$ and the attention context vector $\mathbf{d}_t$. Here, we make use of the Luong attention
mechanism:

$$r_t = \hat{\mathbf{H}}^{p\mathbf{T}} W^a h_t$$
$$a_t^h = softmax(r_t)$$
$$d_t = \hat{\mathbf{H}}^p \cdot a_t^h \qquad (4)$$
$$\mathbf{c}_t = tanh(W^b[h_t; d_t])$$

For the out-of-vocabulary problem, we apply a max-out pointer network to copy words from the input directly [29]. We use raw attention scores $r_i = \{r_{i,k}\}_{k=1}^{M}$ over the input sequence which has a vocabulary Ω. At every step, the word is regarded as a unique copy target and the final score is calculated as the maximum value of all scores pointing to the same word:

$$
\text{sc}^{copy}(y_i) = \begin{cases} \max\limits_{k,\text{where}x_k=y_i} r_{i,k}, & y_i \in \Omega \\ -\inf, & otherwise \end{cases}
\tag{5}
$$

Here, x_k is the word vocabulary index of the kth word in the input and y_i denotes the ith word in the decoded sequence. Scores of non-occurring words are set to negative infinity. Then, we concatenate $\text{sc}^{copy}(y_i)$ and $\text{sc}^{gen}(y_i)$ and perform *softmax* on the concatenated vectors. Non-occurring words are masked out in this step.

3.3 Reinforcement Learning

We use the self-critical sequence training (SCST) algorithm [21] for RL. SCST is an efficient reinforcement algorithm that directly utilizes the test-time inference output to normalize the rewards it experiences. At each training iteration, the model generates two output sequences: the sampled output Y^s, produced by multinomial sampling, that is, each word y_t^s is sampled according to the likelihood $P(y_t|X, y_{<t})$ predicted by the generator, and the baseline output $\hat{Y}$, obtained by greedy search, that is, by maximizing the output probability distribution at each decoding step. We define $r(Y)$ as the reward of an output sequence Y, computed by comparing it to corresponding ground-truth sequence Y^* with some reward metrics. The loss function is defined as:

$$
\mathbf{L}_{rl} = (r(\hat{Y}) - r(Y^s)) \sum_t \log \mathbf{P}(y_t^s|X, y_{<t}^s)
$$

Using this reinforcement loss alone does not result in correctly learnt word probabilities. For this reason, we follow the mixed objective approach [1], combining both cross-entropy loss (language model loss) and the RL loss:

$$
\mathbf{L}_{mixed} = \lambda \mathbf{L}_{rl} + (1-\lambda)\mathbf{L}_{ml}
$$

where λ is a mixing ratio to control the balancing between RL loss and model loss. We experiment with different automatic evaluation metrics as our reward function: BLEU, METEOR and Rouge-L.

4 Experimental Setup

In this section, we first introduce the dataset we use for model evaluation and then outline implementation details, evaluation metrics and our baselines to compare against.

Table 2. Question generation evaluation results as reported on the SQuAD test sets as defined in Sect. 4.1 ("split 1" and "split 2"). Evaluation metrics not reported in the respective papers are marked as '-'. The reported metrics are BLEU-3 (B-3), BLEU-4 (B-4), Meteor (MT) and Rouge-L (RGL).

Models	Split1				Split2			
	B-3	B-4	MT	RGL	B-3	B-4	MT	RGL
S2S-MCP	21.60	16.38	20.25	44.48	22.16	16.85	20.25	44.99
SemQG	-	18.37	22.65	46.68	-	20.76	24.20	48.91
G2S-RLQG	-	17.94	21.76	46.02	-	18.30	21.70	45.98
ours-basic	24.97	19.18	22.56	47.44	26.25	20.46	23.15	48.57
ours-RL-B4	26.39	20.39	23.60	48.65	27.46	21.49	**24.45**	49.61
ours-RL-MT	**26.73**	**20.69**	**23.72**	48.56	**28.01**	**22.02**	24.35	49.66
ours-RL-RGL	25.60	19.85	22.95	**48.66**	26.68	20.95	23.41	**49.76**

4.1 Datasets

We test our proposed QG model on the SQuAD [20] dataset. It contains over 100K question-answer pairs generated by crowdworkers from 536 Wikipedia articles. The answers are selected word spans from article sentences. The dataset contains publicly accessible train and development splits and a privately hosted test split. Following [4], we split the original training dataset into training and development set with a 90%-10% ratio, and use the whole original development set as our test set (we refer to this as "split 1"). In addition, we also conduct experiments on another data split ("split 2") following [29], which uses the whole original training data as training set and splits the original development set as development set and test set with a 50%-50% ratio. Providing results on both types of splits tells us something about the robustness of our model and allows a fair comparison to a range of prior works.

4.2 Implementation Details

We implement the proposed QG model in PyTorch 1.4 [18]. We set the hyperparameters based on the literature and an empirical evaluation of data split 2. We select the model that performs best on the development set as the final model. The encoder uses a 2 layer bi-directional LSTM. The LSTM hidden cell size is 300. A dropout layer with a probability 0.3 is applied between two bi-directional LSTM layers. We keep the 45K most frequent words in SQuAD as vocabulary. The decoder uses a 2 layer LSTM with a hidden cell size 600. We use SGD with momentum for optimization (momentum value is 0.8). The initial learning rate is 0.1 and decreases linearly after half of the training steps. We use beam search (beam size 10) for the decoding. Decoding stops when the <EOS> token is generated or the length of generated question exceeds the maximum allowed length. We set the mini-batch size to 64 and train the model with 2 GTX 1080

Ti GPUs for 40 epochs. We truncate all paragraphs to 400 words by keeping the sentences closest to the target sentence. The minimum and maximum decoding lengths are set to 5 and 32 words respectively. The mixing ratio λ in RL is set to 0.2.

4.3   Evaluation Metrics

Following [4, 12, 29], we compare the performance of our proposed model to a number of baselines along with three automatic evaluation metrics: BLEU, Meteor and Rouge-L, which are commonly used in text generation tasks. We calculate these metrics using the evaluation package released by [4]. **BLEU** [17] is a widely used automatic text evaluation metric especially for machine translation task. It is computed with the geometric average of the modified n-gram precision and the brevity penalty. In our experiments, we consider the BLEU-3 and BLEU-4 scores. **Meteor** [2] is a language-specific evaluation metric that compares the candidate with the reference text in terms of exact, stem, synonym, and paraphrase matches between words and phrases. Lastly, **Rouge** [9] measures the number of overlapping units such as n-gram, word sequences, and word pairs between the candidates and the references. Rouge-L calculates the longest common sub-sequence shared by the candidate and reference text.

In addition to the automatic metrics, we also conducted a human evaluation on split-2. We randomly sampled 100 questions generated by the baseline model S2S-MCP and our meteor-rewarded RL model. Our annotator received the context paragraphs, the answers, and the two types of generated questions plus the gold standard questions. The annotator rated the (generated) questions on a 3-point scale along two dimensions: their syntax correctness and their relevance (i.e. is the question relevant to the context and the answer). For syntax, 1 means major syntax issues; 2 means a small mistake (e.g. lacking an article or pronoun); 3 is correct. In the relevance category, 1 means the question is not relevant to the context and the answer; 2 means partially relevant (e.g. question may be more general than what the answer is about); 3 means the question is relevant and has the answer span as the answer.

4.4   Baseline Methods

We compare our proposed model with the following baselines: S2S-MCP [29], SemQG [28], and G2S-RLQG [1]. S2S-MCP is a paragraph-level end-to-end question generation model using LSTM, max-out copy network and gated self-attention networks. The SemQG model addresses semantic drift in question generation using reinforcement learning with hybrid rewards and deep context word vectors like BERT and ELMo. G2S-RLQG proposes a reinforcement learning-based graph-to-sequence model for QG. We report the results as found in the respective papers.

5   Results and Analysis

In this section, we report the evaluation results of our proposed model, conduct model analysis, and compare our results with state-of-art baselines.

Table 2 presents a comparison of our proposed model along with the just-introduced baselines. We conducted our experiments with four variants of our model: one without RL ("ours-basic") and three variants with RL and each time a different metric as reward function: BLEU-4, Meteor, and Rouge-L respectively. In terms of model effectiveness, we can see our basic model without reinforcement learning to achieve better results than all baseline methods. By applying reinforcement learning with BLEU-4, Meteor, or Rouge-L as the reward, we achieve further improvements on all these metrics. On both dataset splits, RL using METEOR as reward overall yields the best results.

Table 3. Ablation study on SQuAD split-1 test set.

Model	B-3	B-4	MT	RGL
ours-basic	24.97	19.18	22.56	47.44
Without answer tag	24.29	18.59	22.47	46.28
Without bert encoding	22.87	17.45	21.30	44.34
Without attention fusion	24.55	18.78	22.22	46.37

Next, we perform an ablation study to assess the impact of different model components. The results are shown in Table 3. We here compare the performance of our model without BERT embeddings, without answer tags, and without attention-fusion. Without answer tags, the BLEU-4 score of our model drops from 19.18 to 18.59, which indicates the importance of tagging answer spans in the context for QG. Without BERT's context encoding, the model performance in BLEU-4 scores drops from 19.18 to 17.45. Given the extent to which BERT has improved state-of-the-art models, this drop is not surprising. The model performance without BERT encoding still outperforms baseline model S2S-MCP, which indicates our model architecture's effectiveness. We also compare our model's performance without attention-fusion of multi-level encoding. In this instance, the BLEU-4 score drops from 19.18 to 18.78. This shows that the attention-fusion captures the alignment information from the target sentence and paragraph. We also conduct a human evaluation in terms of syntax and relevance on 100 randomly sampled ground-truth questions and questions generated by the baseline model S2S-MCP and our model. Table 4 shows the human evaluation results. Importantly, we find our model to outperform our baseline in terms of relevance (2.42 vs. 2.04) while having a comparable level of syntax correctness (2.48 vs. 2.50).

To gain an intuition of the questions the different models produce, we provide two examples in Table 1. For the latter example, we also visualize the alignment scores of the target sentence and paragraph in Fig. 3. We can see the words that

Table 4. Human evaluation (mean and standard deviation) on split-2. The evaluation adopted a 3-point scale. Higher is better.

Model	Syntax	Relevance
Gold	2.91 (0.35)	2.94 (0.28)
ours-RL-MT	2.48 (0.77)	2.42 (0.78)
S2S-MCP	2.5 (0.745)	2.04 (0.88)

neighbor the answer span (such as *cytotoxic, immunosuppressive, drugs, anti-inflammatory*) receive greater scores. This alignment indicates the encoder can capture most useful knowledge for decoding.

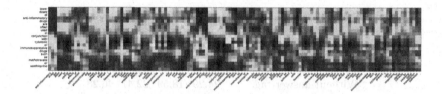

Fig. 3. Attention fusion alignments map: each row represents an alignment vector from target sentence to the context paragraph. Cold blue color means lower score and the hot red colors means higher scores. (Color figure online)

6   Conclusions

In this paper, we propose a novel sequence to sequence model for paragraph-level question generation. In this model, we encode the paragraph and target sentence separately and use attention-fusion to learn the alignment of the paragraph and the target sentence. We demonstrate that the proposed model can effectively learn the alignment between the paragraph the reference question, and outperform existing baseline models. We further conduct RL on the model and show that with the automatic evaluation metrics such as METEOR, BLEU and Rouge-L as the reward, the application of RL can further improve the model's performance. A human evaluation confirms this finding. While in this work we are focusing on generating factual questions, in future work, we aim to generate more diverse and complicated questions for education purposes, that cover different levels of learning (not just questions for remembering facts, but also for knowledge understanding and analyzing).

Acknowledgments. This research has been supported by the China Scholarships Council (No. 201906340170).

References

1. Chen, Y., Wu, L., Zaki, M.J.: Reinforcement learning based graph-to-sequence model for natural question generation. In: 8th International Conference on Learning Representations, ICLR 2020, Addis Ababa, Ethiopia, 26–30 April 2020. OpenReview.net (2020). https://openreview.net/forum?id=HygnDhEtvr

2. Denkowski, M., Lavie, A.: Meteor universal: language specific translation evaluation for any target language. In: Proceedings of the Ninth Workshop on Statistical Machine Translation, pp. 376–380 (2014)

3. Dong, L., et al.: Unified language model pre-training for natural language understanding and generation. In: Advances in Neural Information Processing Systems, pp. 13042–13054 (2019)

4. Du, X., Shao, J., Cardie, C.: Learning to ask: neural question generation for reading comprehension. arXiv preprint arXiv:1705.00106 (2017)

5. Fabbri, A.R., Ng, P., Wang, Z., Nallapati, R., Xiang, B.: Template-based question generation from retrieved sentences for improved unsupervised question answering. arXiv preprint arXiv:2004.11892 (2020)

6. Gong, Y., Bowman, S.R.: Ruminating reader: reasoning with gated multi-hop attention. arXiv preprint arXiv:1704.07415 (2017)

7. Heilman, M.: Automatic factual question generation from text. Language Technologies Institute School of Computer Science Carnegie Mellon University 195 (2011)

8. Heilman, M., Smith, N.A.: Good question! statistical ranking for question generation. In: Human Language Technologies: The 2010 Annual Conference of the North American Chapter of the Association for Computational Linguistics, pp. 609–617. Association for Computational Linguistics (2010)

9. Lin, C.Y.: Rouge: a package for automatic evaluation of summaries. In: Text Summarization Branches Out, pp. 74–81 (2004)

10. Lindberg, D., Popowich, F., Nesbit, J., Winne, P.: Generating natural language questions to support learning on-line. In: Proceedings of the 14th European Workshop on Natural Language Generation, pp. 105–114 (2013)

11. Liu, B., et al.: Learning to generate questions by learning what not to generate. In: The World Wide Web Conference, pp. 1106–1118 (2019)

12. Ma, X., Zhu, Q., Zhou, Y., Li, X., Wu, D.: Improving question generation with sentence-level semantic matching and answer position inferring. arXiv preprint arXiv:1912.00879 (2019)

13. Manning, C.D., Surdeanu, M., Bauer, J., Finkel, J.R., Bethard, S., McClosky, D.: The Stanford corenlp natural language processing toolkit. In: Proceedings of 52nd Annual Meeting of the Association for Computational Linguistics: System Demonstrations, pp. 55–60 (2014)

14. Mazidi, K., Nielsen, R.: Linguistic considerations in automatic question generation. In: Proceedings of the 52nd Annual Meeting of the Association for Computational Linguistics (Volume 2: Short Papers), pp. 321–326 (2014)

15. Mitkov, R., et al.: Computer-aided generation of multiple-choice tests. In: Proceedings of the HLT-NAACL 2003 Workshop on Building Educational Applications Using Natural Language Processing, pp. 17–22 (2003)

16. Mostow, J., Chen, W.: Generating instruction automatically for the reading strategy of self-questioning. In: AIED, pp. 465–472 (2009)

17. Papineni, K., Roukos, S., Ward, T., Zhu, W.J.: BLEU: a method for automatic evaluation of machine translation. In: Proceedings of the 40th annual meeting of the Association for Computational Linguistics, pp. 311–318 (2002)

18. Paszke, A., et al.: Pytorch: an imperative style, high-performance deep learning library. In: Wallach, H., Larochelle, H., Beygelzimer, A., d'Alch'e Buc, F., Fox, E., Garnett, R. (eds.) Advances in Neural Information Processing Systems, vol. 32, pp. 8024–8035. Curran Associates, Inc. (2019). http://papers.neurips.cc/paper/9015-pytorch-an-imperative-style-high-performance-deep-learning-library.pdf
19. Pennington, J., Socher, R., Manning, C.D.: Glove: global vectors for word representation. In: Proceedings of the 2014 Conference on Empirical Methods in Natural Language Processing (EMNLP), pp. 1532–1543 (2014)
20. Rajpurkar, P., Zhang, J., Lopyrev, K., Liang, P.: Squad: 100,000+ questions for machine comprehension of text. arXiv preprint arXiv:1606.05250 (2016)
21. Rennie, S.J., Marcheret, E., Mroueh, Y., Ross, J., Goel, V.: Self-critical sequence training for image captioning. In: Proceedings of the IEEE Conference on Computer Vision and Pattern Recognition, pp. 7008–7024 (2017)
22. Tang, D., Duan, N., Qin, T., Yan, Z., Zhou, M.: Question answering and question generation as dual tasks. arXiv preprint arXiv:1706.02027 (2017)
23. Tang, D., et al.: Learning to collaborate for question answering and asking. In: Proceedings of the 2018 Conference of the North American Chapter of the Association for Computational Linguistics: Human Language Technologies, vol. 1 (Long Papers), pp. 1564–1574 (2018)
24. Vaswani, A., et al.: Attention is all you need. In: Advances in Neural Information Processing Systems, pp. 5998–6008 (2017)
25. Wang, Z., Lan, A.S., Nie, W., Waters, A.E., Grimaldi, P.J., Baraniuk, R.G.: QG-Net: a data-driven question generation model for educational content. In: Proceedings of the Fifth Annual ACM Conference on Learning at Scale, pp. 1–10 (2018)
26. Xie, Z.: Neural text generation: a practical guide. arXiv preprint arXiv:1711.09534 (2017)
27. Yuan, X., et al.: Machine comprehension by text-to-text neural question generation. arXiv preprint arXiv:1705.02012 (2017)
28. Zhang, S., Bansal, M.: Addressing semantic drift in question generation for semi-supervised question answering. arXiv preprint arXiv:1909.06356 (2019)
29. Zhao, Y., Ni, X., Ding, Y., Ke, Q.: Paragraph-level neural question generation with maxout pointer and gated self-attention networks. In: Proceedings of the 2018 Conference on Empirical Methods in Natural Language Processing, pp. 3901–3910 (2018)

Learning Vietnamese-English Code-Switching Speech Synthesis Model Under Limited Code-Switched Data Scenario

Cuong Manh Nguyen[1,2(✉)], Lam Viet Phung[1(✉)], Cuc Thi Bui[1,2],
Trang Van Truong[1], and Huy Tien Nguyen[1,3,4]

[1] Zalo Group - VNG Corporation, Ho Chi Minh City, Vietnam
{cuongnm5,lampv,cucbt,trangtv}@vng.com.vn
[2] Post and Telecommunication Institute of Technology, Ha Noi City, Vietnam
[3] Vietnam National University, Ho Chi Minh City, Vietnam
[4] Faculty of Information Technology, University of Science,
Ho Chi Minh City, Vietnam
ntienhuy@fit.hcmus.edu.vn

Abstract. Recent advances in deep learning facilitate the development of end-to-end Vietnamese text-to-speech (TTS) systems that produce Vietnamese voices with high intelligibility and naturalness. However, enabling these systems to speak Vietnamese and English words in the same utterance fluently remains a challenge known as the code-switching (CS) problem in speech synthesis. The main reason is that it is not easy to obtain a large amount of high-quality CS corpus from a Vietnamese speaker. In this paper, we explore the efficacy of three approaches, which are based on the Tacotron-2 end-to-end framework, to build such a Vietnamese TTS system under a limited code-switched data scenario: (1) CS synthesis based on grapheme-to-syllable (G2S), (2) CS synthesis based on speaker embedding, and (3) CS synthesis based on speaker embedding and language embedding. We handle English and Vietnamese words in the code-switched input text by converting them into Vietnamese syllables using our G2S model. For the speaker-embedding based approach, we combine Vietnamese monolingual data in our dataset with an English public dataset to train a multi-speaker Tacotron-2 system. The experimental results show that adding language embedding is effective, and training with character input representations outperforms phonemes. Thus, the speaker and language-embedding based approach achieves strong results in naturalness for CS speech. Besides, the G2S-based CS synthesis also has good results, with almost absolute English pronunciation accuracy.

Keywords: Speech synthesis · Multi-speaker · Tacotron-2 · Code-switching

---

C.M. Nguyen and L.V. Phung—Equal contribution.

D. N. Pham et al. (Eds.): PRICAI 2021, LNAI 13032, pp. 153–163, 2021.
https://doi.org/10.1007/978-3-030-89363-7_12

1   Introduction

Text-to-Speech (TTS) is a technology that converts any text into a speech signal. With TTS, human-machine communication is easier and more natural than ever. As a result, it has great potential and can be applied to many different purposes, e.g., audiobooks, movie narrations, response services in telecommunications, and virtual assistants. Through decades of research and development, end-to-end speech synthesis systems for a single language have achieved outstanding results and produced natural human-like voices even in real-time. Based on these advances, recent end-to-end neural TTS models have been extended to enable control of speaker identity, controllability, or multilingual.

In the last two decades, there have been many attempts to build high-quality Vietnamese TTS systems. A data processing scheme proved its efficacy in optimizing the naturalness of end-to-end TTS systems trained on Vietnamese found data [12]. Text normalization methods were explored, utilizing regular expressions and language model [17]. New prosodic features (e.g., phrase breaks) were investigated, which showed their efficacy in improving the naturalness of Vietnamese hidden Markov models (HMM)-based TTS systems [2]. Different types of acoustic models were investigated, such as HMM [9], deep neural networks (DNN) [8], and sequence-to-sequence models [12]. For post-filtering, it was shown that a global variance scaling method might destroy the tonal information; therefore, exemplar-based voice conversion methods were utilized in post-filtering to preserve the tonal information [18]. Moreover, recently, Phung has applied new data processing method to generate natural Vietnamese human-like voices; and achieved good results in Vietnamese speech synthesis [12]. To our knowledge, there is little to no study on CS TTS systems involving Vietnamese. In linguistics, the interlacing of languages in text or speech is known as code-switching (CS). Along with the rise of globalization, code-switching is a common phenomenon that occurs in social media text, informal messages, and voice navigation [16]. The CS phenomenon poses a significant challenge for modern TTS systems to generate corresponding sounds of foreign words in CS texts. A typical foreign language in the CS synthesis system is probably English because of its popularity. Mac showed that among the top 10000 foreign words, which cover up 83% foreign word tokens in his Vietnamese corpus text, 70% of these words are in the English dictionary [6]. Therefore, we can see building a Vietnamese TTS system, which can pronounce English in code-switched utterances fluently, as building a CS bilingual Vietnamese-English system. Those two languages use two different sets of phonemes. If we have a large amount of code-switched data, then that problem is relatively trivial. However, it is not easy to obtain a bilingual CS TTS dataset from a single Vietnamese speaker who achieves native-level fluency in both languages. In this work, our Vietnamese dataset consists of mostly Vietnamese monolingual utterances, and only 12% are Vietnamese-English code-switched utterances (e.g., " dịch bùng phát, nên mình đang work from home").

In order to manage the alphabetic inputs from multiple languages, two types of encoders were examined in the context of CS TTS: shared multilingual encoder with explicit language embedding and separated monolingual encoder [1]. Using the encoders created more natural code-switched utterances than Tacotron [19]. Xue proposed a robust Mandarin-English mixed-lingual TTS system using solely monolingual data in [21]. In summary, E2E TTS introduces one of the most successful implementations for CS speech content [23].

We explore the efficacy of three approaches, which are based on the Tacotron-2 end-to-end framework [15], to build a Vietnamese TTS system under a limited bilingual code-switched data scenario. (1) Grapheme-to-Syllable-based CS synthesis, (2) Speaker-embedding based CS synthesis, (3) Speaker-embedding and language-embedding based CS synthesis. With the grapheme-to-syllable (G2S) model, we convert all English words into Vietnamese syllables and some self-defined syllables to describe features of English pronunciation, such as voiceless consonants. In this approach, we take advantage of the efficiency of the Tacotron-2 model for monolingual syllables, and we utilize the code-switched data contained in our Vietnamese dataset to learn the features of English pronunciation. Using the G2S model, however, does not guarantee the naturalness of the voice because the pronunciation of Vietnamese syllables is probably different from that of English syllables. This limitation of G2S model motivates us to adopt a speaker-embedding based approach that should improve the naturalness of pronunciation. Specifically, we combine Vietnamese monolingual data from our Vietnamese dataset with an English public dataset to train a multi-speaker Tacotron-2 system. We expect that this speaker-embedding model can learn the native pronunciation of English words from English speakers. Our last approach, which is the speaker embedding and language-embedding based CS synthesis, combines speaker-based CS synthesis and language embedding. In our intuition, by providing explicit language information for each input character, our system can learn to handle the code-switched data better.

2 Vietnamese-English Code-Switching Synthesis Systems

Our systems are based on Tacotron 2, which comprises a sequence-to-sequence acoustic model, followed by a neural vocoder to generate waveform from the acoustic feature. We used WaveGlow [14] vocoder instead of WaveNet [10] vocoder as in the original Tacotron 2 architecture. WaveGlow is a deep generative model for audio that integrates Glow [5], a generative model for image processing, with WaveNet. The acoustic model has an encoder and an autoregressive decoder with attention. The encoder converts an input text into a hidden linguistic feature representation which the decoder consumes to predict an acoustic feature. Thus, to solve the code-switched synthesis problem, we focus on the feature prediction part.

2.1 Grapheme-to-Syllable-Based Code-Switching Synthesis

In this approach, we convert all English words into Vietnamese syllables and some self-defined syllables to describe features of English pronunciation.

Vietnamese is a monosyllabic language where each Vietnamese word contains a syllable, a complete block in pronunciation. Meanwhile, English is a multi-syllable language. Therefore, many words in English are composed of more than one syllable. Nevertheless, English syllables and Vietnamese syllables are quite similar, especially in the pronunciation of Vietnamese people.

The most obvious difference is the presence of voiceless consonants in English syllables (e.g., final fricative consonants), which is absent in Vietnamese syllables. To read English words more naturally, the model needs to read voiceless consonants. With the small number of English words in the dataset, our solution is to borrow Vietnamese syllables and voiceless consonants to read the English words. For examples, 'studio' is split into ' x-tiu-đi-ô ', 'speech' becomes ' x-pích-ch '. In the examples above, the voiceless consonants are the 'x' sound and 'ch' sound. We link syllables with hyphens, so the model knows they are syllables of an English word and are not separate Vietnamese syllables, making the duration and pronunciation of an English word more accurate.

To do so, we build a specific G2S converter where the input is the English word (such as "studio") and the corresponding syllables (such as " x-tiu-đi-ô" with hyphens separating the four syllables). We use the G2S converter to normalize English words in the input text of our Tacotron-2 system to phonetic form. Our G2S converter is a seq2seq model with 2 BiLSTM encoders and 2 LSTM decoders with attention as described in Fig. 1. Our implementation is based on [11] but we use character input representations instead of phoneme. We also train the Tacotron-2 system with character-level input.

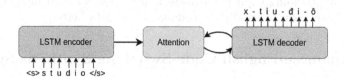

Fig. 1. An overview of the components of the G2S model

2.2 Speaker-Embedding Based Code-Switching Synthesis

In this approach, we utilize speaker embedding to address the CS phenomenon. We build a multi-speaker TTS system by prepending a speaker embedding module, making the system share the vast majority of parameters between speakers to a traditional Tacotron-2 system. Thus, the multi-speaker speech synthesis model is a single model that can generate speech from many different voices of different speakers.

Unlike Deep Voice 3 [13] which learned low-dimensional site-specific speaker embedding for each training speaker, we use a channel-wise speaker embedding. Figure 2 shows an overview of speaker embedding code-switching synthesis system, but we do not use the language embedding module. One-hot speaker identity vector is converted to a 32-dimensional speaker embedding vector by the speaker embedding network. The embedded vector is concatenated with each element of the Tacotron-2 encoded sequence attended by the Tacotron-2 attention and decoder network while generating a spectrogram.

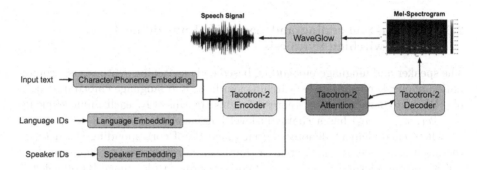

Fig. 2. An overview of speaker-embedding and language-embedding based code-switching synthesis system

With this approach, we do not need the CS data. In our experiment, we only use the Vietnamese monolingual data in our Vietnamese dataset to remove the effect of CS data. We combine Vietnamese monolingual data with an English monolingual public dataset to train the speaker-embedding based CS synthesis system. We have two speakers, so the input one-hot speaker identity vector is [0, 1] or [1, 0]. We expect the model to learn the pronunciation of English words from a native speaker. When we apply the model on CS input text to synthesize Vietnamese voice, the model knows how to pronounce the English words as English speakers.

The original Tacotron-2 system uses character input representations [15]. However, some other end-to-end TTS systems also achieve good results when used phoneme input representations [20], or hybrids between character and phoneme [4]. Another study showed that phoneme input representation gives better results than the character in multi-lingual TTS [22]. This paper also evaluates the effect of using different text input representations in our speaker-embedding based CS synthesis system. The input text is represented by a 512-dimensional character embedding or phoneme embedding.

Speaker-Embedding and Character-Representation Based CS Synthesis. Vietnamese characters originated from Latin characters, so Vietnamese characters were most similar to English. So for extending a character-based input vocabulary to a multilingual setting is straightforward; we concatenate character sets in the training corpus for each language. Equivalent characters are shared across languages. We keep all English words in origin included in the dataset.

Speaker-Embedding and Phoneme-Representation Based CS Synthesis. We use grapheme-to-phoneme (G2P) models to convert input text to the corresponding phoneme sequence. For Vietnamese input text, we use a dictionary built by a language expert to map Vietnamese syllables with the corresponding Vietnamese phonemes. For English input text, we use a pre-trained English G2P model from Montreal Forced Aligner [7].

2.3   Speaker-Embedding and Language-Embedding Based Code-Switching Synthesis

The speaker and language-embedding based code-switching synthesis is a combination of speaker-based code-switching synthesis and language embedding module. We use character input representations. In this way, each input sequence $x = [x_1, x_2, ..., x_n]$ has a character-level language ID sequence $l = [l_1, l_2, ..., l_n]$ where each element denotes the language ID of corresponding character in the input sequence. In our system, a character corresponding to language ID of 1 if it is from Vietnamese words and corresponding to language ID of 2 if it is from English words. We obtain language-embedded information for each character of the input text by a learned 4-dimensional language embedding network. We concatenate the language embedded information with the character embedded information from a learned 512-dimensional character embedding to form the input of the Tacotron-2 encoder (see Fig. 2). In our intuition, by providing explicit language information for each input character, our system can learn to handle the code-switched data better.

3   Experiments

3.1   Dataset

The data we build for training the G2S model are Out-Of-Vietnamese-Vocabulary (OOV) words collect from a news website[1], which are primarily English words. Our dataset consists of 20000 pairs of OOV words and corresponding spelling. We also use a method of concatenating short words to long words to generate more data for the model.

Our Vietnamese internal TTS dataset contains 21 h of voice recording from a northern Vietnamese female speaker, including 11900 utterances, and only 12% are CS utterances. In the CS utterances, English words only account for 8.29%, with most English words like famous people's names, teams, or places.

Due to the limited number of English words in our Vietnamese dataset, we utilize an additional English database to learn English pronunciation. We use LJSpeech public database that consists of 13,100 short audio clips of a female speaker reading passages from 7 non-fiction books and have a total length of approximately 24 h [3].

---

[1] baomoi.com.

3.2 Training Setup

For the G2S-based CS synthesis system, we first train the G2S model with a batch size of 32, using the Adam optimizer configured with an initial learning rate of 0.001. Then we use the G2S model to convert the English words contained in the original Vietnamese dataset to phonetic form. Finally, we train the Tacotron-2 system on a Vietnamese normalized dataset with batch size 32 on a single GPU.

For systems based on speaker embedding and speaker-language embedding, we remove the CS data in the original Vietnamese dataset to obtain the Vietnamese monolingual dataset, combined with the LJSpeech dataset for training. The systems are all trained with a batch size of 32, using the Adam optimizer configured with an initial learning rate of 10^{-3}. After 15k steps, an exponential decay halves the learning rate every 10k steps.

4 Evaluation and Discussion

This section evaluates the efficacy of four CS TTS systems in terms of speech quality, English word pronunciation quality, and English pronunciation accuracy test. In Sect. 4.1, we conduct a MOS test to evaluate the overall sound quality. In Sect. 4.2, we also conduct a MOS test to evaluate the pronunciation quality of English words. Finally, in Sect. 4.3, we evaluate the pronunciation accuracy of English words. The pronunciation assessment set of English words that we use has 20 sentences, with 671 words, of which 15% are English words, and the rest is in Vietnamese. We have used English words that are not included in the training dataset and are not ordinary words. 40% of them are English words that contain voiceless consonants. The tests can be found here [2].

4.1 Speech Quality Test

We evaluate the overall sound quality, including both English and Vietnamese languages. We have eight participants in the assessment. Each participant listened to 20 test sentences once and rated the quality of each sentence on a 5-point scale, including "very bad" (1), "bad" (2), "fair" (3), "good" (4), and "very good" (5). In total, there are 80 (sentences) × 4 (systems) = 320 (trials). The results are presented in Table 1.

The evaluation results show that the G2S-based model produces the best natural voice. Speaker and language-embedding based model is also close to achieving the best results.

4.2 English Pronunciation Quality Test

We conduct the second MOS test to evaluate how well English words are pronounced. In this section, we only evaluate the pronunciation quality of English

---

[2] Samples are available at: https://proptitclub.github.io/paper/sample.html.

Table 1. The average MOS of four systems.

Systems	MOS
G2S-based CS synthesis	4.03
Speaker-embedding and character-representation based CS synthesis	3.95
Speaker-embedding and phoneme-representation based CS synthesis	3.33
Speaker and language-embedding based CS synthesis	3.96

words in the test set and exclude Vietnamese words. Eight participants listened to 20 test sentences and rated the quality of the pronunciation in a 5-point scale: "very bad" (1), "bad" (2), "fair" (3), "good" (4), and "very good" (5). The results are presented in Table 2.

Table 2. The average MOS of four systems focus on English words pronounced.

Systems	MOS
G2S-based CS synthesis	3.75
Speaker-embedding and character-representation based CS synthesis	3.82
Speaker-embedding and phoneme-representation based CS synthesis	3.22
Speaker and language-embedding based CS synthesis	3.97

As expected, the best performance is obtained when using the speaker and language-embedding based model, the addition of language embedding to provide language information about input characters helps the model pronounce English words more naturally.

4.3 English Pronunciation Accuracy Test

We estimate the percentage of English words that can be pronounced correctly, in other words, that the participants can recognize the word. We have 4 participants with an average English background. They will see the vocabulary first and then listen to all 80 sentences. For each English word, the participant will rate '1' if they can recognize it and '0' if they cannot. We then sum up the percentage of correctly pronounced words achieved by the models, the final result is averaged. Table 3 show that the number of English words pronounced correctly, in percentage.

The G2S-based model gave the best results with 96.41% of English words recognizable by the participants. Speaker and language-embedding based model and speaker-embedding and character-representation based model also have good results with more than 90% accuracy. Speaker-embedding and phoneme-representation based model have much worse results when participants can only recognize 71.01% of English words.

Table 3. Percent of the number of English words pronounced correctly.

Systems	Accuracy
G2S-based CS synthesis	96.41
Speaker-embedding and character-representation based CS synthesis	90.81
Speaker-embedding and phoneme-representation based CS synthesis	71.01
Speaker and language-embedding based CS synthesis	92.61

4.4 Discussion

G2S-Based CS Synthesis: The pronunciation of the English words has the same tone as Vietnamese ones, so Vietnamese people can understand and be closer. We can also customize the pronunciation of some of the new words that appear in the world (e.g., "Covid-19") or manually modify the pronunciation of words that are less likely to appear in the dictionary. Thus, it gives us more controllable. However, the pronunciation of English word is occasionally vietnameselized too much, which results in an unnatural pronunciation. Furthermore, this is not an automatic method. This G2S system requires linguistic experts to manage the Vietnamese pronunciation of English words manually.

We found that the end-to-end model Tacotron-2 produces stable audio, low noise, good sound quality, and a natural voice for Vietnamese monolingual sentences. Furthermore, with the normalization of English words in the data, the model shows that the ability to learn voiceless consonants is quite good while the code-switched data is limited. With the G2S converter, our CS synthesis system can read almost all English words, but pronunciation accuracy depends heavily on the G2S model.

Speaker-Embedding and Character-Representation Based CS Synthesis: On the English word pronounced, this model gives the best quality according to the participants' rating. Due to not using code-switched data, the model can learn how to pronounce English words from the LJSpeech dataset; reading English words is much more natural. The LJSpeech dataset includes many common English words, but no dataset can cover all the English words, such as "Covid-19", which is a recent emerging word. This approach also has limitations: English words that are not in the dataset sound unnatural, and word stress is often misread.

Speaker-Embedding and Phoneme-Representation Based CS Synthesis: This approach produces quite lousy audio. This result comes from the model's inability to generalize the phoneme mix between Vietnamese and English; moreover, the two sets of phonemes of English and Vietnamese do not share the same information as to characters. With Vietnamese words still retaining a quite good voice, clear sound, and accurate pronunciation. Nevertheless, the synthesized English words sound bad. In addition, many words could not be pronounced, especially words that were not in the training dataset, which made the rating of the model underestimated by participants.

Speaker and Language-Embedding Based CS Synthesis: In this approach, the synthesized voice is not as soft and natural as the previous approaches. However, the ability to pronounce unseen English words is better than character-representation based CS synthesis.

5   Conclusion and Future Works

We presented three approaches to create a code-switching synthesis system under a limited code-switched data scenario. We used a public dataset of English [3], and a Vietnamese dataset contains 12% of CS data, and our model is based on Tacotron-2. The results of our evaluation verified the effectiveness of the three methods. In the first approach using G2S, our model can read most English words with pleasing naturalness; however, the pronunciation of English words still has some disadvantages, e.g., the pronunciation of words with voiceless consonants. In the second approach using speaker-embedding, Our model showed that the pronunciation quality of English words was better than that of the G2S-based model, and using character input representations outperforms phonemes. Moreover, for the third approach using both language embedding and speaker embedding, our model can read English words more naturally and stably than the above two approaches. The above results showed that we can ultimately create a robust bilingual speech synthesis model using limited code-switched training data, which have only a small number of English words in the dataset. Furthermore, this method promises to apply to other languages to create a natural multilingual speech synthesis model.

References

1. Cao, Y., et al.: End-to-end code-switched TTS with mix of monolingual recordings. In: ICASSP 2019 IEEE International Conference on Acoustics, Speech and Signal Processing (ICASSP), pp. 6935–6939 (2019). https://doi.org/10.1109/ICASSP.2019.8682927
2. Dinh, A.T., Phan, T.S., Vu, T.T., Luong, C.M.: Vietnamese HMM-based speech synthesis with prosody information. In: Eighth ISCA Workshop on Speech Synthesis, Barcelona, Spain (2013)
3. Ito, K., Johnson, L.: The LJ speech dataset (2017). https://keithito.com/LJ-Speech-Dataset/
4. Kastner, K., Santos, J.F., Bengio, Y., Courville, A.C.: Representation mixing for TTS synthesis. CoRR abs/1811.07240 (2018). http://arxiv.org/abs/1811.07240
5. Kingma, D.P., Dhariwal, P.: Glow: Generative flow with invertible 1x1 convolutions (2018)

6. Mac, D.K., Nguyen, V.H., Nguyen, D.N., Nguyen, K.A.: How to make text-to-speech system pronounce "voldemort": an experimental approach of foreign word phonemization in Vietnamese. In: ICASSP 2021 IEEE International Conference on Acoustics, Speech and Signal Processing (ICASSP), pp. 6483–6487 (2021). https://doi.org/10.1109/ICASSP39728.2021.9414386

7. McAuliffe, M., Socolof, M., Mihuc, S., Wagner, M., Sonderegger, M.: Montreal forced aligner: trainable text-speech alignment using Kaldi. In: INTERSPEECH (2017)

8. Nguyen, T., Nguyen, B., Phan, K., Do, H.: Development of Vietnamese speech synthesis system using deep neural networks. J. Comput. Sci. Cybern. **34**, 349–363 (2019). https://doi.org/10.15625/1813-9663/34/4/13172

9. Ninh, D.K., Yamashita, Y.: F0 parameterization of glottalized tones for HMM-based Vietnamese TTS. In: INTERSPEECH-2015, pp. 2202–2206 (2015)

10. van den Oord, A., et al.: WaveNet: a generative model for raw audio. CoRR abs/1609.03499 (2016). http://arxiv.org/abs/1609.03499

11. Park, K., Kim, J.: G2PE. https://github.com/Kyubyong/g2p (2019)

12. Phung, V.L., Kinh, P.H., Dinh, A.T., Nguyen, Q.B.: Data processing for optimizing naturalness of Vietnamese text-to-speech system. In: 2020 23rd Conference of the Oriental COCOSDA International Committee for the Co-ordination and Standardisation of Speech Databases and Assessment Techniques (O-COCOSDA), pp. 1–6 (2020)

13. Ping, W., et al.: Deep voice 3: 2000-speaker neural text-to-speech. CoRR abs/1710.07654 (2017). http://arxiv.org/abs/1710.07654

14. Prenger, R., Valle, R., Catanzaro, B.: Waveglow: a flow-based generative network for speech synthesis. CoRR abs/1811.00002 (2018). http://arxiv.org/abs/1811.00002

15. Shen, J., et al.: Natural TTS synthesis by conditioning WaveNet on MEL spectrogram predictions. CoRR abs/1712.05884 (2017). http://arxiv.org/abs/1712.05884

16. Sitaram, S., Chandu, K.R., Rallabandi, S.K., Black, A.W.: A survey of code-switched speech and language processing. CoRR abs/1904.00784 (2019). http://arxiv.org/abs/1904.00784

17. Tuan, D.A., Lam, P.T., Hung, P.D.: A study of text normalization in Vietnamese for text-to-speech system. In: Proceedings of Oriental COCOSDA Conference, Macau, China (2012)

18. Akagi, M., Nguyen, T.-T., Vu, D.-T., Phung, T.-N., Huynh, V.-N. (eds.): ICTA 2016. AISC, vol. 538. Springer, Cham (2017). https://doi.org/10.1007/978-3-319-49073-1

19. Wang, Y., et al.: Tacotron: towards end-to-end speech synthesis (2017)

20. Wang, Y., et al.: Style tokens: unsupervised style modeling, control and transfer in end-to-end speech synthesis. CoRR abs/1803.09017 (2018). http://arxiv.org/abs/1803.09017

21. Xue, L., Song, W., Xu, G., Xie, L., Wu, Z.: Building a mixed-lingual neural TTS system with only monolingual data (2019)

22. Zhang, Y., et al.: Learning to speak fluently in a foreign language: multilingual speech synthesis and cross-language voice cloning. In: Interspeech (2019). https://arxiv.org/abs/1907.04448

23. Zhou, X., Tian, X., Lee, G., Das, R.K., Li, H.: End-to-end code-switching TTS with cross-lingual language model. In: ICASSP 2020 IEEE International Conference on Acoustics, Speech and Signal Processing (ICASSP), pp. 7614–7618 (2020). https://doi.org/10.1109/ICASSP40776.2020.9054722

Multi-task Text Normalization Approach for Speech Synthesis

Cuc Thi Bui[1,2]($\boxtimes$), Trang Van Truong[1], Cuong Manh Nguyen[1,2], Lam Viet Phung[1], Manh Tien Nguyen[3], and Huy Tien Nguyen[1,4,5]

[1] Zalo Group - VNG Corporation, Ho Chi Minh city, Vietnam
{cucbt,trangtv,cuongnm5,lampv}@vng.com.vn
[2] Post and Telecommunication Institute of Technology, Ha Noi city, Vietnam
[3] Hanoi University of Science and Technology, Hanoi, Vietnam
[4] Faculty of Information Technology, University of Science,
Ho Chi Minh city, Vietnam
ntienhuy@fit.hcmus.edu.vn
[5] Vietnam National University, Ho Chi Minh city, Vietnam

Abstract. Text normalization for Text-To-Speech includes several challenging tasks in natural language processing such as verbalizing abbreviations, Out-Of-Vocabulary (OOV) words, and chunking phrases for long sentences without punctuation. Instead of dealing with these tasks independently, we propose a multi-task end-to-end model based on a denoising auto-encoder. As enriching information via multi-task learning and text denoising, the proposed approach shows improvement in the text normalization task, especially for complicated cases which require context and language understanding. In addition, we also design a novel process of data prepossessing to leverage annotated data for training. According to experiments on a handcrafted test set of 200,000 sentences in Vietnamese, our model achieves an overall accuracy of 95.5%.

Keywords: Text normalization · End-to-end model · Handle OOV words · Handle abbreviation · Speech synthesis · Prosodic phrasing · Machine translation

1 Introduction

Text normalization plays a significant role in building a good Text-To-Speech (TTS) system. This process is usually the first step for any TTS system, which aims to translate written form words (i.e., non-standard word (NSW)) to "spoken" form. There are various types of NSWs in text that should be normalized: date, number, digit, expression, OOV words, etc. They can be divided into two main classes: (i) basic NSWs and (ii) ambiguous NSWs. Basic NSWs which have only one meaning are easily modeled by handcrafted rules. For ambiguous NSWs, the normalization process has to deal with a high degree of ambiguity where words have more than one pronunciation. Therefore, the correct word has to be distinguished from the surrounding context.

© Springer Nature Switzerland AG 2021
D. N. Pham et al. (Eds.): PRICAI 2021, LNAI 13032, pp. 164–176, 2021.
https://doi.org/10.1007/978-3-030-89363-7_13

Recently, text normalization for TTS applications has attracted a large number of Natural Language Processing (NLP) research [9,11,14]. However, this task also has faced several challenges. Firstly, verbalization of numbers has several ways to express such as time, score readers in the sports domain, measurement, fraction, day range, monetary amounts. For example, "3/5" can be read as "mùng ba tháng năm" (the 3rd of May) as a date, or "ba trên năm" (three fifths) as a fraction; "12:30" could be time "mười hai giờ ba mươi" (half past twelve) or the score of a game "mười hai ba mươi" (twelve thirty). In addition, OOV words and abbreviations are also complex issues. The former is how to convert from a foreign word to proper syllable sequences in Vietnamese (e.g., Barcelona, Arsenal). The latter requires additional information to translate a shortened form to the original one correctly. For example, an abbreviation "TT" can be expanded as "Thông tin" (information), "Thị trường" (market) or "Trọng tài" (arbitration). Some prior works [12] proposed to expand OOV words and abbreviations via dictionaries, which made it impossible to deal with unseen words and ambiguity of abbreviations in different contexts. Finally, long sentences without punctuation make speech synthesis systems generate unnatural speech results. Therefore, prosodic phrasing is a necessary and challenging phase in text normalization for TTS systems.

Previous studies on text normalization focus on rule-based methods [9,12] with labor-intensive sets of additional rules for individual cases despite the ambiguity of the actual text. This work typically classifies NSWs into different pattern groups such as date, time, numbers, and then into sub-groups such as phone numbers, year, and corresponding NSWs transformations. However, the rule-based method generally encounters time-consuming and labor-intensive analysis or labeling processes with linguistic expertise. In addition, a large number of added rules lead to difficulties in maintaining comprehension and consistency.

Recently, deep learning has achieved much success in computer science, especially in computer vision [3,5] and natural language processing [2,13]. Especially, sequence-to-sequence (seq2seq) tasks for Machine Translation, Auto-Tagging, Speech-To-Text, Text-To-Speech, Handwriting recognition, and Text Normalization are among them. The advantage of seq2seq models lies in the fact that these models can map sequences of different lengths to each other.

In this paper, we propose a multi-task end-to-end text normalization model with automatically prepared data from our processing technique for NSWs. This solution handles OOV words and abbreviations to make training data reliable without manually labeling. To process OOV words, we introduce a Grapheme-To-Phoneme (G2P) model for text normalization without requiring post-processing OOV words. Our module handles OOV words as an independent component of the rule-based system in existing systems. After being processed by a rule-based system, the word detected as OOV is converted to spelling (i.e., how to read the word) via the G2P model. The G2P model has the same idea as the G2P model in English [10]. However, instead of using phonemes to represent an OOV spelling, we split it into first sounds and rhymes in Vietnamese. We come up with the convenience of integrating the G2P model for handling OOV spelling to the text normalization model while keeping the result reasonable as the G2P model works independently. For abbreviation, it is challenging to collect sufficiently abbreviation data for deep learning models. We propose a strategy to achieve abbreviation data automatically and efficiently for training robustness models. In addition, we employ speech synthesis data to tune the phrase prediction task for handling long-sentence synthesis problems. Dealing with these above tasks in an end-to-end model via multi-task training shows impressive results compared to individual models. According to our experiments, applying denoising auto-encoder [6] significantly improves performance compared to models without this pretrain phase.

The rest of this paper is organized as follows: Sect. 2 reviews related work. Section 3 introduces our solution to build an end-to-end text normalization with pre-processing for NSWs and speech synthesis data. After the processing phase, we describe the proposed LSTM-based machine translation model. Section 4 shows the results of experiments, and Sect. 5 concludes our work and discusses future work.

2   Related Work

This section briefly reviews related work, including Text normalization for the TTS system and Prosodic phrasing for the TTS system.

Neural Network-Based Text Normalization: several research works have applied neural networks for text normalization and achieved impressive results. Trang et al. [11] propose a two-step model for text normalization, including: (i) classify NSWs into different categories using Random Forest, (ii) expand them via a seq2seq model. The seq2seq model shows 96.53% for abbreviations and 96.25% for loanwords with a post-adjustment for some completely wrong cases. Junhui Zhang et al. [14] focus on building a hybrid text normalization system combining a rule-based model and a neural model. NSWs are firstly extracted from the input text by regular expressions. The remaining NSWs pass to multi-head self-attention to predict pattern classifications, where the label is one of 36 categories that are the inheritance from the rule-based system. Overall, the performance is improved by over 1.9% on sentence level.

Prosodic Phrasing for TTS System: several studies have been conducted to resolve prosodic phrasing. Trang et al. [8] proposed a phrasing model using syntactic information: structure based on syntactic rules, final lengthening linked to syllabic structures and tone types. Break levels (including significant breaks, minor breaks) and relative positions of syllables are used to train VTed, an HMM-based TTS system for Vietnamese. Ngoc [7] present a study on prosodic models using CaPu (Capitalization and Punctuation model) model using the ViBert embedding for generating fixed vectors to GRU layer followed by conditional random field and the final one is a layer to classify punctuation-tag, with data collected from several domains. All data has to be converted to the normalized format of TTS and remove punctuation for recovery task using CaPu. They also model the phase of OOV to spelling as a machine translation problem by an encoder-decoder-based transformer with data collected from the English vocabulary.

3 The Proposed Approach

3.1 Pre-processing Method

Instead of attempting to classify the various types of NSWs, we group them into three main classes: (i) OOV, (ii) abbreviation and (iii) the others.

An overview process of the pre-processing method is shown in Fig. 1.

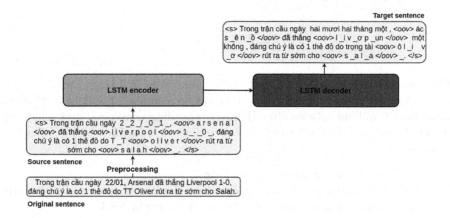

Fig. 1. An overview process of system

Handle OOV Words: Based on the idea that pronouncing OOV is context-independent, we break OOV words into characters and wrap them with OOV tags to make the model focus on OOV words, for example:

– *Original sentence:* Chân sút bukayo saka ghi bàn thắng duy nhất.
– *Source sentence:* chân sút <OOV> b u k a y o </OOV> <OOV> s a k a </OOV> ghi bàn thắng duy nhất.
– *Target sentence:* chân sút <OOV> b _u c _a d _ô </OOV> <OOV> s_a c _a </OOV> ghi bàn thắng duy nhất .

Our implementation is based on [10], but we do not use phonemes for representation. Instead, we split each Vietnamese syllable by first sounds and rhymes. The OOV spelling is generated by a previously trained G2P model.

Model G2P for OOV words in Vietnamese. We collect OOV words from a news aggregator website in Vietnam[1]. With a dataset of more than 20.000 data pairs of OOV words and corresponding spelling, the OOV words are not only English but also come from different languages such as Japanese, Chinese, German, Thai. Most of them are proper names, technical terms, movie titles, or quotes in foreign languages. We use a simple seq2seq model including a BiLSTM encoder and a LSTM decoder with attention as described in Fig. 2. To avoid an error of duplicating end of a word in conventional seq2seq models, we do some post-processing methods.

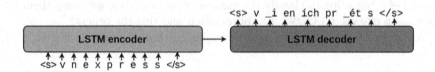

Fig. 2. G2P system

Handle Abbreviation. We collect abbreviation data in a large available news corpus text of Vietnamese [1]. The text corpus contains 25 GB of data with more than 9 million articles after character encoding conversion and removing duplicate articles. For each article, abbreviations are identified by the following assumption:

- NSWs have characters in uppercase form.
- A NSW is followed by an annotation where the first character of each word in the annotation is corresponding to the character in NSW.

Identified abbreviations will be substituted for the entire article. Finally, we have 6 million sentences with reliable labeled abbreviations.

Remaining NSWs. For tokens not in Vietnamese syllable, we break it into characters:

- *Original sentence:* "ngày 20/10 là ngày phụ nữ việt nam"
- *Source sentence:* "ngày 2 _0 _/ _1 _0 là ngày phụ nữ việt nam"

Each character in NSWs has prefix "_" for additional information about its position against the others.

---

[1] baomoi.com.

3.2 Prosodic Phrasing

Chunking phrases for long sentences plays an essential role in improving the naturalness of the TTS system. Our solution is to build a dataset by combining output data from the normalization tool and the data with breaks using the word time-stamp of an Automatic Speech Recognition (ASR) system. If the quiet time in audio is more than 0.5 s, we put a break mark at this silent position. The output of the system are described in the following example:

- *Original sentence:* "Suốt nhiều tháng trong năm người dân phải đi đò vì con đường duy nhất vào thôn bị ngập nước."
- *Source sentence:* "suốt nhiều tháng trong năm người dân phải đi đò vì con đường duy nhất vào thôn bị ngập nước"
- *Target sentence:* "suốt nhiều tháng trong năm * người dân phải đi đò * vì con đường duy nhất vào thôn bị ngập nước"

The punctuation "*" means break, which is silence detected from ASR alignment. When combining with target sentence, we keep both origin punctuation break in normalization tool and break phrase from ASR. As a result, we have more than 20.000 sentences from two recorded voices (i.e., male and female). This data is relatively small compared to all data we trained for the text normalization task; thus, it is used for the last fine-tuning phase.

3.3 Neural Machine Translation Model

Model Architecture. In machine translation tasks, a neural machine translation is a solution using neural networks. Recently, transformer-based architectures are dominant in this area. However, we have some constraints on speed and hardware, so instead of using the transformer-based model, we use a LSTM model with transfer learning techniques. As shown in Fig. 3, our model consists of 3 transfer learning schemes: (i) denoising auto-encoder pre-train model with BART transform, which is described in the next section, (ii) text normalization model trained with directly rule-based system data and (iii) the final model with prosodic phrasing trained with TTS data including break punctuation generated by ASR alignment.

Each LSTM-based machine translation model has 3 Bi-LSTM layers encoder and 2 Bi-LSTM layers decoder with attention, which totally has 10 million parameters. Our model uses an adam optimizer with a learning rate of 0.001, label smoothing of 0.1, which makes the model smooth with wrong cases generated by the rule-based system.

Denoising Auto-encoder Model. To make the model quickly understands the sentence context, we have experimented with BART: a pre-trained denoising auto-encoder [6]. BART is a pretext task with two stages: (i) text is corrupted with an arbitrary noising function, and (ii) a sequence-to-sequence model is learned to reconstruct the original text. However, unlike BART original, we make text corrupted with span token mask and token replace, not using token drop

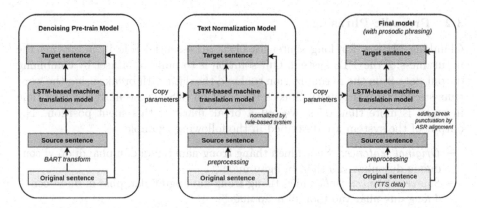

Fig. 3. An overview of the proposed approach

and processing text with sent pair like swap sentence position. Moreover, we add an option for position mask to word in sentence focus on punctuation because the context of punctuation will bring more information for the downstream task to predict ambiguous NSWs, like date-time, score readers in sport domain, measure expressions. An overview process of denoising auto-encoder is shown in Fig. 4.

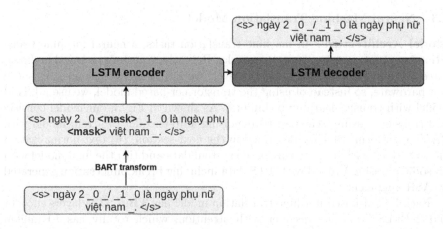

Fig. 4. Denoising auto-encoder

We experiment with the following BART configuration: random ratio: 0.02, mask ratio: 0.15, including the probability of mask punctuation, is 0.3, and all other tokens share 0.7.

4 Experiment

4.1 Dataset

We experiment in a large available news corpus text of Vietnamese [1]. The training dataset has more than 66 million sentences converted by the rule-based normalized system and improved by the self-training feedback model. The cases containing OOV words and abbreviations are handled by the proposed processing method.

For the test dataset, we manually label 200.000 sentences in Vietnamese collected from 13 fields: technology, life, entertainment, education, science, economic, real estate, legal, world, sports, cultural, social, vehicle. The sentence-level accuracy of the rule-based system for the test set is 92.5%. Table 1 shows statistics of our test set consisting of sentences in 31 primary classes.

4.2 Experimental Settings

In our experiments, we use OpenNMT-py, an open-source machine translation toolkit developed by Guillaume Klein et al. [4]. It is a robust framework to support for implementing several research in the machine translation field. In experiments 1 and 2, we compared the effectiveness of the pretext denoising task for training text normalization. Table 2 summarizes the performance for each model. Experiment 3 is to use the text normalization model for the downstream phrase prediction task.

Experiment 1: Training Model with Directly Data Generated by the Rule-Based System. Firstly, we train a model without a pre-train denoising auto-encoder. The result shows 93.2% in the test set, although the accuracy in the valid set is nearly 96.7%. It means our model is quite fitted to data generated by the rule-based system for both correct and incorrect cases. For example:

- *Source sentence:* "cuộc khảo sát được \<oov\> m e r d e k a \</oov\> tiến hành từ ngày 2 _4 tới 3 _0 _- _3 ."
- *Target sentence (ground truth label):* "cuộc khảo sát được \<oov\> m _ơ đ _ê c _a \</oov\> tiến hành từ ngày hai mươi tư **tới ngày ba mươi tháng ba** ."
- *Target sentence (predict by model):* "cuộc khảo sát được \<oov\> m _ơ đ _ê c _a \</oov\> tiến hành từ ngày hai mươi tư **tới ba mươi đến ba** ."

Because the rule-based system does not cover a case where the word after "tới" (to) is date-time, so it wrongly converts "-" to range pattern. If our model understands more about the sentence context, it can correctly convert this case.

Experiment 2: Training Pretext Task Denoising Then Transfering to the Text Normalization Task. This experiment includes two steps: (i) train the denoising auto-encoder task with the objective described in Sect. 3.3, (ii) use

Table 1. Statistic category of test set

Category	Example	Quantity
address	Số nhà 16, ngách 61/521 (No. 16, 61/521 Alley)	10473
license_plates	29V51234	380
date	12/12/2020	7340
date_range	20/11-21/12/2019	119
day	4/4, 05/12	22076
day_range	12-15/08	272
digit	VJ12098	3970
expression	1+1=2	2114
fraction	12:5, 1/25	351
frequency	10 cuốn/tháng (10 copies/month)	4776
ip_address	192.168.14.1	16
measurement	1024MB, 40-50km/h	52783
money	20,5USD, 100.000$	50
month	07/2018, 9-2018	5553
month_range	02/2020-02/2021	32
number	1685747383, -12,5	189063
percentage	15%-30%, 15.4-30%	1505
phone	18008198, +33-1-4455-3990	559
quarter	IV/2018, Q1.2019	372
decree	558-TB/UBKTTW	2406
range	từ 12-24 chiếc (from 12-24 items)	4575
roman_number	XXVIII	2349
score	tỉ số 1-3 (score 1-3)	2520
time	07:50 AM, 05:32:32	5752
time_range	2-3h, 8h15-10h15	56
year_range	2004/2005, 2019-2020	199
abbreviation	TPHCM - thành phố Hồ Chí Minh (Ho Chi Minh city)	74602
OOV	liverpool : li-vơ-pun	312866
special_char	an toàn & vệ sinh (safety & hygiene)	4131
special_code	TFSI 3.0	59289
url_and_email	https://baomoi.com/	50

Table 2. Accuracies of Text normalization models

Experiment	Validation	Test
Model trained with directly data generated by the rule-based system	96.7	93.2
Model trained with transfer from the pretext denoising task	94.1	95.5

this model to the downstream text normalization task. The amount of data used for the downstream task is 10 million sentences, which just contain NSWs. Our model reaches 94.1% accuracy on the validation set but nearly 95.5% on the test set. We have analyzed some sentences with ambiguous NSWs:

Example 1:

- *Source sentence:* "ngược lại , **C _Đ _C _S** ở D _N thuê lại L _Đ cũng không có quyền tập hợp họ vào tổ chức **C _Đ**".
- *Target sentence (ground truth label):* "ngược lại , **công đoàn cơ sở** ở doanh nghiệp thuê lại lao động cũng không có quyền tập hợp họ vào tổ chức **công đoàn**"
- *Target sentence (parsed by rules):* "ngược lại , **cao đẳng cơ sở** ở doanh nghiệp thuê lại lao động cũng không có quyền tập hợp họ vào tổ chức **cao đẳng** "
- *Target sentence (predicted by the model in Exp 1):* "ngược lại , **cao đẳng cơ sở** ở doanh nghiệp thuê lại lao động cũng không có quyền tập hợp họ vào tổ chức **cao đẳng**"
- *Target sentence (predicted by the model in Exp 2) :* "ngược lại , **công đoàn cơ sở** ở doanh nghiệp thuê lại lao động cũng không có quyền tập hợp họ vào tổ chức **công đoàn**"

Example 2:

- *Source sentence:* "trường hợp khác là bệnh nhân **U _T** phổi , đã hoá trị , xạ trị song khối u vẫn to ra , được dùng thuốc **M _D _**, hiện bệnh nhân vẫn sống sau 7 tháng."
- *Target sentence (ground truth label):*"trường hợp khác là bệnh nhân **ung thư** phổi , đã hoá trị , xạ trị song khối u vẫn to ra , được dùng thuốc **miễn dịch** , hiện bệnh nhân vẫn sống sau bảy tháng"
- *Target sentence (parsed by rules) :* "trường hợp khác là bệnh nhân **u tê** phổi , đã hoá trị , xạ trị song khối u vẫn to ra , được dùng thuốc **mờ đê** , hiện bệnh nhân vẫn sống sau bảy tháng"
- *Target sentence (predicted by the model in exp 2) :* "trường hợp khác là bệnh nhân **ung thư** phổi , đã hoá trị , xạ trị song khối u vẫn to ra , được dùng thuốc **miễn dịch** , hiện bệnh nhân vẫn sống sau bảy tháng

Abbreviation "C _Đ" in example 1 has many alternative words such as: "Cao Đẳng" (college), "Công Đoàn" (federation), "Cổ Đông'" (shareholder), etc. In the second example, the abbreviation "U _T" and "M _D" are too hard if we just use 2, or 3 words around to predict. With the efficiency of understanding context after training with the pretext denoising task, our model has predicted correctly abbreviation for this situation. However, the rule-based system has the wrong label in some instances:

- *Source sentence:* "người dùng trước đây đã thể hiện mong muốn màn hình <oov> i p h o n e </oov> lớn hơn , nhưng <oov> i p h o n e </oov> 4 _S cũng chỉ mất với màn hình như của <oov> m o d e l </oov> trước đó ."

– *Target sentence (ground truth label):* "người dùng trước đây đã thể hiện mong muốn màn hình <oov> ai ph _ôn </oov> lớn hơn , nhưng <oov> ai ph _ôn </oov> **bốn ét** cũng chỉ mắt với màn hình như của <oov> m _ô đ _ồ </oov> trước đó"

– *Target sentence (predicted by the model in exp 2):* "người dùng trước đây đã thể hiện mong muốn màn hình <oov> ai ph _ôn </oov> lớn hơn , nhưng <oov> ai ph _ôn </oov> **bốn giây** cũng chỉ mắt với màn hình như của <oov> m _ô đ _ồ </oov> trước đó"

When analyzing the data train, we recognize the rule-based system has failed for converting "S" in the phrase "iphone 4 _S" to "iphone 4 giây" (iphone four seconds) and that made our model failed in this case.

Our model does not work well in all cases. Some sentences containing NSWs about score reading in the sport domain are confused between range pattern and ratio as follow:

– *Source sentence:* "thông tin tay vợt nguyễn tiến minh (hạng 7 _4 thế giới) xuất sắc đánh bại tay vợt kém anh 1 _3 tuổi người <oov> i n d o n e s i a </oov> <oov> i s h a n </oov> <oov> m a u l a n a </oov> <oov> m u s t a f a </oov> với tỉ số thuyết phục 2 _1 _- _1 _5 , 2 _1 _- _1 _5 ở trận tứ kết giải <oov> s i n g a p o r e </oov> mở rộng 2 _0 _1 _8 thực sự là điều thú vị ."

– *Target sentence (ground truth label):* "thông tin tay vợt nguyễn tiến minh hạng bảy mươi tư thế giới   xuất sắc đánh bại tay vợt kém anh mười ba tuổi người <oov> in đ _ô n _ê s _i a </oov> <oov> i s _an </oov> <oov> m _au l _a n _a </oov> <oov> m _ót x t _a ph _a </oov> với tỉ số thuyết phục **hai mươi mốt mười lăm** , **hai mươi mốt mười lăm** ở trận tứ kết giải <oov> s _inh g _a p _o </oov> mở rộng hai nghìn không trăm mười tám thực sự là điều thú vị"

– *Target sentence (predict by model):* "thông tin tay vợt nguyễn tiến minh hạng bảy mươi tư thế giới   xuất sắc đánh bại tay vợt kém anh mười ba tuổi người <oov> in đ _ô n _ê s _i a </oov> <oov> i s _an </oov> <oov> m _au l _a n _a </oov> <oov> m _ót x t _a ph _a </oov> với tỉ số thuyết phục **hai mươi mốt mười lăm** , **hai mươi mốt đến mười lăm** ở trận tứ kết giải <oov> s _inh g _a p _o </oov> mở rộng hai nghìn không trăm mười tám thực sự là điều thú vị"

With phrase "2 _1 _- _1 _5 , 2 _1 _- _1 _5", our model is just correct to convert it to score reading in the first sub phrase: "2 _1 _- _1 _5", and wrong to convert score reading in the second sub phrase instead of range expression.

Experiment 3: Using the Text Normalization Model for the Downstream Phrase Prediction Task. The final text normalization model is employed for the phrase prediction task. We train with 20.000 sentences parsed from the output data of TTS audio aligned by ASR. Our model gets accuracy 81% F1 for punctuation break compared to the ASR output. The major drawback is that our model does not add break compared to break recognition by the

ASR alignment. It is easy to understand because the TTS audio records are not consistent across two people, so breaking phrases from different people can be not the same. We generate some cases to analyze the model for phrase prediction as follow:

- *Source sentence:* "cần phải hiểu hệ thống đào tạo nghề của C _Đ là nằm trong hệ thống đào tạo nghề chung của cả nước."
- *Target sentence:* "cần phải hiểu hệ thống đào tạo nghề của cao đẳng là nằm trong hệ thống đào tạo nghề chung của cả nước"
- *Target sentence(predicted by the model):* "cần phải hiểu * hệ thống đào tạo nghề của CĐ là nằm trong hệ thống đào tạo nghề chung của cả nước"

The model added token "*" for break after phrase: "cần phải hiểu" (it is necessary to understand that), it is reasonable as "cần phải hiểu" is used to introduce the next content and not depend on the next phrase that makes TTS systems more naturalness.

5   Conclusion and Future Works

We presented a multi-task end-to-end text normalization model based on a denoising auto-encoder. In addition, we proposed a novel process of data prepossessing to take advantage of labeled data for training. Our model achieved impressive results with a handcrafted test set of 200,000 sentences in Vietnamese, especially for complicated cases which require surrounding context. Furthermore, integrating prosodic phrasing which inserts punctuation into long sentences makes speech synthesis more naturalness. In the future, we plan to improve data provided by the rule-based system by comparing to data generated by the text normalization model to identify mismatched samples for reviewing.

References

1. Binh, V.Q.: Vietnamese news corpus. https://github.com/binhvq/news-corpus (2018)
2. Goldberg, Y., Hirst, G.: Neural Network Methods in Natural Language Processing. Morgan & Claypool Publishers, San Rafael (2017)
3. He, K., Zhang, X., Ren, S., Sun, J.: Deep residual learning for image recognition. In: 2016 IEEE Conference on Computer Vision and Pattern Recognition (CVPR), pp. 770–778 (2016)
4. Klein, G., Kim, Y., Deng, Y., Senellart, J., Rush, A.: OpenNMT: open-source toolkit for neural machine translation. In: Proceedings of ACL 2017, System Demonstrations, pp. 67–72. Association for Computational Linguistics, Vancouver, Canada, July 2017. https://www.aclweb.org/anthology/P17-4012
5. LeCun, Y., Bengio, Y., Hinton, G.: Deep learning. Nature **521**(7553), 436–444 (2015). https://doi.org/10.1038/nature14539

6. Lewis, M., et al.: BART: denoising sequence-to-sequence pre-training for natural language generation, translation, and comprehension. In: Proceedings of the 58th Annual Meeting of the Association for Computational Linguistics, pp. 7871–7880. Association for Computational Linguistics, Online, July 2020. https://aclanthology.org/2020.acl-main.703

7. Ngoc, P.P., Quang, C.T., Nguyen, Q.M., Do, Q.T.: Improving prosodic phrasing of Vietnamese text-to-speech systems. In: Proceedings of the 7th International Workshop on Vietnamese Language and Speech Processing, pp. 19–23. Association for Computational Linguistics, Hanoi, Vietnam, December 2020. https://www.aclweb.org/anthology/2020.vlsp-1.4

8. Nguyen, T.T.T., Rilliard, A., Tran, D., d'Alessandro, C.: Prosodic phrasing modeling for Vietnamese TTS using syntactic information. In: INTERSPEECH (2014)

9. Nguyen, T.T.T., Pham, T.T., Tran, D.D.: A method for Vietnamese text normalization to improve the quality of speech synthesis. In: Proceedings of the 2010 Symposium on Information and Communication Technology, pp. 78–85, SoICT 2010. Association for Computing Machinery, New York, NY, USA (2010). https://doi.org/10.1145/1852611.1852627

10. Park, K., Kim, J.: G2PE (2019). https://github.com/Kyubyong/g2p

11. Trang, N.T.T., Bach, D.X., Tung, N.X.: A hybrid method for Vietnamese text normalization. In: Proceedings of the 2019 3rd International Conference on Natural Language Processing and Information Retrieval, pp. 104–109, NLPIR 2019. Association for Computing Machinery, New York, NY, USA (2019). https://doi.org/10.1145/3342827.3342851

12. Tuan, D.A., Lam, P.T., Hung, P.D.: A study of text normalization in Vietnamese for text-to-speech system. In: Proceedings of Oriental COCOSDA Conference, Macau, China (2012)

13. Young, T., Hazarika, D., Poria, S., Cambria, E.: Recent trends in deep learning based natural language processing [review article]. IEEE Comput. Intell. Mag. **13**, 55–75 (2018)

14. Zhang, J., et al.: A hybrid text normalization system using multi-head self-attention for mandarin. In: ICASSP 2020 IEEE International Conference on Acoustics, Speech and Signal Processing (ICASSP), pp. 6694–6698 (2020)

Performance-Driven Reinforcement Learning Approach for Abstractive Text Summarization

Trang-Phuong N. Nguyen$^{(\boxtimes)}$(ID), Nam-Chi Van, and Nhi-Thao Tran(ID)

Vietnam National University, University of Science, Ho Chi Minh City, Vietnam
nnptrang@apcs.vn, vcnam@fit.hcmus.edu.vn, tttnhi@mso.hcmus.edu.vn

Abstract. Recently, the use of *Reinforcement Learning* with Neural Networks in *Abstractive Summarization* is getting more popular, but still currently restricted. In this paper, we propose PEARL as a novel framework to expand the proficiency of *Reinforcement Learning* approach in *Abstractive Text Summarization*. PEARL consists of two out-of-the-box *Reinforcement Learning* algorithms: F_{Rouge} and $D_{Threshold}$, where F_{Rouge} reconstructs the training objective, and $D_{Threshold}$ helps to improve the flexibility for the arbitrary data. We evaluate PEARL in the large-scale *CNN/DailyMail* and the medium-scale *VNTC-Abs* datasets. Results show that our PEARL produces significantly greater ROUGE scores than baselines as well as achieves the new state-of-the-art model without either pre-trained models or extra training data. This research provides proof of validity based on data analysis.

Keywords: Abstractive Text Summarization · Reinforcement Learning · REINFORCE · Performance-driven · PEARL · Cohesion threshold

1 Introduction

Text Summarization is the act of shortening sentences or documents where the grammar and the content from the original text are guaranteed. There are two approaches: *Extractive* and *Abstractive*. The *Extractive* way collects a subset of words from the source text to form the output summary. On the other hand, *Abstractive Summarization* is free to choose the words that may or may not appear in the input, then interprets valuable information in a new way. This study focuses on *Abstractive* summarizing only.

With the Encoder-Decoder design, Sequence-to-Sequence [17] is a popular framework used in various tasks, including *Abstractive Text Summarization*. The Encoder processes the input words sequentially to have an abstract representation. This information is then used as initial data for Decoder to make a sequence of output's word predictions. The Recurrent Neural Networks (RNNs) is applied along with the Encoder-Decoder design to significantly improve the *Summarization* task by [3,10,15]. However, the primary Sequence-to-Sequence with RNNs faces the out-of-vocabulary (OOV) issue and the long sequences scaling.

© Springer Nature Switzerland AG 2021
D. N. Pham et al. (Eds.): PRICAI 2021, LNAI 13032, pp. 177–190, 2021.
https://doi.org/10.1007/978-3-030-89363-7_14

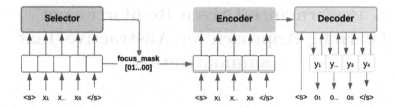

Fig. 1. The general Sequence-to-Sequence with SELECTOR architecture

To solve the OOV issue, Pointer Generator Network [16] *(PG Network)* observes words in the vocabulary and also considers words from source text via a switching gate. In detail, the switching gate decides to select one word in the vocabulary or extract exactly one word from the input at each Decoder step. Besides, to deal with the long sequences, SELECTOR [2] raises a *focus mask* to mark crucial words along with the input that needs to be paid more attention to. Figure 1 visualizes the main idea of the Encoder-Decoder associated with SELECTOR. Although these methods are proven to provide positive updates, there are still problems of flexibility and weak rigor caused by the hyperparameters.

Along with Neural Networks, the Reinforcement Learning *(RL)* is gaining significant notice in Natural Language Processing [9,19]. The principle elements of *RL* are (1) Agent: a trainable input-output system, (2) Action: agent's behaviors, and (3) Reward: value received after a specified number of completed actions. Besides, three primary categories of *RL* tasks are to (1) train an *Actor* to produce the best *Action*, (2) train a *Critic* to estimate the *Reward* value correctly among a fixed *Actions set*, and (3) the mixed *Actor-Critic*. As a general-purpose framework, *RL* aims to maximize the *Reward* along a sequential Action-making. However, previous works showed that *RL* is limited to small-scale corpora [19].

The early works on *Abstractive Summarization* applied *RL* with the sentence-level's feedback as *Reward*. [12] combined the supervised Neural Network model with *Self-Critical Sequence Training (SCST)* [14]. *SCST* is the idea of preferring the inference procedure rather than the uncontrollable *Critic* model to estimate *Reward*. Besides, [7] also made use of *SCST*, but combined the semantic assessment with *Reward* calculation. However, current algorithms for *RL* approach applied in *Abstractive Summarization* are not diverse when most of the research is directing to solve certain problems. By the ability to exploit feedbacks from the environment for the final output result, it is worth expanding *RL* to uncertain corners in *Abstractive Summarization*. For example, receiving feedbacks on the quality of the output summary, the model is not only able to update the labeled word probability but also another unlabeled tasks.

In response, we propose the Performance-driven Reinforcement Learning (PEARL) approach to (1) **reconstruct the training objective** to produce summaries that are close to human-action, (2) provide a **dynamic cohesion estimator** on the document unit to be **adaptable with arbitrary data**. We tested PEARL on the large-scale *CNN/DailyMail* [5] and the medium-scale *VNTC-Abs* [11] datasets. Our methods not only significantly outperform baselines but also achieve the state-of-the-art result with neither a pre-trained model nor extra training data. This research proves the validity based on data analysis.

2   Background

In general, the *Abstractive Summarization* task is the many-to-many form of Sequence-to-Sequence. In Encoder-Decoder framework, the Encoder receives a sequence of $x = (x_1, x_2, ..., x_S)$ as S words in the source text. Then, the Decoder generates $\hat{y} = (\hat{y_1}, \hat{y_2}, ..., \hat{y_N})$ as N words for the summary. Specifically, $\hat{y_i}$ is selected from a conditional *Multinomial distribution* $p(y|x) = \mathbb{E}[p_\theta(y|x)]$, where θ is the trainable parameters.

2.1   Related Works

Pointer Generator Network. *(PG Network)* [16] desires to solve the *OOV* problem which is one of Encoder-Decoder's issues. A word is considered to be *OOV* if it appears in the input but is not listed in the fixed vocabulary built from the most popular words. Practically, *OOV* could store the key information such as names, dates, or numeric data. Therefore, ignoring *OOV* leads to the lack of content or a misleading summary. To deal with *OOV*, at each Decoder step, *PG Network* selects one word for the summary by considering picking out **from the fixed vocabulary** or extracting **from the input**.

First, the probability of each word in the fixed vocabulary set is represented by P_{vocab}. Applying the Attention Mechanism [18] in P_{vocab} computation, the *Attention Score* e^t is calculated to store the importance of each word in the input based on the Encoder's (h_i) and Decoder's output (s_t), then normalized to get the *Attention Distribution* a^t. The e^t and a^t calculation given by [1] are presented in Eq. 1, where ν, W_h, W_s, and b_{attn} are learnable parameters. In Eq. 2, a context vector $h_t^\star$ is produced by making use of a^t and hidden states h, and then normalized by *Softmax* function to achieve P_{vocab}, where V', V are learnable variables.

$$e_i^t = \nu^T \tanh(W_h h_i + W_s s_t + b_{attn})$$
$$a^t = Softmax(e^t)$$
$$h_t^\star = \sum_i a_i^t h_i \tag{1}$$

$$P_{vocab} = Softmax(V'(V[s^t, h_t^\star])) \tag{2}$$

Next, the probability of words in both input and vocabulary set is denoted as $P(w)$. To construct $P(w)$, *PG Network* generates p_{gen} as a switching gate to modify words probability, which is showed in Eq. 3, with trainable parameters w_h, w_s, and w_x. In Eq. 4, the output $\hat{y}$ is the highest value's index in P. Then, the training objective is to minimize the maximum-likelihood

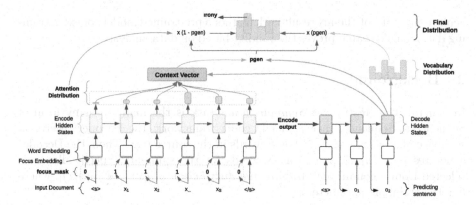

Fig. 2. The baseline Sequence-to-Sequence with *PG Network* and SELECTOR (Color figure online)

$L_{ml} = -\sum_{t=1}^{N} log(p(\hat{y}_t|\hat{y}_1,\ldots,\hat{y}_{t-1},x))$. Figure 2 visualizes the main concept of *PG Network*.

$$p_{gen} = \sigma(w_h^T h_t^\star + w_s^T s_t + w_x^T x_t)$$

$$P(w) = p_{gen} \star P_{vocab}(w) + (1 - p_{gen}) \sum_{i:w_i=w} a_i^t \tag{3}$$

$$\hat{y} = Argmax(P) \tag{4}$$

SELECTOR [2] generates a binary *focus mask* to emphasize the crucial words along the input. According to SELECTOR, a word is crucial if it appears in the referenced summary created by humans. By this assumption, SELECTOR constructed the *focus mask*'s ground-truth by setting value *one* at indices caring words that appear both in the source text and the referenced summary, the value *zero* marks for otherwise. To train, the input document is fed to a Bidirectional Gated Recurring Units *(BiGRU)* to form the focus logit *(logit)*. Following Eq. 5, a *fixed threshold* is used to transform *logit* to a binary mask *m*. The blue part in Fig. 2 visualizes how the binary *focus mask* is concatenated to word embedding as an extra information before going through the Encoder-Decoder.

$$(h_1...h_S) = BiGRU(x)$$

$$logit_t = \sigma(FC([h_t; h_1; h_S])) \tag{5}$$

$$m = (binary)(logit > threshold)$$

Previous Reinforcement Learning approaches in *Summarization* task are to maximize the *Reward* of the predicted summary, after a sequence of *Actions* on every single step in predicting word. Where the *Agent* is the Sequence-to-Sequence model, the *Action* is the summary and the *Reward* is determined by the *Summarization* metrics such as ROUGE [8] scores. *RL* defines the policy p_θ in respect of parameter θ, to map *Actions* to words probability. Then, the training purpose is to minimize the negative *expected Reward*, which is formularized as $L_{rl}(\theta) = -E_{w_s \sim p_\theta}[R_{func}(w_s)]$, via *Policy Gradient* optimization, where w_s is the predicted word in the output summary. $L_{rl}(\theta)$ is estimated with a single sample in p_θ that $L_{rl}(\theta) \approx -R_{func}(w_s)$, $w_s \sim p_\theta$.

Policy Gradient with REINFORCE Algorithm computes and adjusts the expected gradient $\nabla_\theta L_{rl}(\theta)$. According to [20], $\nabla_\theta L_{rl}(\theta)$ could be calculated as $\nabla_\theta L_{rl}(\theta) = -E_{w_s \sim p_\theta}[R_{func}(w_s)\nabla_\theta log(p_\theta(w_s))]$. In practical, by using *Monte-Carlo* [13] random sample, the expected gradient is approximated as described in Eq. 6. On another note, REINFORCE provides a simple-to-conduct solution, however, the high variance of *Reward* could lead to a less-than-desirable result in some situations.

$$\nabla_\theta L_{rl}(\theta) \approx -R_{func}(w_s)\nabla_\theta log(p_\theta(w_s)) \tag{6}$$

Moreover, term *baseline* (denoted as b) in REINFORCE is defined as the preferred *Reward* value that helps to reduce the variance. Since the *baseline* calculation is designed independent of *Action*, it does not affect to the expected gradient. The REINFORCE with *baseline* is shown in Eq. 7.

$$\nabla_\theta L_{rl}(\theta) \approx -(R_{func}(w_s) - b)\nabla_\theta log(p_\theta(w_s)) \tag{7}$$

Self-critical Sequence Training *(SCST)* [14] is a branch of REINFORCE with *baseline*. *SCST* obtains its *baseline* from the procedure used in the inference time. In more detail, w_s and $\hat{w}_s$ are defined as output word that generated by the **RL** model and the **inference procedure**, respectively. In [12]'s work, with the same parameter θ, the words logit is sampled by the *Multinomial distribution* to produce w_s and passed through the *Softmax* to form $\hat{w}_s$ as in the test-time. Following the Eq. 8, $R_{func}(\hat{w}_s)$ is then used as the *baseline* in the *SCST* structure. In reality, the *SCST* is trained parallel with maximum-likelihood training objective ($L_{ml}(\theta)$), which is introduced as a mixed learning objective [12]. Equation 9 defines the mixed of $L_{rl}(\theta)$ and $L_{ml}(\theta)$, where α is the scaling factor to divide the magnitude between them.

$$\nabla_\theta L_{rl}(\theta) \approx -(R_{func}(w_s) - R_{func}(\hat{w}_s))\nabla_\theta log(p_\theta(w_s)) \tag{8}$$

$$\nabla_\theta L_{mixed}(\theta) = \alpha\nabla_\theta L_{rl}(\theta) + (1 - \alpha)\nabla_\theta L_{ml}(\theta) \tag{9}$$

2.2 Materials

Evaluation Metric. We evaluate our work by ROUGE [8], which is the typical assessment for *Abstractive Text Summarization*. ROUGE calculates the similarity between the two summaries by counting the words overlapping on them. In details, there are three ROUGE points: ROUGE-1 *(R-1)* - the unigram overlapping, ROUGE-2 *(R-2)* - the bigram overlapping, ROUGE-L *(R-L)* - the longest common subsequence. The high value of ROUGE points means the high level of similarity between the reference and the predicted summary.

Datasets. We conduct PEARL on two datasets, which are the *CNN/DailyMail* [5] collected from *CNN News*[1], and the *VNTC-Abs* [11] collected from Vietnamese Online News *VNExpress*[2]. *CNN/DailyMail* contains 287113, 13368, 11490 pairs of input document - referenced summary for the train, validate and test set, respectively. For *VNTC-Abs*, the numbers are 34503, 7422, 7364. Following the prior works [2, 16], we set the maximum length of the input document and the summary to 400 and 100 words for *CNN/DailyMail*. For *VNTC-Abs*, we truncate the length to 650 words for the input and 100 words for the output.

3   PEARL: Performance-Driven Reinforcement Learning

With the *PG Network*, SELECTOR, and *SCST* as the based models, our PEARL produces an out-of-the-box method of performing the *Abstractive Summarization* task by applying two *RL* algorithms, F_{Rouge} and $D_{Threshold}$. We first present in Sect. 3.1 the semantic metrics analysis to explore the *Reward Function* design. Next, Sect. 3.2 is for F_{Rouge} that reconstructs the training objective to expand the quality as well as the ability of *focus mask*. Finally, in Sect. 3.3, the $D_{Threshold}$ is described as a dominant update that increases the flexibility of the whole framework.

3.1   *Reward Function* design and the problem of averaged score

Fundamentally, we use the ROUGE score [8] for the strategy of designing *Reward function* (R_{func}). The general form of R_{func} can be fomularized as:

$$R_{func} = \gamma_1 G(R\text{-}1) + \gamma_2 G(R\text{-}2) + (1 - \gamma_1 - \gamma_2)G(R\text{-}L) \tag{10}$$

where $G(r)$ is the normalize function on the ROUGE point r, γ_1 and γ_2 are hyperparameters for partitioning ROUGE points' contribution in R_{func}. Recent reports [6, 12] simply defined $G(r) = r$ and shared the balance ratio of contribution. In other words, they built R_{func} as the average of the three ROUGE points (denoted as *R-avg*). Then, following the training objective of *RL*, they aimed to maximize this average. However, the average operation could not tightly reply for the quality of the predicted summary. To optimize, we first figure out the causes and then propose a new design for the *Reward function*.

First, we examine the semantic relation from the three ROUGE points on 200 documents collected from *CNN/DailyMail*. Figure 4 displays ROUGE results in

---

[1] CNN News: edition.cnn.com.

[2] VNExpress: vnexpress.net.

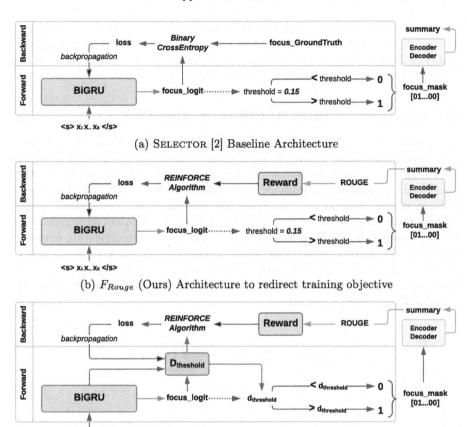

(a) SELECTOR [2] Baseline Architecture

(b) F_{Rouge} (Ours) Architecture to redirect training objective

(c) $D_{Threshold}$ (Ours) Architecture to generate a *Dynamic Threshold*

Fig. 3. The architecture comparison between SELECTOR [2] baseline (Fig. 3a) and our PEARL. PEARL consists of F_{Rouge} (Fig. 3b) and $D_{Threshold}$ (Fig. 3c).

the increasing direction of *R-avg*. Noted that the *R-avg* calculation is depended on the value of *R-1*, *R-2*, and *R-L*, but does not reflect the distance among three of them. The result shows that the high value of *R-avg* comes from the abnormally high value of *R-1* in some situations, which are bounded by the red rectangles. Moreover, the unbalance ROUGE points could lead to the worse quality of the summary due to the lack of structure correction which is qualified by *R-L* [8].

Next, for the design of *Reward Function*, our strategy is to select a metric that is independent in calculating but strongly reflects the tendency of the ROUGE changing. We do the *Pearson Correlation* analysis between ROUGE points, which is performed in Fig. 5. The data for experimenting is the *Validation* results during training SELECTOR, three different epochs for each *CNN/DailyMail* and *VNTC-Abs* dataset. The visualization shows that in all of the cases, *R-L* has the strongest correlation with other ROUGE points. Therefore, we exploit *R-L* as the main component of *Reward Function*, which is $R_{func} = R\text{-}L$. To conclude, the new design of $R_{func} = R\text{-}L$ has two benefits (1) $R\text{-}L$ is able to capture the quality of the summary well by automatically caring assessment of other n-grams [8], (2) $R\text{-}L$ is clear in comparison to other summary's result.

3.2 F_{Rouge}: ROUGE-Based REINFORCE Algorithm

The training objective of SELECTOR is to achieve the high accuracy of predicted *focus mask* (denoted as *F-acc*). *F-acc* is simply calculated by the ratio between the numbers of correct positions and the sequence length, comparing to the *focus mask*'s ground truth. However, our analysis displayed in Fig. 6 shows that in the increasing direction of $R\text{-}L$, *F-acc* does not run on the same tendency but strongly fluctuates. Moreover, we apply the *Pearson Correlation* to examine the data and record the result in Table 1. The result shows the correlation between ROUGE scores and *F-acc* is truly weak. Therefore, our work proposes a *RL* algorithm named F_{Rouge} to reconstruct the training objective from generating a *focus mask* with high accuracy to a *focus mask* that produces the high quality of the final outputted summary.

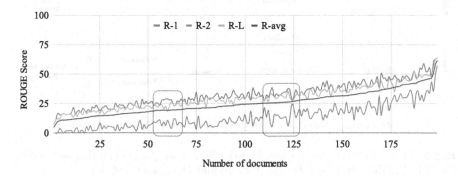

Fig. 4. The relation between ROUGE metrics and ROUGE Average in the increasing direction of the averaged score ($R\text{-}avg$)

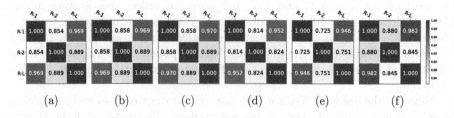

| | (a) | | | (b) | | | (c) | | | (d) | | | (e) | | | (f) | | |

Fig. 5. The *Correlation* between ROUGE metrics. Figures 5a, b, c are collected from *CNN/DailyMail*, Figs. 5d, e, f collected from *VNTC-Abs*

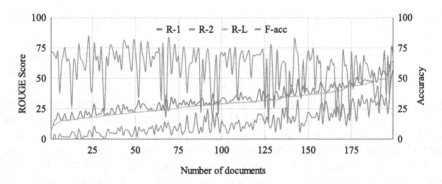

Fig. 6. The relation between ROUGE metrics and the *focus mask* accuracy *(F-acc)* in the increasing direction of *R-L*

Table 1. Correlation between ROUGE and *focus mask* accuracy (*F-acc*)

	R-1	R-2	R-L	R-avg
F-acc	−0.089	−0.0981	−0.0739	−0.0903

F_{Rouge} is designed as a REINFORCE Algorithm that rebuilds the training type from supervised (learning from the *focus mask*'s ground-truth) to unsupervised (directing to the performance of the outputted summary). Mapping to the three main elements of *RL*'s theory, F_{Rouge} is described as following:

- **Agent** is based on the concept of SELECTOR model. Specifically, the *BiGRU* of SELECTOR model is directly trained during the training process.
- **Action** created for each input document is a binary *focus mask*, similar to what the original SELECTOR model did.
- **Reward** is calculated by the *Reward function* R_{func}. R_{func} is constructed from ROUGE score which is described in Sect. 3.1.

Figure 3 visualizes the training processes comparison between F_{Rouge} (Fig. 3b) and the baseline SELECTOR (Fig. 3a). Instead of computing *loss* based on *Binary Cross Entropy* from the *focus mask*'s ground-truth as SELECTOR, our F_{Rouge} calculates *loss* by REINFORCE algorithm that depends on *Action* (the generated *focus mask*) and *Reward value*. The *Reward value* is measured from the *Reward function* which receives the input as the summary generated by feeding the predicted *focus mask* to the Encoder-Decoder. Then, by following the REINFORCE's theory described in Eq. 6, F_{Rouge} updates *Agent* based on the Policy Gradient algorithm.

3.3 $D_{Threshold}$: Dynamic Cohesion Threshold for Document Unit

According to SELECTOR [2], a *fixed threshold* which equals to *0.15* is used to transform the *focus logit* to the *focus mask* for all documents. In Eq. 5, all indices in the *focus logit* whose value is greater than *threshold* will be marked as *one* in the *focus mask*, others are placed with *zero* value. However, the *threshold* value, in this case, is firmly related to the cohesion or the density of informative words in the input, which is different among documents, especially for the genre diversity of texts. This *fixed threshold* is a bottleneck that leads to trouble in specifying and proving the optimization for other datasets. Therefore, we propose a trainable *dynamic threshold* named $D_{Threshold}$ to estimate the proper *threshold* based on document context. $D_{Threshold}$ replaces the fixed *threshold* by a dynamic one to improve the flexibility for each document as well as other arbitrary data.

$D_{Threshold}$ is constructed as a continuous space REINFORCE algorithm which aims to estimate a proper *threshold* for each input document. Aligning to a general *RL* architecture, the three main elements of $D_{Threshold}$ includes:

- **Agent**: we design *Agent* as a *Multilayer Perceptron* model that learns from the context, then determines the cohesion level of the input document.
- **Action**: For each input document, the $D_{Threshold}$'s *Agent* generates $d_{threshold}$ which is a real number in a continuous space $[0, 1]$ for *Action*.
- **Reward**: to observe the compatible of $d_{threshold}$ on the outputted summary's quality, the *Reward function* is built from ROUGE score that also follows the design in Sect. 3.1.

$$d_{threshold} = \sigma(FC([h_S; logit]))$$
$$m = (binary)(logit > d_{threshold})$$

(11)

$D_{Threshold}$'s *Agent* receives two inputs, both are collected from Eq. 5: (1) h_S, which is the SELECTOR Encoder's output as the general context of the whole input document, and (2) the focus logit (*logit*) which rates informative words along the input. The two inputs are concatenated, then added weights via *Linear Layers* and passed through the *Sigmoid Activation Functions*. After that, $D_{Threshold}$ outputs a real number $d_{threshold}$ in range $[0, 1]$ as *Action*. $d_{threshold}$ is then used as the *dynamic threshold* for SELECTOR to normalize *logit* to the *focus mask* m. The Fig. 3c and the Eq. 11 shows our updated process with $D_{Threshold}$.

4 Experiments and Results

4.1 Implementation Detail

Baselines. PEARL is based on three previous works as the initial model: *PG Network* [16], SELECTOR [2], and the *SCST* [12]. In detail, with *PG Network* and SELECTOR, we followed the whole concept and configuration reported by the prior works. With *SCST*, we utilized the main idea but used the *Reward function* described in Sect. 3.1. We also compared the original *Reward function* design with ours. The result is recorded in Table 2, where $SCST(avg)$ denotes the *average operation* as [12]'s work and $SCST$ denotes our form of the *Reward function*.

Table 2. PEARL's sub-methods result and the comparison to baselines. The best scores are bolded

Method	CNN/DailyMail			VNTC-Abs		
	R-1	R-2	R-L	R-1	R-2	R-L
The based models						
baselines	41.72	18.74	38.79	25.72	8.23	21.84
baselines + $SCST(avg)$	41.89	18.92	39.02	32.48	12.72	28.47
PEARL						
baselines + $SCST$	42.30	18.97	39.15	34.73	14.97	31.65
$+F_{Rouge}$	42.89	19.76	39.69	39.14	16.33	37.40
$+F_{Rouge} + D_{Threshold}$	**43.61**	**20.10**	**40.42**	**43.92**	**19.74**	**39.09**

Training Process. We first trained the *PG Network* and SELECTOR models simultaneously until getting the non-increasing result. Then, the *checkpoint* (denoted as *baseline*) that achieved the highest ROUGE score on the *Validation* set continued to be trained with *RL*. Next, the training processes with *RL* are divided into three ordered phases:

1. *SCST*: we froze SELECTOR's parameters and then trained with *SCST* algorithm to improve the Sequence-to-Sequence model.
2. F_{Rouge}: we froze Sequence-to-Sequence's parameters then executed the F_{Rouge} to improve the ability to learn the representation of the focus logit.
3. $D_{Threshold}$: we trained the dynamic threshold generator $D_{Threshold}$ with the non-increasing *checkpoint* collected from F_{Rouge} in the second phase. Meanwhile, we froze all parameters of the Sequence-to-Sequence model and SELECTOR model.

4.2 Result

Our test results for *CNN/DailyMail* and *VNTC-Abs* are shown in Table 2. We observe that PEARL achieves significantly higher ROUGE scores than the based models on both datasets. In particular, the (+1.89 R-1;+1.36 R-2;+1.63 R-L) increased for *CNN/DailyMail* and (+18.20 R-1;+11.51 R-2;+17.25 R-L) for *VNTC-Abs*. Moreover, Table 3 shows that PEARL also produces a better result than other related researches. In addition, PEARL achieves the new state-of-the-art for both *CNN/DailyMail* and *VNTC-Abs* datasets without any pre-trained model or extra-training data.

Analysing further on PEARL's algorithms presented in Table 2, all of our sub-methods are outperforms *baselines*. First, the +0.13 R-L in *CNN/DailyMail* and +3.18 R-L in *VNTC-Abs* that *SCST* performs better than *SCST(avg)* proves the importance of choosing *Reward function* and the reasonable of our design. Next, the +0.54 R-L on *CNN/DailyMail*, especially +5.75 R-L on *VNTC-Abs* improved by F_{Rouge} in the fourth row proves the rationality of the training

Table 3. The comparison of PEARL to related researches. The best results are bolded. The *"-"* symbol stands for the unreported results

Method	CNN/DailyMail			VNTC-Abs		
	R-1	R-2	R-L	R-1	R-2	R-L
PG network [16]	39.53	17.25	36.38	25.21	9.11	21.70
SELECTOR [2]	41.72	18.74	38.79	25.72	8.23	21.84
DEEPREINFORCE [12]	41.16	15.75	39.08	–	–	–
Bottom-Up [4]	41.22	18.68	38.34	–	–	–
CONTOUR [11]	42.08	19.11	39.10	27.27	9.10	23.70
PEARL (*Ours*)	**43.61**	**20.10**	**40.42**	**43.92**	**19.74**	**39.09**

objective that focuses on summary's performance. Finally, $D_{Threshold}$ makes the change of +0.73 R-L on *CNN/DailyMail* and +1.69 R-L on *VNTC-Abs*. This strongly corroborates that our dynamic cohesion estimator helps to generate a better threshold and reforms the quality of *focus mask* as well as enhances the flexibility for the variety of data.

Apart from comparing with *PG Network* [16] and SELECTOR [2], in Table 3, we also measure the full reported result of the DEEPREINFORCE [12] which is the association of *SCST* and intra-attention. Furthermore, we analyze the result of *Bottom-up* [4] and CONTOUR [11] due to the similar idea to take the advantage of informative words in the input. With *CNN/DailyMail* dataset, the highest improved is +4.04 R-L better than *PG Network* and the nearest updates is +1.32 R-L better than CONTOUR. With *VNTC-Abs*, +17.39 R-L is the highest improved better than *PG Network*, and +15.39 R-L is the nearest updates better than CONTOUR.

5   Conclusion

In this paper, we introduce PEARL as a framework that consists of two novel approaches based on *Reinforcement Learning* for *Abstractive Text Summarization*. PEARL helps to enhance the semantic relation, redirect the training objective to the sustainable goal that produces the summary closer to the human's one, considerably improve the flexibility for the arbitrary data. Especially, we explain the validity through data analysis. We set up the experiments with the *CNN/DailyMail* and *VNTC-Abs* datasets. The results show that PEARL is reasonable by significantly outperformed baselines. Moreover, PEARL accomplishes the new state-of-the-art for the *Abstractive Text Summarization* task on both datasets, comparing to other methods that do not use either pre-trained model or extra training data.

Acknowledgement. We thank the anonymous reviewers for their helpful suggestions on this paper. This research was supported by the Department of Knowledge Engineering funded by the Faculty of Information Technology under grant number *CNTT 2020-12* from Vietnam National University, Ho Chi Minh City University of Science.

References

1. Bahdanau, D., Cho, K., Bengio, Y.: Neural machine translation by jointly learning to align and translate. ArXiv 1409, September 2014
2. Cho, J., Seo, M., Hajishirzi, H.: Mixture content selection for diverse sequence generation. In: EMNLP (2019)
3. Chopra, S., Auli, M., Rush, A.M.: Abstractive sentence summarization with attentive recurrent neural networks. In: Proceedings of the 2016 Conference of the North American Chapter of the Association for Computational Linguistics: Human Language Technologies, pp. 93–98. Association for Computational Linguistics, San Diego, California, June 2016. https://doi.org/10.18653/v1/N16-1012, https://www.aclweb.org/anthology/N16-1012
4. Gehrmann, S., Deng, Y., Rush, A.: Bottom-up abstractive summarization. In: Proceedings of the 2018 Conference on Empirical Methods in Natural Language Processing, pp. 4098–4109. Association for Computational Linguistics, Brussels, Belgium, October-November 2018. https://doi.org/10.18653/v1/D18-1443, https://www.aclweb.org/anthology/D18-1443
5. Hermann, K.M., et al.: Teaching machines to read and comprehend. In: Advances in Neural Information Processing Systems, pp. 1693–1701 (2015)
6. Huang, L., Wu, L., Wang, L.: Knowledge graph-augmented abstractive summarization with semantic-driven cloze reward, pp. 5094–5107, January 2020. https://doi.org/10.18653/v1/2020.acl-main.457
7. Li, S., Lei, D., Qin, P., Wang, W.Y.: Deep reinforcement learning with distributional semantic rewards for abstractive summarization. In: Proceedings of the 2019 Conference on Empirical Methods in Natural Language Processing and the 9th International Joint Conference on Natural Language Processing (EMNLP-IJCNLP), pp. 6038–6044. Association for Computational Linguistics, Hong Kong, China, November 2019. https://doi.org/10.18653/v1/D19-1623, https://www.aclweb.org/anthology/D19-1623
8. Lin, C.Y.: ROUGE: a package for automatic evaluation of summaries. In: Text Summarization Branches Out, pp. 74–81. Association for Computational Linguistics, Barcelona, Spain, July 2004. https://www.aclweb.org/anthology/W04-1013
9. Luketina, J., et al.: A survey of reinforcement learning informed by natural language (2019)
10. Nallapati, R., Zhou, B., dos Santos, C., Caglar, G., Xiang, B.: Abstractive text summarization using sequence-to-sequence RNNs and beyond. In: Proceedings of The 20th SIGNLL Conference on Computational Natural Language Learning, pp. 280–290. Association for Computational Linguistics, Berlin, Germany, August 2016. https://doi.org/10.18653/v1/K16-1028, https://www.aclweb.org/anthology/K16-1028
11. Nguyen, T.P.N., Tran, N.T.: Contour: penalty and spotlight mask for abstractive summarization. In: Hong, T.P., Wojtkiewicz, K., Chawuthai, R., Sitek, P. (eds.) Recent Challenges in Intelligent Information and Database Systems, pp. 174–187. Springer Singapore, Singapore (2021)

12. Paulus, R., Xiong, C., Socher, R.: A deep reinforced model for abstractive summarization (2017)
13. Raychaudhuri, S.: Introduction to Monte Carlo simulation. In: 2008 Winter Simulation Conference, pp. 91–100 (2008). https://doi.org/10.1109/WSC.2008.4736059
14. Rennie, S.J., Marcheret, E., Mroueh, Y., Ross, J., Goel, V.: Self-critical sequence training for image captioning (2017)
15. Rush, A.M., Chopra, S., Weston, J.: A neural attention model for abstractive sentence summarization. In: Proceedings of the 2015 Conference on Empirical Methods in Natural Language Processing, pp. 379–389. Association for Computational Linguistics, Lisbon, Portugal, September 2015. https://doi.org/10.18653/v1/D15-1044, https://www.aclweb.org/anthology/D15-1044
16. See, A., Liu, P.J., Manning, C.D.: Get to the point: summarization with pointer-generator networks. In: Proceedings of the 55th Annual Meeting of the Association for Computational Linguistics (Volume 1: Long Papers), pp. 1073–1083. Association for Computational Linguistics, Vancouver, Canada, July 2017. https://doi.org/10.18653/v1/P17-1099, https://www.aclweb.org/anthology/P17-1099
17. Sutskever, I., Vinyals, O., Le, Q.V.: Sequence to sequence learning with neural networks. CoRR abs/1409.3215 (2014). http://arxiv.org/abs/1409.3215
18. Vaswani, A., et al.: Attention is all you need. In: Guyon, I., et al. (eds.) Advances in Neural Information Processing Systems, vol. 30, pp. 5998–6008. Curran Associates, Inc. (2017). http://papers.nips.cc/paper/7181-attention-is-all-you-need.pdf
19. Wang, W.Y., Li, J., He, X.: Deep reinforcement learning for NLP. In: Proceedings of the 56th Annual Meeting of the Association for Computational Linguistics: Tutorial Abstracts, pp. 19–21. Association for Computational Linguistics, Melbourne, Australia, July 2018. https://doi.org/10.18653/v1/P18-5007, https://www.aclweb.org/anthology/P18-5007
20. Williams, R.J.: Simple statistical gradient-following algorithms for connectionist reinforcement learning. Mach. Learn. 8, 229–256 (1992)

Punctuation Prediction in Vietnamese ASRs Using Transformer-Based Models

Viet The Bui[1] and Oanh Thi Tran[2]([✉]) [iD]

[1] FPT School of Business and Technology, FPT University, Hanoi, Vietnam
viet19mse13053@fsb.edu.vn
[2] International School, Vietnam National University, Hanoi, Hanoi, Vietnam
oanhtt@isvnu.vn

Abstract. Punctuation prediction is the task of predicting and inserting punctuation like periods, commas, exclamation marks, etc. into the appropriate positions in transcribed texts in ASR systems. This helps to improve user readability and the performance of many downstream tasks. While most related studies have been performed for popular languages like English and Chinese, there is very little work done for low-resource languages. In order to stimulate the research on these languages, in this paper, we target to improve the quality of punctuation prediction for Vietnamese ASRs. Specifically, we propose a method based on recent advances on pre-trained language models (LMs) for general purposes such as BERT and ELECTRA. The benefit of using these models is that they can be effectively fine-tuned on this punctuation prediction task where only a small amount of training data is available. To further enhance the performance, a simple yet effective technique to provide more context information in predicting punctuation marks for the very left and right words in each segment is also proposed. The experimental results of the proposed model on public benchmark datasets are quite promising. Overall, the proposed architecture substantially enhanced the prediction performance by a large margin and yielded a new state-of-the-art result on these datasets. Specifically, we achieved the F_1 scores of 71.49% and 80.38% on the Novel and Newspaper public datasets, respectively.

Keywords: Punctuation prediction · Vietnamese ASR · viBERT · vELECTRA

1 Introduction

Automatic Speech Recognition (ASR) systems normally generate un-normalized sequences of words (transcripts) which are difficult for human beings to read. It does not contain a proper segmentation into sentences as well as other predicted punctuation symbols like commas, question marks, etc. This also results in the degradation in performance of many further text processing tasks such as question answering, machine translation, etc. because these tasks are normally trained on punctuated texts [13, 21]. Hence, recovering punctuation marks is a

© Springer Nature Switzerland AG 2021
D. N. Pham et al. (Eds.): PRICAI 2021, LNAI 13032, pp. 191–204, 2021.
https://doi.org/10.1007/978-3-030-89363-7_15

very important step towards generating normalized texts [23] in the output of ASR systems. It relates to automatically infer the presence of punctuation and then insert it to the appropriate positions in the transcribed texts.

Detecting punctuation in un-normalized texts requires quite a bit of linguistic sophistication and native speaker intuition [16]. Traditionally, this task was treated as a sequence labelling problem. Based on this approach, researchers exploited different machine learning techniques with different kinds of features to enrich the prediction models. For example, there existed work which used raw speech waveforms with pause duration [6,9,10,20], textual features only [1,4,12,24], or both two feature types in a combination model to build the corresponding prediction models. Most of these studies have been done for popular languages such as Czech, English, French, German, Chinese, and Spanish [2].

While most work so far focused on high resource languages, there is very little work dedicated to low resource languages. In Vietnamese, the research about this field is still very limited. To our knowledge, there is only one work done for punctuator prediction in Vietnamese [15].

In recent years, we have witnessed an increasing interest in using pre-trained LMs based on transformers [25] to improve performances of many NLP tasks [3]. These models have been proposed to deal with the shortage of training data in many NLP tasks by pre-training LMs on a large number of unlabeled datasets. These pre-trained models are then effectively fine-tuned on small labeled datasets of the downstream NLP tasks. They typically result in substantial performance improvements compared to training on these small datasets from scratch [3]. For low-resource languages, this approach is highly effective when it is only possible to collect and annotate very little amount of labeled data for almost every NLP task. For Vietnamese, to the best of our knowledge, these models have not been investigated to address this punctuation prediction task. Hence, in this paper, we aim at exploring these pre-trained LMs for this task in Vietnamese. Two kinds of models which are BERT [3,8] and ELECTRA [3,7] are exploited to boost the accuracy of predicting punctuation in Vietnamese transcribed texts.

In predicting punctuation, the whole transcribed text is usually long, so it is processed by splitting the text into the unit of segments before feeding into the model. For example, we acknowledged that the maximum segment length that BERT can process is 512 tokens. In such cases, it can be seen that the model is prone to make quite bad predictions for the words at the very left and right ends of the segment because there is not enough context information for those words at the boundary positions. To process such cases, we further propose a technique to provide more information about the surrounding words in making prediction of punctuation near those boundary words. This is called surrounding context information (or context information for short) hereafter.

In conclusion, the contribution of this paper is three folds:

- Firstly explore the effectiveness of pre-trained LMs for the task of punctuation prediction in a low-resource language, namely Vietnamese.
- Propose a simple yet effective technique to integrate surrounding contexts in predicting punctuation of the very left and right words in each segment.

– Extensively perform different kinds of experiments on public datasets to make comparisons and provide new SOTA results for future research in this interesting field.

The rest of this paper is organized as follows. Section 2 discusses related work. In Sect. 3, we formally define the problem, and then propose a solution to solve it using pre-trained LMs. Section 4 describes the datasets, experimental setups, experimental results, and some discussions. Finally, we conclude the paper and point out some future lines of work in Sect. 5.

2   Related Work

So far, there have been many studies done for predicting punctuation in post-processing the output of ASR systems. It can be divided into three main approaches based on the type of information available for building prediction models.

The first approach is to use the information of raw speech waveforms with pause duration between words, pitch and intensity as inputs in order to make the prediction. And there is a significant variation in how different researchers use pauses [6,9,10]. However, such information is not always available.

In the case where audio is not provided, researchers have entirely relied on the appearance of texts only. Several methods have already been introduced to deal with this task by using textual information. The first method is to cast it as a sequence labeling problem and then exploit different machine learning algorithms such as conditional random fields (CRFs) [12,24], deep and convolutional neural networks [4], or recently transformer-based models [1] to make punctuation prediction. Another method is to treat the punctuation restoration as a machine translation task, that is, translating from unpunctuated text to punctuated text [5]. There are also other methods which combine both feature types (prosodic features and text features) or build separate models then combined in various ways to further improve the performance.

In the case where the datasets are labeled with not only the information on punctuation marks but also the information on true-casing of words, researchers proposed a variety of joint architectures to jointly learn both punctuation and truecasing information in one go. For example, Sunkara et al., 2020 [19] proposed a joint framework using pre-trained masked LMs such as BERT to build the joint model. Nguyen et al., 2019 [14] proposed a method to restore the normalized texts for long-speech ASR transcription based on Transformer models and chunk merging.

As can be seen that most current work has been extensively studied for high resource languages like English, Spanish, Estonian or Chinese. These languages usually have many public benchmark datasets such as TED talks within IWSLT datasets[1], TDT4 English data[2], Wiki dataset [18], Tsinghua Chinese

---

[1] https://sites.google.com/site/iwsltevaluation2016/.
[2] http://ssli.ee.washington.edu/people/leixin/TDT4.html.

Treebank [26] and Estonian speech transcripts [20]. Unfortunately, there is very little work dedicated to low resource languages. In Vietnamese, the research about this field is still very limited. To our knowledge, there is only one work targeted to punctuator prediction [15]. Encouraging from the effectiveness of recent innovation in pre-trained LMs, in this paper, we propose a learning architecture using BERT [8] and ELECTRA [7], to enhance the performance of punctuation prediction for Vietnamese ASRs. These models are quite effective especially for the NLP tasks with a small amount of labeled data [22]. Additionally, a technique to further boost the performance on predicting the punctuation of boundary words in each segment is also introduced.

3   A Proposed Model to Predict Punctuation

This section first formulates the problem and then introduces a proposed architecture based on pre-trained LMs with extra boundary context information to solve the task.

3.1   Problem Definition

Given an input segment $s_{1:T} = \{x_1, x_2, ..., x_T\}$, of length T and consisting of T syllables x_i. We assume that there are 6 classes corresponding to 6 possible punctuation marks mostly appear in the text documents which are *commas*, *periods*, *colons*, *question marks*, *exclamation marks*, and *semi-colons*.

We need to build a model f to map from each syllable x_i into its class $\hat{y}_i$ that maximize $P(\hat{y}_i|x_i)$ where $\hat{y}_i \in \{comma, period, colon, question\text{-}mark, exclamation\text{-}mark, semi\text{-}colon$ and $Other\}$. The mapping indicates that the punctuation mark $\hat{y}_i$ is located right after the syllable x_i in the recovered form of this text segment. We add one more class, *Other*, to represent that there is no punctuation mark located right after x_i.

This problem can be considered as a sequence labelling task where we make a prediction label for each syllable in the input segment.

3.2   A Proposed Architecture Using Pre-trained LMs
with Boundary Context Information

We first describe the key points of pre-trained LMs, namely BERT [8] and ELECTRA [7]. Then, a proposed framework for learning and predicting punctuation using these LMs is presented. The reason for choosing these models is that many previous works have pointed out that these models normally yielded better performance on many downstream NLP tasks. In fact, the experimental results on the benchmark datasets also prove this statement.

BERT. BERT is trained based on Transformer [25]. Its attention mechanism learns contextual relations between words (or sub-words) in a text. It is basically an encoder-decoder model where an encoder reads the text input and a decoder produces a prediction for the task. The goal of BERT is to generate a language model, therefore, only the encoder mechanism is necessary. Because the encoder reads the entire sequence of words at one time, it allows the model to learn the context of a word based on all of its surroundings (left and right of the word). The detailed workings of Transformer can be found in the paper [8].

When training BERT, there are two prediction goals which are Masked Language Model (MLM) and Next Sentence Prediction (NSP) which are described in more details as follows:

- *MLM*: 15% of the words in each sequence are masked with a [MASK] token. BERT then learns to predict the original one of the masked words, based on the context provided by the other words which are non-masked in this sequence.
- *NSP*: BERT receives pairs of sentences as input and learns to predict if the second one is the subsequent sentence in the original document.

ELECTRA. BERT is trained to correctly predict typically 15% of masked tokens. Therefore, it can only learn from a small portion of text sequences. ELECTRA, which stands for Efficiently Learning an Encoder that Classifies Token Replacements, was proposed to deal with the disadvantage of BERT by learning the task called Replace Token Detection (RTD). It trains the model to distinguish between the real input token from the replaced one. As a consequence, it is more effective in learning from the entire sequence instead of just a small portion of it. ELECTRA consists of two components as described below:

- *Generator*: is a small masked language model trained jointly with the discriminator. It is trained with maximum likelihood to predict masked words. After pre-training, this component is ignored and only the discriminator is fine-tuned on the punctuation prediction task.
- *Discriminator*: trains the model to distinguish between the real and the fake input data. Then, it is used to recognize which token has been replaced or kept the same.

The Proposed Architecture. Figure 1 depicts our proposed architecture to solve the task. This architecture includes three main layers which are described as follows:

Embedding Layer. The input segment is tokenized by the WordPiece tokenizer (Sennrich et al., 2016) [17] and fed into the BERT or ELECTRA encoders. Similar to the work of Pham et al., [15], we also trained the model on segments consisting of 100 syllables. However, for each segment we observe that the token in the middle positions are normally leveraged by the full context information of both left and right words in the input segment. While, the very left or right words at the boundary of the segment only have very little or not enough surrounding context information at the left or right side, respectively. To provide more context for the words at these positions, more contexts are complemented to enrich the information for those words. Specifically, the sequences of k tokens that come before and after the segment are also included before feeding to the BERT/ELECTRA models.

The input segment enriched with the context information at the boundary is tokenized into $s_{1:T+2*k} = x_{-k}, ..., x_1, x_2, ..., x_T, ..., x_{T+k}$, of length $T + 2 * k$ and consisting of tokens x_i. When necessary, context information is padded to the left or to the right with [PAD] tokens.

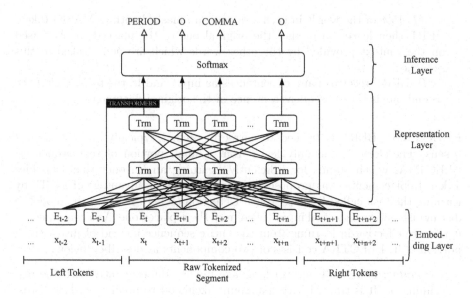

Fig. 1. A proposed architecture using pre-trained LMs with the context information around each segment.

Representation Layer. The lower component exploits BERT or ELECTRA models to encode the context information of s into a representation vector $H = [h_{-k}, ..., h_{T+k}]$. After obtaining the representation, H, we design the decoder architecture on top of the BERT embedding layer for solving the task.

Inference Layer. This layer predicts a probability distribution over punctuation. In more details, the decoder takes in the vector representation h_i for token x_i and passes it through the activation layer L which is calculated as follows:

$$L_i = f(W_o h_i + b_o) \tag{1}$$

where f is a linear function, W_o is the weight matrix, and b_o is the bias vector of two layers. They are learnable parameters of the linear layer.

The prediction for this layer P is calculated using the corresponding sigmoid function which connects the activation layer with the output of this layer.

$$P(y_i|x_i) = softmax(L_i) \tag{2}$$

During training, the model minimizes the loss function of the predictor P over only the tokens of the original segment. We don't predict the labels for extra tokens added as surrounding contexts.

4 Experiments

4.1 Datasets

These two datasets (i.e. Novels and Newspaper) [15] were built from Vietnamese novels and newspapers. There are 6 types of punctuation marks with some statistics given in Table 1.

Table 1. Some statistics about the two Vietnamese benchmark datasets which are Novel and News.

Punctuation	Novel dataset				News dataset			
	Training set		Testing set		Training set		Testing set	
	Number	%	Number	%	Number	%	Number	%
Comma (;)	50909	3.77	21231	4.045	482435	4.041	160472	4.054
Period (·)	66519	4.926	29643	5.648	419580	3.514	138967	3.51
Colon (:)	742	0.055	1153	0.221	32177	0.269	10728	0.271
Qmark (?)	14899	1.103	5271	1.004	13902	0.116	4468	0.113
Exclam (!)	30183	2.235	9167	1.747	7384	0.062	2333	0.059
Semicolon (;)	48	0.004	43	0.008	5675	0.048	2045	0.052
Sentences	**111601**		**44081**		**440866**		**145768**	

These datasets are divided into training, validation and testing with the ratio of 6:2:2. In these datasets, there is no assumption about sentence boundaries inside texts. We also noticed that the distribution of punctuation marks are not equal. Some marks (i.e. *comma, period*) dominate, while the others (i.e. colon, semicolon) only appear very little.

4.2 Experimental Setups

For BERT, we exploited two variants which are mBERT[3] and viBERT[4]. For ELECTRA, we exploited the vELECTRA[5] which is pre-trained for the Vietnamese language. The viBERT and vELECTRA [3] are optimally pre-trained LMs for the Vietnamese language.

---

[3] https://github.com/google-research/bert/blob/master/multilingual.md.
[4] https://github.com/fpt-corp/viBERT.
[5] https://github.com/fpt-corp/vELECTRA.

Our models were implemented in PyTorch[6]. We set the batch size to 32 for both viBERT and vELECTRA. The maximum sequence length is set at 100 which is similar to the previous work [15]. The value of k was set to 50. Our models were trained using the AdamW optimizer [11], a stochastic optimization method that modifies the typical implementation of weight decay in the Adam optimizer by decoupling weight decay from the gradient update. The learning rate was tuned in [1e-5, 1.5e-5, 2e-5, 3e-5, 5e-5, 1e-4] with a linear warm up schedule. To reduce overfitting, we also added dropout with a dropout rate of 0.1 for BERT components and 0.5 for the last layer of fine-tuning.

All experiments were performed on the server where its hardware components are CPU Intel(R) Xeon(R) CPU E5-2698 v4 @ 2.20 GHz, and GPU NVIDIA Tesla V100 32 GB CoWoS HBM2 PCIe 3.0.

4.3   Evaluation Metrics

The system performance is evaluated using precision, recall, and the F_1 score as in many sequence labeling problems as follows:

$$F_1 = \frac{2*precision*recall}{precision+recall}$$
$$precision = \frac{TP}{TP+FP}$$
$$recall = \frac{TP}{TP+FN}$$

where TP (True Positive) is the number of punctuation marks that are correctly identified. FP (False Positive) is the number of punctuation marks that are mistakenly identified as valid ones. FN (False Negative) is the number of punctuation marks that are not identified.

4.4   Experimental Results

This section presents extensive experiments to prove the effectiveness of the proposed architecture and some discussions on the final experimental results.

Firstly, we show experimental results of the proposed architecture with and without using surrounding context information. The results on the NOVEL dataset are illustrated first, followed by the results on the Newspaper dataset. Additionally, to see the impact of the pre-trained models on this downstream task, we performed experiments with different training data sizes to see the performance of the final model on the two datasets. Finally, some discussions on comparison with the previous work and performance on each punctuation mark are also presented.

---

[6] https://pytorch.org/.

Experimental Results on the NOVEL Dataset. Tables 2 and 3 show experimental results of the proposed models on the NOVEL dataset with and without using surrounding contexts. Among three models, the vELECTRA yielded the best F_1 scores and outperformed the other two models by a large margin on all three evaluation metrics. Using vELECTRA, we achieved the F_1 scores of 69.56% without using surrounding contexts, and 71.49% by using surrounding contexts. In comparison with mBERT, the one optimized for Vietnamese, viBERT, boosted the F_1 scores by 4.3% and 3.8% with and without using surrounding contexts, respectively.

Table 2. Experimental results on the NOVEL dataset WITHOUT using surrounding contexts.

Punctuation	mBERT			viBERT			vELECTRA		
	Pre	Rec	F_1	Pre	Rec	F_1	Pre	Rec	F_1
PERIOD	62.77	64.58	63.66	66.32	68.97	67.62	72.05	73.63	72.83
COMMA	61.21	52.58	56.57	63.31	59.67	61.43	68.44	64.48	66.40
COLON	26.21	2.34	4.30	36.84	4.25	7.62	48.39	5.20	9.40
SCOLON	0.00	0.00	0.00	0.00	0.00	0.00	0.00	0.00	0.00
QMARK	77.34	73.17	75.20	77.77	75.81	76.78	80.72	79.53	80.12
EMARK	59.24	58.44	58.84	61.48	60.83	61.15	62.88	66.02	64.41
MICRO AVG.	62.91	59.47	61.14	65.57	64.25	64.90	70.24	68.89	**69.56**

Table 3. Experimental results on the NOVEL dataset using surrounding contexts.

Punctuation	mBERT			viBERT			vELECTRA		
	Pre	Rec	F_1	Pre	Rec	F_1	Pre	Rec	F_1
PERIOD	64.45	66.33	65.37	69.21	70.90	70.05	73.28	76.46	74.84
COMMA	62.88	54.70	58.51	66.76	61.24	63.88	71.18	66.06	68.53
COLON	25.76	2.95	5.29	43.20	4.68	8.45	47.85	6.76	11.85
SCOLON	0.00	0.00	0.00	0.00	0.00	0.00	0.00	0.00	0.00
QMARK	79.18	75.20	77.14	80.27	77.63	78.93	84.11	80.72	82.38
EMARK	59.70	62.27	60.96	62.61	63.90	63.25	64.08	66.96	65.49
MICRO AVG.	64.36	61.62	62.96	68.33	66.19	67.24	72.07	70.91	**71.49**

Experimental Results on the NEWSPAPER Dataset. Tables 4 and 5 show experimental results of the proposed models on the NEWSPAPER dataset with and without using surrounding contexts. Observing the results, we draw the same conclusion as shown on the Novel dataset. Specifically, the vELECTRA outperformed the other two models and yielded new state-of-the-art results. We achieved 78.30% and 80.38% in the F_1 scores without and with using surrounding information, respectively. Because viBERT is optimized on Vietnamese language, this specialized model gave a higher improvement compared to mBERT. It boosts the F_1 scores by 2.8% and 3% with and without using surrounding contexts, respectively.

Table 4. Experimental results on the NEWSPAPER dataset WITHOUT surrounding contexts.

Punctuation	mBERT			viBERT			vELECTRA		
	Pre	Rec	F_1	Pre	Rec	F_1	Pre	Rec	F_1
PERIOD	78.60	80.27	79.43	80.05	84.35	82.14	83.85	86.01	84.92
COMMA	69.92	67.16	68.51	74.51	68.98	71.64	75.46	74.27	74.86
COLON	58.66	47.48	52.48	62.34	48.77	54.73	65.48	56.34	60.56
SCOLON	31.54	12.03	17.42	30.59	19.46	23.79	44.28	10.22	16.61
QMARK	64.86	58.12	61.31	68.81	63.94	66.29	70.12	70.01	70.06
EMARK	38.07	11.36	17.50	38.63	12.30	18.66	38.14	16.67	23.20
MICRO AVG.	73.34	71.32	72.32	76.45	74.19	75.31	78.71	77.89	**78.30**

Table 5. Experimental results on the NEWSPAPER dataset using surrounding contexts.

Punctuation	mBERT			viBERT			vELECTRA		
	Pre	Rec	F_1	Pre	Rec	F_1	Pre	Rec	F_1
PERIOD	80.68	83.12	81.88	82.17	86.67	84.36	85.75	89.03	87.36
COMMA	71.68	69.28	70.46	75.52	71.59	73.50	77.99	74.93	76.43
COLON	62.27	50.14	55.55	66.62	50.57	57.50	69.47	57.87	63.14
SCOLON	34.11	16.53	22.27	33.49	17.11	22.65	42.11	21.12	28.13
QMARK	68.32	62.76	65.42	68.99	71.04	70.00	75.73	72.22	73.94
EMARK	41.60	12.73	19.49	45.83	10.59	17.20	49.21	13.29	20.92
MICRO AVG.	75.31	73.82	74.56	78.11	76.65	77.37	81.12	79.66	**80.38**

Experimental Results with Different Training Sizes. For a better understanding of the performance of the proposed architecture, we performed an empirical comparison taking into consideration the level of different sizes of training sets. On each dataset, we varied the training data sizes by 10% and performed this 10 times. Figure 2 and 3 shows experimental results using the best model, vELECTRA, with surrounding contexts on the Novel and Newspaper datasets.

As we can see, the more training data we have, the better the performance of the model. However, with only very little amount of data, we still achieve quite good performance. For example, with only 10% of original training data size, we could obtain around 62% and 76.7% in the F1 scores on the Novel and Newspaper datasets, respectively.

Discussion

Comparison with the Best Baseline Model. Figure 6 shows experimental results on the two datasets of the best baseline model (i.e. biLSTM without focal losses) and the best proposed model (i.e. vELECTRA) integrated with surrounding

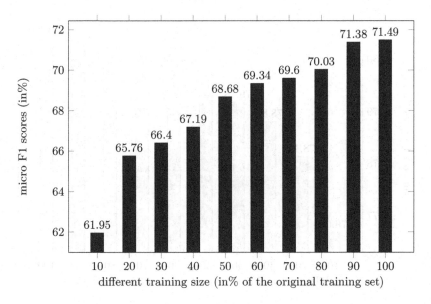

Fig. 2. The F1 scores using different training sizes using vELECTRA with context information on the NOVEL dataset.

contexts. We observed a significant improvement of the proposed model over the baseline one mentioned in [15] on all three evaluation metrics of precision, recall and F_1 scores. Specifically, on the Novel dataset, vELECTRA boosted the F_1 score by 17.71%. On the Newspaper dataset, it boosted the F_1 score by 21.18%. These results set new SOTA results for future work for this task using these benchmark datasets.

Table 6. Experimental results of the best baseline method (biLSTM) and the best proposed model (vELECTRA) integrated with surrounding contexts (micro averaged on all 6 punctuation marks).

Datasets	Models	Pre	Rec	F_1
NEWSPAPER	biLSTM-attention (BAW)	69.63	56.97	62.67
	vELECTRA	**81.12**	**79.66**	**80.38**
NOVEL	biLSTM-attention (BAW)	56.52	45.34	50.31
	vELECTRA	**72.07**	**70.91**	**71.49**

Performance on Each Punctuation Mark. Tables 2, 3, 4, and 5 also show the experimental results of the proposed model on all punctuation marks. We observed that the proposed models yielded relatively high performance on three labels which are *period, comma* and *question marks*. On the Novel dataset, the performance on two labels of *colon* and *semi-colon* are lowest. On the News

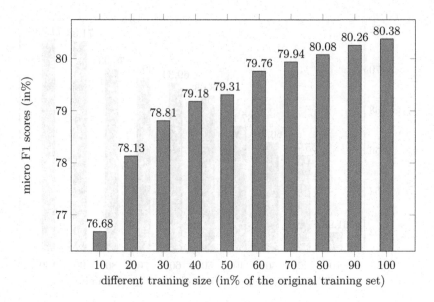

Fig. 3. The F1 scores using different training sizes using vELECTRA with context information on the NEWSPAPER dataset.

dataset, the performance on the two labels of *exclamation* and *semi-colon* are lowest. The reason is that the number of samples in the training datasets on these labels are much smaller in comparison to other labels. This imbalance data problem needs solving in order to improve the performance on these skewed labels.

5   Conclusion

This paper presents an effort to improve the performance of a punctuation prediction model on Vietnamese ASRs. To cope with the data sparsity problem in low-resource languages, we proposed to exploit the recent innovation of pre-trained LMs to solve the task. Trained on a large amount of unlabelled data for general purposes, these pre-trained LMs can be further fine-tuned effectively on many downstream NLP tasks with a small amount of training data. In more detail, we used two LMs, namely BERT and ELECTRA, which are specifically pre-trained for the Vietnamese language. To improve even more, we also proposed a technique to better make the prediction of punctuation marks of the boundary syllables in each segment. The experimental results of these proposed models on two public datasets showed promising results. The best model integrated with surrounding contexts yielded the best performance and established new challenging SOTA results. It outperformed the best baseline model by a large margin. Using the best model with surrounding contexts, we achieved 71.49% and 80.38% in the F_1 scores on the Novel and Newspaper datasets, respectively.

    In the future, we will continue to consider the imbalance data problem to deal with the skewed data of rare punctuation marks.

References

1. Alam, T., Khan, A., Alam, F.: Punctuation restoration using transformer models for high-and low-resource languages. In: Proceedings of the 2020 EMNLP Workshop W-NUT: The Sixth Workshop on Noisy User-Generated Text. Association for Computational Linguistics, pp. 132–142 (2020)
2. Ballesteros, M., Wanner, L.: A neural network architecture for multilingual punctuation generation. In: Proceedings of the 2016 Conference on Empirical Methods in Natural Language Processing, Austin, Texas, 1–5 November, pp. 1048–1053 (2016)
3. Bui, V.T., Tran, O.T., Le, P.H.: Improving sequence tagging for Vietnamese text using transformer-based neural models. In: Proceedings of the 34th Pacific Asia Conference on Language, Information and Computation, pp. 13–20 (2020)
4. Che, X., Wang, C., Yang, H., Meinel, C.: Punctuation prediction for unsegmented transcript based on word vector. In: The 10th International Conference on Language Resources and Evaluation (LREC), pp. 654–658 (2016)
5. Cho, E., Niehues, J., Kilgour, K., Waibel, A.: Punctuation insertion for real-time spoken language translation. In: Proceedings of the Eleventh International Workshop on Spoken Language Translation (2015)
6. Christensen, H., Gotoh, Y., Renals, S.: Punctuation annotation using statistical prosody models. In: ISCA Tutorial and Research Workshop (ITRW) on Prosody in Speech Recognition and Understanding (2001)
7. Clark, K., Luong, M.T., Le, Q.V., Manning, C.D.: ELECTRA: pretraining text encoders as discriminators rather than generators. In: Proceedings of ICLR (2020)
8. Devlin, J., Chang, M.W., Lee, K., Toutanova, K.: BERT: pre-training of deep bidirectional transformers for language understanding. In: Proceedings of NAACL, Minnesota, USA, pp. 1–16 (2019)
9. Igras-Cybulska, M., Ziołko, B., Zelasko, P., Witkowski, M.: Structure of pauses in speech in the context of speaker verification and classification of speech type. EURASIP J. Audio Speech Music Process. **2016**(1), Article ID. 18 (2016)
10. Levy, T., Silber-Varod, V., Moyal, A.: The effect of pitch, intensity and pause duration in punctuation detection. In: IEEE 27th Convention of Electrical and Electronics Engineers in Israel (IEEEI), pp. 1–4. IEEE (2012)
11. Loshchilov, I., Hutter, F.: Decoupled Weight Decay Regularization. In: Proceedings of ICLR (2019)
12. Lu, W., Ng, H.T.: Better punctuation prediction with dynamic conditional random fields proceedings of the 2010 conference on empirical methods in natural language processing, pp. 177–186. MIT, Massachusetts, USA. Association for Computational Linguistics (2010)
13. Ngo, X.B., Tu, M.P.: Leveraging user ratings for resource-poor sentiment classification. Procedia Comput. Sci. **60**, 322–331 (2015). ISSN: 1877-0509, https://doi.org/10.1016/j.procs.2015.08.134
14. Nguyen, B., et al.: Fast and accurate capitalization and punctuation for automatic speech recognition using transformer and chunk merging. In: 22nd Conference of the Oriental COCOSDA International Committee for the Co-ordination and Standardisation of Speech Databases and Assessment Techniques (O-COCOSDA), pp. 1–5 (2019)
15. Pham, T., Nguyen, N., Pham, Q., Cao, H., Nguyen, B.: Vietnamese punctuation prediction using deep neural networks. In: proceedings of the International Conference on Current Trends in Theory and Practice of Informatics: SOFSEM 2020: Theory and Practice of Computer Science, pp. 388–400 (2020)

16. Schutze, H.: Ambiguity Resolution in Language Learning: Computational and Cognitive Models, 176 p. CSLI Publications, Stanford (1997)
17. Sennrich, R., Haddow, B., Birch, A.: Neural machine translation of rare words with subword units. In: Proceedings of the 54th Annual Meeting of the Association for Computational Linguistics (Volume 1: Long Papers), Germany, pp. 1715–1725. Association for Computational Linguistics (2016)
18. Sproat, R., Jaitly, N.: RNN approaches to text normalization: a challenge. arXiv preprint arXiv:1611.00068 (2016)
19. Sunkara, M., Ronanki, S., Dixit, K., Bodapati, S., Kirchhoff, K.: Robust prediction of punctuation and truecasing for medical ASR. In: Proceedings of the 1st Workshop on NLP for Medical Conversations, pp. 53–62. Association for Computational Linguistics (2020)
20. Tilk, O., Alum, T.: Bidirectional recurrent neural network with attention mechanism for punctuation restoration. In: Interspeech, pp. 3047–3051 (2016)
21. Tran, O.T., Ngo, B.X., Le Nguyen, M., Shimazu, A.: Answering legal questions by mining reference information. In: Nakano, Y., Satoh, K., Bekki, D. (eds.) JSAI-isAI 2013. LNCS (LNAI), vol. 8417, pp. 214–229. Springer, Cham (2014). https://doi.org/10.1007/978-3-319-10061-6_15
22. Tran, O.T., Bui, V.T.: A BERT-based hierarchical model for Vietnamese aspect based sentiment analysis. In: 12th International Conference on Knowledge and Systems Engineering (KSE), 2020, pp. 269–274 (2020). https://doi.org/10.1109/KSE50997.2020.9287650
23. Tran, O.T., Bui, V.T.: Neural text normalization in Speech-to-Text systems with rich features. Appl. Artif. Intell. **35**(3), 193–205 (2021)
24. Ueffing, N., Bisani, M., Vozila, P.: Improved models for automatic punctuation prediction for spoken and written text. In: Interspeech, pp. 3097–3101, Lyon, France (2013)
25. Vaswani, A., et al.: Attention is all you need. Adv. Neural Inf. Process. Syst. **30**, 5998–6008 (2017)
26. Zhao, Y., Wang, C., Fu, G.: A CRF sequence labeling approach to Chinese punctuation prediction. In: Proceedings of PACLIC, pp. 508–514 (2012)

Rumor Detection on Microblogs Using Dual-Grained Feature via Graph Neural Networks

Shouzhi Xu, Xiaodi Liu, Kai Ma$^{(\boxtimes)}$, Fangmin Dong, Shunzhi Xiang, and Changsong Bing

College of Computer and Information Technology, China Three Gorges University, Yichang 443002, China
{xsz,makai,fmdong}@ctgu.edu.cn

Abstract. Online social media platforms have been developing rapidly in the era of the Internet and big data, which accelerate rumors being circulated. The spread of rumors might damage citizen rights and disturb social stability. Rumor detection on social media is a challenging task worldwide due to rumor's feature of the high speed, fragmental information, and extensive range. In this paper, we propose a novel model for rumor detection based on Graph Neural Networks (GNN), named *Dual-grained Feature Aggregation Graph Neural Networks* (Du-FAGNN). It applies a Graph Convolutional Network (GCN) with a graph of rumor propagation to learn the text-granularity representations with the spreading of events. We employ a GNN with a document graph to update aggregated features of both word and text granularity, it helps to form final representations of events to detect rumors. Experiments on the Sina Weibo dataset validate the performance of the proposed method for rumor detection.

Keywords: Rumor detection · Graph neural networks · Dual-grained aggregation · Rumor propagation

1 Introduction

In the era of big data, social media platforms have become an indispensable part of our daily life, which increase people's ability to obtain and exchange information significantly. Users can post, forward, and comment on any real-time information through various platforms. Therefore, microblog platforms like Sina Weibo usually have higher flexibility and stronger interactivity, and information can be fully diffused. The explosive growth of data usually leads to fake news and rumors. Since the lack of monitoring mechanisms, harmful information can easily flourish. Rumors on social media have become a serious concern in recent years, especially when disasters like Coronavirus Disease-19 (the COVID-19) outbreak. Peace and order of the society may be affected because of diverse misinformation.

© Springer Nature Switzerland AG 2021
D. N. Pham et al. (Eds.): PRICAI 2021, LNAI 13032, pp. 205–216, 2021.
https://doi.org/10.1007/978-3-030-89363-7_16

Society is taking great efforts to fight against rumors. There are a large number of researches on rumor detection. Most of the traditional methods tend to use classification algorithms with manually extracted features, such as Support Vector Machine (SVM) [22,25], Random Forest [11,20] and Decision Trees [3,27]. Recent researches have employed deep learning methods to explore high-level representations of rumors from text contents, spreading path, users [16] and other features. There are still some challenges. Though plenty of research has been done on text contents, emotional tendency, and user information, the propagation mechanism of rumors has not been studied adequately. How to concretize the propagation patterns is still a problem in terms of rumor diffusion.

In this paper, we propose a novel dual-grained feature aggregation graph neural network (Du-FAGNN)[1], which operates on Graph Convolutional Networks (GCN) and Graph Neural Networks (GNN). The proposed method obtains the text features via GCN and acquires word-text aggregated features via GNN. GCN updates text representations by formulating rumor propagation. GNN generates word-text fused vectors and further updates them to form final representations by constructing co-occurrence graphs of words. We optimize our model components to improve the accuracy of the method. The main contributions of this work are as follows:

- We adopt both GCN and GNN to detect rumors at different grain sizes, which few people would take into account.
- We propose the Du-FAGNN model that considers both word-level representations and text-level updated vectors. Besides, we generate text-granularity features through rumor propagation.
- We concatenate the updated text features of the rumor with the word features of source post at graph neural network module to make comprehensive use of both source posts and retweet posts. Experiments on the Sina Weibo dataset achieve great performance in rumor detection.

The remainder of this paper is organized as follows. Section 2 presents the related work of rumor detection. Section 3 is the statement of variables and data structures and describes GCN and GNN. In Section 4, the proposed model and its modules are elaborated. Section 5 presents the experiments and analyzes the results.

2   Related Work

Automatic detection of rumors aims to identify rumors using series of approaches through plentiful information like text contents, comments, and forwarding patterns on social media. Most previous work focuses on traditional handworked features and classification methods. Yang et al. [25] extracted 19 features from Sina Weibo manually, which exhibited characteristics different from those of Twitter.

---

[1] The Code of our Du-FAGNN model is available and can be accessed via: https://github.com/LXD789/Du-FAGNN.

They sent these features into an SVM classifier with RBF kernel. Considering that traditional rumor detection methods ignored the propagation structure of massages, Wu et al. [22] proposed a hybrid SVM based on a graph kernel to capture the semantic features and high-order propagation patterns. Ma et al. [16] pointed out the present work of detecting rumors neglected the importance of variational features over time, so they proposed a time series method capturing the time-varying features based on the rumor life cycle. Ma et al. [17] also proposed a kernel-based method that captures high-level representations distinguishing different types of rumors by evaluating the similarities between propagation trees. These conventional methods are not only ineffective but also a waste of time and resources.

Several methods based on deep learning were proposed in recent years. Sumeet et al. [10] proposed an approach that represents conversations on social media as binarized constituency trees, which can learn features from source posts and their replies effectively. They used Long Short Term Memory (LSTM) to classify rumors at the root. Ma et al. [15] discovered the continuity of the text stream, and that Recurrent Neural Networks (RNN) could capture the dynamic time signals of rumor forwarding. They proposed a model based on RNN to learn the semantic features of tweet context over time. Using Recursive Neural Networks (RvNN), Ma et al. [18] also proposed top-down and bottom-up tree-structured neural networks that relate text content to propagation clues. It helps to learn rumor representations. Shu et al. [21] found that social context in the process of news spreading on social media has formed inherent relationships among the publisher, the news, and the users. They proposed a framework of modeling publisher-news and user-news interaction relations to classify fake news. Ruchansky et al. [19] proposed the CSI (Capture, Score and Integrate) model in combination with users, texts, and group behavior of spreading fake news. Liu et al. [12] presented a CNN+RNN based time series classifier to detect fake news, its input is time-series in news forwarding paths. Wu et al. [23] put forward a novel method that employs social networks to infer the involvement of users. They used LSTM-RNN to represent and classify the paths of message spreading. Lukasik et al. [14] treated the classification of rumors as a supervised learning task that considers both supervised and unsupervised domain of self-adaption. Gao et al. [6] presented a novel hybrid neural network that combines a task-specific character-based bidirectional language model and stacked LSTM. It can represent text content and the social-time context of source posts to address the early rumor detection task. These deep-learning approaches are more efficient, but cannot learn propagation and high-level representations of rumors well.

Graph Neural Networks (GNN) is very efficient and popular in the past few years. Kipf et al. [9] proposed a CNN-based graph-structured semi-supervised approach in 2016. Bian et al. [2] proposed a new bi-directional graph convolutional model to explore the propagation and dispersion of rumors through the top-down and bottom-up structure. Lu et al. [13] exploited graph-aware co-attention networks based on source posts and series of no-comment retweet users.

It can highlight suspicious retweeters and words to predict whether the source is a rumor. Dong et al. [5] presented a model which can locate several rumor sources in the case of an unknown propagation pattern. Yu et al. [8] created a GCN-based model that takes both static characteristics like user information, text content and dynamic features such as rumor diffusion. Han et al. [7] adopted GNN to differentiate spreading mode between fake news and real news. Aiming to solve rumor detection tasks under the framework of representation learning, Wu et al. [24] proposed a novel approach of constructing propagation graph through spreading structure of posts on Twitter, and they applied an algorithm of gated graph neural networks to generate powerful representations for nodes in forwarding graph. Ke et al. [8] exploited a rumor detection framework that provides sufficient knowledge to accurately classify rumors and symmetrically fuses semantic information with propagation heterogeneous graph. Benamira et al. [1] focused on the content-based approach of fake news detection. They considered the problem as a binary text classification task and proposed a graph neural network-based semi-supervised method for fake news detection. Our proposed model is inspired by the GNN.

3   Du-FAGNN Rumor Detection Model

In this section, we propose a GNN-based double-level feature aggregation method for rumor detection, named as *Dual-grained Feature Aggregation Graph Neural Networks* (Du-FAGNN). The core idea of Du-FAGNN is to learn both word and text granularity high-level representations from text content and event propagation to detect rumors.

3.1   Problem Statement

We define a rumor detection dataset as a set of events $C = \{c_1, c_2, ..., c_n\}$, where c_i is the i-th event and n is the number of events. $c_i = \{c_0^i, c_1^i, ..., c_m^i\}$, where c_0^i is the source tweet and each c_j^i is the j-th responsive post of c_0^i. Denote $G_i = (N_i, E_i)$ as the propagation graph of event c_i, where node set $N_i = \{c_0^i, c_1^i, ..., c_m^i\}$ and $E_i = \{e_1^i, e_2^i, ..., e_m^i\}$ represents the set of edges from responded tweet to the retweet post. Denote $A_i \in \{0, 1\}^{m_i \times m_i}$ as the adjacency matrix where

$$A_i = \begin{cases} 1, & if\ e_j^i \in E_i \\ 0, & otherwise. \end{cases} \tag{1}$$

Denote $X_i = [x_0^i, x_1^i, ..., x_m^i]^T$ as the sentence feature matrix extracted from the posts in c_i, where x_0^i represents the sentence feature vector of c_0^i and x_j^i represents the sentence feature vector of c_j^i.

Then we extract source tweets in the rumor detection dataset $S = \{c_0^1, c_0^2, ..., c_0^n\}$. Define a textual document graph $g_i' = (Node_i, Edge_i)$ for source tweet c_0^i, where $Node_i = \{node_1^i, node_2^i, ..., node_p^i\}$ and each $node_j^i$ is a word in the text of source tweet c_0^i. $Edge_i = \{edge_1^i, edge_2^i, ..., edge_{p-1}^i\}$ represents the co-occurrence between words which describes the relationship of words that appear in the same sliding window. Denote $a_i \in \{0, 1\}^{p_i \times p_i}$ as the adjacency matrix where

$$A'_i = \begin{cases} 1 \, , \; if \; edge^i_j \in Edge_i \\ 0 \, , \; otherwise. \end{cases} \tag{2}$$

Denote $F_i = [f^i_1, \; f^i_2, ..., \; f^i_p]$ as the word feature matrix extracted from the words in c^i_0, where f^i_j represents a word feature vector of word $node^i_j$.

In addition, each event c_i is related to a label $y_i \in \{F, \; T\}$ (i.e., False Rumor or True Rumor). Given the dataset, we describe this task as a supervised classification problem that learns a classifier $f : C \rightarrow Y$ to predict the label of an event based on textual content and propagation structure, where C is the event sets and Y is the set of labels.

The rumor detection model consists of three modules, i.e., the text-level feature generation module, the graph neural network module, and the pooling module, as shown in Fig. 1. Specifically, the text-level feature generation module captures textual content features from both source tweets and retweet posts. GCN is used to obtain updated representations of text contents with event propagation structure. The graph neural network module uses Gated GNN to update word-text aggregated representations. We design the pooling module to aggregate node vectors and get the final representation vector of the entire graph.

3.2 Text-Level Feature Generation Module

Adding propagation structure and retweet features, the source tweet feature is enhanced. Based on the retweet relationships, we construct an event graph $G_i = (N_i, \; E_i)$ for event c_i. Then let $A_i \in \mathbb{R}^{m_i \times m_i}$ be its corresponding adjacency matrix of c_i. A_i contains the edges from responded tweets to the retweet posts.

After constructing the event graph G_i, we consider 3-layer GCN to generate text updated representation of event c_i based on A_i and X_i. The propagation function defined in the first-order approximation of ChebNet (1stChebNet) which is applied in GCN is as follows:

$$H^{(l+1)} = F(A, H^{(l)}; \tilde{D}, W^{(l)}) = \sigma(\tilde{D}^{-\frac{1}{2}} \tilde{A} \tilde{D}^{-\frac{1}{2}} H^{(l)} W^{(l)}), \tag{3}$$

where $\tilde{A} = A + I_N$ is the adjacency matrix with added self-connections, $\tilde{D}_{ii} = \sum_j \tilde{A}_{ij}$ and $W^{(l)}$ represents the layer-specific trainable weight matrix. $\sigma(\cdot)$ denotes an activation function, for instance, the $ReLU(\cdot) = max(0, \cdot)$. And the normalized symmetric adjacency matrix $\hat{A} = \tilde{D}^{-\frac{1}{2}} \tilde{A} \tilde{D}^{-\frac{1}{2}}$.

Then we feed the event graph G_i into GCN. The forward propagation function is as follows:

$$Z = f(X, A) = softmax(\hat{A} ReLU(\hat{A} ReLU(\hat{A} X W^{(0)}) W^{(1)}) W^{(2)}). \tag{4}$$

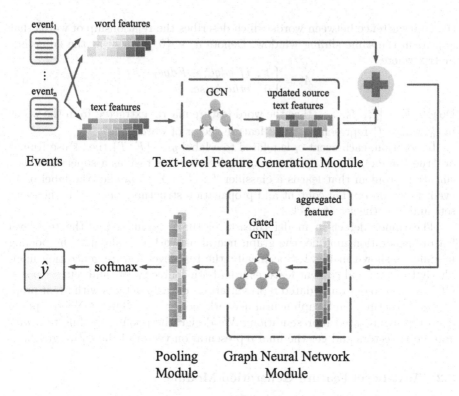

Fig. 1. Our Du-FAGNN rumor detection model

Here, $W^{(0)} \in \mathbb{R}^{C \times H}$ is an input-to-hidden weight matrix for the first hidden layer with H feature maps. $W^{(1)}$ is a hidden weight matrix, while $W^{(2)}$ is a hidden-to-output weight matrix.

We treat the 3-layer GCN model as a pre-trained model that saves parameters after stopping training. Then we use the saved parameters and a modified 3-layer GCN model to generate the source tweet updated representation of event c_i. Dropout is applied to avoid over-fitting.

3.3 Graph Neural Network Module

We consider aggregating word features with updated text features produced in the text-level feature generation module. Base on the textual document graph $g_i' = (Node_i, Edge_i)$ of event c_i, GRU is applied on graph g_i' to learn the embeddings of word nodes. The nodes receive information from their neighbors, then selectively decide which to save and which to get rid of, and finally, merge the stayed information with their own representations to update. The formulas of the operations are:

$$a^t = Ah^{t-1}W_a, \qquad (5)$$

$$z^t = \sigma(W_z a^t + U_z h^{t-1} + b_z), \qquad (6)$$

$$r^t = \sigma(W_z a^t + U_z h^{t-1} + b_z), \tag{7}$$

$$\tilde{h}^t = tanh(W_h a^t + U_h(r^t \odot h^{t-1} + b_h)), \tag{8}$$

$$h^t = \tilde{h} \odot z^t + h^{t-1} \odot (1 - z^t), \tag{9}$$

where $A \in \mathbb{R}^{|\mathcal{V}| \times |\mathcal{V}|}$ is the adjacency matrix, σ is the sigmoid function, z^t is the update gate while r^t is the reset gate. W, U and b are trainable parameters.

By using GRU, we get the updated word features. Then further update the representations. The equation is as follows:

$$h_v = \sigma(f_1(h_v^t)) \odot tanh(f_2(h_v^t)), \tag{10}$$

where h_v^t is the node representation that GRU generates. f_1 and f_2 are multilayer perceptrons (MLP) where the former is an attention weight and the latter is a non-linear feature transformation.

3.4 Pooling Module

Considering that each word plays a certain role in the text, we average the word features. In addition, the role of keywords should be more explicit, we employ the maximum pooling, as shown in (11):

$$h_G = \frac{1}{|\mathcal{V}|} \sum_{v \in \mathcal{V}} h_v + max(h_1, \ldots, h_v). \tag{11}$$

The maximum pooling is selecting the largest value of all nodes in the same dimension as the final output of each dimension. Here, h_G is the graph representation, $\mathcal{V}$ is the node set of a graph and h_j is the ultimate updated word representation of each node.

Then the predicted label of event c_i is calculated by using a softmax layer after obtaining the graph-level vector h_G:

$$\hat{y}_G = softmax(W h_G + b), \tag{12}$$

where W and b are weights and bias, and $\hat{y}_G \in \mathbb{R}^{1 \times C}$ is a probability vector for all the classes used to predict the label of event c_i, C is the number of categories.

4 Experiments and Analysis

4.1 Dataset

We choose the dataset in Weibo [15] to assess our proposed method. It includes two categories of labels: False Rumor (F) and True Rumor (T). In the dataset, nodes in the event propagation graph refer to tweet posts while nodes in the source tweet text graph refer to words in text content. Besides, edges in the event graph represent the forwarding relationship, and edges in the source text graph represent the co-occurrence relationship. The statistics of the dataset are shown in Table 1.

Table 1. Statistics of the dataset

Statistic	Weibo
# of events	4664
# of Rumors	2351
# of Non-rumors	2313
# of Posts	3,805,656
# of Users	2,746,818

4.2 Experiment Settings

The pre-trained BERT [4] model with 12 layers and 256 dimensions is utilized to extract vectors. In the text-level feature generation module, we use it to extract text features for the source tweets and the first 15 retweets of each event. In the graph neural network module, it is applied to extract word vectors in every source tweet. The output of the penultimate layer in BERT is taken as the text and word representations.

In the text-level feature generation module, we use the 3-layer GCN whose dimensions of input and hidden feature vectors are 16 and 128 respectively, and the dimension of output vectors is 32. In the graph neural network module, we concatenate 256-dimension word feature vectors with 32-dimension text representations. 2-layer GGNN is employed to update the word-text aggregated representations to help detect rumors. It has a hidden feature dimension of 96, and it uses stochastic gradient descent to update parameters. Moreover, the Adam algorithm is applied to optimize the model. The dropout rate is 0.5. The graph pooling module uses a maximum pooling algorithm and an average operation.

4.3 Baselines

We compare the proposed model with the following baselines, including:

- SVM-RBF [25]: a rumor detecting method using manual features and SVM classifier with RBF kernel function. The handworked features are extracted from Sina Weibo.
- RvNN [18]: a rumor detecting approach based on tree-structured recursive neural networks. It learns tweet representations via event propagation.
- TextING [26]: a text classification model with GRU, MLP, and graph structure. In the graph, nodes represent words and edges represent word co-occurrence relations.
- TextGCN [9]: a GCN model applied in text classification field. They use word co-occurrence and document word relations to build a text graph. They utilize the one-hot vector as the word features and apply TF-IDF as the edge weight in the text graph.
- PPC_RNN+CNN [12]: an early detection approach of fake news through classifying propagation paths. They construct the paths as multivariate time series and build a time series classifier incorporating RNN and CNN.

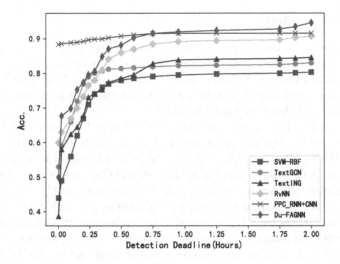

Fig. 2. Comparison of different methods on Weibo dataset

To evaluate the classification model, we generate a confusion matrix between the prediction results and the real label, and we calculate the indicators based on the values in the matrix. We use the four indicators to evaluate the model: Accuracy, Precision, Recall, and F1-score. Accuracy indicates the proportion of correctly classified results in the total results. Precision represents the share of the correctly predicted results among all results predicted to be positive. Recall indicates the proportion of correctly predicted results in all real-positive results. And F1-score represents the comprehensive results of Precision and Recall. It ranges from 0 to 1, 0 means the worst performance while 1 means the best.

Table 2. Results on Weibo dataset (F:False Rumor,T:True Rumor)

Method	Class	Accuracy	Precision	Recall	F1
SVM-RBF*	F	0.818	0.822	0.812	0.817
	T		0.815	0.824	0.819
TextGCN	F	0.837	0.809	0.840	0.824
	T		0.862	0.835	0.848
TextING	F	0.842	0.851	0.844	0.848
	T		0.832	0.839	0.836
RvNN*	F	0.908	0.912	0.897	0.905
	T		0.904	0.918	0.911
PPC_RNN+CNN*	F	0.916	0.884	0.957	0.919
	T		0.955	0.876	0.913
Du-FAGNN	F	**0.957**	**0.949**	**0.983**	**0.966**
	T		**0.970**	**0.917**	**0.943**

4.4 Result Analysis

As shown in Fig. 2, our proposed model yields better than the baseline methods. It is observed that deep learning approaches perform better than those using manually extracted features. The detection speed of Du-FAGNN increases rapidly in the beginning. It can be inferred that the high-level aggregated representations are helpful for model learning.

Results of baseline models and the proposed model are shown in Table 2. In terms of Accuracy, the proposed model improves TextGCN, TextING, RvNN, and PPC_RNN+CNN by 10.9%, 10.4%, 3.8% and 3% respectively on the Weibo dataset. This is because we employ both GCN and GNN structures. We find that the combination of a complex text classification approach and large vectorization models may not be helpful for accuracy. In addition, we find that models with propagation features have higher scores in the evaluation. It is vital of employing different types of features to enhance text vectors for helping to classify the event.

Figure 3(a) shows that our proposed model outperforms the TextING and TextGCN by 5.8% and 6.3% respectively in the case of using only word features. Figure 3(b) shows that the Du-FAGNN model performs better than TextING in the circumstance of using both source-retweet text-granularity features and word-granularity features. The input of TextING is original word-text features without GCN-updating, while the input of Du-FAGNN is the updated word-text features. It can be inferred that word-text aggregated features with propagation structures are conducive for constructing models.

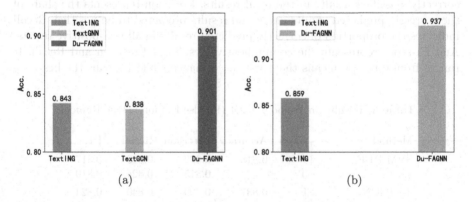

Fig. 3. The comparison of our model and TextING,TextGCN

5   Conclusions

In this paper, we propose an improved GNN-based model named Du-FAGNN for rumor detection on social media. We utilize GCN to generate source text-granularity features by constructing events as graphs. The event graphs help to update source text features by retweet post features. We aggregate text-level features with word-granularity features to make new fused features, they are word representations in events. Besides, we adopt GNN to update and generate the ultimate representations of events and predict. The experimental results on the Sina Weibo dataset demonstrate that the GNN-based method outperforms baselines in terms of both efficiency and accuracy. In particular, the Du-FAGNN model achieves performance by considering both word features and source-retweet features with propagation structure.

Acknowledgment. This work was supported in part by the National Natural Science Foundation of China (Grant No. U1703261). The corresponding author is Kai Ma.

References

1. Benamira, A., Devillers, B., Lesot, E., Ray, A.K., Saadi, M., Malliaros, F.D.: Semi-supervised learning and graph neural networks for fake news detection. In: ASONAM '19: International Conference on Advances in Social Networks Analysis and Mining (2019)
2. Bian, T., et al.: Rumor detection on social media with bi-directional graph convolutional networks. In: Proceedings of the AAAI Conference on Artificial Intelligence, vol. 34, pp. 549–556 (2020)
3. Castillo, C., Mendoza, M., Poblete, B.: Information credibility on twitter. In: Proceedings of the 20th International Conference on World Wide Web, pp. 675–684 (2011)
4. Devlin, J., Chang, M.W., Lee, K., Toutanova, K.: Bert: Pre-training of deep bidirectional transformers for language understanding. arXiv preprint arXiv:1810.04805 (2018)
5. Dong, M., Zheng, B., Quoc Viet Hung, N., Su, H., Li, G.: Multiple rumor source detection with graph convolutional networks. In: Proceedings of the 28th ACM International Conference on Information and Knowledge Management, pp. 569–578 (2019)
6. Gao, J., Han, S., Song, X., Ciravegna, F.: Rp-dnn: A tweet level propagation context based deep neural networks for early rumor detection in social media. arXiv preprint arXiv:2002.12683 (2020)
7. Han, Y., Karunasekera, S., Leckie, C.: Graph neural networks with continual learning for fake news detection from social media. arXiv preprint arXiv:2007.03316 (2020)
8. Ke, Z., Li, Z., Zhou, C., Sheng, J., Silamu, W., Guo, Q.: Rumor detection on social media via fused semantic information and a propagation heterogeneous graph. Symmetry **12**(11), 1806 (2020)
9. Kipf, T.N., Welling, M.: Semi-supervised classification with graph convolutional networks. arXiv preprint arXiv:1609.02907 (2016)
10. Kumar, S., Carley, K.M.: Tree lstms with convolution units to predict stance and rumor veracity in social media conversations. In: Proceedings of the 57th Annual Meeting of the Association for Computational Linguistics, pp. 5047–5058 (2019)
11. Liu, X., Nourbakhsh, A., Li, Q., Fang, R., Shah, S.: Real-time rumor debunking on twitter. In: Proceedings of the 24th ACM International on Conference on Information and Knowledge Management, pp. 1867–1870 (2015)
12. Liu, Y., Wu, Y.F.: Early detection of fake news on social media through propagation path classification with recurrent and convolutional networks. In: Proceedings of the AAAI Conference on Artificial Intelligence, vol. 32 (2018)

13. Lu, Y.J., Li, C.T.: Gcan: Graph-aware co-attention networks for explainable fake news detection on social media. arXiv preprint arXiv:2004.11648 (2020)
14. Lukasik, M., Cohn, T., Bontcheva, K.: Classifying tweet level judgements of rumours in social media. In: Conference on Empirical Methods in Natural Language Processing (2015)
15. Ma, J., et al.: Detecting rumors from microblogs with recurrent neural networks (2016)
16. Ma, J., Gao, W., Wei, Z., Lu, Y., Wong, K.F.: Detect rumors using time series of social context information on microblogging websites. In: Proceedings of the 24th ACM International on Conference on Information and Knowledge Management, pp. 1751–1754 (2015)
17. Ma, J., Gao, W., Wong, K.F.: Detect rumors in microblog posts using propagation structure via kernel learning. Association for Computational Linguistics (2017)
18. Ma, J., Gao, W., Wong, K.F.: Rumor detection on twitter with tree-structured recursive neural networks. Association for Computational Linguistics (2018)
19. Ruchansky, N., Seo, S., Liu, Y.: Csi: a hybrid deep model for fake news detection. In: Proceedings of the 2017 ACM on Conference on Information and Knowledge Management, pp. 797–806 (2017)
20. Sejeong, K., Meeyoung, C., Kyomin, J.: Rumor detection over varying time windows. Plos One 12(1), e0168344 (2017)
21. Shu, K., Wang, S., Liu, H.: Beyond news contents: the role of social context for fake news detection. In: Proceedings of the Twelfth ACM International Conference on Web Search and Data Mining, pp. 312–320 (2019)
22. Wu, K., Yang, S., Zhu, K.Q.: False rumors detection on sina weibo by propagation structures. In: 2015 IEEE 31st International Conference on Data Engineering, pp. 651–662 (2015). https://doi.org/10.1109/ICDE.2015.7113322
23. Wu, L., Liu, H.: Tracing fake-news footprints: characterizing social media messages by how they propagate. In: Proceedings of the Eleventh ACM International Conference on Web Search and Data Mining, pp. 637–645 (2018)
24. Wu, Z., Pi, D., Chen, J., Xie, M., Cao, J.: Rumor detection based on propagation graph neural network with attention mechanism. Expert Syst. Appl. 158, 113595 (2020)
25. Yang, F., Liu, Y., Yu, X., Yang, M.: Automatic detection of rumor on sina weibo. In: Proceedings of the ACM SIGKDD Workshop on Mining Data Semantics, pp. 1–7 (2012)
26. Zhang, Y., Yu, X., Cui, Z., Wu, S., Wen, Z., Wang, L.: Every document owns its structure: inductive text classification via graph neural networks. arXiv preprint arXiv:2004.13826 (2020)
27. Zhao, Z., Resnick, P., Mei, Q.: Enquiring minds: early detection of rumors in social media from enquiry posts. In: Proceedings of the 24th International Conference on World Wide Web, pp. 1395–1405 (2015)

Short Text Clustering Using Joint Optimization of Feature Representations and Cluster Assignments

Liping Sun[1,2], Tingli Du[1,2], Xiaoyu Duan[1,2], and Yonglong Luo[1,2(✉)]

[1] School of Computer and Information, Anhui Normal University, Wuhu 241002, Anhui, China
ylluo@ustc.edu.cn
[2] Anhui Provincial Key Laboratory of Network and Information Security, Anhui Normal University, Wuhu 241002, Anhui, China

Abstract. The application of traditional text clustering methods to short text data is inefficient owing to the high dimensionality and semantic sparseness of such data. Contrastingly, convolutional neural networks can capture the local information between consecutive words in a sentence and extract the semantic features of the text. In this paper, we propose a short text clustering method based on convolutional autoencoders (CAE-STC) that jointly optimizes feature representations and cluster assignments. The proposed method employs a convolutional autoencoder to learn deep text feature representations and preserve the local structure of text generation distribution. By integrating the clustering loss and convolutional autoencoder's reconstruction loss, a unified loss function is formulated to update the network parameters and cluster centers iteratively, improving the performance of the feature learning and clustering tasks. The results of extensive experiments conducted on three public short text datasets demonstrate that the proposed method outperforms several popular clustering methods in terms of the normalized mutual information and clustering accuracy.

Keywords: Short text clustering · Unsupervised learning · Convolutional autoencoder · Feature learning

1 Introduction

With the rapid development of the internet and popularization of social platforms, short text data such as microblogs, online news, and product reviews progressively accumulate every day. Therefore, the extraction of valuable information from these data is of great significance. Short text clustering aims to identify the internal connections between short texts through cluster analysis, which can effectively reduce information redundancy and improve information diversity [1]. In addition, because short text data are rich in emotional vocabulary and user information, short text clustering is widely used in sentiment analysis [2], topic detection [3] and personalized recommendations [4].

In contrast to long texts, the high dimensionality and semantic sparseness of short texts make the application of traditional text clustering methods unsatisfactory [5]. To

© Springer Nature Switzerland AG 2021
D. N. Pham et al. (Eds.): PRICAI 2021, LNAI 13032, pp. 217–231, 2021.
https://doi.org/10.1007/978-3-030-89363-7_17

solve this problem, some researchers have proposed enriching the semantics of words by extending the external information of the short texts. The resulting expanded text feature space can improve the accuracy of the similarity measurement between the short texts, but the selection of an external information database has a degree of subjectivity on the clustering results [6]. Other researchers have solved the problem of text sparseness by mining the information of the short text itself. Specifically, by extracting the features of short text, and then clustering the frequent itemsets in the text. In recent years, owing to the high efficiency of deep learning, numerous researchers have proposed methods that involve combining deep learning and clustering, in which the inherent highly nonlinear transformation characteristics of deep neural networks are used to transform data into a clustering-friendly representation. This approach is widely used in the field of image recognition, and research has also been carried out in the field of natural language processing [7]. Further, with the proposal of the 2013 word vector [8], deep neural networks have exhibited their superiority in constructing text representations, and they have also been applied in text clustering: first, deep neural networks are pre-trained in an unsupervised manner; then, traditional methods are employed to cluster the samples. However, this method is limited because the features learned by neural networks are not modified further during the clustering process, which may cause the learned features to be unreliable during clustering. The effectiveness of feature extraction can directly affect the accuracy of the clustering results; conversely, the quality of the clustering results can provide supervision signals for feature learning.

Among numerous network models, convolutional neural network (CNN) and recurrent neural network are widely used in text processing-related research and rely mainly on automatic machine learning without manual intervention [9, 10]. Compared with recurrent neural network, CNN can not only extract the local information between consecutive words in a sentence but its parameter sharing mechanism also reduces training complexity. In this paper, combined with the Glove word vector model, we propose a short text clustering method based on convolutional autoencoders (CAE-STC) that jointly optimizes feature representations and cluster assignments. Specifically, we first pre-train a convolutional autoencoder (CAE) to obtain network initialization parameters and text latent features. Thereafter, the Kullback-Leibler (KL) divergence of the soft cluster assignment and its auxiliary target distribution are used as the clustering loss function. The clustering loss function is embedded into the CAE to promote the clustering task and guide the feature learning process. Subsequently, the network parameters and cluster centers are iteratively updated by minimizing the loss function. In this manner, cluster-friendly text features and improved clustering results are simultaneously obtained.

Our main contributions can be summarized as follows:

- We construct a CAE for text feature learning and use a CNN to extract local features of the text to eliminate the high dimensionality and high sparseness limitations of short text data.
- We embed the CAE and clustering tasks into a unified learning framework for training to achieve the joint optimization of text feature representations and cluster assignments.

- We conduct numerous experiments on Chinese and English short text datasets. The experimental results reveal that the proposed method achieves a better clustering performance than other models.

2 Related Work

In this section, we review the related work from the following two perspectives: short text clustering and deep neural networks.

2.1 Short Text Clustering

To overcome the dimensionality catastrophe caused by feature sparsity in short text representations, numerous popular approaches have been applied to investigate the semantic extension of short text by introducing external information and mining the information from the short text itself. For the former, Hu et al. [11] combined multiple semantic knowledge bases such as Wikipedia and WordNet to expand the features of short texts and solved the data sparse problem of original short texts. Bouras and Tsogkas [12] exploited the knowledge of WordNet to enhance a K-means algorithm. Chen et al. [13] proposed an improved feature selection method based on HowNet, which redefines the vector space model at the semantic level and uses a new feature generation strategy that incorporates the features of generalized synonyms. Mizzaro et al. [14] employed Wikipedia to enrich the original text with a set of new words. Wei et al. [6] attempted to eliminate word ambiguity by using to WordNet-improved semantic similarity method. Yang et al. [15] modeled the semantics of short texts with the help of a Probase knowledge base and corpus to solve the problem of one word having multiple meanings. However, relying on external knowledge bases causes the clustering results to be subjective, and the quality of the external knowledge base itself has a significant influence on the clustering.

For the latter, Beil et al. [16] employed a topic model to mine sentences topics, and then obtained frequent itemsets of topics and clustered the text. Peng et al. [17] proposed a short text clustering and topic extraction framework based on frequent itemsets, which employs similarity to filter non-important frequent itemsets; thereafter, combines the filtered results with the topic model and spectral clustering algorithm. Finally, it divides the short text into corresponding topic clusters. Cekik and Uysal [18] proved that the use of rough set theory to divide the region according to the value set of the term could more accurately identify documents belonging to a certain category. Although the above-mentioned clustering algorithms can alleviate the sparseness of short text representation, they ignore the sequence of words in the text and cannot capture deep semantic information.

2.2 Deep Neural Networks

Deep learning models have achieved promising results in the field of natural language processing concomitant with the advent of word embeddings. Clustering performance is highly dependent on the data representation quality; word embeddings can represent text as low-dimensional, dense, and continuous vectors that can effectively extract the semantic features of each word. Mikolov et al. [8] introduced the Skip-gram and continuous bag-of-words models, which can map words with similar semantics to similar positions in the vector space. Pennington et al. [19] proposed a new word vector model, named Glove, which considers both corpus local information and overall information. Recently, numerous approaches have combined neural networks with word embeddings to capture truly meaningful syntactic and semantic rules. For example, Xu et al. [20] combined the word2vec word vector model and proposed a CNN-based short text clustering algorithm (STC^2). This algorithm uses a self-learning framework to embed original keyword features into the compressed binary code with local preserving constraints, matches it with deep feature representations using the CNN, and finally, performs K-means clustering on the learned features. Xu et al. [21] attempted to use unsupervised dimensionality reduction methods to replace text hashing to learn unbiased deep text representation on the basis of the above. However, the above-mentioned methods regard feature extraction and clustering as two independent processes and do not consider the clustering results in the provision of supervision signals for feature extraction.

Xie et al. [22] developed a deep embedding clustering (DEC) framework that simultaneously learns feature representations and cluster assignments. The method learns a mapping from the data space to a low-dimensional feature space by using a deep neural network in which the clustering objective is iteratively optimized. Guo et al. [23] employed a CAE structure to learn image features, and preserved the local structure of data generating distribution by integrating the reconstruction and clustering losses. Li et al. [24] proposed a unified clustering framework based on full CAE and soft K-means scoring for image representations and cluster centers joint learning. The effectiveness of the above-mentioned CNN-based deep clustering models has been verified in the field of image recognition, but there are relatively few studies on short text clustering.

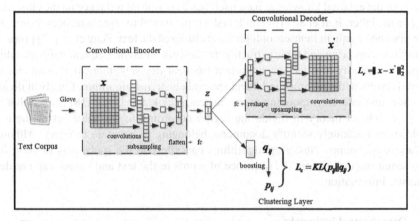

Fig. 1. Architecture of the proposed short text joint optimization clustering model

3 Short Text Clustering Using Joint Optimization of Feature Representations and Cluster Assignments

Figure 1 shows the overall architecture of the proposed CAE-STC model. It combines clustering tasks and deep feature learning in a unified network model for training. Specifically, the model is composed of a convolutional encoder for text feature learning, a convolutional decoder for data reconstruction, and a clustering layer that clusters the features between the encoder and decoder.

3.1 Convolutional Neural Networks (CNN)

For image data, the size of the convolution kernel can theoretically be any value that does not exceed the input size, whereas for text data, it is unreasonable to splice or truncate text or words at will. Figure 2 shows the model architecture, which is a slight variant of the traditional CNN architecture [25]. To ensure minimum granularity of words under natural language processing, the convolution kernel should be at least a complete word vector, and it can only slide along the longitudinal direction of the word vector matrix. Given a dataset of n texts denoted as $X = \{x_1, x_2, \ldots, x_n\}$, let $x_i \in R^{t*d}$, representing a matrix stacked by word vectors, be the input of the network, where t denotes the maximum length of the text. Further, set the number of words in all sentences to t (padded where necessary), and represent each word by a d-dimensional word vector. A convolution operation involves a filter $w_j \in R^{h*d}$ that is applied to a window of h words to produce a new feature. This filter is applied to each possible window of words in the sentence to produce a one-dimensional feature map $c_j \in R^{t-h+1}$. Multiple filters are used to obtain multiple feature maps $c = [c_1, c_2, \ldots, c_a]$, where a denotes the number of filters. Thereafter, we apply the max-over-time pooling operation on each feature map $\hat{c}_j = max\{c_j\}$ and assume that the maximum value captures the most important feature. Subsequently, we pass the result to the fully connected layer. The output of the fully connected layer represents the extracted text feature.

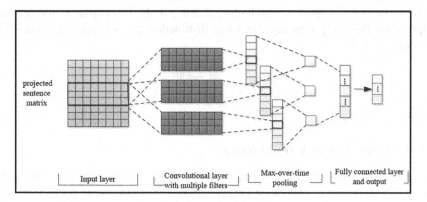

Fig. 2. The convolutional neural network architecture for text

We construct a text-oriented CAE based on the above CNN, which aims to copy the input to its output neural network. First, the input high-dimensional data are transformed into low-dimensional features by employing a convolutional encoder $z = f_w(x)$; thereafter, the original input data are reconstructed by employing a convolutional decoder with a similar structure to the convolutional encoder $\hat{x} = g_{w'}(z)$. The network model is trained by minimizing the mean square error loss function between the input and reconstructed data. The output of the hidden layer z represents text latent features.

$$L_r = \frac{1}{n} \sum_{i=1}^{n} \|x_i - \hat{x}_i\|_2^2 \tag{1}$$

3.2 Clustering Loss

We followed DEC [22] to adapt the soft assignment based on Student's t-distribution to measure the easiness of a sample. Cluster assignment hardening is a commonly used cluster loss function that is composed of the KL divergence between the soft assignment Q and its auxiliary target distribution P. This cluster assignment hardening loss forces the soft assignment to have a stricter probability distribution by promoting the cluster assignment probability distribution Q close to the target distribution P.

$$L_c = KL(P\|Q) = \sum_i \sum_j p_{ij} log \frac{p_{ij}}{q_{ij}} \tag{2}$$

where q_{ij} employs the Student's t-distribution as the kernel to measure the similarity between the embedded point z_i and cluster center u_j.

$$q_{ij} = \frac{\left(1 + \|z_i - u_j\|^2\right)^{-1}}{\sum_{j'} \left(1 + \|z_i - u_{j'}\|^2\right)^{-1}} \tag{3}$$

By squaring the soft cluster assignment and subsequently normalizing them, we aim to learn the cluster assignments with high confidence in the soft cluster assignment and improve the clustering accuracy. The target distribution, p_{ij}, is expressed in Eq. (2) as follows:

$$p_{ij} = \frac{q_{ij}^2 / \sum_i q_{ij}}{\sum_{j'} \left(q_{ij'}^2 / \sum_i q_{ij'}\right)} \tag{4}$$

3.3 CAE-Based Short Text Clustering

Our proposed CAE-STC model consists of two stages: pre-training and fine-tuning. The whole algorithm is summarized in Algorithm 1. The purpose of pre-training is to obtain the initialization parameters for the network. The CAE is pre-trained end-to-end through the reconstruction loss function between the input and reconstructed data. The last layer of the convolutional encoder generates text embedded features and performs

K-means clustering on the pre-trained features to obtain the initial cluster centers. In the fine-tuning stage, the network architecture is composed of CAE and a clustering layer. The network parameters and cluster centers are iteratively updated by minimizing the loss function to extract text features suitable for clustering and learn cluster assignments with high confidence. Equation (5) shows that to minimize damage to the feature space caused only by clustering loss, we set the weighted sum of the CAE's reconstruction loss and the clustering loss as the loss function of the entire network. The CAE is used to learn the embedded features and preserve the local structure of the original text data. The clustering loss guides the embedded features to be prone to forming clusters.

$$L = \alpha L_c + (1 - \alpha)L_r \tag{5}$$

where L_c and L_r are the clustering and reconstruction losses, respectively, and α is the weight parameter of the two loss functions.

Algorithm 1: CAE-Based Short Text Clustering (CAE-STC)

Input: text $:X = \{x_1, x_2, \dots, x_n\}$, $x_i \in R^{t \times d}$; Number of clusters:K; Maximum iterations:T; Stopping threshold:δ

Output: Cluster centers μ, labels y

//**Stage I**:   Train a CAE and clustering with its features
1.   Initialize W and W' via Eq. (1)
2.   Extract features : $Z \leftarrow f_w(X)$
3.   Clustering with the features: $u_z \leftarrow$ K-means (Z)

//**Stage II**: Jointly learn the CAE and cluster centers
4.   **for** $t \leftarrow 1$ to T **do**
5.   Compute all embedded points $\{z_i = f_w(x_i)\}_{i=1}^n$
6.   Compute the soft cluster assignment via Eq. (3)
7.   Update the target distribution via Eq. (4)
8.   Save the last label assignment: $y_{old} \leftarrow y$
9.   Compute the new label assignment y via Eq. (8)
10.   **if** $sum(y_{old} \neq y)/n < \delta$ **then**
11.   stop training
12.   **end if**
13.   Choose a batch of samples $S \in X$
14.   Update μ, W and W' via Eq. (5), Eq. (6) and Eq. (7)
15.   **end for**

Update CAE's Weights and Cluster Centers: Calculate the gradient of clustering loss L_c with respect to the text feature z_i and cluster center u_j by fixing the auxiliary target distribution according to Eqs. (6) and (7). Thereafter, the Adam algorithm is combined with the backpropagation algorithm to directly optimize the network model, and jointly update the cluster centers and the network parameters. The convolutional encoder's weights W is updated by the combined effect of the clustering loss L_c and the reconstruction loss L_r, whereas the convolutional decoder's weights W' is only affected by the reconstruction loss L_r.

$$\frac{\partial L_c}{\partial Z_i} = 2 \sum_{j=1}^{k} \left(1 + \left(\|z_i - u_j\|^2\right)\right)^{-1} \left(p_{ij} - q_{ij}\right)\left(z_i - u_j\right) \tag{6}$$

$$\frac{\partial L_c}{\partial u_j} = 2 \sum_{i=1}^{n} \left(1 + \|z_i - u_j\|^2\right)^{-1} \left(q_{ij} - p_{ij}\right)\left(z_i - u_j\right) \tag{7}$$

Update Target Distribution: The target distribution forces the soft cluster assignment to have a stricter probability distribution. In practice, we update the soft assignment and target distribution using all the embedded points at each iteration. See Eqs. (3) and (4) for our update rules.

After fine-tuning, the final clustering result is that the soft cluster assignment function q_{ij} assigns the text feature z_i to the label of the cluster center u_j with the maximum probability:

$$y_i = \arg\max_j q_{ij} \tag{8}$$

The training process stops if the cluster label assignment change between two consecutive iterations and is less than a threshold of δ.

4 Experiments

4.1 Datasets

We evaluate the proposed method on two English datasets (SearchSnippets and TREC) and one Chinese dataset (Sohu News Headline). Table 1 summarizes the size of the datasets, number of clusters, mean and maximum length of the texts, and vocabulary sizes.

Table 1. Characteristics of the short text datasets.

Datasets	Characteristics			
	Number of clusters	Dataset size	Mean/maximum length of texts	Vocabulary size
SearchSnippets	8	12340	17.88/38	30643
TREC	6	5952	5.93/19	9231
Sohu	10	10000	5.964/14	18713

SearchSnippets[1] is selected from the results of web search transactions using predefined phrases in eight domains, which include Business, Engineering, Culture-Arts-Ent, Politics-Society, Computers, Health, Education-Science and Sports [26].

TREC[2] is a question dataset comprising sentences divided into six question types—specifically, DESC., HUM., ABBR., LOC., ENTY., and NUM.—with a total of 5952 samples.

[1] http://jwebpro.sourceforge.net/data-web-snippets.tar.gz.
[2] https://cogcomp.seas.upenn.edu/Data/QA/QC/.

Sohu[3] consists of text obtained from Sohu News Data from Sogou Lab. The Sohu news data contains real-world news in various aspects such as sports, society and entertainment in 2008. The short text dataset is made up of 10 randomly selected categories, with each category consisting of 1000 news headline compositions.

4.2 Pre-trained Word Vectors

The word vector model represents the text as a low-dimensional, dense, and continuous vector. In our experiment, we use the Glove model to train the word embeddings, and most parameters are set at similar points to those as in [19] to train word vectors, except for using a vector dimensionality of 48, minimum count of five, and window size of five. For the Chinese dataset, we use a large-scale Chinese Wikipedia corpus to train the model to obtain Chinese word vectors. We first use the Jieba tool to segment the sentences; then, we remove the stop words. Subsequently, the words are converted into vectors according to the trained word vectors, and the vectors are used as the input of the network model. For the English dataset, we use a large-scale English Wikipedia corpus to train the model to obtain English word vectors. The English text is directly divided into words using spaces in sentences. The SearchSnippets dataset is processed in advance; thus, there is no need for pre-processing. For the TREC dataset, because it contains numerous words and punctuations that affect semantics, stop words have to be removed.

4.3 Experiment Setting

Comparing Methods. To validate the clustering performance of CAE-STC on the short text datasets, we compare it with the following methods.

- K-means [29] on the original keyword features weighted with term frequency (TF) and term frequency-inverse document frequency (TF-IDF).
- Recursive neural network (RecNN) is proposed in [30]. In the RecNN, a tree structure is first used for greedy approximation with unsupervised recursive autoencoders. Then, semi-supervision is used to capture the semantics of the text based on the predicted structure. To make this recursive method completely unsupervised, we removed the second phase of the cross entropy error to learn the vector, and then averaged all vectors in the tree using K-means.
- DEC [22] first pre-trains the deep autoencoder composed of multilayer perception (MLP), then removes the decoder, employs the encoder to extract text features, and finally optimizes the cluster assignment and feature learning.
- STC^2 [21] represents the text with the word2vec word vector, uses unsupervised dimensionality reduction methods to embed it into a compressed binary code with local preserving constraints, matches it with CNN learning deep feature representations, and performs K-means on the obtained features. In this study, two dimensionality reduction methods, Laplacian Eigenmaps (LE) and Locality Preserving Indexing (LPI), with better clustering performance are selected.

---

[3] https://www.sogou.com/labs/resource/list_pingce.php.

– CAE + K-means uses a CAE to extract text features and thereafter clusters them. Feature learning and clustering are independent of each other.

Hyperparameter Setting. The parameter setting of the clustering method based on deep learning has a significant influence on the learning ability of deep neural networks. For the CNN model, the networks consist of a convolution layer, a max-over-time pooling layer, and a fully connected layer. The number of convolution filters is 256, and the size of the convolution kernels is three, one, and one for SearchSnippets, TREC, and Sohu, respectively. For the CAE-STC model, the networks consist of CAE and a clustering layer. The CAE is pre-trained for 10, 25, and 15 iterations for SearchSnippets, TREC, and Sohu, respectively; the maximum number of iterations in the optimization process is 100, 250, and 250 for SearchSnippets, TREC, and Sohu, respectively. The parameter a, which is used to weigh the clustering loss and reconstruction loss, is 0.9, 0.7, and 0.1 for SearchSnippets, TREC, and Sohu, respectively. The convergence threshold is set to $\delta = 0.1\%$ and the batch size to 200 for all datasets. Our implementation is based on the Keras deep learning framework. To design independent adaptive learning rates for the different parameters, the Adam optimization algorithm is adopted to accelerate the convergence speed of the network.

Evaluation Metric. Clustering performance evaluation is conducted by comparing the labels of the text corpus with the clustering results. Based on the text dataset with a set of labels, two common evaluation criteria are used: accuracy (ACC) [27] and normalized mutual information (NMI) [28].

5   Results and Analysis

Table 2 summarizes the ACC and NMI performances of our proposed method compared with the other methods on the three short text datasets. The experimental results reveal that, with the exception of NMI on the Sohu dataset, the proposed CAE-STC achieves better clustering performance than K-means, STC^2-LE, STC^2-LPI, and CAE + K-means on the three datasets. The reason for the NMI exception of the Sohu dataset may be because that dataset contains a small number of words with a maximum text length of 14. CAE-STC has difficulty capturing rich word order information through CNN using shorter texts, and thus does not yield significant improvement. In contrast, STC^2-LPI uses binary learning objectives constructed by LPI to guide the training of the CNN. The binary code retains the similarity information in the output of LPI, which embeds the text representation with both the word order information and other semantic information. Moreover, we observe that the deep clustering algorithms STC^2-LE, STC^2-LPI, CAE + K-means, and CAE-STC outperform the K-means algorithm based on the vector space model representation by a significant margin on SearchSnippets and Sohu. This is because the traditional vector space model is based on the bag-of-words model at its core, and it ignores the order of the words in the text. When applied to short text data, the traditional vector space model has limitations such as high dimensionality and sparse features, whereas deep neural networks have powerful representation capabilities that can extract text features to obtain low-dimensional and effective text representation.

Table 2. Comparison of clustering performance on the three datasets.

Method	SearchSnippets		TREC		Sohu	
	ACC	NMI	ACC	NMI	ACC	NMI
K-means(TF)	25.44	9.65	52.15	45.99	17.23	12.19
K-means(TF-IDF)	37.84	21.24	60.03	46.68	19.20	13.73
STC^2-LE	75.55	62.80	61.63	41.10	41.52	31.31
STC^2-LPI	75.73	62.91	62.58	44.07	45.75	**32.99**
CAE + K-means	68.03	52.64	57.63	34.85	46.52	29.29
CAE-STC	**82.68**	**66.02**	**63.93**	**48.24**	**47.43**	31.55

To verify that CNN has advantages in text processing, we apply MLP, RecNN, and CNN individually to short text clustering. Figures 3 and 4 show the experimental results. The results demonstrate that CAE-STC, CAE + K-means, and STC^2-LPI are significantly better than DEC and RecNN on SearchSnippets and TREC. This implies that CNN is more suitable for processing short text data than MLP and RecNN, and they can extract local information between text words. In comparison with STC^2-LPI and CAE + K-means, the proposed CAE-STC extracts deep learned representation from the CAE to achieve a large improvement of 6.95%/3.11% and 14.65%/13.38% (ACC/NMI) on SearchSnippets. This is because STC^2-LPI and CAE + K-means first use unsupervised methods to pre-train the neural network, and thereafter perform K-means on the learned features, which results in an inability to further modify the feature representations during the clustering process. Our proposed CAE-STC adopts a framework for the joint optimization of the feature learning and clustering tasks. Feature learning is not only conducive to the improvement of clustering performance but the clustering results can also provide good supervision signals for feature learning.

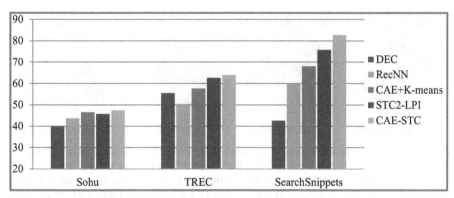

Fig. 3. Comparison of clustering accuracy for DEC, RecNN, CAE + K-means, STC^2-LPI, and CAE-STC on the three datasets, respectively.

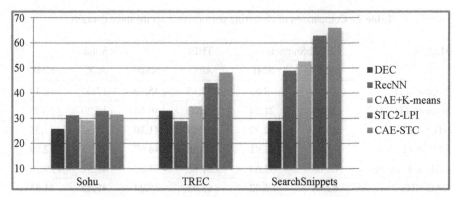

Fig. 4. Comparison of NMI for DEC, RecNN, CAE + K-means, STC^2-LPI, and CAE-STC on the three datasets, respectively.

To explore the representations generated by CAE-STC and the compared methods, we use t-SNE [31] to visualize their short text embedding on SearchSnippets. Figures 5 and 6 respectively show the visualization of the text feature representations on the clustering results and standard labels. We can observe that the clustering results represented by the deep features learned from CAE-STC depict clear boundaries between different clusters, and the samples in the same cluster are highly compact. In addition, the color similarity of the corresponding positions in Figs. 5 (h) and 6 (h) is higher, which illustrates that the clustering performance of the proposed CAE-STC is better.

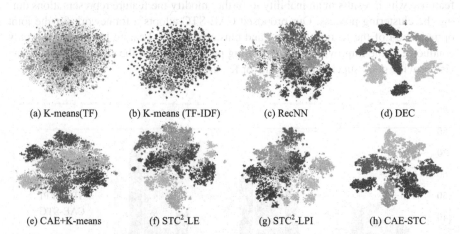

Fig. 5. A 2-dimensional embedding of original keyword features weighted with (a) TF, (b) TF-IDF, (c) average vectors of all tree nodes in RecNN, and deep learned features from (d) DEC, (e) CAE + K-means, (f) STC^2-LE, (g) STC^2-LPI, and (h) CAE-STC. All the above features are respectively used in K-means (TF), K-means (TF-IDF), RecNN, DEC, CAE + K-means, STC^2-LE, STC^2-LPI and our proposed CAE-STC on SearchSnippets. Different colors represent different clusters.

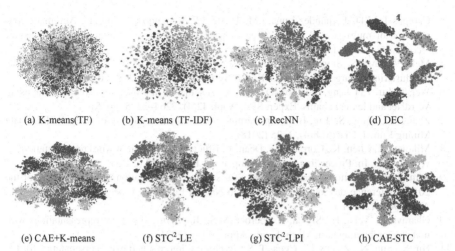

(a) K-means(TF)   (b) K-means (TF-IDF)   (c) RecNN   (d) DEC

(e) CAE+K-means   (f) STC^2-LE   (g) STC^2-LPI   (h) CAE-STC

Fig. 6. A 2-dimensional embedding of original keyword features weighted with (a) TF, (b) TF-IDF, (c) average vectors of all tree nodes in RecNN, and deep learned features from (d) DEC, (e) CAE + K-means, (f) STC^2-LE, (g) STC^2-LPI and (h) CAE-STC. All the above features are respectively used in standard labels on SearchSnippets. Different colors represent different clusters.

6   Conclusion

This paper proposed a method for short text clustering called CAE-STC, which jointly performs clustering and learns representative text features that are suitable for clustering and preserves the local structure of the text in the feature space. CAE-STC extracts text features with the local structure preserved by using a CAE and manipulates the feature space to scatter data by optimizing a KL divergence-based clustering loss. Experimental results reveal that our method achieves better clustering performance than other baseline methods on Chinese and English datasets. Our future work will investigate the incorporation of bidirectional long short-term memory networks into the proposed framework.

Acknowledgments. This research is supported by the Anhui Provincial Natural Science Foundation of China (No. 2108085MF214), the Key Program in the Youth Elite Support Plan in Universities of Anhui Province (No. gxyqZD2020004) and National Natural Science Foundation of China (No. 61972439).

References

1. Jung, H., Lee, B.G.: Research trends in text mining: semantic network and main path analysis of selected journals. Expert Syst. Appl. **162**, 1–12 (2020)
2. Rezaeinia, S.M., Rahmani, R., Ghodsi, A., Veisi, H.: Sentiment analysis based on improved pre-trained word embeddings. Expert Syst. Appl. **117**(1), 139–147 (2019)
3. Chen, J., Gong, Z., Liu, W.: A nonparametric model for online topic discovery with word embeddings. Inf. Sci. **504**, 32–47 (2019)

4. Campos, L.M.D., Fernández-Luna, J.M., Huete, J.F., Redondo-Expósito, L.: Automatic construction of multi-faceted user profiles using text clustering and its application to expert recommendation and filtering problems. Knowl.-Based Syst. **29**, 1–18 (2020)
5. Meht, V., Bawa, S., Singh, J.: Stamantic clustering: combining statistical and semantic features for clustering of large text datasets. Expert Syst. Appl. **174**(15), 1–9 (2021)
6. Wei, T., Lu, Y., Chang, H., Zhou, Q., Bao, X.: A semantic approach for text clustering using WordNet and lexical chains. Expert Syst. Appl. **42**(4), 2264–2275 (2015)
7. Zhang, L., Wang, S., Liu, B.: Deep learning for sentiment analysis: a survey. WIREs Data Mining Knowl. Discov. **8**(4), 1–25 (2018)
8. Mikolov, T., Chen, K., Corrado, G., Dean, J.: Efficient estimation of word representations in vector space. In: Proceedings of Workshop at ICLR, pp. 1–12 (2013)
9. Kim, Y.: Convolutional neural networks for sentence classification. In: Proceedings of the 2014 Conference on Empirical Methods in Natural Language Processing, pp. 1746–1751. ACL, Doha (2014)
10. Gharavi, E., Veisi, H., Silwal, R., Gerber, M.S.: Improving discourse representations with node hierarchy attention. Mach. Learn. Appl. **3**, 1–7 (2021)
11. Hu, X., Sun, N., Zhang, C., Chua, T.-S.: Exploiting internal and external semantics for the clustering of short texts using world knowledge. In: Proceedings of the 18th ACM Conference on Information and Knowledge Management, pp. 919–928. ACM, Hong Kong (2009).
12. Bouras, C., Tsogkas, V.: A clustering technique for news articles using WordNet. Knowl.-Based Syst. **36**, 115–128 (2012)
13. Chen, X., Zhang, Y., Cao, L., Li, D.: An improved feature selection method for chinese short texts clustering based on HowNet. In: Wong, W.E., Zhu, T. (eds.) Computer Engineering and Networking. LNEE, vol. 277, pp. 635–642. Springer, Cham (2014). https://doi.org/10.1007/978-3-319-01766-2_73
14. Mizzaro S., Pavan M., Scagnetto I., Valenti M.: Short text categorization exploiting contextual enrichment and external knowledge. In: Proceedings of the First International Workshop on Social Media Retrieval and Analysis, pp. 57–62. ACL, Gold Coast (2014)
15. Yang, J., Li, Y., Gao, C., Zhang, Y.: Measuring the short text similarity based on semantic and syntactic information. Futur. Gener. Comput. Syst. **114**, 169–180 (2021)
16. Beil, F., Ester, M., Xu, X.: Frequent term-based text clustering. In: Proceedings of the Eighth ACM SIGKDD International Conference on Knowledge Discovery and Data Mining, pp. 436–442. ACM, Edmonton (2002)
17. Peng, M., Huang, J., Zhu, J., Huang, J., Liu, J.: Mass of short texts clustering and topic extraction based on frequent itemsets. J. Comput. Res. Develop. **52**(9), 1941–1953 (2015)
18. Cekik, R., Uysal, A.K.: A novel filter feature selection method using rough set for short text data. Expert Syst. Appl. **160**, 1–15 (2020)
19. Pennington, J., Socher, R., Manning, C.: GloVe: global vectors for word representation. In: Proceedings of the 2014 Conference on Empirical Methods in Natural Language Processing, pp. 1532–1543. ACL, Doha (2014)
20. Xu, J., Wang, P., Tian, G., Xu, B., Zhao, J., Wang, F., Hao, H.: Short text clustering via convolutional neural networks. In: Proceedings of the 1st Workshop on Vector Space Modeling for Natural Language Processing, pp. 62–69. ACL, Denver (2015)
21. Xu, J., et al.: Self-taught convolutional neural networks for short text clustering. Neural Netw. **88**, 22–31 (2017)
22. Xie, J., Girshick, R., Farhadi, A.: Unsupervised deep embedding for clustering analysis. In: Proceedings of the 33rd International Conference on Machine Learning, pp. 1–10. ACM, New York (2016)
23. Guo, X., Liu, X., Zhu, E., Yin, J.: Deep clustering with convolutional autoencoders. In: Liu, D., Xie, S., Li, Y., Zhao, D., El-Alfy, E.-S.M. (eds.) ICONIP 2017, LNCS (LNTCS), vol. 10635, pp. 373–382. Springer, Guangzhou (2017). https://doi.org/10.1007/978-3-319-70096-0_39

24. Li, F., Qiao, H., Zhang, B.: Discriminatively boosted image clustering with fully convolutional auto-encoders. Pattern Recogn. **83**, 161–173 (2018)
25. Collobert, R., Weston, J., Bottou, L., Karlen, M., Kavukcuoglu, K., Kuksa, P.: Natural language processing (almost) from scratch. J. Mach. Learn. Res. **12**, 2493–2537 (2011)
26. Phan, X.-H.., Nguyen, L.-M., Horiguchi, S.: Learning to classify short and sparse text & web with hidden topics from large-scale data collections. In: WWW, pp. 91–100. ACM, Beijing (2008)
27. Zheng, C.T., Liu, C., Sanwong, H.: Corpus-based topic diffusion for short text clustering. Neurocomputing **275**(31), 2444–2458 (2018)
28. Janani, R., Vijayarani, D.S.: Text document clustering using spectral clustering algorithm with particle swarm optimization. Expert Syst. Appl. **134**(15), 192–200 (2019)
29. Wagstaff, K., Cardie, C., Rogers, S., Schroedl, S.: Constrained K-means clustering with background knowledge. In: Proceedings of the Eighteenth International Conference on Machine Learning, pp. 577–584. ACM, San Francisco (2001)
30. Socher, R., Pennington, J., Huang, E.H., Ng, A.Y., Manning, C.D.: Semi-supervised recursive autoencoders for predicting sentiment distributions. In: Proceedings of the 2011 Conference on Empirical Methods in Natural Language Processing, pp. 151–161. ACL, Edinburgh (2011)
31. Maaten, L.V.D., Hinton, G.: Visualizing data using t-SNE. J. Mach. Learn. Res. **9**, 2579–2605 (2008)

Soft-BAC: Soft Bidirectional Alignment Cost for End-to-End Automatic Speech Recognition

Yonghe Wang, Hui Zhang$^{(\boxtimes)}$, Feilong Bao, and Guanglai Gao

College of Computer Science, Inner Mongolia University, Inner Mongolia Key Laboratory of Mongolian Information Processing Technology, Huhhot 010021, China
{cszh,csfeilong,csggl}@imu.edu.cn

Abstract. Connectionist temporal classification (CTC) has gained success in both end-to-end ASR model and as an auxiliary task for attention-based sequence-to-sequence (S2S) system. However, the special topological structure of CTC and the modeling form that a redundant blank symbol to be optionally inserted between each modeling units makes the CTC inclined to model blank symbols, resulting in a worse than expected model alignment effect, and frames are usually aligned with redundant symbols. In this paper, we design a new simple topology and propose a novel smooth alignment optimization method named soft bidirectional alignment cost (soft-BAC), which is an alternative to the CTC. We propose a scheme that only inserts identifiers between consecutive repetitive labels and solve the alignment problem between two time series of speech-transcription pair by minimizing all costs of the left-to-right and right-to-left alignment process. Experiments on the LibriSpeech corpus show that the proposed soft-BAC method achieves significant improvement in word error rate and alignment effect over the CTC-based baseline model.

Keywords: Speech recognition · End-to-end · CTC · Soft bidirectional alignment cost · Multitask learning

1 Introduction

In recent years, end-to-end models have shown promising performance on automatic speech recognition (ASR) tasks. Compared to traditional hybrid systems consisting of separate pronunciation, acoustic and language models, the end-to-end system uses only a single neural network architecture to implicitly model

This research is supported by the National Key Research and Development Program of China (No.2018YFE0122900), China National Natural Science Foundation (No.61773224, No.61866030, No.62066033), Inner Mongolia Natural Science Foundation (No.2018MS06006) and Applied Technology Research and Development Program of Inner Mongolia Autonomous Region (No.2019GG372, No.2020GG0046).

D. N. Pham et al. (Eds.): PRICAI 2021, LNAI 13032, pp. 232–243, 2021.
https://doi.org/10.1007/978-3-030-89363-7_18

all these three to directly transcribe speech to text without requiring predefined alignment between acoustic frame sequences and target labels. For example, the connectionist temporal classification (CTC) [1] and the attention-based sequence-to-sequence (S2S) [2] encoder-decoder architecture are the most commonly used end-to-end ASR models.

Based on the two aforementioned end-to-end methods, various improvements are proposed. For CTC, the original CTC architecture is extended to RNN-transducer [3,4] by combining an independent recursive prediction network trained over the label sequences, which can model the interdependence between the outputs. Also, by integrating with the attention mechanism, CTC shows greater competitiveness [5–7]. For S2S, "listen, attend and spell" (LAS) [8], neural aligner [9], multi-head attention [10,11] and transformer [12–16] were introduced. Recently, hybrid CTC-attention method [17–19] has attracted lots of attention by combining the advantages of the CTC model and the attention model and integrating them together for training. In this architecture, the CTC objective is attached to the attention-based S2S encoder-decoder model as an auxiliary task to guide the attention to perform monotonic alignments. And during decoding, the joint CTC-attention beam search approach has been widely adopted [20].

The advantage of CTC is that it assumes a special topology to monotonically align each label in the target sequence with one or more frame sequences corresponding to the label, which is the right assumption for the ASR task. However, since an additional blank symbol is inserted between each label in the target sequence during the alignment process. The blank symbol is not only used to depict the space label that usually corresponds to the silence between words, but also to segment the continuously repeated label, e.g. double "l" in "hello" should be segmented with the blank symbol to avoid error merging to a single "l". This makes blank symbols assigned with multiple roles. Since the blank symbols have no corresponding fixed acoustic frames, they have more modeling preponderances than other labels, the blank symbol can come from silence frames even any frames. Therefore, CTC inclined to model blank symbols, and produce other labels in very few frames, while most frames correspond to blank symbols, resulting in a worse than expected alignment effect. Recent work [21,22] confirmed that removing the blank symbol is feasible. We believe that the blank symbol is not necessary to insert between each label during the alignment process.

To fix the blank symbol issue, we design a new simple topology and proposed a novel smooth alignment optimization method named soft bidirectional alignment cost (soft-BAC), which is an alternative to the CTC. Specifically, we focus on the left-to-right and right-to-left alignment process of the speech-transcription pair in the end-to-end model, and propose a scheme of inserting an identifier only between consecutive repeated labels and a multitask learning method to train a shared single network by minimizing all the costs of all possible forward and backward alignments. We evaluated and compared our proposal with CTC-based model and CTC loss as an auxiliary task in S2S model, respectively. The experimental results demonstrate that by replacing the CTC with soft-BAC, our proposed method outperforms the CTC baseline and the hybrid CTC-attention architecture both using graphemes or subwords as modeling units.

2   Connectionist Temporal Classification

The CTC-based ASR model directly learns the mapping between acoustic feature sequences $\mathbf{x}$ and transcription sequences $\mathbf{y}$ of different lengths. The key to CTC is that an additional blank symbol is inserted between each label in the target sequence during training. The intention of the blank symbol is not only used to depict the space label that usually corresponds to the silence between words, but also to segment the continuously repeated label. The objective of CTC loss is to maximize the probability distribution over all possible output sequences:

$$P(\mathbf{y}|\mathbf{x}) = \sum_{\pi \in \Phi(\mathbf{y}^*)} P(\pi|\mathbf{x}) = \sum_{\pi \in \Phi(\mathbf{y}^*)} \prod_{t=1}^{T} P(\pi_t|x_t) \tag{1}$$

where $\pi = (\pi_1, ..., \pi_T)$ is a CTC path corresponding to the input sequence $\mathbf{x}$ of length T. $\mathbf{y}^*$ is the label sequence that insert the blank symbol between each subword of $\mathbf{y}$. $\Phi(\mathbf{y}^*)$ is a set of all possible CTC paths. The posterior probabilities $P(\pi_t|x_t)$ are the model outputs for observed labels at each time t.

And minimizing the negative log-probabilities is used in training $L_{CTC} = -\log P(\mathbf{y}|\mathbf{x})$. CTC-based models tend to produce labels in a very few frames, while most frames correspond to blank symbols.

3   Proposed Approach

3.1   Soft Bidirectional Alignment Cost

In end-to-end speech recognition systems, it is assumed that the speech $\mathbf{x}$ with sequence length T is a concatenation of feature vectors generated by transcription $\mathbf{y}$ with sequence length U, which means that there are some correspondences between the speech vector x_i and the subword y_j. Then the score between speech and transcription $S(\mathbf{x}, \mathbf{y})$ is calculated by taking the sum of all corresponding x_i and y_j pairs:

$$S(\mathbf{x}, \mathbf{y}) = \sum_{(i,j) \in A} \delta(x_i, y_j) \tag{2}$$

where $\delta(\cdot)$ is a distance function used to measure the alignment cost. $A \subset \{0,1\}^{T \times U}$ is called alignment, which is a sequence of the corresponding x_i and y_j pairs, denoted with their indexes (i, j). $A_{ij} = 1$ if speech frame x_i is labeled as y_j and $A_{ij} = 0$ otherwise.

There exists a set of possible alignment matrices and is defined as $\mathcal{A}$. The score $S(\mathbf{x}, \mathbf{y})$ is calculated by using the minimum approximation:

$$S(\mathbf{x}, \mathbf{y}) = \min_{A \in \mathcal{A}} \sum_{(i,j) \in A} \delta(x_i, y_j) \tag{3}$$

This problem is a common optimal match with the minimum cost problem. The optimization goal is to consider the cost of all possible alignment matrices to find the best alignment $A^* \in \mathcal{A}$:

$$A^* = \arg\min_{A \in \mathcal{A}} \langle A, S(\mathbf{x}, \mathbf{y}) \rangle, \tag{4}$$

where $\langle A, S(\mathbf{x}, \mathbf{y}) \rangle$ is the inner product between the eligible alignment matrix A and the cost matrix $S(\mathbf{x}, \mathbf{y})$.

Taking these findings into account, in this paper, we propose an alignment optimization method named soft bidirectional alignment cost (soft-BAC) for end-to-end speech recognition system, which is an alternative to the CTC. There are two main points to explain the advantages:

- Our proposed soft-BAC optimization method is much simpler. We abandoned the practice of inserting blank symbols between each label in the model training stage, which is an important characteristic of CTC. Instead, we insert an identifier "#" only between consecutive repeated labels. For example, different label sequences of the same word are expressed as:

$$\left.\begin{array}{l} sta\ g\ \#\ g\ er\ \#\ er \\ sta\ g\ \#\ g\ e\ r\ e\ r \\ sta\ gg\ er\ \#\ er \\ sta\ gg\ e\ r\ e\ r \end{array}\right\} \Rightarrow staggerer \tag{5}$$

- The soft-BAC method can make the model fit faster. Since we use both forward and backward alignment methods to align the input and output of the model based on a frame-by-frame emit/shift strategy without modeling blank symbols, the model will converge quickly.
- The simple topology structure of soft-BAC and redundant blank symbols do not need to be optionally inserted between each modeling unit makes the model strictly implements monotonic alignment of the input speech frames and output labels. The soft-BAC based model can get strict segment alignment labels.

Our soft-BAC optimization method is implemented as a multitask learning (MTL), in which a shared network is trained by using forward and backward alignment cost criteria. The loss function for soft-BAC based MTL architecture is defined as follows:

$$\mathcal{L}_{soft-BAC} = \alpha \mathcal{L}^f_{soft-BAC} + (1 - \alpha) \mathcal{L}^b_{soft-BAC} \tag{6}$$

where $\mathcal{L}^f_{soft-BAC}$ and $\mathcal{L}^b_{soft-BAC}$ are the forward and backward alignment cost loss functions, respectively. The α is a tunable weight smoothing factor, which may be set to be larger than 0.5.

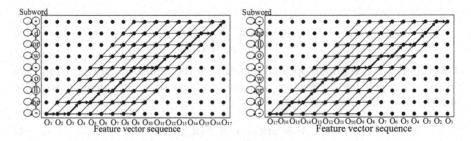

Fig. 1. The alignment procedure in the forward (left) and the backward (right) which represents the subword sequences for the transcription "hello word" over 17 frames. Note that in the alignment approach blank symbols have been discarded, and the subword "-" represent space.

The purpose of alignment is to make each speech frame only be aligned to a single label, so we need to impose rigorous constraints on the eligible warping path to ensure the alignment from $\mathbf{x}$ to $\mathbf{y}$ is strictly one-to-one. Figure 1 shows the alignment procedure in the forward (left) and the backward (right), which is a very simple topology. All paths on the alignment matrices connect the lower-left matrix entry to the upper-right matrix entry using only $\rightarrow \nearrow$ moves. The cost of an alignment is equal to the sum of the distance measurements of entries visited along the path.

At each time step t, the distance measurement value calculated by $\delta(x_i, y_j)$ in Eq. (3) is replaced with the corresponding negative log-probability output by the acoustic model and the probability is calculated by L2 normalization. Therefore, the Eq. (4) is not differentiable. In order to solve this challenge, we propose to use the min function with its soft version to optimize both $\mathcal{L}^f_{soft-BAC}$ and $\mathcal{L}^b_{soft-BAC}$ criteria. Take $\mathcal{L}^f_{soft-BAC}$ for example:

$$\mathcal{L}^f_{soft-BAC}(\mathbf{x}, \mathbf{y}) = \min_\gamma \{\langle A, S(\mathbf{x}, \mathbf{y}) \rangle, A \in \mathcal{A}\}, \tag{7}$$

where the generalized $\min_\gamma \{\}$ operator is formulated as Eq. (8) with a smoothing parameter $0 < \gamma \leq 1$:

$$\min_\gamma \{a_1, ..., a_n\} = -\gamma \log \sum_{i=1}^{n} e^{-a_i/\gamma}. \tag{8}$$

The hyper-parameter γ controls the degree of leakage, and the higher value means mixing more non-minimum values into the output. And $\gamma = 1$ makes the soft-min degenerate to the original min.

During backpropagation, the gradient of Eq. (7) can be derived via the chain rule:

$$\nabla_\mathbf{x} \mathcal{L}^f_{soft-BAC}(\mathbf{x}, \mathbf{y}) = \left(\frac{\partial \Delta(\mathbf{x}, \mathbf{y})}{\partial \mathbf{x}} \right)^T \mathbb{E}_\gamma [A], \tag{9}$$

where $\partial\Delta(\mathbf{x},\mathbf{y})/\partial\mathbf{x}$ is the Jacobian of Δ $w.r.t.$ $\mathbf{x}$. $\mathbb{E}_\gamma[A]$ as shown in Eq. (10), is defined as the average alignment matrix A under the Gibbs distribution $p_\gamma \propto e^{-\langle A, \Delta(\mathbf{x},\mathbf{y})\rangle/\gamma}, \forall A \in \mathcal{A}$.

$$\mathbb{E}_\gamma[A] = \frac{\sum_{A\in\mathcal{A}} e^{-\langle A, \Delta(\mathbf{x},\mathbf{y})\rangle/\gamma} A}{\sum_{A\in\mathcal{A}} e^{-\langle A, \Delta(\mathbf{x},\mathbf{y})\rangle/\gamma}}. \tag{10}$$

3.2 Hybrid Soft-BAC Attention Architecture

In the hybrid CTC-attention based end-to-end ASR architecture, the CTC objective is attached to the attention-based model as an auxiliary task to guide the attention to perform monotonic alignment [17–19]. Our proposed soft bidirectional alignment cost (soft-BAC) is an alternative to CTC. In this paper, we also proposed a hybrid soft-BAC attention architecture. This is implemented as a multitask learning framework, in which the soft-BAC is used as an auxiliary loss to optimize the shared encoder subnetwork. The objective function of MTL is defined as the weighted sum of losses propagated from both soft-BAC and attention model:

$$\mathcal{L}_{MTL} = \lambda\mathcal{L}_{soft-BAC} + (1-\lambda)\mathcal{L}_{Attention} \tag{11}$$

where hyperparameter λ is the weight smoothing factor, and we set to 0.4 in our experiment.

4 Experimental Results

4.1 Datasets

We carry out experiments on the LibriSpeech corpus [23] to verify the performance of the proposed method. The corpus comes with its own train, development and evaluation sets, and are split into "clean" and "other" subsets. Among them, the training set has three subsets with different amounts of transcribed training data: 100 h, 460 h and 960 h. In our experiments, we used 100 h of clean training set and 960 h of mixed data sets for training, respectively. The development data and evaluation data were used to validate our models. For the modeling units, we used graphemes and byte pair encoding (BPE) [24] based subwords, respectively. For the subword sequence of each sentence, the first subword of each word is not marked with a special character. Instead, we use space symbol to separate each word of the sentence.

4.2 Setup

For all experiments, we extracted 80-dimensional log Mel-filterbank plus 3-dimensional pitch from the speech signal based on Kaldi toolkit [25] as the frame-level audio input features. The frame-length is 25 ms with a 10 ms shift. The features were normalized by the mean and the standard deviation on the speaker basis. SpecAugment [26] is applied for data augmentation in the experiment.

Table 1. Comparison of WER using greedy search strategy among CTC-baseline and proposed soft-BAC based Bi-LSTM models with different γ and α values on the LibriSpeech-100 datasets. The modeling units are graphemes and BPE based subwords. None of our experiments used any language model or lexicon information.

No.	Model	LibriSpeech-100			
		Grapheme		BPE-200	
		Test-clean	Test-other	Test-clean	Test-other
1	CTC-baseline	14.8	39.7	15.2	39.5
2	soft-BAC$_{\gamma=1.00,\alpha=1.0}$	14.4	39.8	15.2	38.7
3	soft-BAC$_{\gamma=0.45,\alpha=1.0}$	14.1	36.7	14.2	35.3
4	soft-BAC$_{\gamma=0.55,\alpha=1.0}$	13.5	34.3	13.4	34.6
5	soft-BAC$_{\gamma=0.65,\alpha=1.0}$	13.7	34.5	12.4	33.8
6	soft-BAC$_{\gamma=0.75,\alpha=1.0}$	14.1	35.8	13.5	34.8
7	soft-BAC$_{\gamma=0.55,\alpha=0.5}$	13.6	34.6	12.4	34.2
8	soft-BAC$_{\gamma=0.55,\alpha=0.8}$	13.0	34.0	12.4	33.8
9	soft-BAC$_{\gamma=0.65,\alpha=0.5}$	13.4	34.7	12.1	34.1
10	soft-BAC$_{\gamma=0.65,\alpha=0.8}$	13.4	34.4	12.0	33.2

To verify the effectiveness of our proposed method, two different model structures were used, including Bi-LSTM and LAS. For Bi-LSTM based experiments, we use 5-layer of bi-directional LSTM with 1024 hidden units. For LAS based experiments, we use 2 blocks of VGG [27] layer followed by a 5-layer bi-directional LSTM with 1024 hidden units in the encoder, and 2 unidirectional LSTM layer with 1024 hidden units in the decoder. A location-based attention mechanism with 1024 hidden units was also used in the decoder, where the convolution layer was 10 centered convolution filters. All of the experiments are implemented and performed using the ESPnet [28] end-to-end speech processing toolkit.

In the training phase, the batch size was set to 32 for all tasks. The Adadelta algorithm with the setting described in [29] was used for all tasks. For regularization, label smoothing [30] was applied by weighing the ground truth token at each output step by 0.9, and uniformly distributing the remaining probability mass among other tokens. To speed up the training time and reduce the memory consumption of the training tasks, hierarchical subsampling [31] is used on the second and third bi-directional LSTM layers in the Bi-LSTM task and the encoder network in the LAS task, and the number of time-step factors is set to 2. We trained our models on P40 GPUs and all networks were trained for 50 epochs.

We use the CTC-based model as the baseline. For soft-BAC in the Bi-LSTM model, We conducted a number of experiments in ablation studies and explored several configurations with different γ and α values. As for hybrid CTC/soft-BAC LAS models, MTL hyperparameters $\lambda = 0.4$. Note that, as we did not use any lexicon or language models in the decoding phase, our results were not compared directly with the existing results of the end-to-end model based systems.

Table 2. Comparison of WER using greedy search strategy among CTC-baseline and proposed soft-BAC based Bi-LSTM models with different γ and α values on the LibriSpeech-960 datasets. The modeling units are graphemes and BPE based subwords. None of our experiments used any language model or lexicon information.

No.	Model	LibriSpeech-960			
		Grapheme		BPE-5000	
		Test-clean	Test-other	Test-clean	Test-other
1	CTC-baseline	5.7	14.6	5.3	13.5
2	soft-BAC$_{\gamma=1.00,\alpha=1.0}$	5.5	14.8	5.2	13.7
3	soft-BAC$_{\gamma=0.45,\alpha=1.0}$	4.9	13.1	5.1	13.5
4	soft-BAC$_{\gamma=0.55,\alpha=1.0}$	5.2	13.5	4.6	12.3
5	soft-BAC$_{\gamma=0.65,\alpha=1.0}$	5.1	13.6	4.4	12.1
6	soft-BAC$_{\gamma=0.75,\alpha=1.0}$	5.4	14.0	4.6	12.9
7	soft-BAC$_{\gamma=0.55,\alpha=0.5}$	5.2	13.3	4.6	12.3
8	soft-BAC$_{\gamma=0.55,\alpha=0.8}$	4.9	12.7	4.4	12.1
9	soft-BAC$_{\gamma=0.65,\alpha=0.5}$	5.2	13.5	4.5	12.1
10	soft-BAC$_{\gamma=0.65,\alpha=0.8}$	4.7	12.9	4.3	11.9

4.3 Results

Table 3. Comparison of WER using beam search strategy (beam size = 20) among hybrid CTC/soft-BAC LAS models. The modeling units are graphemes and BPE subwords, where BPE-200 is used for LibriSpeech-100 and BPE-5000 is used for LibriSpeech-960. The hyperparameters γ and α for soft-BAC loss are set to 0.55 and 0.8, respectively. None of our experiments used any language model or lexicon information.

Train data	Model	Grapheme		Subword	
		Test-clean	Test-other	Test-clean	Test-other
100	CTC-LAS	11.5	31.3	10.8	29.5
	soft-BAC LAS	10.9	29.7	10.1	28.2
960	CTC-LAS	4.8	12.9	4.4	11.5
	soft-BAC LAS	4.3	11.6	4.1	10.9

The ablation study of the proposed soft-BAC method based on the Bi-LSTM model and the comparison results with the CTC baseline are presented in Table 1 and 2. We conducted a number of experiments on soft-BAC models with different γ and α values on the LibriSpeech-100 and LibriSpeech-960 datasets. To fully see the effect of the proposed soft-BAC methods, we conduct experiments on different modeling unit tasks including graphemes and BPE-based subwords. We use the simple greedy search strategy to report the 1st pass results

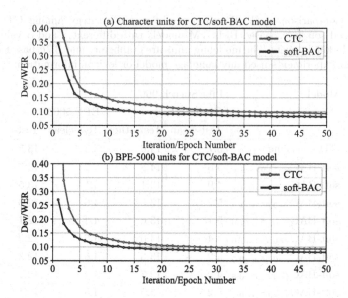

Fig. 2. Word error rate (WER) for the first training epochs of CTC and our soft-BAC based Bi-LSTM model on the LibriSpeech-960 datasets. The hyperparameters γ and α for soft-BAC are set to 0.65 and 1.0, respectively. (a): Grapheme as modeling units. (b): BPE-5000 as modeling units.

directly without using any language model or lexicon dictionary. Table 1 and 2 shows the word error rate (WER) obtained for these experiments. By comparing the results against the baseline CTC, our result shows that the performance is comparable by using the proposed forward alignment cost criterion without the *soft* operation ($\gamma = 1.00, \alpha = 1.0$) as the loss function. We also find that only using the proposed forward alignment cost criterion with the *soft* operation can achieve significant improvements in both tasks. The best performances were obtained by setting the γ in the grapheme and subword tasks to 0.55 and 0.65 on LibriSpeech-100, and 0.45 and 0.65 on LibriSpeech-960. Furthermore, our MTL soft-BAC method yielded consistent improvements for all types of tasks. The weight $\alpha = 0.8$ in the MTL give the best performance.

We also compared the performance of CTC and the proposed soft-BAC as an auxiliary tasks of the LAS model on the LibriSpeech-100 and LibriSpeech-960 datasets. The hyperparameters γ and α of soft-BAC were set to 0.55 and 0.8, respectively. During decoding, we use a beam search strategy similar to [20], which combines the CTC/soft-BAC prefix score (weight = 0.4) and the beam size was set to 20. The results were summarized in Table 3. We can see that using graphemes and BPE-based subword as modeling units, our proposed soft-BAC as an auxiliary task of LAS model has a significant performance improvement compared with CTC. On LibriSpeech-100 datasets, the proposed model improves the CTC baseline model by relative WER reduction 5.2% and 6.5% on test-clean, 5.1% and 4.6% on test-other. On LibriSpeech-960 datasets, the proposed model improved the CTC baseline model by relative WER reduction 10.4% and 6.8% on test-clean, 10.0% and 5.2% on test-other.

In addition to the WER improvements, our proposed soft-BAC is also very helpful in model training. Our soft-BAC criterion is implemented based on PyTorch [32], and the model training takes less time under the same epochs and GPUs compared to the CTC provided by SeanNaren[1]. Figure 2 shows the curves of CTC/soft-BAC based Bi-LSTM model Word Error Rate (WER) on the development sets of LibriSpeech-960 over training epochs. Note that the accuracies of the model were obtained with given gold standard history. We observed that the soft-BAC loss is helpful to the model training with fast convergence and improve the recognition performance achieved by simultaneously using forward and backward alignment optimization methods.

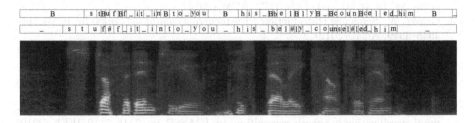

Fig. 3. Comparison of alignments produced by the Bi-LSTM based models with CTC (top) and our soft-BAC (bottom) criterions on audio spectrogram. The modeling units are graphemes and the dataset is LibriSpeech-100.

Figure 3 depicts the alignment of the recognition results of the grapheme-based model in the CTC (top) and soft-BAC (bottom) loss functions. For the CTC result, "B" represent additional blank symbol and "_" represent space. For Soft-BAC result, "#" represent identifier that distinguishes consecutive repeated graphemes and "_" represent space. We observe that our proposed soft-BAC loss can achieve better alignment results, while the CTC based model exhibits 200ms delay and there has been a phenomenon of inserting extra blanks between different characters. In addition, the recognition result of the CTC-based model is worse than that of the soft-BAC based system. For example, an additional blank symbol should be inserted between the red marked graphemes "l" in the figure.

5 Conclusions

We have proposed a new training approach for end-to-end speech recognition by integrating forward and backward alignment optimization methods based on multitask learning architecture. Our method optimizes the model by minimizing

---

[1] https://github.com/SeanNaren/warp-ctc.

all costs of the left-to-right and right-to-left alignment process between two time series of speech-transcription pair. We evaluated and compared our proposal with just CTC loss as the baseline and CTC loss as an auxiliary task in LAS mosel. Our method outperforms CTC in both using graphemes or subwords as modeling units. Future work includes fusing implicit language models to improve performance, and applying our proposal to online models.

References

1. Graves, A., Fernández, S., Gomez, F., Schmidhuber, J.: Connectionist temporal classification: labelling unsegmented sequence data with recurrent neural networks. In: ICML, pp. 369–376. ACM (2006)
2. Graves, A., Jaitly, N.: Towards end-to-end speech recognition with recurrent neural networks. In: ICML, pp. 1764–1772. ACM (2014)
3. Graves, A.: Sequence transduction with recurrent neural networks. In: ICML, pp. 4945–4949. ACM (2012)
4. Graves, A., Mohamed, A.R., Hinton, G.: Speech recognition with deep recurrent neural networks. In: ICASSP, pp. 6645–6649. IEEE (2013)
5. Das, A., Li, J., Zhao, R., Gong, Y.: Advancing connectionist temporal classification with attention modeling. In: ICASSP, pp. 4769–4773. IEEE (2018)
6. Salazar, J., Kirchhoff, K., Huang, Z.: Self-attention networks for connectionist temporal classification in speech recognition. In: ICASSP, pp. 7115–7119. IEEE (2019)
7. Moriya, T., Sato, H., Tanaka, T., Ashihara, T., Masumura, R., Shinohara, Y.: Distilling attention weights for ctc-based asr systems. In: ICASSP, pp. 6894–6898. IEEE (2020)
8. Chan, W., Jaitly, N., Le, Q., Vinyals, O.: Listen, attend and spell: a neural network for large vocabulary conversational speech recognition. In: ICASSP, pp. 4960–4964. IEEE (2016)
9. Sak, H., Shannon, M., Rao, K., Beaufays, F.: Recurrent neural aligner: an encoder-decoder neural network model for sequence to sequence mapping. In: Interspeech, pp. 1298–1302 (2017)
10. Chiu, C.C., et al.: State-of-the-art speech recognition with sequence-to-sequence models. In: ICASSP, pp. 4774–4778 (2018)
11. Hayashi, T., Watanabe, S., Toda, T., Takeda, K.: Multi-head decoder for end-to-end speech recognition. arXiv:1804.08050 (2018)
12. Dong, L., Xu, S., Xu, B.: Speech-transformer: a no-recurrence sequence-to-sequence model for speech recognition. In: ICASSP, pp. 5884–5888. IEEE (2018)
13. Karita, S., Soplin, N.E.Y., Watanabe, S., Delcroix, M., Nakatani, T.: Improving transformer-based end-to-end speech recognition with connectionist temporal classification and language model integration. In: Interspeech, pp. 1408–1412 (2019)
14. Karita, S., et al.: A comparative study on transformer vs rnn in speech applications. In: ASRU, pp. 449–456. IEEE (2019)
15. Pham, N.Q., Nguyen, T.S., Niehues, J., Müller, M., Stüker, S., Waibel, A.: Very deep self-attention networks for end-to-end speech recognition. In: Interspeech, pp. 66–70 (2019)
16. Vaswani, A., et al.: Attention is all you need. In: NIPS, pp. 5998–6008 (2017)
17. Kim, S., Hori, T., Watanabe, S.: Joint ctc-attention based end-to-end speech recognition using multi-task learning. In: ICASSP, pp. 4835–4839 (2017)

18. Watanabe, S., Hori, T., Kim, S., Hershey, J.R., Hayashi, T.: Hybrid ctc/attention architecture for end-to-end speech recognition. IEEE J. Selected Top. Sign. Process. **11**(8), 1240–1253 (2017)
19. Hori, T., Watanabe, S., Yu, Z., Chan, W.: Advances in joint ctc-attention based end-to-end speech recognition with a deep cnn encoder and rnn-lm. In: Interspeech, pp. 949–953 (2017)
20. Hori, T., Watanabe, S., Hershey, J.R.: Joint ctc/attention decoding for end-to-end speech recognition. In: ACL, pp. 518–529 (2017)
21. Collobert, R., Puhrsch, C., Synnaeve, G.: Wav2letter: an end-to-end convnet-based speech recognition system. arXiv:1609.03193 (2016)
22. Liptchinsky, V., Synnaeve, G., Collobert, R.: Letter-based speech recognition with gated convnets. arXiv:1712.09444 (2017)
23. Panayotov, V., Chen, G., Povey, D., Khudanpur, S.: Librispeech: an asr corpus based on public domain audio books. In: ICASSP, pp. 5206–5210 (2015)
24. Sennrich, R., Haddow, B., Birch, A.: Neural machine translation of rare words with subword units. In: ACL, pp. 7–12 (2016)
25. Povey, D., et al.: The kaldi speech recognition toolkit. In: ASRU. IEEE (2011)
26. Park, D.S., et al.: Specaugment: a simple data augmentation method for automatic speech recognition. In: Interspeech, pp. 2613–2617 (2019)
27. Simonyan, K., Zisserman, A.: Very deep convolutional networks for large-scale image recognition. arXiv preprint arXiv:1409.1556 (2014)
28. Watanabe, S., et al.: Espnet: end-to-end speech processing toolkit. In: Interspeech, pp. 2207–2211 (2018)
29. Zeiler, M.D.: Adadelta: an adaptive learning rate method. arXiv:1212.5701 (2012)
30. Chorowski, J., Jaitly, N., Chorowski, J., Jaitly, N.: Towards better decoding and language model integration in sequence to sequence models. In: Interspeech, pp. 2207–2211 (2017)
31. Bahdanau, D., Chorowski, J., Serdyuk, D., Brakel, P., Bengio, Y.: End-to-end attention-based large vocabulary speech recognition. In: ICASSP, pp. 4945–4949 (2016)
32. Paszke, A., et al.: Automatic differentiation in pytorch. In: Conference and Workshop on Neural Information Processing Systems (NIPS) (2017)

Span Labeling Approach for Vietnamese and Chinese Word Segmentation

Duc-Vu Nguyen[1,3]([✉]), Linh-Bao Vo[2,3], Dang Van Thin[1,3],
and Ngan Luu-Thuy Nguyen[2,3]

[1] Multimedia Communications Laboratory, University of Information Technology,
Ho Chi Minh City, Vietnam
{vund,thindv}@uit.edu.vn
[2] University of Information Technology, Ho Chi Minh City, Vietnam
18520503@gm.uit.edu.vn, ngannlt@uit.edu.vn
[3] Vietnam National University, Ho Chi Minh City, Vietnam

Abstract. In this paper, we propose a span labeling approach to model n-gram information for Vietnamese word segmentation, namely SPANSEG. We compare the span labeling approach with the conditional random field by using encoders with the same architecture. Since Vietnamese and Chinese have similar linguistic phenomena, we evaluated the proposed method on the Vietnamese treebank benchmark dataset and five Chinese benchmark datasets. Through our experimental results, the proposed approach SPANSEG achieves higher performance than the sequence tagging approach with the state-of-the-art F-score of 98.31% on the Vietnamese treebank benchmark, when they both apply the contextual pre-trained language model XLM-RoBERTa and the predicted word boundary information. Besides, we do fine-tuning experiments for the span labeling approach on BERT and ZEN pre-trained language model for Chinese with fewer parameters, faster inference time, and competitive or higher F-scores than the previous state-of-the-art approach, word segmentation with word-hood memory networks, on five Chinese benchmarks.

Keywords: Natural language processing · Word segmentation · Vietnamese · Chinese

1 Introduction

Word segmentation is the first essential task for both Vietnamese and Chinese. The input of Vietnamese word segmentation (VWS) is the sequence of syllables delimited by space. In contrast, the input of Chinese word segmentation (CWS) is the sequence of characters without explicit delimiter. The use of a Vietnamese syllable is similar to a Chinese character. Despite deep learning dealing with natural language processing tasks without the word segmentation phase, the research on word segmentation is still necessary regarding the linguistic aspect. Since Vietnamese and Chinese have similar linguistic phenomena such as overlapping ambiguity in VWS [13] and in CWS [26], therefore the research about VWS and CWS is a challenging problem.

Many previous approaches for VWS have been proposed. For instance, in the early stage of VWS, Dinh et al. [6] supposed VWS as a stochastic transduction problem.

© Springer Nature Switzerland AG 2021
D. N. Pham et al. (Eds.): PRICAI 2021, LNAI 13032, pp. 244–258, 2021.
https://doi.org/10.1007/978-3-030-89363-7_19

Therefore, they represented the input sentence as an unweighted Finite-State Acceptor. As a consequence, Le et al. [13] proposed the ambiguity resolver using a bi-gram language model as a component in their model for VWS. After that, Nguyen et al. [16] used conditional random fields (CRFs) and support vector machines (SVMs) for VWS. Recently, Nguyen and Le [22] utilized rules based on the predicted word boundary and threshold for the classifier in the post-processing stage to control overlapping ambiguities for VWS. Besides, Nguyen et al. [18] proposes a method for auto-learning rule based on the predicted word boundary for VWS. Furthermore, Nguyen [17] proposed the joint neural network model for Vietnamese word segmentation, part-of-speech tagging, and dependency parsing. Lastly, Nguyen et al. [20] proposed feature extraction to deal with overlapping ambiguity and capturing word containing suffixes.

From our observation, the number of research and approaches for CWS is greater than VWS. The research [1, 10, 15, 24, 28, 32] treated CWS as a character-based sequence labeling task. The contextual feature extractions were proved helpful in CWS [10]. After that, neural networks were powerful for CWS [1, 10, 15]. The measuring word-hood for n-grams was an effective method for non-neural network model [26] and neural network model [27]. Besides, the multi-criteria learning from many different datasets is a strong method [2, 12, 23]. Remarkably, Tian et al. [27] incorporated the word-hood for n-gram into neural network model effectively.

We have an observation that most of the approaches for VWS and CWS treated word segmentation as a token-based sequence tagging problem, where the token is a syllable in VWS and character in CWS. Secondly, the intersection of VWS and CWS approaches leverages the context to model n-gram of token information, such as measuring the word-hood of the n-gram in CWS. All of the previous approaches in CWS incorporate the word-hood information as a module of their models. Therefore, our research hypothesizes whether we can model a simple model that can simulate measuring word-hood operation.

From our observation and hypothesis, we get the inspiration of span representation in constituency parsing [25] to propose our SPANSEG model for VWS and CWS. The main idea of our SPANSEG is to model all n-grams in the input sentence and score them. Modeling an n-gram is equivalent to find the probability of a span being a word. Via experimental results, the proposed approach SPANSEG achieves higher performance than the sequence tagging approach when both utilize contextual pre-trained language model XLM-RoBERTa and predicted word boundary information on the Vietnamese treebank benchmark with the state-of-the-art F-score of 98.31%. Additionally, we do fine-tuning experiments for the span labeling method on BERT and ZEN pre-trained language model for Chinese with fewer parameters, faster inference time, and competitive or higher F-scores than the previous state-of-the-art approach, word segmentation with word-hood memory networks, on five Chinese benchmarks.

2 The Proposed Framework

Differing from previous studies, we regard word segmentation as a span labeling task. The architecture of our proposed model, namely SPANSEG, is illustrated in Fig. 1, where the general span labeling paradigm is at the top of the figure. This paper is the

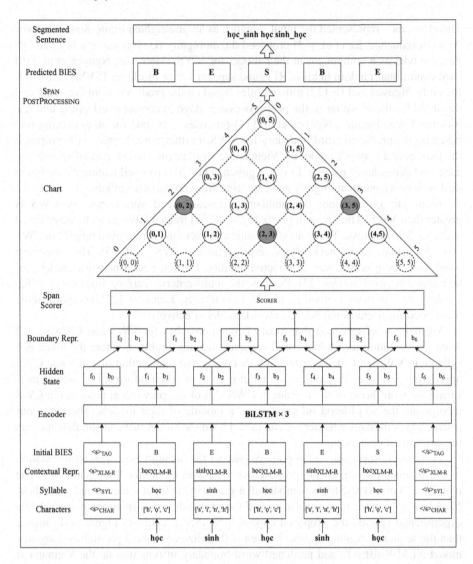

Fig. 1. The architecture of SPANSEG for VWS. The input sentence is "học sinh học sinh học" (*student learn biology*) including five syllables {"học", "sinh", "học", "sinh", and "học"}. The gold-standard segmentation for the input sentence is "học_sinh học sinh_học" including three words {"học_sinh", "học", and "sinh_học"}. The initial BIES (Begin, Inside, End, or Singleton) word boundary tags (differing from gold-standard segmentation) were predicted by an off-the-shelf toolkit RDRsegmenter [18].

first work approach to word segmentation as a span labeling task to the best of our knowledge. Before presenting the details of SPANSEG, we take a first look at problem representation of SPANSEG. In Fig. 1, we consider the input sentence in the form of the index (integer type) and syllable (string type) as an array {0: "học", 1: "sinh", 2: "học",

3: "sinh", 4: "học"}. With this consideration, the gold-standard segmentation "học_sinh học sinh_học" (*student learn biology*) (including three words {"học_sinh", "học", and "sinh_học"}) is presented by three spans $(0,2)$ ("học_sinh"), $(2,3)$ ("học"), and $(3,5)$ ("sinh_học"). By approaching word segmentation as a span labeling task, we have three positive samples (three circles filled with gray color) for the input sentence in Fig. 1, whereas other circles filled with white color with solid border are negative samples for the input sentence in Fig. 1. Also, in Fig. 1, we note that all circles with dashed border (e.g., spans $(0,0)$, $(1,1)$, ..., (n,n), where n is the length of the input sentence) are skipped in SPANSEG because they do not represent spans.

After presenting SPANSEG, in the rest of this section, we firstly introduce problem representation of word segmentation as a span labeling task (in Subsect. 2.1). Secondly, we introduce the proposed span post-processing algorithm for word segmentation (in Subsect. 2.2). The first and second subsections are two important points of our research. Thirdly, we describe the span scoring module (in Subsect. 2.3). In the last two subsections, we provide the architecture encoder for VWS and CWS. We describe the model SPANSEG for VWS (in Subsect. 2.4). Lastly, we describe SPANSEG for CWS (in Subsect. 2.5).

2.1 Word Segmentation as Span Labeling Task for Vietnamese and Chinese

The input sentence of word segmentation task is a sequence of tokens $\mathcal{X} = x_1 x_2 \ldots x_n$ with the length of n. The token x_i is a syllable or character toward Vietnamese or Chinese, respectively. Given the input $\mathcal{X}$, the output of word segmentation is a sequence of words $\mathcal{W} = w_1 w_2 \ldots w_m$ with the length of m, where $1 \leq m \leq n$. We have a property that the word w_j is constituted by one token or consecutive tokens. So, we use the sequence of tokens $x_i x_{i+1} \ldots x_{i+k-1}$ for denoting the word w_j be constituted by k consecutive tokens beginning at token x_i, where $1 \leq k \leq n$ (concretely, $k = 1$ representing single words and $2 \leq k \leq n$ representing compound words for both Vietnamese and Chinese). Inspired by the work of Stern et al. [25] for constituency parsing, we use the span $(i - 1, i - 1 + k)$ to represent the word constituted by k consecutive tokens $x_i x_{i+1} \ldots x_{i+k-1}$ beginning at token x_i. Therefore, the goal of the span labeling task for both VWS and CWS is to find the list of spans $\hat{S}$ such that every token x_i is spanned, and there is no overlapping between every two spans. Formally, the word segmentation model as span labeling task for both VWS and CWS can be formalized as:

$$\hat{S} = \text{SPANPOSTPROCESSING}(\hat{\mathcal{Y}}) \tag{1}$$

where SPANPOSTPROCESSING$(\cdot)$ simply is a algorithm for producing the word segmentation boundary satisfying non-overlapping between every two spans. The $\hat{\mathcal{Y}}$ is the set of predicted spans as following:

$$\hat{\mathcal{Y}} = \{(l, r) | 0 \leq l \leq n - 1 \text{ and } l < r \leq n \text{ and } \text{SCORER}(\mathcal{X}, l, r) > 0.5\} \tag{2}$$

where n is the length of the input sentence. The SCORER$(\cdot)$ is the scoring module for the span (l, r) of sentence $\mathcal{X}$. The output of SCORER$(\cdot)$ has a value in the range of 0 to 1. In our research, we choose the sigmoid function as an activation function at the last layer of SCORER($\cdot$) module. Lastly, the word segmentation as a span labeling task is the binary classification problem. We use the binary cross-entropy loss for the cost function as following:

$$J(\theta) = -\frac{1}{|\mathcal{D}|} \sum_{\mathcal{X},\mathcal{S} \in \mathcal{D}} \left(\frac{1}{(n(n+1))/2} \sum_{l=0}^{n-1} \sum_{r=l+1}^{n} [(l,r) \in \mathcal{S}] \log \left(\text{SCORER}(\mathcal{X},l,r) \right) \right.$$

$$\left. + [(l,r) \notin \mathcal{S}] \log \left(1 - \text{SCORER}(\mathcal{X},l,r) \right) \right) \quad (3)$$

where $\mathcal{D}$ is the training set and $|\mathcal{D}|$ is the size of training set. For each pair $(\mathcal{X},\mathcal{S})$ in training set $\mathcal{D}$, we compute binary cross-entropy loss for all spans (l,r), where $0 \le l \le n-1$ and $l < r \le n$, and n is the length of sentence $\mathcal{X}$. The term $[(l,r) \in \mathcal{S}]$ has the value of 1 if span (l,r) belongs to the list $\mathcal{S}$ of sentence $\mathcal{X}$ and conversely, of 0. Similarly, the term $[(l,r) \notin \mathcal{S}]$ has the value of 1 if span (l,r) does not belong to the list $\mathcal{S}$ of sentence $\mathcal{X}$ and conversely, of 0. Lastly, we make a note that in our training and prediction progress, we will discard spans with length greater than 7 for both Vietnamese and Chinese (7 is maximum n-gram length following [5] for Chinese, so we decide to choose 7 for Vietnamese according to the statistics in the work of [20]).

2.2 Post-processing Algorithm for Predicted Spans

In the previous Subsect. 2.1, we presented word segmentation as a span labeling task for Vietnamese and Chinese. In this subsection, we present our proposed post-processing algorithm for predicted spans from the span labeling problem. However, we found that in the predicted spans set $\hat{\mathcal{Y}}$ there exists overlapping between some two spans. We deal with the overlapping ambiguity by choosing the spans with the highest score and removing the rest. The overlapping ambiguity phenomenon occurs when our SPANSEG predicts compound words. It occurs in our SPANSEG and other word segmenters on Vietnamese [13] and Chinese [26].

Apart from overlapping ambiguity, our SPANSEG faces the missing word boundary problem. That problem can be caused by originally predicted spans or as a result of solving overlapping ambiguity. We choose the missing word boundary based on all predicted spans $(i-1, i-1+k)$ with $k=1$ for single words to deal with the missing word boundary problem. To sum up, our proposed post-processing algorithm for predicted spans from the span labeling problem, namely SPANPOSTPROCESSING, deals with overlapping ambiguity and missing spans from predicted spans. The detail of our SPANPOSTPROCESSING is presented in Algorithm 1.

2.3 Span Scoring Module

In two previous Subsect. 2.1 and 2.2, we presented two critical points of our research. There we mentioned the SCORER($\cdot$) module many times. In this section, we present SCORER($\cdot$) module. It is based on the familiar module that name Biaffine [7]. While Zhang et al. [33] experimenting with the Biaffine module for constituency parsing, we use the Biaffine module for span labeling word segmentation. The Biaffine module is used in [7] to capture the directed relation between two words in a sentence for

---

Algorithm 1. SPANPOSTPROCESSING

Require:

    The input sentence $\mathcal{X}$ with the length of n;

    The scoring module SCORER($\cdot$) for any span (l, r) in $\mathcal{X}$, where $0 \leq l \leq n-1$ and $l < r \leq n$;

    The set of predicted spans $\hat{\mathcal{Y}}$, sorted in ascending order.

Ensure:

    The list of valid predicted spans $\hat{S}$, satisfying non-overlapping between every two spans.

1:   $\hat{S}_{\text{novlp}} = [(0, 0)]$ $\triangleright$ The list of predicted spans without overlapping ambiguity.

2:   $\hat{S} = []$ $\triangleright$ The final list of valid predicted spans.

3:   **for** $\hat{y}$ **in** $\hat{\mathcal{Y}}$ **do** $\triangleright$ The $\hat{y}[0]$ is the left boundary and $\hat{y}[1]$ is the right boundary of each span $\hat{y}$.

4:      **if** $\hat{S}_{\text{novlp}}[-1][1] < \hat{y}[0]$ **then** $\triangleright$ Check for missing boundary.

5:          $\hat{S}_{\text{novlp}}.\textbf{append}\big((\hat{S}_{\text{novlp}}[-1][1], \hat{y}[0])\big)$ $\triangleright$ Add the missing span to $\hat{S}_{\text{novlp}}$

6:      **end if**

7:      **if** $\hat{S}_{\text{novlp}}[-1][0] \leq \hat{y}[0] < \hat{S}_{\text{novlp}}[-1][1]$ **then** $\triangleright$ Check for overlapping ambiguity.

8:          **if** SCORER$(\mathcal{X}, \hat{S}_{\text{novlp}}[-1][0], \hat{S}_{\text{novlp}}[-1][1]) <$ SCORER$(\mathcal{X}, \hat{y}[0], \hat{y}[1])$ **then**

9:              $\hat{S}_{\text{novlp}}.\textbf{pop}()$ $\triangleright$ Remove the span causing overlapping with the lower score than $\hat{y}$.

10:              $\hat{S}_{\text{novlp}}.\textbf{append}\big((\hat{y}[0], \hat{y}[1])\big)$ $\triangleright$ Add the span $\hat{y}$ to $\hat{S}_{\text{novlp}}$.

11:          **end if**

12:      **else**

13:          $\hat{S}_{\text{novlp}}.\textbf{append}\big((\hat{y}[0], \hat{y}[1])\big)$ $\triangleright$ Add the span $\hat{y}$ to $\hat{S}_{\text{novlp}}$.

14:      **end if**

15:   **end for**

16:   **if** $\hat{S}_{\text{novlp}}[-1][1] < n$ **then** $\triangleright$ Check for missing boundary.

17:      $\hat{S}_{\text{novlp}}.\textbf{append}\big((\hat{S}_{\text{novlp}}[-1][1], n)\big)$ $\triangleright$ Add the missing span to $\hat{S}_{\text{novlp}}$

18:   **end if**

19:   **for** $i, \hat{y}$ **in enumerate**$(\hat{S}_{\text{novlp}})$ **do** $\triangleright$ The $\hat{y}[0]$ is the left boundary and $\hat{y}[1]$ is the right boundary of each span $\hat{y}$, and i is the index of $\hat{y}$ in list $\hat{S}_{\text{novlp}}$.

20:      **if** $0 < i$ **and** $\hat{S}_{\text{novlp}}[i-1][1] < \hat{y}[0]$ **then** $\triangleright$ Check for missing boundary.

21:          $missed\_boundaries = \big[\hat{S}_{\text{novlp}}[i-1][1]\big]$

22:          **for** $bound$ **in range**$\big(\hat{S}_{\text{novlp}}[i-1][1], \hat{y}[0]\big)$ **do**

23:              **if** SCORER$(\mathcal{X}, bound, bound+1) > 0.5$ **then** $\triangleright$ Check for single word.

24:                  $missed\_boundaries.\textbf{append}(bound+1)$

25:              **end if**

26:          **end for**

27:          $missed\_boundaries.\textbf{append}(\hat{y}[0])$

28:          **for** j **in range**$\big(\textbf{len}(missed\_boundaries) - 1\big)$ **do**

29:              $\hat{S}.\textbf{append}\big((missed\_boundaries[j], missed\_boundaries[j+1])\big)$ $\triangleright$ Add the missing span to $\hat{S}$

30:          **end for**

31:      **end if**

32:      $\hat{S}.\textbf{append}\big(\hat{y}[0], \hat{y}[1]\big)$ $\triangleright$ Add the non-overlapping span to $\hat{S}$

33:   **end for**

---

dependency parsing. In the constituency parsing problem, Zhang et al. [33] used the Biaffine module to find the representation of phrases. Our research uses the Biaffine module to model the representation of n-gram for the word segmentation task.

As we can see in Fig. 1, each token x_i in the input sentence has two context-aware word representations including left and right boundary representations except the begin ("<s>") and end ("</s>") tokens. In case we use the BiLSTM (Bidirectional Long Short Term Memory) encoder, the left boundary representation of token x_i is the concatenation of the hidden state forward vector $\mathbf{f}_{i-1}$ and the hidden state backward vector $\mathbf{b}_i$ and the right boundary representation of token x_i is the concatenation of the hidden state forward vector $\mathbf{f}_i$ and the hidden state backward vector $\mathbf{b}_{i+1}$, following Stern et al. [25]. In case we use BERT [4] or ZEN [5] encoder, we chunk the last hidden state vector into two vectors with the same size as forward and backward vectors of the BiLSTM encoder. Even though we use the BiLSTM, BERT, or ZEN encoder, we always have the left and right boundary representation for each token x_i in the input sentence. Therefore, in Fig. 1, we see that the right boundary representation $\mathbf{f}_i \oplus \mathbf{b}_{i+1}$ of token x_i is the left boundary representation of token $\mathbf{x}_{i+1}$. As the work of Zhang et al. [33], we use two MLPs to make the difference between the right boundary representation of token x_i and the left boundary representation of token x_{i+1}. To sum up, we have the left $\mathbf{r}_i^{\text{left}}$ and right $\mathbf{r}_i^{\text{right}}$ boundary representations of token x_i as following:

$$\mathbf{r}_i^{\text{left}} = \text{MLP}^{\text{left}}(\mathbf{f}_{i-1} \oplus \mathbf{b}_i) \tag{4}$$

$$\mathbf{r}_i^{\text{right}} = \text{MLP}^{\text{right}}(\mathbf{f}_i \oplus \mathbf{b}_{i+1}) \tag{5}$$

Finally, inspired by Zhang et al. [33], given the input sentence $\mathcal{X}$, the span scoring module $\text{SCORER}(\cdot)$ for span (l, r) in our SPANSEG model is computed by using a biaffine operation over the left boundary representation of token x_l and the right boundary representation of token x_r as following:

$$\text{SCORER}(\mathcal{X}, l, r) = \text{sigmoid}\left(\begin{bmatrix} \mathbf{r}_l^{\text{left}} \\ 1 \end{bmatrix}^{\text{T}} \mathbf{W} \mathbf{r}_r^{\text{right}} \right) \tag{6}$$

where $\mathbf{W} \in \mathbb{R}^{d \times d}$. To sum up, the $\text{SCORER}(\mathcal{X}, l, r)$ gives us a score to predict whether a span (l, r) is a word.

2.4 Encoder and Input Representation for VWS

In three previous Subsect. 2.1, 2.2, and 2.3, we describe three mutual parts of the SPANSEG model for Vietnamese and Chinese. In this subsection, we present the encoder and the input representation for VWS of the SPANSEG model. Firstly, the default configuration of SPANSEG for the input representation of token x_i is composed as following:

$$\begin{aligned} \textbf{default\_embedding}_i = \big(&\textbf{static\_syl\_embedding}_i \\ &+ \textbf{dynamic\_syl\_embedding}_i\big) \oplus \textbf{char\_embedding}_i \end{aligned} \tag{7}$$

where the symbol $\oplus$ denotes the concatenation operation. The **static_syl_embedding**$_i$ is extracted from the pre-trained Vietnamese syllable embedding with the dimension of 100 provided by Nguyen et al. [19]. So, the dimension of vector **dynamic_syl_**

embedding$_i$ also is 100. We initialize randomly and update the value of **dynamic_syl_embedding$_i$** in the training progress. We do not update the value of **static_syl_embedding$_i$** during training model. Besides, we also use a character embedding for the input representation by using BiLSTM network for sequence of characters in token x_i to obtain **char_embedding$_i$**.

The default configuration does not utilize the Vietnamese predicted word boundary information as many previous works on VWS did. Following the work of Nguyen [17], we additionally use the boundary BIES tag embedding for the input representation of token x_i. Therefore, the second configuration of SPANSEG, namely SPANSEG (TAG) is presented as following:

$$\textbf{default\_tag\_embedding}_i = \textbf{default\_embedding}_i \oplus \textbf{bies\_tag\_embedding}_i$$
(8)

where the value of **bies_tag_embedding$_i$** (with the dimension of 100) is initialized randomly and updated; and the boundary BIES tag is predicted by the off-the-shelf toolkit RDRsegmenter [18].

Recently, many contextual pre-trained language models were proposed inspired by the work of Devlin et al. [4]. However, our research utilizes contextual pre-trained multilingual language model XLM-Roberta (XLM-R) [3] with the *base* architecture for VWS since there is no contextual pre-trained monolingual language model for Vietnamese at this time. So, the third configuration of SPANSEG, namely SPANSEG (XLM-R), is presented as following:

$$\textbf{default\_xlmr\_embedding}_i = \textbf{default\_embedding}_i \oplus \textbf{xlmr\_embedding}_i$$ (9)

where the **xlmr_embedding$_i$** is the projected vector from the hidden state of *the last four layers* of the XLM-R model. The dimension of **xlmr_embedding$_i$** is 100. We do not update parameters of the XLM-R model during the training process.

Lastly, we make the fourth configuration for SPANSEG, namely SPANSEG (TAG + XLM-R). This configuration aims to combine all syllables, characters, predicted word boundaries, and contextual information for VWS.

$$\textbf{default\_tag\_xlmr\_embedding}_i = \textbf{default\_embedding}_i$$
$$\oplus \textbf{bies\_tag\_embedding}_i \oplus \textbf{xlmr\_embedding}_i$$ (10)

After we have the input representation for each token x_i of the input sentence $\mathcal{X}$, we feed them into the BiLSTM network to obtain the forward f_i and backward b_i vectors. The forward f_i and backward b_i vectors is used in the SCORER($\cdot$) module in Subsect. 2.3.

2.5 Encoder and Input Representation for CWS

To make a fair comparison to the state-of-the-art model for CWS, we used the same encoder as the work of Tian et al. [27]. Following the work [27], we choose two BERT [4] and ZEN [5] encoders with the *base* architecture. The BERT and ZEN are two famous encoders utilizing contextual information for Chinese language processing, in which the ZEN encoder enhances n-gram of characters information. For each character x_i in the input sentence $\mathcal{X}$, we chunk the hidden state vector of *the last layer* of BERT or ZEN into two vectors with the same size as the forward f_i and backward b_i vectors in the BiLSTM network. Finally, the forward f_i and backward b_i vectors are used in the SCORER($\cdot$) module in Subsect. 2.3. We update the parameters of BERT and ZEN in training progress following the work of Tian et al. [27].

3 Experimental Settings

3.1 Datasets

The largest VWS benchmark dataset[1] is a part of the Vietnamese treebank (VTB) project [21]. We use the same split as the work of Nguyen et al. [18]. The summary of the VTB dataset for the word segmentation task is provided in Table 1.

Table 1. Statistics of the Vietnamese treebank dataset for word segmentation. We provide the number of sentences, characters, syllables, words, character types, syllable types, word types. We also compute the out-of-vocabulary (OOV) rate as the percentage of unseen words in the development and test set.

	VTB		
	Train	Dev	Test
# sentences	74,889	500	2,120
# characters	6,779,116	55,476	307,932
# syllables	2,176,398	17,429	96,560
# words	1,722,271	13,165	66,346
# character types	155	117	121
# syllable types	17,840	1,785	2,025
# word types	41,355	2,227	3,730
OOV Rate	–	2.2	1.6

For evaluating our SPANSEG on CWS, we employ five benchmark datasets including MSR, PKU, AS, CityU (from SIGHAN 2005 Bakeoff [8]), and CTB6 [31]. We convert traditional Chinese characters in AS, and CityU into simplified ones following previous studies [1,23,27]. We follow the official training/test data split of MSR, PKU, AS, and CityU, in which we randomly extract 10% of the training dataset for development as many previous works. For CTB6, we the same split as the work of Tian et al. [27]. For pre-processing phase of all CWS dataset in our research, we inherit the process[2] of Tian et al. [27]. The summary of five Chinese benchmark datasets for the word segmentation task is presented in Table 2.

[1] The details of VTB dataset are presented at https://vlsp.org.vn/vlsp2013/eval/ws-pos.
[2] https://github.com/SVAIGBA/WMSeg.

Table 2. Statistics of five Chinese benchmark dataset for word segmentation. We provide the number of sentences, characters, words, character types, word types. We also compute the out-of-vocabulary (OOV) rate as the percentage of unseen words in the test set.

	MSR		PKU		AS		CITYU		CTB6		
	Train	Test	Train	Test	Train	Test	Train	Test	Train	Dev	Test
# sentences	86,918	3,985	19,054	1,944	708,953	14,429	53,019	1,492	23,420	2,079	2,796
# characters	4,050,469	184,355	1,826,448	172,733	8,368,050	197,681	2,403,354	67,689	1,055,583	100,316	134,149
# words	2,368,391	106,873	1,109,947	104,372	5,449,581	122,610	1,455,630	40,936	641,368	59,955	81,578
# character types	5,140	2,838	4,675	2,918	5,948	3,578	4,806	2,642	4,243	2,648	2,917
# word types	88,104	12,923	55,303	13,148	140,009	18,757	68,928	8,989	42,246	9,811	12,278
OOV Rate	–	2.7	–	5.8	–	4.3	–	7.2	–	5.4	5.6

3.2 Model Implementation

The Detail of SPANSEG for Vietnamese. For the encoder mentioned in the Subsect. 2.4, the number of layers of BiLSTM is 3, and the hidden size of BiLSTM is 400. The size of MLPs mentioned in the Subsect. 2.3 is 500. The dropout rate for embedding, BiLSTM, and MLPs is 0.33. We inherit hyper-parameters from the work of [7]. We trained all models up to 100 with the early stopping strategy with patience epochs of 20. We used AdamW optimizer [11] with the default configuration and learning rate of 10^{-3}. The batch size for training and evaluating is up to 5000.

The Detail of SPANSEG for Chinese. For the encoder mentioned in the Subsect. 2.5, we do fine-tuning experiments based on BERT [4] and ZEN [5] encoders. The size of MLPs mentioned in the Subsect. 2.3 is 500. The dropout rate for BERT and ZEN is 0.1. We trained all models up to 30 with the early stopping strategy with patience epochs of 5. We used AdamW optimizer [11] with the default configuration and learning rate of 10^{-5}. The batch size for training and evaluating is 16.

4   Results and Analysis

4.1   Main Results

For VWS, we also implement the BiLSTM-CRF model with the same backbone and hyper-parameters as our SPANSEG. The overall results are presented in Table 3. On the default configuration, our SPANSEG gives a higher result than BiLSTM-CRF with the F-score of 97.76%. On the configuration with pre-trained XLM-R, our SPANSEG (XLM-R) gives a higher result than BiLSTM-CRF (XLM-R) with the F-score of 97.95%. On the configuration with predicted boundary BIES tag from off-the-shelf toolkit RDRsegmenter [18], the BiLSTM-CRF (TAG) gives a higher result than our SPANSEG (TAG) with the F-score of 98.10%. Finally, on the configuration with a combination of all features, our SPANSEG (TAG+XLM-R) gives a higher result than BiLSTM-CRF (TAG+XLM-R) with the F-score of 98.31%, which is also the state-of-the-art performance on VTB. We can see that the contextual information is essential for SPANSEG since SPANSEG models the left and right boundary of a word rather than the between to consecutive tokens.

Table 3. Performance (F-score) comparison between SPANSEG (with different configurations) and previous state-of-the-art models on the test set of VTB dataset.

	VTB			
	P	R	F	R_{OOV}
vnTokenizer [13]	96.98	97.69	97.33	–
JVnSegmenter-Maxent [16]	96.60	97.40	97.00	–
JVnSegmenter-CRFs [16]	96.63	97.49	97.06	–
DongDu [14]	96.35	97.46	96.90	–
UETsegmenter [22]	97.51	98.23	97.87	–
RDRsegmenter [18]	97.46	98.35	97.90	–
UITsegmenter [20]	97.81	**98.57**	98.19	–
BiLSTM-CRF	97.42	97.84	97.63	72.47
SPANSEG	97.58	97.94	97.76	**74.65**
BiLSTM-CRF (XLM-R)	97.69	97.99	97.84	72.66
SPANSEG (XLM-R)	97.75	98.16	97.95	70.01
BiLSTM-CRF (TAG)	97.91	98.28	98.10	69.16
SPANSEG (TAG)	97.67	98.28	97.97	65.94
BiLSTM-CRF (TAG+XLM-R)	97.94	98.44	98.19	68.87
SPANSEG (TAG+XLM-R)	**98.21**	98.41	**98.31**	72.28

For CWS, we presented the performances of our SPANSEG in Table 4. We do not compare our method with previous studies approaching multi-criteria learning since simply the training data is different. Our research focuses on the comparison between our SPANSEG and sequence tagging approaches. Firstly, we can see that our SPANSEG (BERT) achieves higher results than state-of-the-art methods WMSEG (BERT-CRF) [27] on four datasets including MSR (98.31%), PKU (96.56%), AS (96.62%), and CTB6 (97.26%) except CityU (97.74%). Our SPANSEG (ZEN) do not achieve the stable performance as SPANSEG (BERT). The potential reason for this problem is that both ZEN [5] encoder and our SPANSEG try to model n-gram of Chinese characters causing inconsistency.

Lastly, we test the WMSEG and our SPANSEG when dealing with the largest benchmark dataset AS on Chinese to discuss the size of the model and the inference time. The statistics are presented in Table 5, showing that our SPANSEG has the smaller size and faster inference time than WMSEG. The statistics can be explained by WMSEG [27] containing word-hood memory networks to encode both n-grams and the word-hood information, while our SPANSEG encodes n-grams information via span representation.

Table 4. Performance (F-score) comparison between SPANSEG (BERT and ZEN) and previous state-of-the-art models on the test set of five Chinese benchmark datasets. The symbol [★] denotes the methods learning from data annotated through different segmentation criteria, which means that the labeled training data are different from the rest.

	MSR		PKU		AS		CITYU		CTB6	
	F	R_{OOV}	F	R_{OOV}	F	R_{OOV}	F	R_{OOV}	F.	R_{OOV}
Chen et al. [1]	97.40	–	96.50	–	–	–	–	–	96.00	–
Xu and Sun [30]	96.30	–	96.10	–	–	–	–	–	95.80	–
Zhang et al. [32]	97.70	–	95.70	–	–	–	–	–	95.95	–
Chen et al. [2] [★]	96.04	71.60	94.32	72.64	94.75	75.34	95.55	81.40	–	–
Wang and Xu [29]	98.00	–	96.50	–	–	–	–	–	–	–
Zhou et al. [34]	97.80	–	96.00	–	–	–	–	–	96.20	–
Ma et al. [15]	98.10	80.00	96.10	78.80	96.20	70.70	97.20	87.50	96.70	85.40
Gong et al. [9]	97.78	64.20	96.15	69.88	95.22	77.33	96.22	73.58	–	–
Higashiyama et al. [10]	97.80	–	–	–	–	–	–	–	96.40	–
Qiu et al. [23] [★]	98.05	78.92	96.41	78.91	96.44	76.39	96.91	86.91	–	–
WMSEG (BERT-CRF) [27]	98.28	**86.67**	96.51	**86.76**	96.58	78.48	97.80	87.57	97.16	88.00
WMSEG (ZEN-CRF) [27]	**98.40**	84.87	96.53	85.36	**96.62**	**79.64**	97.93	**90.15**	**97.25**	**88.46**
METASEG [12] [★]	98.50	–	96.92	–	97.01	–	98.20	–	97.89	–
SPANSEG (BERT)	98.31	85.32	**96.56**	85.53	**96.62**	79.36	97.74	87.45	**97.25**	87.91
SPANSEG (ZEN)	98.35	85.66	96.35	83.66	96.52	78.43	**97.96**	90.11	97.17	87.76

Table 5. Statistics of model size (MB) and inference time (minute) of WMSEG [27] and our SPANSEG dealing with the training set of the AS dataset on Chinese. We use the same batch size as the work of Tian et al. [27]. The inference time is done by using Tesla P100-PCIE GPU with memory size of 16,280 MiB via Google Colaboratory.

	BERT Encoder		ZEN Encoder	
	WMSEG	SPANSEG	WMSEG	SPANSEG
Size (MB)	704	397	1,150	872
Inference Time (minute)	28	15	46	32

4.2 Analysis

Table 6. Error statistics of the overlapping ambiguity problem involving three consecutive tokens on VWS dataset. The symbols ✓ and ✗ denote predicting correctly and incorrectly, respectively.

BiLSTM-CRF	SPANSEG	Configuration			
		Defalut	XLM-R	TAG	TAG+XLM-R
✗	✗	15	5	19	7
✓	✗	7	**0**	4	0
✗	✓	7	**0**	18	1

To explore how our SPANSEG learns to predict VWS and CWS, we select the statistics of the overlapping ambiguity problem involving three consecutive tokens. The first case is that given the gold standard tags "**B E** S", the prediction is incorrect if its tags "S **B E**", and is correct if its tags "**B E** S". The second case is that given the gold standard tags "S **B E**", the prediction is incorrect if its tags "**B E** S", and is correct if its tags "S **B E**". Notably, we do not count the case that is not one in two cases we describe. We present the error statistics for Vietnamese in Table 6. We can see that the contextual information from XLM-R helps both BiLSTM-CRF and our SPANSEG in reducing ambiguity. However, according to Table 3, the predicted word boundary information helps both BiLSTM-CRF and our SPANSEG in increasing overall performance but causes the overlapping ambiguity problem. Our SPANSEG (TAG) solves overlapping ambiguity better than BiLSTM-CRF (TAG) when utilizing predicted word boundary information. Lastly, we also provide error statistics for Chinese in Table 7. We can see that overlapping ambiguity is the crucial problem for both WMSEG [27] and our SPANSEG on MSR, PKU, and AS datasets.

Table 7. Error statistics of the overlapping ambiguity problem involving three consecutive tokens on five Chinese benchmark datasets. The symbols ✓ and ✗ denote predicting correctly and incorrectly, respectively.

WMSEG [27]	SPANSEG	MSR	PKU	AS	CITYU	CTB6
✗	✗	14	13	12	2	3
✓	✗	2	2	2	1	2
✗	✓	2	1	5	0	0

5 Conclusion

This paper proposes a span labeling approach, namely SPANSEG, for VWS. Straightforwardly, our approach encodes the n-gram information by using span representations. We evaluate our SPANSEG on the Vietnamese treebank dataset for the word segmentation task with the predicted word boundary information and the contextual pre-trained embedding from the XLM-RoBerta model. The experimental results on VWS show that our SPANSEG is better than BiLSTM-CRF when utilizing the predicted word boundary and contextual information with the state-of-the-art F-score of 98.31%. We also evaluate our SPANSEG on five Chinese benchmark datasets to verify our approach. Our SPANSEG achieves competitive or higher F-scores through experimental results, fewer parameters, and faster inference time than the previous state-of-the-art method, WMSEG. Lastly, we also show that overlapping ambiguity is a complex problem for VWS and CWS. Via the error analysis on the Vietnamese treebank dataset, we found that utilizing the predicted word boundary information causes overlapping ambiguity; however, our SPANSEG is better than BiLSTM-CRF in this case. Finally, our SPANSEG will be made available to the open-source community for further research and development.

References

1. Chen, X., Qiu, X., Zhu, C., Liu, P., Huang, X.: Long short-term memory neural networks for chinese word segmentation. In: Proceedings of EMNLP, pp. 1197–1206 (2015)
2. Chen, X., Shi, Z., Qiu, X., Huang, X.: Adversarial multi-criteria learning for chinese word segmentation. In: Proceedings of ACL, pp. 1193–1203 (2017)
3. Conneau, A., et al.: Unsupervised cross-lingual representation learning at scale. In: Proceedings of ACL, pp. 8440–8451 (2020)
4. Devlin, J., Chang, M.W., Lee, K., Toutanova, K.: BERT: pre-training of deep bidirectional transformers for language understanding. In: Proceedings of NAACL, pp. 4171–4186 (2019)
5. Diao, S., Bai, J., Song, Y., Zhang, T., Wang, Y.: ZEN: pre-training chinese text encoder enhanced by N-gram representations. In: Findings of EMNLP, pp. 4729–4740 (2020)
6. Dinh, D., Hoang, K., Nguyen, V.T.: Vietnamese word segmentation. In: Proceedings of the Sixth Natural Language Processing Pacific Rim Symposium, pp. 749–756 (2001)
7. Dozat, T., Manning, C.D.: Deep biaffine attention for neural dependency parsing. In: Proceedings of ICLR (2017)
8. Emerson, T.: The second international chinese word segmentation bakeoff. In: Proceedings of the Fourth SIGHAN Workshop on Chinese Language Processing (2005)
9. Gong, J., Chen, X., Gui, T., Qiu, X.: Switch-LSTMs for multi-criteria chinese word segmentation. In: Proceedings of AAAI, pp. 6457–6464 (2019)
10. Higashiyama, S., et al.: Incorporating word attention into character-based word segmentation. In: Proceedings of NAACL, pp. 2699–2709 (2019)
11. Ilya, L., Frank, H.: Decoupled weight decay regularization. In: Proceedings of ICLR (2019)
12. Ke, Z., Shi, L., Sun, S., Meng, E., Wang, B., Qiu, X.: Pre-training with meta learning for chinese word segmentation. In: Proceedings of NAACL, pp. 5514–5523 (2021)
13. Hông Phuong, L., Thi Minh Huyên, N., Roussanaly, A., Vinh, H.T.: A hybrid approach to word segmentation of vietnamese texts. In: Martín-Vide, C., Otto, F., Fernau, H. (eds.) LATA 2008. LNCS, vol. 5196, pp. 240–249. Springer, Heidelberg (2008). https://doi.org/10.1007/978-3-540-88282-4_23
14. Luu, T.A., Yamamoto, K.: Ung dụng phuong pháp Pointwise vào bài toán tách tu cho tieng Viet (2012). http://www.vietlex.com/xu-li-ngon-ngu/117-Ung_dung_phuong_phap_Pointwise_vao_bai_toan_tach_tu_cho_tieng_Viet
15. Ma, J., Ganchev, K., Weiss, D.: State-of-the-art chinese word segmentation with Bi-LSTMs. In: Proceedings of EMNLP, pp. 4902–4908 (2018)
16. Nguyen, C.T., Nguyen, T.K., Phan, X.H., Nguyen, L.M., Ha, Q.T.: Vietnamese word segmentation with CRFs and SVMs: an investigation. In: Proceedings of PACLIC, pp. 215–222. Tsinghua University Press (2006)
17. Nguyen, D.Q.: A neural joint model for Vietnamese word segmentation, POS tagging and dependency parsing. In: Proceedings of the The 17th Annual Workshop of the Australasian Language Technology Association, pp. 28–34 (2019)
18. Nguyen, D.Q., Nguyen, D.Q., Vu, T., Dras, M., Johnson, M.: A fast and accurate vietnamese word segmenter. In: Proceedings of LREC, pp. 2582–2587 (2018)
19. Nguyen, D.Q., Vu, T., Nguyen, D.Q., Dras, M., Johnson, M.: From word segmentation to POS tagging for vietnamese. In: Proceedings of the Australasian Language Technology Association Workshop 2017, pp. 108–113 (2017)
20. Nguyen, D.-V., Van Thin, D., Van Nguyen, K., Nguyen, N.L.-T.: Vietnamese word segmentation with SVM: ambiguity reduction and suffix capture. In: Nguyen, L.-M., Phan, X.-H., Hasida, K., Tojo, S. (eds.) PACLING 2019. CCIS, vol. 1215, pp. 400–413. Springer, Singapore (2020). https://doi.org/10.1007/978-981-15-6168-9_33

21. Nguyen, P.T., Vu, X.L., Nguyen, T.M.H., Nguyen, V.H., Le, H.P.: Building a large syntactically-annotated corpus of vietnamese. In: Proceedings of the Third Linguistic Annotation Workshop (LAW III), pp. 182–185 (2009)
22. Nguyen, T.P., Le, A.C.: A hybrid approach to Vietnamese word segmentation. In: Proceeding of IEEE-RIVF, pp. 114–119 (2016)
23. Qiu, X., Pei, H., Yan, H., Huang, X.: A concise model for multi-criteria chinese word segmentation with transformer encoder. In: Findings of EMNLP, pp. 2887–2897 (2020)
24. Song, Y., Guo, J., Cai, D.: Chinese word segmentation based on an approach of maximum entropy modeling. In: Proceedings of the Fifth SIGHAN Workshop on Chinese Language Processing, pp. 201–204 (2006)
25. Stern, M., Andreas, J., Klein, D.: A minimal span-based neural constituency parser. In: Proceedings of ACL, pp. 818–827 (2017)
26. Sun, M., Shen, D., Tsou, B.K.: Chinese word segmentation without using lexicon and hand-crafted training data. In: Proceedings of ACL-COLING, pp. 1265–1271 (1998)
27. Tian, Y., Song, Y., Xia, F., Zhang, T., Wang, Y.: Improving chinese word segmentation with wordhood memory networks. In: Proceedings of ACL, pp. 8274–8285 (2020)
28. Tseng, H., Chang, P., Andrew, G., Jurafsky, D., Manning, C.: A conditional random field word segmenter for sighan bakeoff 2005. In: Proceedings of the Fourth SIGHAN Workshop on Chinese Language Processing (2005)
29. Wang, C., Xu, B.: Convolutional neural network with word embeddings for chinese word segmentation. In: Proceedings of IJCNLP, pp. 163–172 (2017)
30. Xu, J., Sun, X.: Dependency-based gated recursive neural network for chinese word segmentation. In: Proceedings of ACL, pp. 567–572 (2016)
31. Xue, N., Xia, F., Chiou, F.D., Palmer, M.: The penn chinese treebank: phrase structure annotation of a large corpus. Nat. Lang. Eng. 11(2), 207–238 (2005)
32. Zhang, M., Zhang, Y., Fu, G.: Transition-based neural word segmentation. In: Proceedings of ACL, pp. 421–431 (2016)
33. Zhang, Y., Zhou, H., Li, Z.: Fast and accurate neural CRF constituency parsing. In: Proceedings of IJCAI, pp. 4046–4053 (2020)
34. Zhou, H., Yu, Z., Zhang, Y., Huang, S., Dai, X., Chen, J.: Word-context character embeddings for chinese word segmentation. In: Proceedings of EMNLP, pp. 760–766 (2017)

VSEC: Transformer-Based Model for Vietnamese Spelling Correction

Dinh-Truong Do[1]([✉]), Ha Thanh Nguyen[2], Thang Ngoc Bui[1], and Hieu Dinh Vo[1]

[1] VNU University of Engineering and Technology, Hanoi, Vietnam
{17021090,thangbn,hieuvd}@vnu.edu.vn
[2] Japan Advanced Institute of Science and Technology, Ishikawa, Japan
nguyenhathanh@jaist.ac.jp

Abstract. Spelling error correction is one of topics which have a long history in natural language processing. Although previous studies have achieved remarkable results, challenges still exist. In the Vietnamese language, a state-of-the-art method for the task infers a syllable's context from its adjacent syllables. The method's accuracy can be unsatisfactory, however, because the model may lose the context if two (or more) spelling mistakes stand near each other. In this paper, we propose a novel method to correct Vietnamese spelling errors. We tackle the problems of mistyped errors and misspelled errors by using a deep learning model. The embedding layer, in particular, is powered by the byte pair encoding technique. The sequence to sequence model based on the Transformer architecture makes our approach different from the previous works on the same problem. In the experiment, we train the model with a large synthetic dataset, which is randomly introduced spelling errors. We test the performance of the proposed method using a realistic dataset. This dataset contains 11,202 human-made misspellings in 9,341 different Vietnamese sentences. The experimental results show that our method achieves encouraging performance with 86.8% errors detected and 81.5% errors corrected, which improves the state-of-the-art approach 5.6% and 2.2%, respectively.

Keywords: Vietnamese spell correction · Deep learning · Subword level · Vietnamese realistic dataset

1 Introduction

Spelling error correction [4] is an important task, which aims to detect and correct spelling errors in a document. It is used for a variety of natural language applications, including search queries [1,6,10], message filtering systems [7,23,24], and optical character recognition (OCR) [16,19,20]. In this paper, we consider Vietnamese spelling correction in general.

In most cases, there are two kinds of errors in the Vietnamese language: mistyped errors and misspelled errors [11]. Mistyped errors are errors that occur during the typing process. The majority of these mistakes are caused by the

© Springer Nature Switzerland AG 2021
D. N. Pham et al. (Eds.): PRICAI 2021, LNAI 13032, pp. 259–272, 2021.
https://doi.org/10.1007/978-3-030-89363-7_20

typist's unintentional actions, such as pressing the wrong key between two adjacent characters on the keyboard. Furthermore, these errors typically stop at the syllable level, and they can be detected if the typist carefully reviews the text. Mistyped errors can be classified into two smaller categories: non-word errors and real-word errors. Non-word errors mean that the words completely do not exist in the dictionary. Real-word errors, on the other hand, are errors that the words that are still in the dictionary but used in the wrong contexts.

A misspelled error is one that the typists did not realize was incorrect. This type of error is caused by regional pronunciation mistakes or the difficulty of some Vietnamese words. Compared to mistyped errors, misspelled errors are harder to detect since we not only need to rely on the context but also have knowledge of the standard dialect to detect these errors. Table 1 shows some examples of spelling errors in Vietnamese.

Table 1. Examples of Vietnamese spelling errors.

Non-word mistyped	Original: **Trời** hôm nay đẹp quá. Today's **???** is so beautiful. Correct: **Trời** hôm nay đẹp quá Today's **weather** is so beautiful.
Real-word mistyped	Original: **Sướng** còn đọng trên lá. **Pleasure** remains on the leaves. Correct: **Sương** còn đọng trên lá. **Dew lingers** remains on the leaves
Misspelled	Original: Thuyền của tôi đang **leo** trong bến. My boat **is climbing** in the dock Correct: Thuyền của tôi đang **neo** trong bến. My boat **is anchored** in the dock.

Spelling error correction is a problem that has received a lot of attention from the natural language processing community. In the Vietnamese language, there were a large number of studies approaching this problem by adopting statistical language models [9, 12–14], such as N-gram. These traditional models learn the context by training on a large dataset. This method, however, has its limitation: the context of a syllable can only be grasped by the adjacent syllables. For sentences that have two or more spelling mistakes next to each other, it is harder for the model to identify errors. In recent years, the application of deep learning models to the Vietnamese spelling check is a new trend that interests researchers [11]. The advantage of this approach is that the context of a syllable is not constrained by surrounding syllables, allowing the model to detect spelling errors more accurately. Although some positive results have been obtained, almost all studies on this method primarily focus on correcting certain types of spelling errors, making it difficult to apply in the real world.

In this paper, we propose a subword-level Transformer based model for Vietnamese spelling correction and evaluate it with a realistic dataset. The contributions of the paper include:

- A deep learning method for Vietnamese spelling correction, where both mistyped errors and misspelled errors are considered;
- A process of generating Vietnamese spelling errors, which artificially add errors to a non-error sentence; this process is used to produce a large number of artificial mistakes for deep learning models to learn from;
- A public dataset of human-made spelling errors, which includes 9,341 sentences in 4,582 different types of errors; this dataset is a benchmark for evaluating various approaches.

The rest of the paper is organized as follows. The next section briefly introduces some related works. Section 3 details each step of the proposed method. Section 4 presents the experimental results of the models, and we draw some conclusions in Sect. 5.

2   Related Work

Spelling error correction is an essential part of natural language processing (NLP). In the Vietnamese language, many methods have been proposed for this problem. Previous approaches can be primarily divided into two categories. One employs traditional statistical language models and the other uses machine learning.

In 2008, Phuong H. Nguyen et al. [12] proposed a statistical method that used POS Bigram (Part Of Speech Bigram) to detect suspected syllables. Minimum Edit Distance and SoundEx algorithms have been applied to generate suggestion candidates in the correcting phase. To rank these candidates, some heuristics in relevant criteria are also used.

Nguyen Thi Xuan Huong et al. [9] developed an N-gram language model for Vietnamese spell correction. A large unlabeled dataset is used to learn the context of syllables. Specifically, the N-gram score for each syllable in the candidate set is calculated based on the frequency of occurrence in unigram, bigram, and trigram. The model creates the candidate set based on changing characters in syllables corresponding to typing errors, consonant errors, etc. The current syllable is considered an error if a syllable in the candidate set has a higher N-gram score than the current one. This approach is currently state-of-the-art with approximately 94% F1 score on their experimental data.

By detecting and correcting spelling errors, Nguyen Hong Vu et al. [14] proposed a method to normalize Vietnamese tweets. The words with spelling errors were detected based on a dictionary. The model corrected the errors by combining the Vietnamese vocabulary structure with a language model based on improved Dice and SRILM (A language model).

Spelling error correction is an important step in improving the accuracy of OCR-generated text. For Vietnamese OCR errors, Quoc-Dung Nguyen et al. [13] developed an approach for generating and scoring correction candidates based on linguistic features. The spelling errors will be detected based on the unigram, bigram, and trigram dictionaries. After the detecting phase, a candidate set for each syllable error will be generated by applying insertion, deletion, and substitution operators. The candidates with high score which is calculated based on linguistic features such as Syllable Similarity, Bigram frequency, Trigram frequency, and Edit Probability will be included in the suggestion list.

In 2018, Nguyen Ha Thanh et al. [11] proposed a deep learning method to solve Vietnamese consonant misspell errors. To identify and correct error positions, the model employs misspell direction encoding and bidirectional stacked LSTM architecture.

Spelling error correction can be formulated as a problem of translating a misspelling sequence to a corrected one. This type of problem can be solved with typical methods used for machine translation. Some researchers have applied Neural Machine Translation (NMT) models [2,8,25] to correct spelling errors in popular languages such as English and Chinese. Their positive results demonstrate that this is a viable solution to the problem of spelling error correction.

One of challenges with NMT is the out-of-vocabulary problem. Increasing the model's vocabulary size is a simple way to solve this problem. However, if the vocabulary is too large, the dimension of the vector embedding will be too high. It increases the computation time and adds complexity to the model's training. To address this problem, some studies [3,18] applied Byte Pair Encoding (BPE), which tokenizes sentences at subword level [17]. This technique keeps input length to a reasonable level while handling unseen and rare words.

3   Methodology

3.1   Problem Statement

Vietnamese spelling correction can be formulated as follows. Given a set of syllable sequences $X = \{x^i = (x_1^i, x_2^i ..., x_n^i)\}$ with some errors in x^i, and a set of syllable sequences $Y = \{y^i = (y_1^i, y_2^i ..., y_m^i)\}$, where y^i is error-free. The goal is to transform each sequence x^i into corresponding sequence y^i. Following that, the task can be considered as a problem of learning a function $f: X \rightarrow Y$ that satisfies $f(x^i) = y^i$.

3.2   Model Overview

The state-of-the-art method for Vietnamese spelling correction is to use a statistical language model. Although the method is trainable on a large dataset, it uses a limited context. This motivates us to create a new model which exploits broad context.

Figure 1 illustrates an overview of our proposed model, called VSEC, in training and testing processes. The pipeline of VSEC is composed of three components: a preprocessing module, a tokenization module, and a Transformer-based model. The original data is first preprocessed to remove any noise that might appear in the sentence. The BPE tokenizer then converts each sentence into a sequence of tokens. Finally, the Data Loader feeds the sequence into the Transformer-based model for training.

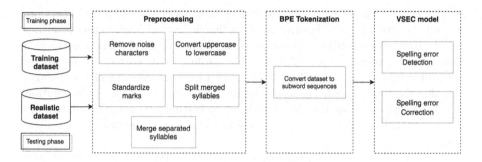

Fig. 1. Model pipeline

3.3 Preprocessing

To ensure that the results are reliable, data quality assurance is critical. Each input sequence needs to be removed noise before proceeding to the next phase. Our preprocessing module, in particular, consists of five steps:

- **Step 1: Remove noise characters** - In this step, we remove characters that are not useful for learning the context of a sentence such as emojis, line break characters.
- **Step 2: Convert uppercase to lowercase** - Using both upper and lower case can affect the model's data density. Therefore, all uppercase characters are converted to lowercase.
- **Step 3: Standardize marks** - In this step, each syllable is converted to the syllable in the telex typing form. Following that, the data is standardized using a mapping set between the telex syllable and the correct mark syllable. *For example: Syllable " "cuả" " => Telex syllable "cuar" => Standardized syllable " "của" ".*
- **Step 4: Split merged syllables** - The appearance of merged syllables in the dataset may have a detrimental effect on the model's learning. We use the Peter Norvig word segmentation algorithm to solve this problem [15]. When syllables are merged in the Vietnamese language, they transform into the syllables in the telex typing form. This occurs as a result of the Vietnamese typing tools' mechanism. Therefore, while calculating probability using the Peter Norvig algorithm, it is critical to convert the telex syllable to the standard Vietnamese syllable.

- **Step 5: Merge separated syllables** - A syllable that has spaces between its characters is known as a separated syllable. The model is also more difficult to converge due to the appearance of these strange syllables. To solve this problem, we employ the Trie structure [21], which has demonstrated its ability to browse prefixes.

3.4   Tokenization

In Vietnamese, each space-separated token is in monosyllabic form. Therefore, we call the word level in English as the syllable level in Vietnamese from now on. At first glance, using syllable level as the input seems like a good idea. However, this level is not well suited for spelling error correction, as we can have difficulties with misspelling syllables or rare syllables (out of vocabulary). It makes the model harder to learn the sentence's context. One of the solutions to this problem is to use the character level. Nevertheless, breaking syllables into characters will increase the sequence length. As a result, the model is large and slow to converge.

Subword level is between syllable level and character level. It keeps the input length at a reasonable level while addressing the out-of-vocabulary problem. For example, we can split a Vietnamese misspelling syllable "nghành" into two tokens: "ngh" and "ành", and present "nghành" by vectors of these tokens. The BPE algorithm is used to construct a subword dictionary [17]. Given a large corpus, this tokenization technique groups characters into frequent sequences. It is totally unsupervised and requires no information about the context of the sentence. An example of how BPE obtains vocabulary from raw text is shown in Table 2.

Table 2. An example of how BPE obtains vocabulary given a raw sequence

Iteration	Sequence	Vocabulary
0	a t e /w a t /w	{a, t, e, /w}
1	at e /w at /w	{a, t, e, /w, at}
2	at e /w at/w	{a, t, e, /w, at, at/w}
3	at e/w at/w	{a, t, e, /w, at, at/w, e/w}
4	ate/w at/w	{a, t, e, /w, at, at/w, e/w, ate/w}

The algorithm of BPE is as follows. Firstly, a special token $/w$ is appended to each syllable to indicate the end position of a syllable. Then, we split all sentences in the corpus into characters. At this point, the vocabulary only contains single characters. After that, we iteratively count all token pairs and merge each occurrence of the most frequent pair (Y, Z) into a new token YZ and add it to the vocabulary. The size of the final vocabulary is equal to the total number of merge operations and initial characters. The number of merge operations is the only parameter of the BPE algorithm. We will have a large vocabulary if this number is large. An example of the BPE tokenization result is in Fig. 2.

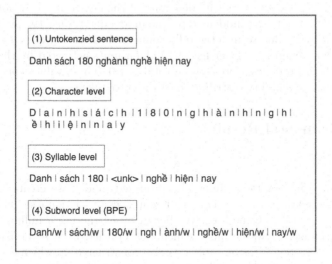

Fig. 2. Comparison of different tokenization levels. Tokens are separated by "|". "nghành" is not a Vietnamese syllable.

3.5   Transformer Model

Based on the idea of treating Vietnamese spelling error correction as a machine translation problem, the proposed model learns to translate the sentence having spelling errors to the corrected one. Specifically, we use the Seq2seq architecture based on Transformer [22] as our baseline. The Transformer encodes a misspelling sentence to a context hidden state using a stack of L encoder blocks, each of which employs a multi-head self-attention layer and a feed-forward network. The decoder uses the encoder's hidden states and the sequence of previous target tokens to generate the target hidden state by applying a stack of L decoder blocks. The decoder block has the same architecture as the encoder one, except it has an extra attention layer over the encoder's hidden states.

The goal of Transformer is to predict the next token y_t, given the source tokens $(x_1, x_2, ..., x_n)$. The formulas of this process are:

$$\mathbf{h}^{src}_{1..n} = encoder(\mathbf{E}^{src}_{x_{1..n}}) \tag{1}$$

$$\mathbf{h}_t = decoder(\mathbf{E}^{trg}_{y_{1..t-1}}, \mathbf{h}^{src}_{1..n}) \tag{2}$$

$$\mathbf{P}_t(w) = softmax(\mathbf{W}^T \mathbf{h}_t) \tag{3}$$

The embedding matrix is represented by $\mathbf{E} \in \mathbf{R}^{d \times |V|}$, where d is the embedding dimension, and $|V|$ is the size of the vocabulary. The value of x_i represents the position of the i-th token in the vocabulary. The encoder's hidden states are denoted by $\mathbf{h}_{1..n}^{src}$ and the target hidden state of the next token is denoted by $\mathbf{h}_t$. After obtaining the target hidden state, the model determines the next token to be generated by feeding $\mathbf{h}_t$ into the fully connected (dense) layer behind. Particularly, the fully connected layer has $|V|$ hidden units activated by the Softmax function, which produces scores whose total is 1.0. These values correspond to the generation probability distribution of the next token.

4 Experimental Results

4.1 Dataset

To generate a dataset for training the proposed model, we created a process for artificially adding errors to non-error sentences in Vietnamese. This process is referred to as Error Generator. We began by extracting 5 million sentences from a Vietnamese news corpus[1], which was crawled from several prominent Vietnamese websites. A fusion table was also constructed, in which each syllable is linked to a group of other candidates, to present common types of Vietnamese spelling errors such as mistyped errors, consonant errors. Then, at random, we selected 8% of the syllables in the sentences to artificially generate errors, with 90% of them being replaced with other syllables, 5% being removed, and 5% being duplicated. The difference between VSEC Error Generator and others is the use of add and delete operators, which represents errors when the typists often use copy and paste.

In addition, we developed a realistic dataset for testing. We sampled the contents of 618 documents at Tailieu[2], an educational material website. To ensure that the dataset includes a significant amount of incorrect sentences, we sampled documents from lower quality texts, and thus the error rate of the dataset higher. Three people handled three phases of labeling to carefully correct spelling errors in the texts. The dataset includes 9,341 sentences, which contain 11,202 spelling errors in 4,582 different types[3].

4.2 Evaluation Metric

We utilized syllable-level precision, recall, and F1 score which are common in the community [9,12,14]. In addition, we evaluated the accuracy of both detection and correction tasks. Specifically, we used six metrics:

$$Detection\ Precision = \frac{\#\ of\ true\ detections}{\#\ of\ error\ detected} \qquad (DP) \qquad (4)$$

---

[1] https://github.com/binhvq/news-corpus.
[2] https://tailieu.vn.
[3] https://github.com/VSEC2021/VSEC.

$$Detection\ Recall = \frac{\#\ of\ true\ detections}{\#\ of\ actual\ errors} \qquad (DR) \qquad (5)$$

$$Detection\ F1\text{-}score = \frac{2 * DR * DP}{DR + DP} \qquad (DF) \qquad (6)$$

$$Correction\ Precision = \frac{\#\ of\ true\ corrections}{\#\ of\ error\ detected} \qquad (CP) \qquad (7)$$

$$Correction\ Recall = \frac{\#\ of\ true\ corrections}{\#\ of\ actual\ errors} \qquad (CR) \qquad (8)$$

$$Correction\ F1\text{-}score = \frac{2 * CR * CP}{CR + CP} \qquad (CF) \qquad (9)$$

4.3 Experimental Setting

The BPE Tokenizer is used in the experiments based on HuggingFace's library.[4] Specifically, the BPE Tokenizer was trained on news corpus to build a subword-level vocabulary. We set the vocab size to 30,000 and kept other default hyperparameters.

In the training phase, we use Adam optimizer with Cross-Entropy Loss to train the neural network model with Transformer architecture. Through the experiment, the model achieved the best results with hyperparameters are shown in Table 3.

Table 3. Parameters

Parameters	Value
Embedding dimension	512
Sequence length	200
Number of head in multi-head attention	8
Number of encoder/decoder layers	3
Batch size	32
Learning rate	0.0003
Drop out rate	0.1

To conduct an informative experiment, we rebuild the N-gram model as a single baseline for comparison. Comparison to other approaches [11,13,14] is not conducted due to two main reasons. First, they are proposed for domains different from ours [13,14]. Some studies only focus on OCR spelling correction. Apparently, it is not directly comparable to the methods for general solutions

---

[4] https://github.com/huggingface/tokenizers.

like VSEC. Second, some studies primarily focus on a specific sort of Vietnamese spelling errors, such as consonant misspell errors [11]. Thus, it is unfair to compare VSEC with methods in these studies. For the above reasons, we evaluate and analyze the current state-of-the-art method, N-gram, to ensure fairness and generality of the experiment.

In addition, the BiLSTM Seq2seq model with attention mechanism and the Transformer models at different token levels are also trained and tested according to the same process. The Vietnamese news corpus is still being used to build these baseline methods.

4.4   Main Results

Table 4 shows the experimental results of all methods on the test dataset. From the table, we can see that the proposed model substantially outperforms the baseline methods. Particularly, in the detection phase, our proposed method performs much better than the baselines in terms of all metrics. The result for recall of correction task on the test dataset is greater than 76%, implying that more than 76% of errors will be fixed.

Table 4. Performances of Different Methods on Vietnamese spelling correction

Method	Detection			Correction		
	DP	DR	DF	CP	CR	CF
N-gram	0.912	0.731	0.812	**0.891**	0.714	0.793
Seq2seq with attention	0.310	0.752	0.439	0.222	0.539	0.315
Character-level Transformer	0.775	0.367	0.498	0.612	0.290	0.393
Syllable-level Transformer	0.719	0.776	0.746	0.636	0.686	0.661
VSEC	**0.931**	**0.813**	**0.868**	0.874	**0.763**	**0.815**

The N-gram method achieves the highest precision of correction because it can reduce false corrections by using an additional parameter, *error_threshold*. The use of this parameter is effective with more than 89% of precision in both evaluation criteria. However, precision and recall are a tradeoff. Increasing the precision of the N-gram method entails lowering the recall. On the other hand, the proposed method shows more balance, when the values of the precision and recall measurements are not significantly different. Specifically, the proposed method reaches 86.8% with the F1 score measure in the error detection task and 81.5% in the error correction task, while the N-gram method only reaches 81.2% and 79.3%, respectively.

For the methods of using Seq2seq architecture, the subword-level Transformer model performs better than the other baselines, while the method of the BiLSTM Seq2seq model with attention mechanism performs fairly poorly. This indicates that, despite ignoring traditional recurrent architectures, the Transformer-based models are still able to outperform the LSTM-based models. Furthermore, the subword-level model can beat the models at other token levels. This demonstrates that the subword-level model can handle the out of vocabulary problem better than one at the syllable level and it also performs effectively than the character-level model.

4.5 Effect of Hyperparameter

We also investigate the effect of the vocabulary size and the data size. Table 5 shows that the proposed method reaches its best performance with the data size is 5 million. This indicates that the more training data the higher performance can achieve.

Table 5. Impact of different sizes of training data

Training Set	Detection			Correction		
	DP	DR	DF	CP	CR	CF
500K	0.880	0.679	0.767	0.777	0.599	0.676
1M	0.896	0.729	0.804	0.817	0.665	0.733
2M	0.891	0.769	0.826	0.826	0.713	0.765
5M	**0.931**	**0.813**	**0.868**	**0.874**	**0.763**	**0.815**

A larger vocabulary size means fewer syllables split into two or more tokens. Table 6 presents the results of the proposed method in different values of the hyperparameter vocabulary size. The highest F1 score is obtained at the vocabulary size equal to 30,000. That is to say, having a larger vocabulary does not guarantee a higher F1 score.

Table 6. Impact of different values of vocabulary size

Vocabulary size	Detection			Correction		
	DP	DR	DF	CP	CR	CF
1K	0.886	0.585	0.705	0.771	0.509	0.613
10K	0.935	0.793	0.858	**0.878**	0.745	0.806
30K	0.931	**0.813**	**0.868**	0.874	**0.763**	**0.815**
50K	**0.937**	0.773	0.847	0.874	0.721	0.790

4.6 Discussion

We observed that the proposed method is able to make more effective use of context information than the N-gram method. When there are two or more errors next to each other in a sentence, N-gram usually detects one and leaves the others undetected. The proposed method, on the other hand, can detect both of the errors. For example, there are 2 two errors in the sentence "Chuẩn bị sãn sang hợp đồng ký kết" (Prepare the contract to be signed). The syllables "sãn" and "sang" are incorrect and they should be written as "sẵn" "sàng", which form a word meaning "ready". The N-gram method only corrects one syllable that is "sãn" while the proposed method can correct both of them. It is because the N-gram method relies on the context provided by nearby syllables, specifically two syllables before and two syllables after the target.

We also found that the proposed method has three major types of false detections. For statistics of errors, we sampled 100 false detections from the test set. We noticed that 32% of errors are foreign words and acronym words, 28% of errors are due to a lack of domain-specific knowledge, and the remaining 40% of errors have no specific type.

Foreign words and acronym words are the first type of false detection. These words are sometimes converted to Vietnamese syllables by the model. For example, in the sentence "TH đã luôn tiếp cận sản xuất theo chuỗi đồng cỏ sạch" (TH has always approached clean grassland chain production), the acronym word "TH" (a Vietnamese company) is converted to "Thì" syllable. This indicates that in order to make more reliable detections, the models must have a stronger way to determine what the special syllables are.

The second type of false detection is due to a lack of domain-specific knowledge. For example, in the sentence "Đồ thị của hàm số bậc hai" (Graph of quadratic function). The model turned the word "Đồ thị" (Graph) into "Đô thị" (City). This happens due to the fact that the test set is inclined to scholarly language while it is not much in the training data created from the news corpus. This problem is still very challenging for the existing model to determine this type of error.

5 Conclusions

In this paper, we propose a neural network approach for Vietnamese spelling correction. Our method is powered by applying a deep learning subword-level model based on Transformer. The technique of subword tokenization is general and potentially useful for dealing with the out-of-vocabulary problem. The Transformer model takes the sequence of subword tokens containing spelling errors as the source and the corrected one as the target. Experimental results on the realistic dataset show that our method outperforms the state-of-the-art model using the N-gram method. For further research, we plan to extend the Error Generator to capture more types of Vietnamese spelling errors and explore pre-trained models such as multilingual BERT [5] to apply to this task.

Acknowledgement. This work has been supported by Vietnam National University, Hanoi (VNU), under Project No. QG.18.61.

References

1. Ahmad, F., Kondrak, G.: Learning a spelling error model from search query logs. In: Proceedings of Human Language Technology Conference and Conference on Empirical Methods in Natural Language Processing, pp. 955–962 (2005)
2. Büyük, O.: Context-dependent sequence-to-sequence turkish spelling correction. ACM Trans. Asian Low-Resource Lang. Inform. Process. (TALLIP) **19**(4), 1–16 (2020)
3. Choudhary, H., Pathak, A.K., Saha, R.R., Kumaraguru, P.: Neural machine translation for english-tamil. In: Proceedings of the Third Conference on Machine Translation: Shared Task Papers, pp. 770–775 (2018)
4. Church, K.W., Gale, W.A.: Probability scoring for spelling correction. Stat. Comput. **1**(2), 93–103 (1991)
5. Devlin, J., Chang, M.W., Lee, K., Toutanova, K.: Bert: Pre-training of deep bidirectional transformers for language understanding. arXiv preprint arXiv:1810.04805 (2018)
6. Gao, J., Quirk, C., et al.: A large scale ranker-based system for search query spelling correction (2010)
7. Gong, H., Li, Y., Bhat, S., Viswanath, P.: Context-sensitive malicious spelling error correction. In: The World Wide Web Conference, pp. 2771–2777 (2019)
8. Gu, S., Lang, F.: A chinese text corrector based on seq2seq model. In: 2017 International Conference on Cyber-Enabled Distributed Computing and Knowledge Discovery (CyberC), pp. 322–325. IEEE (2017)
9. Thi Xuan Huong, N., Dang, T.-T., Nguyen, T.-T., Le, A.-C.: Using large N-gram for vietnamese spell checking. In: Nguyen, V.-H., Le, A.-C., Huynh, V.-N. (eds.) Knowledge and Systems Engineering. AISC, vol. 326, pp. 617–627. Springer, Cham (2015). https://doi.org/10.1007/978-3-319-11680-8_49
10. Li, M., Zhu, M., Zhang, Y., Zhou, M.: Exploring distributional similarity based models for query spelling correction. In: Proceedings of the 21st International Conference on Computational Linguistics and 44th Annual Meeting of the Association for Computational Linguistics, pp. 1025–1032 (2006)
11. Nguyen, H.T., Dang, T.B., Nguyen, L.M.: Deep learning approach for vietnamese consonant misspell correction. In: Nguyen, L.-M., Phan, X.-H., Hasida, K., Tojo, S. (eds.) PACLING 2019. CCIS, vol. 1215, pp. 497–504. Springer, Singapore (2020). https://doi.org/10.1007/978-981-15-6168-9_40
12. Nguyen, P.H., Ngo, T.D., Phan, D.A., Dinh, T.P., Huynh, T.Q.: Vietnamese spelling detection and correction using bi-gram, minimum edit distance, soundex algorithms with some additional heuristics. In: 2008 IEEE International Conference on Research, Innovation and Vision for the Future in Computing and Communication Technologies, pp. 96–102. IEEE (2008)
13. Nguyen, Q.D., Le, D.A., Zelinka, I.: Ocr error correction for unconstrained vietnamese handwritten text. In: Proceedings of the Tenth International Symposium on Information and Communication Technology, pp. 132–138 (2019)
14. Nguyen, V.H., Nguyen, H.T., Snasel, V.: Normalization of vietnamese tweets on Twitter. In: Abraham, A., Jiang, X.H., Snášel, V., Pan, J.-S. (eds.) Intelligent Data Analysis and Applications. AISC, vol. 370, pp. 179–189. Springer, Cham (2015). https://doi.org/10.1007/978-3-319-21206-7_16

15. Norvig, P.: Natural language corpus data. Beautiful Data, pp. 219–242 (2009)
16. Reynaert, M.W.: Character confusion versus focus word-based correction of spelling and ocr variants in corpora. Int. J. Document Anal. Recogn. (IJDAR) **14**(2), 173–187 (2011)
17. Sennrich, R., Haddow, B., Birch, A.: Neural machine translation of rare words with subword units. arXiv preprint arXiv:1508.07909 (2015)
18. Tacorda, A.J., Ignacio, M.J., Oco, N., Roxas, R.E.: Controlling byte pair encoding for neural machine translation. In: 2017 International Conference on Asian Language Processing (IALP), pp. 168–171. IEEE (2017)
19. Taghva, K., Stofsky, E.: Ocrspell: an interactive spelling correction system for ocr errors in text. Int. J. Document Anal. Recogn. **3**(3), 125–137 (2001)
20. Takahashi, H., Itoh, N., Amano, T., Yamashita, A.: A spelling correction method and its application to an ocr system. Pattern Recogn. **23**(3–4), 363–377 (1990)
21. Thue, A.: Uber die gegenseitige lage gleicher teile gewisser zeichenreihen. Kra. Vidensk. Selsk. Skrifer, I. Mat. Nat. Kl, pp. 1–67 (1912)
22. Vaswani, A., et al.: Attention is all you need. In: Advances in Neural Information Processing Systems, pp. 5998–6008 (2017)
23. Wint, Z.Z., Ducros, T., Aritsugi, M.: Spell corrector to social media datasets in message filtering systems. In: 2017 Twelfth International Conference on Digital Information Management (ICDIM), pp. 209–215. IEEE (2017)
24. Wint, Z.Z., Ducros, T., Aritsugi, M.: Non-words spell corrector of social media data in message filtering systems. Journal of Digital Information Management, vol. 16, no. 2 (2018)
25. Zhou, Y., Porwal, U., Konow, R.: Spelling correction as a foreign language. arXiv preprint arXiv:1705.07371 (2017)

What Emotion Is Hate? Incorporating Emotion Information into the Hate Speech Detection Task

Kosisochukwu Judith Madukwe$^{(\boxtimes)}$ (ID), Xiaoying Gao (ID), and Bing Xue (ID)

School of Engineering and Computer Science, Victoria University of Wellington,
P.O. Box 600, Wellington 6012, New Zealand
{kosisochukwu.madukwe,xiaoying.gao,bing.xue}@ecs.vuw.ac.nz

Abstract. Finding ethical, platform-independent, computationally efficient methods of adding contextual information to the hate speech detection task is difficult. Methods that rely only on the text for successful classification are of extreme importance. Emotion information extracted from text has been shown to be effective for sentiment analysis and thus we hypothesize that it could have a potential for hate speech. In this study, we propose several methods of introducing emotions into the task of hate speech detection. Using an emotion lexicon, we counter-fitted pre-trained word embeddings (Word2Vec, GloVe, FastText) and also generated a binary and a weighted emotional embedding vector. These were used as features for classification on four publicly available hate speech datasets. Our results and analysis demonstrate that the inclusion of emotion information especially anger, sadness, disgust, fear are helpful for hate speech detection.

Keywords: Hate speech detection · Emotion information · Emotion lexicon · Text classification · Word embedding · Natural language processing

1 Introduction

The detection of hateful speech (*"language that attacks or diminishes, that incites violence or hate against groups, based on specific characteristics"*) on social media platforms is an important task because the implications of the presence of hate speech translate negatively to real life. The research community has mostly framed this detection task as a text classification task, where given a sentence, a classification model decides if it's hateful or not depending on the sentences' innate features. Studies on feature extraction for hate speech detection have taken various forms, from n-grams to word embeddings to language models [4,16,17].

In a lot of text classification tasks, word embeddings are a staple feature. They are usually used as the first layer of a deep learning network. The word embedding of choice differs depending on the designer's preference or the task at hand. Popular choices are Word2Vec (W2V) [20], Glove (GLV) [26] and FastText (FT) [3]. The information learnt while creating these embeddings are transferred

© Springer Nature Switzerland AG 2021
D. N. Pham et al. (Eds.): PRICAI 2021, LNAI 13032, pp. 273–286, 2021.
https://doi.org/10.1007/978-3-030-89363-7_21

to the downstream task under consideration. In recent years, there have been some criticisms to the robustness of these embeddings for numerous downstream tasks. For instance, in the sentiment analysis task which houses negative and positive sentiment polarities, pre-trained word embedding based on co-occurrence and distributional theory might find it difficult to distinguish between synonyms and antonyms (two paradigms that belong to the negative and positive classes respectively). Therefore, some studies [10,25,32,34] have looked into various ways of improving/counter-fitting/retro-fitting existing embeddings to better suit specific downstream tasks with the help of external knowledge sources such as a lexicon. Using an existing embedding instead of training one from scratch is more computationally efficient, less time consuming and excellent for lack-of-data domains. In [34], they use a synonym and antonym lexicon to counter-fit the W2V embedding for the task of sentiment analysis. They coax synonymous words in a word representation model to move closer to one another and antonymous words to move further away. Apart from lexical information, [10] used demographic information for retrofitting embedding for increasing within-class similarity.

It has been shown that hate speech is hard to detect without additional contextual information [12]. However, these additional contextual information are difficult to extract, can be platform dependent, or severely go against ethical norms. Therefore, better sources of contextual information are required. We hypothesise that emotion information could be an excellent source. This is because, as has been shown in literature [1,2,8,19,30], emotions are pertinent information that exists in and can be extracted from hateful text. However, not all the emotion types are "hateful" emotions and thus have the potential to negatively affect or be passive in improving the performance. In [1], they demonstrated that tweets from suspended accounts showed more disgust, fear, sadness emotions. Also, they showed that negative sentiment were higher in tweets that were deemed neutral than tweets deemed hateful from active accounts. Thus, the presence of negative sentiment does not always translate to "hateful" emotions. Therefore, more investigations are needed in using emotions for the task of detecting hate speech in text.

Hence, we propose and investigate the use of specific emotions without using sentiment polarities for including emotion information into the hate speech detection task. The overall aim of this work is to demonstrate how the incorporation of emotion information affects the task of hate speech detection. Specifically, we design linguistic constraints to support the hypothesis and we compare the performance of the proposed methods to the baselines (pre-trained regular embeddings [3,20,27] and existing studies in [8,19,31]. The specific goals of this work are to:

- Propose new methods of incorporating emotion information into the task of detecting textual hate speech and evaluate their performance on four hate speech datasets.
- Design an appropriate emotion linguistic constraint for the embedding refinement process.

- Evaluate the impact of using particular "hateful" emotions for detecting hate in text with and without a classification task.
- Compare the performance of using all eight emotions and sentiment polarities to the performance of a reduced emotion set.

The rest of this paper is organized as follows: Sect. 2 provides a background and an overview of related literature. Section 3 describes the proposed approaches and methods. Section 4 discusses the chosen experiment design while Sect. 5 shows the results and analysis. Section 6 concludes the work and highlights limitations and future plans.

2 Background and Related Work

Distributional word representations [3,20,26] are a very crucial aspect of a lot of natural language processing tasks. These representations assume that similar words appear in the same context. This similarity could be a semantic or relatedness similarity. Despite their success in many intrinsic and downstream tasks, these representations are limited by the fact that they depend on co-occurrence information which in turn conflates or confuses "semantic similarity" and "conceptual association" [9]. This issue has been tackled by studies such as [13]. A limitation that still persisted is the inability of these representations to distinguish between synonyms and antonyms or more generally, words that co-occur in texts and thus have similar context but have different relationships. Hence, words will be considered as similar to their antonyms in these vector representation spaces. To combat this, post-processing vector space specialization methods [25,31–33], which aims to pull representations of desired words in one group together and push undesired/unrelated words in the other group away from themselves, were developed. These methods can be applied to an already pre-trained embedding vectors.

Emotion information has been used in hateful and abusive language detection studies in a few different ways. In [29], they used a multitask learning approach to incorporate emotion into the abusive language detection. The abuse detection task was the primary task and the emotion detection task was the auxiliary task. No external lexicons were used. The study in [30] captured emotions for detecting abusive language from emojis in the text. The study in [19] used the NRC emotion lexicon [22]. They generated an 8-d representation which was added to negative and positive sentiment polarity binary vector, anger emotion intensity vector and other vectors to provide a 14-d feature. In [8], they used the NRC emotion lexicon to generate a 10-d (positive and negative sentiment polarities and Plutchik's [28] eight emotion types) emotional vector which was used as input into a logistic regression model. The study in [11] showed the effectiveness of retro-fitting or counter-fitting while using domain specific embedding and a sentiment lexicon. In our work, we used a pre-trained embeddings which we postulate is computationally less expensive as it does not require a domain specific fine-tuning. Our method counter-fits pre-trained embeddings using only specific emotions proven to be hate related. Also we do not use negative and positive sentiment polarities.

3   The Proposed Approach

Different methods of incorporating emotion information into pre-trained 300-dimensional (300-d) distributed representations of words (word embeddings) - Word2Vec, GloVe, FastText for hate speech detection are proposed and evaluated. They can be divided into three major categories. The first category is the counter-fitting method. Counter-fitting has been shown as a computationally effective method of introducing external information into an embedding space. The second category is a horizontal concatenation, which contrary to the first category does not require additional training or refining of an embedding space thus, is more computationally efficient. The third category exploits the power of ensembles. This category offers the least amount of interaction between the pre-trained embeddings and the emotion information. These are depicted in Fig. 1 and described in detail below.

(A) First, we counter-fit an existing pre-trained word embedding using an external lexical resource. The counter-fitting technique is based on Mrkšić's' [25] model because it is closely related to our counter-fitting objective functions. Generally, the aim of Mrkšić's' model is to improve the capability of a vector space representation of words' semantic similarity inference by introducing antonymy and synonymy constraints into the said space. It uses a three-termed objective function which are Antonym Repel (pushes antonymous word vectors away from each other), Synonym Attract (pushes known synonymous words pairs closer) and Vector Space Preservation (preserves original semantic information by bending the transformed vector space towards the original). We refer the readers to [25] for more details.

The choice of the lexical resource depends on the purpose of the downstream task. In this work, we use NRC emotion lexicon since the emotion information is the key factor while carrying out the task of this paper, i.e. to harness the emotions in text as pertinent contextual information for detecting hateful speech. The NRC emotion lexicon created by [22] contains 14k English words. Each word has at least one of the eight emotions from Plutchik's [28] model of basic emotions - *joy, trust, fear, surprise, sadness, disgust, anger, anticipation*.

To create the linguistic constraints from the NRC emotion lexicon [22,23], we select only words that have at least one indication to the presence of either disgust, fear, anger and sadness emotion as opposed to the pre-trained emotional embedding [31] that used all 8 emotions in the Plutchik's emotion model for counter-fitting. The *emotion attract* constraint contains word pairs we intend to push together while the *emotion repel* constraint contains word pairs we intend to push further apart. The *emotion attract* constraint is represented by word pairs (w_i, e_i). Each word left in the lexicon after dropping the "positive" emotion (*joy, trust, surprise, anticipation*) words, will become w_i and its corresponding emotion will make up the second part of the word pair e_i. For example; the word *cry* is associated with the emotion *sadness* from the lexicon. The constraint will become (*cry, sadness*).

Similarly, the *emotion repel* constraint word pairs are represented as (w_i', e_i), where w_i' represents the antonym of w_i generated from NLTK [14] package. For example; the antonym of the word *cry* is *laugh*, the constraint will become (*laugh*, *sadness*). A single word can be associated with more than one emotion. In cases like this, multiple constraints are created for that word. For the *emotion attract* constraint, we created 4972 word pairs and the *emotion repel* constraint we created 1972 word pairs. This discrepancy is because not all words in the lexicon has its antonym present in the NLTK package. This method is denoted as **HateEmoEmb**. This method tests the performance of altering the pre-trained embedding with additional information.

(B) Using the NRC emotion lexicon, we generate a binary 8-d embedding for all the words present in the lexicon. Each dimension represents one of Plutchik's eight emotion. 1 represents an emotions' presence and 0 represents its absence. This was concatenated with each of the 3 pre-trained regular embeddings. This method is denoted as **EmbConcat8Bin** and will be compared to method A since the pre-trained embeddings are not altered here.

(C) Repeating the above but instead of a binary representation, we weight the vector with the emotion intensity score derived from NRC emotion intensity lexicon [21]. In this lexicon, each word and its emotion has a floating number score ranging from 0 to 1. A score of 1 implies that the word conveys the highest amount of that specific emotion while a 0 score implies that the word conveys the lowest amount of the specific emotion. This 8-d embedding was concatenated with each of the 3 pre-trained regular embedding. This is method denoted as **EmbConcat8Int** and will be compared with method B to determine if the binary information is more or less meaningful than the intensity information.

(D) Then, we repeat EmbConcat8Bin but instead of concatenating with a pre-trained embedding before feeding into the classification model, we feed the emotion and the pre-trained word embedding independently into the model in an ensemble manner. The emotional embeddings are fed into a dense layer and the word embedding is fed into a BiLSTM layer. Their outputs are then concatenated and fed into two more dense layers with the second one being the final layer. This method is denoted this **EmbEnsemble8Bin** and will be used to test the method of introducing the embedding into the classification model i.e. before or after concatenation. It will be compared with method B.

(E) Finally, we repeat EmbConcat8Int the same way as the EmbEnsemble8Bin above. This method is denoted as **EmbEnsemble8Int** and tests the same concept that method D does. It will be compared with method C.

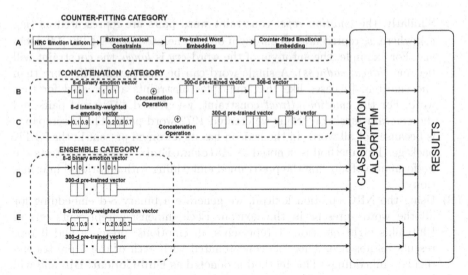

Fig. 1. Illustration showing proposed methods

4 Experiment Design

4.1 Description of Datasets

Hate speech datasets are often plagued with issues which will not be addressed in this work, however, they have been discussed in-depth in [5,18]. The datasets listed below are used as-is for this work with only basic pre-processing (removal of hashtags, usernames, punctuation, and URLS with lower-casing and lemmatization).

1. Davidson[1]: Approximately 25k instances from Twitter in English were labelled Hate, Offensive, or Neither hateful nor offensive [4]. It was made publicly available in text format with no prior train-test split. We randomly split it into Train/Validation/Test sets with ratio 70:15:15.
2. Founta[2]: Approximately 80k instances from Twitter in English were made publicly available in TweetID format [6]. They were labelled Hateful, Abusive, or Normal and Spam with no prior train-test split. After preprocessing, we had about 15k sentences left. We also randomly split this data into Train/Validation/Test sets with ratio 70:15:15.
3. HatEval[3]: The data for the task consists of 9000 tweets in English for training, 1000 for development. For Train set, Class 0 (Hate) has 5217 samples while Class 1 (Non-Hate) has 3783 samples. For the Development Set, Class 0 (Hate) has 573 samples while Class 1 (Non-Hate) has 427 samples. It was

---

[1] https://github.com/t-davidson/hate-speech-and-offensive-language.

[2] https://dataverse.mpi-sws.org/dataset.xhtml?persistentId=doi:10.5072/FK2/ ZDTEMN.

[3] https://competitions.codalab.org/competitions/19935.

curated to predict if a tweet is hateful or not hateful with a particular target (women or immigrants). We randomly split the train set 85:15 to make a validation set and used the development set as the test set.

4. Ethos[4]: This contains 998 comments from YouTube and Reddit in the dataset labelled to either contain hate speech or not [24]. 565 comments are labelled as non hateful while 433 comments are labelled as hateful. It has no prior train-test split. We use 10-fold cross-validation here as was used in the original paper.

5   Results

The classification results when the derived representations were input into a 1-layer BiLSTM network are shown in Table 1. Each reported score is the average of 30 independent runs except for Ethos dataset, where we report the 10 fold cross-validated result. The value in superscript indicates the standard deviation. We use Macro-F1 score for measuring performance because the datasets (Davidson and Founta) are severely unbalanced. Each block in Table 1. contains results for each specific word embedding (W2V, GLV, FT) and its counter-fitted, concatenated or ensemble counterpart. Note that when we refer to pre-trained embeddings (W2V, GLV, FT) collectively we use X_{WGF}. Our experiments have 12 settings i.e. 3 pre-trained regular embeddings with 4 datasets. Overall, the emotion-incorporated methods outperform the methods without emotion information. This is a clear indication that an emotion incorporated representation can improve the detection of hate speech.

For Davidson data, across all three embedding types and their derivatives, method D outperforms. For Founta data, method D outperforms for W2V and FT while method E outperforms for GLV. For HatEval, method B is the best for W2V and FT respectively while method A outperformed for GLV. For Ethos, method E outperformed for GLV and FT while method C outperformed for W2V. Overall, method D had a superior performance for 5 out of 12 settings followed by method E best performing for 3 out of 12 settings. Therefore, 8 out of 12 times, the best performance was by an ensemble of 8-d emotional embedding and 300-d pre-trained embedding. Hence, the results suggest that the ensemble method of incorporating emotion into this task has a higher impact than other methods. The ρ-values from a Friedman test [7] with $\alpha = 0.05$ for each block are reported in italics in Table 1. This shows that there is a significant difference between the methods for 6 out of 12 settings.

Previously, in Sect. 3, we highlighted the concept each one of our proposed method was intended to test for. Here, we discuss the results of these tests using the W2V section only for the four datasets. First, we compare methods A and B. There is no consensus or significant difference between the two methods. Therefore, we can conclude that altering the pre-trained embedding vectors and concatenating emotional information to the pre-trained embedding both have a similar prowess for this task. Next, we compare methods B and C. The results

---

[4] https://github.com/intelligence-csd-auth-gr/Ethos-Hate-Speech-Dataset.

Table 1. Classification results for 4 datasets using W2V, GLV and FT. **A**: X_{WGF}_HateEmoEmb is the hate-only emotional embedding vectors, **B**: X_{WGF}_EmbConcat8Bin is the pre-trained 300-d word embedding concatenated with the 8-d binary emotional embedding from NRC lexicon, **C**: X_{WGF}_EmbConcat8Int is the pre-trained 300-d word embedding concatenated with the 8-d intensity emotional embedding from NRC lexicon, **D**: X_{WGF}_EmbEnsemble8Bin is the ensemble of 8-d emotion binary vector and 300-d embedding vector, **E**: X_{WGF}_EmbEnsemble8Int is the ensemble of 8-d emotion intensity vector and 300-d embedding vector. X_{WGF} refers to the name of the pre-trained embedding of choice. ↑ represents a significant difference in the block

	DAVIDSON	FOUNTA	HATEVAL	ETHOS
–	Macro-F1	Macro-F1	Macro-F1	Macro-F1
W2V	$0.7078^{0.007}$	$0.4994^{0.008}$	$0.7236^{0.007}$	$0.7308^{0.055}$
A	$0.6786^{0.012}$	$0.4542^{0.025}$	$0.7239^{0.009}$	$0.6827^{0.052}$
B	$0.6909^{0.011}$	$0.4076^{0.013}$	$\mathbf{0.7263^{0.008}}$	$0.6153^{0.076}$
C	$0.6919^{0.012}$	$0.4150^{0.019}$	$0.7139^{0.008}$	$\mathbf{0.7376^{0.057}}$
D	$\mathbf{0.7307^{0.005}}$	$\mathbf{0.5068^{0.011}}$	$0.7248^{0.008}$	$0.7321^{0.072}$
E	$0.7258^{0.005}$	$0.4801^{0.027}$	$0.7224^{0.006}$	$0.7242^{0.051}$
$\rho - value$	$0.0109\uparrow$	$0.0071\uparrow$	0.2392	$5.247e\text{-}5\uparrow$
GLV	$0.7231^{0.005}$	$0.5039^{0.007}$	$0.7203^{0.005}$	$0.7314^{0.066}$
A	$0.6824^{0.016}$	$0.4544^{0.024}$	$\mathbf{0.7307^{0.005}}$	$0.6942^{0.051}$
B	$0.6881^{0.012}$	$0.4039^{0.030}$	$0.7278^{0.005}$	$0.7276^{0.060}$
C	$0.6877^{0.014}$	$0.4081^{0.017}$	$0.7263^{0.006}$	$0.7397^{0.053}$
D	$\mathbf{0.7252^{0.005}}$	$0.4930^{0.013}$	$0.7166^{0.005}$	$0.7329^{0.058}$
E	$0.7206^{0.007}$	$\mathbf{0.5050^{0.012}}$	$0.7152^{0.005}$	$\mathbf{0.7472^{0.044}}$
$\rho - value$	$0.0006\uparrow$	0.1062	$0.0007\uparrow$	$0.0001\uparrow$
FT	$0.7028^{0.009}$	$0.4734^{0.017}$	$0.7286^{0.007}$	$0.7034^{0.0431}$
A	$0.6710^{0.023}$	$0.4650^{0.017}$	$0.7281^{0.007}$	$0.6810^{0.028}$
B	$0.7057^{0.007}$	$0.4076^{0.013}$	$\mathbf{0.7305^{0.005}}$	$0.7030^{0.045}$
C	$0.7009^{0.009}$	$0.4108^{0.012}$	$0.7120^{0.010}$	$0.7021^{0.054}$
D	$\mathbf{0.7282^{0.005}}$	$\mathbf{0.4939^{0.021}}$	$0.7273^{0.007}$	$0.6986^{0.052}$
E	$0.7274^{0.004}$	$0.4914^{0.014}$	$0.7267^{0.006}$	$\mathbf{0.7060^{0.041}}$
$\rho - value$	0.1048	0.6320	0.8382	0.0052

show that the intensity information is more informative than the binary information. However, the difference is not extremely significant and in the absence of one, the other can be implemented without a considerable decline in performance. For the method of introducing the embedding to the classification algorithm, we compare methods B and D. The results indicate that the ensemble method performs better than the concatenation method. This could be because the two feature sets do not interact constructively. Hence, the methods that allow

Table 2. Compare the best from our proposed methods (W2V) to AllEmoEmb (W2V) [31]. *superscript* indicates which method produced that score.

	DAVIDSON	FOUNTA	HATEVAL	ETHOS
–	Macro-F1	Macro-F1	Macro-F1	Macro-F1
Our Best(W2V)	**0.7307** [A]	**0.5068** [A]	**0.7263** [B]	0.7376 [C]
AllEmoEmb(W2V) [31]	0.6894	0.4232	0.7210	**0.7438**

Table 3. Compare our proposed methods (W2V) with [8] on Fox News User Comments Data.

	A	B	C	D	E	[8]
Macro-F1	0.458	0.604	0.613	0.612	**0.614**	0.600

each feature to be interpreted without interference from other features performs better. This same pattern is also found while comparing methods C and E.

Next, we discuss the comparisons between the performance of our proposed methods with methods in existing studies. The first study is [31] where they counter-fit existing embeddings with emotion information using all of Plutchik's eight emotions. This was not tested on any downstream classification tasks, therefore we apply the W2V pre-trained emotional embedding (AllEmoEmb) from the study on the four datasets used previously. The results in Table 2 show that our methods performs better in 3 out of 4 datasets.

The next study we compare with is [8] which proposes an ensemble of logistic regression and bi-LSTM models for abusive text detection. The logistic regression model contains word n-gram, an NRC emotion-based vector and a linguistic inquiry and word count feature. We use their data (Fox News User Comments) on our methods because it will provide a fairer comparison instead of attempting to re-implement their method. The results are shown in Table 3. We input only the comment part of their dataset into a bi-LSTM. We compare to their best performing ensemble where their input included the comments, the title and the username from the data. The results show that four of our methods (B, C, D, E) outperform the method in [8] that ensembled two classification models.

Finally, we compare with the work in [19]. They design features using the NRC lexicon for detecting hate speech. Because of some missing information such as a stopword list, pre-defined bi-grams and tri-grams and a changing Hatebase lexicon, we were unable to re-implement their proposed method for comparison. However, the authors graciously shared their dataset, which is an older version of the Davidson dataset containing 11273 samples. They informed us that they down-sampled to the size of the hate class to get a subset of 2459 samples. We used this subset on our methods for comparison. In their study, the authors reported per class precision and recall. We use this to calculate the macro-F1 for

Table 4. Compare our proposed methods (W2V) with [19] on a subset of Davidson data.

	A	B	C	D	E	[19]
Macro-F1	0.77	**0.80**	0.78	0.63	**0.80**	0.77

their best performing results and compare with ours in Table 4. The results show that 3 of our methods (B, C, E) outperform theirs while A performs comparably.

Overall, the size of the datasets and more importantly the imbalance in its classes seem to affect, to a large extent, the performance of methods. To further illustrate, for the original Davidson dataset (about 25k instances) the method D is the best performing while for the Davidson subset (about 11k instances) with an even further reduction in the hate class and hence, a further increase in the imbalance ratio, method D is the least performing. Thus, it is difficult to draw a stronger conclusion on which method(s) is unanimously the best choice. Nevertheless, methods B, C, D and E are strong contenders.

5.1 Further Analysis on the Counter-Fitted Embeddings (HateEmoEmb and AllEmoEmb)

In this analysis section, we attempt to analyse the embeddings without a classification task, in order to provide another viewpoint to the results. The analysis looks into the HateEmoEmb and AllEmoEmb embeddings to further highlight their performance and to compare them.

During the counter-fitting process, we noticed a vast reduction in the vocabulary size of the resulting counter-fitted embedding. This occurrence was most likely due to the small size of the linguistic constraint used. To demonstrate, the original pre-trained W2V has a vocabulary size of approximately 400k while the HateEmoEmb (W2V_A/Ours) has a vocabulary size of approximately 79k. Interestingly, they outperform or perform competitively with the much larger vocabulary sized embeddings. The vocabulary sizes of the GLV and FT counterparts also follow a similar trend. This further points to the usefulness of the incorporated emotion information.

Analysing the embedding without a classification task (Table 5), we measure the similarity between randomly selected words for the pre-trained embeddings, the pre-trained emotion embedding (AllEmoEmb) and the hate emotion counter-fitted embedding (HateEmoEmb) using cosine similarity. Words on the upper half of the table are required to be closer to one another while words on the lower half of the table are required to be far apart from one another. For cosine similarity scores, the closer the score is to 1, the closer or more similar the words are in the embedding vector space. From Table 5, it is clear that the HateEmoEmb (W2V_A/Ours) vectors have higher cosine similarity for the upper half of the table and a lower cosine similarity for the lower half of the table across all the embeddings. This demonstrates that this embedding successfully pushed the words associated with the emotions of interest closer together and their unrelated words far apart even better than the W2V-based AllEmoEmb vector space did. GLV and FT also follow a similar trend.

The next analysis without a classification task, involves t-distributed stochastic neighbor embedding (tSNE) [15] plots of the embeddings. The plots shown in Figs. 2, 3 and 4 (for W2V only) also support the results in Table 5. More specifically, we can see that the words related to "negative" emotions are mixed in with the words related to the "positive" emotions for the original pre-trained embeddings. There is no clear divide. One interesting discovery was even though the two sets of words were mixed, the words *"disgust"*, *"fear"*, *"sadness"*, *"anger"* were close together. For the emotion counter-fitted embedding vector spaces, the demarcation between the two sets of words becomes even clearer. For AllEmoEmb (Fig. 3), there is a clear demarcation except one or two rouge words while for the HateEmoEmb (Fig. 4), the demarcation is much more clearer. This shows that the counter-fitting was successful in moving emotionally similar words closer together in the embedding space. Contrary to the observation for the original pre-trained embedding tSNEs, the words *"disgust"*, *"fear"*, *"sadness"*, *"anger"* were not close together even though they were separate from the other set. GLV and FT (not shown for space reasons) show consistent results too.

Table 5. Cosine Similarity Scores for embedding vectors from W2V, W2V_AllEmoEmb [31], HateEmoEmb (W2V_A/Ours). We want the top half to have a higher cosine similarity and the bottom half to have a lower cosine similarity. GLV and FT also follow a similar trend

word1	word2	W2V	[31]	Ours
wound	fear	0.032	0.010	**0.940**
horror	disgust	0.428	0.412	**0.953**
idiotic	anger	0.214	0.770	**0.965**
normal	disgust	0.014	0.183	**−0.041**
unarmed	fear	0.098	0.160	**−0.062**
flatter	anger	−0.017	0.101	**−0.060**

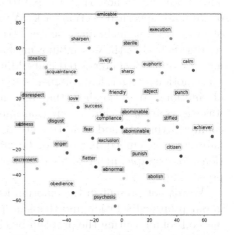

Fig. 2. Pre-trained Word Embedding (W2V)

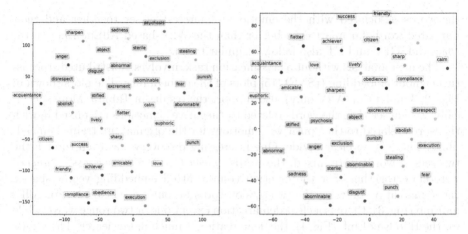

Fig. 3. W2V_AllEmoEmb [31]   **Fig. 4.** HateEmoEmb (W2V_A/Ours)

6   Conclusion

This study shows how the incorporation of emotion improves the performance
of the hate speech detection task. We proposed and evaluated many methods
of incorporation including counter-fitting, concatenation and ensembling. The
results show that the ensembling method is superior than the rest. Our further
analysis on the counter-fitted embedding also showed that using specific "hateful" emotions (anger, fear, disgust, sadness) were more effective than using a host
of emotions. We also show that our tailor-made emotion linguistic constraint
was successful in including emotion information into the embedding during the
counter-fitting method. Additionally, due to the considerably smaller size of the
hate emotion embedding, it can be efficiently used in space-constraint situations, for example, in a real-life detection of online hate speech that requires fast
processing.

Words not present in the emotion lexicon we used will lack a representation
in our proposed solution and this is a limitation. Future studies will investigate
methods of alleviating the problem by either updating the un-represented words
during counter-fitting or increasing the coverage of the lexicon. Future endeavors
will also involve discovering other types of information that can serve as a source
of context for improving hate speech detection. Finally, note that this study used
only a shallow neural network and we believe that a deeper neural network design
might produce even better results.

References

1. Alorainy, W., Burnap, P., Liu, H., Javed, A., Williams, M.L.: Suspended accounts: a source of tweets with disgust and anger emotions for augmenting hate speech data sample. In: 2018 International Conference on Machine Learning and Cybernetics (ICMLC), vol. 2, pp. 581–586 (2018)
2. Bilewicz, M., Soral, W.: Hate speech epidemic. the dynamic effects of derogatory language on intergroup relations and political radicalization. Political Psychol. **41**(S1), 3–33 (2020)
3. Bojanowski, P., Grave, E., Joulin, A., Mikolov, T.: Enriching word vectors with subword information (2017)
4. Davidson, T., Warmsley, D., Macy, M., Weber, I.: Automated hate speech detection and the problem of offensive language. In: Proceedings of the 11th International AAAI Conference on Web and Social Media, pp. 512–515. ICWSM '17 (2017)
5. Fortuna, P., Soler, J., Wanner, L.: Toxic, hateful, offensive or abusive? what are we really classifying? an empirical analysis of hate speech datasets. In: Proceedings of the 12th Language Resources and Evaluation Conference, pp. 6786–6794. ELRA, France (2020)
6. Founta, A.M., et al.: Large Scale Crowdsourcing and Characterization of Twitter Abusive Behavior (2018)
7. Friedman, M.: A comparison of alternative tests of significance for the problem of m rankings. Ann. Math. Statist. **11**(1), 86–92 (1940)
8. Gao, L., Huang, R.: Detecting online hate speech using context aware models. In: Proceedings of the International Conference Recent Advances in Natural Language Processing, RANLP 2017, pp. 260–266. INCOMA Ltd., Bulgaria (2017)
9. Hill, F., Reichart, R., Korhonen, A.: SimLex-999: evaluating semantic models with (genuine) similarity estimation. Comput. Linguist. **41**(4), 665–695 (2015)
10. Hovy, D., Fornaciari, T.: Increasing in-class similarity by retrofitting embeddings with demographic information. In: Proceedings of the 2018 Conference on Empirical Methods in Natural Language Processing, pp. 671–677. ACL, Belgium (2018)
11. Koufakou, A., Scott, J.: Lexicon-enhancement of embedding-based approaches towards the detection of abusive language. In: Proceedings of the Second Workshop on Trolling, Aggression and Cyberbullying, pp. 150–157. ELRA, France (2020)
12. Kwok, I., Wang, Y.: Locate the hate: detecting tweets against blacks. In: AAAI (2013)
13. Levy, O., Goldberg, Y.: Dependency-based word embeddings. In: Proceedings of the 52nd Annual Meeting of the Association for Computational Linguistics, pp. 302–308. ACL, Maryland (2014)
14. Loper, E., Bird, S.: Nltk: the natural language toolkit. In: Proceedings of the ACL-02 Workshop on Effective Tools and Methodologies for Teaching Natural Language Processing and Computational Linguistics - Volume 1, pp. 63–70. ETMTNLP '02, ACL, USA (2002)
15. van der Maaten, L., Hinton, G.: Visualizing data using t-sne. J. Mach. Learn. Res. **9**, 2579–2605 (2008)
16. Madukwe, K.J., Gao, X., Xue, B.: A ga-based approach to fine-tuning bert for hate speech detection. In: 2020 IEEE Symposium Series on Computational Intelligence (SSCI), pp. 2821–2828 (2020)
17. Madukwe, K.J., Gao, X.: The thin line between hate and profanity. In: 32nd Australasian Joint Conference on Artificial Intelligence, pp. 344–356. Australia (2019)

18. Madukwe, K.J., Gao, X., Xue, B.: In data we trust: a critical analysis of hate speech detection datasets. In: Proceedings of the Fourth Workshop on Online Abuse and Harms, pp. 150–161. ACL, Online (2020)
19. Martins, R., Gomes, M., Almeida, J.J., Novais, P., Henriques, P.: Hate speech classification in social media using emotional analysis. In: 2018 7th Brazilian Conference on Intelligent Systems (BRACIS), pp. 61–66 (2018)
20. Mikolov, T., Chen, K., Corrado, G., Dean, J.: Efficient estimation of word representations in vector space (2013)
21. Mohammad, S.M.: Word affect intensities. In: Proceedings of the 11th Edition of the Language Resources and Evaluation Conference (LREC). Japan (2018)
22. Mohammad, S.M., Turney, P.D.: Emotions evoked by common words and phrases: using mechanical turk to create an emotion lexicon. In: Workshop on Computational Approaches to Analysis and Generation of Emotion in Text, pp. 26–34. CAAGET '10, ACL, USA (2010)
23. Mohammad, S.M., Turney, P.D.: Crowdsourcing a word-emotion association lexicon. Comput. Intell. **29**(3), 436–465 (2013)
24. Mollas, I., Chrysopoulou, Z., Karlos, S., Tsoumakas, G.: Ethos: an online hate speech detection dataset (2020)
25. Mrkšić, N., et al.: Counter-fitting word vectors to linguistic constraints. In: Proceedings of the 2016 Conference of the North American Chapter of the Association for Computational Linguistics: Human Language Technologies, pp. 142–148. ACL, San Diego, California (2016)
26. Pennington, J., Socher, R., Manning, C.: GloVe: global vectors for word representation. In: Proceedings of the 2014 Conference on Empirical Methods in Natural Language Processing (EMNLP), pp. 1532–1543. ACL, Doha, Qatar (2014)
27. Pennington, J., Socher, R., Manning, C.D.: Glove: global vectors for word representation. In: Empirical Methods in Natural Language Processing (EMNLP), pp. 1532–1543 (2014)
28. Plutchik, R.: Chapter 1 - a general psychoevolutionary theory of emotion. In: Theories of Emotion, pp. 3–33. Academic Press (1980)
29. Rajamanickam, S., Mishra, P., Yannakoudakis, H., Shutova, E.: Joint modelling of emotion and abusive language detection (2020)
30. Safi Samghabadi, N., Hatami, A., Shafaei, M., Kar, S., Solorio, T.: Attending the emotions to detect online abusive language. In: Proceedings of the Fourth Workshop on Online Abuse and Harms, pp. 79–88. ACL, Online (2020)
31. Seyeditabari, A., Tabari, N., Gholizade, S., Zadrozny, W.: Emotional embeddings: Refining word embeddings to capture emotional content of words (2019)
32. Vulić, I.: Injecting lexical contrast into word vectors by guiding vector space specialisation. In: Proceedings of The Third Workshop on Representation Learning for NLP, pp. 137–143. ACL, Melbourne, Australia (2018)
33. Wieting, J., Bansal, M., Gimpel, K., Livescu, K.: From paraphrase database to compositional paraphrase model and back. Trans. ACL **3**, 345–358 (2015)
34. Yu, L.C., Wang, J., Lai, K.R., Zhang, X.: Refining word embeddings for sentiment analysis. In: Proceedings of the 2017 Conference on Empirical Methods in Natural Language Processing, pp. 534–539. ACL, Copenhagen, Denmark (2017)

Enhanced Named Entity Recognition with Semantic Dependency

Peng Wang[1,2], Zhe Wang[3], Xiaowang Zhang[1,2(✉)], Kewen Wang[3], and Zhiyong Feng[2]

[1] State Key Laboratory of Communication Content Cognition, Beijing, China
[2] College of Intelligence and Computing, Tianjin University, Tianjin, China
xiaowangzhang@tju.edu.cn
[3] School of Information and Communication Technology, Griffith University, Brisbane, Australia

Abstract. Dependency-based models for the named entity recognition (NER) task have shown promising results by capturing long-distance relationships between words in a sentence. However, while existing models focus on the syntactic dependency between entities, we are unaware of any work that considers semantic dependency. In this work, we study the usefulness of semantic dependency information for NER. We propose a NER model that is guided by semantic dependency graphs instead of syntactic dependency trees. The extensive experiments illustrate the effectiveness of the proposed model and the advantages of semantic dependency over syntactic dependency for NER. Also, it shows correlations between the NER performance and the semantic dependency annotations qualities.

Keywords: Named entity recognition · Syntactic dependency · Semantic dependency · Graph neural network

1 Introduction

Named Entity Recognition is one of NLP tasks to recognize named entities from texts belonging to pre-defined semantic types such as person, date, events, location, etc. [21,23]. NER has attracted wide interest not only as a standalone task of information extraction, but also as an essential semantic information extraction step for downstream Natural language processing(NLP) tasks such as entity linking [25], entity relationship extraction [16], and semantic parsing [4].

Meanwhile, research in linguistic dependency theory shows that there exists a subject-subordinate relationship between words, and such a dependency structure could also capture useful semantic information within sentences. Based on such insight, there have been quite some research efforts in enhancing NER models through grammar dependency features, with several valuable features proposed based on syntactic dependency structures [9,10,24]. As highlighted in [9], there is a clear correlation between the entity types and the dependency relations, which can enhance the prediction of named entities with various dependency types.

© Springer Nature Switzerland AG 2021
D. N. Pham et al. (Eds.): PRICAI 2021, LNAI 13032, pp. 287–298, 2021.
https://doi.org/10.1007/978-3-030-89363-7_22

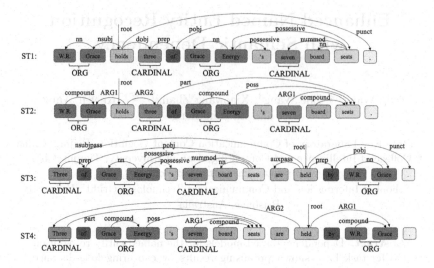

Fig. 1. Examples annotated with linguistic dependencies and named entities.

Figure 1 contains two sentences adapted from the SemEval-2015 task 18 English dataset (DM) [18], and it illustrates the relationship between language dependency structures and named entity types. Some words or phrases in the sentences are annotated with named entity types, such as ORG for organization and CARDINAL for numerals that do not fall under another type [21]. Also, the dependency relationship between words is expressed as labeled arcs. In particular, arcs in sentences ST1 and ST3 describe the syntactic dependency between words, with tags such as nn for noun compound modifier and nsubj for a nominal subject. On the other hand, the arcs in sentences ST2 and ST4 describe the semantic dependency between words, with tags such as poss for possession relations and part for measuring partitives(vague part-whole) relations.

There are several differences between syntactic and semantic dependency. First, it is obvious that the arcs and the tags in these two types of dependency convey different information. Secondly, as shown in the above example, syntactic dependency (in ST1 and ST3) always forms a dependency tree, where each word has only one head parent node. On the other hand, semantic dependency (in Fig. 1 ST2 and ST4) is a directed acyclic graph (DAG). For instance, the word seats in ST2 and ST4 has multiple head words three, Energy, seven, and board. Thirdly, semantic dependency structure is often preserved under simple rephrasing, whereas it is not the case for syntactic dependency. Note that ST3 and ST4 are rephrasing of ST1 and ST2, and hence the semantic dependency graph is preserved from ST2 and ST4, but the syntactic dependency tree changes from ST1 to ST3. This is an advantage of semantic dependency. Finally, each word in a syntactic dependency tree (e.g., ST1 and ST3) has an arc, but it is not the case for semantic dependency graphs (e.g., ST2 and ST4).

The long-distance dependency has been found valuable for capturing non-local structural information [5], and distributed hybrid representation deep learning models have been deployed to capture both syntactic and semantic features of words. As discussed before, syntactic dependency has been applied to increase the performance of NER, whereas we are unaware of any work on using semantic dependency for NER. Hence, the usefulness of semantic dependency and the complex long-distance interactions conveyed in such structures are unexplored, and how to use such information to enhance the word embedding in NER remains an open question.

In this work, we present the first study on leveraging semantic dependency for NER to the best of our knowledge. The significant contributions are as follows. We propose a BiLSTM-GCN-CRF model to capture the contextual information and the long-distance semantic relationship between words for enhancing the representation of the words for the NER task. Nevertheless, there is no existing NER dataset that contains semantic dependency annotations. Hence, we apply existing semantic parsing models to predict semantic dependency relations for OntoNotes 5.0 Chinese and English datasets [21], the CoNLL-2003 English dataset [23]. Finally, our extensive experiments result on these corpora shows the effectiveness of the proposed model and the advantage of semantic dependency features over syntactic dependency for NER. Also, it shows correlations between the NER performance and the semantic dependency annotations qualities.

2   Related Work

Existing works focus on learning distributed representations that capture semantic and syntactic properties of words. Besides word-level (e.g., GloVe [19], FastText [26], ELMo [20]) and character-level [2] representations, additional information is often incorporated into the representations before feeding them into context encoding layers. For example, the BiLSTM-CRF model [8] uses four types of features: spelling, context, and gazetteer features, as well as word embeddings. Some recent works make use of linguistic dependency information as an additional feature [10,13]. Jie et al. [9] incorporate syntactic dependency structures to capture long-distance syntactic interactions between words. Aguilar et al. [1] also consider syntactic tree structures with relative and global attentions, and Nie et al. [17] incorporate syntactic information into neural models. These approaches all make use of the syntactic dependency information, but have not considered semantic dependency.

Syntactic and semantic dependency can be extracted by dependency parsing, using bi-lexicalized dependency grammar [27]. Syntactic dependency parsing reveals shallow semantic information in sentences [7]. In contrast, we could regard semantic dependency parsing (SDP), based on dependency graph parsing, as an extension of syntactic dependency parsing that characterizes more semantic relations [18]. Hence, in this paper, we study NER models with semantic dependency information.

As we are unaware of any dataset with both human annotated named entities and their semantic dependency, we need to obtain semantic dependency using existing SDP models. Through comparing the performance of existing models on SDP corpora, including the task 9 of SemEval 2016 [3], and the task 18 of SemEval 2015 [18], we selected two SDP models provided by NLP toolkits HanLP[1] and SuPar[2].

3   Model

This section first briefly introduces the BiLSTM-CRF model [12], which is the base for our model. Then we introduce our NER model Sem-BiLSTM-GCN-CRF, which builds a GCN on top of the linear-chain structure in BiLSTM-CRF to process complex semantic dependency graphs.

3.1   BiLSTM-CRF

The BiLSTM-CRF model turns the NER problem into a sequence labeling problem. For an input sequence $\mathbf{x} = x_1, x_2, \ldots, x_i, \ldots, x_n$ with n tokens, we need to predict the corresponding label sequence $\mathbf{y} = y_1, y_2, \ldots, y_i, \ldots, y_n$, defined according to the BIO, IOBES or IOB tagging schemes [22]. The CRF [11] tags the entity types, i.e., given $\mathbf{x}$, scoring the label sequence $\mathbf{y}$:

$$P(\mathbf{y} \mid \mathbf{x}) = \frac{\exp\left(score(\mathbf{x}, \mathbf{y})\right)}{\sum_{\mathbf{y}'} \exp\left(score(\mathbf{x}, \mathbf{y}')\right)}$$

The label prediction sequence has the highest output score [12], which means the final prediction is the sequence $\mathbf{y}$ with the highest score in all output label sequences. We can get the output score by summing the transitions score and emissions score from the Bi-LSTM:

$$score(\mathbf{x}, \mathbf{y}) = \sum_{i=1}^{n-1} T_{y_i, y_{i+1}} + \sum_{i=1}^{n} E_{i, y_i},$$

where $\mathbf{T}$ is the transitions matrix with $T_{y_i, y_{i+1}}$ being the transition parameter from y_i to y_{i+1}, and $\mathbf{E}$ is the emissions matrix obtained by the hidden layer of the BiLSTM with E_{i, y_i} being the score of the label y_i in the sentence's i-th position.

3.2   Sem-BiLSTM-GCN-CRF

To guide the BiLSTM-CRF model with semantic dependency information, we use GCN to process such dependency graphs. Unlike [28], which uses only adjacency matrices to capture dependency edges between words, our model also processes

[1] HanLP: https://github.com/hankcs/HanLP.
[2] SuPar: https://github.com/yzhangcs/parser.

dependency tag information. GCN has also been considered in [9] to incorporate syntactic dependency information. Processing semantic dependency graphs are more involved than syntactic ones, as the latter are tree-shaped, whereas the former is not necessarily so. This is why using an MLP layer instead of GCN in the model [9] improves its performance, as MLP is sufficient to capture dependency trees, but it cannot handle multi-head relationships in semantic dependency graphs. On the other hand, the dependency graphs need to be cleaned before being input to the GCN. This is because some of the edges are often erroneous or irrelevant, which is common in automatically constructed dependency graphs. To address this issue, we employ the edge-wise gating parameters for specific dependency relations. Hence, we use GCN with edge-wise gating for encoding semantic dependency, and our model combines BiLSTM with directed GCN, using CRF as the final layer. The architecture of our model Sem-BiLSTM-GCN-CRF is shown in Fig. 2.[3] To represent the input, each word is represented by the concatenation $\mathbf{u}$ of the word embedding $\mathbf{w}$, its context-based word vector $\mathbf{v}$ from ELMO [20], and its character-based representation $\mathbf{t}$ from GloVe [19] for English and FastText [6] for Chinese. That is, $\mathbf{u} = \mathbf{w} \oplus \mathbf{t} \oplus \mathbf{v}$. And then, the BiLSTM layer captures the contextual information of in $\mathbf{u}$.

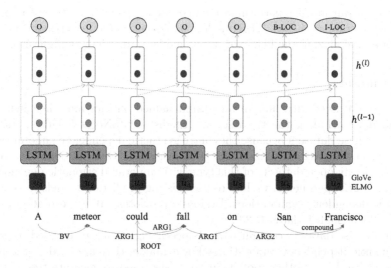

Fig. 2. BiLSTM-GCN-CRF. Dashed connections mimic the dependency edges.

Following most of the implementation for context-based GCN [9,14,28], we stack the GCN layer on top of LSTM to capture the semantic dependency relationship between the words to enrich the representation of words. As discussed before, some semantic-dependency prediction models use directed acyclic graphs

---

[3] The named entity tags use the BIO labeling scheme: B-LOC labels the beginning of a location entity, I-LOC represents the inside word of the named entity, and O-LOC means outside a named entity.

(DAG) for dependency parsing. Thus in a dependency graph, each node (word) may have more than one head node (word) (as shown in Fig. 1). Using GCN allows our model to effectively capture global information and gives substantial speedup as it does not involve recursive operations that are difficult to parallelize. We treat the dependency graph as undirected and build a symmetric adjacency matrix during the GCN update. The final GCN computation is formulated as:

$$\mathbf{h}_i^{(l)} = ReLU \Big(\sum_{j=1}^{n} A_{ij}(\mathbf{W}_1^{(l)}\mathbf{h}_j^{(l-1)} + \mathbf{W}_2^{(l)}\mathbf{h}_j^{(l-1)}w_{r_{ij}} + \mathbf{b}_{r_{ij}}^{(l-1)}) \Big) \qquad (1)$$

where $\mathbf{h}_i^{(l)}$ is the output vector at the i-th position in the l-th layer, $A_{i,j}$ is a value in the adjacency matrix A, and $w_{r_{ij}}$ is the weight of the dependency relation $r_{i,j}$. We use parameter matrix $\mathbf{W}_1$ for self connections and matrix $\mathbf{W}_2$ for dependency. For L layers of GCN in the model, $\mathbf{h}_1^{(L)}, \dots, \mathbf{h}_n^{(L)}$ are the output word representations. Finally, the last layer is CRF.

4 Experiment

We evaluate our model's performance on commonly used datasets by comparing it with the state-of-the-art NER models based on syntactic dependency information and analyzing the behavior of our model in different configurations.

4.1 Datasets

There are datasets with human annotated named entities and their syntactic dependency, including the Chinese and English OntoNotes 5.0 datasets [21]. We chose these datasets because they have syntactic dependency annotation, so that we can compare our model with those using such information. Yet, we are unaware of any open datasets of this type with annotated semantic dependency. Hence, in our experiments, we had to use existing prediction models to generate semantic dependency annotations. Besides OntoNotes 5.0, we also adopted the CoNLL 2003 English dataset [23].

All of these datasets contain part-of-speech tags that can be used to generate semantic dependency annotations. For example, they are used as the input feature of HanLP. Another toolkit SuPar is also used to generate the semantic dependency tags for evaluating the effect of different semantic dependency information (predicted by different models) on our performance. The English SDP models of SuPar are trained on the DM, PAS, and PSD datasets from SemEval-2015 task 18 [18], while Chinese models are trained on TEXT domain data of corpora from SemEval-2016 Task 9 [3].

4.2 Experimental Setup

We used BiLSTM-CRF [12] as the baseline model, which incorporates either syntactic or semantic dependency information. At the same time, we also feed syntactic dependency to our BiLSTM-GCN-CRF model, denoted Syn-BiLSTM-GCN-CRF model, as another baseline for comparing the benefits of syntactic and semantic dependency. In addition, we also compared our model to the DGLSTM-CRF model [9], the state-of-the-art syntactic dependency NER model.

The system configurations are based on [9] and our parameter tunings. The hidden layer size is set to 200 in the LSTM and GCN models. We use the GloVe [19] with 100-d word embeddings for English text, and FastText [6] word embeddings for Chinese text. ELMo [20] is used for both English and Chinese texts in our experiments for deep contextualized word representations. Our models are optimized by mini-batch stochastic gradient descent, which learning rate is 0.01. The L2 regularization parameter is 1e-8. We train for 300 epochs with a clipping rate of 3.

4.3   Main Results

Our model are compared with existing models on the three datasets, OntoNotes 5.0 Chinese (OntoNotes CN), English (OntoNotes EN), and CoNLL-2003 English (CoNLL). For each compared model, we used the numbers of LSTM/GCN layers that gave the best performance; for instance, BiLSTM(2)-CRF has a 2 LSTM layers and BiLSTM(1)-GCN(1)-CRF has 1 LSTM lay and 1 GCN layer. All the inputs are concatenated with the ELMo representations. We used SuPar to generate the semantic dependency tags. The Dependency column shows whether dependency information is not included (-), or it is provided with the datasets (gold), or it is generated. If the dependency is generated, we record the F1 score of the generating models and the text corpus they are trained on[4]. Table 1 shows the results, where those for BiLSTM-CRF and DGLSTM-CRF are from [9,12].

On all the three datasets, Sem-BiLSTM-GCN-CRF outperforms the baseline BiLSTM-CRF and Syn-BiLSTM-GCN-CRF in most of the metrics. Note that Sem-BiLSTM-GCN-CRF and Syn-BiLSTM-GCN-CRF have similar model architecture, and the only difference is the type of dependency used. Also, on OntoNotes CN and EN, Syn-BiLSTM-GCN-CRF uses dependency information that comes from the datasets, where Sem-BiLSTM-GCN-CRF uses dependency generates. Furthermore, on OntoNotes CN and CoNLL, the performance of Syn-BiLSTM-GCN-CRF is not as good as BiLSTM-CRF, which shows the GCN encoding of syntactic dependency may not always benefit the NER task. Hence, overall it suggests the advantages of semantic dependency compared to syntactic dependency in NER.

Compared to DGLSTM-CRF, Sem-BiLSTM-GCN-CRF achieves the state-of-the-art recall performance on OntoNotes CN. Furthermore, while its performance is closely after DGLSTM-CRF with "gold" dependency, it consistently outperforms DGLSTM-CRF with generated dependency in all the other cases.

---

[4] TEXT is the textbook corpus from SemEval-2016 Task 9, DM is the DELPH-IN corpus from SemEval-2015 Task 18, PAS is the Enju corpus from SemEval-2015 Task 18, PSD is the Prague corpus from SemEval-2015 Task 18, and LAS is the English Penn Treebank (PTB) corpus [15].

Table 1. Comparison on OntoNotes 5.0 Chinese/English and CoNLL-2003 English.

Dataset	Model (+ELMo)	Dependency	Prec.	Rec.	F1
OntoNotes CN	BiLSTM(1)-CRF	-	**79.20**	79.21	79.20
	Syn-BiLSTM(1)-GCN(1)-CRF	Gold	78.71	79.29	79.00
	Sem-BiLSTM(1)-GCN(1)-CRF	80.41 (TEXT)	78.30	**81.05**	79.65
	Sem-BiLSTM(1)-GCN(2)-CRF		<u>79.10</u>	80.60	<u>79.84</u>
	DGLSTM(2)-CRF	89.28	-	-	79.59
	DGLSTM(2)-CRF	Gold	78.86	<u>81.00</u>	**79.92**
OntoNotes EN	BiLSTM(2)-CRF	-	88.25	89.71	88.98
	Syn-BiLSTM(1)-GCN(2)-CRF	Gold	<u>89.40</u>	89.71	89.55
	Sem-BiLSTM(1)-GCN(1)-CRF	92.32 (DM)	89.22	90.10	<u>89.65</u>
	Sem-BiLSTM(1)-GCN(2)-CRF		88.78	89.90	89.34
	Sem-BiLSTM(1)-GCN(1)-CRF	93.43 (PAS)	89.18	90.04	89.61
	Sem-BiLSTM(1)-GCN(2)-CRF		88.98	89.77	89.37
	Sem-BiLSTM(1)-GCN(1)-CRF	82.64 (PSD)	88.73	**90.25**	89.49
	Sem-BiLSTM(1)-GCN(2)-CRF		88.00	89.10	88.55
	DGLSTM(2)-CRF	94.89	-	-	89.64
	DGLSTM(2)-CRF	Gold	**89.59**	<u>90.17</u>	**89.88**
CoNLL	BiLSTM(2)-CRF	-	92.10	92.30	92.20
	Syn-BiLSTM(1)-GCN(1)-CRF	95.86 (LAS)	91.93	92.26	92.09
	Sem-BiLSTM(1)-GCN(1)-CRF	92.32 (DM)	**92.21**	<u>92.49</u>	<u>92.35</u>
	DGLSTM(2)-CRF	94.00	<u>92.20</u>	**92.50**	**92.35**

This shows the competitiveness of our model compared to DGLSTM-CRF on generated dependency.

For the configurations of GCN layers, when it is increased from 1 to 2, in most of the cases, the NER performance of our model decreases. Hence, it seems GCN with a single layer is sufficient to capture the semantic dependency. We have also evaluated our model jointly with syntactic and semantic dependency features in a naive manner, which gave a suboptimal performance as compared to the semantic based NER model. It is potentially due to the inequality of the two types of information, as semantic dependency edges are often orders of magnitude more than those syntactic ones. Hence, the syntactic dependency information may not be effectively utilized. We leave the study of a joint model as future work.

4.4 Effect of Dependency Quality

The previous set of experiments shows the difference between gold-standard and predicted syntactic dependency in NER performance. To evaluate the impact of the quality of semantic dependency on the NER performance, we used the SuPar and Hanlp toolkits for comparison. As a result, semantic dependency tags with different accuracy, measured by their F1 scores, are generated for OntoNote 5.0 and ConLL-2003 datasets. Also, SuPar and Hanlp have different data pre-processing methods, and their dataset segmentation sizes are different. Figure 3 shows the NER accuracy (NER F1 scores) of our model using semantic dependency of various quality (dependency parsing F1 scores). A strong correlation between the NER accuracy and dependency accuracy, which shows the potential of our model with high-quality dependency annotations.

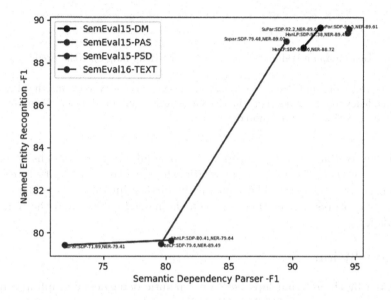

Fig. 3. Correlations between NER performance and semantic dependency quality.

5   Analysis

To further analyze why a NER model could benefit from semantic dependency information, we show the heat maps in Fig. 4) on the named entity types and the corresponding semantic dependency edges in the OntoNotes Chinese dataset. The x-axis lists various semantic dependency annotations, the y-axis is the named entity annotations, and each value shows the percentage (%) of semantic dependency edges with annotation x associated with the named entity type y.

Figure 4(a) shows the correlation between the entity types and the prediction of dependency relations on the OntoNotes Chinese test dataset. Specifically, each entry denotes the percentage of the entities with a parent dependency with a specific dependency relation. We can see that most of the entities relate to the Desc, Nmod, Quan dependencies. Especially the dependency relationship Quan (i.e., Quantity) have more than 80% of the entity type CARDINAL and 58% of the entity type QUANTITY associated to it, which suggests the semantic correlations.

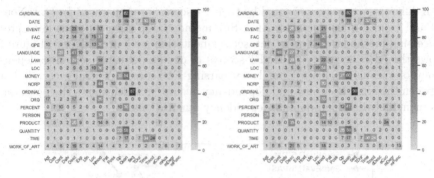

(a) Heap map on training data.   (b) Heap map on NER prediction.

Fig. 4. Correlations and Percentage between the entity types (y axis) and the of semantic dependency relations (x axis) in the OntoNotes Chinese dataset. Columns with percentage less than 5% are ignored for brevity.

We can see that Fig. 4(a) and Fig. 4(b) are similar in terms of density. Moreover, both of them show consistent relationships between the entity types and the dependency relations. The comparison further illustrates that our model effectively captures the relations between the named entities and the semantic dependency.

6   Conclusion

Motivated by the relationships between semantic dependency graph and name entities, we propose a BiLSTM-GCN-CRF model to encode semantic information from the semantic dependency toolkits effectively and then enhanced the word representations. Through extensive experiments on multiple corpora, the proposed model effectively uses and captures the long-distance semantic dependency relationships between the words for improving NER performance. Our experiment analysis shows that NER benefits more from semantic dependency relations than syntactic dependency based on the same model. In addition, we find the high-quality dependency parsing will positively affect the improvement of NER. We leave studying a multi-feature fusion mechanism of syntactic and semantic of full dependencies for NER and other information extraction domains as future work.

Acknowledgements. This work is supported by the funding of State Key Laboratory of Communication Content Cognition (A32002) and Key Research and Development Program of Hubei Province (No. 2020BAB026).

References

1. Aguilar, G., Solorio, T.: Dependency-aware named entity recognition with relative and global attentions (2019)

2. Akbik, A., Blythe, D., Vollgraf, R.: Contextual string embeddings for sequence labeling. In: Proceedings of COLING-18, pp. 1638–1649 (2018)
3. Che, W., Shao, Y., Liu, T., Ding, Y.: SemEval-2016 task 9: Chinese semantic dependency parsing. In: Proceedings of the 10th International Workshop on Semantic Evaluation, SemEval@NAACL-HLT 2016, San Diego, CA, USA, 16–17 June 2016, pp. 1074–1080. ACL (2016)
4. Dong, L., Lapata, M.: Coarse-to-fine decoding for neural semantic parsing. In: Proceedings of ACL-18, pp. 731–742 (2018)
5. Finkel, J.R., Grenager, T., Manning, C.D.: Incorporating non-local information into information extraction systems by Gibbs sampling. In: Proceedings of ACL-05, pp. 363–370 (2005)
6. Grave, E., Bojanowski, P., Gupta, P., Joulin, A., Mikolov, T.: Learning word vectors for 157 languages. In: Proceedings of LREC-18 (2018)
7. Hajic, J., et al.: The CoNLL-2009 shared task: syntactic and semantic dependencies in multiple languages. In: Proceedings of CoNLL-09, pp. 1–18 (2009)
8. Huang, Z., Xu, W., Yu, K.: Bidirectional LSTM-CRF models for sequence tagging (2015)
9. Jie, Z., Lu, W.: Dependency-guided LSTM-CRF for named entity recognition. In: Proceedings of EMNLP-19, pp. 3860–3870 (2019)
10. Jie, Z., Muis, A.O., Lu, W.: Efficient dependency-guided named entity recognition. In: Proceedings of AAAI-17, pp. 3457–3465 (2017)
11. Lafferty, J.D., McCallum, A., Pereira, F.C.N.: Conditional random fields: probabilistic models for segmenting and labeling sequence data. In: Proceedings of ICML-01, pp. 282–289 (2001)
12. Lample, G., Ballesteros, M., Subramanian, S., Kawakami, K., Dyer, C.: Neural architectures for named entity recognition. In: Proceedings of NAACL-HLT-16, pp. 260–270 (2016)
13. Ling, X., Weld, D.S.: Fine-grained entity recognition. In: Proceedings of AAAI-12 (2012)
14. Marcheggiani, D., Titov, I.: Encoding sentences with graph convolutional networks for semantic role labeling. In: Proceedings of EMNLP-17, pp. 1506–1515 (2017)
15. Marcus, M.P., Santorini, B., Marcinkiewicz, M.A.: Building a large annotated corpus of English: the penn treebank. Comput. Linguistics **19**(2), 313–330 (1993)
16. Miwa, M., Bansal, M.: End-to-end relation extraction using LSTMs on sequences and tree structures. CoRR abs/1601.00770 (2016)
17. Nie, Y., Tian, Y., Song, Y., Ao, X., Wan, X.: Improving named entity recognition with attentive ensemble of syntactic information (2020)
18. Oepen, S., et al.: SemEval 2015 task 18: broad-coverage semantic dependency parsing. In: Proceedings of SemEval@NAACL-HLT-15, pp. 915–926 (2015)
19. Pennington, J., Socher, R., Manning, C.D.: Glove: global vectors for word representation. In: Proceedings of EMNLP-14, pp. 1532–1543 (2014)
20. Peters, M.E., et al.: Deep contextualized word representations. In: Proceedings of NAACL-HLT-18, pp. 2227–2237 (2018)
21. Pradhan, S., et al.: Towards robust linguistic analysis using OntoNotes. In: Proceedings of CoNLL-13, pp. 143–152 (2013)
22. Ratinov, L., Roth, D.: Design challenges and misconceptions in named entity recognition. In: Proceedings of CoNLL-09, pp. 147–155 (2009)
23. Sang, E.F.T.K., Meulder, F.D.: Introduction to the CoNLL-2003 shared task: language-independent named entity recognition. In: Proceedings of CoNLL-03, pp. 142–147 (2003)

24. Sasano, R., Kurohashi, S.: Japanese named entity recognition using structural natural language processing. In: Proceedings of IJCNLP-08, pp. 607–612 (2008)
25. Shen, W., Han, J., Wang, J., Yuan, X., Yang, Z.: SHINE+: a general framework for domain-specific entity linking with heterogeneous information networks. IEEE Trans. Knowl. Data Eng. **30**(2), 353–366 (2018)
26. Wang, C., Cho, K., Kiela, D.: Code-switched named entity recognition with embedding attention. In: Proceedings of Workshop on Computational Approaches to Linguistic Code-Switching, pp. 154–158 (2018)
27. Zhang, M.S.: A survey of syntactic-semantic parsing based on constituent and dependency structures. SCIENCE CHINA Technol. Sci. **63**(10), 1898–1920 (2020). https://doi.org/10.1007/s11431-020-1666-4
28. Zhang, Y., Qi, P., Manning, C.D.: Graph convolution over pruned dependency trees improves relation extraction. In: Proceedings of EMNLP-18, pp. 2205–2215 (2018)

Improving Sentence-Level Relation Classification via Machine Reading Comprehension and Reinforcement Learning

Bo Xu, Zhengqi Zhang, Xiangsan Zhao, Hui Song, and Ming Du$^{(\boxtimes)}$

School of Computer Science and Technology, Donghua University, Shanghai, China
{xubo,songhui,duming}@dhu.edu.cn, {2202405,2191948}@mail.dhu.edu.cn

Abstract. Distant supervision (DS) has been proposed to automatically annotate data and achieved significant success in relation classification. However, despite its efficiency, distant supervision often suffers from the *noisy labeling* problem. To solve the problem, existing methods can be divided into two major approaches: (1) Some works adopt multi-instance learning (MIL) for relation classification to reduce the impact of noisy data. However, they do not perform well at the sentence level. (2) Other works focus on finding the noisy instances directly. They mainly use reinforcement learning to filter out the noisy instances. The key component is the instance selector, which is used to select the correct instances from the noisy data. However, current instance selectors usually use simple neural network models and initialize the models with random parameters, which leads to limited improvement and slower convergence. In this paper, we propose a novel instance selector to directly select the high-quality instances from DS-generated data as the refined training data to improve the performance of sentence-level relation classification. Specifically, the instance selector consists of a machine reading comprehension (MRC) estimator and an instance sampler. The MRC estimator is used to evaluate the quality of the instances, and the instance sampler is used to select the high-quality instances. Moreover, due to the lack of explicit knowledge about which instances are mislabeled, we use reinforcement learning to train the MRC estimator. Experiments show that our method achieves state-of-the-art performance on two human-annotated NYT10 datasets. The source code of this paper can be found in https://github.com/xubodhu/MRCRL.

1 Introduction

The task of relation classification (RC) is to predict the semantic relation between two entities from plain text. These relational facts are helpful for many downstream applications, such as knowledge graph completion [18] and question answering [2]. Recently, neural relation classification with minimal feature

This paper was supported by the National Natural Science Foundation of China (61906035), Shanghai Sailing Program (19YF1402300) and National Natural Science Foundation of China (61972081).

D. N. Pham et al. (Eds.): PRICAI 2021, LNAI 13032, pp. 299–310, 2021.
https://doi.org/10.1007/978-3-030-89363-7_23

engineering has made a great success [4]. However, it heavily relies on a large amount of annotation data, which is expensive and time-consuming.

To obtain large-scale annotated data, distant supervision has been proposed to automatically annotate data from the knowledge base [11]. The basic idea is that if two entities have a semantic relation in the knowledge base, then all sentences containing the two entities can be labeled as this relation. Despite its efficiency, distant supervision often suffers from the *noisy labeling* problem.

For example, given a fact (`Bill Gates`, `place_of_birth`, `Seattle`) in the existing knowledge base. The sentence *'Microsoft founder Bill Gates was born in Seattle'* will be correctly labeled as the `place_of_birth` relation. While another sentence, *'Bill Gates moved into the house he bought in Seattle'* will be wrongly labeled as the `place_of_birth` relation.

The existing methods to alleviate the *noisy labeling* problem can be divided into two major approaches: (1) Some works adopt multi-instance learning (MIL) for relation classification to reduce the impact of noisy data [5,9,16,20]. Multi-instance learning is a form of supervised learning where a label is given to a bag of instances, rather than a single instance [7]. In the context of relation classification, each entity pair defines a bag and the bag consists of all the sentences mentioning the entity pair. The main idea is to select informative instances from the bags. These methods perform well in bag-level relation classification but perform poorly in sentence-level relation classification [3]. (2) Other works focus on finding the noisy instances directly. They mainly use reinforcement learning [3,13] to filter out the noisy instances. The key component is the instance selector, which is used to select the correct instances from the noisy data. For example, [3] constructs a CNN-based instance selector for all relations, and [13] constructs a binary CNN-based instance selector for each relation. However, current instance selectors usually use simple neural network models and initialize the models with random parameters, which leads to limited improvement and slower convergence.

In this paper, we study how to directly select the high-quality instances from DS-generated data to improve the performance of sentence-level relation classification. Specifically, we propose a novel instance selector to select the high-quality instances, which consists of a machine reading comprehension (MRC) estimator and an instance sampler. The MRC estimator is used to evaluate the quality of the instances, and the instance sampler is used to select the high-quality instances.

Conventional MRC task aims to extract a correct span to answer the question regarding a given context, which can be formalized as two multi-class classification tasks, i.e., predicting the starting and ending positions of the answer spans [8]. Unlike the conventional MRC model, we use the MRC estimator to evaluate the quality of the instance. For example in Fig. 1, there are two DS-generated instances with the same relational fact and different texts. For each instance, we first use a template-based method to convert the relational fact into a question and a candidate span. Then, we input the question, the candidate span, and the context into the MRC estimator. The MRC estimator predicts the

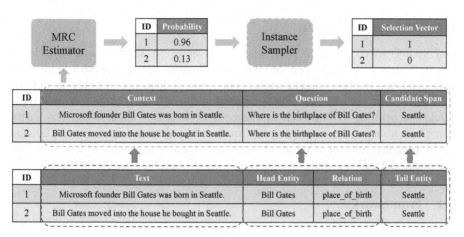

Fig. 1. An example of our instance selector selects the high-quality instances from DS-generated data. An instance contains a relational fact (head entity, relation, tail entity) and a text, and the text contains head entity and tail entity in the relational fact.

probability of the given candidate span as the correct answer. As shown in the figure, the output probabilities of these two instances are 0.96 and 0.13, respectively. We use the output probabilities as the quality of the two instances. After that, we use the instance sampler to select the high-quality instances based on their probabilities. Finally, only the first instance is selected for sentence-level relation classification.

Moreover, due to the lack of explicit knowledge about which instances are mislabeled, we use reinforcement learning to train the MRC estimator. Specifically, the instance selector selects some instances and uses the performance of the relation classification model as feedback (or reward) to update the parameters of the MRC estimator. The main contributions of this paper are as follows:

- Firstly, to the best of our knowledge, we are the first to use the machine reading comprehension model to evaluate the quality of the instances.
- Secondly, due to the lack of explicit knowledge about which instances are mislabeled, we use the reinforcement learning method to train the MRC estimator.
- Finally, experiments conducted on two human-annotated NYT10 datasets show that our instance selector can effectively select high-quality instances from DS-generated data and learn better parameters for the MRC estimator through reinforcement learning method.

2 Overview

In this section, we define our problem and introduce our framework.

2.1   Problem Definition

Our goal is to construct a good instance selector to directly select the high-quality instances from DS-generated data as the refined training data to improve sentence-level relation classification. The task of instance selector is defined as follows: Let D^S be the DS-generated data, which contains N instances $\{(h_i, r_i, t_i, text_i)\}_{i=1}^{N}$. For each instance, $text_i$ is a text mentioning the entity pair (h_i, t_i), and r_i is a relation label produced by distant supervision. The goal of the instance selector is to select some high-quality instances D from the DS-generated data D^S.

2.2   Framework

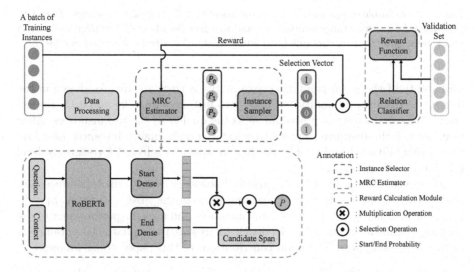

Fig. 2. The Reinforcement Learning Framework for Training the Instance Selector.

Our reinforcement learning framework for training the instance selector is shown in Fig. 2, which contains two main components, namely instance selector and reward calculation module. The instance selector consists of an MRC estimator and an instance sampler. The MRC estimator is used to evaluate the quality of the instances, and the instance sampler is used to select the high-quality instances. The reward calculation module is an indicator used to evaluate the action of the selection, which consists of a relation classifier and a reward function. The relation classifier is trained on the selected instances, and the reward function calculates the reward based on the performance of the relation classifier on the validation set. The reward is served as a reinforcement signal to update the parameters of the MRC estimator in the instance selector.

3   Method

In this section, we first introduce the processing of the input data and then describe each component in detail. Finally, we introduce how to train the framework.

3.1   Data Processing

In order to use the MRC estimator to evaluate the quality of the instances, we need to process the training instances into the input-form (question, context, candidate span) of the MRC estimator.

Specifically, for each instance, we need to convert the data format from $(h_i, r_i, t_i, text_i)$ to $(question_i, context_i, cspan_i)$. The process is as follows: we first convert the $text_i$ into the $context_i$ without any operation. Then we generate a *question slot* $((h_i, r_i, ?)$ or $(?, r_i, t_i))$ and its corresponding candidate span $cspan_i$ $(t_i$ or $h_i)$ from the relational fact (h_i, r_i, t_i). For each question slot with the same relation, we design a question template. Finally, we generate a natural language question $question_i$ based on the question template. Table 1 shows some examples of the question slots and their corresponding question templates.

Table 1. Examples of some question slots and corresponding question templates.

Question slot	Question template
$(h_i,$/location/country/capital, ?)	Where is the capital of h_i?
$(?,$/location/location/contains, $t_i)$	Where does t_i contain?
$(h_i,$/people/person/nationality, ?)	Where is the nationality of h_i?
$(h_i,$/people/person/place_lived, ?)	Where is the lived place of h_i?

3.2   MRC Estimator

The MRC estimator is used to evaluate the quality of the instance. As shown in Fig. 2, the MRC estimator mainly consists of a *RoBERTa* layer [10], two dense layers, a multiplication operation, and a selection operation.

Specifically, for each processed instance $(question_i, context_i, cspan_i)$, the input x_i of the *RoBERTa* layer is a pair of sequence with two different special tokens: "$\langle s \rangle$ $question_i$ $\langle /s \rangle$ $\langle /s \rangle$ $context_i$ $\langle /s \rangle$", and the output representation of the context is $\boldsymbol{H}_i \in \mathbb{R}^{l \times d}$, where l is the length of the $context_i$ and d is the vector dimension of the last layer of *RoBERTa*. Then, we use two dense layers to predict the probability distributions of each token index being the start position and end position of the answer given the question. The prediction process is as follows:

$$P_i^{start} = Softmax(\boldsymbol{H}_i \boldsymbol{W}_{start} + b_{start}) \qquad (1)$$

$$P_i^{end} = Softmax(\boldsymbol{H}_i \boldsymbol{W}_{end} + b_{end}) \qquad (2)$$

where $\boldsymbol{W}_{start} \in \mathbb{R}^{d \times 1}$ and $\boldsymbol{W}_{end} \in \mathbb{R}^{d \times 1}$ are the weights, $b_{start} \in \mathbb{R}$ and $b_{end} \in \mathbb{R}$ are the biases. $\boldsymbol{P}_i^{start} \in \mathbb{R}^{l \times 1}$ and $\boldsymbol{P}_i^{end} \in \mathbb{R}^{l \times 1}$ are the probability distributions.

After that, we use a multiplication operation to calculate the probabilities of all spans $\boldsymbol{P}_i^{span}$ in the $context_i$. As shown in Eq. 3, the probability of each span being the correct answer is equal to the probability of the start position of the span multiplied by the probability of the end position of the span.

$$P_i^{span} = P_i^{start}(P_i^{end})^T, \tag{3}$$

where $\boldsymbol{P}_i^{span} \in \mathbb{R}^{l \times l}$ is the probability matrix. Finally, we use the selection operation to obtain the probability of the given candidate span P_i^{cspan} from $\boldsymbol{P}_i^{span}$ through the start index and end index of the given candidate span $cspan_i$. The selection process is as follows: let I_{start} and I_{end} be the start index and the end index of the given candidate span $cspan_i$ in the $context_i$, the probability of the given candidate span P_i^{cspan} is the value of the I_{start}-th row and the I_{end}-th column of $\boldsymbol{P}_i^{span}$. Finally, we use the probability P_i^{cspan} as the quality of the instance $(h_i, r_i, t_i, text_i)$. The greater the probability, the higher the quality.

3.3   Instance Sampler

The instance sampler is used to select high-quality instances. In this paper, we propose two sampling strategies. In the training phase, in order to encourage exploration based on the uncertainty in the exponentially large selection space, following [19], we use *Bernoulli* sampling to sample the instances. Each instance will be selected with its probability, which is provided by the MRC estimator. While in the prediction phase, we first sort the instances in descending order by their probabilities and then select the top p% instances as high-quality instances.

3.4   Reward Calculation Module

The reward calculation module is an indicator used to evaluate the action of the selection, which consists of a relation classifier and a reward function.

Relation classification has been widely studied in recent years [9,21]. In this paper, we adopt the CNN architecture proposed by [3] for relation classifier, which consists of an input layer, a convolution layer, a max-pooling layer, and an output layer. We denote the relation classifier as f_θ, where θ is the parameters. Given a selected instance $(h_{i'}, r_{i'}, t_{i'}, text_{i'})$, the input of the relation classifier is $z_{i'} = (h_{i'}, t_{i'}, text_{i'})$, and the output is the probability for all relations is $p(\mathbf{r}|z_{i'})$. This can be briefly described as follows:

$$p(\mathbf{r}|z_{i'}) = f_\theta(z_{i'}) \tag{4}$$

We use the *cross-entropy* as the loss function [1], and use the stochastic gradient descent (SGD) optimizer [17] to update the parameters θ according to Eq. 5:

$$\theta \leftarrow \theta + \frac{\alpha}{B_{rc}} \sum_{k=1}^{B_{rc}} \nabla_\theta \log p(r_k|z_k), \tag{5}$$

where α is the learning rate of the relation classifier, B_{rc} is the batch size for training the relation classifier.

The reward function calculates the reward based on the performance of the trained relation classifier on the validation set $D^v = (z^v, r^v)$. Specifically, the calculation of the reward R is as follows:

$$R = F1(f_\theta(z^v), r^v) - \delta, \tag{6}$$

where $F1(f_\theta(z^v), r^v)$ is the micro averaged $F1$ score on the validation set. δ is the moving average, which is used to improve the stability of reinforcement learning based on policy gradient. We will explain how to calculate it in the following subsection.

3.5   MRC Estimator Training

Finally, we introduce how to train the MRC estimator based on the reward. Similar to [19], the training process of the MRC Estimator is shown in Algorithm 1.

Algorithm 1. The Training Process of MRC Estimator

Inputs: DS-generated data $D^S = \{(h_i, r_i, t_i, text_i)\}_{i=1}^N$, batch size B_s and B_{rc}, learning rate α and β, moving average window size T, validation set D^v.
Outputs: the MRC estimator g_ϕ.
1: **Initialize** parameters ϕ for the MRC model g_ϕ, and moving average $\delta = 0$;
2: **while** until convergence **do**
3:     Randomly sample a batch of instances $D_B^S = \{(h_j, r_j, t_j, text_j)\}_{j=1}^{B_s}$ from D^S;
4:     $\{(question_j, context_j, cspan_j)\}_{j=1}^{B_s} = DataProcessing(D_B^S)$;
5:     **for** $j = 1$ to B_s **do**
6:         Calculate probability $P_j^{cspan} = g_\phi(question_j, context_j, cspan_j)$
7:     **end for**
8:     Obtain selected instances $D_{B'}^S$ from D_B^S by using *Bernoulli* sampling
9:     Initialize a relation classifier f_θ, and use $D_{B'}^S$ to learn θ according to Equation 5
10:    Calculate reward R according to Equation 6
11:    Update ϕ according to Equation 7;
12:    Update δ according to Equation 9;
13: **end while**

We first initialize the parameters ϕ for the MRC estimator g_ϕ and set the moving average δ to 0. For each iteration, we randomly select a batch of instances D_B^S from D^S, the batch size is B_s, and process the original data into the input format of the MRC estimator. Then we use the MRC estimator to evaluate the quality of each processed instance $(question_j, context_j, cspan_j)$ and obtain selected instances $D_{B'}^S$ from D_B^S by using *Bernoulli* sampling. After that, we initialize a relation classifier f_θ with random parameters and use $D_{B'}^S$ to learn the parameters θ of the relation classifier according to Eq. 5. Then we calculate the reward R according to Eq. 6, and update the parameters ϕ of the MRC estimator g_ϕ as follows:

$$\phi \leftarrow \phi + \beta \cdot R \cdot \nabla_\phi \log \pi_\phi(D_B^S, (s_1, ..., s_{B_s})) \tag{7}$$

$$\pi_\phi(D_B^S, (s_1, ..., s_{B_s})) = \prod_{j=1}^{B_s} (P_j^{cspan})^{s_j} \cdot (1 - P_j^{cspan})^{1-s_j}, \tag{8}$$

where $\pi_\phi(D_B^S, (s_1, ..., s_{B_s}))$ is the probability that the selection vector $(s_1, ..., s_{B_s})$ is selected based on g_ϕ and $s_j = \{0, 1\}$ is an indicator variable, indicating whether to select this instance. Finally, we update the moving average δ according to Eq. 9.

$$\delta \leftarrow \frac{T-1}{T}\delta + \frac{1}{T}F1(f_\theta(z^v, r^v)) \tag{9}$$

4 Experiment

In this section, we present the experimental results.

4.1 Dataset

We conducted experiments on the DS-generated NYT10 dataset [15], which is widely used for bag-level relation classification. In this paper, we need to evaluate the performance of selected instances on sentence-level relation classification. Therefore, we decided to use the NYT10 training set as our training data, and then use two human-annotated NYT10 test sets as our test data. We refer to the two human-annotated datasets of NYT10 [15] as *NYT-T1* [22] and *NYT10-T2* [12], respectively.

The original NYT10 training set contains 53 relations, one of which is the special label *NA*, which means that the given entity pair does not belong to the remaining 52 relations or has no relationship. However, the test data in the two human-annotated datasets do not contain *NA* relation. Therefore, for a fair comparison, we drop the *NA* relations in the training data. The statistics about these datasets are listed in Table 2.

Table 2. Statistics of the datasets

Training data			Test data		
Source	Relations	Instances	Source	Relations	Instances
NYT10	52	136,379	NYT-T1	22	5,202
			NYT-T2	28	4,288

In our experiments, we follow the previous work [3] and use the *accuracy* metric to evaluate the performance of sentence-level relation classification on non-*NA* relations.

4.2 Parameter Settings

We conduct all the experiments on NVIDIA GTX 2080 Ti GPUs. The parameter settings of our framework are as follows.

For the MRC estimator, we use *RoBERTa* in our model[1], which is pre-trained in a large-scale reading comprehension dataset, SQuAD 2.0 [14]. It contains 12 layers of transformer blocks, 12 self-attention heads, and the hidden size of 768. The batch size of the training instances is 5,120. The maximum length of the input text is 132, the output size of the start dense layer and the end dense layer are both 1. Other parameters in it are initialized with the pre-trained *RoBERTa* model.

For the relation classifier, we use the same hyperparameter settings as in [3] during training and testing. Specifically, the batch size is 4, the dimensions of word embedding and position embedding are 50 and 5, respectively. The window size of the convolutional layer is 3, the number of feature maps is 230. The learning rate α of the relation classifier is 0.1.

For training the reinforcement learning framework, we randomly select 10% from the *NYT10* training data as the validation set. We use the adaptive moment estimation (Adam) optimizer [6] to update the parameters of the MRC estimator, and the learning rate β is 0.005. The moving window size T is 6.

4.3 Baselines

Our goal is to construct a good instance selector. In order to evaluate the quality of the instance selector, we need to train the relation classifier with selected instances and evaluate the performance of sentence-level relation classification on the test set. To demonstrate the effect of our MRC-based instance selector and the reinforcement learning training framework, we compare with several instance selectors:

- DS. We train the relation classifier with the DS-generated training data.
- CNN-RL [3]. The state-of-the-art reinforcement learning denoising method for relation classification, which constructs a CNN-based instance selector for all relations. We adopt *TensorFlow* implementation[2] in our experiment.
- CNNs-RL [13]. Another state-of-the-art reinforcement learning denoising method for relation classification, which constructs a binary CNN-based instance selector for each relation. We adopt *PyTorch* implementation[3] in our experiment.
- MRC-RL. Our MRC-based instance selector proposed in this paper.
- MRC-Static. A variant of our instance selector that using the initialize parameters of *RoBERTa* and without training.
- MRC-Non-Static. Another variant of our instance selector that using the initialize parameters of *RoBERTa* and fine-tuning the parameters by using the DS-generated training data.

---

[1] https://huggingface.co/deepset/roberta-base-squad2.
[2] https://github.com/xuyanfu/TensorFlow_RLRE.
[3] https://github.com/Panda0406/Reinforcement-Learning-Distant-Supervision-RE.

4.4 Performance Comparison and Analysis

The instance sampler component is used to select the top p% instances with the highest probabilities. In our experiments, we first compare the performance of MRC-based methods under different p values, and then choose the optimal sampling rate (90%) for each MRC-based method. Table 3 shows the performance of different instance selectors on two human-annotated test data. The detailed analysis is as follows.

Table 3. The performance of different instance selectors on two human-annotated test data.

Test data	DS	CNN-RL	CNNs-RL	MRC-Static	MRC-Non-Static	MRC-RL
NYT10-T1	86.45	81.37	85.99	86.63	86.93	**87.01**
NYT10-T2	79.62	74.43	79.28	79.78	80.27	**80.50**

Firstly, we compare the MRC-based methods (*MRC-Static, MRC-Non-Static,* and *MRC-RL*) with *DS*. From the table, we find that all the MRC-based methods perform better than *DS*, which shows that the prior knowledge in the pre-trained model (*RoBERTa*) used by the MRC estimator can be used to find high-quality instances. This shows the effectiveness of the MRC estimator for the instance selector.

Secondly, we compare *MRC-RL* with *MRC-Static* and *MRC-Non-Static*. From the table, we find that *MRC-Non-Static* is better than *MRC-Static*, which shows that fine-tuning is a good way to learn the parameters for the MRC estimator. *MRC-RL* achieves the best performance, which shows that reinforcement learning is a better way to learn the parameters.

Finally, we compare *MRC-RL* with *CNN-RL* and *CNNs-RL*. From the table, we find that *MRC-RL* is better than *CNN-RL* and *CNNs-RL*, which indicates that our MRC-based instance selector is better than other instance selectors.

5 Conclusion

In this paper, we propose a novel instance selector to directly select the high-quality instances from DS-generated data as the refined training data to improve the performance of sentence-level relation classification and use the reinforcement learning method to train the instance selector. Experiments conducted on two human-annotated NYT10 datasets show that our instance selector can effectively select high-quality instances from DS-generated data and can learn better parameters for the MRC estimator through the reinforcement learning method.

References

1. De Boer, P.T., Kroese, D.P., Mannor, S., Rubinstein, R.Y.: A tutorial on the cross-entropy method. Ann. Oper. Res. **134**(1), 19–67 (2005)
2. Dong, L., Wei, F., Zhou, M., Xu, K.: Question answering over freebase with multi-column convolutional neural networks. In: Proceedings of the 53rd Annual Meeting of the Association for Computational Linguistics and the 7th International Joint Conference on Natural Language Processing (Volume 1: Long Papers), pp. 260–269 (2015)
3. Feng, J., Huang, M., Zhao, L., Yang, Y., Zhu, X.: Reinforcement learning for relation classification from noisy data. In: Proceedings of the Thirty-Second AAAI Conference on Artificial Intelligence, (AAAI-18), New Orleans, Louisiana, USA, 2–7 February 2018, pp. 5779–5786 (2018)
4. Han, X., et al.: More data, more relations, more context and more openness: A review and outlook for relation extraction. In: Proceedings of the 1st Conference of the Asia-Pacific Chapter of the Association for Computational Linguistics and the 10th International Joint Conference on Natural Language Processing, pp. 745–758 (2020)
5. Ji, G., Liu, K., He, S., Zhao, J.: Distant supervision for relation extraction with sentence-level attention and entity descriptions. In: Proceedings of the AAAI Conference on Artificial Intelligence, vol. 31, pp. 3060–3066 (2017)
6. Kingma, D.P., Ba, J.: Adam: a method for stochastic optimization. arXiv preprint arXiv:1412.6980 (2014)
7. Kumar, S.: A survey of deep learning methods for relation extraction. arXiv preprint arXiv:1705.03645 (2017)
8. Li, X., Feng, J., Meng, Y., Han, Q., Wu, F., Li, J.: A unified MRC framework for named entity recognition. In: Proceedings of the 58th Annual Meeting of the Association for Computational Linguistics, pp. 5849–5859 (2020)
9. Lin, Y., Shen, S., Liu, Z., Luan, H., Sun, M.: Neural relation extraction with selective attention over instances. In: Proceedings of the 54th Annual Meeting of the Association for Computational Linguistics (Volume 1: Long Papers), pp. 2124–2133 (2016)
10. Liu, Y., et al.: RoBERTa: a robustly optimized BERT pretraining approach. arXiv preprint arXiv:1907.11692 (2019)
11. Mintz, M., Bills, S., Snow, R., Jurafsky, D.: Distant supervision for relation extraction without labeled data. In: Proceedings of the Joint Conference of the 47th Annual Meeting of the ACL and the 4th International Joint Conference on Natural Language Processing of the AFNLP, pp. 1003–1011 (2009)
12. Phi, V., Santoso, J., Tran, V., Shindo, H., Shimbo, M., Matsumoto, Y.: Distant supervision for relation extraction via piecewise attention and bag-level contextual inference. IEEE Access, 103570–103582 (2019)
13. Qin, P., Xu, W., Wang, W.Y.: Robust distant supervision relation extraction via deep reinforcement learning. In: Proceedings of the 56th Annual Meeting of the Association for Computational Linguistics, ACL 2018, Melbourne, Australia, 15–20 July 2018, vol. 1, Long Papers, pp. 2137–2147 (2018)
14. Rajpurkar, P., Jia, R., Liang, P.: Know what you don't know: Unanswerable questions for squad. In: Proceedings of the 56th Annual Meeting of the Association for Computational Linguistics (Volume 2: Short Papers), pp. 784–789 (2018)

15. Riedel, S., Yao, L., McCallum, A.: Modeling relations and their mentions without labeled text. In: Balcázar, J.L., Bonchi, F., Gionis, A., Sebag, M. (eds.) ECML PKDD 2010. LNCS (LNAI), vol. 6323, pp. 148–163. Springer, Heidelberg (2010). https://doi.org/10.1007/978-3-642-15939-8_10
16. Surdeanu, M., Tibshirani, J., Nallapati, R., Manning, C.D.: Multi-instance multi-label learning for relation extraction. In: Proceedings of the 2012 Joint Conference on Empirical Methods in Natural Language Processing and Computational Natural Language Learning, EMNLP-CoNLL 2012, 12–14 July 2012, Jeju Island, Korea, pp. 455–465 (2012)
17. Sutskever, I., Martens, J., Dahl, G., Hinton, G.: On the importance of initialization and momentum in deep learning. In: International Conference on Machine Learning, pp. 1139–1147. PMLR (2013)
18. Wang, Z., Zhang, J., Feng, J., Chen, Z.: Knowledge graph embedding by translating on hyperplanes. In: Proceedings of the AAAI Conference on Artificial Intelligence, vol. 28, pp. 1112–1119 (2014)
19. Yoon, J., Arik, S., Pfister, T.: Data valuation using reinforcement learning. In: International Conference on Machine Learning, pp. 10842–10851. PMLR (2020)
20. Zeng, D., Liu, K., Chen, Y., Zhao, J.: Distant supervision for relation extraction via piecewise convolutional neural networks. In: Proceedings of the 2015 Conference on Empirical Methods in Natural Language Processing, EMNLP 2015, Lisbon, Portugal, 17–21 September 2015, pp. 1753–1762 (2015)
21. Zeng, D., Liu, K., Lai, S., Zhou, G., Zhao, J.: Relation classification via convolutional deep neural network. In: COLING 2014, 25th International Conference on Computational Linguistics, Proceedings of the Conference: Technical Papers, 23–29 August 2014, Dublin, Ireland, pp. 2335–2344 (2014)
22. Zhu, T., et al.: Towards accurate and consistent evaluation: a dataset for distantly-supervised relation extraction. In: Proceedings of the 28th International Conference on Computational Linguistics, pp. 6436–6447 (2020)

Multi-modal and Multi-perspective Machine Translation by Collecting Diverse Alignments

Lin Li[1(✉)], Turghun Tayir[1], Kaixi Hu[1], and Dong Zhou[2]

[1] School of Computer and Artificial Intelligence, Wuhan University of Technology,
Wuhan, China
{cathylilin,hotpes,issac_hkx}@whut.edu.cn
[2] School of Computer Science and Engineering, Hunan University of Science
and Technology, Xiangtan, China
dongzhou@hnust.edu.cn

Abstract. Multi-modal machine translation (MMT) is one of the most active research directions in the natural language processing. Recently, Seq2Seq translation model with images shows promising performance in enhancing translation quality. However, the existing technologies inadequately consider diverse multi-modal alignments when using different ways of adding images. We observe that this diversity can produce differentiated knowledge and further generates distinct translation outputs. In order to address the above problem, this paper proposes a Multi-perspective and Multi-modal Machine Translation Method by Collecting Diverse Alignments (M^3-CoDA) which introduces different granularities of image features to the attention mechanism, aiming at forming diverse implicit multi-modal alignments. Moreover, those implicit alignments will produce MMT results from different perspectives. This paper further designs a sequence ensemble to aggregate multiple translation results. The experimental results on the Multi30k dataset show that our proposed method significantly improves translation quality compared with several popular baselines in terms of BLEU.

Keywords: Multi-modal machine translation · Multi-perspective · Diverse alignments · Multi-modal attention

1 Introduction

With the increasingly close communication between different languages and countries, machine translation (MT) has advantages over manual translation in efficiency and cost. The development of computer technology such as deep learning provides promising solutions for the end-to-end model MT. In recent years, multi-modal machine translation (MMT) can effectively use the image information corresponding to the source text and improve the translation quality. One of the most popular frameworks is so called Seq2Seq based on Transformer [8,22].

D. N. Pham et al. (Eds.): PRICAI 2021, LNAI 13032, pp. 311–322, 2021.
https://doi.org/10.1007/978-3-030-89363-7_24

Since text and image belong to different data modality, how to bridge the modality gap between them is one of the challenges of MMT. In the translation task, if multi-modal alignment is performed as a latent intermediate step, the task can usually be improved [3] and an effective way to address this is to use attention [2]. The key problem is how to introduce images to enhance the alignment. Adding extracted image features to the attention structure of Transformer is an effective way to improve multi-modal translation [11]. However, the alignment of text and image is affected by the granularity of features, thus producing diverse alignments. How to make good use of the diverse alignments is a challenge for improving the performance of MMT.

To address the above problem, this paper proposes a Multi-perspective and Multi-modal Machine Translation Method by Collecting Diverse Alignments (M^3-CoDA). Firstly, on the decoder of Transformer, a diverse alignments module is designed to combine the output from encoder with one-dimensional global features or two-dimensional local features of image to achieve diverse alignments. And then, multi-perspective probability distributions over vocabulary are derived from diverse alignments, all of which will jointly take effect on the next-step prediction. Finally, sequence ensemble is designed in the multi-perspective module to improve the traditional way of directly fusing the probability outputs from translated sentences, and further optimize the translation results.

In summary, this paper makes the following contributions:

- Our M^3-CoDA method can produce diverse alignments and further output multi-perspective translation results, thereby improving the quality of MMT.
- The diverse alignments module is proposed by considering the different features granularity of images in the attention mechanism, so that the decoder will be allowed to focus on different parts of image when generating each successive word.
- The experimental results on the open multi-modal dataset Multi30k show that our proposed method effectively improves the translation quality of baseline in terms of BLEU.

2 Related Work

MMT aims to build translation models that can process and correlate information from multiple modalities [1]. Caglayan et al. [5] have deeply discussed on whether multi-modal information is helpful to MT. Their experimental results show that the MMT model with image features is better than the text-only MT. In addition, in order to select the optimal image representation layer, Caglayan et al. studied the accuracy of different image features on the image classification task, extracted features from each layer of ResNet-50 [10] and evaluated the classification performance.

Caglayan et al. [4] have added image features to the head or tail of the original text sequence, and a transformation matrix is used to address embedding dimension mismatch between image and text. Helcl et al. [3] have introduced

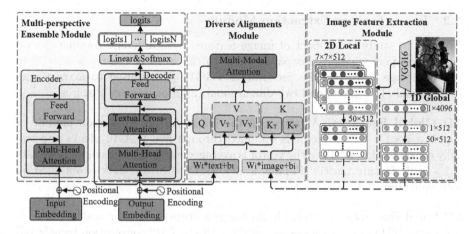

Fig. 1. The structure of our M^3-CoDA. It contains three modules: image feature extraction module, diverse alignments module and multi-perspective ensemble module. Image feature extraction module extracts two kinds of image features with different granularity and outputs them to diverse alignments module to form diverse alignments. Diverse alignments are input into the decoder of Transformer in the multi-perspective ensemble module to generate multi-perspective translation results. Some detailed network structures within the Transformer, like layer normalization, are omitted for clarity.

an additional layer of attention structure on the decoder end of Transformer to receive image features as input. Grönroos et al. [8] have used the Gate mechanism that applies image features to encoder or decoder to improve the ability of model to understand ambiguous words and phrases, and achieved the best results in English-German translation in WMT18. Kiros et al. [14] and Han et al. [9] have improved the attention mechanism through coordinated representation learning.

The existing MMT approaches pay little attention on the diversity of multi-modal alignments. What's more, the results of different alignments of text and image should be processed effectively. This paper proposes an end-to-end diverse alignments MMT method from the aspects of attention mechanism, image feature extraction and sequence data prediction fusion, which provides a feasible way for improving multi-modal translation quality.

3   Methodology

3.1   The Framework of Our M^3-CoDA

The core idea of our M^3-CoDA model is to embed a diverse alignments module that aligns image and text features to improve the vectorized representation quality of multi-modal information. This paper uses Transformer as the basic network structure and designs three modules, namely image feature extraction module, diverse alignments module and multi-perspective ensemble module. Its overall structure is shown in Fig. 1.

3.2 Image Feature Extraction Module

In order to study the impact of image features with different granularities on translation performance, this paper refers to the work of Huang et al. [12] to extract image features. The pre-trained VGG16 [18] is used to extract one-dimensional (1D) global and two-dimensional (2D) local image features.

1D Global Features. As shown in the image feature extraction module in Fig. 1, a $1 \times 1 \times 4096\text{D}$ vector is obtained through five VGG16 blocks and two fully connected layers. Then the vector is averaged every 8 dimensions to generate a $1 \times 512\text{D}$ feature matrix. Finally, a $50 \times 512\text{D}$ feature matrix is obtained by self-replication.

2D Local Features. As shown in the image feature extraction module of Fig. 1, a $7 \times 7 \times 512\text{D}$ vector is obtained after three times of 512 convolution kernels and one pooling layer. Then the vector is transformed into a $49 \times 512\text{D}$ matrix by linear transformation, and zeros are added at the last row to make it a $50 \times 512\text{D}$ feature matrix.

3.3 Diverse Alignments Module

Text and Image Representation. This paper fuses the text features from the encoder and the image features from the image feature extraction module by designing linear weighting in multi-modal attention. The text feature $x_t \in \mathbb{R}^{b \times d}$ and the image feature $x_i \in \mathbb{R}^{b \times d}$ are linearly transformed into $W_t \cdot x_t + b_t$ and $W_i \cdot x_i + b_i$, where b and d are the sentence length and embedding size, W_t, W_i, b_t and b_i are the weights and biases of the linear transformation of text and image features, respectively. Then they are sent to multi-modal attention for fusion.

Through linear transformation, the text and image features are mapped to a common semantic space and effective semantic complementarity is realized, and they satisfy the addition and subtraction operations. For example, an image feature vector of a dog - a text feature vector of a dog + a text feature vector of a cat = an image feature vector of a cat.

Diverse Alignments. In multi-modal works, alignment is defined as the relationship and correspondence between sub-components that find instances from two or more modalities [3]. Attention mechanism allows models to learn alignments between different modalities such as image and text description [23]. As shown in the middle block of Fig. 1, we use multi-modal attention to align text and image features with different granularities and produce different alignments. Attention function A and context vector C are calculated as follows:

$$A(Q, K, V) = softmax\left(\frac{QK^T}{\sqrt{d}}\right)V \tag{1}$$

$$C = \sum_{i=1}^{h} A\left(QW_i^Q, KW_i^K, VW_i^V\right)W_i^O \tag{2}$$

where h is the number of attention heads, $W_i^Q, W_i^K, W_i^V \in \mathbb{R}^{d \times d}$ and $W_i^O \in \mathbb{R}^{hd \times d}$ are trainable parameter matrices.

The input of multi-modal attention is as follows: Query matrix Q always comes from the text cross-attention in the decoder. The Key matrix K always contains both the linearly transformed text feature K_T and image feature K_V. K_V can be a 1D global image features K_{1D} or a 2D local image features K_{2D}. Value matrix V is similar to K, the difference is that there are also cases where V only includes text features V_T. For the above Eqs. (1) and (2), the four input forms shown below produce diverse alignments.

(1) when K includes the text features K_T and the 1D global image features K_{1D}, and V only includes the text features V_T, the corresponding attention function A and context vector C are calculated as follows:

$$A(Q, K_T + K_{1D}, V_T) = softmax\left(\frac{Q(K_T + K_{1D})^T}{\sqrt{d}}\right) V_T \qquad (3)$$

$$C = \sum_{i=1}^{h} A\left[QW_i^Q, (K_T + K_{1D})W_i^{(K_T + K_{1D})}, V_T W_i^{V_T}\right] W_i^O \qquad (4)$$

(2) when K includes the text features K_T and the 2D local image features K_{2D}, and V only includes the text features V_T, A and C are calculated as follows:

$$A(Q, K_T + K_{2D}, V_T) = softmax\left(\frac{Q(K_T + K_{2D})^T}{\sqrt{d}}\right) V_T \qquad (5)$$

$$C = \sum_{i=1}^{h} A\left[QW_i^Q, (K_T + K_{2D})W_i^{(K_T + K_{2D})}, V_T W_i^{V_T}\right] W_i^O \qquad (6)$$

(3) when K includes the text features K_T and the 1D global image features K_{1D}, and V also includes the text features V_T and the 1D global image features V_{1D}, the corresponding A and C are calculated as follows:

$$A(Q, K_T + K_{1D}, V_T + V_{1D}) = softmax\left(\frac{Q(K_T + K_{1D})^T}{\sqrt{d}}\right)(V_T + V_{1D})$$

$$\tag{7}$$

$$C = \sum_{i=1}^{h} A\left[QW_i^Q, (K_T + K_{1D})W_i^{(K_T + K_{1D})}, (V_T + V_{1D})W_i^{(V_T + V_{1D})}\right] W_i^O$$

$$\tag{8}$$

(4) when K includes the text features K_T and the 2D local image features K_{2D}, and V also includes the text features V_T and the 2D local image features V_{2D}, the corresponding A and C are calculated as follows:

$$A(Q, K_T + K_{2D}, V_T + V_{2D}) = softmax\left(\frac{Q(K_T + K_{2D})^T}{\sqrt{d}}\right)(V_T + V_{2D})$$

$$\tag{9}$$

$$C = \sum_{i=1}^{h} A \left[QW_i^Q, (K_T + K_{2D}) W_i^{(K_T + K_{2D})}, (V_T + V_{2D}) W_i^{(V_T + V_{2D})} \right] W_i^O$$

$$(10)$$

3.4 Multi-perspective Ensemble Module

Recently, the idea of ensemble learning has appeared on the decoding side of the model to improve the translation performance [17, 21, 25]. As shown in the leftmost block of Fig. 1, this paper designs sequence ensemble in the multi-perspective module to improve the different traditional results formed by diverse alignments and further optimize the translation results.

Algorithm 1. Multi−perspective ensemble algorithm

Input: Model probability distribution tables are $logits1$, $logits2$, ..., $logitsN$. Maximum length of sentence is MAX_LEN
Output: Probability distribution table of fusion model
1: $MAX\_LEN = 50$; $i = 1$
2: **for** $i < MAX\_LEN$ **do**
3:      $logits\_s = 0$; $n = 1$
4:      **for** $n < N$ **do**
5:          $logits[i][n] = decoder[n](logits[i-1])$
6:          $logits\_s[i] \mathrel{+}= logits[i][n]$
7:          $n{+}{+}$
8:          $logits[i] = logits\_s[i] / N$
9:      **end for**
10:     $i{+}{+}$
11: **end for**
12: **return** $logits$

Considering the different effects of different alignments on translation quality, we further calculate the average probability distribution inferred from sub-models that input text and image information to obtain a new distribution table [20]. The word corresponding to the maximum probability value in this table is taken as the output word of our model. For example, the multi-perspective ensemble process of the source language sentence "a boy stands with three girls" is shown in Fig. 2. The four model prediction probabilities of the first word are averaged to obtain a new probability distribution table, in which the maximum probability corresponds to "ein", so the translation result of "a" in the current time series prediction is "ein". Then re-input "ein" into the decoders of the four models to get the translation result of the next word in the same way, and repeat this process until the last word is predicted. The pseudo code of multi-perspective ensemble is descripted in Algorithm 1.

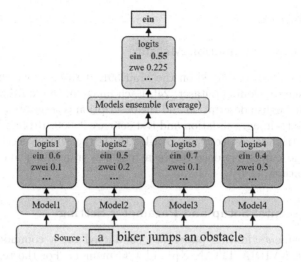

Fig. 2. Model fusion process. This figure shows the fusion of predicted values of the first word in the four models.

3.5   Loss Function

In this paper, *mean_loss* is used as the objective function in our model training. The first step is to make a *softmax* calculation on the j-th source sentence word prediction vector x_j output by the model decoder, as shown in Eq. (11):

$$y_j = softmaxt(x_j) \tag{11}$$

The second step is to use the vector y_j and its standard answer representation vector $\acute{y}_j$ to calculate cross-entropy, as shown in Eq. (12):

$$H(y_j) = -\sum_{j=1}^{|J|} y_j log(\acute{y}_j) \tag{12}$$

where $|J|$ represents the dimension of the vector x_j. The third step is to use Eq. (13) to calculate *mean_loss*:

$$mean\_loss = \frac{\sum_{j=1}^{L} H(y_j) \cdot is\_target_j}{\sum_{j=1}^{L} is\_target_j} \tag{13}$$

where L represents the length of the source sentence, this paper sets the sentence length to 50, *is_target* is a vector representing the actual length of the source sentence, and *is_target$_j$* is the j-th value of the vector. For example, there is a source sentence with 35 words and its *is_target* vector is $(w_1, w_2, \ldots, w_{35}, w_{36}, \ldots, w_{50})$, where $w_1, w_2, \ldots, w_{35} = 1$, $w_{36}, \ldots, w_{50} = 0$.

4 Experiment

4.1 Dataset and Evaluation Measure

Our experiments are conducted on the Multi30K dataset [7] which extends the Flickr30k image captioning dataset [24]. Each image in the Multil30k dataset is paired with an English description and the description is translated into German. The size of the training, validation and test sets are 29000, 1014 and 1000 image-source-target triplets respectively. BLEU [15] is the widely accepted measure to evaluate the correspondence between machine translation and professional human translation.

4.2 Experimental Setup and Parameter Setting

All the experiments in this paper are conducted on a commodity machine equipped with NVIDIA TITAN Xp and 12G memory. For the text processing like WMT18[1], words are used as the minimum segmentation unit with lower-case and punctuation normalization, and finally a training vocabulary table for English and German is obtained. In order not to block any words that appear less frequently, the length of the sentence and the number of occurrences of each word in the training set are set to 50 and 1, respectively.

The main network parameters of our method are as follows: Encoder and decoder are 6 layers, multi-head is 8, embedding and hidden layer dimensions are 512. Dropout and learning rates are 0.2 and 0.0001, and the filter size of feed-forward neural network is 2048. The warm-up steps and epoch are set at 4000 and 30. Batch-size and label smoothing [19] are set to 32 and 0.1 respectively. The Adam optimizer [13] is used for parameter optimization and the beam-search strategy is used for prediction in the decoding stage.

4.3 Baselines

In the WMT18 MMT task competition, models with good translation performance [6,8] works on optimizing the utilization of image features by the introduced Gate Layer structure. In addition, Helcl et al. [11] set an attention unit at the decoder, which gets the weighted sum of the image representation and a layer of attention to the image feature is added between the self-attention layer and the feedforward neural network in each decoder layer of Transformer. [9] is the most recent work in the baselines.

4.4 Experimental Results

Performance Comparisons. Based on Transformer, this paper reproduces the experimental results of decoder gate, decoder gate, decoder & decoder gate in [8], double attentive decoder in [11], and CVSR [9], as listed in Table 1.

---

[1] http://www.statmt.org/wmt18/multimodal-task.html.

Table 1. Comparisons with baselines

Model	BLEU
Text-only Transformer [22]	30.28
Encoder gate [8]	30.01 ↓
Decoder gate [8]	29.98 ↓
Encoder-Decoder gate [8]	30.36 ↑
Double attentive decoder [11]	30.65 ↑
CVSR [9]	31.41 ↑
Ours	**34.07** ↑

Table 2. Results of different diverse alignments experiment

Model number	Model	BLEU
①	Text-only Transformer	30.28
②	$(K \neq V)$ + 1D global features	31.41 ↑
③	$(K \neq V)$ + 2D local features	31.50 ↑
④	$(K = V)$ + 1D global features	30.96 ↑
⑤	$(K = V)$ + 2D local features	30.43 ↑

In Table 1, it can be found that, compared to the text-only neural MT model, the multi-modal model fused with image is not always better. For example, adding the gate structure after encoder or decoder [8] does not improve translation performance, and even the accuracy of the model is reduced.

For the multi-modal translation model based on the gate structure, the experimental results show that adding a gate layer at both ends of decoder and decoder at the same time (30.36) is better than adding one of them separately (30.01 and 29.98). The two gate structures can filter out some irrelevant information by using image features at the decoder and decoder stages simultaneously, thereby improving the accuracy of the model. In the CVSR method, a linear layer is added on the decoder side to combine the image feature representation based on collaborative learning, and a BLEU 31.41 is obtained.

Our M³-CoDA shows the best performance, and the BLEU score is 34.07. Compared with latest CVSR (31.41), our M³-CoDA gains translation improvement by introducing image features of different granularities and combines them with the attention mechanism to form diverse alignments.

Results of Diverse Alignments. In Table 2, experiments ②③④⑤ correspond to the four alignments in Sect. 3.3, it is observed that our M³-CoDA with aligning two different granular image features with text features has better translation performance than the MT model based on text-only ①. In our M³-CoDA, K always includes the image features K_V and text features K_T. $K \neq V$ means that

V only includes the encoder output V_T, $K = V$ means that V includes the image features V_V and text features V_T.

Compared with the results of ② and ③, the model performance of 2D local image features is better than that of 1D global features (31.50 vs 31.41), because 2D local image features extracted based on different channels can express deeper semantic information, thereby increasing the effect of image features in the model prediction stage. Compared with the experimental results of ④ and ⑤, the model performance of 2D local image features does not always have advantages. The possible reason is that when both K and V include the image and text features ($K=V$), the effect of the text information in the multi-modal attention is reduced to a certain extent.

Results of Multi-perspective Ensemble. As shown in Table 3, this paper uses the multi-perspective ensemble method to fuse the experimental results of the four models ②③④⑤ produced by the diverse multi-modal alignments shown in the previous section, and the four experiments are regarded as single models of the fusion model.

Table 3. Results of multi-perspective ensemble

Ensemble	Combination	Number of models	BLEU
Com-1	②④	2	32.48
Com-2	③⑤	2	32.14
Ours	②③④⑤	4	**34.07**

Comparing the results of Com-1 and Com-2 in Table 3 and the experimental results in Table 2, it is found that the effect of fusing two models with different granularities is better than that of any single model. The fusion of the four models achieves the best result (M^3-CoDA) with BLEU 34.07, which is 18.18% higher than the text-only baseline model, and the performance improvement about 8–11% on a single MMT model. The main reason for the result of the fusion model is greatly improved as shown in the Fig. 2. The translation result of the current word "a" in Model4 is incorrect, but the correct result is obtained after fusion with the other three models. The performance of the fusion model can be improved by fusing different models with differences.

5   Conclusion and Future Work

This paper proposes the M^3-CoDA MMT method, which can produce diverse alignments and further output multi-perspective translation results, thereby improving the quality of MT. Experiments results show that this method greatly improved the translation quality of the existing translation methods. With more pubic MMT datasets, future work can test the generation of the proposed method.

In the future, we plan to use a neural network with better performance such as Faster R-CNN [16] to extract the region image features and align them with their corresponding text word features. Meanwhile, since the main work of this paper focuses on the decoder, we will try to study the encoder in the future.

Acknowledgement. This work was supported by the National Natural Science Foundation of China under Project No. 61876062.

References

1. Arthur, P., Neubig, G., Nakamura, S.: Incorporating discrete translation lexicons into neural machine translation. In: EMNLP, pp. 1557–1567 (2016)
2. Bahdanau, D., Cho, K., Bengio, Y.: Neural machine translation by jointly learning to align and translate. In: ICLR (2015)
3. Baltrusaitis, T., Ahuja, C., Morency, L.: Multimodal machine learning: a survey and taxonomy. IEEE Trans. Pattern Anal. Mach. Intell. **41**(2), 423–443 (2019)
4. Caglayan, O., et al.: LIUM-CVC submissions for WMT17 multimodal translation task. In: WMT, pp. 432–439 (2017)
5. Caglayan, O., Aransa, W., Wang, Y.: Does multimodality help human and machine for translation and image captioning? In: WMT, pp. 627–633 (2016)
6. Cao, Q., Xiong, D.: Encoding gated translation memory into neural machine translation. In: EMNLP, pp. 3042–3047 (2018)
7. Elliott, D., Frank, S., Sima'an, K., Specia, L.: Multi30K: multilingual English-German image descriptions. In: VL@ACL (2016)
8. Grönroos, S., et al.: The MeMAD submission to the WMT18 multimodal translation task. In: WMT (shared task), pp. 603–611 (2018)
9. Han, Y., Li, L., Zhang, J.: A coordinated representation learning enhanced multimodal machine translation approach with multi-attention. In: ICMR, pp. 571–577 (2020)
10. He, K., Zhang, X., Ren, S., Sun, J.: Deep residual learning for image recognition. In: CVPR, pp. 770–778 (2016)
11. Helcl, J., Libovický, J., Varis, D.: CUNI system for the WMT18 multimodal translation task. In: WMT (shared task), pp. 616–623 (2018)
12. Huang, P., et al.: Attention-based multimodal neural machine translation. In: Proceedings of the First Conference on Machine Translation, WMT, pp. 639–645. The Association for Computer Linguistics (2016)
13. Kingma, D.P., Ba, J.: Adam: a method for stochastic optimization. In: ICLR (2015)
14. Kiros, R., Salakhutdinov, R., Zemel, R.S.: Unifying visual-semantic embeddings with multimodal neural language models. CoRR abs/1411.2539 (2014)
15. Papineni, K., Roukos, S., Ward, T., Zhu, W.: BLEU: a method for automatic evaluation of machine translation. In: ACL, pp. 311–318 (2002)
16. Ren, S., He, K., Girshick, R.B., Sun, J.: Faster R-CNN: towards real-time object detection with region proposal networks. In: NIPS, pp. 91–99 (2015)
17. Sennrich, R., Haddow, B., Birch, A.: Edinburgh neural machine translation systems for WMT 16. In: WMT, pp. 371–376 (2016)
18. Simonyan, K., Zisserman, A.: Very deep convolutional networks for large-scale image recognition. In: ICLR (2015)
19. Szegedy, C., Vanhoucke, V., Ioffe, S., Shlens, J., Wojna, Z.: Rethinking the inception architecture for computer vision. In: CVPR, pp. 2818–2826 (2016)

20. Tan, L., et al.: An empirical study on ensemble learning of multimodal machine translation. In: BigMM, pp. 63–69 (2020)
21. Tan, Z., Wang, B., Hu, J., Chen, Y., Shi, X.: XMU neural machine translation systems for WMT 17. In: WMT, pp. 400–404 (2017)
22. Vaswani, A., et al.: Attention is all you need. In: NIPS, pp. 5998–6008 (2017)
23. Xu, K., et al.: Show, attend and tell: neural image caption generation with visual attention. In: ICML, vol. 37, pp. 2048–2057 (2015)
24. Young, P., Lai, A., Hodosh, M., Hockenmaier, J.: From image descriptions to visual denotations: new similarity metrics for semantic inference over event descriptions. Trans. Assoc. Comput. Linguistics **2**, 67–78 (2014)
25. Zhou, L., Hu, W., Zhang, J., Zong, C.: Neural system combination for machine translation. In: ACL, pp. 378–384 (2017)

Simplifying Paragraph-Level Question Generation via Transformer Language Models

Luis Enrico Lopez, Diane Kathryn Cruz, Jan Christian Blaise Cruz, and Charibeth Cheng$^{(\boxtimes)}$

De La Salle University Manila, Taft Ave., Malate, 1004 Manila, Philippines
{luis_lopez,diane_cruz,jan_christian_cruz,charibeth.cheng}@dlsu.edu.ph

Abstract. Question Generation (QG) is an important task in Natural Language Processing (NLP) that involves generating questions automatically when given a context paragraph. While many techniques exist for the task of QG, they employ complex model architectures, extensive features, and additional mechanisms to boost model performance. In this work, we show that transformer-based finetuning techniques can be used to create robust question generation systems using only a single pretrained language model, without the use of additional mechanisms, answer metadata, and extensive features. Our best model outperforms previous more complex RNN-based Seq2Seq models, with an 8.62 and a 14.27 increase in METEOR and ROUGE_L scores, respectively. We show that it also performs on par with Seq2Seq models that employ answer-awareness and other special mechanisms, despite being only a single-model system. We analyze how various factors affect the model's performance, such as input data formatting, the length of the context paragraphs, and the use of answer-awareness. Lastly, we also look into the model's failure modes and identify possible reasons why the model fails.

Keywords: Question generation · Delimiters · Transformer networks

1 Introduction

Question Generation (QG) [13], while not as prominent as its sibling task Question Answering (QA), still remains relevant in NLP. The ability to ask meaningful questions is closely related to *comprehension* [9], making QG important in the bigger picture of AI.

Over the years, many successful models for QG have been produced. Basic Sequence-to-Sequence (Seq2Seq) models [5] provided early baselines, eventually adding improvements such as: the use of linguistic features [18], introduction of answer-awareness [2,17], application of Reinforcement Learning [16], and the shift to Transformer [15] models to replace RNNs [2].

L. E. Lopez, D. K. Cruz and J. C. B. Cruz—Equal contribution. Order determined by drawing lots.

D. N. Pham et al. (Eds.): PRICAI 2021, LNAI 13032, pp. 323–334, 2021.
https://doi.org/10.1007/978-3-030-89363-7_25

While all of these techniques are robust, they all employ complex models, extra features, and additional mechanisms that make them harder to train and expensive to reproduce. In this work, we show that transformer-based finetuning techniques can be used to create robust question generation systems using only a single pretrained language model, without the use of additional mechanisms, answer metadata, and extensive features.

We show that our method, albeit simpler, produces results on par with the state-of-the-art. We benchmark standard language model finetuning on a reformatting of the SQuAD [12] v.1.1 dataset and evaluate generation performance with standard language generation metrics. In addition, we perform a variety of analyses in order to isolate performance indicators within our model and identify its weaknesses and failure modes.

2   Methodology

2.1   Data Preparation

We train the QG model on version 1.1 of the Stanford Question Answering Dataset (SQuAD) [12]. SQuAD contains context paragraphs, each with sets of questions and corresponding answer spans related to the contents of these paragraphs; in total, SQuAD contains more than 100,000 crowdsourced questions. While originally intended for the task of question answering, previous works on question generation [4,17] have repurposed SQuAD as a training and test dataset, designating the questions as the target output rather than the answer spans.

We then frame QG as a Language Modeling task. Each training example consists of a context paragraph and its associated question(s) transformed into a single continuous sequence with a delimiter in between. Training examples are separated by the newline character \n. Figure 1 shows an example of a single training example in this form.

Super Bowl 50 was an American football game to determine the champion of the National Football League (NFL) for the 2015 season. The American Football Conference (AFC) champion... [SEP] Which NFL team represented the AFC at Super Bowl 50?

Fig. 1. A sample training example with the ARTIFICIAL delimiter and the OQPL format. The context, delimiter, and question are highlighted in red, green, and blue respectively. (Color figure online)

Additionally, we experiment with two factors in reformatting the input data this way: the delimiter used, and the representation method for multiple questions per context paragraph. Figure 2 illustrates the six data formats we use for model training.

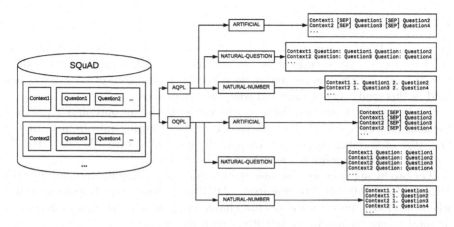

Fig. 2. Data preparation pipeline for SQuAD.

Delimiters. We experiment with three different delimiting schemes: 1) ARTIFI-CIAL, or a delimiter in the form of the token `[SEP]`, 2) NATURAL-QUESTION, or a delimiter in the form of the word `Question`, and 3) NATURAL-NUMBER, or a delimiting scheme in the form of a numbered list, where each item is a question.

The ARTIFICIAL delimiter was not present in the original model's vocabulary, and its weights are learned from scratch during the finetuning phase, while the NATURAL delimiting schemes rely on token weights already learning during the pretraining phase, thus making it possible for the model's pretrained knowledge to affect performance through these delimiters. Similar keywords have been shown to be effective in invoking certain pretrained model behaviors (e.g. `TL;DR:` for summarization), even in a zero-shot setting [11].

Questions Per Line. There can be several questions associated with a single paragraph. We experiment with two ways to flatten this many-to-one relationship in the formatted data:

All Questions Per Line (AQPL). A single training example consists of a context paragraph with all of its associated questions placed immediately after it, separated from one another with the selected delimiter. While this avoids duplication of context and thus results in faster training time, it may potentially result in the model no longer being able to attend to earlier tokens as its context window moves further away from the beginning of the input paragraph.

One Question Per Line (OQPL). Each context paragraph is duplicated for each of its associated questions, such that for a single training example, there is only one context and one question. For many cases, this may alleviate the moving context window problem raised with AQPL. However, this format does result in a longer training time due to the duplicated contexts increasing the size of the final formatted dataset.

2.2   Experiments

We use the 124M parameter GPT-2, the smallest of the four available sizes, as our base model. We then finetune six QG models, each using one of the data format combinations enumerated in Sect. 2.1. Larger versions of GPT-2 was not used in this study due to time and compute limitations.

Each model was trained for 3 epochs using the Adam optimizer [7] with a learning rate of 5×10^{-4}, linearly increasing the learning rate from 0 for the first 10% of training steps, then linearly decaying afterward. We use GPT-2's full 1024 maximum sequence length and a batch size of 32.

For producing questions, we use the top-p nucleus sampling method [6] with a value of $p = 0.9$ and a temperature of 0.6. Each generation loop stops either when the model generates the newline character \n, or when the model generates 32 total tokens, signalling an infinite generation loop.

Similar to the work of [17], we perform automatic evaluation metrics such as BLEU_1, BLEU_2, BLEU_3, BLEU_4 [10], ROUGE_L [8] and METEOR [1]. We used the evaluation package made by [14] to quantify the models' performance.

3   Results and Discussion

The best performing model is the One Question Per Line (OQPL) model with number delimiters, achieving the highest score for BLEU_2, BLEU_3, BLEU_4 and METEOR. For BLEU_1 and ROUGE_L, the One Question Per Line (OQPL) model with artificial delimiters performed the best. A summary of the finetuning results can be found on Table 1.

Table 1. Model finetuning scores

Format	Delimiter	BLEU_1	BLEU_2	BLEU_3	BLEU_4	METEOR	ROUGE_L
AQPL	Artificial	54.83	30.13	15.72	7.31	20.53	43.88
	Number	54.98	30.31	15.79	7.57	20.69	43.83
	Question	55.03	30.46	16.20	7.74	20.71	44.039
OQPL	Artificial	**55.60**	31.03	16.56	7.89	21.03	**44.41**
	Number	55.51	**31.17**	**16.79**	**8.27**	**21.2**	44.38
	Question	55.28	30.81	16.55	8.21	21.11	44.27

It is interesting to note, however, that the best OQPL models are on average only 0.6917 points better than their corresponding All Questions Per Line (AQPL) counterparts. We hypothesize that this is because not enough of SQuAD's context paragraphs combined with their questions are long enough to cause the moving context window problem (refer to Sect. 2.1) to occur. This means that the choice between data formatting (OQPL vs AQPL) only matters marginally, provided that the context length does not approach the maximum sequence length of the model.

For further analysis, we also extracted post-finetuning features from the generated questions such as question length, paragraph context length, and longest sub-sequence (between the paragraph context and generated question) on the best performing model. These features yielded some interesting observations, which we touch on in the following subsections.

3.1 Evaluating Context-Copying

From the initial results, we observe that a number of generated questions seem to be *simply pulled from the given context, with phrase order reversed.* In order to quantify how frequent this behavior is present in the model, we calculate the longest common subsequence (LCS) between the generated questions and its corresponding context paragraph.

We find that, on average, the model tends to take 6.25 tokens from the context paragraph it was given. In cases where this happens, the generated questions tend to be identification type questions (who/what/when/where), which comprise 91.67% of the total generated samples.

We hypothesize that the model learned this mode (context-copying) as its most common generation style because of the frequency of identification type questions in the training dataset. As we suspected, SQuAD contains 88.26% identification type questions in the training set, which lends empirical evidence to our hypothesis.

To diversify the model's question generation style, we hypothesize that the training dataset should also have a move diverse question style beyond simple identification-type questions.

3.2 Failed Generations

We observe that 19 of the generated questions using SQuAD's test set were "non-questions" falling in two distinct categories: Generations where *the last 3 words keep repeating,* and; Generations where *the question was cut prematurely.* Example generations from these two categories can be found on Table 2.

For the first category, we look at the model's attention visualization for clues on why the model repeatedly generates the same three words. A sample attention visualization can be found in Fig. 3.

In all the failed generations falling under the first category, we find that attention weights tend to be evenly distributed over a number of random positions as it generates the question. Instead of aiding the model to output the best next token, attention ends up "confused," providing noise to the model. We hypothesize that this is due to either insufficient training or a problem with the sampling mechanism.

In the second category, we surmise that the reason why the model cuts generation is simply because it reached the maximum generation length while copying text from the context. This is a consequence of the model's context-copy mechanism, which it learned as its most common generation mechanism.

Table 2. Examples of failed generations from the best performing model's failure modes.

Case	Question	Context
1	What is a profession of the profession of the profession of the profession of the profession of the profession of the profession of the profession of the profession of the profession of the profession	Teaching may be carried out informally, within the family, which is called homeschooling, or in the wider community. Formal teaching may be carried out by paid professionals. Such professionals enjoy a status in some societies on a par with physicians, lawyers, engineers, and accountants (Chartered or CPA)
2	Which newspaper in the United States defined Southern California as including the seven counties of Los Angeles, San Bernardino, Orange, Riverside, San Diego, Ventura and Sant	In 1900, the Los Angeles Times defined southern California as including "the seven counties of Los Angeles, San Bernardino, Orange, Riverside, San Diego, Ventura and Santa Barbara." In 1999, the Times added a newer county–Imperial–to that list

Layer 1 Head 11

0.02 0.02   0.01   0.01

Teaching may be carried out informally,   within the family,   which is called homeschooling,   or in the wider

community.   Formal teaching may be carried out by paid professionals.   Such professionals enjoy a status in

some societies on a par with physicians,   lawyers,   engineers,   and accountants (Chartered or CPA). 1 .

What is a profession of the profession of the profession of the profession of the profession of the profession of the

profession of the profession of the profession of the profession of the profession of the profession of the profession

of the profession of the profession of the profession of the profession of the profession of the profession of the

profession of the

Fig. 3. Sample attention visualization for generated outputs of failure mode 1. This example shows the words and the attention values to those words when focusing on the word "profession," which is highlighted in red. (Color figure online)

3.3 Optimal Context Length

In order to understand the limits of the model's robustness, we also look at varying the length of the context paragraph, which we surmise is a performance indicator for the model.

For every context paragraph in the test set with at least 30 sentences, we perform the following:

1. The context is fed to the model to generate outputs.
2. The outputs are scored via BLEU, the results are logged.
3. We then sentence-split the context paragraph using SpaCy, removing the last sentence, and reconstructing the now-modified context paragraph.
4. We repeat from step 1 until the modified context paragraph now only has one sentence.

We remove entire sentences instead of reducing the number of words as this interferes with how intact the information is in the context. The model should also be able to produce a question, disregarding performance, even with just one sentence as a context paragraph. We also only test context paragraphs with at most 30 sentences as, on average, this is the most that fit in GPT-2's 1024 maximum sequence length restriction for inputs.

An example of the sentence reduction scheme is shown on Table 3.

Table 3. Sample context paragraph after sentence reduction generation, all of the context in the figure above would be fed to the best performing model. The first sentence, second sentence, third sentence, and fourth sentence highlighted in black, blue, green, and red respectively

Sentence number	Context
1	Proportionality is recognised one of the general principles of European Union law by the European Court of Justice since the 1950s
2	Proportionality is recognised one of the general principles of European Union law by the European Court of Justice since the 1950s. According to the general principle of proportionality the lawfulness of an action depends on whether it was appropriate and necessary to achieve the objectives legitimately pursued
3	Proportionality is recognised one of the general principles of European Union law by the European Court of Justice since the 1950s. According to the general principle of proportionality the lawfulness of an action depends on whether it was appropriate and necessary to achieve the objectives legitimately pursued.When there is a choice between several appropriate measures the least onerous must be adopted, and any disadvantage caused must not be disproportionate to the aims pursued
4	Proportionality is recognised one of the general principles of European Union law by the European Court of Justice since the 1950s. According to the general principle of proportionality the lawfulness of an action depends on whether it was appropriate and necessary to achieve the objectives legitimately pursued. When there is a choice between several appropriate measures the least onerous must be adopted, and any disadvantage caused must not be disproportionate to the aims pursued.The principle of proportionality is also recognised in Article 5 of the EC Treaty, stating that" any action by the Community shall not go beyond what is necessary to achieve the objectives of this Treaty

From this analysis, we show that the optimal number of sentences in the context is more or less 10. As the number of sentences increase from 1 to 10, we see that the performance also increases. However, as we increase the number of sentences in the context all the way to 30, the performance is shown to degrade. A graph showing the BLEU scores in relation to the number of sentences in the context paragraph is shown in Fig. 4.

We hypothesize that this is because the model needs to look at more information in order to identify relevant attention positions as the number of sentences increase. From an interpretative perspective, the performance degradation when the number of sentences increase makes sense because there will be more possible questions to produce from a longer context paragraph than a shorter one.

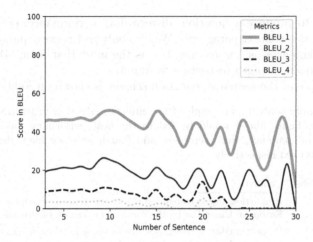

Fig. 4. BLEU scores for each length

A short context paragraph will have a more apparent subject, which can be directly used by the model's context-copy mechanism in order to generate good questions. On the other hand, if the model encounters a long context paragraph where the subject is not apparent (or if the context paragraph has multiple topics/subjects), the context-copy mechanism that the model usually employs will have a hard time pinpointing exact attention positions from where it bases its generated questions from.

Further analyzing the results, we see that BLEU_1 unsurprisingly degrades the slowest as it only looks at unigram correspondence, while BLEU_4 degrades the fastest, reaching a score of 0 as early as the 17 sentence mark.

From this analysis, we learn that a higher number of sentences in the context paragraph will give the model more information to generate a question from, too many sentences will confuse the model and cause its performance to degrade.

3.4   Answer-Awareness

Given that a number of well-performing previous studies on question generation use answer-awareness, we also test if our single-transformer method will benefit from this additional feature. Answer-awareness refers to the usage of the answer's position or the answer to the question itself, alongside the context paragraph, as input to the model for question generation.

In order to test this, we employ a OQPL artificial-based formatting scheme, marking the start position of the answer within the context with a special answer start ([ANSS]) token, and marking the end of the answer with a special answer-end ([ANSE]) token.

A sample input context paragraph with answer-awareness tokens can be found in Fig. 5.

Super Bowl 50 was an American football game to determine the champion of the National Football League (NFL) for the 2015 season. The American Football Conference (AFC) champion [ANSS] Denver Broncos [ANSE] defeated the National Football Conference (NFC) champion Carolina Panthers 2410 to earn their third Super Bowl title. The game was played on February 7, 2016, at Levi's Stadium in the San Francisco Bay Area at Santa Clara, California. As this was the 50th Super Bowl, the league emphasized the "golden anniversary" with various gold-themed initiatives, as well as temporarily suspending the tradition of naming each Super Bowl game with Roman numerals (under which the game would have been known as "Super Bowl L"), so that the logo could prominently feature the Arabic numerals 50. [SEP] Which NFL team represented the AFC at Super Bowl 50?

Fig. 5. A sample training example for answer-aware question generation training. The marked answer span is highlighted in red. Uses the ARTIFICIAL delimiter and the OQPL format. Text adapted from SQuAD dataset [12]. (Color figure online)

We then follow the same finetuning setup as the original OQPL artificial model, evaluating on BLEU and ROUGE_L scores. A summary of the finetuning results for the answer-aware model can be found on Table 4.

Table 4. Summary of Answer-Aware finetuning results.

Model	BLEU_1	BLEU_2	BLEU_3	BLEU_4	ROUGE_L
OQPL Standard	55.60	31.03	16.56	7.89	44.41
OQPL Answer-Aware	36.07	18.83	10.95	6.40	39.80

From these results, we can see that the answer-aware models perform significantly worse in terms of BLEU score, and marginally worse than the standard OQPL artificial model in terms of ROUGE_L.

We surmise that this is because the model has no inherent idea what to do with the answer-awareness information, and unlike true answer-aware models like UniLM [2], no explicit mechanism that puts importance to the answer-awareness is present in the model. While it is possible for the model to inherently learn to attend to the answer information, this is not deterministic. An explicit, separate mechanism to incorporate answer-awareness in order to help the model learn the feature's significance is still important to have. In the end, the model still performs better without answer-awareness.

4   Related Literature

The most prevalent technique for question generation studies is the usage of a sequence-to-sequence (Seq2Seq) model [2–4,17] in addition to a variety of other features and mechanisms. Attention is also a widely used technique, used by works that employ both standard RNN architectures and Transformer models [2,17].

Other studies employ widely different techniques such as using a policy gradient for reinforcement learning [16], various linguistic features [18], and answer awareness [3,16–18].

While most of these works produce robust results, they are complex (Seq2Seq naturally using two neural networks instead of one) and use a lot of extra techniques in order to boost performance. Our work, in comparison, simply uses a single model (one transformer) instead of two in a Seq2Seq setup. It also uses a simple finetuning setup, and does not use any extensive modifications or techniques. However, it produces robust results that are on par with the state of the art in question generation (Table 5).

Table 5. Previous Works with Paragraph Level Input

Model	Answer	BLEU_4	METEOR	ROUGE_L
Du et al. (2017) [4]	–	12.28	16.62	39.75
Du et al. (2018) [3]	✓	15.16	19.12	–
Zhao et al. (2018) [17] (s2s+a)	–	4.8	12.52	30.11
Zhao et al. (2018) [17] (s2s-a-at-mcp-gsa)	✓	16.38	20.25	44.48
Dong et al. (2019) [2]	✓	22.12	25.06	51.07
GPT2 + attention (ours)	–	8.26	21.2	44.38

Our model outperforms prior RNN-based Seq2Seq works [3,4,17] in terms of METEOR and ROUGE_L score. It is worth noting that, in addition to a more complex model setup, [17] uses other techniques such as a maxout pointer mechanism and gated self attention mechanisms. Other previous work also use answer awareness, using the positions of the answers in the paragraph, or the answers themselves, as additional features for the model. Our transformer uses none of these extra features, yet still achieves robust METEOR and ROUGE_L scores that outperform these studies.

Our model performs worse in terms of BLEU_4 and ROUGE_L, and slightly worse in terms of METEOR when compared with the recent UniLM work of [2]. It is important to note that [2] is also the only other work that uses a Transformer for their question generation model. Their incorporation of an answer-awareness mechanism, in addition to the multiple modes of finetuning on a Seq2Seq transformer produces the best results in recent literature.

While our model performs worse than UniLM, we note that UniLM uses a Seq2Seq-based approach, necessitating the use of two separate Transformers: an encoder and a decoder. In contrast, our model relies only on a single Transformer-decoder-based language model, effectively halving model complexity. In addition, our model does not require any sort of answer tagging, making it suitable for situations where this information is not available in the input context. Our model is smaller, less complex, and faster to operate, making it an ideal alternative for a variety of use cases related to question generation.

5   Conclusion

Previous attempts at paragraph-level question generation have relied on several additional features and techniques in order to produce state-of-the-art results.

In this paper, we demonstrate that a simple single Transformer-based question generation model is able to outperform more complex Seq2Seq methods without the need for additional features, techniques, and training steps. For future work, we plan to evaluate performance on more difficult datasets that pose "why" or "how" questions as opposed to SQuAD's factoid-only questions. We also look towards training with larger model sizes and evaluating the cost-benefit of using larger models as opposed to more efficient ones.

References

1. Denkowski, M., Lavie, A.: Meteor universal: language specific translation evaluation for any target language. In: Proceedings of the EACL 2014 Workshop on Statistical Machine Translation (2014)
2. Dong, L., et al.: Unified language model pre-training for natural language understanding and generation. CoRR arXiv:1905.03197 (2019)
3. Du, X., Cardie, C.: Harvesting paragraph-level question-answer pairs from Wikipedia. In: Proceedings of the 56th Annual Meeting of the Association for Computational Linguistics (Volume 1: Long Papers), pp. 1907–1917. Association for Computational Linguistics, Melbourne, July 2018. https://doi.org/10.18653/v1/P18-1177. https://www.aclweb.org/anthology/P18-1177
4. Du, X., Shao, J., Cardie, C.: Learning to ask: neural question generation for reading comprehension. CoRR (2017). arXiv:1705.00106
5. Duan, N., Tang, D., Chen, P., Zhou, M.: Question generation for question answering. In: Proceedings of the 2017 Conference on Empirical Methods in Natural Language Processing, pp. 866–874. Association for Computational Linguistics, Copenhagen, Denmark, September 2017. https://doi.org/10.18653/v1/D17-1090. https://www.aclweb.org/anthology/D17-1090
6. Holtzman, A., Buys, J., Forbes, M., Choi, Y.: The curious case of neural text degeneration. CoRR arXiv:1904.09751 (2019)
7. Kingma, D.P., Ba, J.: Adam: a method for stochastic optimization. In: Bengio, Y., LeCun, Y. (eds.) 3rd International Conference on Learning Representations, ICLR 2015, San Diego, CA, USA, 7–9 May 2015, Conference Track Proceedings (2015). arXiv:1412.6980
8. Lin, C.Y.: ROUGE: a package for automatic evaluation of summaries. In: Text Summarization Branches Out, pp. 74–81. Association for Computational Linguistics, Barcelona, July 2004. https://www.aclweb.org/anthology/W04-1013
9. Nappi, J.S.: The importance of questioning in developing critical thinking skills. Delta Kappa Gamma Bull. **84**(1), 30 (2017)
10. Papineni, K., Roukos, S., Ward, T., Zhu, W.J.: BLEU: a method for automatic evaluation of machine translation. In: Proceedings of the 40th Annual Meeting of the Association for Computational Linguistics, pp. 311–318. Association for Computational Linguistics, Philadelphia, July 2002. https://doi.org/10.3115/1073083.1073135. https://www.aclweb.org/anthology/P02-1040
11. Radford, A., Wu, J., Child, R., Luan, D., Amodei, D., Sutskever, I.: Language models are unsupervised multitask learners. OpenAI Blog (2019)
12. Rajpurkar, P., Zhang, J., Lopyrev, K., Liang, P.: SQuAD: 100,000+ questions for machine comprehension of text. In: Proceedings of the 2016 Conference on Empirical Methods in Natural Language Processing, pp. 2383–2392. Association for Computational Linguistics, Austin, November 2016. https://doi.org/10.18653/v1/D16-1264

13. Rus, V., Cai, Z., Graesser, A.: Question generation: example of a multi-year evaluation campaign. In: Proceedings WS on the QGSTEC (2008)
14. Sharma, S., El Asri, L., Schulz, H., Zumer, J.: Relevance of unsupervised metrics in task-oriented dialogue for evaluating natural language generation. CoRR arXiv:1706.09799 (2017)
15. Vaswani, A., et al.: Attention is all you need. In: Advances in Neural Information Processing Systems, pp. 5998–6008 (2017)
16. Yuan, X., et al.: Machine comprehension by text-to-text neural question generation. In: Proceedings of the 2nd Workshop on Representation Learning for NLP, pp. 15–25. Association for Computational Linguistics, Vancouver, August 2017
17. Zhao, Y., Ni, X., Ding, Y., Ke, Q.: Paragraph-level neural question generation with maxout pointer and gated self-attention networks. In: Proceedings of the 2018 Conference on Empirical Methods in Natural Language Processing, pp. 3901–3910. Association for Computational Linguistics, Brussels, October–November 2018
18. Zhou, Q., Yang, N., Wei, F., Tan, C., Bao, H., Zhou, M.: Neural question generation from text: a preliminary study. CoRR arXiv:1704.01792 (2017)

Neural Networks and Deep Learning

ABAE: Utilize Attention to Boost Graph Auto-Encoder

Tianyu Liu, Yifan Li, Yujie Sun, Lixin Cui$^{(\boxtimes)}$, and Lu Bai

Engineering Research Center of State Financial Security, Ministry of Education,
Central University of Finance and Economics, Beijing 102206, China
`cuilixin@cufe.edu.cn`

Abstract. Graph Auto-Encoder(GAE) emerged as a powerful node embedding method, has attracted extensive interests lately. GAE and most of its extensions rely on a series of encoding layers to learn effective node embeddings, while corresponding decoding layers trying to recover the original features. Promising performances on challenging tasks have demonstrated GAE's powerful ability of representation. On the other hand, Subgraph Convolutional Networks(SCNs), as an extension of Graph Convolutional Networks(GCNs), can aggregate both tagged and local structural features in an artful way. In this paper, we show that SCNs can be improved (AttSCNs) by an attention mechanism to acquire better representational capability, which is competent for the duty of encoder. Then we develop inversed AttSCNs and propose a novel auto-encoder, i.e., Attention-Based Auto-Encoder(ABAE). This architecture utilizes attention mechanism to get insight of the data. We perform experiments on some challenging tasks to show the effectiveness of our models. Moreover, we construct AttSCNs for *Node Classification*. The results demonstrate that AttSCNs can produce considerable embeddings. Furthermore, we launch *Link Prediction* task for the proposed ABAE. Experimental results show that our ABAE has its fantastic power and achieves state-of-the-art in *Link Prediction*.

Keywords: Subgraph Convolutional Networks · Graph Auto-Encoder · Learning graph representation · Node embeddings

1 Introduction

Graphs are universal data structure in non-Euclidean space, thanks to their powerful modeling capabilities. Among various challenging tasks in the graph domain, learning node embeddings is a basic but crucial difficulty. It aims at integrating existing features and topological structures, and forming effective node representations. Consequently, the extracted representations can provide support for downstream tasks while boosting the performance.

Several shallow embedding techniques like DeepWalk [1], Node2vec [2] were earlier introduced. However, such methods have the shortcoming of enormous

---

Y. Li and Y. Sun—Equally Contributed.

© Springer Nature Switzerland AG 2021
D. N. Pham et al. (Eds.): PRICAI 2021, LNAI 13032, pp. 337–348, 2021.
https://doi.org/10.1007/978-3-030-89363-7_26

parameters to be optimized and fail to take both features and structural information into consideration. To overcome these shortcomings, graph neural networks(GNNs) [3] have recently emerged. Readers can refer to [4] for a whole review. These approaches can consider information diffusion using message passing. Nonetheless, some of them still face the offensive problems such as over-smoothing.

Among these deep graph neural networks, Graph Auto-Encoder(GAE) and Variation Graph Auto-Encoder(VGAE) [5] arose as excellent approaches to achieve interpretable node embeddings. [6] developed Subgraph Convolutional Neural Networks(SCNs) as a depth-based representation method of graph structure. This architecture captures both global topological structure and local connection within graph in an ingenious way. However, though SCNs alleviate the influences of the over-smoothing problem, there is still some unreasonableness existing in the architecture. For more details, we will introduce them in Sect. 2.

In this paper, we first analyze the aforementioned models and give our comprehension. Then we develop AttSCNs with an attention mechanism to learn useful information. Finally, we combine them with an inversed version throughout encoder-decoder architecture and propose our ABAE model. Our contributions are threefold.

- We analyse advantages and limitations of previous works, mainly about GAE and SCNs.
- We develop the improved AttSCNs and Attention-Based Auto-Encoder, which is able to capture structural features and local connectivity.
- We empirically evaluate the performance of our models and show that our models are competitive even compared with other SOTA methods.

The rest of this paper is organized as follows. Section 2 illustrates the mentioned GAE and SCNs while analyzing these components. Section 3 proposed the improved AttSCNs, which are proved to be more powerful for information aggregation. Section 4 describes the inversed AttSCNs and gives the whole architecture of our new ABAE model. Section 5 explores the performance of our models on challenging tasks respectively and gives an experimental evaluation. Finally, we conclude our works and discuss future work in Sect. 6.

2 Related Work

In this section, we will introduce GAE and SCNs and analyse their architectures from a unique perspective. More specifically, $G = (V, E)$ denotes graph, where V denotes the set of vertices and $E \subseteq V \times V$ denotes the set of edges. $X \in \mathbb{R}^{N \times d}$ is the feature matrix of the graph.

2.1 Graph Auto-Encoders

Graph Auto-Encoders transferred the encoder-decoder architecture to graph domain, and achieved a great success. The encoding layers try to extract potent features while the decoding layers try to recover as much as possible signals from the encoded vectors. [7] proved that even simple linear encoding layer with an inner-product decoding layer can achieve compelling results for plain graphs, which inspires us that the encoder-decoder architecture has a strong potential to learn vast information. Meanwhile, when it comes to complicated graphs, [8] and [11] suggest that decoder is also a significant component of Auto-Encoders. Paired encoder and decoder [11] may contribute to prominent progress for graph-based tasks.

Empirically paired encoder-decoder hold similar capabilities of encoding and decoding. In this way, the more signal decoders recover, the more information is packed into the representational vectors. This leads to a significant improvement of the performance of the model. In this time the decoder can probably strengthen the encoder intuitively.

2.2 Subgraph Convolutional Networks

Inspired by Graph Convolutional Networks [12], [6] proposed a novel model QS-CNNs based on quantum-walk. This model first decomposes a graph into a family of K-layer m-ary expansion trees for each unique vertex, then scans a subgraph based window defined over an m-ary tree. The whole model can be divided into three parts as follows.

Rank. QS-CNNs score each node with a quantum-based rank. The quantum-walk method provides better efficiency. However, it may be too complicated and our experiments show even degree rank can obtain similar effectiveness. So we replace this ranking with sorted degree. In this regard, we call the model SCNs, not QS-CNNs.

Construct. QS-CNNs establish subtrees for each vertex, which is crucial for extracting structural features reflecting the local connectivity. The model uses graph grafting and pruning to standardize the neighborhood subgraph for constructing an m-ary tree. Following this, the leaf nodes of each subtree are further replaced by their own subtrees. Figure 1 shows the concrete reproduction.

Convolute. Sliding the fixed-size window over the subtrees. After several operations, the subtrees degenerate as the origin nodes. However, the sliding window cannot distinguish the root with its child. In other words, if two nodes are linked with the root, they have an equal status. Though the weight of filters are alterable, they may not be appropriate for every m-are tree. We will use an attention mechanism to solve this problem.

In our perspective, SCNs can be considered as the limited expansion of GCNs cause every root has a fixed number of children, and the networks benefit from the tree-shape structure to alleviate the effect of over-smoothing. However, although SCNs can effectively capture local connectivity, they still lose the latent

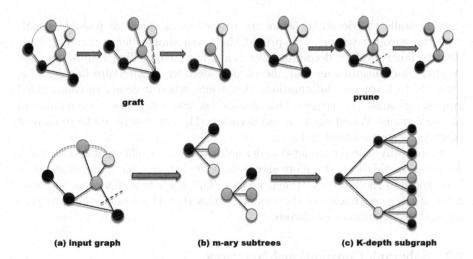

(a) input graph   (b) m-ary subtrees   (c) K-depth subgraph

Fig. 1. Graph grafting crops of excess nodes if the neighbor is larger than required and graph pruning pads with dummy nodes if it is smaller than required. Concrete process is shown in figure.

distant connectivity. Meanwhile, when combining with GAE [11], it seems that the inversed SCNs do not make sense.

3   Proposed Improved AttSCNs

In this section, we first transform the convolutional process of SCNs into another form, and further develop the improved AttSCNs.

3.1   Insight of Subgraph Convolution

In this subsection, we show that convolution in SCNs is another form on grid data of node-wise method.

Given previous subtree T with height K and m-ary, note that T is a full m-ary tree, so T has the node number of $\frac{m^K-1}{m-1}$ while the non-leaf node number is $\frac{m^{K-1}-1}{m-1}$. We can grade the nodes of T with $1, 2, ..., \frac{m^K-1}{m-1}$. Here, each node denotes a feature vector $p_{node} \in R^{1 \times d}$ where d is the dimension.

When preforming the convolutional operation, we first construct a node matrix $M \in R^{(m+1) \times \frac{m^{K-1}-1}{m-1}}$. Each column of M indicates the root with its children. See Fig. 2 for more details. Then the fixed-sized Conv1d filter can slide the matrix and form the new matrix $M_{new} \in R^{1 \times \frac{m^{K-1}-1}{m-1}}$. After that, M_{new} can be realigned as a new subtree T_{new} with height $K - 1$ and m-ary.

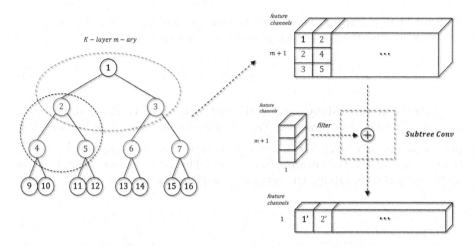

Fig. 2. We translate subgraph convolution into another form. First construct node matrix for a subtree. Then a Conv1d filter will slide over the matrix and reform a new shrunken subtree.

In this way, it seems unreasonable as the filter weight is shared for each column. Empirically different child nodes should have different status and contribute different impact. Therefore, we consider to use an attention mechanism to distinguish the filter weights.

3.2 Attention-Based SCNs

To address the shared weight problem, we employ the attention mechanism as below.

Let c_0 be one non-leaf node of one subtree, and $c_1, c_2...c_m$ be its child nodes. Similar to [13], we can compute the attention coefficients between root and child nodes as follows.

$$e_j = a(\mathbf{W}c_0, \mathbf{W}c_j) \qquad where \quad j = 0, 1, 2, ..., m \qquad (1)$$

Here, a is a shared attentional mechanism $a : \mathbb{R}^d \times \mathbb{R}^d \to \mathbb{R}$ for computing attention coefficients. To make coefficients easily comparable, we normalize them using the softmax function.

$$\alpha_j = softmax(e_j) = \frac{exp(e_j)}{\sum_{i=0}^{m} exp(e_i)} \qquad where \quad j = 0, 1, 2, ..., m \qquad (2)$$

Then the root can be updated as follows.

$$\boldsymbol{n}_{new} = \sigma(\sum_{i=0}^{m} \alpha_i \mathbf{W}c_i) \qquad (3)$$

To learn hierarchical information for integration, we employ multi-head attention. Specifically, H independent attention execute as follows.

$$\boldsymbol{n}_{new} = \|_{h=1}^{H} \; \sigma(\sum_{i=0}^{m} \alpha_i^h \mathbf{W}^h \boldsymbol{c}_i) \tag{4}$$

Hitherto, we successfully combine the root with its child nodes and generate a new root. We show this process in Fig. 3. For each column of M, we perform this process and obtain $M_{new} \in R^{1 \times \frac{m^{K-1}-1}{m-1}}$. After several attention-based convolutions, a subtree will be converted into a node. This node contains more features and structural connectivity, which can be considered as the node representations.

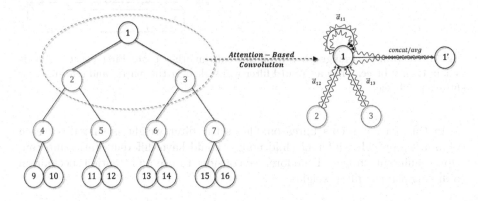

Fig. 3. The attention-based subgraph convolution. For each non-leaf node, we will conduct attention-based subgraph convolution and form a new node which represents the new embedding. Consequently, when we finish all the convolution, the whole subtree will shrink with height K-1.

4   Attention-Based Auto-Encoder

With promising encoding capabilities, AttSCNs can probably take the duty of encoder. Meanwhile, we should consider the paired decoder to boost encoder. [11] uses 1×1 *Conv* to construct inversed SCNs, which may lead to structural information loss. However, thanks to the exquisite construction, we can obtain the inversed AttSCN by caching the attention coefficients.

4.1   Inversed AttSCNs

Reviewing the equations above, we find that W in Eq. 3 plays the role of linear transformation, hence we can first perform this process. Given $m + 1$ nodes $c_0, c_1, ..., c_m$ and the linear transfer parameters W, we can derive the new $m + 1$ nodes by applying W to each node.

$$c_i' = W c_i \tag{5}$$

Therefore, we can rewrite Eq. 3 in vector form as below.

$$n_{new} = \sigma(AC^T) \tag{6}$$

Here, $A = (\alpha_0, \alpha_1, ..., \alpha_m)$ denotes the attention coefficients vector and $C = (c'_0, c'_1, ..., c'_m)$ denotes the transformed signal for $m + 1$ nodes. We can cache A for further computation.

In the inversed AttSCN, when we obtain n_{new}, we need inversed process to acquire recovery with low loss. Therefore, we can obtain an approximate solution by this equation. Here, A^g is pseudoinverse matrix.

$$C' = \sigma'(A^g \ n_{new}) \tag{7}$$

Because A^g can be computed by cached A, we can represent a node vector ascent as a subtree T'. After several similar operations, T' will grow as the same size of the original subtree.

Mathematically, A^g is computed by applying a series of operations of A^T and A, and it costs too much time of at least $O(n^3)$, which is unaffordable. Therefore, we try to find an approximate solution. As A^g is a transformation of A^T, we set $A^g = \sigma(A^T W')$ to accelerate the computation and mitigate the computational burden. In this situation, the formula can be written as follows.

$$C' = \sigma'(A^T W' \ n_{new}) \tag{8}$$

4.2   Proposed ABAE

After defining encoders and decoders, we compose these components and propose a novel architecture, i.e., Attention-Based Auto-Encoder. The total process can be summarized as follows.

First, we construct subtrees for each vertex as mentioned above.

Second, the encoders perform attention-based subgraph convolution for each subtree. The subtrees will shrink gradually which means information is aggregated in steps. Ultimately the subtrees will degenerate as nodes and form the final representations. Meanwhile, the encoders will give attention coefficients for decoders' computation.

Finally, the decoders take in the encoded nodes and help these nodes grow as the same size of the original subtrees. Then, ABAE will compute the loss and make optimization. Figure 4 illustrates the whole process.

Due to the superiority of the attention mechanism and auto-encoder architecture, our AttSCNs encoders can learn vast information from well-designed subtree structure and give hierarchical representations. Meanwhile, inversed AttSCNs have powerful decoding capabilities both theoretically and practically, which contributes to the promising performance.

Note that training process of our AttSCNs does not rely on the adjacency matrix, which is used only in constructing, and this structure gives us a mass of flexibility. When a node is dynamically added into the graph, we only need to construct the subtree for the node and implement attention-based convolution.

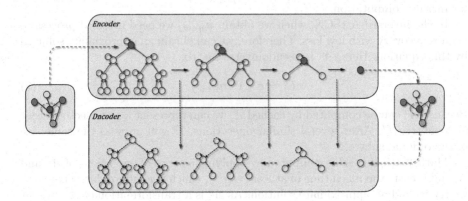

Fig. 4. The whole process of ABAE. After constructing subtrees for each vertex, these subtrees are input of our model. AttSCNs as encoders perform attention-based subgraph convolution and inversed AttSCNs as decoders perform recovery devolution. After optimization, the ourput of last AttSCNs represents the node embeddings.

4.3 Loss of ABAE

In this section, we will determine the loss function used for optimization. Note that decoder's duty is to recover signals from node embeddings, therefore we compute the loss between T and T'. The process of reducing the loss is equivalent to recover more signals, and expect more encoding capabilities. In this paper, we choose $MSELoss$ as below.

$$Loss1 = \sum_{nodeNum} \sum_{i=1}^{d} (T_{node,i} - T'_{node,i}) \tag{9}$$

In *Link Prediction* task, we should add another part of loss for better performance. We utilize the *inner-product* decoder to compute A_{pred} : $A_{pred} = \sigma(ZZ^T)$. Where Z is the node embeddings output of the last AttSCNs and σ denotes the sigmoid function. We use A_{pred} to compute another CrossEntropyLoss with adjacency matrix A. This part of loss is described as follows.

$$Loss2 = BinaryCrossEntropyLoss(A_{pred}, A) \tag{10}$$

Along with loss shown in Eq. 9, we assign weights and use the loss to optimize our ABAE.

$$loss = \alpha Loss1 + \beta Loss2 \tag{11}$$

Here, α and β are loss weighted hyperparameters for adjustment.

5 Experiments

In this section, we evaluate the performance of our models, AttSCNs and Attention-Based Auto-Encoder, and compare them with state-of-the-art methods. We choose three citation network datasets including Cora, CiteSeer and Pubmed as benchmark. Concretely, we first construct AttSCNs for *Node Classification* task to prove their effectiveness. Then we perform ABAE methods on *Link Prediction* and show its excellent performance. Finally, we use these results to analyze our models. Our code is available at https://github.com/smart-lty/ABAE.

5.1 Dataset Description

In this part, we briefly introduce the three datasets we will use in further evaluation. Specifically, these benchmarks are citation networks. These datasets are composed of machine learning papers, and are very popular in recent years for graph deep learning. Details are shown in Table 1.

Table 1. Details of Graph Benchmark

Datasets	Nodes	Edges	Features	Classes
Cora	2708	5409	1433	7
CiteSeer	3327	4732	3703	6
Pubmed	19717	44338	500	3

5.2 Node Classification with AttSCNs

First, we focus on *Node Classification*. We tackle this problem with simple AttSCNs. This model simply constructs subtrees and implements attention-based subgraph convolution without linear transformation. We compare this model with a) some classical methods , including GCN [12], GAT [13], QS-CNNs [6] and b) some latest powerful approaches including Graph U-Nets [14], Graph-Bert [15], DifNet [16], NodeNet [17] and AS-GCN [18]. Note that, the experimental results of these methods are reported from their original papers. Total comparison is shown in Table 2.

For the evaluation, we adjust a number of hyperparameters to obtain the best performance of each dataset. The dataset is randomly divided into three parts of training, validation and testing set to evaluate the classification performance. We evaluate prediction accuracy on a testing set of 300 examples, and we choose a validation set of 300 examples from the same dataset. We take the test accuracy as the final result. The parameters for the different datasets are set as follows. a) for Cora: 3(K), 2(m), 0.145(learning rate), 64(hidden nums), 0.6(dropout), and 5(multi heads); b) for Citeseer: 3(K), 3(m), 0.045(learning rate), 32(hidden nums), 0.7(dropout), and 5(multi heads); c) for Pubmed: 3(K),

Table 2. Node Classification Accuracy(In % ± Standard Error)

Models	Cora	CiteSeer	Pubmed
GCN	81.5	70.3	79.0
GAT	83.0 ± 0.7	72.5 ± 0.7	79.0 ± 0.3
QS-CNNs	85.95 ± 1.58	–	89.63 ± 1.67
g-U-nets	84.4 ± 0.6	73.2 ± 0.5	79.6 ± 0.2
Graph-BERT	84.3	71.2	79.3
DifNet	85.1	72.7	79.5
Nodenet	86.8	80.09	90.21
AS-GCN(full-supervised)	87.44	79.66	**90.60**
AttSCNs(ours)	$\mathbf{88.7} \pm 1.2$	$\mathbf{80.5} \pm 0.7$	87.0 ± 0.1

2(m), 0.0958(learning rate), 64(hidden nums), 0.2(dropout), and 1(multi heads). From the experimental results we observe that our AttSCNs models perform better on Cora and CiteSeer. When compared with classical methods and latest methods, AttSCNs get better grades which shows its strong encoding ability. On pubmed, we also obtain a result that have been greatly improved. The results show that our model has certain research significance on node classification tasks.

It is distinct that our model performs better than QS-CNNs and a series of classical methods. Meanwhile, our AttSCNs show great power in node aggregation area even compared with latest approaches. The results empirically demonstrate the effectiveness of the proposed AttSCNs.

5.3 Link Prediction with AttSCN-Based Auto-Encoder

Moreover, we pay attention to *Link Prediction* task to evaluate our proposed ABAE model. We compare our model with some SOTA approaches including s-VGAE [19], sGraphite-VAE [20], GIC [21] and BANE [22] in citation network datasets. We compare these models based on their ability to correctly classify edges and non-edges, therefore we report AUC and AP scores for each model on the test set. The comparison is shown in Table 3. For the evaluation, we also conduct parameter optimization. We first split the dataset into validation and testing sets, i.e., 10% for validation and 5% for test. We report the average accuracy of 100 experiments. We adjust a number of hyperparameters to obtain the best performance of each dataset as below. a) for Cora: 2(K), 2(m), 0.0004(learning rate), 16(hidden nums), 0.1(dropout), and 5(multi heads); b) for Citeseer: 2(K), 2(m), 0.005(learning rate), 64(hidden nums), 0.05(dropout), and 8(multi heads); c) for Pubmed: 3(K), 2(m), 0.001(learning rate), 64(hidden nums), 0.05(dropout), and 8(multi heads).

The result demonstrates that our ABAE achieves state-of-the-art for these datasets and this strongly inspired us that ABAE has a strong potential in *Link Prediction*.

Table 3. Link Prediction with AUC and AP scores

Models	Cora		Citeseer		Pubmed	
	AUC	AP	AUC	AP	AUC	AP
s-VGAE	94.1 ± 0.1	94.1 ± 0.3	94.7 ± 0.2	95.2 ± 0.2	96.0 ± 0.1	96.0 ± 0.1
sG-VAE	93.7	93.5	94.1	95.4	94.8	96.3
GIC	93.5 ± 0.6	93.3 ± 0.7	97.0 ± 0.5	96.8 ± 0.5	94.8 ± 0.1	96.3 ± 0.1
BANE	93.5	–	95.59	–	–	–
AttSCNs(ours)	$\mathbf{98.3 \pm 0.3}$	$\mathbf{98.5 \pm 0.3}$	$\mathbf{98.6 \pm 0.3}$	$\mathbf{98.4 \pm 0.4}$	$\mathbf{98.2 \pm 0.1}$	$\mathbf{98.2 \pm 0.1}$

6 Conclusion and Future Work

Node Embedding is a universal difficulty lying in graph domain. With great representations, we can solve many problems and get insight of graphs. In this paper, we first improve SCNs and develop a powerful architecture, AttSCNs, which is proved to have amazing capabilities for obtaining node embeddings. Furthermore, we propose a novel model with encoder-decoder structure named the ABAE. It achieves start-of-the-art than lastest link prediction methods. This model has a strong potential in *Link Prediction* and it shows the advantages of attention mechanism and auto-encoder architecture.

For future work, we can further improve the proposed ABAE model. First, it is worthwhile trying combining other useful methods with our AttSCNs and ABAE to tackle other challenging tasks e.g. *Graph Classification*. Second, AttSCNs can be updated with advanced methods and we can take edge features into consideration as well. Moreover, AttSCNs as effective encoding method may be transplanted to other graph tasks. We believe that with detailed supplement, our models can achieve better performance.

Acknowledgments. This work is supported by the National Natural Science Foundation of China (Grant no. T2122020, 61976235 and 61602535), the program for innovation research in Central University of Finance and Economics, the Emerging Interdisciplinary Project of CUFE.

References

1. Perozzi, B., Al-Rfou, R., Skiena, S.: Deepwalk: online learning of social representations. In: Proceedings of the 20th ACM SIGKDD International Conference on Knowledge Discovery and Data Mining (2014)
2. Grover, A., Leskovec, J.: node2vec: scalable feature learning for networks. In: Proceedings of the 22nd ACM SIGKDD International Conference on Knowledge Discovery and Data Mining (2016)
3. Gori, M., Monfardini, G., Scarselli, F.: A new model for learning in graph domains. In: Proceedings. 2005 IEEE International Joint Conference on Neural Networks, 2005, vol. 2. IEEE (2005)
4. Joshi, R.B., Mishra, S.: Learning Graph Representations. arXiv preprint arXiv:2102.02026 (2021)

5. Kipf, T.N., Welling, M.: Variational graph auto-encoders. arXiv preprint arXiv:1611.07308 (2016)
6. Zhang, Z., et al.: Quantum-based subgraph convolutional neural networks. Pattern Recogn. **88**, 38–49 (2019)
7. Salha, G., Hennequin, R., Vazirgiannis, M.: Simple and effective graph autoencoders with one-hop linear models. arXiv preprint arXiv:2001.07614 (2020)
8. Li, J., et al.: Graph Autoencoders with Deconvolutional Networks. arXiv preprint arXiv:2012.11898 (2020)
9. Shi, H., Fan, H., Kwok, J.T.: Effective decoding in graph auto-encoder using triadic closure. In: Proceedings of the AAAI Conference on Artificial Intelligence, vol. 34. no. 01 (2020)
10. Flam-Shepherd, D., Wu, T., Aspuru-Guzik, A.: Graph deconvolutional generation. arXiv preprint arXiv:2002.07087 (2020)
11. Bai, L., Cui, L., Bai, X., Hancock, E.R.: Deep depth-based representations of graphs through deep learning networks. Neurocomput. **336**, 3–12 (2019)
12. Kipf, T.N., Welling, M.: Semi-supervised classification with graph convolutional networks. arXiv preprint arXiv:1609.02907 (2016)
13. Velikovi, P., et al.: Graph attention networks. arXiv preprint arXiv:1710.10903 (2017)
14. Gao, H., Shuiwang, J.: Graph u-nets. In: International Conference on Machine Learning. PMLR (2019)
15. Zhang, J., et al.: Graph-bert: Only attention is needed for learning graph representations. arXiv preprint arXiv:2001.05140 (2020)
16. Zhang, J.: Get Rid of Suspended Animation Problem: Deep Diffusive Neural Network on Graph Semi-Supervised Classification. arXiv preprint arXiv:2001.07922 (2020)
17. Dabhi, S., Parmar, M.: NodeNet: A Graph Regularised Neural Network for Node Classification. arXiv preprint arXiv:2006.09022 (2020)
18. Huang, W., et al.: Adaptive sampling towards fast graph representation learning. arXiv preprint arXiv:1809.05343 (2018)
19. Davidson, T.R., et al.: Hyperspherical variational auto-encoders. arXiv preprint arXiv:1804.00891 (2018)
20. Di, X., et al.: Mutual information maximization in graph neural networks. In: 2020 International Joint Conference on Neural Networks (IJCNN). IEEE (2020)
21. Mavromatis, C., Karypis, G.: Graph InfoClust: Leveraging cluster-level node information for unsupervised graph representation learning. arXiv preprint arXiv:2009.06946 (2020)
22. Yang, H., et al.: Binarized attributed network embedding. In: 2018 IEEE International Conference on Data Mining (ICDM). IEEE (2018)

Adversarial Examples Defense via Combining Data Transformations and RBF Layers

Jingjie Li[1], Jiaquan Gao[1], and Xiao-Xin Li[2(✉)]

[1] Nanjing Normal University, Nanjing 210023, China
{192202027,gaojiaquan}@njnu.edu.cn
[2] Zhejiang University of Technology, Hangzhou, China
mordekai@zjut.edu.cn

Abstract. Convolutional Neural Networks (CNNs) are vulnerable to adversarial attacks. By adding imperceptible perturbations to the input images, adversarial attack methods can fool CNN models with a high confidence. The main reason is that existing CNN models usually use softmax-like linear classifiers. Recent researches indicate that Radial Basis Function (RBF) network can effectively improve the nonlinearity classification capability and demonstrates robustness against white-box attacks, while data transformations can smooth the classification boundary and show high efficacy for countering black-box attacks. We propose to incorporate data transformations and RBF together to simultaneously enhance the robustness of CNNs against white-box and black-box attacks. However, applying RBF to a very deep CNN will lead to a difficult convergence during training, while data transformations might reduce classification accuracy due to introducing noises. To solve these issues, we further propose a deep supervision strategy and a novel dual loss function. Experiments on two public available datasets demonstrate that applying the proposed methods to the existing CNN models greatly improve their abilities against adversarial attacks while keeping their original recognition performance.

Keywords: RBF networks · Data transformations · Deep supervision

1 Introduction

In recent years, CNNs have recently achieved state-of-the-art performance in many computer vision tasks, such as image classification [1,2], object detection [3,4], and speech recognition [5,6]. However, it has been demonstrated that deep learning methods can be easily fooled by small imperceptible perturbations in the input images [7,8]. The main reason lies in the softmax-like linear classifiers used by many deep-learning methods. While linear classifiers are very effective

This work was supported by the Natural Science Foundation of China under grant number 61872422.

D. N. Pham et al. (Eds.): PRICAI 2021, LNAI 13032, pp. 349–361, 2021.
https://doi.org/10.1007/978-3-030-89363-7_27

for classification, they force the model to assign high confidences to the regions far from the decision boundary. Due to the vulnerability of linear classifiers, an adversary can easily add some visually imperceptible changes into the input images and migrate the perturbed images across the classification boundary.

In order to improve the non-linearity of a model, Goodfellow *et al.* [8] explored a variety of methods, including shallow and deep RBF network. They used the shallow RBF network to decrease the error rate on MNIST using adversarial examples generated with the fast gradient sign method. Vidnerová *et al.* [9] also demonstrated the robustness of the RBF unit against adversarial perturbations for shallow CNNs. However, deploying a *deep* RBF network is still a challenging problem due to the vanishing gradient problem during training. In addition, an RBF network usually has a decreased generalization ability, which leads to its low robustness against the black-box attacks. In this work, we use the black-box attacks to denote the attacks generating adversarial samples without knowing the architecture and the parameters of the target network, whereas the white-box attacks knows both the architecture and the parameters of the target network. On the other hand, we noticed that using input data transformation methods, such as Gaussian noise injection (GNI) [10] and input feature squeezing (IFS) [11], can destroy the adversarial perturbation structure to some extent, and such defense strategy has a good effect in defending against black-box attack. Unfortunately, the data transformation methods have poor efficacy against white-box attacks. We therefore suggest increasing the robustness of the underlying network by combining data transformation and RBF together.

Our contributions are as follows. First, we devise a novel dual loss function to overcome the vanishing gradient problem caused by deep RBF network. Second, we propose to incorporate data transformation methods (i.e., GNI and IFS) into the deep RBF network to simultaneously enhance the robustness of the underlying networks against both white-box attacks and black-box attacks. Third, in order to improve the accuracy of legitimate datasets and impose intermediate features better, we also integrate deep supervision into the network. Extensive experiments on two baseline networks, six attack methods and two public datasets demonstrate that our proposed model can effectively defend the adversarial examples generated by white-box attacks and black-box attacks.

2 Related Works

2.1 Attack Methods

Fast Gradient Sign Method (FGSM). Goodfellow *et al.* [8] proposed the Fast Gradient Sign Method (FGSM) for crafting adversarial examples. FGSM is an untargeted attack method and it uses the same attack strength at every dimension. Let X be the input image, y_{true} the target class of X and $J(X, y_{true})$ the cost used to train the neural network. FGSM generates the adversarial example as follows

$$X^{\text{adv}} = X + \epsilon \text{sign}\left(\nabla_X J\left(X, y_{true}\right)\right), \tag{1}$$

where ϵ is a hyper-parameter used to determine the perturbation size.

Basic Iterative Method (BIM). BIM [12] is an iterative variant of FGSM. By applying iteratively FGSM multiple times with smaller steps β, BIM generates the adversarial example as follows

$$X_0^{\mathrm{adv}} = X,\ X_{N+1}^{\mathrm{adv}} = \mathrm{clip}_{X,\epsilon}\left(X_N^{\mathrm{adv}} + \beta\mathrm{sign}\left(\nabla_X J\left(X_N^{\mathrm{adv}}, y_{true}\right)\right)\right), \qquad (2)$$

where clip() is used to clip pixel values of intermediate results after each step to ensure that they are in an ϵ-neighbourhood of the original image. BIM was found to produce superior results to fast gradient sign [12].

Carlini and Wagner's Method (CW). The CW method [13] is an optimization-based attack method with a high success rate and can craft targeted or untargeted adversarial samples with very low distortions. CW has three versions: CW_0, CW_2 and CW_∞, which are based on ℓ_0 norm, ℓ_2 norm, and ℓ_∞ norm, respectively. The author point out that the untargeted CW_2 version has the best performance. In our paper, we select CW_2 attack.

2.2 Defense Methods

Papernot *et al.* [14] provided a comprehensive summary of work on defending against adversarial samples, grouping work into two broad categories: adversarial training and gradient masking, which we discuss further below. Recently, researchers [10,11] also contributed a third approach, transforming the input data so that the model is not sensitive to small perturbations.

Defense via Data Transformation. Data transformation methods is a kind of method to preprocess the input images before feeding them to a CNN, including Gaussian noise injection (GNI) [10] and input feature squeezing (IFS) [11]. And this kind of method can destroy the adversarial perturbation structure to some extent.

Feature Squeezing. Xu *et al.* [11] observed that the feature input spaces are often unnecessarily large, which provides large degrees of freedom for an adversary to construct adversarial examples. To shrink the input space, Xu *et al.* [11] proposed two feature squeezing methods: reducing the color bit depth of each pixel and spatial smoothing. Due to its simplicity and efficacy against adversarial samples, feature squeezing can be complementary to other defense methods.

Gaussian Noise Injection. In digital images, noise mainly come from the process of image acquisition and transmission. In the space domain and frequency domain, Gaussian noise (also known as normal noise) is commonly used in practice due to its mathematical ease of handling. Because perturbation has the characteristics of extremely small, Gu and Rigazio [10] consider the Gaussian noise can help move the adversarial examples input outside the network blind-spots and smooth the classification boundary, which can be explained that the addition of Gaussian noise destroys the structure of adversarial perturbation. Experimental results also show that GNI can defend adversarial examples to some extent. However, this method only has good defensive performance against black-box attacks, but has poor defensive performance against white-box attacks. At the same time, since adding the tiny perturbation, the model will have a impact on the performance on the clean samples.

RBF Networks. RBF networks [15,16] are neural networks with one hidden layer of RBF units and a linear output layer. An RBF unit means a neuron with multiple real input $X = (X_1, \cdots, X_n)$ and a output y. The output y is computed as:

$$y = \varphi \left(\gamma \|X - C\|^2 \right) \tag{3}$$

where $\varphi: \mathbb{R} \rightarrow \mathbb{R}$ is suitable activation function, C is the center for neurons. Typically Gaussian $\varphi(Z) = \exp\{-z^2\}$ and $\gamma > 0$ corresponds to the width of the Gaussian. Thus the network computes the following function $f:\mathbb{R} \rightarrow \mathbb{R}$:

$$f(X) = \sum_{i=1}^{h} \eta_i \varphi \left(\gamma_i \| X - C_i \| \right), \tag{4}$$

where $\eta_i \in \mathbb{R}$ is weight of the output of neuron, h is the number of neuron in the hidden layer.

When RBF is combined with shallow CNN [9], the RBF unit can resist perturbation effectively. However, applying RBF to a very deep CNN will lead to a difficult convergence during training. The main reason is that the clustering operations in RBF slow down the learning process.

3   Proposed Method

3.1   Network Design

In this section, we devise an defense model incorporating both data transformation and RBF to enhance the robustness of CNNs. The proposed network model architecture is shown in Fig. 1.

In the proposed model, we first calculate the information entropy of the input image. If the entropy is less than a certain threshold, feature squeezing [11] is used to transform the image. Information entropy [17] measures the information quantity contained in an image, and can be calculated as follows

$$H = -\sum_{i} \sum_{j} P_{i,j} \cdot \log P_{i,j}. \tag{5}$$

Gaussian noises are then added to the image to destroy the crafted adversarial perturbation structure. Finally, we use the RBF layer to further mitigate the problem of misclassification. Due to the nonlinearity characteristic of RBF, adding an RBF layer after the softmax layer can correct the confidence caused

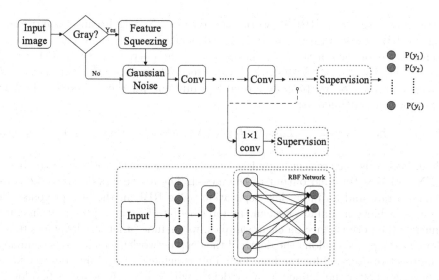

Fig. 1. Illustration of the proposed model. Blue dotted frame is the added RBF network, while the red dotted frame is the supervision. (Color figure online)

by perturbation to some extent. Therefore, the distance between the sample and the classification boundary can be further widened. Meanwhile, to enhance the nonlinearity of the network classifier, we suggest stacking multiple RBF layers after the softmax layer. In terms of the question that Gaussian noise injection might reduce the classification accuracy on the clean image samples, we further use deep supervision for the model. The intermediate supervision modules adopt the similar configuration of the RBF network structure. Next, we discuss the shallow and deep networks respectively.

For the shallow CNN, we consider adding one RBF network after the softmax layer. In addition, the proposed model has no intermediate supervision since the basic CNN network is shallow. More importantly, for the deep CNN, we consider add some intermediate supervisions on CNN except adding Gaussian noise and RBF networks. The supervision architectures are well-designed for image classification task. The supervision select a feature map as the input, and then use 1×1 convolution to compress features. After that, supervision network flatten the feature map to a one-dimensional vector, and softmax is used to map to a confidence vector. Finally the RBF are added to the end of the supervision for classification. The interpretation of supervision structure and position selection would be discussed in the Sect. 4.2.

3.2 Loss Function

For the shallow CNN, the loss function is based on cross-entropy. While more noteworthy, for deep CNN, our experiments show that it is difficult for the network to converge after the addition of RBF network to the deep network. We noticed that the deep RBF network converges slowly only because of introducing the RBF layer. In order to train the deep RBF model more effectively, we combine the output of the basic network and the output of the RBF layer as the weighted sum of the losses, which can effectively improve the convergence of training process. So we propose a dual loss function for the deep network. The loss function is defined as:

$$Loss_{output} = \omega \cdot Loss_{CE}(f_{CNN}(X), Y) + Loss_{CE}\left(\hat{Y}, Y\right), \qquad (6)$$

Here, $loss_{CE}$ is the cross-entropy loss function, f_{CNN} is the output of the basic CNN and $\hat{Y}$ is the final output of the model. The above loss enforces the convergence rate and an inter-class separation using RBF in the output space. In order to achieve a similar effect in the intermediate feature representations and enhance the performance on clean samples, we include other auxiliary loss functions $Loss_{supervision}$ along the depth of the deep networks, which act as companion objective function for the final loss. This is achieved by adding intermediate supervisions after the defined network depth, which maps the features to a lower dimension output, and is then used in the loss definition. And the number of supervision can be determined according to the length of the network.

The structure of supervision is similar to the added part of the backbone network. Therefore, the loss function of the supervision is the same as the loss function Eq. (6). The loss function of the overall network is the sum of the final network output loss and the supervised output loss, which can be expressed as loss function Eq. (7).

$$Loss_{final} = \lambda_0 \cdot Loss_{output} + \sum_{i=1}^{m} \lambda_i \cdot Loss_{supervision_i}, \qquad (7)$$

These functions avoid the difficult convergence problem and act as regularization that encourage features belonging to the same class to come together and the ones belonging to different classes to pushed apart.

4 Experiments

4.1 Experimental Setting

In this section, we report the results of several experiments on two public datasets: MNIST [18] and CIFAR10 [19]. For the MNIST, we choose LeNet-5 [18] as the baseline network. For the CIFAR10, we choose VGG16 [20] as the baseline network.

Three untargeted attack methods, i.e., FGSM [8], BIM [12] and CW_2 [13], are selected to craft adversarial examples. The perturbation size ϵ of FGSM is set to 0.3 on MNIST and set to 0.05 on CIFAR10. The two hyper-parameters β and ϵ in BIM are set 0.1 and 0.3 on MNIST, and set to 0.01 and 0.03 on CIFAR10. The information entropy H is set to 3.

Six defense methods are chosen for comparison: (1) the RBF network (CNN_RBF) [9] where the number of the centers is set to 300; (2) a CNN model using GNI with standard deviation 0.3 on MNIST and 0.05 on CIFAR10 (GNI_CNN) [10]; (3) Adversarial training (AT) [8]: we train the LeNet-5 and VGG16 models on clean and adversarial samples, which are generated by CW_2; (4) Feature Squeezing [11]; (5) Spatial smoothing [11]; (6) AuxBlocks [21].

In our experiments, we also set four types of test sets to compare defense ability against black-box attacks: Clean, TestSet I, TestSet II and TestSet III. In the defense experiments of LeNet-5 and VGG16, we first set the clean test set images of the MNIST and CIFAR10 datasets as Clean test set, respectively. Next, we generate adversarial examples test set by attacking three models (CNN, CNN_RBF, GNI_CNN), which are set as TestSet I, TestSet II and TestSet III. For the shallow CNN experiments, the CNN model represents LeNet-5, while for the deep CNN experiments, the CNN model represents VGG16. The four test set samples from MNIST and CIFAR10 are shown in Fig. 2.

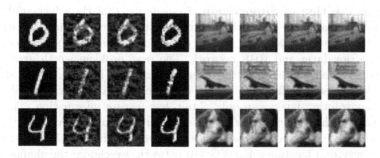

Fig. 2. Set of legitimate and adversarial samples from MNIST and CIFAR10 datasets: For each dataset, legitimate samples, which are correctly classified by CNNs, are found on the leftmost column. Adversarial samples, which are misclassified by CNNs, are on the next three columns.

4.2 Ablation Study

In view of the loss and supervision mentioned in Sect. 3, instinctively, there are three questions need to be discussed. In this section, we discuss the ablation experiments on VGG16 network, and since VGG16 only has 16 layers, we consider adding one supervision for proposed model.

Different Values of ω. In this section, we carried out a series of experiments to analyze the ω in proposed Eq. (6), and obtained the accuracy of the model with different ω values on clean and adversarial samples. The specific results are shown in Fig. 3. From the figure, we can observe that the value of 0.2 performs better than other values in comprehensive defense effect on clean and adversarial examples (generated by FGSM, BIM and CW). Thereby, we propose that ω should not be too large and we choose the $\omega = 0.2$ for the following experiment.

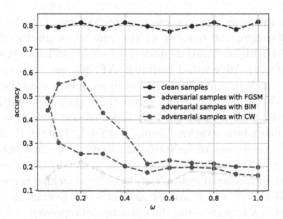

Fig. 3. Accuracy on different values of ω under three white-box attacks.

Different Position of Supervision. Considering that the adversarial examples misclassification is due to high-dimensional linear operation, we set up a simple structure to expand the feature graph, and then classify it through the full connection layer and RBF network. The next problem worth exploring is where supervision will have better defense effect. The instinct is that supervision at low layer is difficult to obtain better classification accuracy since the shallow convolution layers can only obtain less feature information. Therefore, we investigate the impact of our proposed supervision on different position. We conduct the defense experiments on clean and adversarial samples based on different supervision locations. For VGG16 network, we choose the shallow layer, the middle layer and the deep layer three representative positions to add supervision, which are after the fourth convolutional layer, the seventh convolutional layer and the eleventh convolutional layer. Then we set to supervision1, supervision2 and supervision3 respectively. The super parameter λ_0 and λ_1 in Eq. (7) are set 1. The specific results are shown in Table 1. Considering the comprehensive defense performance both on legitimate and adversarial examples, the result proposes that the supervision3 is the better. Therefore, we propose that low layers are not a wise election for an supervision position and we choose the supervision3 for the following experiment.

Table 1. Defense accuracy (%) on different supervision position for VGG16 against white-box FGSM attack on CIFAR10.

	Clean	FGSM
Supervision1	79.96	56.34
Supervision2	80.29	66.47
Supervision3	81.57	63.46

Different Centers of RBF. Considering enhancing the nonlinear of the network classifier, we choose to set the one RBF as a superposition of multiple RBF networks. We conduct experiments based on VGG16 with two RBF networks and three RBF networks, and the results show that the network defense effect with two-layer RBF is better. On the analysis of the model with adding two RBF networks, we thought that the center number should not be selected too small, because of the cluster operation and linear mapping is a kind of operation similar to kernel function mapping from low dimension to high dimension. Meanwhile, the number of centers should not be too large, because the CIFAR10 dataset has only 10 categories. Therefore, we made the contrast experiments under the various attacks, according to two RBF layers selection of different number of centers. Observing these curves in Fig. 4, we can confirm that accuracy is better for comprehensive defense, when the parameter C is set 30.

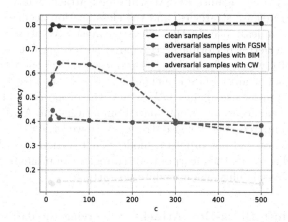

Fig. 4. Accuracy on different values of RBF center under three white-box attacks.

At the same time, we also provide more acceptable evaluation measures for classification such as precision, recall and F1 score. The defense results is displayed in Table 2. Due to the characteristic of two public datasets that the uniform distribution of category data, we still take the accuracy as the main evaluation standard in the next experimental results.

Table 2. Comparisons of different evaluation measures(%) against FGSM white-box attack on CIFAR10.

	Accuracy	Precision	Recall	F1
CNN	21.58	21.18	20.47	20.82
CNN_RBF	55.38	58.67	56.4	57.51
GNI_CNN	19.48	18.77	17.93	18.34
Proposed	64.19	65.68	63.73	64.69

4.3   Defense Results

In order to demonstrate the advantages of the proposed model with GNI and RBF clearly, we carried out experiments on MNIST and CIFAR10 datasets. We compare the defense ability for our proposed model and other defense strategies against white-box and black-box attacks. For MNIST, since LeNet-5 is only has 5 layers, we consider adding only one RBF network without supervision. While for CIFAR10, we choose use one supervision on VGG16.

Defense Against White-Box Attacks. In this section, we compare the defense ability for our proposed model and other defense strategies against three white-box attacks in Table 3.

Observing the data in Table 3, for MNIST, the proposed model has 91.00% classification accuracy against FGSM white-box attack, which is better than other compared defense strategies, and the classification accuracy against BIM is improved by at least 5%. In the defense against CW attack, the proposed model also has a better performance compared with other defense strategies.

For CIFAR10, we can deem that the proposed model has the optimal classification accuracy against FGSM, increasing 10%-40% compared other defense strategies. And for defense against CW attack, the proposed model also has the better classification accuracy except Spatial Smoothing and AuxBlocks, increasing 10%-40% compared other defense strategies. However, for the defense against BIM attack, accuracy of our proposed model is not obvious, which is needed to study further. Therefore, the incorporated strategies can promote each other and improve the defense ability against white-box attacks.

Defense Against Black-Box Attacks. Observing the data in Table 4, for MNIST, the proposed model is better than other defense strategies against FGSM and BIM attacks, increasing about 20%-40% compared to adversarial training. Noteworthy, the best defense strategy is adversarial training in defense against CW attack, which is because the part of training dataset are adversarial examples generated by CW attack. However, the proposed model also achieve similar effects to adversarial training. Moreover, the experiments results show that the defense ability of proposed model is better than GNI_CNN and CNN_RBF defense strategies against black-box attacks.

In terms of the defense performance against CW attack on MNIST dataset, we consider that the proposed strategy achieve similar effects to adversarial training, while this is not obvious from the results. Therefore, significant experiments were conducted. We imposed paired t-tests to compare defense performance of the two defense strategies. Specifically, we calculated the performance difference according to the three test sets, and then test the hypothesis that the performance of two defense strategies is similar according to the difference. We calculate the mean μ and variance σ^2 of the difference are 2.15 and 6.10, respectively. When the significance α is 0.95, the variable τ_t is less than the critical

Table 3. Comparisons of accuracy(%) against three white-box attacks on MNIST and CIFAR10.

	MNIST				CIFAR10			
	Clean	FGSM	BIM	CW	Clean	FGSM	BIM	CW
CNN	99.04	8.12	0.74	5.99	81.15	21.58	14.21	0.38
CNN_RBF	98.88	16.25	2.59	98.80	81.14	55.38	15.98	17.91
GNI_CNN	99.07	24.06	0.96	11.42	78.45	19.48	16.74	6.23
AT	99.06	23.74	1.03	10.97	83.62	20.78	16.94	0.88
Feature Squeezing	98.57	83.09	85.15	84.04	81.15	20.99	23.89	20.75
Spatial Smoothing	98.76	12.80	0.75	86.98	81.15	19.72	14.00	65.60
AuxBlocks	98.40	68.65	5.51	62.90	82.34	27.00	14.34	66.80
Proposed	98.72	91.00	89.86	98.70	81.57	64.19	15.27	41.44

value $t_{\frac{\alpha}{2}, k-1}$, and the hypothesis cannot be rejected. The variable τ_t is computed as $\tau_t = \left| \frac{\sqrt{k}\mu}{\sigma} \right|$, where k is the number of test sets.

Next, we compare the defense ability for our proposed model and other defense strategies against black-box attacks on three type of test sets in Table 4. For CIFAR10, we can deem that the proposed model has the better classification accuracy against FGSM, which is significantly improved 5%–20% compared with other defense strategies. For defense against BIM attack, the proposed has obtained the optimal result on different adversarial examples. Like the MNIST experiments, since we used the adversarial examples generated by CW attack to train the VGG16 model, adversarial training has better performance in iden-

Table 4. Comparisons of accuracy (%) against three black-box attacks on MNIST and CIFAR10.

		TestSet	CNN	CNN_RBF	GNI_CNN	AT	AuxBlocks	Proposed
MNIST	FGSM	I	–	39.87	68.63	56.92	52.69	95.15
		II	60.65	–	85.39	69.16	40.97	96.66
		III	47.66	45.32	–	48.35	47.46	93.65
	BIM	I	–	30.74	66.68	46.50	53.92	95.61
		II	59.96	–	86.71	72.91	47.45	97.22
		III	30.34	32.25	–	36.28	41.45	93.84
	CW	I	–	94.70	96.92	98.56	76.63	97.41
		II	99.04	–	99.09	99.07	79.29	98.72
		III	87.96	86.93	–	95.47	70.88	90.50
CIFAR10	FGSM	I	–	30.02	47.66	34.90	30.68	51.53
		II	55.54	–	70.44	35.50	50.26	70.26
		III	37.23	35.65	–	39.35	37.71	45.23
	BIM	I	–	23.71	52.73	49.76	33.14	66.46
		II	27.58	–	54.36	52.52	30.50	66.45
		III	28.75	26.72	–	53.27	38.45	55.27
	CW	I	–	75.95	76.65	83.22	79.18	79.01
		II	76.24	–	76.82	83.07	78.37	78.92
		III	75.01	75.31	–	82.43	77.93	76.19

tifying the adversarial examples. In addition, under the CW black-box attack, the proposed model achieves the optimal defense accuracy except the adversarial training model. Meanwhile, due to the high accuracy of CNN_RBF against CW black-box attack, the improvement of the proposed defense strategies is only about 3%. Further research is needed to improve the defense ability against CW attack.

5 Conclusion

In this paper, we propose a scalable defense strategy, which selects whether to use feature squeezing according to the information entropy of the input image, and then incorporate data transformations and RBF together to simultaneously enhance the robustness of CNNs against white-box attacks and black-box attacks. However, applying RBF to a very deep CNN will lead to the vanishing gradient problem during training, while data transformation might reduce classification accuracy due to introducing noises or squeezing the feature space. To solve these issues, we further proposed a deep supervision strategy and a novel dual loss function. Experiments on two public available datasets demonstrate that applying the proposed methods to the existing CNN models greatly improve their defense ability against adversarial attacks while keeping their recognition performance on legitimate dataset.

References

1. He, K., Zhang, X., Ren, S., Sun, J.: Deep residual learning for image recognition. In: IEEE Conference on Computer Vision and Pattern Recognition, CVPR, pp. 770–778. IEEE Computer Society (2016)
2. Zoph, B., Vasudevan, V., Shlens, J., Le, Q.V.: Learning transferable architectures for scalable image recognition. In: IEEE Conference on Computer Vision and Pattern Recognition, pp. 8697–8710. IEEE Computer Society (2018)
3. Ren, S., He, K., Girshick, R.B., Sun, J.: Faster R-CNN: towards real-time object detection with region proposal networks. In: Advances in Neural Information Processing Systems, pp. 91–99 (2015)
4. He, K., Gkioxari, G., Dollár, P., Girshick, R.B.: Mask R-CNN. In: IEEE International Conference on Computer Vision, pp. 2980–2988. IEEE Computer Society (2017)
5. Bahdanau, D., Chorowski, J., Serdyuk, D., Brakel, P., Bengio, Y.: End-to-end attention-based large vocabulary speech recognition. In: IEEE International Conference on Acoustics, Speech and Signal Processing, pp. 4945–4949. IEEE (2016)
6. Chiu, C., et al.te-of-the-art speech recognition with sequence-to-sequence models. In: IEEE International Conference on Acoustics, Speech and Signal Processing, pp. 4774–4778. IEEE (2018)
7. Szegedy, C., et al.: Intriguing properties of neural networks. In: International Conference on Learning Representations (2014). http://arxiv.org/abs/1312.6199
8. Goodfellow, I.J., Shlens, J., Szegedy, C.: Explaining and harnessing adversarial examples. In: International Conference on Learning Representations (2015). http://arxiv.org/abs/1412.6572

9. Vidnerová, P., Neruda, R.: Deep networks with RBF layers to prevent adversarial examples. In: Rutkowski, L., Scherer, R., Korytkowski, M., Pedrycz, W., Tadeusiewicz, R., Zurada, J.M. (eds.) ICAISC 2018. LNCS (LNAI), vol. 10841, pp. 257–266. Springer, Cham (2018). https://doi.org/10.1007/978-3-319-91253-0_25

10. Gu, S., Rigazio, L.: Towards deep neural network architectures robust to adversarial examples. In: International Conference on Learning Representations (2015). http://arxiv.org/abs/1412.5068

11. Xu, W., Evans, D., Qi, Y.: Feature squeezing: detecting adversarial examples in deep neural networks. In: Annual Network and Distributed System Security Symposium. The Internet Society (2018). http://wp.internetsociety.org/ndss/wp-content/uploads/sites/25/2018/02/ndss2018_03A-4_Xu_paper.pdf

12. Kurakin, A., Goodfellow, I.J., Bengio, S.: Adversarial examples in the physical world. In: International Conference on Learning Representations. OpenReview.net (2017)

13. Carlini, N., Wagner, D.A.: Towards evaluating the robustness of neural networks. In: IEEE Symposium on Security and Privacy, pp. 39–57. IEEE Computer Society (2017)

14. Papernot, N., McDaniel, P., Sinha, A., Wellman, M.: Towards the science of security and privacy in machine learning. arXiv preprint arXiv:1611.03814 (2016)

15. Peng, J.X., Li, K., Irwin, G.W.: A novel continuous forward algorithm for RBF neural modelling. IEEE Trans. Autom. Control. $52(1)$, 117–122 (2007)

16. Moody, J.E., Darken, C.J.: Fast learning in networks of locally-tuned processing units. Neural Comput. $1(2)$, 281–294 (1989)

17. Li, Q., Wang, H., Li, B., Tang, Y., Li, J.: IIE-SegNet: deep semantic segmentation network with enhanced boundary based on image information entropy. IEEE Access 9, 40612–40622 (2021). https://doi.org/10.1109/ACCESS.2021.3064346

18. LeCun, Y., Bottou, L., Bengio, Y., Haffner, P.: Gradient-based learning applied to document recognition. Proc. IEEE $86(11)$, 2278–2324 (1998)

19. Krizhevsky, A., Hinton, G., et al.: Learning multiple layers of features from tiny images (2009)

20. Simonyan, K., Zisserman, A.: Very deep convolutional networks for large-scale image recognition. In: International Conference on Learning Representations (2015). http://arxiv.org/abs/1409.1556

21. Yu, Y., Yu, P., Li, W.: Auxblocks: defense adversarial examples via auxiliary blocks. In: International Joint Conference on Neural Networks, pp. 1–8. IEEE (2019)

An Improved Deep Model for Knowledge Tracing and Question-Difficulty Discovery

Huan Dai, Yupei Zhang$^{(\boxtimes)}$, Yue Yun, and Xuequn Shang$^{(\boxtimes)}$

Northwestern Polytechnical University, Xi'an, China
{daihuan,yundayue}@mail.nwpu.edu.cn, {ypzhaang,shang}@nwpu.edu.cn

Abstract. Knowledge Tracing (KT) aims to analyze a student's acquisition of skills over time by examining the student's performance on questions of those skills. In recent years, a recurrent neural network model called deep knowledge tracing (DKT) has been proposed to handle the knowledge tracing task and literature has shown that DKT generally outperforms traditional methods. However, DKT and its variants often lead to oscillation results on a skill's state may due to it ignoring the skill's difficulty or the question's difficulty. As a result, even when a student performs well on a skill, the prediction of that skill's mastery level decreases instead, and vice versa. This is undesirable and unreasonable because student's performance is expected to transit gradually over time. In this paper, we propose to learn the knowledge tracing model in a "simple-to-difficult" process, leading to a method of Self-paced Deep Knowledge Tracing (SPDKT). SPDKT learns the difficulty of per question from the student's responses to optimize the question's order and smooth the learning process. With mitigating the cause of oscillations, SPDKT has the capability of robustness to the puzzling questions. The experiments on real-world datasets show SPDKT achieves state-of-the-art performance on question response prediction and reaches interesting interpretations in education.

Keywords: Knowledge tracing · Self-paced learning · Deep learning · Personalized education

1 Introduction

Knowledge tracing (KT) is one of the key research areas for empowering personalized education and a fundamental part of intelligent tutoring systems [1, 14]. It is a task to model students' mastery level of the knowledge components (KCs) based on their historical learning trajectories, where KC is a generic term for skill, concept, exercise, etc. With the estimated students' knowledge state, teachers or tutors can gain a better understanding of the attainment levels of their students and can tailor the learning materials accordingly. Moreover, students

© Springer Nature Switzerland AG 2021
D. N. Pham et al. (Eds.): PRICAI 2021, LNAI 13032, pp. 362–375, 2021.
https://doi.org/10.1007/978-3-030-89363-7_28

may also take advantage of the learning analytics tools to come up with better learning plans to deal with their weaknesses and maximize their learning efficacy [2,3]. Many approaches have been developed to solve the KT problem, such as using the hidden Markov model (HMM) in Bayesian knowledge tracing (BKT) which applies hidden Markov models to learn each student's guess, slip, and learn probabilities for each skill [4]. The disadvantage of BKT model is that it assumes the binary level of student mastery of skills and independence of student interaction with question which is not consistent with the learning process. Meanwhile, the large amount of data produced by a growing number of online education platforms and recent advances of machine learning technology provide us with unprecedented opportunities to build advanced models for accurate knowledge tracing [5]. Deep Knowledge Tracing (DKT), a deep neural networks model, has shown its superior performance in comparison with traditional knowledge tracing models [6]. More subsequent variants of the DKT models [10,11,13] aimed at improving the accuracy of the prediction but failed to explain for why students would answer this question correctly. However, DKT and its successor algorithms produced unstable performance, with oscillating predictions that sometimes went down after producing a correct answer. When a student performs well in a learning task related to a skill s_i, the model's predicted performance for the skill s_i may drop instead, which leads to a low prediction accuracy. As depicted in Fig. 1, there are sudden surges and plunges in the predicted performance of some skills across time-steps. For example, the probabilities of correctly answering skill 2, skill 7 fluctuate when the student answers skill 9 in the middle of the learning sequence. This is intuitively undesirable and unreasonable as students' knowledge state is expected to transit gradually over time, but not to alternate between mastered and not-yet-mastered [7,8]. Chun-Kit Yeung *et. al* address this problem by introducing regularization terms that correspond to reconstruction and waviness to the loss function of the original DKT model [9]. However, these regularization terms are complex and hard to explain the meaning. In this paper, we introduce more simple term and also can make learning process more smooth. To this end, in this paper, we propose a deep model named Self-paced Deep Knowledge Tracing (SPDKT), which introduce self-paced regularization term to the loss function of the DKT model. The proposed method is based on the intuition that learning process of a student generally starts with learning easier questions and then gradually takes more complex questions into consideration. Difficulty of questions differs from student to student. SPDKT visualizes the difficulty of the question for students and explains why the student answered the wrong question. To our best knowledge, question's difficulty ranking is not given in advance, which makes it very challenging to measure them. Specifically, SPDKT reflects the easiness or difficulty of the questions by assigning different weights to questions. The experiments have been conducted on four public datasets to evaluate the performance of SPDKT, which shows that SPDKT could get better performance through modeling difficulty of questions in student learning process. Our major contributions are: 1) First, we consider the difficulty feature of questions to model the learning

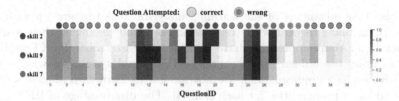

Fig. 1. A student from the Math dataset is used to plot the heatmap illustrating the oscillation problem in DKT. The label in the vertical dimension corresponds to the skill tag. The label in the horizontal dimension refers to the input fed into the DKT at each time-step. The color of heatmap indicates the predicted probability that the student will answer next question correctly, i.e., $p(a_{t+1} = 1 | q_{t+1} = s_i)$. The darker the color, the higher the probability.

process of the student, which lead to a smooth knowledge tracing of the student. 2) Second, we propose a simple-to-difficult process algorithm of ranking the difficulty of questions for students automatically, which we dub Self-paced Deep Knowledge Tracing (SPDKT). 3) Third, SPDKT incorporates the difficulty regularization into the DKT framework for enhancing the learning robustness of DKT. Theoretical studies show that SPDKT converges to a stationary solution and is robust to the noisy and confusing data. Experimental results on public datasets demonstrate the effectiveness and robustness of the proposed method.

2   Related Work

2.1   Deep Knowledge Tracing

Deep knowledge tracing (DKT) which was first introduced by Piech *et al.* [6] consists in performing knowledge tracing (KT) by means of neural networks. DKT model outperforms logistic models in predicting the results of future exams. DKT uses a long short-term memory networks (LSTM), a variant of recurrent neural networks, to model student performance learning and uses large numbers of artificial neurons for representing latent knowledge state along with a temporal dynamic structure. LSTM allows a model to learn the latent knowledge state from data. It is defined by the following equations:

$$h_t = \tanh\left(W_{hx}x_t + W_{hh}h_{t-1} + b_h\right)$$
$$y_t = \sigma\left(W_{yh}h_t + b_y\right) \tag{1}$$

In DKT, both tahn and the sigmoid function are applied element wise and parameterized by an input weight matrix W_{hx}, recurrent weight matrix W_{hh}, initial state h_0, and readout weight matrix W_{yh}. Biases for latent and readout units are represented by b_h and b_y.

However, DKT models only predict the correctness of the next question for a student. It does not consider any educational features into models, which makes the interpretation of such models a strenuous task [15,16]. Therefore, in this paper, we consider the interaction between students and questions and automatically find the difficulty of questions from the student response sequence.

2.2   Self-Paced Learning

Humans and animals often learn from the examples which are not randomly presented but organized in a meaningful order which gradually includes from easy items with fewer concepts to complex items with more concepts. Inspired by this principle, Bengio *et. al.* proposed a learning paradigm called curriculum including samples from easy to complex for training so as to increase the entropy of training samples [17]. Then, Kumar *et. al.* proposed a practical model named Self-paced Learning (SPL) which embeds curriculum design as a regularization term into the learning objective [18]. Due to its generality, the SPL theory has been widely applied to various task, such as object tracking [19], image classification [20, 22], and multimedia event detection [21].

Inspired by the idea of SPL, we use SPL to improve the robustness of DKT model by reassigning the weights of questions. In addition, SPL learns these question records from easy to difficult, which could provide the interpretation of question difficulty in knowledge tracing.

3   The Proposed Model

3.1   Problem Definition

Generally, KT is formulated as a supervised sequence learning problem that is to, given a student's records $X = \{(s_1, a_1), (s_2, a_2), \ldots, (s_{t-1}, a_{t-1})\}$, predict the probability of correct response to a new question, *i.e.*, $P(a_t = 1 | s_t, X)$. With this KT framework, the time series data consist of student skill interaction sequences, given by $X_i = \left\{ \left(s_t^i, a_t^i \right) \right\}_{t=1}^{T}$ where s_t^i is the skill index attempted by the i_{th} student at discrete time step t, while $a_t^i \in \{0, 1\}$ is the assessment of the student's response, with 0 indicating an incorrect response and 1 indicating a correct response.

3.2   SPDKT Model

The goal of SPDKT is to discover the difficulty of questions and achieve a high prediction accuracy. We now introduce our proposed method SPDKT.

In order to model the difficulty of the question, we introduce a set of latent variables v to represent the difficulties of questions. The object function of our proposed SPDKT model is formulated as

$$\min_{\mathbf{w}, v} E(\mathbf{w}, v) = \sum_{i=1}^{n} v_i \ell_i^t(\mathbf{w}) + \lambda^t f(v; t) \tag{2}$$

where $\ell_i^t = \ell \left(y^T \delta \left(s_{t+1} \right), a_{t+1} \right)$ is the loss for given prediction of student i in t-th iteration. $\delta \left(s_{t+1} \right)$ is the one-hot encoding of which question is answered at time $t + 1$, a_{t+1} represents the ground truth of question's response, y represents the predicted response of the question, $\mathbf{w}$ is the knowledge learning model parameters and ℓ be binary cross entropy. In formula (2), $f(v; t)$ is a SP-regularizer and $v = [v_1, ..., v_n]^T$ is the latent weight variable induced from $f(v; t)$, and λ is the age parameter.

Objective (2) of SPDKT in each step is to minimize a weighted loss together with a self-paced regularizer. Without introduce vector $\mathbf{v}$, the loss function is directly minimized and outliers whose losses are usually very large are easy to be paid more attention to. SPDKT overcomes this problem by considering student noise data and assigning different weights v to the losses of training samples. Therefore, the self-paced function should satisfy the following conditions:

$$\lim_{\ell \to 0} v(\ell, \lambda) = 1, \quad \lim_{\ell \to \infty} v(\ell, \lambda) = 0 \tag{3}$$

$$\lim_{\lambda \to 0} v(\ell, \lambda) \leq 1, \quad \lim_{\lambda \to \infty} v(\ell, \lambda) = 0 \tag{4}$$

These two conditions ensure that v will always be zero when the loss is very large, which means that the corresponding sample is very likely to be outlier [29]. The large loss of student response data indicates that the question is difficulty to the student. Thus, SPDKT can eliminate the negative influence of outliers in training data to a large extent and improve the robustness of DKT. Figure 2 presents the schematic diagram to illustrate SPDKT model. We adopt a majorization minimization (MM) algorithm to learn the difficulty and the knowledge based on formula (2). MM algorithms have been widely used in machine learning and aim to convert a complicated optimization problem into an easy one by alternatively iterating the majorization step and the minimization step [24]. We denote w^t as the model parameters in the t-th iteration of the MM algorithm.

(1) Difficulty Learning

The particular useful property is that SPDKT estimates the difficulty of questions, which can recommends proper questions to students to improve the quality of online education.

SPDKT learns the difficulty of the question by solving the following problem:

$$E = v_i^* \left(\lambda; \ell_i \left(w^t \right) \right) = \arg \min_{v_i \in [0,1]} v_i \ell_i \left(w^t \right) + \lambda^t f(v_i; t) \tag{5}$$

The self-paced function in Eq. (5) is $\lambda^t f(v; t) = \lambda^t \left(\frac{1}{2}v^2 - v \right)$ which is the smooth function of learning continuous question's difficulty. The Eq. (5) is a convex function of v in [0,1] and thus the global minimum can be obtained at $\nabla_v E(\mathbf{v}) = 0$. We have

$$\frac{\partial E}{\partial v_i} = \ell_i + \lambda^t(v - 1) = 0 \tag{6}$$

The closed-form optimal solution for v_i $(i = 1, 2, ..., n)$ can be written as:

$$v_i = \begin{cases} 1 - \frac{\ell_i^t}{\lambda^t} & \ell_i^t < \lambda^t \\ 0 & \ell_i^t \geq \lambda \end{cases} \tag{7}$$

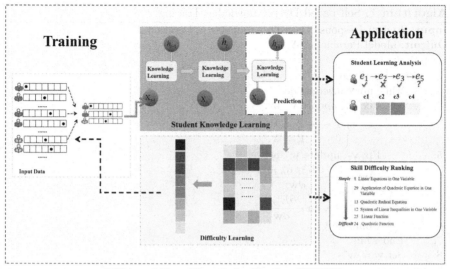

Fig. 2. The overview of SPDKT model.

From the Eq. (7), v_i is decreasing with respect to ℓ_i and we have that $\lim_{\ell_i \to 0} v_i = 1, \lim_{\ell \to \infty} v_i = 0$. It indicates that the SPDKT model favors easy samples because the easy samples have lower loss values and larger weights. Finally, each individual v_i increases with respect to λ^t in the closed-form solution in Eq. (7). In an extreme case, when λ^t approaches positive infinity, we have $\lim_{\ell_i \to 0} v = 1$. Similarly, when λ^t approaches 0, we have $\lim_{\ell \to \infty} v = 0$. When the model "age" gets larger, it tends to incorporate more samples into training.

(2) Knowledge Learning

Knowledge learning aims to calculate **w** by

$$w^{t+1} = \arg\min_w \sum_{i=1}^{n} v_i \ell_i \left(w^t\right) \tag{8}$$

Then the cost function of SPDKT is

$$w_{spdkt} = \arg\min_w \sum_{i=1}^{n} v_i \ell \left(y^T \delta \left(q_{t+1}\right), a_{t+1}\right) \tag{9}$$

We chose the deep-learning based model to train **w** of function ℓ. For a single pattern, the two error functions have the following relationship:

$$\Delta \mathbf{w} = -\alpha \frac{\partial E^i_{SPDKT}}{\partial \mathbf{w}}$$

$$= -v_i \cdot \alpha \cdot \frac{\partial E^i_{DL}}{\partial \mathbf{w}} \tag{10}$$

Algorithm 1. Self-paced Deep Knowledge Tracing

Input: Student Response Data D, parameter λ, iteration T
Output: Model Parameter $\mathbf{W}$

1: Initialize $\mathbf{w}^*$
2: for $t = 1$ to T do
3:     while not converged do
4:         Fix $\mathbf{w}_t$, update $\mathbf{v}^*$ by:
$$v_i^* = \begin{cases} 1 - \frac{l_i^t}{\lambda^t} & l_i^t < \lambda^t \\ 0 & l_i^t \geq \lambda \end{cases}$$
5:         Fix $\mathbf{v}_t$, update $\mathbf{w}^*$ by:
$$\Delta \mathbf{w} = -\alpha \frac{\partial E_{SPDKT}^i}{\partial \mathbf{w}}$$
$$= -v_i \cdot \alpha \cdot \frac{\partial E_{DL}^i}{\partial \mathbf{w}}$$
6:         Compute $\mathbf{v}_{t+1}$
7:     End while.
8:     Set $\mathbf{w} = \mathbf{w}^*$
9: End for

---

where $\mathbf{w}$ is the weights in a certain layer of the network, and α is the learning rate. E_{SPDKT} and E_{DL} are the error function of the proposed SPDKT model and loss function without self-paced vector, respectively. It is observed that SPDKT modifies the sample weights to be $v_i \alpha$ by introducing the latent weight variable $\mathbf{v}$. It could be the reason why SPDKT is more robust. When the samples are easy, the learning rates are high values and the network can update the parameters in a large step. The samples have small learning rates when the samples are difficult. With the small learning rates, the network is able to update the parameters slowly for converging to a better value. The details of SPDKT are summarized in Algorithm 1.

3.3   Theoretical Analysis

In this section, we provide some theoretical analysis of SPDKT to clarify the reason why SPDKT is capable of performing robustness and can converge to a stationary solution. In [23], Hao Li et $al.$ have proved that

$$E\left(\mathbf{w}^t, \mathbf{v}^t\right) \leq E\left(\mathbf{w}^{t-1}, \mathbf{v}^{t-1}\right) \tag{11}$$

where $\mathbf{w}^t$ and $\mathbf{v}^t$ indicate the values of $\mathbf{w}$ and $\mathbf{v}$ in the t-th iteration.

Obviously, the objective values decrease in every iteration in SPDKT algorithm. Therefore Algorithm 1 can converge to a stationary solution.

The solving strategy on SPL exactly accords with a MM algorithm implemented on a latent objective and the loss function contained in this latent objective has a similar configuration with a non-convex regularized penalty. In SPDKT, we obtain the solution $\mathbf{v}^*$ as follows:

$$\mathbf{v}^*\left(\lambda^t; \ell\right) = \arg\min_{\mathbf{v}} \mathbf{v}\ell + \lambda^t f(\mathbf{v}, t) \tag{12}$$

Table 1. AUC scores for each algorithm on four datasets. We see that SPDKT obtains the higher results in each dataset.

Data sets	AUC			
	ASSISment2009	ASSIStent2015	Statics2011	Math
DKT	74.1	72.5	77.0	80.6
DKVMV-CA	73.6	72.6	72.4	73.2
qDKT	76.2	77.0	83.4	83.5
SPDKT	**83.4**	**85.2**	**86.4**	**85.5**

We get the integrative function of $\mathbf{v}^*(\lambda; \ell)$ calculated by Eq. (12) as:

$$F_{\lambda^t}(\ell) = \int_0^\ell \mathbf{v}^* \left(\lambda^t; \ell\right) dl + c \tag{13}$$

where c is a constant.

Now we calculate the latent losses with the linear soft weighting function as follows:

$$F_{\lambda^t}(\ell) = \begin{cases} -\frac{1}{2\lambda^t}\ell^2 + \ell + c & \ell < \lambda \\ c & \ell \geq \lambda^t \end{cases} \tag{14}$$

Note that when $\lambda_t = \infty$, the latent loss $F_{\lambda^t}(\ell)$ will degenerate to the original loss ℓ. There is an evident suppressing effect of $F_{\lambda^t}(\ell)$ on large losses as compared with the original loss function ℓ. When ℓ is larger than a certain threshold, $F_{\lambda^t}(\ell)$ will become a constant thereafter, which rationally explains why SPLDKT shows good robustness to the noises. The difficulty samples with very large margins will have constant SPLDKT losses and thus have no effect on the model training due to their zero gradients. Corresponding to the original SPL model, these samples with large losses will be with 0 importance weights v_i, and thus have no effects on the optimization of model parameters.

4   Experiment

In this section, we evaluate SPDKT model on four public datasets. To convince our method, we compare with the related methods, *i.e.*, Deep Knowledge Tracing (DKT), Concept-Aware Deep Knowledge Tracing (DKVM-CA), and Question-centric Deep knowledge Tracing (qDKT). All experiment codes are implemented by Python and could be available at https://github.com/ypzhaang.

4.1   Data Sets

To evaluate performance, we consider four datasets for our experiments: ASSIST-ments2009, ASSISTments2015, Statics 2011, and a dataset from AICFE—an online learning platform.

ASSISTments2009[1]. This dataset was gathered in the year 2009–2010 from the ASSISTments platform. ASSISTments is an online tutoring platform that evaluates students with prebuild problem sets. The "skill-builder" data set is a large, standard benchmark [25]. Due to duplicated record issues [26], an updated version was released and all previous results on the old data set were conducted using the updated data set. 4,151 students answered 325,637 exercises along with 110 distinct exercise tags.

ASSISTments2015[2]. This dataset is from ASSISTments, but gathered in the year of 2015. ASSISTments2015 only contains student responses on 100 skill builders with the highest number of student responses. After preprocessing (removing the value of correct $\notin \{0, 1\}$), this data set remains 683,801 effective records from 19,840 students. Each problem set in this data set has only one associated skill. Although this data set has the largest number of records, the average records for each student is also the lowest.

Statics2011[3]. Statics is from a college-level engineering statics course with 189297 trials, 333 students and 1223 exercises tags, available from the PSLC DataShop web site [27,28].

Math[4]. This dataset is from AICFE collecting K-12 stage student test. The Math test data consists of 1499 students, 33 skills and total response data are 54285.

4.2 Comparison Methods

Our idea is to find the difficulty level of questions from student response data. The baseline methods are DKT, DKVM-CA, and qDKT. The brief introduction of these four methods shows following:

1) DKT: This model is the base model of KT research. This comparison is to convince that our model improves the DKT performance [6]. 2) DKVMN-CA: This method is based on dynamic key-value memory network which embeds the question difficulty information into DKVMN [12,30]. 3) qDKT: This method uses the new NLP algorithm to improve DKT performance, which leverages the semantic of question text [31].

4.3 Student Performance Prediction

We measure the Area Under the Curve (AUC) to evaluate the prediction accuracy on each dataset. An AUC of 50% represents the score achievable by random guess. A higher AUC score accounts for a better prediction performance. We

---

[1] https://sites.google.com/site/assistmentsdata/home/assistment-2009-2010-data/skill-builder-data-2009-2010.

[2] https://sites.google.com/site/assistmentsdata/home/2015-assistments-skill-builder-data.

[3] https://pslcdatashop.web.cmu.edu/DatasetInfo?datasetId=507.

[4] http://www.bnu-ai.cn/data.

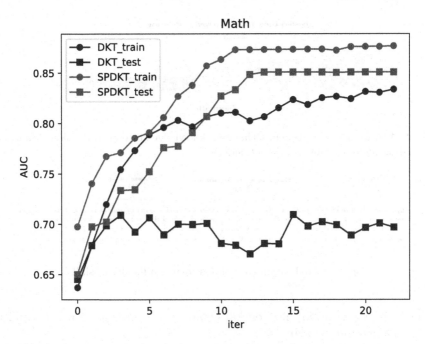

Fig. 3. The AUC results of DKT and SPDKT.

divide 80% of data as training data and the remain as testing set on all datasets. Then we compute the AUC of each method. We compare the SPDKT model with the DKT, DKVMN-CA and qDKT. Results of the test AUC on all data sets are shown in Table 1. As shown in Table 1, SPDKT gets the better AUC result than others. On ASSISment2009, SPDKT achieves average test AUC of 83.4% which is better than 74.1% for DKT. On other datasets, SPDKT also performs better than DKT. Compared with other methods adding question information, like DKVMN-CA and qDKT, SPDKT gets better AUC than these methods.

Moreover, the DKT model suffers severe overfitting, while our SPDKT model does not confront with such a problem. As indicated in Fig. 3, we test on Math dataset which is a small dataset. There is no huge gap between the training AUC and testing AUC of SPDKT and AUC increase steady then converging a stable solution.

In summary, SPDKT performs better than other methods across all the datasets, in particular on the Statics20011 dataset whose number of distinct questions is large. This result demonstrates that our SPDKT can model student learning process well when the number of questions is very large.

4.4   Analysis Knowledge State of Student

Our SPDKT model demonstrates a smooth prediction transition notably. In difficulty learning step, SPDKT selects the questions with similar difficulty to

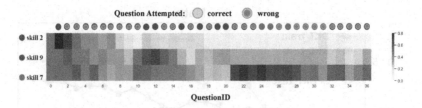

Fig. 4. An example of a student's changing knowledge state on three skills. Skills are marked in different colors on the left side.

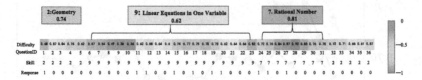

Fig. 5. Visualization case of a student's difficulty of skills.

train. This process avoids most of skill's mastery level decreasing when a student answers a question wrongly.

Figure 4 shows an example of depicting a student's three changing skills. The first column represents the initial state of each skill before the student answers any question. From the Fig. 4, student's skill mastery level transforms smoothly. For example, when student answers the first question correctly, the knowledge state of the skill 2 increase and the last four questions incorrectly, the knowledge state of the skill 2 decrease; when student answers the sixth question incorrectly, the knowledge state of the skill 9 decrease. After answering thirty-six questions, the student is shown to fail to understand the skill 2.

4.5   Analysis Difficult of Skills

Our SPDKT model has the power to discover the difficulty of skills using the paced weight **v**. This section provides the results of analyzing difficulty of skills on Math dataset. According to the weight **v**, we visualize a student's skills difficulty rank. Figure 5 gives the knowledge skills that different questions are corresponding to. As indicated in Fig. 5, SPDKT analyses the difficulty of each question of student s_1 and then computes mean value of the difficulty of skills. From Fig. 5, we obtain some useful suggestions for student s_1, for instance, practising "Linear Equations in One Variable" first. The exercises involved in "Geometry" and "Rational Number" skills can recommend later.

According to all students analysis, we obtained the difficulty level of 33 skills as shown in Fig. 6. From Fig. 6, The red box could arrive at several useful conclusions. "Linear Equations in One Variable" is easier than "Quadratic Equation in One Variable", and "Linear Function" is easier than "Quadratic Function".

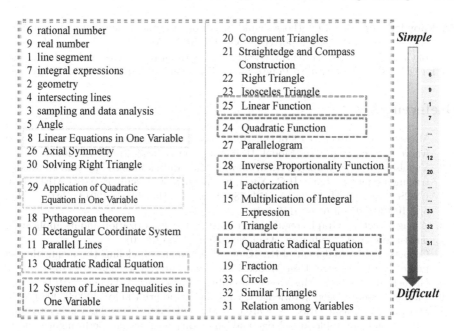

Fig. 6. Visualization of 33 skills difficulty in Math dataset. The skill difficulty is ranked along the direction of the arrow.

5 Discussion and Conclusion

In this paper, we propose a new learning-based method of student modeling, called Self-paced Deep Knowledge Tracing (SPDKT) in education. Recent researches mostly attempt to define the difficulty to the DKT model, such as leveraging NLP models to mine the question text and then using item response theory (IRT) models to estimate the question's difficulty. However, IRT model has strong condition assumption. SPDKT incorporates the difficulty feature of questions and then makes the learning process smooth by adding the SP-regularizer. Therefore, three particularly interesting novel properties of our new model are that (1) it does not need prior expert annotations (it can learn difficulty of skills in its own) by incorporating SP-regularization into DKT model and (2) it makes the learning process more smooth and it could discover each student's different levels of these skills to achieve personalized education. (3) it improves the robustness of DKT with assigning different weights of samples. Experiment results show SPDKT achieves sate-of-the-art performance on several datasets. In future works, more student learning features could be considered to improve the prediction accuracy and novel methods might be developed to improve the interpretability of DKT models.

Acknowledgments. All authors thank the editors and the reviewers for their helpful comments. This work was supported in part by the National Natural Science Foundation of China (Grant No. 61802313, U1811262), the Reformation Research on Education and Teaching at Northwestern Polytechnical University (Grant No. 2021JGY31).

References

1. Mitrovic, A.: Fifteen years of constraint-based tutors: what we have achieved and where we are going. User Model. User-Adap. Inter. **22**(1–2), 39–72 (2012)
2. Yudelson, M.V., Koedinger, K.R., Gordon, G.J.: Individualized bayesian knowledge tracing models. In: Lane, H.C., Yacef, K., Mostow, J., Pavlik, P. (eds.) AIED 2013. LNCS (LNAI), vol. 7926, pp. 171–180. Springer, Heidelberg (2013). https://doi.org/10.1007/978-3-642-39112-5_18
3. Zhang, Y., et al.: Graphs regularized robust matrix factorization and its application on student grade prediction. Appl. Sci. **10**(5), 1755 (2020)
4. Corbett, A.T., Anderson, J.R.: Knowledge tracing: modeling the acquisition of procedural knowledge. User Model. User-Adap. Inter. **4**(4), 253–278 (1994)
5. Gaebel, M.: MOOCs: Massive Open Online Courses. EUA, Geneva (2014)
6. Piech, C., et al.: Deep knowledge tracing. arXiv preprint arXiv:1506.05908 (2015)
7. Scruggs, R., Baker, R.S., McLaren, B.M.: Extending deep knowledge tracing: inferring interpretable knowledge and predicting post-system performance. arXiv preprint arXiv:1910.12597 (2019)
8. Zhang, L., et al.: Incorporating rich features into deep knowledge tracing. In: Proceedings of the Fourth (2017) ACM Conference on Learning@scale (2017)
9. Yeung, C.-K., Yeung, D.-Y.: Addressing two problems in deep knowledge tracing via prediction-consistent regularization. In: Proceedings of the Fifth Annual ACM Conference on Learning at Scale (2018)
10. Wang, Z., Feng, X., Tang, J., Huang, G.Y., Liu, Z.: Deep knowledge tracing with side information. In: Isotani, S., Millán, E., Ogan, A., Hastings, P., McLaren, B., Luckin, R. (eds.) AIED 2019. LNCS (LNAI), vol. 11626, pp. 303–308. Springer, Cham (2019). https://doi.org/10.1007/978-3-030-23207-8_56
11. Benedetto, L., et al.: R2DE: a NLP approach to estimating IRT parameters of newly generated questions. In: Proceedings of the Tenth International Conference on Learning Analytics & Knowledge (2020)
12. Zhang, J., et al.: Dynamic key-value memory networks for knowledge tracing. In: Proceedings of the 26th International Conference on World Wide Web (2017)
13. Baker, F.B.: The basics of item response theory. For full text (2001). http://ericae.net/irt/baker
14. Zhang, Y., et al.: Meta-knowledge dictionary learning on 1-bit response data for student knowledge diagnosis. Knowl. Based Syst. **205**, 106290 (2020)
15. Khajah, M., Lindsey, R.V., Mozer, M.C.: How deep is knowledge tracing?. arXiv preprint arXiv:1604.02416 (2016)
16. Liu, Q., et al.: EKT: exercise-aware knowledge tracing for student performance prediction. IEEE Trans. Knowl. Data Eng. **33**(1), 100–115 (2019)
17. Bengio, Y., et al.: Curriculum learning. In: Proceedings of the 26th Annual International Conference on Machine Learning (2009)
18. Kumar, M.P., Packer, B., Koller, D.: Self-paced learning for latent variable models. In: NIPS, vol. 1 (2010)
19. Tang, K., et al.: Shifting weights: adapting object detectors from image to video. In: Advances in Neural Information Processing Systems (2012)

20. Lin, L., et al.: Active self-paced learning for cost-effective and progressive face identification. IEEE Trans. Pattern Anal. Mach. Intell. **40**(1), 7–19 (2017)
21. Kumar, M.P., et al.: Learning specific-class segmentation from diverse data. In: 2011 International Conference on Computer Vision. IEEE (2011)
22. Pi, T., et al.: Self-paced boost learning for classification. In: IJCAI (2016)
23. Li, H., Gong, M.: Self-paced convolutional neural networks. In: IJCAI (2017)
24. Hunter, D.R., Lange, K.: A tutorial on MM algorithms. Am. Stat. **58**(1), 30–37 (2004)
25. Feng, M., Heffernan, N., Koedinger, K.: Addressing the assessment challenge with an online system that tutors as it assesses. User Model. User-Adap. Inter. **19**(3), 243–266 (2009)
26. Xiong, X., et al.: Going deeper with deep knowledge tracing. International Educational Data Mining Society (2016)
27. Khajah, M., et al.: Integrating latent-factor and knowledge-tracing models to predict individual differences in learning. In: Educational Data Mining 2014 (2014)
28. Koedinger, K.R., et al.: A data repository for the EDM community: the PSLC DataShop. In: Handbook of Educational Data Mining, vol. 43, pp. 43–56 (2010)
29. Jiang, L., et al.: Self-paced curriculum learning. In: Proceedings of the AAAI Conference on Artificial Intelligence. vol. 29, no. 1 (2015)
30. Ai, F., et al.: Concept-aware deep knowledge tracing and exercise recommendation in an online learning system. International Educational Data Mining Society (2019)
31. Sonkar, S., et al.: qDKT: question-centric deep knowledge tracing. arXiv preprint arXiv:2005.12442 (2020)

ARNet: Accurate and Real-Time Network for Crowd Counting

Yinfeng Xia, Qing He, Wenyue Wei, and Baoqun Yin[✉]

Department of Automation, University of Science and Technology of China,
Hefei 230027, China
{julyxia,heqing2020,wywei}@mail.ustc.edu.cn, bqyin@ustc.edu.cn

Abstract. Taking into account the problem of the redundant structure and excessive parameters in the current crowd counting network, we propose an end-to-end encoder-decoder architecture called Accurate and Real-time Network (ARNet) for high-accuracy and real-time crowd counting. The encoder adopts lightweight SqueezeNet as the backbone network to extract multi-level features, the decoder can integrate contextual information to enhance the semantic representation capabilities of low-level features. In addition, we design the Parameter-Sharing Context-Aware Module (PSCAM) and the Mask Density Generator (MDG). Without adding excessive parameters, the PSCAM can capture the global context by applying multiple dilated convolutional layers with the same convolution parameters and different dilation rates. The MDG based on multi-task learning can generate accurate density maps by introducing semantic segmentation to suppress background interference. Extensive experiments on four benchmark crowd datasets, which indicate our ARNet can achieve the optimal trade-off between counting accuracy and computation efficiency.

Keywords: Crowd counting · Counting accuracy · Computation efficiency

1 Introduction

The crowd counting task, which aims to obtain the global counts from the image, plays an important role in crowd monitoring, public safety, emergency evacuation and other fields. With the rapid development of deep learning and convolutional neural networks (CNN), networks based on density regression have gradually replaced traditional methods based on handcrafted features in the field of crowd counting, and have attracted widespread attention from researchers. The value of each pixel in the density map reflects the density of the corresponding area in the image, and estimated people count can be obtained by accumulating the values of all pixels.

Early networks [1,2] apply the basic CNN layers to construct counting networks, but their simple structure design resulted in poor counting performance. Some networks with deeper structures are proposed in order to adapt to the

© Springer Nature Switzerland AG 2021
D. N. Pham et al. (Eds.): PRICAI 2021, LNAI 13032, pp. 376–389, 2021.
https://doi.org/10.1007/978-3-030-89363-7_29

complexity of the scene. CSRNet [3] utilizes dilated convolution layers to expand the receptive field while maintaining the resolution as a backend network. CAN [4] adaptively encode the scale of the contextual information required to accurately predict crowd density, which can compensate for perspective distortion. Although the counting performance is improved, the redundant structure and parameters limit their application in the real world.

In order to ensure qualifications of accuracy and speed in counting tasks, as well as the application conditions that can be deployed in mobile or embedded systems. In our work, we propose a lightweight structure for real-time crowd counting, named ARNet. ARNet based on an encoder-decoder framework can generate high-resolution density estimation maps. The encoder adopts lightweight SqueezeNet [5] as the backbone for extracting multi-level features; the decoder can strengthen the semantic representation capabilities of low-level features. In addition, the Parameter-Sharing Context-Aware Module (PSCAM) is designed for capturing global contexts without adding excessive parameters, the Mask Density Generator (MDG) is proposed to suppress the background interference problem in the process of regressing the density maps. Due to the reasonable network structure, ARNet can achieve the requirements of accuracy and real-time simultaneously.

In summary, the key contributions of this work are as follows:

1. We propose a novel lightweight encoder-decoder architecture named ARNet, which can achieve the optimal trade-off between counting accuracy and computation efficiency.
2. We establish PSCAM and MDG to alleviate the problem of context omission and background interference in the lightweight counting network.
3. Various experiments are conducted on four challenging datasets, the results show that ARNet can achieve the best trade-off between counting accuracy and efficiency compared to recent technologies.

The rest of this paper is organized as follows. Firstly, we briefly review the related work in Sect. 2. Secondly, we introduce various modules and loss functions in the ARNet in Sect. 3. Afterward, we discuss the specific implementation details of the experiments in Sect. 4. Then, the performance comparison between our approach and the state-of-the-art method is presented in Sect. 5, we also verify the effectiveness of various modules in this section. Finally, we conclude the paper in Sect. 6.

2 Related Work

2.1 Crowd Counting and Density Estimation

Early counting methods are usually detection-based [6,7], which apply sliding window detectors to identify pedestrians and count the number. Some object detectors [8,9] based on deep learning can achieve excellent detection accuracy in sparse scenes. However, their counting performance is limited by the scene, and it is difficult to apply in the situation of dense crowds. The regression-based method [10,11] has been proposed to directly learn the mapping from an image patch to count, which can alleviate the above problems. Firstly, they usually extract features including texture and gradient; then some regression techniques such as linear regression and Gaussian mixture regression are used to learn the mapping function of crowd counting. However, the regression-based method cannot perceive the spatial distribution of the population, and it was gradually replaced by the CNN-based density estimation approaches.

The CNN-based density estimation approaches can be divided into multi-column methods and single-column methods according to the network architecture. The multi-column method [1,2] can capture multi-scale information by applying sub-column networks with different receiving fields, which can effectively deal with the problem of the scale variation. However, its further development has been restricted due to problems such as training difficulty and parameter redundancy. Different from the structure of the multi-column method, the single-column method [3,4] usually adopts a single and deeper CNN. Due to their architectural simplicity and training efficiency, the single-column network architecture has received more and more attention in recent years.

2.2 Lightweight Networks

It is a research hotspot that how can achieve the optimal balance between accuracy and performance by tuning neural model architectures in the field of deep learning. The SqueezeNet [5] composed of several fire modules achieve AlexNet-level [12] accuracy based on the bottleneck approach. Depthwise separable convolution was proposed in MobileNetv1 [13], which uses between 8 to 9 times less computation than standard convolutions at only a small reduction in accuracy. ShuffleNet [14] can achieve higher efficiency than MobileNetV1 by applying group convolution and channel shuffle. MobileNetV2 [15] based on the inverted residual structure with liner bottleneck can reach high performance effective and efficient. In addition, the network compression approaches and the Neural architecture search (NAS) are also applied to the design of lightweight networks.

3 Proposed Method

As shown in Fig. 1, the fundamental idea of our approach is to deploy an end-to-end CNN-based model to generate density estimation maps, which can achieve the optimal trade-off between counting accuracy and computation efficiency. The network architecture of ARNet will be discussed in Sect. 3.1; the loss function of the ARNet will be analyzed in Sect. 3.2.

3.1 Network Architecture

The proposed ARNet consists of four components: Encoder, Parameter-Sharing Context-Aware Module (PSCAM), Decoder and Mask Density Generator (MDG).

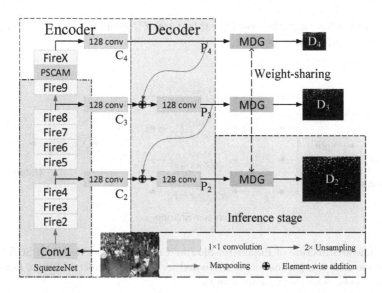

Fig. 1. The architecture of our propose network. C_2–C_4 represents the feature maps generated by the encoder, P_2–P_4 represents the feature maps processed by the decoder, D_2–D_4 represents the density estimation maps.

Encoder. As we mentioned earlier, the counting model requires a sufficiently deep structure to cope with the complexity of the scene. Although VGG [16] can be applied as the backbone to extract in-depth feature information, its huge parameters amount consume more terminal memory and computing resources in the mobile systems, making it difficult to achieve the real-time requirements of counting. Therefore, we apply the lightweight pre-trained SqueezeNet as the encoder to extract multi-level features. On the one hand, the Fire module in SqueezeNet is composed of a squeezed convolutional layer and an expanded convolutional layer, which can significantly reduce parameters and calculations. On the other hand, the SqueezeNet pre-trained on the ImageNet can overcome overfitting caused by images insufficiency of crowd datasets.

Parameter-Sharing Context-Aware Module. Moreover, we add an additional Parameter-Sharing Context-Aware Module (PSCAM) at the end of encoder to capture global contextual features. As shown in Fig. 2, the feature map is first divided into four sub-feature maps with the same channel dimension, and then fed into the dilated convolutional layer with different expansion rates to obtain contextual information in multiple receptive fields, the four sub-feature maps are concatenated in the final stage. It is worth noting that the dilated convolutional layer we designed achieves the parameter sharing of the filters, only slightly different in the expansion rate. This design of parameter-sharing not only avoids an obvious increase in the parameters amount, but also prevents network overfitting. We select the features C_2, C_3 generated by Fire4 and Fire8 of the SqueezeNet, and the contextual features C_4 generated by PSCAM as the input of our subsequent decoder.

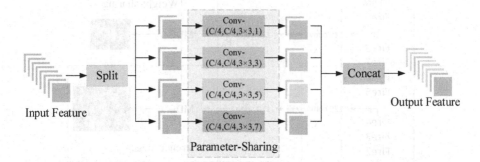

Fig. 2. The architecture of Parameter-Sharing Context-Aware Module (PSCAM), the convolutional layer's parameters are denoted as "Conv-(number of filters, number of input channels, kernel size, dilation rate)".

Decoder. The crowd density estimation map generated by the crowd counting network in real-world applications needs to contain two measures: high counting accuracy and detailed spatial distribution. However, each sub-features of the encoder can not meet those measures simultaneously due to the imbalance of spatial and semantic information in feature maps of different levels. The low-level features have rich spatial information yet lack semantic information due to their small receptive fields, and vice versa. So we introduce the Feature Pyramid Network [17] structure to the decoder for developing a top-down architecture with lateral connections for building high-level semantic feature maps of all scales. Formally, the feature map generated by the decoder can be described as:

$$P_i = \begin{cases} C_i, & i = 4 \\ f(C_i + up(P_{i+1})), & i = 2, 3 \end{cases} \tag{1}$$

where $up()$ denotes up-sampling by a factor of $2\times$ via bilinear interpolation. f represents the convolution operation on each merged map used to generate the final feature map for reducing the aliasing effect of upsampling.

Mask Density Generator. The task-related prediction network composed of several convolutional layers was often adopted by the previous counting network for regressing density maps. This simple density generator is susceptible to background interference factors, which results in more faint bright pixels appearing in the background regions. To deal with this problem, we design the Mask Density Generator (MDG) [18] as the back-end prediction network. It can be seen from Fig. 3 that MDG consists of two sub-prediction modules named the Semantic-Aware module (SAM) and the Density-Aware Module (DAM). The SAM can achieve full-pixel foreground-background semantic segmentation from the crowd image, and provide relevant attention masks to DAM. The DAM is exploited to generate rough density maps, which are multiplied by attention masks from SAM to obtain individual foreground or background density maps. The density maps of foreground and background are summed pixel-wise to give the final density map. Based on the concept of weight-sharing, we perform density map prediction on all levels of features by adopting a single MDG, which not only forces the middle layer of the network to learn task-related features, but also enhances the robustness of the network. After MDG processing, a series of density maps with different resolutions D_2–D_4 are obtained.

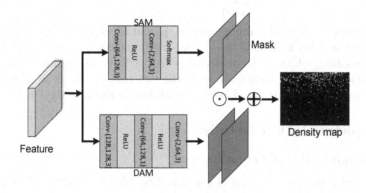

Fig. 3. The architecture of the Mask Density Generator (MDG), the convolutional layer's parameters are denoted as "Conv-(number of filters, number of input channels, kernel size)"

3.2 Loss Functions

The network we designed can generate foreground-background masks and density estimation maps at each level layers, so that multiple losses can be applied to each intermediate output under distributed supervision. The propagation flow originating from each distributed supervision will aggregates into the overall gradient flow during the backpropagation process, so that the gradient disappearance can be avoided.

The loss function distributed at each layer is a combination of classification loss and regression loss. As shown in Fig. 3, the loss of the density map generated by the MDG is calculated by applying the Euclidean distance between the estimated map and the ground-truth density map, the classification loss of the mask generated by the SAM is calculated by applying the cross-entropy between the predicted foreground-background mask and the ground-truth label. Let $M^i(X_j; \Theta)$ and $C^i_{sm}(X_j; \Theta)$ denote the estimated density map and predicted foreground-background mask generated by the i-th layer of ARNet with the parameter Θ, respectively, X_j represents the input image. The classification loss function $\mathcal{L}_{ce}^i$ and the density map estimation loss function $\mathcal{L}_{mse}^i$ of i-th layer are defined as follows:

$$\mathcal{L}_{mse}^i(\Theta) = \frac{1}{N}\sum_{j=1}^{N}\left\|M^i\left(X_j;\Theta\right) - M_j^i\right\|_2^2 \tag{2}$$

$$\mathcal{L}_{ce}^i(\Theta) = -\frac{1}{N}\sum_{j=1}^{N}y_j^i\log\left(C_{sm}^i\left(X_j;\Theta\right)\right) \tag{3}$$

$$\mathcal{L} = \sum_{i\in\{2,3,4\}}\left(\mathcal{L}_{mse}^i(\Theta) + \gamma\times\mathcal{L}_{ce}^i(\Theta)\right) \tag{4}$$

where N is the number of training samples, y_j^i and M_j^i represent the ground-truth label in the one-hot form and the ground-truth density map for image X_j after average pooling, which is conducted over a $2^i\times 2^i$ pixel window, respectively. γ is a ratio factor that aims to balance the two tasks, γ is set to 1 after cross-validation. Equation (4) is used as the overall loss function in the training phase.

4   Implementation Details

4.1   Ground Truth Generation

The ground truth density map is generated by blurring each head annotation with a normalized 2D Gaussian kernel. Supposing there is a head annotation at pixel x_i in a labeled crowd image, it can be formalized as a unit impulse function $\delta(x - x_i)$. Hence, the ground truth density map $F(x)$ can be calculated as follows:

$$F(x) = \sum_{i=1}^{N}\delta(x - x_i) * G_\sigma(x) \tag{5}$$

where, N is the number of people and x denotes two dimensional coordinates of a pixel at the head location. The sum of all pixel values gives the crowd count of the input image. In our experiments, we use a fixed spread Gaussian kernel with $\sigma = 15$ to generate density maps.

In particular, the ground truth segmentation map of the SAM is generated based on the threshold applied to the corresponding ground truth density map due to the lack of precise labels. It is sufficient for the rough pixel classification of backgrounds and crowds, since we focus on density map estimation and mainly employ classification for auxiliary learning. The ground-truth label map can be generated by the following formula:

$$y_i(x) = \begin{cases} 0, \, ap_i[F(x)] = 0 \\ 1, \, ap_i[F(x)] \neq 0 \end{cases} \tag{6}$$

where, $y_i(x)$ denotes the value of position x in ground truth label at i-th layer; ap_i is the average pooling, which is conducted over a $2^i\times 2^i$ pixel window. The digital label 0 and 1 represent the background and foreground, respectively.

4.2   Data Augmentation

Firstly, We augment the training data by cropping nine image patches at random locations in one image, each image patch is one-fourth of the size of the original image. Then, we crop fixed-size image patches of 256×256 pixels at random locations in each image patch. Finally, we apply the following data augmentation methods to the image: (1) Horizontal flip; (2) Gamma transformation; (3) Grayscale processing; (4) Switch RGB channels; (5) Add Gaussian noise. This data augmentation strategy is extremely important for the counting networks, especially for networks trained on small-scale datasets.

4.3   Training Process and Inference Process

The backbone network is initialized from a pre-trained SqueezeNet and the rest convolutional layers are initialized by a Gaussian distribution with the mean of 0 and the standard deviation of 0.01. The Adam algorithm is used to optimize the model and the network is trained with the batch size of 16. We multiply the density map by a magnification factor of 100 according to Gao's proposal [19]. The neural network could get faster convergence and achieve lower estimation error, this can also balance the classification loss and the density map estimation loss. The implementation of our method is based on the PyTorch framework.

Since the network we designed is a fully convolutional network, images of any size can be input in the inference stage. It's worth noting that we can reduce Flops by 8.9% in the inference stage by turning off the prediction of density map on feature maps P_2 and P_3, because it only provides gradient flow in the training stage.

4.4   Counting Performance Evaluation Metrics

Following some previous works [20], we mainly adopt three metrics to evaluate the counting performance, which are Mean Absolute Error (MAE), Mean Squared Error (MSE) and mean Normalized Absolute Error (NAE). They can be formulated as follows:

$$MAE = \frac{1}{N} \sum_{i=1}^{N} |c_i - \hat{c}_i| \tag{7}$$

$$MSE = \sqrt{\frac{1}{N} \sum_{i=1}^{N} |c_i - \hat{c}_i|^2} \tag{8}$$

$$NAE = \frac{1}{N} \sum_{i=1}^{N} \frac{|c_i - \hat{c}_i|}{c_i} \tag{9}$$

where N is the number of images in the test set. $\hat{c}_i$ is the estimated count and c_i is the corresponding actual count. Moreover, MAE is an indicator for evaluating the accuracy of predicted crowd counts and MSE demonstrates the robustness of the estimated counts.

5   Experiments

5.1   Datasets

It is prone to overfit the data due to the smaller scales of ShanghaiTech [1] and UCF-QNRF datasets [11], so we conduct experiments on the two large-scale datasets: JHU-CROWD++ [21] and NWPU-Crowd [20]. Compared with the above small-scale datasets, they have more complex environmental scene transformations, which can be more effective in holistically evaluating the accuracy and robustness of crowd counting networks.

ShanghaiTech. The ShanghaiTech dataset is divided into two parts: Part_A (SHT_A) and Part_B (SHT_B). SHT_A contains 482 images randomly crawled from the Internet. The training set has 300 images and the testing set has 182 images. SHT_B contains 716 images taken from the busy streets of the metropolitan areas in Shanghai. The training set has 400 images, and the testing set has 316 images. The density of SHT_A is higher than SHT_B, and the density varies significantly.

UCF-QNRF. The UCF-QNRF contains 1.25 million humans marked with dot annotations and consists of 1,535 crowd images with wider a variety of scenes containing the most diverse set of viewpoints, densities and lighting variations. We use 1,201 images for training and 334 images for testing.

JHU-CROWD++. A new large-scale unconstrained dataset named JHU-CROWD++ introduced by Sindagi *et al.* with a total of 4,372 images (containing 1,515,005 head annotations). The dataset is split into train, val and test sets, which contain 2722, 500 and 1600 images respectively.

NWPU-Crowd. NWPU-Crowd is the most challenging crowd counting datasets at present, which requires our network to have extremely high performance. It consists of 5,109 images and a total of 2,133,375 annotated heads with dots and frames. For fair evaluation, an online evaluation benchmark website was developed to allow researchers to submit their estimation results.

Figure 4 shows the samples of crowd datasets and their corresponding density maps estimated by our ARNet together with ground truth maps. It can be seen that ARNet shows strong robustness to deal with the variation of crowd density levels, but the counting accuracy of the high-density level is still inferior to that of the low-density level.

5.2   Results and Analysis

In this section, we conduct three comparative experiments (counting performance, calculation efficiency, and component composition) to verify the effectiveness of the model.

Comparison of Counting Performance: In this section, we evaluate our approach against currently reported methods on four benchmark datasets. Table 1 indicates that ARNet can achieve the lowest counting error in small-scale

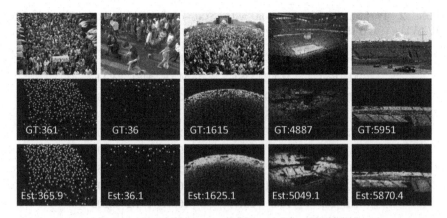

Fig. 4. Results of the proposed model on datesset. The first column: SHT_A dataset; the second column: SHT_B dataset; the third column: UCF-QNRF dataset; the fourth column: JHU-CROWD++ dataset; the last column: NWPU-Crowd dataset.

Table 1. Performance comparison with State-of-the-art methods on the ShanghaiTech and the UCF-QNRF datatsets.

Dtaset	SHT_A		SHT_B		UCF-QNRF	
Method	MAE	MSE	MAE	MSE	MAE	MSE
MCNN [1]	110.2	173.2	26.4	41.3	277	426
CMTL [22]	101.3	152.4	20.0	31.1	252	514
Switch-CNN [2]	90.4	135.0	21.6	33.4	228	445
CSRNet [3]	68.2	115.0	10.6	16.0	–	–
SANet [23]	67.0	104.5	8.4	13.6	–	–
CAN [4]	62.3	100.0	7.8	12.2	107	183
BL [24]	62.8	101.8	7.7	12.7	88.7	154.8
S-DCNet [25]	58.3	95.0	6.7	10.7	104.4	176.1
1/4-CSRNet + SKT [26]	71.6	114.4	7.5	11.7	144.4	234.6
PaDNet [27]	59.2	98.1	8.1	12.2	96.5	170.2
MobileCount [28]	98.6	162.9	9.1	15.1	137.8	238.2
SACCN [29]	59.2	98.0	6.8	10.5	96.1	167.8
ARNet	62.5	101.4	7.5	12.6	111.0	207.9

datasets compared to lightweight models (MCNN, CMTL, Switch-CNN, SANet, 1/4-CSRNet + SKT, MobileCount), and has a 12.7% MAE improvement for the SHT_A dataset compared with the second-best approach, 1/4-CSRNet + SKT. Moreover, ARNet also shows competitive counting performance compared with depth models on small-scale datasets. It can be seen in Table 2 that ARNet can show better accuracy and robustness of the estimated counts on large-scale datasets.

Table 2. Performance comparison with State-of-the-art methods on the JHU-CROWD++ and the NWPU-Crowd test sets.

Dtaset	JHU-CROWD++		NWPU-Crowd		
Method	MAE	MSE	MAE	MSE	NAE
MCNN [1]	188.9	483.4	232.5	714.6	1.063
CMTL [22]	157.8	490.4	–	–	–
CSRNet [3]	85.9	309.2	121.3	387.8	0.604
SANet [23]	91.1	320.4	190.6	491.4	0.991
SCAR [30]	–	–	110.0	485.3	0.288
CAN [4]	100.1	314.0	106.3	386.5	0.295
BL [24]	75.0	297.9	105.4	454.2	0.203
SFCN [31]	77.5	297.6	105.7	424.1	0.254
ARNet	78.2	276.8	89.3	332.8	0.222

Comparison of Computation Efficiency: The critical goal of this work is to achieve model efficiency, so we compare our method with the existing crowd counting models on inference efficiency for verifying its superiority. In Table 3, we compare ARNet with state-of-the-art methods on the following indicators: MAE, MSE, Params (number of parameters), Flops and FPS. The execution code is computed on RTX 2080 GPU, the size of input image is 1024×768 and the batch size is 8.

Although the number of parameters of MCNN is the smallest, it shows the largest counting error due to its simple network structure. SANet can improve the representation ability of features by employing scale aggregation modules, but such fragmented operators severely reduce the degree of parallelism and prolongs the inference time. MobileCount shows extremely short inference time, yet it do not perform well in counting performance. Compared with CSRNet and CAN, our proposed model shows better counting performance and only has about 10% of the parameters. In general, ASNet can achieve the best trade-off between counting accuracy and computation efficiency.

Ablation Experiment for Component Composition: We analyze the effects of different components of ARNet on SHT_A dataset in the following four aspects:

1. **Baseline:** The proposed baseline consists of two components: the encoder-decoder network and the simple density generator.
2. **Baseline + PSCAM:** In this configuration, we only embed PSCAM on the baseline to verify the performance improvement by capturing the global context.
3. **Baseline + MDG:** In this configuration, we only replace simple density generator with MDG to verify performance improvement by suppressing image background interference.
4. **ARNet:** In this configuration, we embed PSCAM and DHN on the baseline simultaneously to verify the overall performance improvement.

Table 3. The comparison of our proposed method with state-of-the-arts in terms of Params(MB), FLOPs(G), inference Time(ms) and FPS.

Methods	MAE	MSE	Params	FLOPs	Time	FPS
MCNN [1]	26.4	26.4	0.13	21.32	10.08	99.2
CMTL [22]	20.0	31.1	2.46	95.70	22.11	45.2
MobileCount [28]	9.1	15.1	3.34	6.32	4.88	204.9
SANet [23]	8.4	13.6	1.39	71.54	24.74	40.3
CSRNet [3]	10.6	16.0	16.26	325.34	48.71	20.5
CAN [4]	7.8	12.2	18.10	218.20	57.01	17.5
ARNet	7.5	12.6	1.77	36.20	10.25	97.6

Table 4. The effects of different components in ARNet on the SHT_A dataset.

Method	MAE	MSE
Baseline	71.82	114.68
Baseline + PSCAM	68.00	110.82
Baseline + MDG	65.25	105.38
ARNet	**62.54**	**101.42**

The results of these experiments are shown in Table 4. It can be found that the worst MAE and MSE are obtained on the baseline network. The PSCAM and MDG we designed can achieve certain performance improvements. When they are embedded simultaneously, ARNet can obtain the lowest MAE and MSE, compared to the baseline network, the counting performance has increased by 12.9%.

6 Conclusion

In this paper, we propose a novel end-to-end encoder-decoder framework called ARNet for high-accuracy and real-time crowd counting. Specifically, the encoder can extract multi-level features by applying SqueezeNet as backbone and the decoder is able to enhance semantic context representation capabilities. In addition, the Parameter-Sharing Context-Aware Module (PSCAM) can capture context information to improve the robustness of the network without significantly increasing the number of parameters, the Mask Density Generator (MDG) based on multi-task learning can regress accurate density map by suppressing background interference. Meanwhile, the loss calculation under the distributed supervision can avoid the disappearance of gradients and urge the network to generate high-resolution density estimation maps. Extensive experiments conducted on four benchmark datasets indicated that ARNet can achieve the optimal trade-off between counting accuracy and computation efficiency.

References

1. Zhang, Y., Zhou, D., Chen, S., Gao, S., Ma, Y.: Single-image crowd counting via multi-column convolutional neural network. In: Proceedings of the IEEE Conference on Computer Vision and Pattern Recognition, pp. 589–597 (2016)
2. Sam, D.B., Surya, S., Babu, R.V.: Switching convolutional neural network for crowd counting. In: 2017 IEEE Conference on Computer Vision and Pattern Recognition (CVPR), pp. 4031–4039. IEEE (2017)
3. Li, Y., Zhang, X., Chen, D.: CSRNet: dilated convolutional neural networks for understanding the highly congested scenes. In: Proceedings of the IEEE Conference on Computer Vision and Pattern Recognition, pp. 1091–1100 (2018)
4. Liu, W., Salzmann, M., Fua, P.: Context-aware crowd counting. In: Proceedings of the IEEE/CVF Conference on Computer Vision and Pattern Recognition, pp. 5099–5108 (2019)
5. Iandola, F.N., Han, S., Moskewicz, M.W., Ashraf, K., Dally, W.J., Keutzer, K.: SqueezeNet: AlexNet-level accuracy with 50x fewer parameters and < 0.5 MB model size. arXiv preprint arXiv:1602.07360 (2016)
6. Dollar, P., Wojek, C., Schiele, B., Perona, P.: Pedestrian detection: an evaluation of the state of the art. IEEE Trans. Pattern Anal. Mach. Intell. **34**(4), 743–761 (2011)
7. Enzweiler, M., Gavrila, D.M.: Monocular pedestrian detection: survey and experiments. IEEE Trans. Pattern Anal. Mach. Intell. **31**(12), 2179–2195 (2008)
8. Ren, S., He, K., Girshick, R., Sun, J.: Faster R-CNN: towards real-time object detection with region proposal networks. IEEE Trans. Pattern Anal. Mach. Intell. **39**(6), 1137–1149 (2016)
9. Liu, W., et al.: SSD: single shot multibox detector. In: Leibe, B., Matas, J., Sebe, N., Welling, M. (eds.) ECCV 2016. LNCS, vol. 9905, pp. 21–37. Springer, Cham (2016). https://doi.org/10.1007/978-3-319-46448-0_2
10. Chan, A.B., Liang, Z.S.J., Vasconcelos, N.: Privacy preserving crowd monitoring: counting people without people models or tracking. In: Proceedings of the IEEE Conference on Computer Vision and Pattern Recognition, pp. 1–7 (2008)
11. Idrees, H., et al.: Composition loss for counting, density map estimation and localization in dense crowds. In: Ferrari, V., Hebert, M., Sminchisescu, C., Weiss, Y. (eds.) ECCV 2018. LNCS, vol. 11206, pp. 544–559. Springer, Cham (2018). https://doi.org/10.1007/978-3-030-01216-8_33
12. Krizhevsky, A., Sutskever, I., Hinton, G.E.: ImageNet classification with deep convolutional neural networks. In: Advances in Neural Information Processing Systems, vol. 25, pp. 1097–1105 (2012)
13. Howard, A.G., et al.: MobileNets: efficient convolutional neural networks for mobile vision applications. arXiv preprint arXiv:1704.04861 (2017)
14. Zhang, X., Zhou, X., Lin, M., Sun, J.: ShuffleNet: an extremely efficient convolutional neural network for mobile devices. In: Proceedings of the IEEE Conference on Computer Vision and Pattern Recognition, pp. 6848–6856 (2018)
15. Howard, A., Zhmoginov, A., Chen, L.C., Sandler, M., Zhu, M.: Inverted residuals and linear bottlenecks: Mobile networks for classification, detection and segmentation (2018)
16. Simonyan, K., Zisserman, A.: Very deep convolutional networks for large-scale image recognition. arXiv preprint arXiv:1409.1556 (2014)
17. Lin, T.Y., Dollár, P., Girshick, R., He, K., Hariharan, B., Belongie, S.: Feature pyramid networks for object detection. In: Proceedings of the IEEE Conference on Computer Vision and Pattern Recognition, pp. 2117–2125 (2017)

18. Xia, Y., He, Y., Peng, S., Hao, X., Yang, Q., Yin, B.: EdeNet: elaborate density estimation network for crowd counting. Neurocomputing **459**, 108–121 (2021)
19. Gao, J., Lin, W., Zhao, B., Wang, D., Gao, C., Wen, J.: C$^\wedge$ 3 framework: an open-source pytorch code for crowd counting. arXiv preprint arXiv:1907.02724 (2019)
20. Wang, Q., Gao, J., Lin, W., Li, X.: NWPU-Crowd: a large-scale benchmark for crowd counting and localization. IEEE Trans. Pattern Anal. Mach. Intell. **43**(6), 2141–2149 (2020)
21. Sindagi, V., Yasarla, R., Patel, V.M.: JHU-CROWD++: large-scale crowd counting dataset and a benchmark method. IEEE Trans. Pattern Anal. Mach. Intell., 1 (2020). https://doi.org/10.1109/TPAMI.2020.3035969
22. Sindagi, V.A., Patel, V.M.: CNN-based cascaded multi-task learning of high-level prior and density estimation for crowd counting. In: 2017 14th IEEE International Conference on Advanced Video and Signal Based Surveillance (AVSS), pp. 1–6. IEEE (2017)
23. Cao, X., Wang, Z., Zhao, Y., Su, F.: Scale aggregation network for accurate and efficient crowd counting. In: Ferrari, V., Hebert, M., Sminchisescu, C., Weiss, Y. (eds.) ECCV 2018. LNCS, vol. 11209, pp. 757–773. Springer, Cham (2018). https://doi.org/10.1007/978-3-030-01228-1_45
24. Ma, Z., Wei, X., Hong, X., Gong, Y.: Bayesian loss for crowd count estimation with point supervision. In: Proceedings of the IEEE/CVF International Conference on Computer Vision, pp. 6142–6151 (2019)
25. Xiong, H., Lu, H., Liu, C., Liu, L., Cao, Z., Shen, C.: From open set to closed set: counting objects by spatial divide-and-conquer. In: Proceedings of the IEEE/CVF International Conference on Computer Vision, pp. 8362–8371 (2019)
26. Liu, L., Chen, J., Wu, H., Chen, T., Li, G., Lin, L.: Efficient crowd counting via structured knowledge transfer. In: Proceedings of the 28th ACM International Conference on Multimedia, pp. 2645–2654 (2020)
27. Tian, Y., Lei, Y., Zhang, J., Wang, J.Z.: PaDNet: pan-density crowd counting. IEEE Trans. Image Process. **29**, 2714–2727 (2019)
28. Wang, P., Gao, C., Wang, Y., Li, H., Gao, Y.: MobileCount: an efficient encoder-decoder framework for real-time crowd counting. Neurocomputing **407**, 292–299 (2020)
29. Yi, Q., Liu, Y., Jiang, A., Li, J., Mei, K., Wang, M.: Scale-aware network with regional and semantic attentions for crowd counting under cluttered background. arXiv preprint arXiv:2101.01479 (2021)
30. Gao, J., Wang, Q., Yuan, Y.: SCAR: spatial-/channel-wise attention regression networks for crowd counting. Neurocomputing **363**, 1–8 (2019)
31. Wang, Q., Gao, J., Lin, W., Yuan, Y.: Pixel-wise crowd understanding via synthetic data. Int. J. Comput. Vision **129**(1), 225–245 (2021)

Deep Recommendation Model Based on BiLSTM and BERT

Changwei Liu$^{(\boxtimes)}$ and Xiaowen Deng

Information Engineering College, Guangzhou Nanyang Polytechnic College,
Guangzhou 510900, China
2181471@s.hlju.edu.cn

Abstract. Recommendation models based on rating behavior often fail to properly deal with the problem of data sparsity, resulting in the cold-start phenomenon, which limits the recommendation effect. A model based on user behavior and semantics can better describe user preferences and item features to improve the performance of a recommender system, but is usually shallow and ignores deep features between the user and item. This paper proposes a deep neural network and self-attention mechanism (DSAM) model to solve these problems. The DSAM model introduces a two-way LSTM unit and a self-attention mechanism, combined with a large-scale pretrained BERT model to mine deep nonlinear features and hidden vectors in user comment information and perform score prediction. In comparative experiments carried out on the Amazon product dataset, the error of DSAM prediction results was lower than that of a reference group, and the average error was reduced by 4%.

Keywords: Deep learning · Cold start · Preliminary training · Rating matrix

1 Introduction

The rapid development of the internet has exponentially increased the amount of data, bringing about information overload and a sharp drop in information quality and utilization. As an effective tool to alleviate information overload, the recommendation system came into being, and has been widely used in the fields of financial investment [1], online education, e-commerce [2], and medical treatment [3,13]. A recommendation system filters data through information processing and data analysis to obtain user preferences and find their favorite products. How to provide high-quality recommendation services is the most important problem.

The most widely used recommendation model is based on collaborative filtering, which groups based on preference and recommends products with similar characteristics. Collaborative filtering can approximately partition implicit semantics and neighborhood-based methods. Algorithms based on matrix factorization can well solve the implicit semantic model, and have received much

D. N. Pham et al. (Eds.): PRICAI 2021, LNAI 13032, pp. 390–402, 2021.
https://doi.org/10.1007/978-3-030-89363-7_30

attention. The most common include the neural factorization machine (NFM) [4,14], deep factorization machine (DFM) [5], and latent factor model (LFM) [6]. Although matrix-based decomposition collaborative algorithms can find the correlation characteristics between hidden factors, the recommendation quality cannot be improved due to the sparseness of the score data.

Extracting the information from the review text to alleviate the sparsity of the scoring matrix is the most effective solution [7,11], and diversified information fusion is also a popular research direction. Comment text data contain rich and valuable information. Users have very different evaluations and likes of the same item. Therefore, comment information can better portray user preferences.

Deep learning technology has been applied in various industries [10]. Due to its strong learning and anti-interference abilities, it has performed well in recommendation systems. Many recommendation algorithms are integrated with deep nonlinear network structures. For example, DeepCoNN [8] has a bidirectional nerve section. One network is used to train users' comments, and the other learns the corresponding features from the items. Experiments showed that DeepCoNN performed better than the traditional recommendation model. DeepCoNN uses a CNN encoding method whose convolution kernel has a fixed value, resulting in the loss of long-distance features. DeepCoNN considers that the contribution of each comment to the user is the same, which is not necessarily the case. To further distinguish the contribution of each comment will continue to improve the recommendation effect. To solve the above problems, our paper proposed a deep neural network and self-attention mechanism (DSAM) based on deep neural networks and self-attention mechanisms.

The main contributions of this article are as follows.

(1) A deep DSAM recommendation model is proposed, which fuses the review text and scoring matrix. Owing to the integration of comment text data, the phenomenon of data cold-start is effectively alleviated, and the user's deep preferences and advanced features of items can be better learned, thereby ameliorating the accuracy of the model.
(2) The BERT model is used instead of traditional pre-training to overcome the problem of polysemous words in the text. The BiLSTM unit and self-attention mechanism are introduced to effectively capture contextual connections so that the model can more accurately understand the semantic and emotional characteristics of comments and mine the deep connections between users, items, and ratings to enhance the recommendation effect.
(3) We conduct comparative experiments on Amazon datasets and analyze the performance of mainstream recommendation models. The root mean square error (RMSE) obtained from the experiment is lower, which demonstrates that the DSAM model is feasible, has better recommendation quality, and alleviates the problem of data sparsity.

2   DSAM Model

2.1   Problem and Symbol Definition

The traditional latent factor model (LFM) algorithm only relies on the $U - I$ rating matrix, ignoring rich semantic and emotional information in the review text. The review information has deeply hidden features that cannot be expressed by the rating, and the text is often unstructured, bringing difficulty to processing.

The comment text is rich in user semantic information, which can be combined with the evaluation matrix to capture deeply hidden characteristics of users and items. The fusion of deep features can enhance the interpretability of the model and overcome data sparsity. The BERT-BiLSTM model can be combined to process unstructured text and extract deep semantic features.

Assume that a dataset T is composed of N tuples (u, i, w_{ui}, r_{ui}), each representing user comment w_{ui} and corresponding rating information r_{ui} of item i. The DSAM model uses this information to obtain the predicted score $\hat{r}_{ui}$ and minimize the error between this value and the real score r_{ui}. Table 1 lists the symbols and operations.

Table 1. Symbols

Symbol	Description
w_{ui}	user u comment text on review item i
r_{ui}	user u rating of item i
N_u	user neural network
N_i	item neural network
d	maximum comment set
U	deep features of user
I	deep features of item
U_{bert}	user comments implicitly
I_{bert}	item comments implicitly
R_u	user preference
R_i	item preference
LFM_u	user latent vector
LFM_i	item latent vector
$\odot$	add operation
$\otimes$	interactive operations involving multiplication and addition
$\oplus$	vector superposition operation
Y	predicted value
S	scoring matrix

2.2   DSAM Model Structure

We structure of the proposed DSAM model is shown in Fig. 1 The model has three modules: characteristic fusion, LFM matrix decomposition, and feature extraction based on BERT and BiLSTM. The text processing module obtains the semantic representation of the input text through the BERT pretraining layer, obtains the vector representation of each word in the sentence, and transmits these to the BiLSTM layer for further semantic coding to obtain user and item comment trait vectors R_u and R_i. We obtain the hidden vectors LFM_u and LFM_i of $U - I$ through the matrix decomposition module. In the fusion layer, R_u and R_i are fused to obtain the user's and item's deep traits U and I, respectively. The prediction score is gained by the full connection layer.

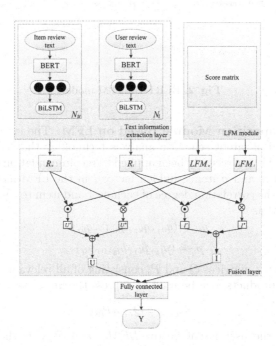

Fig. 1. DASM model

Feature Extraction Module Based on BERT and BiLSTM. The text processing module is shown in Fig. 2 The input layer contains two parallel neural networks N_u and N_i, to process user and item information, respectively. After entering the item and user comment data, the data are modeled through N_u, N_i, and the input is mapped to the corresponding word vector sequence through the BERT model,

$$h_i = h_{forward} \oplus h_{backward} \tag{1}$$

where h_i represents the hidden state of U_{bert} or I_{bert}, and the hidden state of the BiLSTM unit can be represented by $\{h_1, h_2, \ldots, h_d\}$.

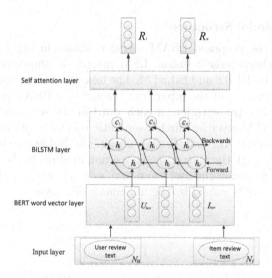

Fig. 2. BERT-BiLSTM model

Matrix Decomposition Module Based on LFM. The latent factor model (LFM) is a kind of latent semantic analysis technology that was first used in data mining, and it has recently been applied to recommendation and prediction. Assuming m users and n items, hidden factor l in the LFM model, and initial score matrix S, the correlation degree of each user and item to each hidden factor can be expressed as

$$q_u = (q_{u_1}, q_{u_2}, q_{u_3} ..., q_{u_l}) \qquad (2)$$

$$p_i = (p_{i_1}, p_{i_2}, p_{i_3} ..., p_{i_l}) \qquad (3)$$

The implicit vector matrices Q and P, consisting of all relevance vectors q_u and p_i of users and products, can be used to express the initial score as

$$S_{m \times n} = Q_{m \times l} P_{l \times n} \qquad (4)$$

where $Q_{m \times l}$ is the user latent vector LFM_u, and $P_{l \times n}$ is the item's hidden feature, LFM_i.

Feature Fusion Module. In the first module layer, the deep nonlinear features R_u and R_i of the review text are obtained through Bert-BiLSTM and the self-attention mechanism. In the second module, the hidden features LFM_u and LFM_i of users and items are obtained through LMF matrix decomposition. The trait fusion module combines the deep and hidden features in the review text and predicts the score. Inspired by DeepCoNN and factorization machine [11,15], the low-order hidden features LFM_u and LFM_i can interact with first-order features to obtain high-order features. First-order features corresponding to users and items are respectively calculated as

$$U^1 = R_u \odot LFM_u \qquad (5)$$

$$I^1 = R_i \odot LFM_i \qquad (6)$$

where $\odot$ represents the addition operation of vectors R_u and LFM_u whose dimensions are both l.

R_u, R_i, LFM_u, and LFM_u are spliced into first-order features U^1 and I^1, and second-order features are calculated using the idea of a FM. The quadratic term can be changed to improve calculation efficiency:

$$\sum_{i=1}^{n} \sum_{j=i+1}^{n} \langle v_i, v_j \rangle x_i x_j = \frac{1}{2} \sum_{f=1}^{k} \left(\left(\sum_{i=1}^{n} v_{i,f} x_i \right)^2 - \sum_{i=1}^{n} v_{i,f}^2 x_i^2 \right) \qquad (7)$$

We decompose x_i into an l-dimensional vector v_i x_i and calculate the second-order features as

$$U^2 = \frac{1}{2} \sum_{f=1}^{k} \left(\left(\sum_{i=1}^{n} v_{i,f} x_i \right)^2 - \sum_{i=1}^{n} v_{i,f}^2 x_i^2 \right) \qquad (8)$$

The first-order features U^2 and I^2 contain all of the information of the quadratic term results, and the first- and second-order features can be fully mined through the fully connected layer. We obtain the first-order features U^1, I^1 and second-order features U^2, I^2, and continue to merge them to obtain the deep high-level features of users and items.

$$U = U^1 \oplus U^2 \qquad (9)$$

$$I = I^1 \oplus I^2 \qquad (10)$$

Score Prediction. Linear regression is performed on the depth characteristics and related parameters of the fusion layer in the fully connected layer to obtain the scoring prediction formula,

$$Y = W * (U \otimes I) + b_u + b_i + \mu \qquad (11)$$

where $\otimes$ denotes the phase operation of the corresponding elements of the depth feature vector, W is the weight of the FC layer, b_u is the user offset, b_i is the item offset, and μ is the global offset. If there are new users and only b_u and U are 0, the DSAM model can still be trained with other parameters, making full use of the score and comment text for learning to further reduce prediction error and avoid the cold-start phenomenon.

To model users and products and then score predictions is actually a regression problem, and the objective function is a square loss function,

$$L = \sum_{u,i \in T} (\widehat{r_{ui}} - r_{ui})^2 \qquad (12)$$

where T is a sample in the training set, $\widehat{r_{ui}}$ is the predicted score, and r_{ui} is the true score. Adaptive moment estimation is used to optimize the objective function, which can automatically adjust the learning rate, speed up convergence, and simplify model learning. The learning process of the DSAM model is as follows.

(1) The user and item rating and review data are preprocessed to obtain the user and product review dataset, and feature extraction is performed with BERT-BiLSTM to form a vector matrix to obtain the hidden features of the review text.
(2) LMF technology is used to decompose the scoring data and add bias items.
(3) The obtained features are merged in the fusion layer to form the deep features of users and products.
(4) Training is performed according to the loss function, and the result of previous Training is reconstructed into a scoring matrix and then recommended.

3 Experiment

3.1 Dataset

An Amazon review dataset was selected to verify the effectiveness and accuracy of the DSAM model. The dataset includes user information, ratings, comments, and the timestamp of an item.

Three sub-category datasets with different topics and sizes were selected: Movies and TV (MT), Digital Music (DM), and Toys and Games (TG). MT has the largest data volume, and DM the smallest. We needed to use four features: user number, product number, user's product rating, and user's comment information on the product. The statistical results are shown in Table 2.

Although there are many users and goods, the number of goods purchased by users is only a small fraction of the total. Therefore, it is necessary to calculate statistics on commodity rating data, whose results are shown in Table 3.

After preprocessing, the sparseness of the scoring data was very large. Experiments showed that the fusion of review information can effectively alleviate sparsity to further improve the accuracy of scoring prediction.

Table 2. Dataset information

Data	Users	Items	Samples	Average word count
MT	231096	84017	2173892	2161.38
DM	14538	9362	139781	2161.38
TG	209516	121191	1720971	1646.92
Average	151716	71523	692711	1514.93

Table 3. Commodity score statistical results

Data	Less than 10	Less than 20	Less than 30
MT	0.514	0.683	0.727
DM	0.499	0.639	0.695
TG	0.603	0.738	0.833
Average	0.538	0.687	0.751

The model was evaluated by the $RMSE$, whose smaller value indicates a more accurate prediction, and which is calculated as

$$RMSE = \sqrt{\frac{1}{N} \sum_{i=1}^{N} (r_{ui} - \widehat{r_{ui}})^2} \tag{13}$$

where N is the total number of samples, r_{ui} is the true score, and $\widehat{r_{ul}}$ is the predicted score.

3.2 Comparative Experiment

This article sets up this experiment for two purposes. First, it is verified whether the combination of review text and scoring matrix can effectively alleviate the adverse effects of data sparseness. The second is to compare the DSAM combined with the review text to verify that the DSAM model described in this article can further reduce the error by fusing deep features.

We compared the DSAM model with five prediction models, as shown in Table 4. LFM [6], SVD++ [9], and DeepCoNN [8] are discussed above. HFT inputs comment information and fuses the obtained text topic with the hidden factor obtained by matrix decomposition. The author proves through experiments that the item feature topic distribution is more accurate than the prediction produced by the user topic distribution. CDL [12] combined the Bayesian formula of PMF based on collaborative deep learning, and verified the excellent ability of the CDL model on three datasets.

Table 4. Prediction model

Model	Use scoring matrix	Use comment text	Use deep learning algorithms
LFM	True	False	False
SVD++	True	False	False
DeepCoNN	True	True	True
HFT	True	True	False
CDL	True	True	True
DSAM	True	True	True

3.3 Experimental Detailed Settings

The dataset was randomly divided into 70% for training, 20% for validation, and 10% for testing. Arguments were confirmed on the verification set, and the capability of the model was evaluated on the test set. Comparison models such as LFM and SVD++ used grid search to determine the number of hidden factors and regular term coefficients. Parameters of DeepCoNN, CDL, HFT, and other models were adjusted according to the corresponding literature to obtain the best performance, and other environmental factors were as consistent as possible.

The proposed DSAM model has many parameters, and it was necessary to experiment with parameter sensitivity on datasets such as MT and DM, with results as shown in Fig. 3 We concluded that DSAM, when combined with the score and comment text, performed best when the number of hidden factors was 16. The errors of LFM and SVD++ gradually increased with the number of hidden factors. We believe this is because too many parameters caused overfitting. After the parameter sensitivity experiment, the model combined with deep learning could be concluded to be more stable than the model based on matrix factorization, and it was hard to conclude that there was overfitting. To prevent overfitting, a dropout unit was added in the learning process. The experimental results of exploring the influence of different dropout ratios on the model are shown in Fig. 4 From the results, it can be determined that the model performs best when the dropout is set to 0.5 in the MT dataset, because overfitting is alleviated and the generalization ability of the model is improved.

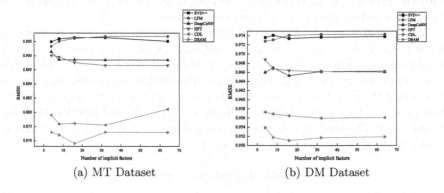

(a) MT Dataset   (b) DM Dataset

Fig. 3. Influence of hidden factors on RMSE

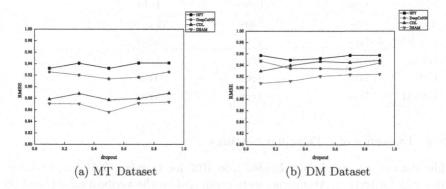

(a) MT Dataset   (b) DM Dataset

Fig. 4. Effect of dropout ratio on model

HFT, DeepCoNN, and CDL performed more stably on the MT dataset than on the DM dataset, because MT had simpler semantics and larger data volume, and DM had insufficient samples to learn stable parameters. As the dropout ratio increased, the performance of all of the models decreased to varying degrees, which is consistent with the previous statement that models with matrix decomposition are more likely to produce overfitting.

3.4   Experimental Analysis

The model performance was optimized to the extent possible according to the parameter comparison experiment. The word vector dimension of DSAM and DeepCoNN was set at 300, the dimension of attention weight was set at 400, and the model parameters were adjusted according to the corresponding literature to form a control group. Experiments were performed on the DM, MT, and TG datasets, where D_L, D_C, and D_D represent the RMSE improvement rates of DSAM relative to LFM, CDL, and DeepCoNN, respectively, as shown in Table 5. The following conclusions can be drawn from Table 5.

(1) Traditional models such as LFM and SVD++, which only rely on scoring data, are not as effective as models based on review text, such as Deep-CoNN, HFT, CDL, and DSAM. Information in the review text can effectively improve the expressiveness of hidden factors.

(2) In models that introduce the scoring matrix and review text, the error accuracy of CDL and DSAM is less than that of HFT. We believe that the dropout and batch normalization in CDL and DSAM mainly alleviate overfitting. Traditional models can only learn shallow linear features, while deep learning-based models can effectively learn deep nonlinear features to further improve accuracy.

Table 5. RMSE results

Model	MT	DM	TG
LFM	0.898	0.922	0.971
SVD++	0.895	0.914	0.972
HFT	0.894	0.897	0.967
DeepCoNN	0.892	0.898	0.959
CDL	0.857	0.877	0.879
DSAM	0.799	0.804	0.833
D_D	4.02%	3.05%	3.12%
D_C	2.24%	1.96%	2.12%

(3) DSAM performed best in the experiments on three datasets. In terms of RMSE parameters, it is about 3.05% 4.02% relative to DeepCoNN, and 1.92% 3.05% relative to CDL. The RMSE improvement rate shows that the DSAM model can more fully extract the deep and advanced features between users and items compared with models that only rely on review text and deep learning (DeepCoNN). Unlike DCL, DSAM uses pretrained BERT to deal with static word vector problems and combines two-way long- and short-term memory neural networks to generalize comment data. In short, in-depth recommendations that integrate ratings and review text perform better.

To verify the ability of DSAM to deal with cold-start problems, we constructed user and commodity models and conducted model cold-start experiments on the DM and MT datasets. We constructed a cold-start dataset based on user-item modeling, and conducted comparative experiments on DSAM and LFM, with results as shown in Fig. 5 The Y-axis represents the difference between the RMSE of the DSAM and LFM models, where a positive number indicates that DSAM performs better. As the number of samples increases, the advantages of DSAM slowly decay. When the number of training samples is 5, the curve is still positive, indicating that DSAM can better alleviate the cold-start phenomenon than LFM. We constructed a cold-start dataset based on user-item modeling, and conducted comparative experiments on DSAM and LFM, with results as shown in Fig. 5 The Y-axis represents the difference between the RMSE of the DSAM and LFM models, where a positive number indicates that DSAM performs better. As the number of samples increases, the advantages of DSAM slowly decay. When the number of training samples is 5, the curve is still positive, indicating that DSAM can better alleviate the cold-start phenomenon than LFM.

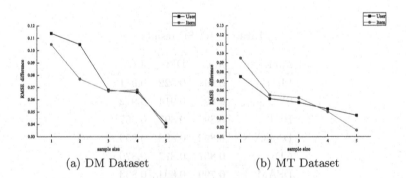

(a) DM Dataset   (b) MT Dataset

Fig. 5. Cold-start experiment results

4   Conclusion

We proposed a DSAM prediction model based on deep learning and fusion of comment text.

DSAM can extract the deeply hidden characteristics of users and items from the rating matrix and review text, and fuse the first- and second-order features to obtain high-order features. Comparative experiments showed that the method and model in this article can effectively reduce the prediction error. Related experiments were carried out for the cold-start phenomenon, and through comparison with the LFM model, it was confirmed that the DSAM model fused with the scoring matrix and review text can more effectively deal with this problem.

References

1. Naranjo, R., Santos, M.: A fuzzy decision system for money investment in stock markets based on fuzzy candlesticks pattern recognition. Expert Syst. Appl. **133**, 34–48 (2019)
2. Li, H., Li, H., Zhang, S., Zhong, Z., Cheng, J.: Intelligent learning system based on personalized recommendation technology. Neural Comput. Appl. **31**(9), 4455–4462 (2019)
3. Nakashima, N., et al.: Recommended configuration for personal health records by standardized data item sets for diabetes mellitus and associated chronic diseases: a report from collaborative initiative by six Japanese associations. J. Diab. Investig. **10**(3), 868–875 (2019)
4. Luo, X., Zhou, M., Xia, Y., Zhu, Q.: An efficient non-negative matrix-factorization-based approach to collaborative filtering for recommender systems. IEEE Trans. Industr. Inf. **10**(2), 1273–1284 (2014)
5. Lara-Cabrera, R., González-Prieto, Á., Ortega, F., et al.: Deep matrix factorization approach for collaborative filtering recommender systems. Appl. Sci. **10**(14), 4926 (2020)
6. Nguyen, J., Zhu, M.: Contentboosted matrix factorization techniques for recommender systems. Stat. Anal. Data Mining **6**(4), 286–301 (2013)
7. Jiang, S., Qian, X., Shen, J., Mei, T.: Travel recommendation via author topic model based collaborative filtering. In: 21st International Conference on MultiMedia Modeling, pp. 392–402 (2015)
8. Zheng, L., Noroozi, V., Yu, P.S.: Joint deep modeling of users and items using reviews for recommendation. In: Proceedings of the 10th ACM International Conference on Web Search and Data Mining, pp. 425–434 (2017)
9. Zhao, J., et al.: Attribute mapping and autoencoder neural network based matrix factorization initialization for recommendation systems. Knowl.-Based Syst. **166**, 132–139 (2019)
10. Li, W., Qi, F., Tang, M., Yu, Z.: Bidirectional LSTM with self-attention mechanism and multi-channel features for sentiment classification. Neurocomputing **387**, 63–77 (2020)
11. Xu, M., Wu, J., Wang, H., Cao, M.: Anomaly detection in road networks using sliding-window tensor factorization. IEEE Trans. Intell. Transp. Syst. **20**(12), 4704–4713 (2019)
12. Wang, H., Wang, N., Yeung, D.-Y.: Collaborative deep learning for recommender systems. In: Proceedings of the 21th ACM SIGKDD International Conference on Knowledge Discovery and Data Mining, pp. 1235–1244 (2015)
13. Sengupta, S., Basak, S., Saikia, P., Paul, S., Tsalavoutis, V., Atiah, F., et al.: A review of deep learning with special emphasis on architectures, applications and recent trends. Knowl.-Based Syst. **194**(12), 105596 (2020)

402   C. Liu and X. Deng

14. Shi, C., Hu, B., Zhao, X., Yu, P.: Heterogeneous information network embedding
    for recommendation. IEEE Trans. Knowl. Data Eng. **31**(2), 357–370 (2019)
15. Brunton, S.L., Noack, B.R., Koumoutsakos, P.: Machine learning for fluid mechan-
    ics. Ann. Rev. Fluid Mech. **52**(1), 477–508 (2020)

GCMNet: Gated Cascade Multi-scale Network for Crowd Counting

Jinfang Zheng[1], Panpan Zhao[1], Jinyang Xie[1], Chen Lyu[1,2], and Lei Lyu[1,2(✉)]

[1] School of Information Science and Engineering, Shandong Normal University,
Jinan 250358, China
{lvchen,lvlei}@sdnu.edu.cn
[2] Shandong Provincial Key Laboratory for Distributed Computer Software Novel
Technology, Jinan 250358, China

Abstract. With the rapid development of convolutional neural networks, many CNN-based methods have emerged and made promising progress in the field of crowd counting. However, dealing with extremely scale variation remains a challenging but attractive issue. In this paper, we propose an innovative Gated Cascade Multi-scale Network (GCM-Net) to tackle with the issue by taking full advantage of the representation of multi-scale features in a multi-level network. First of all, we implement such an idea by obtaining rich contextual information with a multi-scale contextual information enhancement module. Then, considering the pixel-level image detail information that is lost during the successive feature extraction process, we propose a hopping cascade module to refine this detail information. However, naively refining all the detail information is sub-optimal. Therefore, a gated information selection delivery module is designed to adaptively control the delivery of information between multi-level features. Combined with our proposed module, our method can effectively generate high-quality crowd density maps. The superiority of our method over current methods is demonstrated through extensive experiments on four challenging datasets.

Keywords: Crowd counting · Hopping cascade · Gated information ·
Multi-scale feature · Deep learning

1 Introduction

Crowd counting based on computer vision aims at generating high-quality density maps of crowd scenes, thereby calculating the total number of the crowd. It is widely used in public safety and video surveillance. What's more, the proposed methods for crowd counting can be extended to other fields with similar tasks, including traffic control, agricultural monitoring, and cell counting.

With the rapid growth of deep learning, many CNN-based methods have made amazing improvements in crowd counting. However, crowd counting is still a difficult task due to the complexity of the scenes, especially the large scale variation (Fig. 1).

© Springer Nature Switzerland AG 2021
D. N. Pham et al. (Eds.): PRICAI 2021, LNAI 13032, pp. 403–417, 2021.
https://doi.org/10.1007/978-3-030-89363-7_31

Fig. 1. Scale variation in crowd scenes.

In recent years, numerous methods have been proposed to tackle with the problem of scale variation. MCNN [31] uses filters with different sizes to solve the size variation of the human head. CSRNet [12] adopts dilated convolutions as the back-end part to extract deeper features by expanding the receptive fields. Kang et al. [11] propose an adaptive fusion feature pyramid to handle multiple scales. CAN [14] combines multiple receptive fields with different sizes and learns the correct context for each image location.

Although above methods have achieved better performance, there are still some deficiencies to be improved. On the one hand, the crowd scene has large scale variations in size, shape, and location, and using a simple multi-column structure does not effectively extract multi-scale contextual information. On the other hand, features captured by earlier layers in the deep network contain less semantic information, so naively cascading multi-level features in the network does not effectively solve large scale variation.

To this end, we introduce an innovative deep learning framework named Gated Cascade Multi-scale Network (GCMNet) to take full advantage of the representation of multi-scale features. The architecture of GCMNet is shown in Fig. 2. To perform more comprehensive multi-scale representations and overcome the drawbacks of multi-branch structure, we design a multi-scale contextual information enhancement module to capture the global context. We employ four parallel convolutional layers with different filter sizes and combine the features generated by these convolutions. By doing this, the representation capability of the network is greatly improved. In addition, with the successive feature extraction process, a large amount of detail information is lost, so we have integrated various pixel-level detail through a hopping cascade module, thus ensuring the completion of multi-level feature fusion. Furthermore, the utilization of hopping cascade module to integrate multi-level features does not weight the importance of the information contained therein. While a gated information selection delivery module is adopted, we can determine the turn-on and turn-off of information in multi-level features to perform adaptive and effective delivery of useful information.

In summary, the main contributions of our work are as follows:

- We design a multi-scale contextual information enhancement module with multiple different sizes of convolutional filters to extract multi-scale contextual information.
- We put forward a hopping cascade module that cascades multi-level features to reconstruct pixel-level image detail.
- We propose a gated information selection delivery module to adaptively control information delivery between multi-level features.

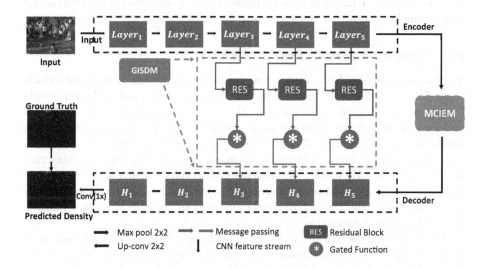

Fig. 2. The overall framework of our GCMNet.

2   Related Works

In recent years, significant improvements have been achieved in crowd counting from traditional methods [3,7] to CNN-based methods [9,28]. In this paper, we mainly focus on three categories of CNN-based methods: multi-scale feature extraction methods, multi-level feature fusion methods, and feature-wise gated convolution methods.

2.1   Multi-scale Feature Extraction Methods

This kind of method aims to address the scale variation in crowd counting with multi-scale contextual information. Zhang et al. [31] propose a multi-column convolutional neural network to extract multi-scale features. Similarly, Sam et al. [20] put forward the Switching-CNN, which uses the density variation to improve the accuracy and localization of crowd counting. Cao et al. propose the SANet [1] for extracting multi-scale features based on the Inception architecture of encoders. ADCrowdNet [13] combines multi-scale deformable convolution with an attention mechanism to construct a cascade framework. Jiang et al. [10] design a grid coding network that captures multi-scale features by integrating multiple decoding paths. In addition, the spatial pyramid pooling (SPP) [5] uses pooling layers with different sizes to extract multi-scale feature maps and finally aggregates them into a fixed-length vector, thus improving robustness and accuracy. Therefore, it is widely used in SCNet [26], PaDNet [25], and CAN [14] for extracting multi-scale features.

In this paper, we utilize four parallel convolutional layers to extract multi-scale features and fuse features to improve the redundancy arising from the multi-branch structure.

2.2 Multi-level Feature Fusion Methods

Several recent works for complex and intensive prediction tasks have demonstrated that features from multiple layers are favorable to produce better results. Deeply encoded features contain semantic information of the object, while shallowly encoded features conserve more spatially detailed information. Several studies on crowd counting [15,23,31] have attempted to use features from multilevel convolutional neural networks for more accurate information extraction. Many studies [15,31] predict the independent results of each stage and finally fuse them to obtain multi-scale information. Sindagi et al. [23] introduce a multilevel bottom-top and top-bottom fusion method to combine shallower information with deeper information.

Different from the above methods, we propose a hopping cascade module to perform multi-level feature fusion with hopping cascade, thereby the pixel-level image details lost during extraction can be regained.

2.3 Feature-Wise Gated Convolution Methods

The introduction of gating mechanisms in convolutions has also been extensively studied in language, vision, and speech. Dauphin et al. [2] effectively reduce gradient dispersion by using linear gating units and also retain the ability to be nonlinear. Oord et al. [18] employ a selected-pass mechanism to improve performance and convergence speed. Yu et al. [29] propose an end-to-end gated evolution-based generative image restoration system to improve the restoration of free-form masks and user-guided inputs. WaveNet [17] applies gated activation units to audio sequences to simulate audio signals and obtains better results.

In this study, we propose a gated information selection delivery module to adaptively control the information delivery between multi-level features during the hopping cascade.

3   Proposed Algorithm

In this section, we will outline the overall framework of our GCMNet and give a detailed introduction of the theory to realize each module.

3.1 Overview of Network Architecture

The overall framework is shown in Fig. 2. Following the practice of most previous work, we adopt VGG-16 [22] as the backbone network and choose the first five stages ($Layer_1 - Layer_5$) of the pre-trained VGG-16 to generate the hopping features at five levels, which are represented as $F^e = \{f_i^e, i = 1, \ldots, 5\}$. After $Layer_5$, we add the Multi-scale Contextual Information Enhancement Module (MCIEM) consisting of multiple convolutional layers with different sizes of filters to capture global context information. Afterwards, to reconstruct the pixel-level image detail information that is lost in the successive feature extraction, we propose the hopping cascade module to cascade the hopping features F^e with the upsampling features $F^d = \{f_i^d, i = 1, \ldots, 5\}$ generated by upsampling operations. Moreover, we design the Gated Information Selection Delivery Module (GISDM) to control the delivery of the pixel-level image detail information in F^e with the aim of effectively integrating the multi-level features in the cascade process.

3.2 Multi-scale Contextual Information Enhancement Module

It is observed that the output features fused by using parallel convolution contain more image details than the features generated by successive convolution operations. Therefore, we come up with the MCIEM to capture global context information. The module consists of four parallel convolutional layers with filters of different sizes $k \in \{3, 7, 11, 15\}$ and four max-pooling layers. The details of the MCIEM is given in Fig. 3.

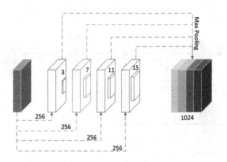

Fig. 3. Details of MCIEM.

Firstly, the multi-level features f_5^e extracted by the backbone network are taken as the input to the MCIEM. Then the four parallel convolutions with the receptive field of 3×3, 7×7, 11×11, and 15×15 are used to extract multi-scale features. Finally, these features are fed into a 2×2 max-pooling layer and then fused together to extract more comprehensive contextual features. With the MCIEM, multi-scale features can encode richer contextual information.

3.3 Hopping Cascade

Though MCIEM can extract effective contextual information through multiscale features, some pixel-level image detail information is lost in this extraction process. Therefore, we introduce the hopping cascade module to reconstruct the lost pixel-level image detail information.

Specifically, after the MCIEM, we choose the $H_1 - H_5$ with 32-fold bilinear upsampling operations to generate upsampling features $F^d = \{f_i^d, i = 1, \ldots, 5\}$. Meanwhile, the lost pixel-level image detail information is reconstructed by cascading F^e with F^d. Our cascade module takes the hopping features f_3^e, f_4^e, f_5^e and upsampling features f_3^d, f_4^d, f_5^d as input. The cascade process is implemented by the following equation.

$$H_i = ReLU(Conv(f_i^e; \theta)) + ReLU(Conv(f_i^d; \theta)) \tag{1}$$

where $Conv(*; \theta)$ is a convolutional layer with parameter $\theta = \{W, b\}$, $ReLU()$ is an activation function. f_i^e is parallel to the multi-level feature f_i^d and they have the same size.

3.4 Gated Information Selection Delivery Module

The pixel-level image detail information is reconstructed with the hopping cascade module, but not all of the pixel-level detail information contributes to the realization of accurate crowd counting. Therefore, we propose the GISDM to deliver this information from adaptive selection, which consists of a residual block and a gated function, as shown in Fig. 4.

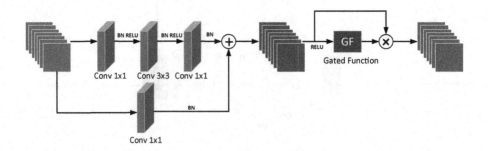

Fig. 4. Details of GISDM.

In our implementation, we feed the hopping features into a residual block to improve the representation ability of hopping features, which is expressed as G_i:

$$G_i = Res(ReLU(Conv(f_i^e; \theta))) \tag{2}$$

where $Res(*)$ represents the residual block.

Additionally, we introduce the gated function to further calibrate this information and achieve adaptive delivery of pixel-level detail information instead of indiscriminately delivering all information among multi-level features. The gated function is essentially a convolutional layer with sigmoid activation in the range of $[0, 1]$. Let $GF(x; \theta)$ denotes the gated function:

$$GF(x; \theta) = Sig(Conv(x; \theta)) \tag{3}$$

where $Sig()$ represents sigmoid function, $Conv(x; \theta)$ is a 1×1 convolutional layer of channels with x.

With the gated function, G_i can be rewritten as:

$$G_i = GF(G_i; \theta) \otimes Res(ReLU(Conv(f_i^e; \theta))) \tag{4}$$

where $\otimes$ represents an element-wise product.

Therefore, the H_i is summarized as:

$$H_i = Conv(G_i; \theta) + ReLU(Conv(f_i^d; \theta)) \tag{5}$$

where G_i is the updated features after performing the GISDM.

4   Experiments

In this section, we first give the description of the four widely used datasets and the implementation settings. Additionally, we compare our method with state-of-the-art methods by evaluating counting performance and density map quality. Finally, we perform an extensive ablation study to demonstrate the effectiveness of each component of our method.

4.1   Datasets

ShanghaiTech Dataset [31]. The ShanghaiTech dataset is composed of Part A and Part B datasets. Part A dataset includes 482 images, which are randomly crawled from the Internet and represent highly crowded scenes. It is divided into the training sets and test sets. Part B dataset is acquired from the surveillance cameras of commercial streets, representing relatively sparse scenes, with 400 images in the training sets and 316 images in the test sets.

UCF_CCF_50 Dataset [7]. The UCF_CCF_50 dataset is full of challenges. The training sample is limited and it only collects 50 annotated images of complex scenes from the Internet. These images have a large number of different people, ranging from 94 to 4543. There are a total of 63,974 head annotations, with an average of 1,280 per image.

UCF-QNRF Dataset [8]. The dataset contains 1535 high-resolution images with 1,251,642 head annotations, which has more head annotations than the previous datasets. The number of people in each image varies from 49 to 12,865. And the training and test sets have 1,201 and 334 images, respectively.

WorldExpo'10 Dataset [30]. This dataset includes 1,132 annotated video sequences collected from 103 different scenes captured by 108 surveillance cameras at the 2010 Shanghai World Expo. There are 3,980 annotated frames with a total of 199,923 annotated pedestrians, of which 3,380 annotated frames are used for model training and the other 600 frames are used for model testing.

4.2   Settings

Ground Truth Generation. We generate ground truth density maps following the same theory as in MCNN [31]. We use a normalized Gaussian kernel to blur each human head annotation thus generating the ground truth density maps $F(x)$.

$$F(x) = \sum_{i=1}^{N} \delta(x - x_i) \times G_{\sigma_i}(x), with \ \sigma_i = \beta \overline{d^i} \tag{6}$$

where N represents the number of people in the image, x is the position of the pixel in the image, x_i represents the labeled position of the ith individual, $\delta(x-x_i)$ denotes a head annotation at pixel x_i, G_{σ_i} represents a Gaussian kernel with standard deviation σ_i, and $\overline{d^i}$ represents the average distance between x_i and its nearest k heads. In our implementation, we set $\beta = 0.3$ and $\sigma_i = 3$.

Evaluation Metrics. To evaluate the performance of our method, we adopt the Mean Absolute Error (MAE) and Root Mean Square Error (RMSE), which are denoted as Eq. (7) and Eq. (8), respectively.

$$MAE = \frac{1}{N} \sum_{i=1}^{N} |C_i^{ES} - C_i^{GT}| \tag{7}$$

$$RMSE = \sqrt{\frac{1}{N} \sum_{i=1}^{N} (C_i^{ES} - C_i^{GT})^2} \tag{8}$$

where N is the total number of the test images, C_i^{ES} and C_i^{GT} are the estimated and ground-truth counts of the ith image, respectively.

MAE and RMSE determine the accuracy and the robustness of the crowd counting, respectively. The lower their values, the better performance of the count results.

In addition, the Peak Signal-to-Noise Ratio (PSNR) and Structural Similarity (SSIM) in images are exploited to evaluate the quality of the output density maps.

The PSNR is defined as:

$$PSNR = 10 \times \log_{10}(\frac{MAX_I^2}{MSE}) \tag{9}$$

where MAX_I is the maximum possible pixel value of the images.

$$SSIM(x,y) = \frac{(2\mu_x\mu_y + C_1)(2\sigma_{xy} + C_2)}{(\mu_x^2 + \mu_y^2 + C_1)(\sigma_x^2 + \sigma_y^2 + C_2)} \tag{10}$$

where μ_x and μ_y denote the mean values of images x and y, respectively. σ_x and σ_y denote the variance of images x and y, respectively. σ_{xy} is the covariance of images x and y. C_1 and C_2 are two constants and defined as:

$$\begin{cases} C_1 = (K_1 \times L)^2 \\ C_2 = (K_2 \times L)^2 \end{cases} \tag{11}$$

where $K_1 = 0.01$, $K_2 = 0.03$, $L = 255$.

PSNR essentially represents the error between the corresponding pixels. The higher its value, the better the quality of the density map. SSIM measures the similarity between the predicted density map and the ground truth in terms of brightness, contrast and structure. The higher its value, the smaller the image distortion.

Implementation Details. We utilize the pre-trained VGG-16 to initialize the parameters of the first five stages of our model, and parameters of the other convolutional layers are initialized randomly using a Gaussian distribution with $\delta = 0.01$. Both upsampling and downsampling operations are simulated using bilinear interpolation. We use Adam optimizer to train our network for 200 epochs, and the learning rate is initially set to $1e-5$. And the network is trained by minimizing the Euclidean distance between the estimated density map and the ground truth. The loss function is defined as:

$$L(\Theta) = \frac{1}{2N} \sum_{i=1}^{N} ||F(X_i; \Theta) - D_i||_2^2 \tag{12}$$

where N is the number of training images, X_i is the ith input image, $F(X_i; \Theta)$ denotes the estimated density map, D_i represents the ground truth density map.

4.3   Comparisons with the State-of-the-Art

ShanghaiTech. We compare our method with several state-of-the-art methods and the comparison results are listed in Table 1. On Part A, our method obtains the MAE improvement by 4.28% and RMSE improvement by 4.46% compared to the second-best result. On Part B, our method achieves the MAE and RMSE improvements by 4.31% and 4.61%, respectively, compared to the second-best result.

UCF_CC_50. The UCF_CC_50 dataset has a huge challenge and we evaluate our method according to 5-fold cross-validation [12]. As shown in Table 1, we compare our method with the current state-of-the-art methods. Our method has a very significant improvement, with MAE and RMSE improved by 18.57% and 18.69%, respectively, compared to the latest CFANet method. Despite the limited training samples, our method converges well in this dataset.

Table 1. Comparisons of GCMNet and state-of-the-art methods on three datasets.

Dataset	Part A		Part B		UCF_CC_50		UCF-QNRF	
Method	MAE	RMSE	MAE	RMSE	MAE	RMSE	MAE	RMSE
MCNN [30]	110.2	173.2	26.4	41.3	377.6	509.1	277.0	426.0
CSRNet [12]	68.2	115.0	10.6	16.0	266.1	397.5	120.3	208.5
TEDNet [10]	64.2	109.1	8.2	12.8	249.4	354.5	113	188
BL [16]	62.8	101.8	7.7	12.7	229.3	308.2	88.7	154.8
ASNet [9]	57.78	90.13	–	–	174.84	251.63	91.59	159.71
AMSNet [6]	56.7	93.4	6.7	10.2	208.4	297.3	101.8	163.2
AMRNet [15]	61.59	98.36	7.02	11.00	184.0	265.8	86.6	152.2
CFANet [19]	56.1	89.6	6.5	10.2	203.6	287.3	89.0	152.3
GCMNet(ours)	**53.7**	**85.6**	**6.22**	**9.73**	**165.8**	**233.6**	**84.7**	**148.1**

UCF-QNRF. Table 1 shows the MAE and RMSE of our method as well as the state-of-the-art methods on UCF-QNRF dataset. The proposed method is compared with eight methods. It can be observed that the proposed method is able to yield the best performance on this dataset. The MAE exceeds the second-best method by 2.19% and RMSE improves over the second-best method by 2.69%.

WorldExpo'10. Our method is compared with six state-of-the-art methods. In Table 2, we give the comparison results of MAE for each scene. Our proposed method obtains the best performance in scene 1 (sparse crowd S1), scene 4 (dense crowd S4). Moreover, the best average MAE performance is also achieved.

Table 2. Comparisons of GCMNet and state-of-the-art methods on WorldExpo'10.

Dataset	WorldExpo'10					
Method	S1	S2	S3	S4	S5	Ave
TEDNet [10]	2.3	10.1	11.3	13.8	2.6	8.0
ADCrowdNet [13]	1.6	13.2	8.7	10.6	2.6	7.3
CAN [14]	2.9	12.0	10.0	7.9	4.3	7.4
PGCNet [27]	2.5	12.7	8.4	13.7	3.2	8.1
RPNet [28]	2.4	10.2	9.7	11.5	3.8	8.2
ASNet [9]	2.22	10.11	8.89	7.14	4.84	6.64
GCMNet (ours)	**1.43**	**10.22**	**8.47**	**7.04**	**2.84**	**6.00**

In this section, we first conduct experiments on four datasets and then compare our model quantitatively with several state-of-the-art methods. It is clearly seen from the results that our method achieves the best performance on Shang-haiTech, UCF_CC_50 and UCF-QNRF datasets, and outperforms some of the

Fig. 5. Sample results of the GCMNet on ShanghaiTech dataset. The first row shows the samples of the input image. The second row shows the ground truth for each sample while the third row presents the density map generated by GCMNet. The number in each density map denotes the count number.

current state-of-the-art methods on WorldExpo'10 dataset. And the predicted density maps on ShanghaiTech dataset is also given and compared with the ground truth, as shown in Fig. 5. It can be obviously seen from the figures that our method is advanced for crowd counting in different scenes. Regardless of highly crowded or sparse crowd counting scenes, we effectively address the scale variation in crowd counting. Our method effectively uses multi-scale features for accurate crowd counting.

4.4 Comparison of Density Map Quality

In this section, we compare our method with other representative methods: MCNN, CP-CNN, CSRNet, CFF and SCAR in PSNR and SSIM.

Table 3. Comparisons of PSNR and SSIM of GCMNet and representative methods on ShanghaiTech Part A.

Method	PSNR	SSIM
MCNN [31]	21.4	0.52
CP-CNN [24]	21.72	0.72
CSRNet [12]	23.79	0.76
CFF [21]	25.4	0.78
SCAR [4]	23.93	0.81
GCMNet(ours)	**28.66**	**0.84**

As shown in Table 3, our GCMNet achieves the highest SSIM and PSNR. In particular, we get PSNR of 28.66 and SSIM of 0.84 on ShanghaiTech Part A dataset. Compared with SCAR, the PSNR and SSIM are improved by 19.77% and 3.70%, respectively. The results show that our method has a significant advantage in generating high-quality density maps.

4.5 Ablation Study

In this section, we conduct ablation study on ShanghaiTech dataset to verify the effectiveness of each module in our network and analyze the impact of different network combinations on the counting performance.

Table 4. Results of ablation study on ShanghaiTech Part A and Part B datasets.

Dataset	Part A		Part B	
Configuration	MAE	RMSE	MAE	RMSE
VGG-16	78.3	120.1	18.3	22.9
VGG-16+MCIEM	66.8	102.3	14.7	17.9
VGG-16+MCIEM+Hopping Cascade	57.1	90.7	8.5	11.6
VGG-16+MCIEM+Hopping Cascade+GISDM	**53.7**	**88.6**	**6.22**	**9.73**

We use four different combinations to test our model:

(1) VGG-16: VGG-16 first 13-layer network with 32-fold upsampling operations at the end.
(2) VGG-16+MCIEM: VGG-16 first 13-layer network with MCIEM for extracting multi-scale contextual information and 32-fold upsampling operations at the end.
(3) VGG-16+MCIEM+Hopping Cascade: VGG-16 first 13-layer network with MCIEM for extracting multi-scale contextual information and hopping cascade module for cascading the hopping features f_3^e, f_4^e, f_5^e with the upsampling features f_3^d, f_4^d, f_5^d.
(4) VGG-16+MCIEM+Hopping Cascade+GISDM: our proposed method.

We give the experimental results of ablation study in Table 4. It can be seen that directly using VGG-16 for feature extraction does not necessarily yield the best performance. After injecting MCIEM into the network for multi-scale feature extraction, the counting error is greatly reduced compared to the previous stage. Further improvements are made by adding the hopping cascade module, and the results show that, as with MCIEM, the performance of the model is substantially improved and the counting error is substantially reduced. Finally, the embedded GISDM adaptively performs information delivery, which further optimizes the effect of crowd counting. In conclusion, our proposed final model achieves the best performance and further accuracy in estimating the crowd. Each of the structures added to our model is effective and complementary to each other. The counting results are significantly better in the case of both high-density and low-density scenes. Figure 6 gives the stage density maps of the ShanghaiTech Part B dataset during the ablation study, and it is observed that our final model improves on the previous missing (yellow circles) and redundant (red circles) counts, effectively addressing the problem of scale variation. Our model achieves accurate density estimation and produces high-quality density maps.

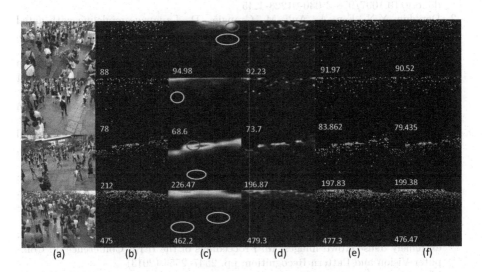

Fig. 6. Stage results of ablation study on ShanghaiTech Part B dataset. (a) Input image, (b) Ground Truth, (c) Baseline (VGG-16), (d) VGG-16+MCIEM, (e) VGG-16+MCIEM+Hopping Cascade, (f) Ours. The number in each density map denotes the count number. The yellow and red circles label the missing and redundant counts of the Baseline method, respectively.

5   Conclusion

This paper proposes a novel end-to-end Gated Cascade Multi-scale Network (GCMNet), which effectively solves the problem of rapid scale variation in crowd counting. With the MCIEM, our GCMNet can capture global context at multiple scales. Then we introduce a hopping cascade module to make full use of the pixel-level image detail information. Subsequently, we design a GISDM to selectively integrate multi-level features by adaptively delivering valid information. Finally, the multi-level features are used to generate the final density maps. Extensive experimental results on four datasets show that our GCMNet is superior under different evaluation metrics. In the future, we will explore better methods to perform multi-scale feature extraction and effective integration of multi- level features.

Acknowledgement. This work is supported by the National Natural Science Foundation of China (61976127).

References

1. Cao, X., Wang, Z., Zhao, Y., Su, F.: Scale aggregation network for accurate and efficient crowd counting. In: Ferrari, V., Hebert, M., Sminchisescu, C., Weiss, Y. (eds.) ECCV 2018. LNCS, vol. 11209, pp. 757–773. Springer, Cham (2018). https://doi.org/10.1007/978-3-030-01228-1_45
2. Dauphin, Y.N., Fan, A., Auli, M., Grangier, D.: Language modeling with gated convolutional networks. In: International Conference on Machine Learning, pp. 933–941. PMLR (2017)
3. Dollar, P., Wojek, C., Schiele, B., Perona, P.: Pedestrian detection: an evaluation of the state of the art. IEEE Trans. Pattern Anal. Mach. Intell. **34**(4), 743–761 (2011)
4. Gao, J., Wang, Q., Yuan, Y.: SCAR: spatial-/channel-wise attention regression networks for crowd counting. Neurocomputing **363**, 1–8 (2019)
5. He, K., Zhang, X., Ren, S., Sun, J.: Spatial pyramid pooling in deep convolutional networks for visual recognition. IEEE Trans. Pattern Anal. Mach. Intell. **37**(9), 1904–1916 (2015)
6. Hu, Y., et al.: NAS-count: counting-by-density with neural architecture search. In: Vedaldi, A., Bischof, H., Brox, T., Frahm, J.-M. (eds.) ECCV 2020. LNCS, vol. 12367, pp. 747–766. Springer, Cham (2020). https://doi.org/10.1007/978-3-030-58542-6_45
7. Idrees, H., Saleemi, I., Seibert, C., Shah, M.: Multi-source multi-scale counting in extremely dense crowd images. In: Proceedings of the IEEE Conference on Computer Vision and Pattern Recognition, pp. 2547–2554 (2013)
8. Idrees, H., et al.: Composition loss for counting, density map estimation and localization in dense crowds. In: Ferrari, V., Hebert, M., Sminchisescu, C., Weiss, Y. (eds.) ECCV 2018. LNCS, vol. 11206, pp. 544–559. Springer, Cham (2018). https://doi.org/10.1007/978-3-030-01216-8_33
9. Jiang, X., et al.: Attention scaling for crowd counting. In: Proceedings of the IEEE/CVF Conference on Computer Vision and Pattern Recognition, pp. 4706–4715 (2020)
10. Jiang, X., et al.: Crowd counting and density estimation by trellis encoder-decoder networks. In: Proceedings of the IEEE/CVF Conference on Computer Vision and Pattern Recognition, pp. 6133–6142 (2019)
11. Kang, D., Chan, A.B.: Crowd counting by adaptively fusing predictions from an image pyramid. In: British Machine Vision Conference 2018, BMVC 2018, Newcastle, UK, 3–6 September 2018, p. 89 (2018)
12. Li, Y., Zhang, X., Chen, D.: CSRNet: dilated convolutional neural networks for understanding the highly congested scenes. In: Proceedings of the IEEE Conference on Computer Vision and Pattern Recognition, pp. 1091–1100 (2018)
13. Liu, N., Long, Y., Zou, C., Niu, Q., Pan, L., Wu, H.: ADCrowdNet: an attention-injective deformable convolutional network for crowd understanding. In: Proceedings of the IEEE/CVF Conference on Computer Vision and Pattern Recognition, pp. 3225–3234 (2019)
14. Liu, W., Salzmann, M., Fua, P.: Context-aware crowd counting. In: Proceedings of the IEEE/CVF Conference on Computer Vision and Pattern Recognition, pp. 5099–5108 (2019)
15. Liu, X., Yang, J., Ding, W., Wang, T., Wang, Z., Xiong, J.: Adaptive mixture regression network with local counting map for crowd counting. In: Vedaldi, A., Bischof, H., Brox, T., Frahm, J.-M. (eds.) ECCV 2020. LNCS, vol. 12369, pp. 241–257. Springer, Cham (2020). https://doi.org/10.1007/978-3-030-58586-0_15

16. Ma, Z., Wei, X., Hong, X., Gong, Y.: Bayesian loss for crowd count estimation with point supervision. In: Proceedings of the IEEE/CVF International Conference on Computer Vision, pp. 6142–6151 (2019)
17. van den Oord, A., et al.: WaveNet: a generative model for raw audio. In: The 9th ISCA Speech Synthesis Workshop, Sunnyvale, CA, USA, 13–15 September 2016 (2016)
18. Oord, A.v.d., Kalchbrenner, N., Vinyals, O., Espeholt, L., Graves, A., Kavukcuoglu, K.: Conditional image generation with pixelCNN decoders, pp. 4790–4798 (2016)
19. Rong, L., Li, C.: Coarse-and fine-grained attention network with background-aware loss for crowd density map estimation. In: Proceedings of the IEEE/CVF Winter Conference on Applications of Computer Vision, pp. 3675–3684 (2021)
20. Sam, D.B., Surya, S., Babu, R.V.: Switching convolutional neural network for crowd counting. In: 2017 IEEE Conference on Computer Vision and Pattern Recognition (CVPR), pp. 4031–4039. IEEE (2017)
21. Shi, Z., Mettes, P., Snoek, C.G.: Counting with focus for free. In: Proceedings of the IEEE/CVF International Conference on Computer Vision, pp. 4200–4209 (2019)
22. Simonyan, K., Zisserman, A.: Very deep convolutional networks for large-scale image recognition. In: 3rd International Conference on Learning Representations, ICLR 2015, San Diego, CA, USA, 7–9 May 2015, Conference Track Proceedings (2015)
23. Sindagi, V., Patel, V.M.: Multi-level bottom-top and top-bottom feature fusion for crowd counting. In: 2019 IEEE/CVF International Conference on Computer Vision (ICCV), pp. 1002–1012 (2019)
24. Sindagi, V.A., Patel, V.M.: Generating high-quality crowd density maps using contextual pyramid CNNs. In: Proceedings of the IEEE International Conference on Computer Vision, pp. 1861–1870 (2017)
25. Tian, Y., Lei, Y., Zhang, J., Wang, J.Z.: PaDNet: pan-density crowd counting. IEEE Trans. Image Process. **29**, 2714–2727 (2019)
26. Wang, Z., Xiao, Z., Xie, K., Qiu, Q., Zhen, X., Cao, X.: In defense of single-column networks for crowd counting. In: British Machine Vision Conference 2018, BMVC 2018, Newcastle, UK, 3–6 September 2018, p. 78 (2018)
27. Yan, Z., et al.: Perspective-guided convolution networks for crowd counting. In: Proceedings of the IEEE/CVF International Conference on Computer Vision, pp. 952–961 (2019)
28. Yang, Y., Li, G., Wu, Z., Su, L., Huang, Q., Sebe, N.: Reverse perspective network for perspective-aware object counting. In: Proceedings of the IEEE/CVF Conference on Computer Vision and Pattern Recognition, pp. 4374–4383 (2020)
29. Yu, J., Lin, Z., Yang, J., Shen, X., Lu, X., Huang, T.S.: Free-form image inpainting with gated convolution. In: Proceedings of the IEEE/CVF International Conference on Computer Vision, pp. 4471–4480 (2019)
30. Zhang, C., Li, H., Wang, X., Yang, X.: Cross-scene crowd counting via deep convolutional neural networks. In: Proceedings of the IEEE Conference on Computer Vision and Pattern Recognition, pp. 833–841 (2015)
31. Zhang, Y., Zhou, D., Chen, S., Gao, S., Ma, Y.: Single-image crowd counting via multi-column convolutional neural network. In: Proceedings of the IEEE Conference on Computer Vision and Pattern Recognition, pp. 589–597 (2016)

GIAD: Generative Inpainting-Based Anomaly Detection via Self-Supervised Learning for Human Monitoring

Ning Dong and Einoshin Suzuki[✉] [iD]

ISEE, Kyushu University, Fukuoka 819-0395, Japan
suzuki@inf.kyushu-u.ac.jp

Abstract. Detecting anomalies in human monitoring is an important task in many real-world applications. In addition to typical anomalies of objects or actions which have never been observed before, there are also anomalous combinations where we need to consider the relations of items. Existing methods for visual anomaly detection predominantly rely on global level comparisons for computing anomaly scores without focusing on local differences or relations. Some anomalous combination detection methods usually need labels to obtain good context models, which is not suitable for human monitoring task as being aware of all possible anomalies beforehand is usually impossible. As one of our baselines, there is also a clustering-based method which can detect anomalous combinations of two overlapping regions. However, we consider a more general situation that the regions do not necessarily overlap and propose a different way to detect anomalies. Specifically, we propose a self-supervised learning method, Generative Inpainting-based Anomaly Detection (GIAD), to detect not only typical anomalies but also anomalous combinations. The proposed method employs unmasked areas in the salient regions and the information around them (contextual information) with a designed local and global inpainting loss for recovering masked areas in the regions so as to detect anomalies. We also propose a novel attention-based Gaussian weighting anomaly score by considering the importance of each salient region. Experimental evaluations on two real-world datasets demonstrate that our method outperforms the baselines by 6.07%–21.46% on AUC scores.

Keywords: Anomaly detection · Generative inpainting · Gaussian weighting anomaly score · Human monitoring · Self-supervised learning

1 Introduction

Human monitoring, especially that of human's activities or behaviors, has drawn attention in many research fields [1–3]. Detecting anomalies from human's activities is one of the most fundamental and yet important areas for surveillance [4], healthcare [5], and so on in artificial intelligence. However, due to the rareness

© Springer Nature Switzerland AG 2021
D. N. Pham et al. (Eds.): PRICAI 2021, LNAI 13032, pp. 418–432, 2021.
https://doi.org/10.1007/978-3-030-89363-7_32

(a) Normal examples   (b) Abnormal examples

Fig. 1. Several examples with salient regions generated by Densecap [20]. The red rectangles show the anomalous parts or their combinations. The left image in (b) is considered as an anomalous combination between playing with a phone (action) and the current environment (a working area), though we observe such an action in another place (a resting area) which is considered as normal in the training set. For the right image in (b), a man holding a teddy bear could be anomalous if he never held it in the training set. (A woman held it in the training set instead, which is shown at the right in (a).) The right images in (a) and (b) are from [18]. (Color figure online)

of anomalies, an anomaly detection problem is usually seen as one-class classification in which only normal data is accessible to learn an anomaly detection model [6].

Lots of efforts have been made for one-class anomaly detection, and the idea of reconstructing normal training data is a commonly used strategy [6–8]. The abnormal data is expected to have a high reconstruction error during the test phase. With the development of generative adversarial networks (GANs) [9], recent methods [10–13] employ adversarial training, which enhances the data regeneration quality [14], for better anomaly detection systems.

Despite their favorable performance, existing methods for visual anomaly detection [10–13,15] predominantly rely on global level comparisons for computing anomaly scores without focusing on local differences or relations of items. They are effective in detecting single-region anomalies. Here, single-region anomalies represent actions or objects, which are usually a part of images and are never observed in the training set. However, in real-world applications, although some actions or objects have already been observed, they might not be expected to appear in their current scenes or have relations with other items in the scenes [16–18]. In this paper, we define such typical situations as anomalous combinations. It is also important to detect this kind of anomalies in real-world applications, such as developing an intelligent mobile robot which monitors at different places [11,18,19].

There are two main challenges to detect anomalous combinations. The first one is that the discriminative parts can only occupy small portions of the image. See the left example in Fig. 1 (b) and the captions. The reason to recognize this image as anomalous is the phone in the man's hand in such an environment, which only occupies a small part (about 30×30 pixels) of the image. The second one is that to detect anomalous combinations we need to consider the contextual information around items. Current context models [16,21] which detect anomalous combinations need accurate labels for items in the images. This requirement deviates from the setting of one-class anomaly detection. Although splitting an image into many patches is a commonly used strategy [6,11,13], these methods still cannot detect anomalous combinations because they cannot capture the contextual information of items.

A recent method [18] explored dual process theory [22] with an incremental clustering method, which can detect anomalous combinations of two overlapping regions. However, in this paper, we explore more general combination anomalies, where overlapping is a special case. Also, we propose a different way to detect the mentioned anomalies.

More specifically, inspired by the recent progress of inpainting [14,23,24], which recovers the missing parts from the contextual information of known pixels, we propose a self-supervised learning method, Generative Inpainting-based Anomaly Detection (GIAD), to detect not only the single-region anomalies but also the anomalous combinations for human monitoring. The key idea of our method is that the items in either single-region anomalies or anomalous combinations cannot be recovered to their original shapes if we mask them because they have conflicts with their contextual information (contextual violations). On the other hand, inpainting the non-anomalous items is not hampered, since we train our network with only anomaly-free data. To achieve this goal, we mask salient regions generated by Densecap [20] in the images and recover them with a local and global similarity loss. We propose a novel anomaly score function based on an attention mechanism and a multivariate normal distribution to adjust the contribution of each region in the score.

In summary, the contributions of our paper are as follows.

- We partially mask the salient regions in an image and recover the missing parts with a local and global similarity loss. This approach focuses on not only the entire image but also the salient regions for better reconstruction, so as to well detect anomalies.
- Given the similarities of multiple salient regions within an image, we explore an attention-based Gaussian weighting anomaly score to allocate different weights for each region.
- We show that our proposed method GIAD outperforms all baselines on two real-world datasets, which contain not only single-region anomalies but also anomalous combinations, in terms of several evaluation metrics.

2   Related Work

Our work is related to generative reconstruction and anomalous combination detection. Thus, we introduce related works from the two aspects.

2.1   Generative Reconstruction Approaches

The assumption of detecting anomalies based on generative reconstruction is that normal data instances can be better reconstructed than anomalies from a latent space [8]. For example, [10,12,25] compute the reconstruction errors of the inputs and the corresponding outputs to predict whether images are anomalous.

Kimura et al. [26] proposed a self-supervised masking method which specifically focuses on the discriminative parts of the images to enable robust anomaly detection. They used the discriminator's class activation maps for improving robustness against the background noise.

However, the above methods compute the reconstruction error at the image (global) level, which cannot always guarantee a large reconstruction error for anomalies and tend to make false negatives when the anomalies occupy only small portions of the image [8,27]. A commonly used setting is to split an image into many patches with a sliding window [6,11,13]. However, it assumes no relation between patches, which is not suitable for detecting anomalous combinations.

With the development of inpainting techniques [14,23,24], which aim to fill missing pixels of an image with contextual information from known areas, there are also some research to detect anomalies based on inpainting recent years. Nguyen et al. [28] proposed to generate a coarse heatmap using image inpainting for region-based anomaly detection. They adversarially trained a deep convolutional network to locate and inpaint missing brain regions. The network will fail to reconstruct unhealthy data that it has not observed in training. Vitjan et al. [29] also considered anomaly detection as a self-supervised reconstruction-by-inpainting problem by employing a convolutional encoder-decoder structure, which reconstructs the missing parts with masks of multi-scales. However, their smoothing operation results in blurry inpainting results. It can overlook anomalies which occupy only a small part of the image. Thus, based on Structural Similarity Index Measure [30], we propose a local and global similarity loss, which focuses on not only the entire image but also its local parts.

2.2 Anomalous Combinations Detection

Anomalous combinations detection, sometimes referred to out-of-context detection [16,21], considers the relations between items in images. Choi et al. [21] proposed a graphical model which integrates different sources of contextual information and computes the probability of each item's presence and the likelihood of each detection being correct. Oh et al. [16] proposed a model using fully-connected conditional random fields to integrate the contextual information such as the co-occurrence and the geometric relationships between objects. However, these methods need labels to obtain the normal relations between objects at the training phase. For the purpose of one-class anomaly detection and human monitoring, this setting is unrealistic. Fadjrimiratno et al. [18] proposed a real-time autonomous mobile robot based on "Fast and Slow Thinking" from the dual process theory [22] with an incremental clustering method, which can detect not only single-region anomalies but also an anomaly of a pair of overlapping regions. Compared with their approach, we consider more general combination anomalies in which the regions do not necessarily overlap each other, and we also explore a

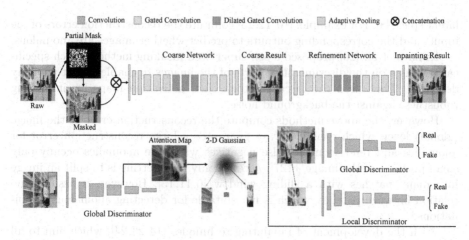

Fig. 2. Overview of our method. Top right: the generative inpainting network with global and local discriminators. The generator contains a coarse network and a refinement network, which has the same structure in [23] except we use gated convolution because the partial mask is irregular. We also design an adaptive local discriminator for predicting whether each salient region is real or fake. Bottom left: Gaussian local region weighting from an attention map. (Color figure online.)

different way to detect anomalous combinations by recovering the missing parts in salient regions with inpainting and a new anomaly score function.

3   Methodology

3.1   Problem Formulation

We target at detecting whether an input image is abnormal by considering its salient areas and the contextual information around them. The input dataset $\mathcal{D}$ is composed of a training set $\mathcal{D}^{\text{tra}} = \{(\mathbf{I}_1, y_1), \ldots, (\mathbf{I}_n, y_n)\}$ and a test set $\mathcal{D}^{\text{tst}} = \{(\mathbf{I}_1^*, y_1^*), \ldots, (\mathbf{I}_m^*, y_m^*)\}$, where $\mathcal{D}^{\text{tra}} \cap \mathcal{D}^{\text{tst}} = \varnothing$. y and y^* are the labels to the corresponding inputs. In the case of a one-class anomaly detection problem, $\mathcal{D}^{\text{tra}}$ contains only normal images $y_i = 0$, $i = 1, 2, \ldots, n$, and $\mathcal{D}^{\text{tst}}$ contains both normal and abnormal images $y^* \in \{0, 1\}$. Here, 0 and 1 represent the class labels of normal and abnormal images, respectively. The goal is to train a network with samples in $\mathcal{D}^{\text{tra}}$ to detect the anomalies in $\mathcal{D}^{\text{tst}}$.

We predict whether an image $\mathbf{I}_j^*$, $j = 1, 2, \ldots, m$, is abnormal by combining the inpainting results of its k most salient regions $\mathbf{R}_j^* = \{\mathbf{R}_{j1}^*, \mathbf{R}_{j2}^*, \ldots \mathbf{R}_{jk}^*\}$ in the image. Salient region $\mathbf{R}_{jt}^*$ is obtained by a pre-trained dense captioning model, such as Densecap [20], and have the form of $(x_{jt}^*, y_{jt}^*, w_{jt}^*, h_{jt}^*)$, where x_{jt}^* and y_{jt}^* represent the coordinates of the top-left vertex, while w_{jt}^* and h_{jt}^* are the width and the height, respectively.

Following [18,19], we consider three kinds of anomalies which are single-region anomalies, background-region anomalies, and dual-region anomalies.

- A **single-region anomaly** is an object or an action which has never been observed in the training set. Such an anomaly only occupies a part of the image and has been tackled in many previous works [10,11,13,15].
- A **background-region anomaly** is an action or object which is not supposed to be in its current environment, such as the left image in Fig. 1 (a). The action in the red rectangle never takes place in this environment, but we observe it in another environment in the training set.
- A **dual-region anomaly** is a kind of anomaly which is composed of a pair of image regions. It refers to the items in the two regions which are not supposed to appear at the same time, e.g., the right image in Fig. 1 (b).

The last two are considered as kinds of anomalous combinations, since we cannot determine whether there is an anomaly from just one region.

The performance of our method is evaluated in terms of Receiver Operator Characteristic Curve (ROC), that plots the true positive rate (TPR) against the false positive rate (FPR) at various threshold settings, Area Under Curve (AUC) score, accuracy, recall, and precision.

3.2 Local Salient Region and Global Similarity Loss

As shown in many inpainting tasks [23,24], the result of inpainting a totally masked object will be prone to removing the object instead of recovering it. Thus, for our purpose of detecting anomalies from the inputs and the corresponding inpainting results, we use partial masks which randomly keeps some areas visible in a salient region to recover the masked areas.

Given a partial mask $\mathbf{M}$ shown in Fig. 2, where white (value equals 1) means the area that needs to be inpainted and black (value equals 0) is the unmasked area, the input is defined as

$$\mathbf{I}_{in} = \mathbf{I} \odot (1 - \mathbf{M}) \otimes \mathbf{M}, \tag{1}$$

where $\mathbf{I}$ is the raw image, $\odot$ and $\otimes$ represent element-wise multiplication and concatenation operation, respectively.

Let $\mathbf{I}'$ be a coarse result and $\mathbf{I}''$ be a final inpainting result, where $(\mathbf{I}', \mathbf{I}'') = G(\mathbf{I}_{in})$, and G represents the generator. Although ℓ_2-loss is widely used in reconstruction tasks [10,11,13], it correlates poorly with image quality as perceived by a human observer and it assumes that each pixel is independent [31]. As suggested in [31,32], a combination loss of ℓ_1 and SSIM (Structural Similarity Index Measure) function [30] helps reconstruct images better, which is defined as

$$\mathcal{L}_{mix}(\mathbf{I}, \hat{\mathbf{I}}) = \alpha(1 - \text{SSIM}(\mathbf{I}, \hat{\mathbf{I}})) + (1 - \alpha)||\mathbf{I} - \hat{\mathbf{I}}||_1, \tag{2}$$

where $\hat{\mathbf{I}}$ is the reconstructed image. α is a trade-off hyperparameter that controls the relative importance of the two items.

Typical inpainting methods usually consider the global loss only and utilize ℓ_1- or ℓ_2-loss on the entire image. In our task of detecting anomalies from salient regions, we need to pay more attention to the inpainting results of the regions because we obtain a local anomaly score for each region. Thus, other than the improved global similarity loss $\mathcal{L}_{global}$,

$$\mathcal{L}_{global} = \mathbb{E}_{\mathbf{I},\mathbf{I}',\mathbf{I}''}[\mathcal{L}_{mix}(\mathbf{I},\mathbf{I}') + \mathcal{L}_{mix}(\mathbf{I},\mathbf{I}'')], \quad (3)$$

we also consider a local salient region loss $\mathcal{L}_{local}$ of a salient region in the image,

$$\mathcal{L}_{local} = \mathbb{E}_{\mathbf{R},\mathbf{R}',\mathbf{R}''}[\mathcal{L}_{mix}(\mathbf{R},\mathbf{R}') + \mathcal{L}_{mix}(\mathbf{R},\mathbf{R}'')], \quad (4)$$

where $\mathbf{R}, \mathbf{R}', \mathbf{R}''$ represent the corresponding region in the raw, coarse, and final inpainting images given the region coordinates, respectively. The final similarity loss is the summation of the above two loss functions.

$$\mathcal{L} = \mathcal{L}_{global} + \mathcal{L}_{local}. \quad (5)$$

3.3   Attention-Based Gaussian Weighting Anomaly Score

During the test phase, each salient region is masked and then inpainted by our trained network. For the single-region anomalies or the anomalous combinations, there exist contextual violations. Thus, some of the salient regions cannot be recovered well because we train our inpainting network with only normal data. In order to determine the contribution of each salient region in the final anomaly score, we propose an attention-based Gaussian weighting anomaly score function.

Take Fig. 3 (a) as an example. Only the red rectangle contains anomalous action and we expect that it can contribute more to the final anomaly score than other normal regions. Hence, we propose a novel way to calculate the anomaly score of an image with these regions. Given the jth image $\mathbf{I}_j^*$, which contains k regions, in the test set, we calculate the local anomaly score $A_{jt}, t = 1, 2, \ldots, k$, of each region $\mathbf{R}_{jt}^*$ by $\mathcal{L}_{mix}$:

$$A_{jt} = \mathcal{L}_{mix}(\mathbf{R}_{jt}^*, \mathbf{R}_{jt}^{*''}), \quad (6)$$

where $\mathbf{R}_{jt}^{*''}$ is the final inpainting result of the tth region $\mathbf{R}_{jt}^*$.

Given the multivariate normal distribution function

$$p(\mathbf{x}|\boldsymbol{\mu},\boldsymbol{\Sigma}) = \frac{1}{\sqrt{(2\pi)^d |\boldsymbol{\Sigma}|}} \exp(-\frac{1}{2}(\mathbf{x} - \boldsymbol{\mu})^T \boldsymbol{\Sigma}^{-1}(\mathbf{x} - \boldsymbol{\mu})), \quad (7)$$

we allocate different weights for different regions by taking the coordinates of the center of a region as the input.

Since the most salient region is not at a fixed position, we propose a biased mean vector for Eq. 7 to determine the region with the highest weight according to the attention mechanism. As shown in Fig. 3, we first obtain the center position $C_{jt} = (x_{jt}, y_{jt})$ of each region $\mathbf{R}_{jt}^*$. Then the highest activation point $T_j = (x_j, y_j)$ is obtained from an attention map which is generated by a commonly used approach named Grad-CAM [33] from an intermediate layer in the

$$(a) \qquad\qquad (b) \qquad\qquad (c)$$

Fig. 3. Overview of selecting mean vector μ for Gaussian function. (a) Image with several regions. (b) Attention map. (c) The position with the highest activation score (marked as a blue dot), the nearest region (marked as a red rectangle) to the blue dot, and the center (marked as a red dot) of the region. (Color figure online)

Table 1. Statistics of the two datasets.

	Robotic$^+$		HAM	
	Training	Test	Training	Test
Normal	5114	416	11777	466
Abnormal	0	28	0	34

global discriminator. We select the closest region center $C_{jt_{min}}$ to T_j by Euclidean distance $d(\cdot,\cdot)$ as the mean vector $\mu = C_{jt_{min}}$ in the Gaussian function, where

$$t_{min} = \operatorname*{arg\,min}_{t \in \{1,2,...,k\}} d(T_j, C_{jt}). \tag{8}$$

The weight $\gamma_{jt} = p(C_{jt}|C_{jt_{min}}, \Sigma)$ of $\mathbf{R}_{jt}^*$ is calculated by its center position given Eq. 7. The final anomaly score $\hat{A}_j$ for $\mathbf{I}_j^*$

$$\hat{A}_j = \sum_{t=1}^{k} \frac{\gamma_{jt}}{\sum_{t=1}^{k} \gamma_{jt}} A_{jt}. \tag{9}$$

4 Experiments

4.1 Datasets

To evaluate our proposed method GIAD, we conduct experiments on two human monitoring datasets which are both taken by an autonomous robot. The statistics of the two datasets are shown in Table 1 and several examples are shown in Fig. 4.

Robotic$^+$ Dataset. This dataset is an extension of a previous robotic dataset which was introduced in [19]. It contains 4768 training and 358 test images including 15 abnormal images that only include single-region anomalies. We add some background-region anomalies, examples of which are shown in the two rightmost columns in Fig. 4 (a), to this dataset. Such a kind of anomalies need to take both the actions and the environment into consideration. The dataset has 346 and 86 additional training and test samples, respectively.

(a) Robotic$^+$ (b) HAM

Fig. 4. Examples of the Robotic$^+$ dataset and the HAM dataset [18]. The examples in the top row and bottom row are normal and anomalous, respectively. In (a), the leftmost column contains samples from the original Robotic dataset [19], where holding an umbrella is an unseen action in the training set. The two rightmost columns in (a) are several added samples in the Robotic$^+$ dataset. Playing with a cellphone or sleeping is abnormal when the man is in this environment (a working area), but normal when he is in another environment (see the top middle sample). In the HAM dataset, the man holding a teddy bear or a handbag, which belongs to another person in the training set, is considered as anomalous.

HAM Dataset. The samples in HAM (**H**uman **A**ctivities **M**onitoring) dataset [18] are taken at several designated positions in a room to monitor human activities and find anomalies. It contains 11777 training and 500 test samples. In addition to the single-region anomalies, it also contains dual-region anomalies, e.g., holding a teddy bear or a bag belonging to another person, and playing with a basketball in a room.

4.2   Experimental Setup

Following [18,19], we use a pre-trained Densecap [20] as the saliency region extractor and set $k = 10$ as the number of detected regions for each image. For stable GAN training, we adopt spectral normalization and hinge loss as the adversarial loss [34]. We optimize $\mathcal{L}$ and the adversarial loss by Adam [35] optimizer with an initial learning rate 2×10^{-3}, $\beta_1 = 0.5$, and $\beta_2 = 0.999$, which are common settings used in previous works [10,25,34]. The hyperparameter α in the $\mathcal{L}_{mix}$ loss function was set to 0.85, which is the same setting in [31,32]. We implemented our approach using the Pytorch[1] framework and Python on Ubuntu 20.04 equipped with an NVIDIA RTX TITAN GPU and an i9-7900X CPU.

As the baselines, we compare our approach GIAD with GAN-based methods, including a variant of Lawson's work [11] named FA-GAN [36], GANomaly [10], and skip-GANomaly [25].[2] We also compare a state-of-the-art inpainting-based

---

[1] https://pytorch.org/.

[2] The codes of GANomaly and skip-GANomaly are from the official implementations on Github.

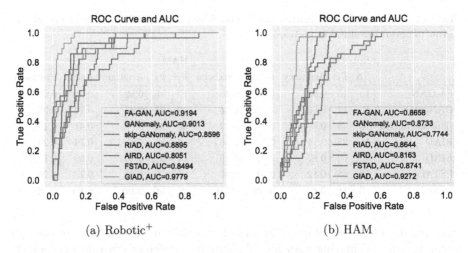

(a) Robotic+   (b) HAM

Fig. 5. ROC curves and AUCs on the two datasets.

anomaly detection approach RIAD [29].[3] All the networks are trained for 500 epochs by resizing the inputs to 256 × 256. Moreover, we take two region-based approaches as our baselines, which are named AIRD [19] (Anomalous Image Region Detection) and FSTAD [18] (Fast-and-Slow-Thinking Anomaly Detection) here. For the last two methods, an anomalous image is defined as an image which contains at least one anomalous region [18]. For the baseline methods, we keep the hyperparameter values as suggested in their original papers.

4.3 Results and Analysis

As shown in Fig. 5, we first examine the performance of our proposed method by comparing the baselines through ROC curves and AUCs. According to the previous experiments [36], FA-GAN and GANomaly achieve AUC scores of 1.0 and 0.967 on the original Robotic dataset, respectively. The AUC scores drop 8.06% and 6.79% for the two methods on the Robotic+ dataset, which shows the additional samples are more challenging. Both plots in Fig. 5 show that our method consistently outperforms the baselines. The AUC scores of GIAD are 0.9779 and 0.9272 on the two datasets, which correspond to 6.36%–21.46% and 6.07%–19.73% improvements over the baseline methods, respectively. Table 2 shows the numbers of the false negative and the false positive samples, as well as those of several evaluation metrics. From Table 2, we see that our method can suppress the numbers of both false negatives and false positives compared with the other methods on both datasets.

The top row in Fig. 6 shows a true positive example in the Robotic+ dataset by our method but overlooked by other baselines except FSTAD. Note that in

---

[3] https://github.com/plutoyuxie/Reconstruction-by-inpainting-for-visual-anomaly-detection.

Table 2. Number of false negatives (FN) and false positives (FP), as well as results in terms of several evaluation metrics.

	Robotic[+]					HAM				
	FN	FP	Accuracy	Recall	Precision	FN	FP	Accuracy	Recall	Precision
FA-GAN	13	16	0.93	0.54	0.48	12	75	0.82	0.65	0.23
GANomaly	15	14	0.93	0.46	0.48	9	75	0.83	0.74	0.25
skip-GANomaly	16	43	0.87	0.43	0.22	20	92	0.78	0.41	0.13
RIAD	14	25	0.91	0.50	0.36	9	80	0.82	0.74	0.24
AIRD	12	69	0.82	0.57	0.19	14	88	0.80	0.59	0.19
FSTAD	13	65	0.82	0.54	0.19	7	76	0.83	0.79	0.26
GIAD	**5**	**10**	**0.97**	**0.82**	**0.70**	**2**	**50**	**0.90**	**0.94**	**0.39**

the training phase, we observe the man is working at his computer in such an environment and playing with his cellphone in a different environment (a resting area). Compared with other samples in this scenario, playing a cellphone only occupies a small area (about 30×30 pixels), which can be seen as a small abnormal action in this environment. We see that FA-GAN and GANomaly can reconstruct the background well but fail in the area of the man holding a cellphone. The two methods make wrong predictions because the high-level features in CNNs tend to neglect details of small regions. For skip-GANomaly, due to its use of U-net structure, the output can combine the low-level features of the input for better reconstruction, which results in false negative predictions. The result of RIAD is blurry due to its use of ℓ_2-loss and the smoothing operation, which results in a relatively low anomaly score. This example is also overlooked by AIRD because it assumes that each region is independent and cannot detect such combinations. Our method obtains the position with the highest activation score, which is marked as a blue dot in (f), and the red rectangle, which is the nearest region to the blue dot and is used to compute the center of the Gaussian weight.

We also show another abnormal example in the HAM dataset detected by our method in the bottom row in Fig. 6. The woman touches the basketball and she never did it in the training set. Although the reconstructed images by FA-GAN and GANomaly look blurry, the anomaly scores of these images are much smaller than those of the abnormal samples.[4] That is because they calculate the anomaly score of the latent vectors. Small changes at latent vectors may not yield a large anomaly score in the two methods, but they can produce significant visual differences. The evidence can be also found in [36].

Figure 7 shows abnormal examples in the two datasets, which are overlooked by our method.[5] When predicting these examples, the attention maps provide wrong positions, which mislead the Gaussian weighting function. Thus, although the anomalous regions (marked as red rectangles) are assigned relatively high anomaly scores in the two examples, the weights of the two regions are small,

---

[4] The other two region-based methods successfully detect this example.

[5] The two examples are detected by FSTAD only.

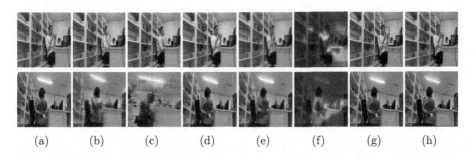

(a)   (b)   (c)   (d)   (e)   (f)   (g)   (h)

Fig. 6. Examples of the anomalies in the Robotic$^+$ (top row) and HAM (bottom row) datasets. Our method successfully detects these examples. (a) Original inputs. (b)-(e) are reconstructed images by FA-GAN, GANomaly, skip-GANomaly, and RIAD, respectively. (f) Attention maps. (g) The positions with the highest activation scores (marked as blue dots) and the nearest regions (marked as red rectangles). (h) The inpainting results from the images obtained by masking the regions in (g). (Color figure online)

(a) An example from Robotic$^+$ (b) An example from HAM

Fig. 7. False negative examples with our method in the Robotic$^+$ (a) and the HAM datasets (b). The leftmost image in (a) is the input, and the middle one is the attention map. The rightmost image in (a) shows the position with the highest activation score (marked as a blue dot), the nearest region (marked as a green rectangle), and an anomalous region (marked as a red rectangle). (Color figure online)

which makes the final anomaly score of these examples much smaller than other abnormal examples.

Previous methods [6,11,13] usually detect small anomalies in real-world scenarios by splitting an image into many patches with a sliding window. To see whether our approach still outperforms the three GAN-based baselines which use such a setting, we explore two different sizes of the sliding window for them. Note that these sliding windows are larger enough to cover the combinations of objects in images. Table 3 shows the results of the three GAN-based baselines. We see that although the three GAN-based baselines have different degrees of improvement on AUC scores with the sliding windows, our method still outperforms them. The reason lies in the fact that although the size of the sliding window increases, there is still no relation between patches available. For example, they still cannot detect the examples in Fig. 6.

Table 3. Comparisons of AUC scores. For the three GAN-based baselines, we take two different settings of the sliding window which are determined by the size of anomalies. A '70p-20s' represents the sliding window has the size of 70 × 70 pixels and the step size of 20 pixels.

	FA-GAN			GANomaly			skip-GANomaly			RIAD	AIRD	FSTAD	GAID
	Image-level	70p-20s	140p-20s	Image-level	70p-20s	140p-20s	Image-level	70p-20s	140p-20s				
Robotic+	0.919	0.936	0.919	0.901	0.918	0.939	0.860	0.880	0.908	0.890	0.805	0.849	**0.978**
HAM	0.866	0.887	0.884	0.873	0.880	0.873	0.774	0.806	0.832	0.864	0.816	0.874	**0.927**

5   Conclusion

In this paper, we proposed a generative inpainting-based model to detect both single-region anomalies and anomalous combinations in human monitoring tasks. By utilizing inpainting, the model is capable of making use of contextual information of known areas in each salient region to reconstruct the missing parts. Moreover, we explore an attention-based Gaussian weighting anomaly score to allocate different importance weights for salient regions according to the attention map from the discriminator to obtain the final anomaly score. Experiments on two real-world robotic datasets show the superiority of our proposed method compared with other baselines in terms of detecting unseen anomalies or small anomalies, as well as anomalous combinations.

The limitation is that the Gaussian center could not be accurate if the background is different from the previous observations, which makes the discriminator generate misleading attention maps. Our future work will explore a more robust discriminator with additional pretext tasks, e.g. rotation task, to learn feature representations for better localization of the Gaussian center.

References

1. Sargano, A.B., Angelov, P., Habib, Z.: A comprehensive review on handcrafted and learning-based action representation approaches for human activity recognition. Appl. Sci. **7**(1), 110 (2017)
2. Liang, Q., et al.: Research on non-contact monitoring system for human physiological signal and body movement. Biosensors **9**(2), 58 (2019)
3. Mahbub, U., Rahman, T., Ahad, M.A.R.: Contactless human monitoring: challenges and future direction. Contactless Hum. Act. Anal. **200**, 335 (2021)
4. Morais, R., Le, V., Tran, T., Saha, B., Mansour, M., Venkatesh, S.: Learning regularity in skeleton trajectories for anomaly detection in videos. In: Proceedings of CVPR, pp. 11996–12004 (2019)
5. Deguchi, Y., Takayama, D., Takano, S., Scuturici, V.M., Petit, J.M., Suzuki, E.: Skeleton clustering by multi-robot monitoring for fall risk discovery. J. Intell. Inf. Syst. **48**(1), 75–115 (2017)
6. Zaheer, M.Z., Lee, J.h., Astrid, M., Lee, S.I.: Old is gold: redefining the adversarially learned one-class classifier training paradigm. In: Proceedings of CVPR, pp. 14183–14193 (2020)
7. Liu, W., Luo, W., Lian, D., Gao, S.: Future frame prediction for anomaly detection-a new baseline. In: Proceedings of CVPR, pp. 6536–6545 (2018)

8. Pang, G., Shen, C., Cao, L., Hengel, A.V.D.: Deep learning for anomaly detection: a review. ACM Comput. Surv. (CSUR) **54**(2), 1–38 (2021)
9. Goodfellow, I.J., et al.: Generative adversarial nets. In: Proceeding of NIPS, pp. 2672–2680 (2014)
10. Akcay, S., Atapour-Abarghouei, A., Breckon, T.P.: GANomaly: semi-supervised anomaly detection via adversarial training. In: Jawahar, C.V., Li, H., Mori, G., Schindler, K. (eds.) ACCV 2018. LNCS, vol. 11363, pp. 622–637. Springer, Cham (2019). https://doi.org/10.1007/978-3-030-20893-6_39
11. Lawson, W., Bekele, E., Sullivan, K.: Finding anomalies with generative adversarial networks for a PatrolBot. In: Proceedings of CVPR Workshops, pp. 12–13 (2017)
12. Schlegl, T., Seeböck, P., Waldstein, S.M., Langs, G., Schmidt-Erfurth, U.: f-AnoGAN: fast unsupervised anomaly detection with generative adversarial networks. Med. Image Anal. **54**, 30–44 (2019)
13. Sabokrou, M., Khalooei, M., Fathy, M., Adeli, E.: Adversarially learned one-class classifier for novelty detection. In: Proceedings of CVPR, pp. 3379–3388 (2018)
14. Pathak, D., Krahenbuhl, P., Donahue, J., Darrell, T., Efros, A.A.: Context encoders: feature learning by inpainting. In: Proceedings of CVPR, pp. 2536–2544 (2016)
15. Schlegl, T., Seeböck, P., Waldstein, S.M., Schmidt-Erfurth, U., Langs, G.: Unsupervised anomaly detection with generative adversarial networks to guide marker discovery. In: Proceedings of IPMI, pp. 146–157 (2017)
16. Oh, J., Kim, H.I., Park, R.H.: Context-based abnormal object detection using the fully-connected conditional random fields. Pattern Recogn. Lett. **98**, 16–25 (2017)
17. Park, S., Kim, W., Lee, K.M.: Abnormal object detection by canonical scene-based contextual model. In: Fitzgibbon, A., Lazebnik, S., Perona, P., Sato, Y., Schmid, C. (eds.) ECCV 2012. LNCS, vol. 7574, pp. 651–664. Springer, Heidelberg (2012). https://doi.org/10.1007/978-3-642-33712-3_47
18. Fadjrimiratno, M.F., Hatae, Y., Matsukawa, T., Suzuki, E.: Detecting anomalies from human activities by an autonomous mobile robot based on "fast and slow" thinking. In: Proceedings of VISIGRAPP, Subvolume for VISAPP, vol. 5. pp. 943–953 (2021)
19. Hatae, Y., Yang, Q., Fadjrimiratno, M.F., Li, Y., Matsukawa, T., Suzuki, E.: Detecting anomalous regions from an image based on deep captioning. In: Proceedings of VISIGRAPP, Subvolume for VISAPP, vol. 5, pp. 326–335 (2020)
20. Johnson, J., Karpathy, A., Fei-Fei, L.: DenseCap: fully convolutional localization networks for dense captioning. In: Proceedings of CVPR, pp. 4565–4574 (2016)
21. Choi, M.J., Torralba, A., Willsky, A.S.: Context models and out-of-context objects. Pattern Recogn. Lett. **33**(7), 853–862 (2012)
22. Kahneman, D.: Thinking, Fast and Slow. Macmillan, Basingstoke (2011)
23. Yu, J., Lin, Z., Yang, J., Shen, X., Lu, X., Huang, T.S.: Generative image inpainting with contextual attention. In: Proceedings of CVPR, pp. 5505–5514 (2018)
24. Yu, J., Lin, Z., Yang, J., Shen, X., Lu, X., Huang, T.S.: Free-form image inpainting with gated convolution. In: Proceedings of ICCV, pp. 4471–4480 (2019)
25. Akcay, S., Atapour-Abarghouei, A., Breckon, T.P.: Skip-GANomaly: skip connected and adversarially trained encoder-decoder anomaly detection. In: Proceedings of IJCNN, pp. 1–8 (2019)
26. Kimura, D., Chaudhury, S., Narita, M., Munawar, A., Tachibana, R.: Adversarial discriminative attention for robust anomaly detection. In: Proceedings of WACV, pp. 2172–2181 (2020)
27. Tang, Y., Zhao, L., Zhang, S., Gong, C., Li, G., Yang, J.: Integrating prediction and reconstruction for anomaly detection. Pattern Recogn. Lett. **129**, 123–130 (2020)

28. Nguyen, B., Feldman, A., Bethapudi, S., Jennings, A., Willcocks, C.G.: Unsupervised region-based anomaly detection in brain MRI with adversarial image inpainting. arXiv preprint arXiv:2010.01942 (2020)
29. Zavrtanik, V., Kristan, M., Skočaj, D.: Reconstruction by inpainting for visual anomaly detection. Pattern Recogn. **112**, 107706 (2021)
30. Wang, Z., Bovik, A.C., Sheikh, H.R., Simoncelli, E.P.: Image quality assessment: from error visibility to structural similarity. IEEE Trans. Image Process. **13**(4), 600–612 (2004)
31. Zhao, H., Gallo, O., Frosio, I., Kautz, J.: Loss functions for image restoration with neural networks. IEEE Trans. Comput. Imaging **3**(1), 47–57 (2017)
32. Godard, C., Mac Aodha, O., Brostow, G.J.: Unsupervised monocular depth estimation with left-right consistency. In: Proceedings of CVPR, pp. 270–279 (2017)
33. Selvaraju, R.R., Cogswell, M., Das, A., Vedantam, R., Parikh, D., Batra, D.: Grad-CAM: visual explanations from deep networks via gradient-based localization. In: Proceedings of ICCV, pp. 618–626 (2017)
34. Miyato, T., Kataoka, T., Koyama, M., Yoshida, Y.: Spectral normalization for generative adversarial networks. In: Proceedings of ICLR (2018)
35. Kingma, D.P., Ba, J.: Adam: a method for stochastic optimization. In: Proceedings of ICLR (2015)
36. Dong, N., Hatae, Y., Fadjrimiratno, M.F., Matsukawa, T., Suzuki, E.: Experimental evaluation of GAN-based one-class anomaly detection on office monitoring. In: Helic, D., Leitner, G., Stettinger, M., Felfernig, A., Raś, Z.W. (eds.) ISMIS 2020. LNCS (LNAI), vol. 12117, pp. 214–224. Springer, Cham (2020). https://doi.org/10.1007/978-3-030-59491-6_20

Heterogeneous Graph Attention Network for User Geolocation

Xuan Zhang⑩, FuQiang Lin, DiWen Dong, WangQun Chen, and Bo Liu⁽✉⁾

College of Computer Science, National University of Defense Technology,
Changsha, China
{zhangxuan,linfuqiang13,ddw_bak,chenwangqun19,kyle.liu}@nudt.edu.cn

Abstract. Identifying the geographic location of online social media
users, also known as User Geolocation (UG), plays an essential part in
many Internet application services. One main challenge is the scarcity of
users' public geographic information. To overcome it, most works focus
on user geolocation prediction with posts and interactions on social
media. However, they do not consider the distinction of variant social
connections, which may impair the performance of the UG models. To
address this issue, we propose a multi-view model, Heterogeneous graph
Attention networks for user Geolocation (HAG), which introduces the
attention mechanism to mine valuable cues in social networks and text
contexts jointly. In the network module, we creatively apply a heterogeneous graph to model various social interactions and introduce a heterogeneous graph attention network to learn network structure information.
In the text module, we propose a context attention network to extract
geo-related text information. Extensive experiments conducted on three
Twitter datasets show that HAG achieves state-of-the-art performance
compared to strong baselines.

Keywords: User geolocation · Heterogeneous graph · Attention
mechanism

1 Introduction

As one of the social media users' attributes, geographic location has become
crucial information for many online application services, such as event detection
[23] and location-based recommendation [3]. Despite the broad applications of
users' locations, user geolocation remains challenging due to the scarce and noisy
clues in publicly available information. For example, the data on Twitter shows
that only 5% of users provide the coordinates of their home in profile [6], and
1% of tweets are geotagged [5]. Therefore, it is a burning question to predict the
locations of users on social media.

Users' public information on social media, e.g., published posts and social
interactions, provides clues to UG. Early works focus on mining location clues
in user media posts, such as location-related words and language habits. Representative text-based methods include word distribution comparison [22,33]

© Springer Nature Switzerland AG 2021
D. N. Pham et al. (Eds.): PRICAI 2021, LNAI 13032, pp. 433–447, 2021.
https://doi.org/10.1007/978-3-030-89363-7_33

and location indicative words extraction [13, 20]. In addition, social networks extracted from social interactions can also reveal the distance between users. Most network-based methods utilize label propagation or node embedding [8, 30] to process network structure data. More recently, hybrid methods [10, 21] absorb both advantages of the previous two to improve further performance, fusing text and network features to infer users' location.

Previous work has achieved promising results thanks to well-designed models; however, there remain some shortcomings. The dominant approaches [21, 36] simply treat various types of interaction in social networks as the same, without distinguishing the importance of varied social connections. Such simplification ignores the correlation of different types of social interaction and may impair performance. Besides, during text processing, commonly used indicative words [13] and bag-of-words features [20] can not sufficiently capture the overall semantics of given textual content. Further, static embedding methods, such as doc2vec [10], are tricky to capture users' location-related language habits.

To address the above problems, we propose a multi-view model for UG. First, to finely handle the various types of social connections, our method applies a heterogeneous social graph to represent social interactions between users and employs a heterogeneous graph attention network (HAN) [32] to learn user network embedding. Next, inspired by the superiority of recurrent neural network (RNN) on modeling overall context semantics, we adopt a context attention network (CAN) that combines RNN with the attention mechanism to obtain the context embedding. Finally, a geolocation prediction layer combines the above two embeddings to identify the locations of social media users.

The main contributions of our work are summarized as follows:

- We utilize heterogeneous graphs to model social interaction with considering the difference of varied connections and apply HAN to learn user node representations. To the best of our knowledge, it is the first attempt to distinguish the importance of different social interactions for UG.
- We adopt CAN to dynamically learn features of context semantics instead of traditional static representations, in which the use of attention mechanisms is beneficial to capture user location-related language habits.
- Experimental results on three real Twitter datasets show that our model consistently outperforms all baselines in all evaluation metrics.

2   Related Work

2.1   User Geolocation

According to different types of users' social media information used to make predictions, we can roughly divide most existing works into three paradigms.

Text-Based Approach. The first text-based method uses place name detection and heuristic algorithms to determine the geographic scope of web pages [9].

After that, plenty of text-based methods have been proposed for geo-locating online users. The word distribution model identifies users' location by comparing the similarity of the word distribution between the target text and the label text [22,33]. An alternative approach predicts users' locations by searching for location indicative words [13]. Subsequently, bag-of-words models such as TF-IDF [15] and LDA [4] are widely used in text feature extraction [19,20]. Although the text-based approach has achieved some success, problems such as noisy text and limited text are still troublesome.

Network-Based Approach. Backstrom et al. [1] apply the maximum likelihood method to estimate the users' locations and report that the possibility of friend relation decreases monotonously with distance. In addition to reciprocal friendships, social interactions such as mention and repost can also reveal the distance between users [16]. In a social network constructed by user interactions, methods such as label propagation [8] and node embedding [30] are used to predict users' locations. Generally, network-based approaches provide a new clue for UG. However, this line of approaches still performs unsatisfactorily because isolated users cannot benefit from network information.

Hybrid Approach. Combing text and network can effectively solve the disadvantages mentioned above. Therefore, most recent works utilize deep learning techniques to integrate various user characteristics related to geographic location. For example, Do et al. [10] fuse features of TF-IDF, doc2vec, and node2vec to infer users' locations. In addition to text and network features, more user meta-data such as time zone, profile location can be aggregated for prediction through attention mechanisms [14]. Further, graph neural networks have made remarkable achievements in processing non-euclidean spatial data. So graph convolutional networks (GCN) and graph attention networks are widely used to leverage multiple views of user data [21,36].

2.2   Heterogeneous Graph Neural Network

Heterogeneous graph neural networks (HGNN) aim to deal with heterogeneous graphs, which have multiple types of nodes or edges [11]. One of the early attempts to model heterogeneous graphs is the relation graph convolutional network [24], which focuses on multiple relational graphs. In addition, heterogeneous graph neural network [35] adopts bidirectional LSTM to aggregate the features of different types of nodes. To improve the performance and interpretability of HGNN, the heterogeneous graph attention network (HAN) [32] incorporates the attention mechanism to model the importance of each meta-path-defined edge. Inspired by their work, we conduct the first attempt to construct a heterogeneous graph representing different social interactions and adopt HAN to model the heterogeneous graph.

3   Preliminary

In this section, we formally describe the UG task. Before that, we define a heterogeneous graph, meta-path, and meta-path-based neighbors as follows.

Definition 1 (Heterogeneous Graph [26]). *A heterogeneous graph is a graph that consists of multiple types of nodes or edges. The formal representation of a heterogeneous graph is $\mathcal{G} = (\mathcal{V}, \mathcal{E})$, where the node-set $\mathcal{V}$ and the edge-set $\mathcal{E}$ are associated with the node type mapping function $\phi : \mathcal{V} \longrightarrow \mathcal{A}$ and the edge type mapping function $\psi : \mathcal{E} \longrightarrow \mathcal{R}$. $\mathcal{A}$ and $\mathcal{R}$ represent the set of node types and edge types, where $|\mathcal{A}| + |\mathcal{R}| > 2$.*

Example 1. A heterogeneous graph $\mathcal{G} = (\mathcal{V}, \mathcal{E})$ on the Twitter social network consists of user nodes $\mathcal{V}$ and various social connections $\mathcal{E}$ such as mention, retweet, and reply. In this case, we have $\mathcal{A} = \{\text{User}\}$ and $\mathcal{R} = \{\text{Mention}, \text{Retweet}, \text{Reply}\}$.

Definition 2 (Meta-path [27]). *A meta-path is defined as a path composed of a series relations between various nodes. The formal description is $\Phi = A_1 \xrightarrow{R_1} A_2 \xrightarrow{R_2} \cdots \xrightarrow{R_l} A_{l+1}$, where $A \in \mathcal{A}$ and $R \in \mathcal{R}$.*

Example 2 Interactions between users in Twitter social networks can be represented by various meta-paths, such as User $\xrightarrow{\text{Retweet}}$ User and User $\xrightarrow{\text{Mention}}$ User.

Definition 3 (Meta-path-based Neighbors [35]). *Meta-path-based neighbors N_v^{Φ} is a set of nodes connected with node v through a meta-path Φ.*

In summary, we give the formal definition of the problem as follows. Suppose we have a set of social media users $\mathcal{V}$ and each user $v \in \mathcal{V}$ has a set of media posts $T_v = \{t_1, t_2, \ldots, t_N\}$ published by v. We extract social interactions (such as mention and retweet) between users from posts to construct a heterogeneous graph $\mathcal{G} = (\mathcal{V}, \mathcal{E})$ with different types of edges. Based on the posts and social interactions, our task aims to predict the geographic locations of users.

4   Approach

In this section, we propose the heterogeneous graph attention network for user geolocation (HAG). As shown in Fig. 1, the HAG model consists of three parts: heterogeneous graph attention network, context attention network, and geolocation prediction. In detail, the first two parts generate network embeddings and context embeddings, respectively, and the last part aggregates these two embeddings for prediction. Next, we start with the construction of a heterogeneous graph and follow with a detailed introduction of the above three components.

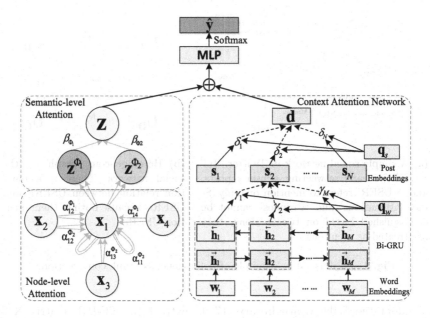

Fig. 1. The framework of HAG.

4.1 Heterogeneous Graph Construction

We extract interactions from users' tweets to construct a heterogeneous graph $\mathcal{G} = (\mathcal{V}, \mathcal{E})$. The heterogeneous graph treats users as nodes and various interactions as different types of edges. Specifically, if one mentions another or both mention the third user, the two user nodes will be connected by a bidirectional mention (M) edge, and the same deal for the retweet (R) relation. In addition, we add all types of self-loops to each node. Figure 2(a) provides an illustrative example. Note that although $USER_A$ retweets the tweet that mentions $USER_C$ (in the form of @$USER_C$), a mention relation is not linked between $USER_A$ and $USER_C$. Instead, we treat this mention operation as only a social interaction between $USER_C$ and the original author $USER_B$. According to the above processing, we generate a heterogeneous graph of the social network as Fig. 2(b). Further, if a user is mentioned or retweeted by more than k users, the user is treated as a 'celebrity' [19]. We filter out all 'celebrity' nodes to reduce network edges with low geolocation utility. In the constructed heterogeneous graph, the mention and retweet interaction between users can also be represented by meta-paths $U \xrightarrow{M} U$ and $U \xrightarrow{R} U$, respectively.

4.2 Heterogeneous Graph Attention Network

We adopt HAN to model a heterogeneous graph $\mathcal{G} = (\mathcal{V}, \mathcal{E})$ for learning the network structure information. Specifically, given a set of user nodes $\mathcal{V}$ paired with their published posts T, we regard a user's posts as one user document

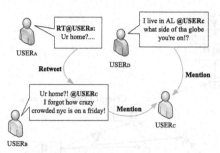
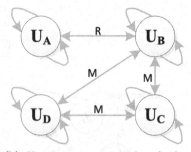

(a) A simple social network in Twitter. 'RT @USER' means retweeting a user's posts, and '@USER' refers to mention or reply. Since '@mentions' and '@replies' cannot be distinguished based on tweets alone, they are treated as mentions

(b) Heterogeneous graph of the social network. There is a mention relation between USER$_B$ and USER$_D$ because both of them mention USER$_C$

Fig. 2. An illustrative example of heterogeneous graph construction.

and adopt the Scikit-Learn library [17] to extract the TF-IDF matrix $\mathbf{X}$ for all user documents. Then, considering a user node $v \in \mathcal{V}$, we take the feature vector $\mathbf{x}_v \in \mathbf{X}$ of the user v's document as the initial node features. After that, a node-level attention layer generates the node-level features based on different meta-paths by joint modeling the information from meta-path-based neighbors. The learned features are then fed into a semantic-level attention layer to generate the user network embeddings.

Node-Level Attention. Since there is only one type of node in our heterogeneous graph, we adopt a share matrix $\mathbf{W}_x$ to learn hidden node features $\tilde{\mathbf{x}}_v$:

$$\tilde{\mathbf{x}}_v = \mathbf{W}_x \cdot \mathbf{x}_v. \tag{1}$$

Then, we perform self-attention [28] on the nodes to model the correlations between users. Specifically, for a pair of users (v, u) linked by a meta-path Φ, we compute the attention coefficient e_{vu}^{Φ} to measure the influence strength of user u to user v:

$$e_{vu}^{\Phi} = \sigma(\mathbf{a}_{\Phi}^{\mathrm{T}} \cdot [\tilde{\mathbf{x}}_v \| \tilde{\mathbf{x}}_u]), \tag{2}$$

where $\|$ denotes the concatenate operation of the vector, $\mathbf{a}_{\Phi}$ is the node-level attention vector of meta-path Φ, and $\sigma(\cdot)$ represents a nonlinear activation function (LeakyReLU$(\cdot)$ in our experiments). To convert the coefficients into node-level attention scores α_{vu}^{Φ}, we normalize the attention coefficients by softmax function:

$$\alpha_{vu}^{\Phi} = \frac{\exp(e_{vu}^{\Phi})}{\sum_{u \in N_v^{\Phi}} \exp(e_{vu}^{\Phi})}, \tag{3}$$

where N_v^{Φ} denotes the meta-path-based neighbors of user v. Next, we aggregate the hidden features of the neighbor nodes based on node-level attention scores:

$$\mathbf{z}_v^{\Phi} = \sigma(\sum_{u \in N_v^{\Phi}} \alpha_{vu}^{\Phi} \cdot \tilde{\mathbf{x}}_u), \qquad (4)$$

where $\mathbf{z}_v^{\Phi}$ denotes the node-level embedding of user v.

We further apply a multi-head attention mechanism to attend to node-level information from different representation subspaces jointly. Specifically, we concatenate K independent learned embeddings generated by different $\mathbf{a}_\Phi^k$ and $\mathbf{W}_x^k$ as follows:

$$\mathbf{z}_v^{\Phi} = \overset{K}{\underset{k=1}{\|}} \; \sigma(\sum_{u \in N_v^{\Phi}} \alpha_{vu}^{\Phi,k} \cdot \tilde{\mathbf{x}}_u^k). \qquad (5)$$

After that, we can learn all nodes' node-level embeddings $\{\mathbf{Z}^{\Phi_1}, \mathbf{Z}^{\Phi_2}, \ldots, \mathbf{Z}^{\Phi_L}\}$ for different meta-paths $\{\Phi_1, \Phi_2, \ldots, \Phi_L\}$.

Semantic-Level Attention. Given the node-level embeddings $\{\mathbf{Z}^{\Phi_1}, \mathbf{Z}^{\Phi_2}, \ldots, \mathbf{Z}^{\Phi_L}\}$, we first apply a fully connected layer to learn hidden representations of $\mathbf{Z}_{\Phi_i}$ for each meta-path Φ_i. Then, to measure the importance of meta-path Φ_i, we calculate the correlation coefficients between the hidden representations and the semantic-level attention vectors $\mathbf{q}_z$ and average them to get the importance coefficients w_{Φ_i} as follows:

$$w_{\Phi_i} = \frac{1}{|\mathcal{V}|} \sum_{v \in \mathcal{V}} \mathbf{q}_z^{\mathrm{T}} \cdot \tanh(\mathbf{W}_z \cdot \mathbf{z}_v^{\Phi_i} + \mathbf{b}_z), \qquad (6)$$

where $\mathbf{W}_z$ is the weight matrix and $\mathbf{b}_z$ is the bias vector. Next, we normalize the importance coefficients of meta-path to obtain the semantic-level attention score β_{Φ_i} as:

$$\beta_{\Phi_i} = \frac{\exp(w_{\Phi_i})}{\sum_{i=1}^{L} \exp(w_{\Phi_i})}, \qquad (7)$$

where L is the number of meta-paths. Next, the semantic attention scores are used to obtain network embeddings $\mathbf{Z}$ as follows:

$$\mathbf{Z} = \sum_{i=1}^{L} \beta_{\Phi_i} \cdot \mathbf{Z}_{\Phi_i}. \qquad (8)$$

To learn information of higher-order neighbors, we stack several HAN layers to learn the final network embedding vector $\mathbf{z}_v$ of user v.

4.3   Context Attention Network

In addition to social interaction, we also extract geo-related text information by incorporating a context attention network to enhance our model performance.

In detail, given the published posts $T = \{t_1, t_2, \ldots, t_N\}$ of a user, our CAN first applies the post encoder to obtain the representation of each post independently. Then a text encoder jointly learns the final context representation by aggregating all post embeddings.

Post Encoder. Considering the superiority of GRU [2] in learning contextual information compared to static embedding methods, we adopt bidirectional GRU (Bi-GRU) to learn the latent representation of each word. In practice, given a post $t = \{w_1, w_2, \ldots, w_M\}$, we first adopt GloVe's Twitter vectors [18] to obtain word embeddings $\{\mathbf{w}_1, \mathbf{w}_2, \ldots, \mathbf{w}_M\}$. After that, Bi-GRU takes the word embeddings as input to generate the hidden states of each word, represented by the following formula:

$$\mathbf{H} = \text{GRU}(\mathbf{w}_1, \mathbf{w}_2, \ldots, \mathbf{w}_M), \tag{9}$$

where $\mathbf{H} = \{\mathbf{h}_1, \mathbf{h}_2, \ldots, \mathbf{h}_M\}$ denotes the contextual representation of each word, which concatenates the forward and backward hidden states.

To distinguish the contribution of different words to geo-related features, we introduce a word-level attention vector $\mathbf{q}_w$ and aggregate the contextual representations of these words to generate the post embedding $\mathbf{s}$ as follows:

$$c_i = \mathbf{q}_w^{\text{T}} \cdot \tanh(\mathbf{W}_w \cdot \mathbf{h}_i + \mathbf{b}_w), \tag{10}$$

$$\gamma_i = \frac{\exp(c_i)}{\sum_{i=1}^{M} \exp(c_i)}, \tag{11}$$

$$\mathbf{s} = \sum_{i=1}^{M} \gamma_i \cdot \mathbf{h}_i, \tag{12}$$

where $\mathbf{W}_w$ and $\mathbf{b}_w$ are the weight matrix and the bias vector, respectively. We compute the correlation coefficients c_i to represent the importance of each word and adopt a softmax function to get the normalized attention score γ_i.

Text Encoder. Considering the differences in the location-related clues between posts, we use the attention mechanism to measure the contribution of each post to user geolocation. In practice, given the posts embeddings $\{\mathbf{s}_1, \mathbf{s}_2, \ldots, \mathbf{s}_N\}$ of user v, we adopt a post-level attention vector $\mathbf{q}_s$ to learn the weight of posts and aggregate those posts embeddings to obtain the final context embedding $\mathbf{d}_v$:

$$o_i = \mathbf{q}_s^{\text{T}} \cdot \tanh(\mathbf{W}_s \cdot \mathbf{s}_i + \mathbf{b}_s), \tag{13}$$

$$\delta_i = \frac{\exp(o_i)}{\sum_{i=1}^{N} \exp(o_i)}, \tag{14}$$

$$\mathbf{d}_v = \sum_{i=1}^{N} \delta_i \cdot \mathbf{s}_i, \tag{15}$$

where $\mathbf{W}_s$ denotes the weight matrix and $\mathbf{b}_s$ is the bias vector.

4.4 Geolocation Prediction

To combine the features extracted from user texts and social interactions, we transform these features into the same feature space and then fuse network embedding $\mathbf{z}_v$ with context embedding $\mathbf{d}_v$ to obtain the hybrid feature vector. Next, we adopt a multilayer perceptron (**MLP**) to predict the probability $\hat{\mathbf{y}}_v$:

$$\hat{\mathbf{y}}_v = \text{Softmax}(\mathbf{MLP}(\mathbf{M}_z \cdot \mathbf{z}_v \oplus \mathbf{M}_d \cdot \mathbf{d}_v)), \tag{16}$$

where $\oplus$ denotes the element-wise sum operator, $\mathbf{M}_z$ and $\mathbf{M}_d$ are the mapping matrix. The element $\hat{y}_{vi} \in \hat{\mathbf{y}}_v$ represents a user's predicted probability of being located at the region i, and the region with the maximum probability is the final predicted region.

Finally, towards learning and optimization of the model, we employ cross-entropy to calculate the loss for classification as follows:

$$\text{Loss} = - \sum_{v \in \mathcal{V}_{\text{label}}} \sum_i y_{vi} \cdot \log(\hat{y}_{vi}), \tag{17}$$

where $\mathcal{V}_{\text{label}}$ is a set of nodes with geotags, and y_{vi} represents the probability that the actual location of the user v belongs to the region i.

5 Experiment

5.1 Dataset

To evaluate the effectiveness of our method, we conduct experiments on three popular Twitter datasets: GeoText [12], Twitter-US [22], and Twitter-World [13]. All these datasets are pre-partitioned into training, development, and test sets. Social media users in these datasets contain their published posts, also tagged with their location in the form of latitude and longitude. Our experiments only use the raw data in these Twitter datasets. To treat the UG task as a classification task, we discretize the geographic coordinates of training users into small regions through the k-d tree [22] method. Considering the unbalanced distribution of users in a region, we choose the centroid of all training users' coordinates in the region as the coordinates it represents. For the input of our model, we lowercase each of the tweets, remove stop words and extract interactions between users from tweets. Table 1 reports some quantitative statistics on users, tweets, mention interactions, retweet interactions (removing repeated interactions), and region classes to display these datasets visually.

Table 1. Statistics of datasets.

Dataset	Users	Tweets	Mentions	Retweets	Classes	Train	Dev	Test
GeoText	9,475	377,504	168,911	63,687	129	5,685	1,895	1,895
Twitter-US	449,200	38,036,187	7,168,829	959,276	256	429,650	10,000	10,000
Twitter-World	1,386,766	13,350,229	4,382,850	229,942	930	1,366,766	10,000	10,000

5.2   Baseline

We compare our model with following user geolocation approaches:

1. **HierLR** [34]: A text-based hierarchical classification model that adopts logistic regression (LR) models at each node in a hierarchical grid.
2. **MLP4Geo** [20]: A text-based model that extracts the TF-IDF features of the text as the input of simple MLP.
3. **MADCEL** [19]: A network-based model that performs label propagation on a weighted network.
4. **GCN-LP** [21]: A network-based model that utilizes the graph convolutional networks to convolve one-hot encoding of neighbors.
5. **MADCEL-LR** [19]: A hybrid method that adopts a l_1 regularised LR model to predict textual labels for isolated users before label propagation.
6. **GCN** [21]: A multi-view geolocation model based on GCN, which extracts the bag-of-words feature of the text as input.
7. **MENET** [10]: A multi-entry model that fuses textual information (TF-IDF and doc2vec), social network (node2vec), and metadata (timestamp).

5.3   Metrics

To evaluate the quality of the model, we utilize the Haversine formula [25] to calculate the error measured in kilometers between the predicted coordinate $\hat{c}$ and the real coordinate c, and adopt three distance-based metrics as follows:

1. **Acc@161:** The accuracy of location prediction within 161 kilometers or 100 miles from the actual location:

$$acc_{161} = \frac{1}{|\mathcal{V}_{\text{test}}|} \sum_{v \in \mathcal{V}_{\text{test}}} [\text{Haversine}(\hat{c}_v, c_v) \leq 161], \tag{18}$$

where $\mathcal{V}_{\text{test}}$ represents a set of test-set users.
2. **Mean:** The average of the errors in prediction:

$$mean = \frac{1}{|\mathcal{V}_{\text{test}}|} \sum_{v \in \mathcal{V}_{\text{test}}} \text{Haversine}(\hat{c}_v, c_v). \tag{19}$$

3. **Median:** The median of the errors in prediction:

$$median = \text{median}(\{\text{Haversine}(\hat{c}_v, c_v), c \in \mathcal{V}_{\text{test}}\}). \tag{20}$$

5.4   Implementation

We implement HAG under the PyTorch framework and run it on four GeForce GTX 3090 graphics cards. In the heterogeneous graph construction, 'Celebrity Threshold' is set to $\{5, 15, 5\}$ for different datasets, and the set of meta-paths is $\{U \xrightarrow{R} U, U \xrightarrow{M} U\}$. The heterogeneous graph attention network with two layers is implemented by Deep Graph Library [31], and the hidden state dimension is $\{64, 128, 192\}$ for different datasets. The number of graph attention heads is searched in $\{2, 4, 8, 16\}$. Moreover, in the context attention network, we set the Bi-GRU hidden dimension to $\{50, 100, 200\}$ for different datasets. All activation functions are ELU($\cdot$) [7]. For training, we use the Adam optimizer with the learning rate 1.0×10^{-3}, and the 'patience' of the early stopping method is 25.

5.5   Result

Performance Comparison. Table 2 reports the performance of all models on the three datasets, and the best performances are shown in bold. Compared with network-based methods, two text-based methods HierLR and MLP4Geo, underperform a lot on the GeoText and Twitter-World datasets, indicating that social interaction is more valuable than textual post for user geolocation. The main reason is the limited geo-related cues and noisy text in social media posts. It is worth noting that the text-based methods have competitive performance on the Twitter-Us dataset, which may be due to the sufficient number of tweets in this dataset. In addition, All hybrid methods achieve a considerable performance improvement as compared to network-based methods. Such improvement shows that jointly incorporating the textual information and interactions benefits the UG task. As shown, our model HAG consistently outperforms all baselines, including those hybrid approaches, in all evaluation metrics. We attribute the superiority of our model to the use of the heterogeneous graph attention network and context attention network, which help to distinguish the influence of varied interactions and dynamically extract geo-related cues from textual posts.

Table 2. Twitter user geolocation prediction performance.

Method	GeoText			Twitter-Us			Twitter-World		
	Acc@161	Mean	Median	Acc@161	Mean	Median	Acc@161	Mean	Median
Text-Based									
HierLR	–	–	–	48%	656	191	31.3%	1669	509
MLP4Geo	38%	844	389	54%	554	120	34%	1456	415
Net-Based									
MADCEL	58%	586	60	54%	705	116	45%	2525	279
GCN-LP	58%	576	56	53%	653	126	45%	2357	279
Hybrid									
MADCEL-LR	59%	581	57	60%	529	78	53%	1403	111
GCN	60%	546	45	65%	485	71	54%	1130	108
MENET	62%	532	32	66%	433	45	53%	1044	118
HAG (Ours)	**63.4%**	**518**	**32**	**70%**	**371**	**39**	**59%**	**825**	**53**

Ablation Study. To examine the contributions of different components, we conduct an ablation study by comparing our full model with three variants. The first two remove the heterogeneous graph attention network and the context attention network, respectively. The last variant (denoted as GAT) utilizes a homogeneous graph to represent the social interactions between users and replaces HAN with the multi-head graph attention network [29] to model network structure data. Experimental results on the two datasets (GeoText and Twitter-Us) are shown in Table 3. We find that the heterogeneous graph attention network is essential, and the combination of text and network features is beneficial to improve performance. Moreover, compared with GAT, the proposed HAG achieves higher scores on all datasets because it deeply analyzes the influence of different social interactions for the UG task.

Table 3. Ablation study of HAG on GeoText and Twitter-US.

Method	GeoText			Twitter-Us		
	Acc@161	Mean	Median	Acc@161	Mean	Median
HAG	63.4%	518	32	70%	371	39
w/o HAN	41%	843	411	49%	577	132
w/o CAN	59%	546	45	60%	478	94
GAT	62%	533	39	67%	421	47

Analysis. To better understand the influence of neighbors and interactions on user geolocation prediction, we conduct an in-depth analysis of node-level attention and semantic-level attention. First, we take the user U_{6702} in the GeoText dataset as an example. In the meta-path $U \xrightarrow{R} U$, the attention value between U_{6702} and its neighbors can be calculated through node-level attention, as shown in Fig. 3(a). It is obvious that neighbors with the same geotag as U_{6702} have higher attention scores, which verifies that the closer neighboring users are more critical to U_{6702}'s location prediction. Besides, taking the GeoText dataset as an illustration, we report the Acc@161 scores of the single meta-path models and the corresponding attention scores in Fig. 3(b). The single meta-path model of $U \xrightarrow{M} U$ outperforms that of $U \xrightarrow{R} U$, which may be due to the sufficient mention edges. Further, since there may be many mention edges with low geolocation utility, the attention value of $U \xrightarrow{M} U$ is lower than that of $U \xrightarrow{R} U$.

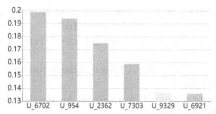
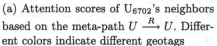
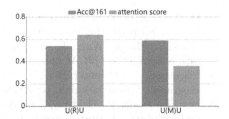

(a) Attention scores of U_{6702}'s neighbors based on the meta-path $U \xrightarrow{R} U$. Different colors indicate different geotags

(b) Performance of single meta-path and corresponding attention value

Fig. 3. In-depth analysis of node-level attention and semantic-level attention.

6 Conclusion

In this paper, we propose a multi-view user geolocation framework, HAG, which combines network features and textual features. On the one hand, through the heterogeneous graph attention network, our model can distinguish different types of social interactions. On the other hand, the context attention network filters out the noise in the text information, thereby extracting features related to geographic location. Extensive experiments on three Twitter datasets verify the superiority of our method. In the future, we plan to apply more user characteristic data such as user metadata to further improve performance.

References

1. Backstrom, L., Sun, E., Marlow, C.A.: Find me if you can: improving geographical prediction with social and spatial proximity. In: WWW 2010 (2010)
2. Bahdanau, D., Cho, K., Bengio, Y.: Neural machine translation by jointly learning to align and translate. CoRR arXiv:1409.0473 (2015)
3. Bao, J., Zheng, Y., Wilkie, D., Mokbel, M.: Recommendations in location-based social networks: a survey. GeoInformatica **19**, 525–565 (2015)
4. Blei, D.M., Ng, A., Jordan, M.I.: Latent Dirichlet allocation. J. Mach. Learn. Res. **3**, 993–1022 (2003)
5. Cheng, Z., Caverlee, J., Lee, K.: You are where you tweet: a content-based approach to geo-locating twitter users. In: Proceedings of the 19th ACM International Conference on Information and Knowledge Management (2010)
6. Cheng, Z., Caverlee, J., Lee, K.: A content-driven framework for geolocating microblog users. ACM Trans. Intell. Syst. Technol. **4**, 2:1–2:27 (2013)
7. Clevert, D.A., Unterthiner, T., Hochreiter, S.: Fast and accurate deep network learning by exponential linear units (ELUs). arXiv: Learning (2016)
8. Davis, C., Pappa, G., de Oliveira, D.R.R., de Lima Arcanjo, F.: Inferring the location of twitter messages based on user relationships. Trans. GIS **15**, 735–751 (2011)
9. Ding, J., Gravano, L., Shivakumar, N.: Computing geographical scopes of web resources. In: VLDB (2000)

10. Do, T., Nguyen, D.M., Tsiligianni, E., Cornelis, B., Deligiannis, N.: Multiview deep learning for predicting twitter users' location. arXiv:1712.08091 (2017)
11. Dong, Y., Hu, Z., Wang, K., Sun, Y., Tang, J.: Heterogeneous network representation learning. In: IJCAI (2020)
12. Eisenstein, J., O'Connor, B.T., Smith, N.A., Xing, E.: A latent variable model for geographic lexical variation. In: EMNLP (2010)
13. Han, B., Cook, P., Baldwin, T.: Geolocation prediction in social media data by finding location indicative words. In: COLING (2012)
14. Huang, B., Carley, K.M.: A hierarchical location prediction neural network for twitter user geolocation. arXiv:1910.12941 (2019)
15. Jones, K.: A statistical interpretation of term specificity and its application in retrieval. J. Doc. **60**, 493–502 (2004)
16. McGee, J., Caverlee, J., Cheng, Z.: Location prediction in social media based on tie strength. In: Proceedings of the 22nd ACM International Conference on Information and Knowledge Management (2013)
17. Pedregosa, F., et al.: Scikit-learn: machine learning in python. J. Mach. Learn. Res. **12**, 2825–2830 (2011)
18. Pennington, J., Socher, R., Manning, C.D.: GloVe: global vectors for word representation. In: EMNLP (2014)
19. Rahimi, A., Cohn, T., Baldwin, T.: Twitter user geolocation using a unified text and network prediction model. arXiv:1506.08259 (2015)
20. Rahimi, A., Cohn, T., Baldwin, T.: A neural model for user geolocation and lexical dialectology. arXiv:1704.04008 (2017)
21. Rahimi, A., Cohn, T., Baldwin, T.: Semi-supervised user geolocation via graph convolutional networks. In: ACL (2018)
22. Roller, S., Speriosu, M., Rallapalli, S., Wing, B., Baldridge, J.: Supervised text-based geolocation using language models on an adaptive grid. In: EMNLP-CoNLL (2012)
23. Sakaki, T., Okazaki, M., Matsuo, Y.: Tweet analysis for real-time event detection and earthquake reporting system development. IEEE Trans. Knowl. Data Eng. **25**, 919–931 (2013)
24. Schlichtkrull, M., Kipf, T.N., Bloem, P., van den Berg, R., Titov, I., Welling, M.: Modeling relational data with graph convolutional networks. In: Gangemi, A., et al. (eds.) ESWC 2018. LNCS, vol. 10843, pp. 593–607. Springer, Cham (2018). https://doi.org/10.1007/978-3-319-93417-4_38
25. Sinnott, R.W.: Virtues of the haversine. Sky Telescope **68**(2), 158–159 (1984)
26. Sun, Y., Han, J.: Mining heterogeneous information networks: a structural analysis approach. SIGKDD Explor. **14**, 20–28 (2013)
27. Sun, Y., Han, J., Yan, X., Yu, P.S., Wu, T.: PathSim: meta path-based top-k similarity search in heterogeneous information networks. Proc. VLDB Endow. **4**, 992–1003 (2011)
28. Vaswani, A., et al.: Attention is all you need. arXiv:1706.03762 (2017)
29. Velickovic, P., Cucurull, G., Casanova, A., Romero, A., Lio', P., Bengio, Y.: Graph attention networks. arXiv:1710.10903 (2018)
30. Wang, F., Lu, C.-T., Qu, Y., Yu, P.S.: Collective geographical embedding for geolocating social network users. In: Kim, J., Shim, K., Cao, L., Lee, J.-G., Lin, X., Moon, Y.-S. (eds.) PAKDD 2017. LNCS (LNAI), vol. 10234, pp. 599–611. Springer, Cham (2017). https://doi.org/10.1007/978-3-319-57454-7_47
31. Wang, M., et al.: Deep graph library: a graph-centric, highly-performant package for graph neural networks. arXiv: Learning (2019)

32. Wang, X., et al.: Heterogeneous graph attention network. In: The World Wide Web Conference (2019)
33. Wing, B., Baldridge, J.: Simple supervised document geolocation with geodesic grids. In: ACL (2011)
34. Wing, B., Baldridge, J.: Hierarchical discriminative classification for text-based geolocation. In: EMNLP (2014)
35. Zhang, C., Song, D., Huang, C., Swami, A., Chawla, N.: Heterogeneous graph neural network. In: Proceedings of the 25th ACM SIGKDD International Conference on Knowledge Discovery and Data Mining (2019)
36. Zheng, C., Jiang, J.Y., Zhou, Y., Young, S., Wang, W.: Social media user geolocation via hybrid attention. In: Proceedings of the 43rd International ACM SIGIR Conference on Research and Development in Information Retrieval (2020)

Hyperbolic Tangent Polynomial Parity Cyclic Learning Rate for Deep Neural Network

Hong Lin, Xiaodong Yang[✉], Binyan Wu, and Ruyan Xiong

ZhejiangGongshang University, Hangzhou 310018, China
{19020090036,20020090023,20020090037}@pop.zjgsu.edu.cn,
xdyang@zjgsu.edu.cn

Abstract. With the development of artificial intelligence technology, optimizing the performance of deep neural network model has become a hot issue in the field of scientific research. Learning rate is one of the most important hyper-parameters for model optimization. In recent years, some learning rate algorithms with cycle mechanism have been proposed. Most of them adopt warm restart and cycle mechanism to make the learning rate value cyclically change between two boundary values and prove their effectiveness by practicing in image classification task. In order to further improve the performance of neural network model and prove the effectiveness in different training task, the paper proposes a novel learning rate schedule called hyperbolic tangent polynomial parity cyclic learning rate (HTPPC), which adopts cycle mechanism and combines the advantages of warm restart and polynomial decay. In addition, the performance of HTPPC is demonstrated on image classification and object detection tasks.

Keywords: Deep neural network · Learning rate · Warm restart · Cycle mechanism

1 Introduction

In recent years, there have been abundant research results on deep neural networks. It has been successfully applied in many fields such as video detection, image classification, object detection, face recognition, text translation and driverless cars [9]. Many scholars are dedicated to studying how to optimize neural networks to improve the performance of the model.

Learning rate [29] is one of the most important hyper-parameters that affects model convergence [18]. The neural network model forms a loss function according to the internal parameters. The convergence of model depends on the minimization of the loss function.

At present, Gradient Descent [4] is the most commonly used optimization strategy in model training, which is used to update parameter in the neural network model to minimize the loss function. In the process of parameter updating,

© Springer Nature Switzerland AG 2021
D. N. Pham et al. (Eds.): PRICAI 2021, LNAI 13032, pp. 448–460, 2021.
https://doi.org/10.1007/978-3-030-89363-7_34

the learning rate determines updating pace, thus affecting the effect of minimizing the loss function greatly [2,28]. Therefore, choosing an appropriate learning rate schedule is extremely important for model training [6].

In order to improve the performance of neural network model, this paper proposes a novel algorithm called hyperbolic tangent polynomial parity cyclic learning rate (HTPPC). It adopts the shape of hyperbolic tangent function (tanh) and polynomial function to divide the learning rate rise and fall periods. At the same time, the method adopts the way of odd-even high-low cycle, sets two cycle maximums. Through the high and low alternating learning rate value, saddle point and local minimum are better crossed, which improves the generalization ability and effective capacity of the model. Although the current popular adaptive learning rate algorithm can automatically adjust learning rate of each iteration through complex and precise calculations, existing studies have proved that the final result is usually worse than the cyclic methods [12,16].

This article demonstrated the effectiveness of HTPPC on the CIFAR-10 and CIFAR-100 datasets [10] with image classification model such as ResNet50 [10], Vgg16 [24], GoogleNetv2 [26], MobileNetv2 [23] and the Pascal Voc dataset [27] with object detection model such as ShuffleNetV2-YOLOv3 [17,21].

2 Related Work

Initially, monotonic decay learning rate such as exponential decay learning rate [1] and piecewise decay learning rate (Piecewise Decay LR) were widely used in the training of advanced DNN architecture [5]. Through a lot of experiments and attempts, attenuation of learning rate can improve the performance of model, but it will result in a slower training speed. In order to effectively improve convergence speed and accuracy of the model, some non-traditional learning rate methods have been proposed in recent years.

In 2016, Loshchilov et al. proposed the stochastic gradient descent method with warm restart [15]. This method no longer monotonically decays learning rate, but initializes learning rate to a preset value after a period of interval, and then gradually decays.

Inspired by the method, Leslie N. Smith proposed cyclical learning rate (CLR) in 2017, which makes learning rate increase and decrease periodically within two reasonable learning rate boundary values [25]. It is proved that the increase and decrease of learning rate are effective in the overall training, which can make the model jump out of the local minimum point and saddle point during the training process.

In 2019, Purnendu Mishra et al. proposed polynomial learning rate policy with warm restart (poly with restart) [19]. Learning rate is initialized to a certain value in each cycle and performed polynomial decays. Experiments prove that the combination of warm restart and polynomial decay is effective in improving the accuracy of the model.

In 2020, a scholar proposed trapezoidal decay cyclic learning rate (TDL) [14], the learning rate of each cycle rises linearly, keeps a fixed value and then declines linearly. Research has shown that keeping a stationary maximum value of each learning rate cycle can help improve accuracy.

The above learning rates with cyclic mechanism are only practiced in image classification task. In the article, the effectiveness of HTPPC is demonstrated on image classification and object detection tasks, and further improve the training effect of the model. HTPPC combines the characteristics of cyclic mechanism, stationary value and polynomial decay. It is effective improved classification accuracy and convergence speed.

3   Hyperbolic Tangent Polynomial Parity Cyclic Learning Rate (HTPPC)

This section introduces a novel learning rate method called hyperbolic tangent polynomial parity cyclic learning rate.

3.1   The HTPPC

According to the analysis of random matrix theory and neural network theory, an important reason that makes it difficult to optimize neural networks is that there are a large number of saddle points in high-dimensional non-convex optimization problems [3]. The saddle point is usually surrounded by a plane with the same error value and the plane is different in size, which makes it difficult for SGD algorithm to escape from saddle point. The core idea of HTPPC is to consider the problems of saddle points and local minimum points in the parameter space.

As Rong Ge discussed, adding occasional random noise to the gradient helps to escape from saddle points. [7]. A lot of work has shown that for non-convex optimization, the inherent noise helps in convergence. When interference noise no longer has enough power to escape the saddle point, learning rate can be increased to enhance the effect of the noise [8]. The method is similar to the effect of Eq. (1) as follow:

$$w_{t+1} = w_t - \eta \cdot \bigtriangledown f(w_t) + \varepsilon, \tag{1}$$

Where ε is a noise parameter. The parameters of each training sample are updated by stochastic gradient descent, and each execution is updated once [22]. The formula of updating parameters w is:

$$w_{t+1} = w_t - \eta \cdot \bigtriangledown f(w_t), \tag{2}$$

where η represents learning rate, $\bigtriangledown f(w_t)$ as a gradient function. HTTPC studied in this paper uses momentum optimizer [20]. Stochastic gradient descent not only increases the speed in the direction of the gradient, but also increases noise interference, μ determines the size of the inertia:

$$z_{t+1} = \mu \cdot z_t + \bigtriangledown f(w_t) \tag{3}$$

$$w_{t+1} = w_t - \eta \cdot z_{t+1}. \tag{4}$$

That is equivalent to subtracting an $\eta \cdot \mu \cdot z_t$ from the original formula:

$$w_{t+1} = w_t - \eta \cdot \nabla f(w_t) - \eta \cdot \mu \cdot z_t, \qquad (5)$$

where z_t represents direction and size of the last update, $\eta \cdot \mu \cdot z_t$ is equivalent to the noise parameter ε in Eq. (1).

During the training process, there are a large number of different saddle points in the high-dimensional non-convex function, and the flat area near the saddle point is not uniform in size. In this paper, we consider changing the maximum cycle range to increase the randomness. Through the experimental comparison, the effect of setting maximum value randomly is worse than setting two best maximum values.

Therefore, our method sets two optimal maximum values in the cycle period. In the odd period, learning rate value of this method is in a larger range. In the even period, it is in a smaller range. Through alternating high and low transformations, the model is more effective to jump out of different local minimums and cross gradient flat areas of different areas.

Another reason why HTPPC works is that, by following the "LR parity range determination" method in Sect. 3.2, three most suitable learning rate values are selected. It is likely that near optimal learning rates will be used throughout training [25].

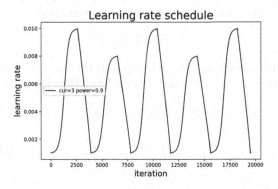

Fig. 1. Hyperbolic tangent polynomial parity cyclic learning rate

In addition to the alternating cycle method, the rising of HTPPC accounts for 2/3 of each cycle, and the curve is a deformed hyperbolic tangent function. The shape characteristics of this function enables HTPPC to have a small learning rate at the beginning, then rise rapidly, and maintain a gentle upward trend when it is close to the maximum value. The decline of HTPPC accounts for the last 1/3 of each cycle, and the curve adopts polynomial decay. It can adapt to different network models through adjustable deformation parameters [19]. Figure 1 shows the model of HTPPC.

The steps of the hyperbolic tangent polynomial parity cyclic learning rate algorithm are as follows:

(1) Set the parameters for model training: the maximum boundary of the odd period L_{odd}, the maximum boundary of the even period L_{even}, the minimum boundary L_{min}. Number of epochs per cycle is s, and cur controls the curvature of learning rate. Polynomial decay shape parameter is $power$.

(2) Determine the number of cycles: we get the current epochs T_e by integrated function. g indicates the current cycle, which is calculated by T_e and s, the formula is as follows:

$$g = T_e \% s. \tag{6}$$

(3) Divide the period range: o indicates a node of two-thirds of a cycle, which is calculated by g and s. a and b control the rise and fall of functions in each cycle. When HTPPC is in the rise phase, a is 1 and b is 0. When HTPPC is in the declined phase, a is 0 and b is 1.

$$o = (3 \cdot g)/(2 \cdot s) \tag{7}$$

$$a = |o - 1| \tag{8}$$

$$b = o. \tag{9}$$

(4) Determine the parity period: p is a parameter for controlling the parity period, it will alternate between 0 and 1 depending on the number of cycles, the value of p is 1 for odd cycles and 0 for even cycles.

$$p = (1 + g)\%2. \tag{10}$$

(5) Calculation the learning rate: when p is 1, the learning rate formula is Eq. (11), and when p is 0, the learning rate formula is Eq. (12).

$$\eta_J = (L_{odd} - L_{min}) \cdot \left(a \cdot \left(\frac{tanh(\frac{3 \cdot cur \cdot g}{s} - 3)}{2 \cdot tanh(cur)} + \frac{1}{2} \right) + b \cdot \left(\frac{-3 \cdot g}{s} + 3 \right)^{power} \right) + L_{min} \tag{11}$$

$$\eta_O = (L_{even} - L_{min}) \cdot \left(a \cdot \left(\frac{tanh(\frac{3 \cdot cur \cdot g}{s} - 3)}{2 \cdot tanh(cur)} + \frac{1}{2} \right) + b \cdot \left(\frac{-3 \cdot g}{s} + 3 \right)^{power} \right) + L_{min}. \tag{12}$$

These parameters (g, o, a, b and p) are parameters in the algorithm, not hyper-parameters for tuning. The learning rate algorithm with cycle mechanism realizes the loop transformation of learning rate η between the minimum learning rate boundary L_{min} and two maximum learning rate boundary L_{even} and L_{odd}.

3.2   LR Parity Range Determination

Leslie N. Smith introduced the "LR range test" method [25] in CLR to estimate the maximum and minimum boundaries of the learning rate. On the basis of this method, we propose the "LR parity range measurement" method to determine the three boundary lines of alternating parity. Before formal training, we continuously increase the learning rate from a minimum in a few epochs or iterations.

As learning rate continues to increase, the accuracy rate begins to rise. After a period of time, the increase in accuracy begins to decrease and jitter. Usually after the accuracy rate begins to fall, if the learning rate increases a little bit, the accuracy rate will increase slightly or more. Therefore, the maximum value of even period ($even\_lr$) is corresponding learning rate when accuracy rate drops for the first time, and the minimum value ($base\_lr$) is 1/4 of $even\_lr$, with three decimal places. The maximum value of odd period (odd_lr) is corresponding learning rate when accuracy rate drops for the second time. Compared with the "LR range test" method, the "LR parity range measurement" method has more accurate boundary determination. For other deep learning training tasks, accuracy can be changed to corresponding evaluation index. For example, ShuffleNetV2-YOLOv3 object detection model in the experiment in Sect. 4.3, the accuracy rate can be changed to mAP to determine learning rate loop range.

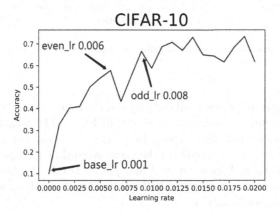

Fig. 2. Resnet50 LR range test; classification accuracy as a function of increasing learning rate for 8 epochs (LR parity range measurement).

Figure 2 shows an example of making this type of run with the CIFAR-10 dataset. When $lr = 0.006$ the model accuracy rate drops for the first time, so set $even\_lr = 0.006, base\_lr = even\_lr/4 \approx 0.001$. Then accuracy rate drops for the second time at $lr = 0.008$, so set $odd\_lr = 0.008$. When using a new model or dataset, this method can quickly confirm the three changing ranges of learning rate.

3.3   Cycle Period Stepsize

The stepsize refers to the number of epochs contained in each cycle. Experiments show that running for 4 or more cycles will achieve even better performance. Moreover, it is best to stop training at the end of a cycle, which is when the learning rate is at its minimum [25].

3.4   Curvature Parameter and Polynomial Shape Parameter

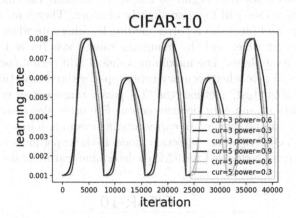

Fig. 3. An illustrations of the effect of different values of *cur* and *power* on the learning rate curve for HTTP.

The curvature parameter *cur* and the polynomial decay parameter *power* control the shape of learning rate decay, as shown in Fig. 3. The larger *cur*, the more smooth areas before and after hyperbolic tangent function. *cur* and *power* make learning rate change more flexible in the cycle. According to experimental results are shown in Table 1. When *cur* is 3 and *power* is 0.9, the model could learn faster and the accuracy rate could be higher. Therefore, all experiments in this paper adopt this combination.

Table 1. Experimental results of HTPPC with multiple parameter training CIFAR-10 dataset on Resnet50.

Network	Parameter	Accuracy
Resnet50	cur = 3, power = 0.3	78.71
	cur = 3, power = 0.6	78.76
	cur = 3, power = 0.9	**80.10**
	cur = 5, power = 0.3	78.87
	cur = 5, power = 0.6	78.78
	cur = 5, power = 0.9	78.01

4   Experiments

In this section, we train CIFAR-10 and CIFAR-100 datasets with image classification networks. And we train Pascal Voc dataset with object detection network.

HTPPC is compared with other learning rate methods by training results. All the experiments have been performed on Baidu AI Studio artificial intelligence training platform with NVIDIA Tesla V100 32 GB GPU and PaddlePaddle2.0.2 backend.

4.1   Dataset

The CIFAR-10 [10]and CIFAR-100 [10]are composed of 10 categories and 100 categories respectively, including 60000 images. Among them, 50000 images are used for training and 10000 images are used for testing. Each image is a 32×32 color image.

The Pascal VOC dataset [27]is a set of standardized and excellent dataset for image recognition and classification. The paper uses the union of the training verification sets of VOC2007 and VOC2012 as training set, which contains 16,551 images, and the labeled objects include 20 categories. It uses 4592 pictures of VOC2007 testset for testing.

Table 2. Parameter setting of HTPPC on CIFAR-10 dataset

Network	$base\_lr$	$even\_lr$	odd_lr
Resnet50	0.001	0.005	0.008
Vgg16	0.001	0.006	0.007
GoogleNetv2	0.003	0.015	0.019
MobileNetv2	0.001	0.005	0.009

Table 3. Parameter setting of HTPPC on CIFAR-100 dataset

Network	$base\_lr$	$even\_lr$	odd_lr
Resnet50	0.001	0.007	0.014
Vgg16	0.005	0.023	0.028
GoogleNetv2	0.004	0.016	0.02
MobileNetv2	0.001	0.005	0.007

4.2   Experiment on CIFAR-10 and CIFAR-100

In this section, We train CIFAR-10 and CIFAR-100 datasets with different learning rate schedulers, such as HTPPC, constant learning rate (constant LR), Piecewise Decay LR, CLR, poly with restart, TDL and Adam [13]. The network are trained by SGD with momentum 0.9, using L2 regularization with 0.001, batch size is 128. For data enhancement, we fill 4 pixels as padding, then randomly cut each picture to 32×32, then adjust the picture size to 96×96, and finally perform horizontal flip and random angle flip.

The stepsize of learning rate with cycle mechanism is 40 epochs. Set L_{even}, L_{odd} and L_{min} of HTPPC through "LR parity range determination" mentioned in 3.2. More parameter settings are shown in Table 2 and Table 3; the maximum and minimum values of CLR, TDL and poly with restart in different networks are min_lr and $even\_lr$ in Table 2 and Table 3. For Piecewise Decay LR, the initial learning rate is 0.01, and it is decayed by 0.5 times after 50 epochs. For poly with restart, we set $power = 0.9$. For constant LR and Adam, the learning rate is 0.001. All training are trained for 200 epochs, each epoch has 391 iterations.

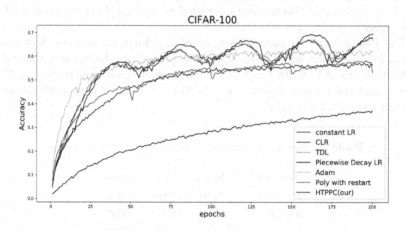

Fig. 4. Test accuracy on MobileNetv2 with different learning rate schemes: constant LR (black line), CLR (green line), TDL (skyblue line), Piecewise Decay LR (blue line), Adam (orange line), poly with restart (purple line) and our approach (red line). (Color figure online)

Observing the accuracy curve in Fig. 4, although HTPPC learning rate is not as high as Adam in the initial stage, but it has shown a clear advantage in the later stage of training. When training to 80 epochs, HTPPC reached 69.70% accuracy, and the accuracy of adaptive learning rate Adam was only 63.15%. Compared with other learning rates with circular mechanism, it also has obvious advantages. After training is completed, the highest accuracy of HTPPC reaches 69.70%, which is higher than other learning rate with cycle mechanism, 0.87% higher than CLR, 16.36% higher than poly with restart, and 1.82% higher than TDL.

In order to prove the general effectiveness of HTPPC in image classification task. The experiment is based on different network models to compare the above seven learning rate methods. The specific experimental results are shown in Table 4. We conclude that HTPPC algorithm performs well in these network models. Especially when using MobileNetv2 network training, the highest accuracy rate is significantly greater than other learning rates. The highest test accuracy can reach 92.14% on CIFAR-10 and 69.70% on CIFAR-100.

Table 4. Test average accuracy of 3 runs on CIFAR-10 and CIFAR-100 datasets with multiple networks

Network	Method	CIFAR-10	CIFAR-100
Resnet50	constant LR	84.11	53.67
	Piecewise Decay LR	92.57	64.26
	poly with restart	91.57	66.96
	CLR	92.06	69.18
	TDL	92.13	69.13
	Adam	86.16	67.68
	HTPPC(Ours)	**92.66**	**70.38**
Vgg16	constant LR	69.67	35.78
	Piecewise Decay LR	85.73	50.56
	poly with restart	86.62	55.04
	CLR	91.82	69.66
	TDL	91.15	69.09
	Adam	85.71	61.23
	HTPPC(Ours)	**92.66**	**72.75**
GoogleNetv2	constant LR	78.82	46.51
	Piecewise Decay LR	90.15	61.76
	poly with restart	90.20	60.75
	CLR	89.78	63.88
	TDL	89.81	63.67
	Adam	86.37	50.99
	HTPPC(Ours)	**90.39**	**64.40**
MobileNetv2	constant LR	73.76	37.27
	Piecewise Decay LR	86.43	57.27
	poly with restart	86.60	58.34
	CLR	90.03	68.19
	TDL	90.57	67.88
	Adam	87.73	63.15
	HTPPC(Ours)	**92.14**	**69.70**

4.3 Experiment on Pascal VOC

In this section, we train Pascal VOC dataset with ShuffleNetV2-YOLOv3 network. We compare different learning rates by the evaluation index mean average precision (mAP) of the object detection model [11]. ShuffleNetV2-YOLOv3 uses YOLOv3 as the main framework and replaces backbone network with ShuffleNetv2 to improve performance of network. Compared with original YOLOv3 prediction, the prediction speed can be increased by 10 ms~20 ms, and the model size is less than one-eighth of the original [17,21].

Table 5. Parameter setting of HTPPC learning rate on Pascal VOC dataset

base_lr	even_lr	odd_lr	size
0.002	0.01	0.013	25

The network are trained by SGD with momentum 0.9, using L2 regularization with 0.00005, batch size is 16. For image data enhancement, it performs random adjustment of image brightness, random cropping, random expansion and random flip. L_{even}, L_{odd} and L_{min} of HTPPC are shown in Table 5. $L_{max} = 0.01$, $L_{min} = 0.002$ of CLR and TDL, and the cycle period is 25 epochs. For constant LR and Adam, the learning rate is 0.001. For Piecewise Decay LR, the initial learning rate is 0.01, and it is decayed by 0.5 times after 25 epochs. All training are trained for 100 epochs, each epoch has 1034 iterations.

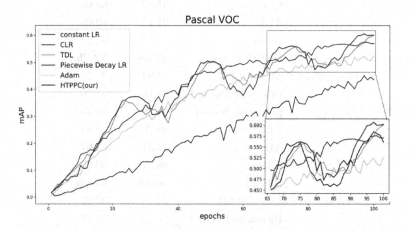

Fig. 5. The mAP on ShuffleNetV2-YOLOv3 with different learning rate schemes: constant LR (black line), CLR (green line), TDL (skyblue line), Piecewise Decay LR (blue line), Adam (orange line) and our approach (red line) (Color figure online)

Figure 5 shows the experimental result. Observing the mAP curve in the figure, it is obvious that the mAP value of HTPPC is higher than other learning rates. At 25 epochs, HTPPC reached 36.99%. At the same time, the mAP of Piecewise Decay LR reached 29.13%, constant LR was 10.69%, CLR was 36.18% and TDL was 35.03%.

The final data result is shown in Table 6. From the table, we can draw that the highest mAP value of HTPPC can reach 60.47%, it is higher than CLR 2.66% and higher than TDL 0.39%. Therefore, compared with the other five learning rate algorithms, the ShuffleNetV2-YOLOv3 object detection network with HTPPC algorithm has better object detection performance.

Table 6. The mAP of different learning rate schemes test on Pascal VOC dataset

Network	Method	Accuracy
ShuffleNetV2-YOLOv3	constant LR	45.21
	Piecewise Decay LR	57.60
	Adam	52.59
	CLR	57.81
	TDL	60.08
	HTPPC(Ours)	**60.47**

4.4 Conclusion

this paper proposes hyperbolic tangent polynomial parity cyclic learning rate, it can better overcome large number of saddle points on the surface of high-dimensional non-convex loss function and improve training effect of the deep learning model. HTPPC combines the advantages of cyclic learning rate, trapezoidal learning rate and polynomial decay learning rate, and proposes a novel alternating parity decay method. Experiments on the image classification model and object detection model prove the effectiveness of HTPPC. Future work includes practicing more parameter combinations of HTPPC algorithm and trying more different deep learning model training tasks.

References

1. An, W., Wang, H., Zhang, Y., Dai, Q.: Exponential decay sine wave learning rate for fast deep neural network training. In: IEEE Visual Communications and Image Processing, pp. 1–4 (2017)
2. Bengio, Y.: Practical recommendations for gradient-based training of deep architectures. Arxiv (2012)
3. Dauphin, Y., Pascanu, R., Gulcehre, C., Cho, K., Ganguli, S., Bengio, Y.: Identifying and attacking the saddle point problem in high-dimensional non-convex optimization. In: NIPS, vol. 27 (2014)
4. Duchi, J., Hazan, E., Singer, Y.: Adaptive subgradient methods for online learning and stochastic optimization. J. Mach. Learn. Res. **12**(7), 2121–2159 (2011)
5. Feng, Y., Li, Y.: An overview of deep learning optimization methods and learning rate attenuation methods. Hans J. Data Mining **8**(3), 186–200 (2018)
6. Fu, Q., et al.: Improving learning algorithm performance for spiking neural networks. In: 2017 IEEE 17th International Conference on Communication Technology (ICCT), pp. 1916–1919 (2017)
7. Ge, R., Huang, F., Jin, C., Yuan, Y.: Escaping from saddle points – online stochastic gradient for tensor decomposition. Mathematics (2015)
8. Goyal, P., et al.: Accurate, large minibatch SGD: training imagenet in 1 hour. Arxiv (2017)
9. Hao, X., Zhang, G., Ma, S.: Deep learning. Int. J. Semant. Comput. **10**(03), 417–439 (2016)

10. He, K., Zhang, X., Ren, S., Sun, J.: Deep residual learning for image recognition, pp. 770–778. IEEE (2016)
11. Hill, L., et al.: Geometric mean average precision, p. 1239. Springer, Heidelberg (2009)
12. Jiao, J., Zhang, X., Li, F., Wang, Y.: A novel learning rate function and its application on the SVD++ recommendation algorithm. IEEE Access **8**, 14112–14122 (2019)
13. Kingma, D., Ba, J.: Adam: a method for stochastic optimization. In: International Conference on Learning Representations (2014)
14. Li, J., Yang, X.: A cyclical learning rate method in deep learning training. In: 2020 International Conference on Computer, Information and Telecommunication Systems (CITS), pp. 1–5 (2020)
15. Loshchilov, I., Hutter, F.: SGDR: stochastic gradient descent with warm restarts. In: ICLR 2017 (5th International Conference on Learning Representations) (2016)
16. Luo, L., Xiong, Y., Liu, Y., Sun, X.: Adaptive gradient methods with dynamic bound of learning rate. In: International Conference on Learning Representations (ICLR) (2019)
17. Ma, N., Zhang, X., Zheng, H.T., Sun, J.: Shufflenet v2: practical guidelines for efficient CNN architecture design. In: European Conference on Computer Vision (2018)
18. Mehta, J.: In Search of Deeper Learning: The Quest to Remake the American High School (2019)
19. Mishra, P., Sarawadekar, K.: Polynomial learning rate policy with warm restart for deep neural network. In: TENCON 2019 (2019)
20. Polyak, B.: Some methods of speeding up the convergence of iteration methods. USSR Comput. Math. Math. Phys. **4**(5), 1–17 (1964)
21. Redmon, J., Farhadi, A.: Yolov3: an incremental improvement. arXiv e-prints (2018)
22. Robbins, H., Monro, S.: A Stochastic Approximation Method. Herbert Robbins Selected Papers (1985)
23. Sandler, M., Howard, A., Zhu, M., Zhmoginov, A., Chen, L.C.: Mobilenetv 2: inverted residuals and linear bottlenecks. In: 2018 IEEE/CVF Conference on Computer Vision and Pattern Recognition (CVPR) (2018)
24. Simonyan, K., Zisserman, A.: Very deep convolutional networks for large-scale image recognition. arXiv:1409.1556 (2014)
25. Smith, L.: Cyclical learning rates for training neural networks. In: 2017 IEEE Winter Conference on Applications of Computer Vision (WACV) (2017)
26. Szegedy, C., et al.: Going deeper with convolutions. In: The IEEE Conference on Computer Vision and Pattern Recognition (CVPR), pp. 1–9 (2015)
27. Vicente, S., Carreira, J., Agapito, L., Batista, J.: Reconstructing pascal VOC. In: Proceedings of the IEEE Computer Society Conference on Computer Vision and Pattern Recognition, pp. 41–48 (2014)
28. Wang, Y., Zhou, P., Zhong, W.: An optimization strategy based on hybrid algorithm of adam and SGD. In: MATEC Web of Conferences, vol. 232 (2018)
29. Xiaohu, Y., Chen, G.A., Cheng, S.X.: Dynamic learning rate optimization of the backpropagation algorithm. IEEE Trans. Neural Netw. **6**(03), 669–677 (1995)

Infrared Image Super-Resolution via Heterogeneous Convolutional WGAN

Yongsong Huang[1], Zetao Jiang[1(✉)], Qingzhong Wang[2,3], Qi Jiang[1], and Guoming Pang[4]

[1] Guilin University of Electronic Technology University, Guilin, China
zetaojiang@guet.edu.cn
[2] City University of Hong Kong, Kowloon, Hong Kong SAR, China
qingzwang2-c@my.cityu.edu.hk
[3] Baidu Research, Beijing, China
[4] ZTE Corporation, Shenzhen, China
pang.guoming@zte.com.cn

Abstract. Image super-resolution is important in many fields, such as surveillance and remote sensing. However, infrared (IR) images normally have low resolution since the optical equipment is relatively expensive. Recently, deep learning methods have dominated image super-resolution and achieved remarkable performance on visible images; however, IR images have received less attention. IR images have fewer patterns, and hence, it is difficult for deep neural networks (DNNs) to learn diverse features from IR images. In this paper, we present a framework that employs heterogeneous convolution and adversarial training, namely, heterogeneous kernel-based super-resolution Wasserstein GAN (HetSRW-GAN), for IR image super-resolution. The HetSRWGAN algorithm is a lightweight GAN architecture that applies a plug-and-play heterogeneous kernel-based residual block. Moreover, a novel loss function that employs image gradients is adopted, which can be applied to an arbitrary model. The proposed HetSRWGAN achieves consistently better performance in both qualitative and quantitative evaluations. According to the experimental results, the whole training process is more stable.

Keywords: Super-resolution · Infrared image · Image processing · Heterogeneous kernel-based convolution · Generative adversarial networks

1 Introduction

Image super-resolution (SR) reconstruction is a very active topic in computer vision as it offers the promise of overcoming some of the limitations of low-cost imaging sensors. Infrared (IR) image super-resolution plays an important role in the military and medical fields and many other areas of vision research. A major problem with IR thermal imaging is that IR images are normally low resolution since the size and precision of IR sensors can be limited. Image super-resolution is a promising and low-cost way to improve the resolution and quality

© Springer Nature Switzerland AG 2021
D. N. Pham et al. (Eds.): PRICAI 2021, LNAI 13032, pp. 461–472, 2021.
https://doi.org/10.1007/978-3-030-89363-7_35

of IR images. Generally, image super-resolution methods based on deep learning can be classified into two categories, namely, models based on generative adversarial networks (GANs) [16,20] and models based on deep neural networks (DNNs) [5,6,8,12,18,21,26,27], both of which have achieved satisfying results on visible images. These methods can achieve a good peak signal-to-noise ratio (PSNR). However, they do not consider the visual characteristics of the human eye. The human eye is more sensitive to contrast differences with a lower spatial frequency. The sensitivity of the human eye to differences in brightness contrast is higher than its sensitivity to color, and the perception of a region by the human eye is affected by the surrounding areas. Situations in which the results of the evaluation are inconsistent with the subjective feeling of a viewer therefore often occur. We recommend using the structural similarity index (SSIM). The learning-based SISR algorithm learns a mapping between low-resolution (LR) and high-resolution (HR) image patches. The prior knowledge used is either explicit or implicit, depending upon the learning strategy. The super-resolution convolutional neural network (SRCNN) [4] algorithm introduced deep learning methods to SISR. A faster model, the faster super-resolution convolutional neural network (FSRCNN) [6], improved upon the SRCNN model and has also been applied to SISR. The efficient subpixel convolutional neural network (ESPCN) algorithm [21] and information multi-distillation network (IMDN) [12] were also proposed to further improve the computational efficiency. A significant advance in the generation of visually pleasing results is the super-resolution generative adversarial network (SRGAN) [16]. A large number of SR methods have been presented, most of which are designed for natural images. Fewer methods have been designed for infrared images. GANs provide a powerful framework for generating plausible-looking natural images. However, they have problems with instability [11,25]. Wasserstein generative adversarial networks (WGAN) [1] was proposed as a solution to this problem. Given the issues that there are few infrared image features and that super-resolution reconstruction is difficult, the building units of the neural network and the loss functions that provide better constraints each play an important role in improving the performance of the GAN.

In this paper, we propose a novel approach for infrared image super-resolution. We revisited the key components of SRGAN and improved the model in two ways. First, we improved the network structure by introducing the heterogeneous kernel-based residual block, which has fewer parameters than previous algorithms, and it is easier to train. HetConv enables multiscale extraction of image features by combining convolutional kernels of different sizes. Second, we developed an improved loss function: the gradient cosine similarity loss function. The traditional loss function does not consider the characteristics of infrared images, and the gradient cosine similarity loss function takes the image gradient as an important feature for better-supervised training. The experimental datasets are publicly available [10], and the experimental effects can be validated.

The remainder of this paper is organized as follows. The related works are presented in Sect. 2. We describe the HetSRWGAN architecture and the gradient cosine similarity loss function in Sect. 3. A quantitative evaluation of new datasets, as well as visual illustrations, is provided in Sect. 4. The paper concludes with a conclusion in Sect. 5.

2   Related Works

2.1   Generative Adversarial Networks

Generative adversarial networks [7] were proposed by Goodfellow, based on game theory. In a pioneering work, C. Ledig et al. [16] used SRGAN to learn the mapping from LR to HR images in an end-to-end manner, achieving performance superior to that of previous work. A low-resolution image I^{LR} is input to a generator network to generate the reconstructed image I^{SR}, while a discriminator network takes the high-resolution images I^{HR} and I^{SR} as input to determine which is the real image and which is the reconstructed image.

2.2   HetConv: Heterogeneous Kernel-Based Convolutions

The heterogeneous kernel-based convolutions algorithm was proposed by Pravendra Singh [22]. Pravendra Singh et al. presented a novel deep learning architecture in which the convolution operation uses heterogeneous kernels. Compared to standard convolution operations, the proposed HetConv reduces the number of calculations (FLOPs) and parameters while still maintaining the presentation efficiency. HetConv is especially different from the depthwise convolutional filter used to perform depthwise convolution (DWC) [3], the pointwise convolutional filter used to perform pointwise convolution (PWC) [24] and the groupwise convolutional filter used to perform groupwise convolution (GWC) [15]. In HetConv, a variable P is used to control how much of the normal convolution kernel is retained in the operation. In addition, the total reduction is R for $K \times K$ kernels. The number of calculations of HetConv is compared with that of the normal convolution, as shown in Eq. 1.

$$R_{HetConv} = \frac{1}{P} + \frac{(1 - 1/P)}{K^2} \tag{1}$$

According to the characteristics of the heterogeneous kernel-based convolutions, we used a skip connection when designing the generator network structure. The HetSRWGAN structure is shown in Fig. 1.

3   HetSRWGAN

3.1   HetSRWGAN Architecture

Our main goal was to improve the overall visual performance of SR. In this section, we describe our improved network architecture. The main difference between the GAN and WGAN [1] is that the sigmoid function and batch normalization (BN) [13] layer of the discriminator network are removed. The entire

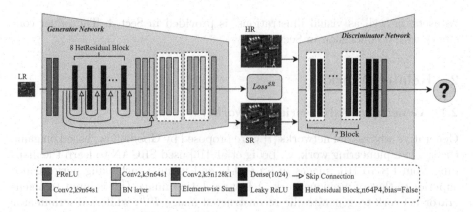

Fig. 1. Architecture of heterogeneous kernel-based super-resolution Wasserstein GAN with the corresponding kernel size (k), number of feature maps (n), stride (s) for each convolutional layer, padding (p) and number of the normal convolution kernel (P) (Best viewed in color). (Color figure online)

neural network is stabilized by gradient punishment [1]. It has been shown that removing the BN layer improves performance and reduces complexity [18,25]. Further, the removal of the BN layer contributes to improving the robustness of the network and reduces the computational complexity and memory consumption. We replaced the original basic block with a heterogeneous kernel-based residual block (HetResidual block), which includes HetConv, as depicted in Sect. 3.2. The HetResidual block is the basic network building unit. This block requires fewer parameters than the original basic block, improves network performance, and reduces computational complexity. More parameters may lead to a higher probability of mode collapse [11,25], so reducing the total number of parameters is beneficial. For the discriminator network, we deepened the network structure and experimentally demonstrated that this modification improves image quality. The detailed experimental results are given in Sect. 4. According to the characteristics of the heterogeneous kernel-based convolutions, we used a skip connection when designing the generator network structure.

3.2   Heterogeneous Kernel-Based Residual Block

Kaiming He et al. [9] first proposed the residual block structure and solved some of the problems caused by deep neural networks by introducing a skip connection and combination. The heterogeneous kernel-based residual block is shown in detail in Fig. 2. The relevant formula is analyzed as follows:

$$\mathbf{y}_i = h(\mathbf{x}_i) + \mathcal{F}(\mathbf{x}_i, \mathcal{W}_i) \tag{2}$$

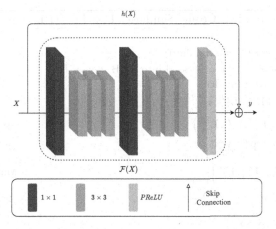

Fig. 2. Architecture of heterogeneous kernel-based residual block.

$$\mathbf{x}_{i+1} = \mathcal{F}(\mathbf{x}_i, \mathcal{W}_i) + h(\mathbf{x}_i) \tag{3}$$

where $\mathcal{F}$ stands for the heterogeneous kernel-based residual block processing. Since $h(\mathbf{x}_l)$ is an identity map, Eq. 3 can be derived:

$$\mathbf{x}_{i+1} = \mathcal{F}(\mathbf{x}_i, \mathcal{W}_i) + \mathbf{x}_i \tag{4}$$

3.3   Gradient Cosine Similarity Loss Function

To make the reconstructed image I^{SR} obtained from the generator network closer to the high-resolution image I^{HR}, it is necessary to provide a neural network loss function with effective constraints. We chose the spatial gradient of the image as the feature that measures the similarity between two images. When there is an edge in the image, there must be a high gradient value. Conversely, when there is a relatively smooth region in an image, the gray value changes little, and the corresponding gradient is also small. Using the gradient as a feature not only captures contours, images, and some texture information but also further weakens the effects of lighting. The gradient of an image at a pixel point (x, y) is a vector with direction and size. G_x is the gradient of I in direction X, and G_y is the gradient of I in direction Y direction. The gradient vector v can be expressed as Eq. 5.

$$v = [G_x, G_y]^T \tag{5}$$

The infrared images in the dataset are RGB images, which are three-channel images [2]. The gradient between the high-resolution three-channel image I^{HR} and the super-resolution reconstructed three-channel image I^{SR} can be expressed as Eqs. 6 and 7.

$$\mathbf{I}_G^{HR} = \left(\mathbf{I}_{G_r}^{HR}, \mathbf{I}_{G_g}^{HR}, \mathbf{I}_{G_b}^{HR} \right) \tag{6}$$

Algorithm 1. Gradient Cosine Similarity Loss Function

Input: I^{SR}, I^{HR}

Output: Gradient Cosine Similarity

1: Infrared images can be processed into RGB images [2].

2: **while** not convergent **do**

3: $\quad I^{HR} \longrightarrow \left(\mathbf{I}_{G_r}^{HR}, \mathbf{I}_{G_g}^{HR}, \mathbf{I}_{G_b}^{HR}\right)$

4: $\quad I^{SR} \longrightarrow \left(\mathbf{I}_{G_r}^{SR}, \mathbf{I}_{G_g}^{SR}, \mathbf{I}_{G_b}^{SR}\right)$ $\qquad\qquad\qquad$ ▷ Gradient matrix.

5: $\quad \mathbf{X}' = \left[\mathbf{I}_{G_r}^{HR}, \mathbf{I}_{G_g}^{HR}, \mathbf{I}_{G_b}^{HR}\right]_{1 \times m}$

6: $\quad \mathbf{Y}' = \left[\mathbf{I}_{G_r}^{SR}, \mathbf{I}_{G_g}^{SR}, \mathbf{I}_{G_b}^{SR}\right]_{1 \times m}$ $\qquad\qquad\qquad$ ▷ Matrix compression.

7: $\quad F_{\cos}\left(\mathbf{X}', \mathbf{Y}'\right) = \frac{\mathbf{X}' \cdot \mathbf{Y}'^{\mathrm{T}}}{\|\mathbf{X}'\| \cdot \|\mathbf{Y}'\|}$ $\qquad\qquad\qquad$ ▷ Cosine similarity.

8: **return** $F_{\cos}\left(\mathbf{X}', \mathbf{Y}'\right)$

$$\mathbf{I}_G^{SR} = \left(\mathbf{I}_{G_r}^{HR}, \mathbf{I}_{G_g}^{HR}, \mathbf{I}_{G_b}^{HR}\right) \tag{7}$$

$\mathbf{I}_G^{HR}$ indicates the gradient vector of the high-resolution image. The subscript of G_g indicates the *green* channel of the high-resolution image. Other subscripts indicate different image channels of *red* and *blue*. For super-resolution reconstructed images I^{SR}, the subscript indicates the same. We use the cosine similarity to measure the similarity between these two vectors, as shown in Eq. 8.

$$\cos_{sim}(\mathbf{X}, \mathbf{Y}) = \frac{\mathbf{X} \cdot \mathbf{Y}}{\|\mathbf{X}\| \cdot \|\mathbf{Y}\|} \tag{8}$$

$\mathbf{X}$ and $\mathbf{Y}$ represent two matrices that can be multiplied by points. The high-resolution image gradient $\mathbf{I}_G^{HR}$ and the SR image gradient $\mathbf{I}_G^{SR}$ can be calculated according to Algorithm 1.

We calculate the cosine similarity by stretching the two matrices into a one-dimensional vector. Likewise, the similarity between the high-resolution image gradient $\mathbf{I}_G^{HR}$ and the SR image gradient $\mathbf{I}_G^{SR}$ can be calculated according to Algorithm 1. The generator loss function of the SRGAN and WGAN includes content loss and adversarial loss. The generator loss function of HetSRWGAN is shown in Eq. 9:

$$\mathrm{Loss}^{SR} = l_X^{SR} + \lambda l_{Gen}^{SR} + \mu \left(1 - F_{cos}\right) \tag{9}$$

where l_X^{SR} and l_{Gen}^{SR} represent the content loss and adversarial loss, respectively.

Table 1. Quantitative evaluation of SR algorithms: Average PSNR/SSIM for scale factors ×4. SRGAN[1] has model collaps.

Algorithm	Params ↓	FLOPs ↓	PSNR/dB ↑		SSIM ↑	
			fusionA-22	fusionC-22	fusionA-22	fusionC-22
HetSRWGAN(Ours)	0.496M	0.095G	30.302	31.987	0.858	0.883
SRMD [27]	1.552M	0.063G	33.210	33.850	0.834	0.852
IMDN [12]	0.893M	91.70G	29.725	30.057	0.735	0.751
DPSR [26]	2.995M	0.052G	32.692	31.662	0.825	0.810
DBPN [8]	10.41M	0.106G	17.438	17.934	0.816	0.842
SRWGAN	0.956M	0.132G	28.319	28.520	0.799	0.805
SRGAN[1] [16]	0.956M	0.132G	5.150	30.444	0.278	0.871
SRCNN [5]	0.148M	0.182M	29.437	30.170	0.754	0.789
FSRCNN [6]	0.013M	0.077M	30.624	31.094	0.797	0.822
ESPCN [21]	0.061M	0.001G	30.814	31.607	0.789	0.819

4   Experiments and Evaluations

4.1   Training Details

Following SRGAN, all experiments were performed with a scaling factor of (4, applied to the 2×2 image) between LR and HR images. We used the PSNR and structural similarity index (SSIM) to evaluate the reconstructed images. Super-resolved images were generated using the reference methods, including SRMD, IMDN, DPSR, DBPN, SRCNN, FSRCNN, ESPCN, SRGAN, and super-resolution Wasserstein GAN (SRWGAN). The generator was trained using the loss function presented in Eq. 9 with $\lambda = 0.001$ and $\mu = 0.001$. The learning rate was set to 0.0001. We observed that a larger batch size benefits training a deeper network. We set the batch size to 64. For optimization, we used Adam [14] with $\beta_1 = 0.9$ in the generator. For the WGAN, we used the Asynchronous SGD (ASGD) [19] in the discriminator. We implemented our models with the PyTorch framework and trained them using NVIDIA TITAN X (Pascal) GPUs.

For training, we primarily used the CVC-09: FIR Sequence Pedestrian Dataset [23]. In CVC-09, a sequence is composed of two sets of images, the day and night sets, a designation which refers to the time of day at which they were acquired. The first set contains 5990 frames, the second set contains 5081 frames, and each sequence was divided into training and testing sets. We performed experiments on two datasets, namely, fusionA-22 and fusionC-22, which contain images obtained by fusing infrared and visible light, using the methods of literature [17] and literature [28], respectively [10]. An image after the fusion of IR and visible light images will have better visual quality, and it will be easier to distinguish details such as characters in the image. The fused image also maintains significant information from the infrared image but makes the performance of the algorithm more easily visualized.

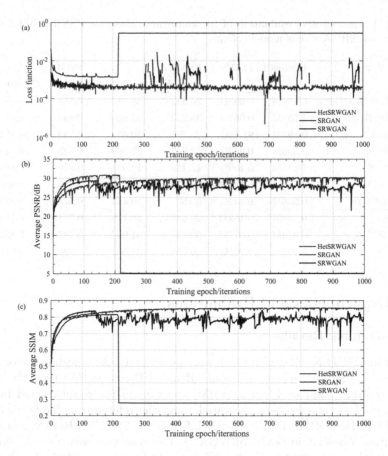

Fig. 3. (a): Changes of loss function with the number of iterations on the dataset CVC-09-1K (b): CVC-09-1K Dataset Training Average PSNR, (c): CVC-09-1K Dataset Training Average SSIM

4.2   Performance of the Final Networks

We compared the performance of three different super-resolution reconstruction algorithms based on generative adversarial networks. Since the GAN cannot simply use the loss function to judge the network training situation, we selected the image after the end of each batch of training to calculate the PSNR and SSIM values. When there are too many model parameters, mode collapse will occur. As the number of iterations increased, SRWGAN was more robust. SRGAN experiences mode collapse. Although the SRWGAN introduces gradient punishment to solve the problem that the network cannot be trained in the later stages, using cross-entropy as a loss function requires considerable time to adjust parameters and still cannot guarantee the stability of the model. Therefore, the loss function will have a negative value, which will cause the curve to be discontinuous. There

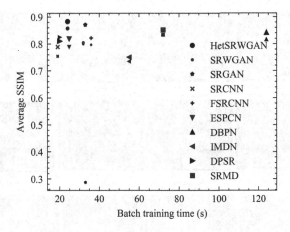

Fig. 4. Time efficiency comparison of all reconstruction methods. The same colour means the same method. The horizontal axis represents the time required for one training session, and the vertical axis represents an objective indicator after the model converges.

was no situation where convergence or instability was not possible. The results are shown in Fig. 3.

The total number of parameters for HetSRWGAN was reduced by 496657 compared to that for SRGAN, a reduction of 52% (Table 1). The significantly reduced total number of parameters helps to reduce the computational complexity of the model and improve robustness.

The SRMD model obtains better performance based on the PSNR; however, it has a large number of parameters, resulting in long training and inference times and greater memory consumption (Table 1, Fig. 4). The objective evaluation indices of the average PSNR and average SSIM were calculated. DNNs have a good effect in reconstructing visible images, but because of the features of single-frame infrared images with few features and high redundancy, the reconstruction effect is not good (Table 1).

SRGAN does not provide control of the generation process, and there is mode collapse (see Fig. 1). The new loss function and HetResidual block make the models faster to train and converge. The HetSRWGAN takes 24 s to train each batch, and the average SSIM is 0.858 and 0.883 (see Table 1). Compared with other methods, HetSRWGAN has the best time efficiency and average SSIM. Figure 5 shows the reconstructions produced by different algorithms.

Figure 5 shows that our proposed HetSRWGAN outperformed previous approaches in both sharpness and amount of detail. Previous GAN-based methods sometimes introduce artifacts. For example, SRGAN adds noise to the entire image. HetSRWGAN removes these artifacts and produces natural results.

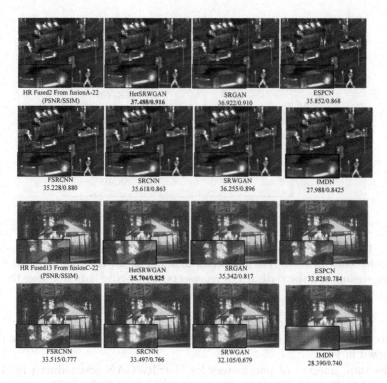

Fig. 5. Super-resolution image reconstruction effect comparison schematic diagram. From left to right: original HR image, HetSRWGAN, SRGAN, ESPCN, FSRCNN, SRCNN, SRWGAN, IMDN, Corresponding PSNR and SSIM are shown below the figure. Red indicates the best. [×4 upscaling] (Color figure online)

5   Conclusions

Our proposed HetSRWGAN method can be well used for infrared image super-resolution reconstruction. We proposed a novel architecture composed of several heterogeneous kernel-based residual blocks without BN layers. A gradient cosine similarity loss function was developed, which can provide stronger supervision of image details, such as edges, and the reconstructed high-resolution images contain more details and realistic textures.

Acknowledgement. This research supported by the Nature Science Foundation of China grants No. 61876049, and No. 61762066.

References

1. Arjovsky, M., Chintala, S., Bottou, L.: Wasserstein GAN. arXiv:1701.07875 [cs, stat], January 2017
2. Bradski, G., Kaehler, A.: Learning OpenCV: Computer Vision with the OpenCV Library. O'Reilly Media Inc., Sebastopol (2008)

3. Chollet, F.: Xception: deep learning with depthwise separable convolutions. In: Proceedings of the IEEE Conference on Computer Vision and Pattern Recognition, pp. 1251–1258 (2017)
4. Dong, C., Loy, C.C., He, K., Tang, X.: Image super-resolution using deep convolutional networks. IEEE Trans. Pattern Anal. Mach. Intell. **38**(2), 295–307 (2016). https://doi.org/10.1109/TPAMI.2015.2439281
5. Dong, C., et al.: Image super-resolution using deep convolutional networks. IEEE Trans. Pattern Anal. Mach. Intell. **38**(2), 295–307 (2015)
6. Dong, C., Loy, C.C., Tang, X.: Accelerating the super-resolution convolutional neural network. In: Leibe, B., Matas, J., Sebe, N., Welling, M. (eds.) ECCV 2016. LNCS, vol. 9906, pp. 391–407. Springer, Cham (2016). https://doi.org/10.1007/978-3-319-46475-6_25
7. Goodfellow, I.J., et al.: Generative Adversarial Networks. arXiv:1406.2661 [cs, stat], June 2014
8. Haris, M., et al.: Deep back-projection networks for super-resolution. In: Proceedings of the IEEE Conference on CVPR, pp. 1664–1673 (2018)
9. He, K., Zhang, X., Ren, S., Sun, J.: Identity Mappings in Deep Residual Networks. arXiv:1603.05027 [cs], March 2016
10. Huang, Y.: Hetsrwgan-dataset, September 2019. https://figshare.com/articles/dataset/HetSRWGAN-dataset/9862184/2
11. Huang, Y., Jiang, Z., Lan, R., Zhang, S., Pi, K.: Infrared image super-resolution via transfer learning and PSRGAN. IEEE Signal Process. Lett. **28**, 982–986 (2021)
12. Hui, Z., et al.: Lightweight image super-resolution with information multi-distillation network. In: Proceedings of the 27th ACM MM, pp. 2024–2032 (2019)
13. Ioffe, S., Szegedy, C.: Batch Normalization: Accelerating Deep Network Training by Reducing Internal Covariate Shift. arXiv:1502.03167 [cs], February 2015
14. Kingma, D.P., Ba, J.: Adam: A Method for Stochastic Optimization. arXiv:1412.6980 [cs], December 2014
15. Krizhevsky, A., Sutskever, I., Hinton, G.E.: ImageNet classification with deep convolutional neural networks. In: Pereira, F., Burges, C.J.C., Bottou, L., Weinberger, K.Q. (eds.) Advances in Neural Information Processing Systems 25, pp. 1097–1105. Curran Associates, Inc. (2012)
16. Ledig, C., et al.: Photo-realistic single image super-resolution using a generative adversarial network. In: Proceedings of the IEEE Conference on CVPR, pp. 4681–4690 (2017)
17. Liu, Y., Chen, X., Cheng, J., Peng, H., Wang, Z.: Infrared and visible image fusion with convolutional neural networks. Int. J. Wavelets Multiresolut. Inf. Process. **16**(03), 1850018 (2017)
18. Nah, S., et al.: Deep multi-scale convolutional neural network for dynamic scene deblurring. In: Proceedings of the IEEE Conference on CVPR, pp. 3883–3891 (2017)
19. Odena, A.: Faster Asynchronous SGD. arXiv:1601.04033 [cs, stat], January 2016
20. Radford, A., et al.: Unsupervised representation learning with deep convolutional generative adversarial networks. arXiv preprint arXiv:1511.06434 (2015)
21. Shi, W., et al.: Real-time single image and video super-resolution using an efficient sub-pixel convolutional neural network. In: Proceedings of the IEEE Conference on CVPR, pp. 1874–1883 (2016)
22. Singh, P., Verma, V.K., Rai, P., Namboodiri, V.P.: HetConv: Heterogeneous Kernel-Based Convolutions for Deep CNNs. arXiv:1903.04120 [cs], March 2019

23. Socarrás, Y., Ramos, S., Vázquez, D., López, A.M., Gevers, T.: Adapting pedestrian detection from synthetic to far infrared images. In: ICCV Workshops, vol. 3 (2013)
24. Szegedy, C., et al.: Going Deeper With Convolutions, pp. 1–9 (2015)
25. Wang, X., et al.: ESRGAN: enhanced super-resolution generative adversarial networks. In: Proceedings of the European Conference on Computer Vision (ECCV) Workshops (2018)
26. Zhang, K., Zuo, W., Zhang, L.: Deep plug-and-play super-resolution for arbitrary blur kernels. In: IEEE Conference on CVPR, pp. 1671–1681 (2019)
27. Zhang, K., et al.: Learning a single convolutional super-resolution network for multiple degradations. In: Proceedings of the IEEE Conference on CVPR, pp. 3262–3271 (2018)
28. Zhang, Y., Zhang, L., Bai, X., Zhang, L.: Infrared and visual image fusion through infrared feature extraction and visual information preservation. Infrared Phys. Technol. **83**, 227–237 (2017)

Knowledge Compensation Network with Divisible Feature Learning for Unsupervised Domain Adaptive Person Re-identification

Jiajing Hong, Yang Zhang, and Yuesheng Zhu$^{(\boxtimes)}$

Shenzhen Graduate School, Peking University, Shenzhen, China
{hjj1901213119,zhangyang310,zhuys}@pku.edu.cn

Abstract. Due to the large domain shift and the discriminative feature learning with unlabeled datasets, unsupervised domain adaptation (UDA) for person re-identification (re-ID) still remains a challenging task. Some current methods adopt a clustering-based strategy to assign pseudo labels to the unlabeled samples in target domains for classification. However, the rich knowledge of the model in different training stages is not fully utilized in those methods and the pseudo labels generated by clustering algorithms inevitably contain noise, which would limit the performance of re-ID models. To tackle this problem, a Knowledge Compensation Network with Divisible feature learning (KCND) is proposed in this paper, which aggregates the past-to-present knowledge of models from training samples for discriminative feature learning and resists the label noise produced by clustering. Also, a novel compensation-guided softened loss is developed to enhance the generalization and robustness of re-ID models. Our experimental results on large-scale datasets (Market-1501, DukeMTMC-reID and MSMT17) have demonstrated the performance of KCND is better than other methods in terms of the mAP and CMC accuracy.

Keywords: Person re-identification · Unsupervised domain adaptation · Knowledge Compensation Network · Divisible feature learning

1 Introduction

Person re-identification (re-ID) aims at matching the images of an individual from one camera with the images captured by other different cameras. Although supervised re-ID methods have achieved great results, they heavily rely on manual labeled data and would result in performance drops while applied to new domains. Unsupervised domain adaptation (UDA) transfers the learned knowledge from a labeled source dataset to an unlabeled target dataset, so it provides a cost-effective solution for cross-domain re-ID applications and becomes an attractive research topic. Due to the domain diversities between different datasets and the unknown person identities in the target domain, it is challengeable for solving the problem of cross-domain unsupervised person re-ID.

© Springer Nature Switzerland AG 2021
D. N. Pham et al. (Eds.): PRICAI 2021, LNAI 13032, pp. 473–486, 2021.
https://doi.org/10.1007/978-3-030-89363-7_36

Most of the existing UDA methods for person re-ID tasks focus on the feature distribution alignment [1, 2], image-style transformation based on GAN [3–5], and the clustering with fine-tuning methods [6–10]. They adopt a two-stage training approach, training the model in the labeled source domain to initialize parameters and then transferring the pre-trained model to the unlabeled target domain for retraining and fine-tuning. Pseudo labels are generated in the target domain by clustering methods to obtain a new labeled dataset, which is used for supervised retraining. However, the label noise generated by clustering and the feature variations caused by domain shift are not well processed in existing methods, limiting the performance of re-ID models.

To effectively overcome the problems mentioned above, in this paper a **K**nowledge **C**ompensation **N**etwork with **D**ivisible feature learning (KCND) is proposed for unsupervised domain adaptive person re-identification. The network aggregates the past-to-present knowledge of models from training samples to perform the cross-camera divisible features learning.

KCND mainly consists of three parts as follows.

(1) **Knowledge Compensation Network (KCN)**. KCN is constructed by a novel approach named Self-ensembling Knowledge Compensation Learning (SKCL). It preserves the weights information of multiple previous networks and combines the complementary knowledge between the models to the next stage. In KCN, soft pseudo labels are generated to alleviate the shortcomings of hard pseudo labels, so that to resist the label noise generated by clustering. As shown in Fig. 1, soft pseudo labels consist of the soft-decision elements which can provide discriminative information from reference samples during the training.

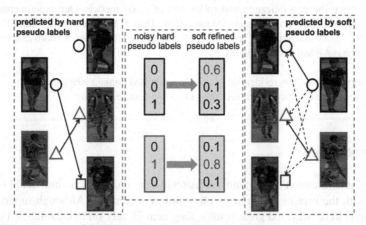

Fig. 1. The generations of the hard and soft pseudo labels. The images with the same color box belong to an identical person, and the left and right parts show the predictions of re-ID models by using the hard and soft pseudo labels respectively.

(2) **Divisible Feature Learning (DFL)**. To deal with the feature variations caused by domain shift and mine the potential similarities and discriminative features of unlabeled samples through KCN, we divide the extracted feature maps of all

samples in the target domain and group them into different parts. And we propose an outliers-aware clustering to assign pseudo labels to unlabeled target samples.

(3) **Compensation-guided Softened Loss (CSL)**. To better utilize the divisible discriminative features and perform the training with the soft and hard pseudo labels jointly, a compensation-guided softened loss is designed, which can enhance the discrimination capability of the proposed re-ID models.

The contributions of this paper are summarized as:

- A novel Knowledge Compensation Network with Divisible feature learning (KCND) is proposed for cross-domain person re-ID task. The past-to-present knowledge of models is creatively aggregated for divisible feature learning and the negative impact of the label noise is reduced simultaneously.
- A compensation-guided softened loss is designed for exploring the potential similarities and discriminative information of reference samples, reducing the feature variations caused by domain shift and enhancing the robustness and generalization of person re-ID models.
- The proposed method achieves the superior performance over other methods in terms of the mAP and CMC accuracy on Market1501, DukeMTMC-reID and MSMT17 datasets.

2 Related Work

There are three main categories of UDA methods for person re-ID, including the feature distribution alignment method, the image-style transformation method and the clustering with fine-tuning method.

2.1 Feature Distribution Alignment Methods

DMLI [1] dynamically aligned the local information between two domains with no extra supervision and then developed AlignedReID++ to improve the performance of global features. [2] developed a camera-aware domain adaptation method to reduce the distribution discrepancy and create discriminative information.

2.2 Image-Style Transformation Methods

PTGAN [12] and SPGAN [3] handled the domain gap problem by transforming the image style of source datasets to match that of target datasets while maintaining the original person identities. SBSGAN [4] addressed the background shift problem by generating images with suppressed backgrounds. But the retrieval performances of these methods based on GAN deeply relied on the image generation quality, and they did not explore the complex relations between different samples in the target domain.

2.3 Clustering with Fine-Tuning Methods

SSG [6] and CVSE [13] combined global-local features of samples and assigned pseudo labels to the unlabeled dataset by clustering algorithms for classification. But the pseudo labels generated by the clustering contain noise, which is not well processed in those methods. MMT [7] and NRMT [9] both adopted a dual-model mutual training strategy by supervising each other to resist the noise of pseudo labels. However, the difference between the two networks would gradually reduce during the training process, and the mutual supervision would be equal to the single network training. DCML [14] designed two metrics to explore credible training samples. However, the threshold adaptive with the credibility of samples is hard to define and DCML simply considered the central and dense samples are credible for training, resulting in the loss of information.

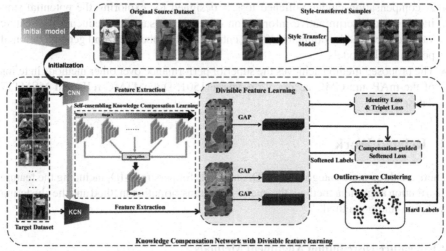

Fig. 2. An illustration of the proposed KCND. The learned style-transferred model is used to generate cross-camera samples and then initialize the CNN model. Different data streams can be distinguished by colors. As shown in the green dotted box, SKCL preserves the weights knowledge of multiple previous networks and aggregates them to the next stage. DFL is designed by dividing the feature maps of all samples and grouping them into different parts. The compensation-guided softened loss is developed to better utilize the soft pseudo labels and explore the discriminative information of reference samples.

3 Proposed Method

A novel Knowledge Compensation Network with Divisible feature learning (KCND) is proposed for unsupervised domain adaptive person re-ID. KCND is shown in Fig. 2. The complementary knowledge between the models is fully utilized to mine discriminative features and resist the label noise produced by clustering, improving the robustness and generalization of re-ID models. Also a compensation-guided softened loss is designed to provide effective guidance for our network. KCND adopts a two-stage training scheme, including the supervised learning in source domains and the unsupervised adaptation to target domains. The labeled source dataset is denoted as $D_s = \{X_s, Y_s\}$, which has N_s samples with P_s unique identities. X_s and Y_s denote the sample images and the identity labels. Each sample x_s in X_s is associated with an identity y_s in Y_s. The target dataset $D_t = \{X_t\}$ consists of N_t samples, and the identity label of each image x_t on the target dataset D_t is unknown.

3.1 Cross-Camera Data Augmentation (CDA)

In order to reduce the image style variations caused by different cameras, we treat each camera as a new domain with different styles to train cycleGAN [15] following [16]. In this manner, the training set is augmented to a combination of the original images and the style-transferred images. Since each style-transferred image preserves the content of its original image, the new sample is considered to be the same identity as the original image. This allows us to leverage the style-transferred images as well as their associated labels to pre-train the re-ID models. As shown in Fig. 3, assuming that training dataset contains K cameras, for images taken by any camera, we use the learned model to augment K-1 images, which have different camera styles but maintain the original identity information.

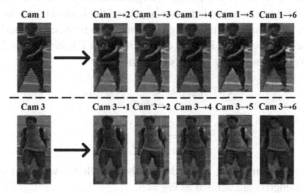

Fig. 3. Examples of style-transferred images in Market-1501.

3.2 Supervised Learning in the Source Domain

In the source domain, a deep neural network model M parameterized by θ trained with cross-entropy loss and hard-batch triplet loss is regarded as the baseline in this paper. We adopt ResNet-50 [17] pre-trained on ImageNet [18] as our backbone. $f\left(x_s^i|\theta\right)$ denotes the feature representation of a sample x_s^i and $p_j\left(x_s^i|\theta\right)$ is the predicted probability of it belonging to the identity j. The cross entropy loss with label smoothing is:

$$L_{s,id}(\theta) = -\frac{1}{N_s}\sum_{i=1}^{N_s}\sum_{j=1}^{P_s} q_j \mathrm{log} p_j\left(x_s^i|\theta\right) \qquad (1)$$

where $q_j = 1 - \varepsilon + \frac{\varepsilon}{P_s}$ if $j = y_s^i$, otherwise $q_j = \frac{\varepsilon}{P_s}$. ε is set as 0.1 following [19]. The triplet loss is defined as

$$L_{s,tri}(\theta) = \frac{1}{N_s}\sum_{i=1}^{N_s}\left[m + \max\|f\left(x_s^i|\theta\right) - f\left(x_s^{i+}|\theta\right)\|_2 - \min\|f\left(x_s^i|\theta\right) - f\left(x_s^{i-}|\theta\right)\|_2\right] \tag{2}$$

where x_s^{i+} and x_s^{i-} are the hardest positive and negative samples of the anchor x_s^i. $\| \bullet \|_2$ denotes the L_2 distance. m is a margin parameter set to 0.5. The overall loss function in the source domain is calculated as

$$L_s(\theta) = L_{s,id}(\theta) + L_{s,tri}(\theta) \tag{3}$$

3.3 Knowledge Compensation Network in the Target Domain

As shown in Fig. 2, in order to build KCN, we propose a novel approach named Self-ensambling Knowledge Compensation Learning (SKCL), which extends the baseline model by taking into account the knowledge of multiple previous networks and exploring the temporal information of models from past to present.

In each training iteration, the images in target domain are fed to M parameterized by θ to predict the classification predictions $p(x_t^i|\theta)$ and the feature representations $f(x_t^i|\theta)$. KCN preserves the complementary weights information between the models to generate reliable soft pseudo labels. The KCN in current iteration T is denoted as $\mathcal{N}^{(T)}(\Theta_T)$ with parameters $\{\Theta_T\}$. The updating of KCN is defined as

$$\mathcal{N}^{(T)}(\Theta_T) \triangleq \sum_{i=0}^{T-1}\lambda_i\mathcal{N}^{(i)}(\Theta_i) \tag{4}$$

$$\Theta_T = \sum_{i=0}^{T-1}\lambda_i\Theta_i \tag{5}$$

where $\sum_{i=0}^{T-1}\lambda_i = 1$, and $\lambda_i \in [0, 1]$ denote the knowledge weights momentum. The initial KCN parameters are defined as $\Theta_0 = \theta$.

3.4 Divisible Feature Learning with Outliers-Aware Clustering

In order to mine the discriminative information from divisible features of KCN, we divide the feature maps of all samples on the target dataset and group them into three different parts: whole bodies, upper and lower parts following SSG [6]. We adopt DBSCAN [11] on each part to obtain a series of clusters. DBSCAN is a density-based clustering method, which assigns pseudo labels for samples in high-density area and regards samples in low-density area as outliers.

Most of the existing pseudo-label-based methods adopted DBSCAN for clustering but simply discarded the outliers from being used for training, limiting the performance of re-ID models. Such outliers might actually be difficult to identify but they contain valuable information. To overcome this problem, we propose an outliers-aware clustering

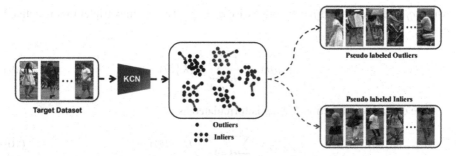

Fig. 4. Outliers-aware clustering.

to further improve DBSCAN. In our experiments, we assign pseudo labels for each outlier according to its nearest neighbor after clustering as shown in Fig. 4.

By assigning the pseudo labels $\tilde{y}_t = \{\tilde{y}_t^{whole}, \tilde{y}_t^{upper}, \tilde{y}_t^{lower}\}$ to each sample x_t in X_t, we can pair each person with different pseudo labels. As a result, we establish a new dataset with pseudo labels, which can be used for normally supervised training.

3.5 Compensation-Guided Softened Loss for Domain Adaptation

By using KCN, the probability for sample x_t^i is predicted as $p(x_t^i|\Theta_T)$, and the feature representation is $f(x_t^i|\Theta_T)$.

In order to provide effective guidance to KCND with the soft pseudo labels, a novel compensation-guided softened loss is designed as follows for optimizing $\{\theta, \Theta\}$:

$$L_{CSL}(\theta|\Theta) = \frac{1}{N_t} \sum_{i=1}^{N_t} \left[\mathcal{K}_t^i(\Theta_T) \log \mathcal{K}_t^i(\theta) + \left(1 - \mathcal{K}_t^i(\Theta_T)\right) \log(1 - \mathcal{K}_t^i(\theta)) \right]$$

$$- \frac{1}{N_t} \sum_{i=1}^{N_t} p\left(x_t^i|\Theta_T\right) \log p\left(x_t^i|\theta\right) \tag{6}$$

where $\mathcal{K}_t^i(\Theta_T)$ is the soft refined label generated by KCN and $\mathcal{K}_t^i(\theta)$ is as

$$\mathcal{K}_t^i(\theta) = \frac{\exp\left(\|f\left(x_t^i|\theta\right) - f\left(x_t^{i-}|\theta\right)\|\right)}{\exp\left(\|f\left(x_t^i|\theta\right) - f\left(x_t^{i+}|\theta\right)\|\right) + \exp\left(\|f\left(x_t^i|\theta\right) - f\left(x_t^{i-}|\theta\right)\|\right)} \tag{7}$$

3.6 Overall Loss and Algorithm

To learn the stable and discriminative knowledge, we joint hard and soft pseudo labels together to optimize our network. The identity loss in target domains is defined as cross entropy with label smoothing mentioned in Sec. III (B), as

$$L_{id}(\theta) = -\frac{1}{N_t} \sum_{i=1}^{N_t} \sum_{j=1}^{P_t} q_j \log p_j\left(x_t^i|\theta\right) \tag{8}$$

where $q_j = 1 - \varepsilon + \frac{\varepsilon}{P_t}$ if $j = \tilde{y}_t^i$, otherwise $q_j = \frac{\varepsilon}{P_t}$. The softmax triplet loss is defined as

$$L_{tri}(\theta) = \frac{1}{N_t} \sum_{i=1}^{N_t} log\mathcal{K}_t^i(\theta) \tag{9}$$

The overall loss function $L_{overall}$ is formulated as

$$L_{overall} = \sum_{k=0}^{split\_num} L^k(\theta|\Theta) \tag{10}$$

$$L^k(\theta|\Theta) = \alpha L_{id}^k(\theta) + \beta L_{tri}^k(\theta) + (1 - \beta)L_{CSL}^k(\theta|\Theta) \tag{11}$$

where α and β are the weighting parameters, *split_num* denotes the number of divided parts.

Algorithm 1 shows the detailed training procedure of the proposed KCND.

Algorithm 1 Knowledge Compensation Network with Divisible Feature Learning

---

Input: $D_s = \{X_s, Y_s\}$, $D_t = \{X_t\}$, $\alpha, \beta, \{\lambda_{T-1}, \lambda_{T-2}, \cdots, \lambda_1, \lambda_0\}$
Output: Fine-tuned model parameters $\{\theta\}$.
Procedure:
1. Initialize pre-trained weights $\{\theta\}$ by optimizing with Eq. 3 on D_s
2. **for each epoch do**
3.   Extract features by KCN on D_t: $f(x_t|\Theta_T)$
4.   Divide the feature maps of all samples on D_t and group them into three different parts
    $f_t = \{f_t^{whole}, f_t^{upper}, f_t^{lower}\}$
5.   Generate hard pseudo labels $\tilde{y}_t = \{\tilde{y}_t^{whole}, \tilde{y}_t^{upper}, \tilde{y}_t^{lower}\}$ of each sample x_t by clustering algorithms.
6.   **for each mini-batch** $\mathcal{B} \in D_t$ **do**
7.   Generate soft pseudo labels on stage T by predicting: $p(x_t^i|\Theta_T), p(x_t^i|\theta), \mathcal{K}_t^i(\Theta_T),$
        $\mathcal{K}_t^i(\theta)$
8.   Jointly update $\{\theta, \Theta\}$ by the gradient descent of the objective function Eq. 10
9.   Update KCN with parameters $\{\Theta_T\}$ following Eq. 4.
10.   **end for**
11. **end for**

---

4   Experiments and Analysis

4.1   Implementation Details

Our implementation is based on PyTorch platform. ADAM optimizer is used for optimizing with a weight decay 0.0005. For both of the source domain pre-training and the target domain fine-tuning, each mini-batch contains 64 person images of 16 identities. Input images are resized to 256×128. Random flipping, random cropping and random erasing are adopted as data augmentation during the training process.

Stage 1: Pre-training in the Source Domain. We pre-train a style-transferred model to generate cross-camera samples and then initialize the baseline on the source dataset as described in Sect. 3.1 and Sect. 3.2. The initial learning rate is 0.00035 and decreased to 1/10 of its previous value on the 40th and 70th epochs in total 80 epochs. Given the mini-batch of images, network parameters are updated by optimizing Eq. 3.

Stage 2: Adaptation with KCND in the Target Domain. For unsupervised domain adaptation in the target dataset, the learning rate is fixed to 0.00035 for overall 40 epochs. In each epoch, the number of training iteration is set to 400. We adopt DBSCAN [11] for clustering and eps is fixed to 0.6 when training with MSMT17 [12] dataset. The network is updated by optimizing Eq. 11 with $\alpha = 0.5$, $\beta = 0.5$.

4.2 Datasets and Evaluation Metrics

We evaluate KCND on three widely used person re-ID datasets: Market-1501 [20], DukeMTMC-reID [21] and MSMT17 [12]. Market-1501 consists of 32668 annotated images of 1501 identities. DukeMTMC-reID contains 16522 images of 702 identities for training, and the remaining images are for testing. MSMT17 is a large-scale dataset consisting of 126441 bounding boxes of 4101 identities.

Evaluation Metrics: In our experiment, the Cumulative Matching Characteristic (CMC) curve and the mean average precision (mAP) are used for performance evaluation. All results in this paper are under the single-query setting.

4.3 Ablation Experiments

We evaluate each component of our proposed KCND method by ablation experiments on Duke-to-Market (D $\rightarrow$ M) and Market-to-Duke (M $\rightarrow$ D). The results are shown in Table 1. "Base" denotes the baseline model introduced in Sect. 3.2.

Effectiveness of KCN. From Table 1, "Base + KCN (w/o L_{CSL})" outperforms "Base $(L_{id}$ & $L_{tri})$" on both datasets. Without KCN, the mAP drops from 64.1% to 58.2% on D $\rightarrow$ M and 54.8% to 49.6% on M $\rightarrow$ D. Experimental results shows that the KCN well utilizes the knowledge of models from training samples and generate reliable soft pseudo labels in the target domain simultaneously.

Effectiveness of CSL. We train the KCN with/without CSL respectively to validate the effectiveness of CSL. As shown in Table 1, without CSL, distinct drops of 9.4% in mAP and 7.4% in top-1 accuracy are observed for D $\rightarrow$ M and 8.5% in mAP and 7.6% in top-1 accuracy are observed for M $\rightarrow$ D. CSL effectively involves the soft refined pseudo labels for training and enhances the discrimination capability of re-ID models.

Effectiveness of DFL. As shown in Table 1, the mAP drops from 77.8% to 73.5% on D $\rightarrow$ M and 66.5% to 63.3% on M $\rightarrow$ D without DFL. It means DFL makes contributions to mining the potential similarities of unlabeled samples including inliers and outliers from global to local features, reducing the feature variations caused by domain shift.

Effectiveness of CDA. As shown in Table 1, the mAP drops from 79.6% to 77.8% on D → M and 67.7% to 66.5% on M → D without CDA. Therefore, our cross-camera data augmentation helps to increase the sample diversity to learn more discriminative features and reduces the impact of camera-variance.

Analysis of Loss Weights. α and β are hyper parameters which are used to trade off the effect between identity loss, triplet loss and temporal-guided softened loss. We evaluate the impact of α and β respectively, which are sampled from {0.3, 0.4, 0.5, 0.6, 0.7, 0.8}, on the task of D → M. The results are shown in Fig. 5 (a) and Fig. 5 (b). We observe the best result is obtained when α and β are both set to about 0.5. Note that large or small value of α and β would limit the improvement of performance.

Table 1. Ablation studies of our proposed KCND method on Duke-to-Market and Market-to-Duke tasks.

Methods	Duke → Market			
	mAP	top-1	mAP	top-10
Supervised model	81.3	93.0	97.5	98.5
Direct Transfer	28.4	56.1	72.8	79.5
Base (L_{id} & L_{tri})	58.2	81.4	90.6	93.0
Base + KCN (w/o L_{CSL})	64.1	82.6	92.3	94.8
Base + KCN (w L_{CSL})	73.5	90.0	96.3	97.7
Base + KCN + DFL	77.8	91.2	97.4	98.4
Base + KCN + DFL + CDA	79.6	92.7	97.5	98.4
Methods	Maket → Duke			
	mAP	top-1	top-5	top-10
Supervised model	70.4	84.9	91.6	93.9
Direct Transfer	26.7	42.5	58.2	64.4
Base (L_{id} & L_{tri})	49.6	67.8	81.2	85.0
Base + KCN(w/o L_{CSL})	54.8	69.2	82.7	86.5
Base + KCN (w L_{CSL})	63.3	76.8	87.4	91.7
Base + KCN + DFL	66.5	80.2	89.1	92.2
Base + KCN + DFL + CDA	67.7	81.3	89.8	92.8

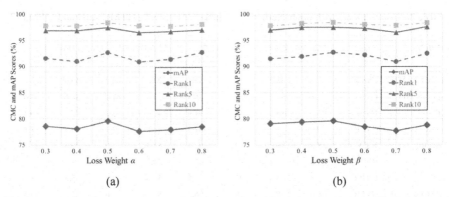

Fig. 5. Analysis of loss weights. (a) The impact of α while fixing β to 0.5. (b) The impact of β while fixing α to 0.5.

4.4 Comparison with the State-of-the-Art Methods

We compare KCND with state-of-the-art methods on four domain adaptation tasks: Duke-to-Market, Market-to-Duke, Duke-to-MSMT and Market-to-MSMT. Table 2 shows the results. We almost achieve fully supervised performances with no annotation and post-processing technique.

Feature Distribution Alignment Methods. Our KCND outperforms the feature alignment unsupervised re-ID models [22–24]. The reason lies in that our network effectively exploits the past-to-present knowledge of models for cross-camera divisible feature learning and performs the training with the soft and hard pseudo labels jointly, taking advantage of the soft pseudo labels to explore the discriminative information of reference samples across domains.

Image-Style Transformation Methods. Image-style transfer methods [3, 5, 25] based on GAN deeply relied on the images generation quality and did not explore the relations between different samples in target domain. Our network can achieve better performance than GAN-based methods, indicating its efficient use of unlabeled samples.

Clustering-Based Methods. These methods [6, 10, 24, 26] assign the pseudo labels to the unlabeled target datasets by clustering algorithms, but the pseudo labels inevitably contain the noise, which is not be well processed, and it will affect the final performance of re-ID models. The mutual supervision training strategy is used to reduce the negative impact of label noise in existing methods (MMT and NRMT). But actually, it quickly converges to a consensus which leads to a local minimum and it gradually becomes equal to single network training due to the bias reduction between two networks, limiting the improvement of performance. DCML simply considered the central and dense samples are credible for training, resulting in the loss of feature information. As shown in Table 2, KCND could achieve better results compared with those methods. Because KCND takes advantage of the complementary knowledge between the models of different training stages for divisible feature learning and the outliers-aware clustering used in KCND can

Table 2. Comparisons with other methods on Market-1501, DukeMTMC-reID and MSMT17.

Methods	Publication	DukeMTMC-reID → Market1501				Market1501 → DukeMTMC-reID			
		mAP	top-1	top-5	top-10	mAP	top-1	top-5	top-10
TJ-AIDL [25]	CVPR	26.5	58.2	74.8	81.1	23.0	44.3	59.6	65.0
SPGAN [3]	CVPR	22.8	51.5	70.1	76.8	22.3	41.1	56.6	63.0
ECN [22]	CVPR	43.0	75.1	87.6	91.6	40.4	63.3	75.8	80.4
MAR [23]	CVPR	40.0	67.7	81.9	87.3	48.0	67.1	79.8	84.2
SSG [6]	ICCV	58.3	80.0	90.0	92.4	53.4	73.0	80.6	83.2
PAST [24]	ICCV	54.6	78.4	–	–	54.3	72.4	–	–
pMR-SADA [8]	CVPR	59.8	83.0	91.8	94.1	55.8	74.5	85.3	88.7
AD-Cluster [5]	CVPR	68.3	86.7	94.4	96.5	54.1	72.6	82.5	85.5
NRMT [9]	ECCV	71.7	87.8	94.6	96.5	62.2	77.8	86.9	89.5
DG-Net++ [10]	ECCV	61.7	82.1	90.2	92.7	63.8	78.9	87.8	90.4
JVTC [26]	ECCV	61.1	83.8	93.0	95.2	56.2	75.0	85.1	88.2
MMT [7]	ICLR	71.2	87.7	94.9	96.9	63.1	76.8	88.0	92.2
DCML [14]	ECCV	72.3	88.2	94.9	96.4	63.5	79.3	86.7	89.5
KCND (Ours)		**79.6**	**92.7**	**97.5**	**98.4**	**67.7**	**81.3**	**89.8**	**92.8**
Methods	Publication	DukeMTMC-reID → MSMT17				Market1501 → MSMT17			
		mAP	top-1	top-5	top-10	mAP	top-1	top-5	top-10
ECN [22]	CVPR	10.2	30.2	41.5	46.8	8.5	25.3	36.3	42.1
SSG [6]	ICCV	13.3	32.2	–	51.2	13.2	31.6	–	49.6
MMT [7]	ICLR	23.3	50.1	63.9	69.8	22.9	49.2	63.1	68.8
DG-Net++ [10]	ECCV	22.1	48.8	60.9	65.9	22.1	48.4	60.9	66.1
NRMT [9]	ECCV	20.6	45.2	57.8	63.3	19.8	43.7	56.5	62.2
KCND (Ours)		**27.5**	**55.4**	**69.0**	**74.3**	**25.3**	**51.6**	**64.3**	**69.7**

efficiently include the valuable information of outliers, demonstrating the effectiveness of our proposed network.

5   Conclusion

In this paper, a Knowledge Compensation Network with Divisible feature learning (KCND) is proposed to tackle the problem that the noise of pseudo labels generated by clustering limits the performance of re-ID models. In KCND the past-to-present knowledge of models is aggregated for cross-camera discriminative feature learning and the soft pseudo labels is generated to resist the label noise. Also, a novel compensation-guided softened loss is developed to enhance the generalization and robustness of re-ID models. The experimental results have demonstrated the effectiveness of the proposed method and show that KCND can achieve higher mAP and CMC accuracy than other methods.

References

1. Luo, H., Jiang, W., Zhang, X., Fan, X., Qian, J., Zhang, C.: AlignedReID++: dynamically matching local information for person re-identification. Pattern Recogn. **94**, 53–61 (2019)
2. Qi, L., Wang, L., Huo, J., Zhou, L., Shi, Y., Gao, Y.: A novel unsupervised camera-aware domain adaptation framework for person re-identification. In: ICCV (2019)
3. Deng, W., Zheng, L., Ye, Q., Kang, G., Yang, Y., Jiao, J.: Image-image domain adaptation with preserved self-similarity and domain-dissimilarity for person re-identification. In: CVPR (2018)
4. Huang, Y., Wu, Q., Xu, J., Zhong, Y.: SBSGAN: suppression of inter-domain background shift for person re-identification. In: ICCV (2019)
5. Zhai, Y., et al.: Ad-cluster: augmented discriminative clustering for domain adaptive person re-identification. In: CVPR (2020)
6. Fu, Y., Wei, Y., Wang, G., Zhou, Y., Shi, H., Huang, T.: Self-similarity grouping: a simple unsupervised cross domain adaptation approach for person re-identification. In: ICCV (2019)
7. Ge, Y., Chen, D., Li, H.: Mutual mean-teaching: pseudo label refinery for unsupervised domain adaptation on person re-identification. In: ICLR (2020)
8. Wang, G., Lai, J., Liang, W., Wang, G.: Smoothing adversarial domain attack and P-memory reconsolidation for cross-domain person re-identification. In: CVPR (2020)
9. Zhao, F., Liao, S., Xie, G.-S., Zhao, J., Zhang, K., Shao, L.: Unsupervised domain adaptation with noise resistible mutual-training for person re-identification. In: Vedaldi, A., Bischof, H., Brox, T., Frahm, J.-M. (eds.) ECCV 2020. LNCS, vol. 12356, pp. 526–544. Springer, Cham (2020). https://doi.org/10.1007/978-3-030-58621-8_31
10. Zou, Y., Yang, X., Yu, Z., Kumar, B.V.K.V., Kautz, J.: Joint disentangling and adaptation for cross-domain person re-identification. In: Vedaldi, A., Bischof, H., Brox, T., Frahm, J.-M. (eds.) ECCV 2020. LNCS, vol. 12347, pp. 87–104. Springer, Cham (2020). https://doi.org/10.1007/978-3-030-58536-5_6
11. Ester, M., Kriegel, H., Sander, J., Xu, X.: A density-based algorithm for discovering clusters in large spatial databases with noise. In: KDD (1996)
12. Wei, L., Zhang, S., Gao, W., Tian, Q.: Person transfer GAN to bridge domain gap for person re-identification. In: CVPR (2018)
13. Zhou, S., Wang, Y., Zhang, F., Wu, J.: Cross-view similarity exploration for unsupervised cross-domain person re-identification. Neural Comput. Appl. **33**(9), 4001–4011 (2021). https://doi.org/10.1007/s00521-020-05566-3
14. Chen, G., Lu, Y., Lu, J., Zhou, J.: Deep credible metric learning for unsupervised domain adaptation person re-identification. In: Vedaldi, A., Bischof, H., Brox, T., Frahm, J.-M. (eds.) ECCV 2020. LNCS, vol. 12353, pp. 643–659. Springer, Cham (2020). https://doi.org/10.1007/978-3-030-58598-3_38
15. Zhu, J.-Y., Park, T., Isola, P., Efros, A.A.: Unpaired image-to-image translation using cycle-consistent adversarial networks. In: ICCV (2017)
16. Zhong, Z., Zheng, L., Zheng, Z., Li, S., Yang, Y.: Camera style adaptation for person re-identification. In: CVPR (2018)
17. He, K., Zhang, X., Ren, S., Sun, J.: Deep residual learning for image recognition. In: CVPR (2016)
18. Deng, J., Dong, W., Socher, R., Li, L., Li, K., Fei-Fei, L.: Imagenet: a large-scale hierarchical image database. In: CVPR (2009)
19. Szegedy, C., Vanhoucke, V., Ioffe, S., Shlens, J., Wojna, Z.: Rethinking the inception architecture for computer vision. In: CVPR (2016)
20. Zheng, L., Shen, L., Tian, L., Wang, S., Wang, J., Tian, Q.: Scalable person re-identification: a benchmark. In: ICCV (2015)

21. Ristani, E., Solera, F., Zou, R., Cucchiara, R., Tomasi, C.: Performance measures and a data set for multi-target, multi-camera tracking. In: Hua, G., Jégou, H. (eds.) ECCV 2016. LNCS, vol. 9914, pp. 17–35. Springer, Cham (2016). https://doi.org/10.1007/978-3-319-48881-3_2
22. Zhong, Z., Zheng, L., Luo, Z., Li, S., Yang, Y.: Invariance matters: Exemplar memory for domain adaptive person re-identification. In: CVPR (2019)
23. Yu, H., Zheng, W., Wu, A., Guo, X., Gong, S., Lai, J.: Unsupervised person re-identification by soft multilabel learning. In: CVPR (2019)
24. Zhang, X., Cao, J., Shen, C., You, M.: Self-training with progressive augmentation for unsupervised cross-domain person re-identification. In: ICCV (2019)
25. Wang, J., Zhu, X., Gong, S., Li, W.: Transferable joint attribute-identity deep learning for unsupervised person re-identification. In: CVPR (2018)
26. Li, J., Zhang, S.: Joint visual and temporal consistency for unsupervised domain adaptive person re-identification. In: Vedaldi, A., Bischof, H., Brox, T., Frahm, J.-M. (eds.) ECCV 2020. LNCS, vol. 12369, pp. 483–499. Springer, Cham (2020). https://doi.org/10.1007/978-3-030-58586-0_29

LoCo-VAE: Modeling Short-Term Preference as Joint Effect of Long-Term Preference and Context-Aware Impact in Recommendation

Jianping Liu[1,2], Bo Wang[1,2(✉)], Ruifang He[1,2], Bin Wu[3], Shuo Zhang[3], Yuexian Hou[1], and Qinxue Jiang[4]

[1] College of Intelligence and Computing, Tianjin University, Tianjin, China
{jianping,bo_wang,rfhe,yxhou}@tju.edu.cn
[2] State Key Laboratory of Communication Content Cognition, People's Daily Online, Beijing, China
[3] Quesoar Co. Ltd., Tianjin, China
{wubin,s}@quesoar.com
[4] School of Engineering, Newcastle University, Newcastle, UK
b9064217@Newcastle.ac.uk

Abstract. User preference modeling is an essential task for online recommender systems. Recently, methods have been applied to model short-term user preferences within a short-term period. These approaches use recent user behavior as the context to determine the current short-term preferences. However, we argue that short-term user preferences are related to more complex contexts, e.g., the seasons or the time of the day. Furthermore, we make the hypothesis that short-term preferences of a user is actually a joint effect of his/her stable long-term preferences and the context-aware impact. Therefore, we propose LoCo-VAE, a unified model of this joint effect with Variational Auto-Encoder (VAE) based strategies. First, we utilize a Multilayer Perceptron(MLP) to capture long-term user preferences. Second, we improve the traditional VAE by distributing user interactions with respect to different contexts to introduce the context-aware impact. Finally, the long-term preferences and context-aware impact are combined with a joint generative training process to generate the embedding of short-term user preferences. Experiments on real-world datasets of Amazon consumption and music selection demonstrate the superiority of our model compare with state-of-the-art methods in recommendation system.

Keywords: Recommender system · Short-term preference · Long-term preference · Context-aware impact · Variational autoencoder

This work was supported by a grant from the National Key Research and Development Program of China(2018YFC0809804), State Key Laboratory of Communication Content Cognition(Grant No.A32003), the Artificial Intelligence for Sustainable Development Goals(AI4SDGs) Research Program, National Natural Science Foundation of China(U1736103, 61976154, 61402323, 61876128), the National Key Research and Development Program(2017YFE0111900).

© Springer Nature Switzerland AG 2021
D. N. Pham et al. (Eds.): PRICAI 2021, LNAI 13032, pp. 487–500, 2021.
https://doi.org/10.1007/978-3-030-89363-7_37

1   Introduction

The recommendation systems are gaining more and more attention and have been broadly utilized in a variety of areas such as online shopping and music. Recommendation systems can provide a personalized user experience by filtering out irrelevant information and selecting a subset of items to maximize the users' satisfaction. Therefore, accurately modeling user preferences is essential to the recommendation systems. Two modeling methods of user preferences are most popular nowadays: static modeling and dynamic modeling. Static modeling aims to learn users' long-term preferences which are presumed to be static or change slightly. Collaborative Filtering (CF) [1] is a classical recommendation technique that is often applied to model static user preferences. CF captures user preferences by finding the latent spaces to encode the user-item interaction matrix which can predict users' preferences. Deep learning models further improve the idea of collaborative filtering, e.g., Variational Autoencoders (VAEs), and have led to substantial progress in the past years, mainly due to their superior ability to capture non-linear user-item relationships [9,13,17]. Instead of modeling users' static preferences with the aforementioned models, temporal-based recommendation focuses on modeling users' dynamic short-term preferences. Recurrent Neural Networks (RNN) and its variants [2,14,27] are popular approaches in temporal-based recommendation models which to capture the temporal evolution of users' preferences over time.

Current temporal-based models, as the mainstream of modeling users' short-term preferences, pay more attention to the transfer between items among a sequence of interactions. However, there are still other factors determining users' short-term interests. Besides the sequential influence of previous items, it has been proved that the relevance of user behavior is highly contextual and short-term preferences depend, such as, on the time of the day or emotion [21], e.g., in the field of music consumption.

At the very beginning of our investigation, we also explored Beauty, a subcategory of the Amazon dataset[1], and defined context as season. We find clear evidence that, for all users, short-term interactions sharing the same context (e.g., transaction happening in Summer) are more similar to each other than interactions from a different context. On the other hand, for a given user, his/her long-term preference is relatively stable, e.g., prefer to specific brand or type. As a result of these two facts, to ensure high user satisfaction, the short-term preference of each user is actually a joint effect of his/her long-term preference and specific context, which is the main hypothesis of this work. Although there have been some attempts at context awareness, they either see context as supplementary to sequence recommendation [4,14] or put it in a factorization machine that requires multiple contextual information [3,26], without emphasizing the combining of long-term preferences and contexts.

Motivated by these observations and subsequent hypotheses, we strive to model the users' short-term preferences with a joint embedding strategy. The

---

[1] http://snap.stanford.edu/data/amazon/.

strategy proposes to represent users' short-term preferences by combing personalized long-term preferences and contextual information. We focus on two key problems: long-term preferences modeling and context-aware short-term preferences modeling. Long-term preferences modeling focuses on the specific and stable preferences of each user. Context-aware short-term preferences modeling focuses on integrating the long-term preferences and specific context information. The general idea is that users' short-term preferences are the results of fluctuations caused by context on the basis of their stable (long-term) preferences. For example, a user who likes Taylor Swift may listen to her different styles of songs at different time of the day or in different moods.

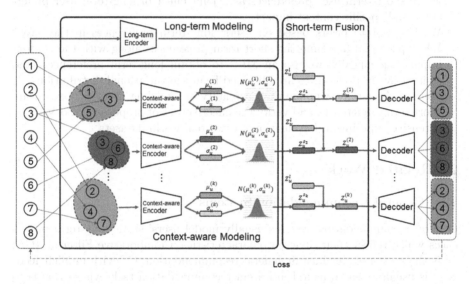

Fig. 1. The overview of our framework. The upper parts correspond to the long-term preferences encoder and the bottom parts correspond to the context-aware impact encoder. The representations of long-term preferences and context-aware impact are combined to get short-term preferences $z_u^{(k)}$. Circles marked with numbers represent items, which is the input of the encoder. Items are divided into k categories marked with different colors according to the context-aware impact of interaction with the user.

To this end, in this work, we propose a novel recommendation model based on VAE [10] for better context-aware modeling of users' short-term preferences, which is motivated by Zhao [17] who improved VAE for capturing the preference of a user regarding the different concepts. We name our model *LoCo-VAE*, which is short for Long-term and Context-aware preference incorporated VAE model for recommendation system. In LoCo-VAE, the long-term preference of a specific user is achieved from his/her behavior records in all contexts and short-term preference is achieved by separately learning the preference of this user from each context. In detail, the prior distribution of all contexts is set as a Gaussian distribution whose mean is the user's long-term preference, rather than a user-agnostic standard Gaussian prior. Through variational analysis, we model users' short-term preferences with context-aware preferences as the posterior distribution and separate long-term preferences from relative entropy penalties, which allows the long-term and context-aware impact to learn simultaneously. This modeling choice leads to representations in an accurate latent space encoding both users' long-term as well as contextual preferences. As users' preferences tend to be dynamic according to the context, harnessing the above information is promising to improve recommendation performance. Our main contributions are summarized as follows:

- We propose LoCo-VAE, which is an unified framework modeling context-aware short-term user preferences as a joint effect of long-term user preferences and specific context impact.
- We incorporate priors based on users' long-term preferences in the latent VAE space and fine-tune the short-term preferences along with the context impact. Specifically, we use an MLP to obtain long-term preferences, and context-aware preferences are obtained from the variational distribution.
- We experimentally examine the rationality of modeling users' context-aware short-term preferences and verify the effectiveness of proposed LoCo-VAE by extensive experimental evaluation on two real-world datasets.

2   Related Work

2.1   General Recommendation Systems

General recommendation systems usually model users' static long-term preferences which reflect their' inherent characteristics. Collaborative Filtering (CF) [1] is the most popular idea in general recommendation. CF with implicit feedback is usually treated as a Top-k item recommendation task, whose goal is to recommend a list of items that users may be interested in [20]. Early CF based works mostly rely on matrix factorization techniques [7,22] to learn latent features of users and items. In recent years, due to the ability of deep learning techniques to learn salient representations, deep learning based methods have been widely applied in recommendation systems. For example, NCF [5] learns a model with non-linear interactions between the latent factors of users and items rather than direct inner product. Autoencoder-based methods [13,16,25] have also been proposed for recommendation systems. MacridVAE [17] learns disentangled representations from user behavior by inferring the high-level concept associated with user preference. Although current general recommendation systems have been widely used in practice, few of these methods take contextual information into consideration, which is essential to further performance improvement.

2.2   Recommendation Systems Based on User Dynamic Preference

To solve the problem of static user preference modeling in general recommendation systems, researchers proposed to model users' dynamic preferences. The earlier work on applying this idea can be traced back to DIVA[19], decision-theoretic agent for recommending movies that distinguishing between a user's general taste in movies and his immediate interests. Later recommendation systems that model users' dynamic preferences focus on the transition process of the state. For example, the factorized personalized Markov chains (FPMC) [23] combined matrix factorization with one-order Markov chain to capture the influence of the last behavior towards the next one. Recently, RNN and its variants are introduced to model dynamic preference. In this direction, Time-LSTM [29] proposes time gates to model time intervals with the goal of capturing both users' long-term and short-term Preferences. SLi-Rec [27] leverages RNN structures for modeling users' short-term preference, and further proposes an attention-based adaptive fusion schema to dynamically combine users' both short-term and long-term preference. MA-GNN [15] proposes a memory augmented graph neural network to capture both the long and short-term user preferences and they apply a graph neural network to model the item contextual information within a short-term period. As mentioned above, current dynamic preferences oriented recommendation systems only consider the sequential temporal feature of the preference, instead of understanding the relation between the complex contextual information and short-term preference.

2.3   Context-Aware Recommendation Systems

To introduce the context information into recommendation systems, point-of-interest (POI) based models are proposed as the main approaches in context-aware recommendation [11,12,28]. POI based recommendation is different from item recommendation and is more sensitive to geographic location. There are also other context-aware recommendation approaches of products, music and books. For example, CA-RNN [14] employs adaptive context-specific input matrices and adaptive context-specific transition matrices to improve conventional RNN models. The adaptive context-specific input matrices capture the context where user behaviors happen. CoSeRNN [4] focused on the dynamic influences of context and learns preference vector based on past consumption history and current context while not apply it into the recommendation system.

3   Methodology

3.1   Notations and Problem Formulation

We assume that a set of N users can interact with the set of M items.(e.g., users purchase products or listen to music) in K contexts. We consider learning with implicit feedback, where the user-item interaction is binary. Specifically, $x_{ui}^{(k)} = 1$ indicates that the interaction of user u with item i in the kth context is observed, whereas $x_{ui} = 0$ means there is no record of such interaction. For convenience, we use $\mathrm{X}_u^{(k)} = \{x_{ui}^{(k)} : x_{ui}^{(k)} = 1\}$ to represent the items adopted by user u in context k. $\mathrm{X}_u = [\mathrm{X}_u^{(1)}, \mathrm{X}_u^{(2)}, \cdots, \mathrm{X}_u^{(k)}] \in \mathbb{N}^{K \times M}$ is the input matrix. Our goal is to suggest top-k items preferred by u in context k.

3.2   Model of LoCo-VAE

Overall Framework. Our framework of LoCo-VAE is presented in Fig. 1. To provide a clear view of our model, we first interpret from the perspective of an autoencoder before derivation. The long-term and context-aware preference is captured by the encoders in the upper and lower parts of Fig. 1, respectively. The decoder takes the combination of the two distributions as input and outputs the probability distribution of the user on item set in the corresponding context.

We start our model by proposing a generative model as VAEs usually do. For a user u in context k, our generative model starts by sampling a d-dimensional latent representation $z_u^{(k)}$ as context-aware short-term preference from a Gaussian prior distribution. The latent representation $z_u^{(k)}$ is then transformed via a non-linear function $g_\psi(\cdot) \in \mathbf{R}^M$ parametrized by ψ to produce a probability distribution over M items:

$$p(z_u^{(k)}) = \mathcal{N}(\mu_u, diag(\sigma_u^2)),$$
$$p_\psi(\mathrm{X}_u^{(k)}) = g_\psi(z_u^{(k)}), \tag{1}$$

where $\mu_u \in \mathbf{R}^d$ and $diag(\sigma_u^2) \in \mathbf{R}^{d \times d}$ denotes the mean and deviation vector of the Gaussian distribution, respectively. As we assume a user's short-term preference is based on the stable long-term preference, coupled with the role of context $z_u^{s_k}$, μ_u is assumed to be the user u's long-term preference $z_u^l \in \mathbf{R}^d$. And the impact of context is fine-tuned by the deviation of the distribution.

Variational Inference. In order to optimize the parameters, we need to maximize $p(\mathrm{X}_u^{(k)})$, which can be rewritten according to the Bayesian formula as:

$$ln[p_\psi(\mathrm{X}_u^{(k)})] = \mathbb{E}_z[ln \frac{p_\psi(\mathrm{X}_u^{(k)}|z_u^{(k)})p(z_u^{(k)})}{p(z_u^{(k)}|\mathrm{X}_u^{(k)})}], \tag{2}$$

where $p_\psi(\mathrm{X}_u^{(k)}|z_u^{(k)})$ is the distribution over M items in context k, and $g_\psi(\cdot)$ can be reached by a neural network to estimate how much a user in the given context is interested in items. To approximate the intractable posterior distribution $p(\mathrm{X}_u^{(k)}|z_u^{(k)})$, we resort to variational inference [8]. Variational inference approximates $(\mathrm{X}_u^{(k)}|z_u^{(k)})$ with a variational distribution $q(z_u^{(k)}) = \mathcal{N}(\mu_u^{(k)}, diag\{(\sigma_u^{(k)})^2\})$. Following the VAE paradigm [10,13,24], we replace the individual variational parameters $\{\mu_u^{(k)}, (\sigma_u^{(k)})^2\}$ with a data-dependent function and set the variational distribution as following:

$$q_\phi(z_u^{(k)}|\mathrm{X}_u^{(k)}) = \mathcal{N}(\mu_\phi(\mathrm{X}_u^{(k)}), diag\{\sigma_\phi^2(\mathrm{X}_u^{(k)})\}), \tag{3}$$

where ϕ is the parameter of the function $f_\phi(\mathrm{x}_u^{(k)}) \equiv [\mu_\phi(\mathrm{x}_u^{(k)}), \sigma_\phi(\mathrm{x}_u^{(k)})] \in \mathbb{R}^{2d}$ that maps $x_u^{(k)}$ to the mean and standard deviation vectors.

After the variational inference, we can further rewrite formula (2) as:

$$ln[p_{\psi,\phi}(\mathrm{x}_u^{(k)})] \geq \mathbb{E}_z[ln p_\psi(\mathrm{x}_u^{(k)}|\mathrm{z}_u^{(k)})] - D_{KL}(q_\phi(\mathrm{z}_u^{(k)}|\mathrm{x}_u^{(k)})||p(\mathrm{z}_u^{(k)})), \qquad (4)$$

where KL is Kullback-Leibler divergence distance measuring the difference between the distribution $q_\phi(\mathrm{z}_u^{(k)}|\mathrm{x}_u^{(k)})$ and the Gaussian distribution $p(\mathrm{z}_u^{(k)})$. We define context-aware preference of user u in context k as $z_u^{s_k}$, and $p(z_u^{s_k}) = \mathcal{N}(0, diag(\sigma_u^2))$. Since

$$D_{KL}(q_\phi(\mathrm{z}_u^{s_k}|\mathrm{x}_u^{(k)})||p(\mathrm{z}_u^{s_k})) \equiv D_{KL}(q_\phi(\mathrm{z}_u^{(k)}|\mathrm{x}_u^{(k)})||p(\mathrm{z}_u^{(k)})),$$

equation (4) is finally transformed into:

$$ln[p_{\psi,\phi}(\mathrm{x}_u^{(k)})] \geq \mathbb{E}_z[ln p_\psi(\mathrm{x}_u^{(k)}|\mathrm{z}_u^{(k)})] - D_{KL}(q_\phi(\mathrm{z}_u^{s_k}|\mathrm{x}_u^{(k)})||p(\mathrm{z}_u^{s_k})). \qquad (5)$$

This lower bound, commonly called *evidence lower bound* (ELBO), is maximized to learn the parameters of ψ and ϕ.

Context-Aware Modeling. The latent representation $\mathrm{z}_u^{s_k}$ is a context-aware preference separated from short-term preference. We map the input $\mathrm{x}_u^{(k)}$ to the mean and standard deviation vectors of the variational distribution $q_\phi(\mathrm{z}_u^{s_k}|\mathrm{x}_u^{(k)})$ through the function $f_\phi(\mathrm{x}_u^{(k)})$, which is obtained through a Multilayer Perceptron(MLP). And $\mathrm{z}_u^{s_k}$ is sampled from Gaussian distribution $q_\phi(\mathrm{z}_u^{s_k}|\mathrm{x}_u^{(k)})$ via reparameterization trick [10].

Long-Term Modeling. Unlike Giannis [9] who obtains the prior distribution in advance, we put it in our model so that the long-term preferences can be optimized with context-aware preferences at the same time. We just apply an MLP which shares a similar construction with the encoder of CDAE [25] with user-specific nodes in the input layer and hidden layer to get z_u^l, transforming the input into a latent representation with the same dimension as $\mathrm{z}_u^{(k)}$ through a function $z_u^l = f_\theta^l(x_u^l)$, where $x_u^l = \Sigma_k \mathrm{x}_u^{(k)}$.

The two distributions of context-aware and long-term preferences are combined into short-term preferences $\mathrm{z}_u^{(k)}$, which are input into the decoder in the right part of Fig. 1. The decoder outputs the probability distribution of the user on item set in the corresponding context. We choose k items with the highest probability as the recommendation results. In practice, the long-term and context-aware preference encoders share parameters (θ can be replaced ϕ), which can effectively alleviate overfitting.

3.3   Objective Function

We optimize the learnable parameters by maximizing the ELBO from Eq. 5, which can be viewed from another perspective: the first part can be understood as reconstruction loss, while the second part is regularization. From this perspective, we make a trade-off between the two parts just like Liang [13] does. Finally, our objective function becomes:

$$\mathcal{L}(x_u; \phi, \psi) = \frac{1}{K} \Sigma_k \{ \mathbb{E}_z [ln p_\psi(x_u^{(k)}|z_u^{(k)})] - \beta \cdot D_{KL}(q_\phi(z_u^{s_k}|x_u^{(k)})||p(z_u^{s_k})) \}. \quad (6)$$

4   Experiments

4.1   Datasets

According to common sense, the user's listening style and purchase of beauty products can be affected by time, which is also proven by Hansen [21] and Sect. 5.1. We conducted our experiments on two largescale user-item datasets from various domains. Specifically, we used the Million Musical Tweets dataset (MMTD)[2], and Amazon consumption dataset[3]. Amazon dataset is a public dataset containing product reviews and metadata from Amazon consumption records, which is widely used as benchmark dataset in recommendation system study. In the experiments, we chose the subcategory of Beauty from Amazon dataset, considering the influence of contexts. MMTD is a largescale source of microblog-based music listening histories that includes temporal and other contextual information. In both Beauty and MMTD datasets, the feature of time was chosen as the context information and divided into seasons and different periods of the day, respectively. Other contexts can also be chosen as long as they count.

We binarized the two datasets by keeping ratings of four or higher while only keeping users who have listened or purchased at least five items. Table 1 summarizes the statistics of both datasets after preprocessing. We split all users into training, validation and test sets. We train the proposed models and baselines using the entire click history of the training users. To evaluate, we take part in the click history from held-out (validation and test) users to learn the necessary user-level representations for the model and then compute metrics by looking at how well each model ranks the rest of the unseen click history from the held-out users. In the last row of Table 1, we list the number of held-out users (we use the same number of users for validation and test). For each held-out user, we randomly choose 80% of the click history as the "fold-in" set to learn the necessary user-level representation and report metrics on the remaining click history.

4.2   Baselines

We compare the performance of proposed LoCo-VAE model with the following state-of-the-art collaborative filtering models and auto-encoder based methods.

Weighted Matrix Factorization (WMF) [6]. WMF is a linear low-rank matrix factorization model. We train WMF with alternating least squares. We

---

[2] http://www.cp.jku.at/datasets/MMTD/.
[3] http://snap.stanford.edu/data/amazon/.

Table 1. Statistics of the datasets.

Dataset	Beauty	MMTD
# Users	35,931	34,051
# Items	95,313	111,629
# Interactions	0.3M	0.8M
Density	0.009%	0.021%
# Held-out users	3000	3000

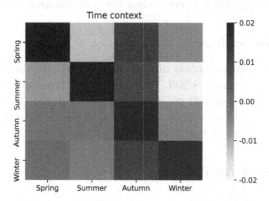

Fig. 2. Visualization of the similarity between the users' preferences of different types of context. In this case, we calculate the similarity between the Beauty consumption records (i.e., user preference) of different seasons (i.e., types of context). A more positive number (i.e., darker red) indicates higher similarity. (Color figure online)

set the weights on all the 0's to 1 and tune the weights on all the 1's in the click matrix among {2, 5, 10, 30, 50, 100} by evaluating recall@10 on validation user.

Neural Collaborative Filtering (NCF) [5]. NCF explores non-linear interactions (via a neural network) between the user and item latent factors. We used the hybrid NeuCF model which gives the best performance in [5]. We selected the latent representation dimension K over {64, 128, 256} by examining the validation recall@10.

Multinomial-Denoising Autoencoder (Mult-DAE) [17]. Mult-DAE augments the standard denoising auto-encoder by replacing the loss function as multinomial likelihood. We search the hidden layer dimension K among {100, 200, 300, 600}, as well as the regularization parameter λ in (0,1).

Multinomial-Variational Autoencoder (Mult-VAE) [17]. Mult-VAE is a generative model with a multinomial likelihood function parameterized by neural network. We set the hidden layer and penalty β by searching for the best recall@10 on validation users.

4.3   Metrics

To evaluate the performance of models, we use two ranking-based metrics: Hit Ratio (HR@R) and Normalized Discounted cumulative gain(NDCG@R). In order to compare proposed LoCo-VAE model with other baselines, for each positive item in the test set we pair it with 99 sampled items that the user has not interacted with as negative items. For each user, both metrics compare the predicted rank of sampled negative items and the positive item with their true rank. HR@R measures whether the Top-R predicted items hit the positive item and NDCG@R gives a higher score when the positive item ranks higher.

4.4   Parameter Settings

We set the latent representation dimension d = 100 and the MLP with a hidden layer whose dimension is 200. We tuned β by Hyperopt [9] and choose 0.5 finally. All the hyper-parameters of our baselines are also tuned by Hyperopt. For learning LoCo-VAE, we used the Adam optimizer with a learning rate of 0.001 as well as a batch size of 500 users.

5   Results and Analysis

5.1   Exploratory Analysis

In order to demonstrate the rationality of our main hypothesis, i.e., users' short-term preferences are a joint effect of long-term preferences and specific context, we investigated the influence of context on the Beauty dataset. we embedded user-item interaction records in a latent semantic space using the *word2vec* continuous bag-of-word model [18] on user-generated reviews. In short, we learn a 100-dimensional real-valued unit-norm embedding of each interaction by calculating the mean of the review embeddings. We randomly select two sets of interactions, each with 400 records. These 400 records consist of 100 records for each season. The similarity between the two sets is obtained by simply computing cosine similarity between their embeddings. Figure 2 displays the results in the form of a heatmap. The positive diagonal with a dark red denotes that records sharing the same context are indeed more similar than records in other contexts. This result highlights our hypothesis that user interactions with the same context do share some similarities. In addition, a similar conclusion in the field of music is also reached by Hansen [4].

5.2   Performance Comparison

Table 2 presents the performance of the proposed LoCo-VAE model with the compared methods in terms of two evaluation metrics at three accuracy levels. The boldface font denotes the winner in that column. For the sake of clarity, the last row of Table 2 also shows the relative improvements achieved by our LoCo-VAE over the baselines. As we can see, LoCo-VAE's relative improvement for

Table 2. The performance metrics of the compared methods. The boldface font denotes the winner in that column. The row 'Impv' indicates the relative performance gain of our LoCo-VAE compared to the best results among baselines.

Dataset	Method	HR@10	HR@5	HR@1	NDCG@10	NDCG@5
Beauty	WMF	0.4565	0.3707	0.2316	0.3316	0.3039
	NCF	0.5366	0.4426	0.2525	0.3833	0.3530
	Mult-DAE	0.6675	0.5912	0.3716	0.5142	0.4895
	Mult-VAE	**0.7020**	0.6021	0.3711	0.5260	0.4938
	LoCo-VAE	0.6999	**0.6079**	**0.3936**	**0.5369**	**0.5071**
	Impv%	−0.30%	0.96%	6.06%	9.48%	2.69%
MMTD	WMF	0.7021	0.6341	0.4666	0.5777	0.5557
	NCF	0.7654	0.6939	0.4474	0.6020	0.5787
	Mult-DAE	0.8499	0.7683	0.4888	0.6665	0.6401
	Mult-VAE	0.8509	0.7690	0.5001	0.6712	0.6445
	LoCo-VAE	**0.8525**	**0.7720**	**0.5236**	**0.6842**	**0.6580**
	Impv%	0.19%	0.39%	4.70%	1.94%	2.09%

NDCG is higher than that for HR, which indicates our model can predict user preferences more accurately to maximize their satisfaction. Besides, LoCo-VAE's overall relative improvement on Beauty is higher than that on MMTD, while the former's data is more sparse, illustrating our superiority on sparse datasets.

Generally speaking, with one exception, LoCo-VAE outperforms compared methods on all datasets for all metrics. The improvement of LoCo-VAE over these baselines is supposed to be attributed to two aspects:

(1) In the real world, users interact with the recommendation in different contexts, and they adaptively make behavioral choices based on the context at the time. Correspondingly, even the same user's interest will vary with different interaction contexts. That is, some music is more likely listened to by users at noon while others are to be played at night. By combining long-term preferences with short-term preferences acted upon by context, LoCo-VAE achieves better performance than those baselines without considering the context;

(2) LoCo-VAE models long-term preferences via an encoder that is trained with context-aware preferences, which is capable of capturing users' short-term preferences in the extinct context.

5.3   Case Study

To validate the second aspect, i.e., LoCo-VAE is capable of capturing users' short-term preferences via context-aware long-term preferences, we randomly sample two users and list their recommended items in the context of noon and night by our model for better understanding, as depicted in Fig. 3.

(a) Items recommended by Loco-VAE for user A at noon. (b) Items recommended by Loco-VAE for user B at noon.

(c) Items recommended by Loco-VAE for user A at night. (d) Items recommended by Loco-VAE for user B at night.

Fig. 3. Two examples randomly sampled from held-out users. For each user, we choose items recommended by the proposed LoCo-VAE in the context of noon and night. For each user, LoCo-VAE tends to recommend soothing music at night, while the rhythm is stronger at noon, which reflects the context-aware impact of each user's short-term interests. The overall recommended music styles of the two users are also different. For user B, LoCo-VAE tends to recommend vigorous music, which reflects the difference in their long-term preference.

By comparing recommended music styles of the same user in two different contexts, we found that LoCo-VAE tends to recommend soothing music at night, while the rhythm is stronger at noon, which reflects the context-aware impact of each user's short-term preferences. In addition, the overall recommended music styles of the two users are also different. For user B, LoCo-VAE tends to recommend vigorous music, which reflects the difference in their long-term preference. This case study not only demonstrates LoCo-VAE's advantage in making a more accurate recommendation but also reveals our advantage in the interpretability of recommendation, which is all benefit from modeling short-term preferences as the joint effect of long-term preferences and context-aware impact.

6 Conclusion

In this work, we consider the task of learning short-term user preferences by combing contextual information with long-term user preferences. To this end, from real-world Amazon consumption datasets, we first verify the essential hypothesis that short-term user preference is a joint effect of long-term preference and specific context.

Driven by this finding, we propose a novel model named LoCo-VAE. LoCo-VAE extends Variational Autoencoders (VAEs) based recommendation model by replacing the standard Gaussian prior with user-dependent priors. The user-dependent priors are defined as long-term preferences and are obtained from user-item interactions. Using this approach, we map users into a latent vector space, which encodes both long-term interests and context-aware preferences. Experiments on Amazon consumption datasets and Musical Tweets datasets show that our proposed LoCo-VAE model achieves the best performance among state-of-the-art baselines.

References

1. Adomavicius, G., Tuzhilin, A.: Toward the next generation of recommender systems: a survey of the state-of-the-art and possible extensions. IEEE Trans. Knowl. Data Eng. **17**(6), 734–749 (2005)
2. Chen, X., Zhang, Y., Qin, Z.: Dynamic explainable recommendation based on neural attentive models. In: Proceedings of the AAAI Conference on Artificial Intelligence, vol. 33, pp. 53–60 (2019)
3. Gan, M., Ma, Y., Xiao, K.: CDMF: a deep learning model based on convolutional and dense-layer matrix factorization for context-aware recommendation
4. Hansen, C., et al.: Contextual and sequential user embeddings for large-scale music recommendation. In: Fourteenth ACM Conference on Recommender Systems, RecSys 2020, pp. 53–62. Association for Computing Machinery, New York (2020)
5. He, X., Liao, L., Zhang, H., Nie, L., Chua, T.S.: Neural collaborative filtering (2017)
6. Hu, Y., Koren, Y., Volinsky, C.: Collaborative filtering for implicit feedback datasets. In: Proceedings of the 8th IEEE International Conference on Data Mining (ICDM 2008), Pisa, 15–19 December 2008
7. Hu, Y., Koren, Y., Volinsky, C.: Collaborative filtering for implicit feedback datasets. In: Eighth IEEE International Conference on Data Mining (2009)
8. Jordan, M.I., Ghahramani, Z., Jaakkola, T.S., Saul, L.K.: An introduction to variational methods for graphical models. Mach. Learn. **37**(2), 183–233 (1999)
9. Karamanolakis, G., Cherian, K.R., Narayan, A.R., Yuan, J., Tang, D., Jebara, T.: Item recommendation with variational autoencoders and heterogeneous priors. In: Proceedings of the 3rd Workshop on Deep Learning for Recommender Systems, DLRS 2018, pp. 10–14. Association for Computing Machinery, New York (2018)
10. Kingma, D.P., Welling, M.: Auto-encoding variational bayes (2014)
11. Li, R., Shen, Y., Zhu, Y.: Next point-of-interest recommendation with temporal and multi-level context attention. In: 2018 IEEE International Conference on Data Mining (ICDM), pp. 1110–1115 (2018). https://doi.org/10.1109/ICDM.2018.00144
12. Lian, D., Wu, Y., Ge, Y., Xie, X., Chen, E.: Geography-aware sequential location recommendation. In: Proceedings of the 26th ACM SIGKDD International Conference on Knowledge Discovery & Data Mining KDD 2020, pp. 2009–2019. Association for Computing Machinery, New York (2020)
13. Liang, D., Krishnan, R.G., Hoffman, M.D., Jebara, T.: Variational autoencoders for collaborative filtering. In: Proceedings of the 2018 World Wide Web Conference WWW 2018, pp. 689–698. International World Wide Web Conferences Steering Committee, Republic and Canton of Geneva (2018)
14. Liu, Q., Wu, S., Wang, D., Li, Z., Wang, L.: Context-aware sequential recommendation. In: 2016 IEEE 16th International Conference on Data Mining (ICDM), pp. 1053–1058 (2016). https://doi.org/10.1109/ICDM.2016.0135
15. Ma, C., Ma, L., Zhang, Y., Sun, J., Coates, M.: Memory augmented graph neural networks for sequential recommendation. In: Proceedings of the AAAI Conference on Artificial Intelligence, vol. 34, no. 4, pp. 5045–5052 (2020)
16. Ma, C., Zhang, Y., Wang, Q., Liu, X.: Point-of-interest recommendation: Exploiting self-attentive autoencoders with neighbor-aware influence. In: Proceedings of the 27th ACM International Conference on Information and Knowledge Management CIKM 2018, p. 697–706. Association for Computing Machinery, New York (2018)

17. Ma, J., Zhou, C., Cui, P., Yang, H., Zhu, W.: Learning disentangled representations for recommendation. In: NeurIPS (2019)
18. Mikolov, T., Chen, K., Corrado, G., Dean, J.: Efficient estimation of word representations in vector space. In: ICLR (2013)
19. Nguyen, H., Haddawy, P.: Diva: applying decision theory to collaborative filtering (1999)
20. Pan, R., et al.: One-class collaborative filtering. In: Proceedings of the 2008 Eighth IEEE International Conference on Data Mining, ICDM 2008, pp. 502–511. IEEE Computer Society (2008)
21. Park, M., Thom, J., Mennicken, S., et al.: Global music streaming data reveal diurnal and seasonal patterns of affective preference. Nat. Hum. Behav. **3**, 230–236 (2019). https://doi.org/10.1038/s41562-018-0508-z
22. Rendle, S., Freudenthaler, C., Gantner, Z., Schmidt-Thieme, L.: Bpr: Bayesian personalized ranking from implicit feedback. In: Proceedings of the Twenty-Fifth Conference on Uncertainty in Artificial Intelligence, UAI 2009, pp. 452–461. AUAI Press, Arlington (2009)
23. Rendle, S., Freudenthaler, C., Schmidt-Thieme, L.: Factorizing personalized markov chains for next-basket recommendation. In: Proceedings of the 19th International Conference on World Wide Web, WWW 2010, pp. 811–820. Association for Computing Machinery, New York (2010)
24. Rezende, D.J., Mohamed, S., Wierstra, D.: Stochastic backpropagation and approximate inference in deep generative models (2014)
25. Wu, Y., DuBois, C., Zheng, A.X., Ester, M.: Collaborative denoising auto-encoders for top-n recommender systems. In: Proceedings of the Ninth ACM International Conference on Web Search and Data Mining, WSDM 2016, pp. 153–162. Association for Computing Machinery, New York (2016)
26. Xin, X., Chen, B., He, X., Wang, D., Ding, Y., Jose, J.: Cfm: Convolutional factorization machines for context-aware recommendation. In: Proceedings of the Twenty-Eighth International Joint Conference on Artificial Intelligence, IJCAI-19, pp. 3926–3932. International Joint Conferences on Artificial Intelligence Organization (2019)
27. Yu, Z., Lian, J., Mahmoody, A., Liu, G., Xie, X.: Adaptive user modeling with long and short-term preferences for personalized recommendation. In: Twenty-Eighth International Joint Conference on Artificial Intelligence IJCAI-19 (2019)
28. Zhao, P., Luo, A., Liu, Y., Zhuang, F., Zhou, X.: Where to go next: a spatiotemporal gated network for next poi recommendation. IEEE Trans. Knowl. Data Eng. **99**, 1 (2020)
29. Zhu, Y., Li, H., Liao, Y., Wang, B., Cai, D.: What to do next: modeling user behaviors by time-lstm. In: Twenty-Sixth International Joint Conference on Artificial Intelligence (2017)

Multi-scale Edge-Based U-Shape Network for Salient Object Detection

Han Sun[1(✉)], Yetong Bian[1], Ningzhong Liu[1], and Huiyu Zhou[2]

[1] Nanjing University of Aeronautics and Astronautics, Nanjing, Jiangsu, China
sunhan@nuaa.edu.cn
[2] School of Informatics, University of Leicester, Leicester LE1 7RH, UK

Abstract. Deep-learning based salient object detection methods achieve great improvements. However, there are still problems existing in the predictions, such as blurry boundary and inaccurate location, which is mainly caused by inadequate feature extraction and integration. In this paper, we propose a Multi-scale Edge-based U-shape Network (MEUN) to integrate various features at different scales to achieve better performance. To extract more useful information for boundary prediction, U-shape Edge Network modules are embedded in each decoder units. Besides, the additional down-sampling module alleviates the location inaccuracy. Experimental results on four benchmark datasets demonstrate the validity and reliability of the proposed method. Multi-scale Edge-based U-shape Network also shows its superiority when compared with 15 state-of-the-art salient object detection methods.

Keywords: Salient object detection · Multi-scale feature · Edge-based

1 Introduction

Saliency Object Detection (SOD) is a significant branch of computer vision. It is involved in plenty of computer vision tasks, such as video summarization [15], visual object tracking [1], semantic segmentation [29]. The salient object is defined as one or more objects that are the most attractive in an image. Saliency Object Detection aims to segment the object with its boundary and background accurately. It can be viewed as a binary classification task to assign foreground pixels to saliency and background pixels to non-saliency.

At the very beginning, SOD models mainly depend on manual features such as texture, color and global contrast [17]. Until 2015, the sudden rise of neural network sets off a wave of wind in the SOD and even the whole field of computer vision. Most scholars turned their attention to neural network models with a great capacity to extract multi-level and multi-scale information, especially after the Fully Convolutional Neural Network (FCN) [14] was proposed.

Although SOD models with convolution neural networks (CNNs) achieved remarkable achievements in recent years, there are still two main problems to be solved. First, predictions around the boundary areas are prone to make mistakes.

© Springer Nature Switzerland AG 2021
D. N. Pham et al. (Eds.): PRICAI 2021, LNAI 13032, pp. 501–514, 2021.
https://doi.org/10.1007/978-3-030-89363-7_38

Besides, the background and foreground have high similarities in some images, making the models confused about object location. These problems are virtually triggered by improper multi-scale feature integration and information loss.

In the past years, most researches are devoted to improving the border region of salient objects, for example, adding some edge information to the framework [2,31], utilizing top local features to refine the saliency map via multiple cycles [5] or raising the weight of edge pixel error punishment in loss function [4]. Recently, a few articles start to refocus on the accuracy of the overall positioning of salient objects [27].

Inspired by these articles, we propose a Multi-scale Edge-based U-shape Network (MEUN), which improves the object location and boundary prediction by additional down-sampling and edge complement. As known, the features extracted from shallow layers usually have high resolution with abundant detailed information. If these features could be fully utilized in the network, the prediction performance around the saliency borders will be greatly promoted. The features drawn from the deep layers contain rich global textual clues. However, too many straight down-sampling operations will lead the features to lose detailed information and influence the prediction of boundary areas. If we simply up-sample the down-sampled features to the size of inputs, the prediction must be too coarse to meet the requirements of SOD nowadays. So we design our module with the encoder-decoder structure called "U-shape Network" [18]. The outputs of each unit in the encoder are transmitted to corresponding unit in the decoder to supply some shallow details for the deep global semantic features. Such a solution could alleviate the problems mentioned above. Besides, we designed the U-shape edge network (UEN) block and the additional down-sampling module (ADM) to further explore the fine details at the bottom sides and the semantic information at the top sides, separately.

In general, to improve the accuracy of the object location and the details of the object boundary, our method properly extracts and merges features from the deep layers and the shallow layers. The main contributions are summarized as following three points:

- We propose the U-shape edge network (UEN) block to fuse the edge information and features extracted by the backbone. Based on the originally advantageous U-shape structure, this module could efficiently add boundary information so that the boundary prediction of saliency maps can be improved.
- An additional down-sampling module (ADM) is designed to further extract useful global structural information. It makes the network proposed going deeper than other networks, so our method can obtain a more accurate saliency object position.
- We build an efficient framework to fully combine and fuse edge information, detailed information and semantic clues. Many experiments are conducted to illustrate the validity of our algorithm and this model could surpass most models on four large-scale salient object detection datasets.

2 Related Work

Because our method designs a novel multi-scale feature integration U-shape Network based on edge information, this part briefly includes three aspects of works, U-shape models, edge-fused models and multi-scale feature aggregation models.

U-Net Based. U-shape network is a variant of Fully Convolutional Networks and is widely used in image segmentation and saliency object detection. This structure has a strong capacity to make the features from different modules interact with each other. It was first proposed in [20] for biomedical image segmentation in 2015. Recently, many saliency models adopt U-structure to obtain multi-scale features and efficient aggregation. Zhou et al. [33] design a module based on U-Net, in which an attention mechanism is taken to jointly enhance the quality of salient masks and reduce the consumption of memory resources. Qin et al. [18] design a two-level nested U-structure without using any pre-trained backbones from image classification. Although these models take advantage of the U-structure, there are still some limitations. For example, U2Net [18] is extremely complex with a large number of parameters up to 176.3 M.

Edge Based. Boundary prediction accuracy is always a problem that most models cannot deal with well. In recent years, edge information is found to be a valuable complement to the salient boundary prediction. EGNet [31] is design to explicitly model complementary salient object information and salient edge information within the network to preserve the salient object boundaries. To supplement semantics and make networks focus on object boundaries, Cen et al. [2] introduce an edge-region complementary strategy and an edge-focused loss function to predict salient maps with clear boundaries accurately. Li et al. [11] propose an edge information-guided hierarchical feature fusion network. Zhou et al. [32] designed a multi-stage and dual-path network to jointly learn the salient edges and regions, in which the region branch network and edge branch network can interactively learn from each other. These methods improve the boundary prediction of the salient object to some extent, but the overall positioning lacks novel improvement.

Multi-scale Feature Aggregation Based. The problems mentioned above are also partly caused by inappropriate aggregation and fusion. Thus, many articles looked for more efficient and effective methods to aggregate low-level features with detailed information and high-level features with semantic clues. Feng et al. [8] employ a Dilated Convolutional Pyramid Pooling (DCPP) module to generate a coarse prediction based on global contextual knowledge. In MINet [16], the aggregate interaction module can efficiently utilize the features from adjacent layers through mutual learning, while the self-interaction module makes the network adaptively extract multi-scale information from data and better deal with scale variation. Li et al. [10] present a residual refinement network with semantic context features, including a global attention module, a multi-receptive block module, and a recurrent residual module. These methods are mainly innovative in feature extraction and fusion, but they do not explore features with more possibilities.

3   Methodology

In this section, the proposed model is discussed in detail. The whole method is further separated into four parts. In the first part, we give an overview of the network architecture. Then we introduce the U-shape edge network block and the additional down-sampling module. Finally, the use of loss function is explained clearly.

3.1   Overview

Figure 1 presents the overall framework, mainly containing the UENs and ADM. The encoder could adopt any common backbone as its encoder, such as ResNet50 [9]. The backbone is divided into five groups according to the size of output features. One group's output is transmitted to the next group and the module with the corresponding scale in the decoder. We suppose that detailed supplement is not enough for promoting edge prediction, so edge information is introduced as a complement for better performance. Firstly, it should be clear that what kind of edge is needed. The background prediction will be disturbed by the background edges marked as saliency. Because in a saliency map, background pixels should be marked as non-salient. To avoid the disturbance from background edges, a salient edge ground truth is used to supervise the edge map generation. The edge

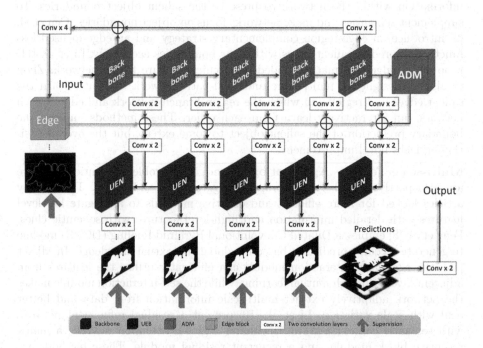

Fig. 1. The overview of the architecture.

features are down-sampled to different scales of the branches. Then processed edge feature is inputted into the UENs.

We also design an Additional Down-sampling Module (ADM) to mine more semantic clues with larger and wider receptive field, which can help locate accurately and precisely. We build the MEUNetwork based on ResNet-50. The final output of ResNet-50 is at 7×7 scale, so ADM down-samples the input feature map by a factor of two. Then, the output of ADM is transmitted to the decoder along with the features from the backbone. The decoder consists of five U-shape edge networks (UEN), and the UENs are connected from the bottom up. The input of the module at the bottom is the element-wise addition of $Feature_{ADM}$ and $Feature_{b5}$. It can be formulated as

$$\text{Input}_5 = \text{Conv\_}2_{3\times3}\left(\text{Conv\_}2_{3\times3}\left(\text{Feature}_{b5}\right) + \text{Feature}_{ADM}\right), \qquad (1)$$

in which $Input_5$ denotes the input of the UEN at the bottom. $Conv\_2_{3\times3}$ is two sets of one 3×3 convolutional layer followed by the batch normalization and ReLU activation, which is used as the basic convolutional unit in this network. $Feature_{ADM}$ and $Feature_{b5}$ are the output of fifth group filters in the encoder and ADM, respectively. The input of other UEN blocks can be written as

$$Input_i = Conv\_2_{3\times3}\left(Conv\_2_{3\times3}\left(Feature_{b_i}\right) + Edge_{sal}\right), \quad i = 1, 2, 3, 4 \quad (2)$$

$Input_i$ is the input of the ith UEN block. $Feature_{b_i}$ represents the output of the ith block in the encoder and $Edge_{sal}$ denotes the edge supplement. It needs to mention that the outputs with different channels from the backbone are squeezed to 128 channels by a 1×1 convolution for the reduction of parameters. Besides, to achieve the best balance between efficiency and quality, edge feature and features in ADM and UENs are all set as 128 channels.

Besides being sent to the next module, the output of each UEN is used to generate a saliency map through two 3×3 convolution layers. Each intermediate prediction is up-sampled to the size of the original image for supervision. In the decoder, the deepest features at 7×7 scale are restored step by step. Compared with other predictions, the last prediction with the highest resolution is the closest to what we want. The final output of the model is the fusion of all the intermediate predictions integrated by convolutional layers. Of course, this step could be skipped because the last saliency map of the decoder is good enough to be the final result.

3.2   UEN Module

Figure 2 shows the overview of different UEN modules, including the UEN_5 and the UEN_A. $DilatedConv_i$ in Fig. 2 denotes the atrous convolution layer with dilation rate i. The 3×3 convolutional layer is heavily used inside this module. Except for the first convolutional layer, each convolutional layer is followed by a down-sampling by a factor of two. In this way, richer information with a global view can be extracted at different scales. We determine the down-sampling times in an UEN_i $(i = 4, 5)$ according to the scale of the input feature.

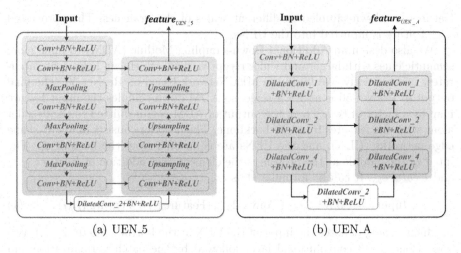

(a) UEN_5   (b) UEN_A

Fig. 2. The structures of UEN5 and UEN_A.

If the input is large enough, such as 112×112, we could down-sample for three times. However, if the input itself is small, excessive down-sampling is redundant and unreasonable. In this situation, two down-sampling operations are enough. For smaller scales, such as 7×7, the module discards the down-sampling. More specifically, we remove the pooling layers and change the original convolutional layer into a dilated convolutional layer. The structure shown in Fig. 2 (a) is the specific settings of UEN_5. Compared to UEN_5, UEN_4 reduces a down-sampling operation and an up-sampling operation followed by a convolutional layer, respectively. After the encoder, a dilated convolutional layer is followed by the batch normalization and ReLU activation function. Here, the input of each convolutional layer is an aggregation of two features. One is the output from the last convolution. The other one is the feature transmitted from the encoder. Here, the two features are aggregated by concatenating. Unlike UEN_i, in Fig. 2 (b), there are three dilated convolution branches in UEN_A with different dilation rates to extract semantic features with different receptive fields. Kernels of the three branches are all 3×3 and dilation rates are 1, 2, 4. The final convolution output $Feature_{UEN}$ is conducted as the output of this module. The input size of each UEN block and the type used in each stage are present in Table 1.

3.3 Additional Down-Sampling Module

In some scenarios of SOD, some salient areas are quite similar to the non-salient areas around them, for example, the salient object and the reflection of itself in the mirror. This problem leads to that sometimes models will treat these easily-confused un-salient regions as salient regions. The purpose of the Additional Down-sampling Module is to explore more global semantic clues as much as possible to assist the model position accurately and eliminate misleading regions. The structure of ADM is shown in Fig. 3. The input is down-sampled after two

Table 1. Input size and the UEN version of each stage in backbone.

Stage	Input size	The type of UEN
Stage1	112×112	UEN_5
Stage2	56×56	UEN_4
Stage3	28×28	UEN_4
Stage4	14×14	UEN_A
Stage5	7×7	UEN_A

convolutional layers. It is reasonable to infer that the more non-zero pixels in a channel, the more information contained. On the contrary, if a channel has comparatively more zero pixels than other channels, we suppose the information content is inadequate. The global average pooling is followed by two fully connected layers to calculate the amount of information in each channel. Each element in the processed vector corresponds to a channel of the down-sampled feature. The down-sampled feature is multiplied by the vector in channel-wise to make a channel enhancement. As a result, the weights of these channels lacking information are weakened and the others are highlighted. The strengthened $Feature_{ADM}$ is used as the final output of ADM.

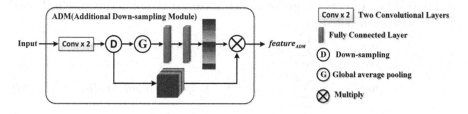

Fig. 3. The structure of ADM.

3.4 Loss Function

Our algorithm supervises five outputs of the model, among which one output is the edge saliency map. Since there is no ground truth of the saliency object edge in the training set, it is necessary to generate the edge labels first. We calculate the gradient for each pixel of the original label. Then, multiply the gradient by itself to get the new value of each pixel:

$$S_{edge} = d_x^2 + d_y^2 \tag{3}$$

S_{edge} is the edge ground truth wanted. d_x and d_y are the gradient values of the pixel in the x-direction and y-direction, respectively. Finally, the non-zero pixels are set as one and then multiply by 255. The edge saliency map is supervised by the edge ground truth generated in this way. The edge loss inspired by [2] is written as:

$$Edge\_Loss = -\sum_{e \in E^+} \log Pr\left(e_n = 1 \mid W\right) - \sum_{e \in E^-} \log Pr\left(e_n = 0 \mid W\right) \qquad (4)$$

e_n represents the pixels in the edge prediction map, and W represents the parameters in the model. $Pr\left(e_n = 1 \mid W\right)$ means the probability that the pixel e_n is calculated as salient edge. E^+ indicates the salient edge pixel set, while E^- is a set that contains all of the pixels except salient edge pixels. Original labels supervise those intermediate saliency maps. For better performance, this method introduces two kinds of loss functions: BCE_Loss and IoU_Loss. BCE Loss is widely used in the training process of binary classifiers. The function is written as:

$$BCE\_Loss = -\sum_{(x,y)} [g(x,y) \log p(x,y) + (1 - g(x,y) \log(1 - p(x,y)))], \qquad (5)$$

where $g(x,y) \in [0,1]$ is the ground truth label of the pixel (x,y) and $p(x,y) \in [0,1]$ is the predicted probability of being salient object. IoU Loss is joint to highlight the prediction error around the salient object boundary. As mentioned before, one of the difficulties in saliency object detection is that the prediction error frequently occurs in the object boundary area, which makes the prediction edge ambiguous and leads to error and missed detection. If the saliency map fails to align with the ground truth, the unaligned part will pay the penalty. The addition of IoU Loss can help the model to correct errors in this specified area. The function is denoted as

$$sum_{inter} = \sum_{y_i \in I} y_i, \quad I = Sal\_map \odot Ground\_Truth, \qquad (6)$$

$$sum_{union} = \sum_{y_j \in J} y_j, \quad J = Sal\_map + Ground\_Truth, \qquad (7)$$

$$IoU\_Loss = \left(1 - \frac{sum_{inter} + 1}{sum_{union} - sum_{inter} + 1}\right) \times \frac{1}{H \times W} \qquad (8)$$

in which H is the height of Sal_map while W is the width. In the experiment, we found that the lower resolution of a saliency map, the more inaccurate the result is. If the losses of all saliency map are given the same weight, it will lead to instability and influence the model performance. Saliency maps generated from deep layers should be weakened with lower weight, so the coefficient is reduced by two. The whole loss function could be written as

$$L_{all} = L_{edge} + BCE\_Loss_{united} + IoU\_Loss_{united}$$
$$+ \sum_{i=1}^{5} \frac{1}{2^{i-1}}(BCE\_Loss_i + IoU\_Loss_i) \qquad (9)$$

$BCE\_Loss_{united} + IoU\_Loss_{united}$ is the loss of united saliency maps. $BCE\_Loss_i + IoU\_Loss_i$ is the loss of the ith intermediate saliency map. The lager i is, the closer the saliency map is to the bottom.

4   Experiment

4.1   Experimental Setting

Datasets and Implementation Details. The model is trained on the DUTS-TR with 10553 images. In detail, we trained the model using the SGD optimizer with initial learning rate 3e-5, 0.9 momentum, 5e-4 weight decay, and batch size 16. Because the ResNet-50 parameters are pre-trained on ImageNet, the learning rate of this part is a tenth of the randomly initialized parts which is set as 3e-5. Then, the trained model is tested on five datasets, including DUTS-TE with 5019 images, DUT-OMROM with 5168 images, HKU-IS with 4447 images and ECSSD with 1000 images.

Metrics. We comprehensively evaluate the model with four metrics widely used in SOD, including mean F-measure (mF), mean absolute error (MAE), structure-measure (Sm) and enhanced-alignment measure (Em). Mean F-measure is the average of F-measures, which is calculated as:

$$F_\beta = \frac{\left(1 + \beta^2\right) \times Precision \times Recall}{\beta^2 \times Precision + Recall} \tag{10}$$

β^2 is usually set as 0.3 to put more emphasis on precision [21]. Mean absolute error is the average of each pixel's absolute error in predictions. Before calculation, each pixel is normalized to $[0, 1]$, and MAE is calculated as

$$MAE = \frac{1}{H \times W} \sum_{i=1}^{H} \sum_{j=1}^{W} |P(i,j) - G(i,j)| \tag{11}$$

H and W is the height and width of the saliency map. $P(i,j)$ is the prediction at location (i,j). $G(i,j)$ denotes the value at location (i,j) in the ground truth. S-measure is a metric proposed to evaluate the structural similarity between the prediction and the corresponding ground truth. S-measure is formulated as

$$S = \alpha S_o + (1 - \alpha)S_r, \tag{12}$$

where S_o represents the object-oriented structural similarity while S_r represents the region-oriented structural similarity. α is set to 0.5, the same as in [6]. E-measure [7] is widely used in SOD as well.

$$E = \frac{1}{W \times H} \sum_{x=1}^{w} \sum_{y=1}^{h} \phi FM(i,j) \tag{13}$$

where $\phi FM(i,j)$ is the enhanced alignment matrix. E-measure considers the performance of both the global average of image and local pixel when evaluating the model.

4.2   Ablation Study

In general, there is no need to down-sample the feature at 7×7 scale because it has a sufficiently large receptive field. However, the experiment results in Table 2 is somewhat counterintuitive. It shows that there is still some different global semantic information waiting to be discovered. The version for comparison is a U-shaped vanilla model, which is trained with the initial learning rate 10^{-4}. Here we use the same learning rate to train the parameters in the backbone and modules designed in our method. The rise of MAE, mF, Sm and Em reflects ADM's reliability and validity. Figure 4 shows the comparison of visualized results between the vanilla network with and without ADM. UENs generate multi-scale features on account of the input level and integrate the features with edge information, which guides the model to pay attention to the boundary areas. The experimental data also reveals that the UENs make greater improvements in various aspects.

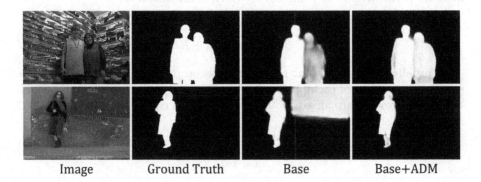

Image   Ground Truth   Base   Base+ADM

Fig. 4. Comparison of predictions between the vanilla network with and without ADM.

Table 2. Comparison of networks with and without the proposed modules, ADM and UENs. Base: a U-structure network with usual U-shape modules.

Datasets			DUTS-TE				DUT-OMROM			
Base	+ADM	+UENs	$mF \uparrow$	$MAE \downarrow$	$Sm \uparrow$	$Em \uparrow$	$mF \uparrow$	$MAE \downarrow$	$Sm \uparrow$	$Em \uparrow$
✓			0.851	0.038	0.894	0.901	0.772	0.065	0.839	0.859
✓	✓		0.860	0.035	0.898	0.907	0.778	0.059	0.843	0.870
✓	✓	✓	0.870	0.031	0.904	0.917	0.790	0.052	0.851	0.881

4.3   Comparison with Other State-of-the-Art Methods

A large number of experiments are conducted to convince the validity of our approach. To make a clear comparison with other state-of-the-art (SOTA) methods, we list all the results in Table 3. There are 15 SOTA methods proposed in the past three years, namely, BMPM [30], RAS [3], PiCANet [13], R3Net [5], BAS-Net [19], PoolNet [12], TDBU [22], PAGE [23], F3Net [24], CPD [28], EGNet [31], MLMSNet [26], U2Net [18], MINet [16], LDF [25]. For a fair comparison, all of the compared saliency maps are provided or generated from released models by the authors. The evaluation codes are all the same. As shown in Table 3 and Fig. 5, our algorithm surpasses most of the methods.

Table 3. Quantitative comparison with state-of-the-art methods on five datasets. The best results are highlighted in bold. The best and the second best results are highlighted in red and green respectively.

Datasets	DUTS-TE				ECSSD				DUT-OMROM				HKU-IS			
Metrics	mF	MAE	Sm	Em	mF	MAE	Sm	Em	mF	MAE	Sm	Em	mF	MAE	Sm	Em
BMPM [30]	.745	.049	.862	.860	.868	.044	.911	.914	.692	.064	.809	.837	.871	.038	.907	.937
RAS [3]	.751	.059	.839	.861	.889	.059	.893	.914	.713	.062	.814	.846	.874	.045	.888	.931
R3Net [5]	.785	.057	.834	.867	.914	.040	.910	.929	.747	.063	.815	.850	.893	.036	.895	.939
PiCANet [13]	.749	.051	.867	.852	.885	.044	.917	.910	.710	.065	.835	.834	.870	.039	.908	.934
MLMSNet [26]	.799	.045	.856	.882	.914	.038	.911	.925	.735	.056	.817	.846	.892	.034	.901	.945
PAGE [23]	.777	.051	.854	.869	.906	.042	.912	.920	.736	.066	.824	.853	.882	.037	.903	.940
CPD [28]	.805	.043	.869	.886	.917	.037	.918	.925	.747	.056	.825	.866	.891	.034	.905	.944
BASNet [19]	.756	.048	.866	.884	.880	.037	.916	.921	.756	.056	.836	.869	.895	.032	.909	.946
F3Net [24]	.840	.035	.888	.902	.925	.033	.924	.927	.766	.053	.838	.870	.840	.062	.855	.859
PoolNet [12]	.799	.040	.879	.881	.910	.042	.917	.921	.739	.055	.832	.858	.885	.032	-	.941
TDBU [22]	.767	.048	.865	.879	.880	.040	.918	.922	.739	.059	.837	.854	.878	.038	.907	.942
EGNet [31]	.815	.039	.875	.891	.920	.041	.918	.927	.755	.052	.818	.867	.898	.031	.918	.948
U2Net [18]	.792	.044	.861	.886	.892	.033	.928	.924	.761	.054	.847	.871	.896	.031	.916	.948
MINet [16]	.828	.037	.884	.917	.924	.033	.925	.953	.756	.055	.833	.873	.908	.028	.920	.961
LDF[25]	.855	.034	.892	.910	.930	.034	.924	.925	.773	.051	.838	.873	.914	.027	.919	.954
Ours	.870	.031	.904	.917	.936	.028	.934	.929	.790	.052	.851	.881	.917	.026	.925	.956

Quantitative Comparison. Table 3 shows the quantitative evaluation results of the SOTA methods mentioned above and our model in terms of mF, MAE, Sm, and Em. The proposed method consistently performs better than all the competitors across four metrics on four datasets. In terms of Em, our method achieves the second best overall performance, which is slightly inferior to MINet. It is worth noting that MEUNet achieves the best performance in terms of the mean F-measure and structure quality evaluation Sm.

Qualitative Comparison. Figure 5 shows the visual comparison between our model and other SOTA methods. The first column is the images and the second column is the corresponding ground truths. Our result is in the third column. It can be observed that our method could locate the salient object accurately and segment the foreground and background around the boundary areas precisely. Predictions in rows 1, 2 and 3 reveal the abilities of the models to deal with detailed extraction, and other lines indicate the location ability. The method proposed in this article is good at keeping as much detail as possible with sharp

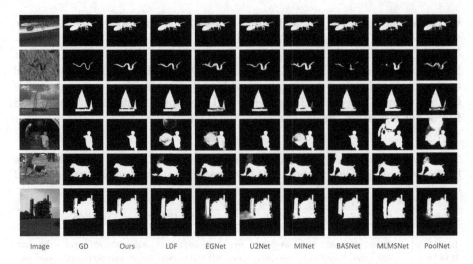

Image   GD   Ours   LDF   EGNet   U2Net   MiNet   BASNet   MLMSNet   PoolNet

Fig. 5. Visual comparison of the previous SOTA methods and our method denoted as 'Ours'.

edges. For example, the legs of the bee in the first picture are clearly present in its prediction, and the snake is continuous and complete only on our map. We suppose that the detail retention ability ascribes to the UENs and the location ability owes to the ADM. In addition to this, the artful structural design allows the features from different layers to complement each other and fuse properly. Our model achieves the best in terms of the overall effect.

5   Conclusion

In this paper, we present a Multi-scale Edge-based U-shape Network with both enhanced high-level semantic features and low-level detail information for SOD. The central architecture of our network is a U-shape encoder-decoder structure which mainly consists of UENs and ADM. The UEN is an outstanding evolution of U-Net, and it contains multi-scale features with rich information and edge information that could assist boundary prediction. ADM can help the network to discover semantic clues from a more global view. Besides, we employ some tricks to improve the performance of the model. For example, the edge saliency map is supervised by salient edges to suppress the edges from the background. The fusion of the parallel four saliency maps is outputed as the final result.

References

1. Borji, A., Frintrop, S., Sihite, D.N., Itti, L.: Adaptive object tracking by learning background context. In: 2012 IEEE Computer Society Conference on Computer Vision and Pattern Recognition Workshops, pp. 23–30. IEEE (2012)

2. Cen, J., Sun, H., Chen, X., Liu, N., Liang, D., Zhou, H.: WFNet: a wider and finer network for salient object detection. IEEE Access **8**, 210418–210428 (2020)
3. Chen, S., Tan, X., Wang, B., Hu, X.: Reverse attention for salient object detection. In: Proceedings of the European Conference on Computer Vision (ECCV), pp. 234–250 (2018)
4. Chen, Z., Zhou, H., Lai, J., Yang, L., Xie, X.: Contour-aware loss: Boundary-aware learning for salient object segmentation. IEEE Trans. Image Process. **30**, 431–443 (2020)
5. Deng, Z., et al.: R^{3}net: recurrent residual refinement network for saliency detection. In: Proceedings of the 27th International Joint Conference on Artificial Intelligence, pp. 684–690 (2018)
6. Fan, D.P., Cheng, M.M., Liu, Y., Li, T., Borji, A.: Structure-measure: a new way to evaluate foreground maps. In: Proceedings of the IEEE International Conference on Computer Vision, pp. 4548–4557 (2017)
7. Fan, D.P., Gong, C., Cao, Y., Ren, B., Cheng, M.M., Borji, A.: Enhanced-alignment measure for binary foreground map evaluation. arXiv preprint arXiv:1805.10421 (2018)
8. Feng, M., Lu, H., Yu, Y.: Residual learning for salient object detection. IEEE Trans. Image Process. **29**, 4696–4708 (2020)
9. He, K., Zhang, X., Ren, S., Sun, J.: Deep residual learning for image recognition. In: Proceedings of the IEEE Conference on Computer Vision and Pattern Recognition, pp. 770–778 (2016)
10. Li, T., Song, H., Zhang, K., Liu, Q.: Learning residual refinement network with semantic context representation for real-time saliency object detection. Pattern Recogn. **105**, 107372 (2020)
11. Li, X., Song, D., Dong, Y.: Hierarchical feature fusion network for salient object detection. IEEE Trans. Image Process. **29**, 9165–9175 (2020)
12. Liu, J., Hou, Q., Cheng, M.M., Feng, J., Jiang, J.: A simple pooling-based design for real-time salient object detection. In: 2019 IEEE/CVF Conference on Computer Vision and Pattern Recognition (CVPR), pp. 3912–3921 (2019)
13. Liu, N., Han, J., Yang, M.H.: Picanet: Learning pixel-wise contextual attention for saliency detection. In: Proceedings of the IEEE Conference on Computer Vision and Pattern Recognition, pp. 3089–3098 (2018)
14. Long, J., Shelhamer, E., Darrell, T.: Fully convolutional networks for semantic segmentation. In: Proceedings of the IEEE Conference on Computer Vision and Pattern Recognition, pp. 3431–3440 (2015)
15. Ma, Y.F., Lu, L., Zhang, H.J., Li, M.: A user attention model for video summarization. In: Proceedings of the tenth ACM International Conference on Multimedia, pp. 533–542 (2002)
16. Pang, Y., Zhao, X., Zhang, L., Lu, H.: Multi-scale interactive network for salient object detection. In: Proceedings of the IEEE/CVF Conference on Computer Vision and Pattern Recognition, pp. 9413–9422 (2020)
17. Perazzi, F., Krähenbühl, P., Pritch, Y., Hornung, A.: Saliency filters: contrast based filtering for salient region detection. In: 2012 IEEE Conference on Computer Vision and Pattern Recognition, pp. 733–740. IEEE (2012)
18. Qin, X., Zhang, Z., Huang, C., Dehghan, M., Zaiane, O.R., Jagersand, M.: U2-Net: going deeper with nested u-structure for salient object detection. Pattern Recogn. **106**, 107404 (2020)
19. Qin, X., Zhang, Z., Huang, C., Gao, C., Dehghan, M., Jagersand, M.: Basnet: boundary-aware salient object detection. In: Proceedings of the IEEE/CVF Conference on Computer Vision and Pattern Recognition, pp. 7479–7489 (2019)

20. Ronneberger, O., Fischer, P., Brox, T.: U-Net: convolutional networks for biomedical image segmentation. In: Navab, N., Hornegger, J., Wells, W.M., Frangi, A.F. (eds.) MICCAI 2015. LNCS, vol. 9351, pp. 234–241. Springer, Cham (2015). https://doi.org/10.1007/978-3-319-24574-4_28

21. Rutishauser, U., Walther, D., Koch, C., Perona, P.: Is bottom-up attention useful for object recognition? In: Proceedings of the 2004 IEEE Computer Society Conference on Computer Vision and Pattern Recognition, 2004. CVPR 2004, vol. 2, p. II. IEEE (2004)

22. Wang, W., Shen, J., Cheng, M.M., Shao, L.: An iterative and cooperative top-down and bottom-up inference network for salient object detection. In: Proceedings of the IEEE/CVF Conference on Computer Vision and Pattern Recognition, pp. 5968–5977 (2019)

23. Wang, W., Zhao, S., Shen, J., Hoi, S., Borji, A.: Salient object detection with pyramid attention and salient edges. In: 2019 IEEE/CVF Conference on Computer Vision and Pattern Recognition (CVPR), pp. 1448–1457 (2019)

24. Wei, J., Wang, S., Huang, Q.: F^3net: Fusion, feedback and focus for salient object detection. In: AAAI (2020)

25. Wei, J., Wang, S., Wu, Z., Su, C., Huang, Q., Tian, Q.: Label decoupling framework for salient object detection. In: 2020 IEEE/CVF Conference on Computer Vision and Pattern Recognition (CVPR), pp. 13022–13031 (2020)

26. Wu, R., Feng, M., Guan, W., Wang, D., Lu, H., Ding, E.: A mutual learning method for salient object detection with intertwined multi-supervision. In: 2019 IEEE/CVF Conference on Computer Vision and Pattern Recognition (CVPR), pp. 8142–8151 (2019)

27. Wu, Y., Liu, Y., Zhang, L., Cheng, M.M.: EDN: salient object detection via extremely-downsampled network. arXiv:abs/2012.13093 (2020)

28. Wu, Z., Su, L., Huang, Q.: Cascaded partial decoder for fast and accurate salient object detection. In: 2019 IEEE/CVF Conference on Computer Vision and Pattern Recognition (CVPR), pp. 3902–3911 (2019)

29. Zeng, Y., Zhuge, Y., Lu, H., Zhang, L.: Joint learning of saliency detection and weakly supervised semantic segmentation. In: Proceedings of the IEEE/CVF International Conference on Computer Vision, pp. 7223–7233 (2019)

30. Zhang, L., Dai, J., Lu, H., He, Y., Wang, G.: A bi-directional message passing model for salient object detection. In: Proceedings of the IEEE Conference on Computer Vision and Pattern Recognition, pp. 1741–1750 (2018)

31. Zhao, J.X., Liu, J.J., Fan, D.P., Cao, Y., Yang, J., Cheng, M.M.: EGNet: edge guidance network for salient object detection. In: Proceedings of the IEEE/CVF International Conference on Computer Vision, pp. 8779–8788 (2019)

32. Zhou, S., et al.: Hierarchical and interactive refinement network for edge-preserving salient object detection. IEEE Trans. Image Process. 30, 1–14 (2020)

33. Zhou, S., et al.: Hierarchical u-shape attention network for salient object detection. IEEE Trans. Image Process. 29, 8417–8428 (2020)

Reconstruct Anomaly to Normal: Adversarially Learned and Latent Vector-Constrained Autoencoder for Time-Series Anomaly Detection

Chunkai Zhang[1]([✉]), Wei Zuo[1]([✉]), Shaocong Li[1], Xuan Wang[1],
Peiyi Han[1,2]([✉]), and Chuanyi Liu[1,2]

[1] Harbin Institute of Technology (Shenzhen), Shenzhen, China
{ckzhang,hanpeiyi,liuchuanyi}@hit.edu.cn, wangxuan@cs.hitsz.edu.cn
[2] Peng Cheng Laboratory, Cyberspace Security Research Center, Shenzhen, China

Abstract. Time-series Anomaly Detection has important applications, such as credit card fraud detection and machine fault detection. Anomaly detection based on the generative model generally detect samples with high reconstruction errors as anomalies. However, some anomalies may get low reconstruction errors, as they can also be well reconstructed due to the strong generalization ability of the model. To ensure the high reconstruction error of anomalies, we propose a novel anomaly detection algorithm named **RAN** (**R**econstruct **A**nomalies to **N**ormal) based on the Autoencoder. We try to force the reconstruction samples of both normal samples and anomaly samples obey the distribution of normal samples, then the difference between normal sample and its reconstruction sample is small while the difference between anomaly sample and its reconstruction sample is large, and higher reconstruction error for anomaly samples is guaranteed. The Autoencoder constructed by 1D-FCN with different kernel sizes is utilized to extract richer features of time-series data. Imitated anomaly samples are feed to the model to provide more information about anomalies. Then, constraints in the latent space and original data space are added to control the reconstruction process. Extensive experiments on real-life time-series datasets also show that **RAN** outperforms some state-of-art algorithms.

Keywords: Anomaly detection · Time-series data · Autoencoder · Reconstruction error · Imitated anomaly samples

1 Introduction

Anomaly detection in time series has been studied in many fields and has practical applications. For example, electrocardiograms anomaly detection can indicate the health status of the heart [6], financial transaction data anomaly detection can detect credit card fraud [1], and network anomaly detection can protect the system from attacks [21]. Since anomalies have different types and labeling real-life data is usually difficult, anomaly detection algorithms are generally unsupervised.

© Springer Nature Switzerland AG 2021
D. N. Pham et al. (Eds.): PRICAI 2021, LNAI 13032, pp. 515–529, 2021.
https://doi.org/10.1007/978-3-030-89363-7_39

Traditional unsupervised anomaly detection algorithms generally use different data-structures to represent data, then calculates the similarity between data objects as anomaly scores. However, most of these algorithms may lose important information in dimension reduction and suffer from the curse of dimension in similarity calculation [22,31]. As the volume and complexity of time-series data grow, deep-learning methods are proposed for anomaly detection, which concluded in [4]. These methods extract features automatically and calculate anomaly scores based on the extracted features.

Recently, deep-learning anomaly detection algorithms based on generative models have been extensively studied [12,26,29,32], which claim normal samples can be well reconstructed and anomaly samples can not. Then input samples with high reconstruction error are tend to be detected as anomalies. However, this statement is not rigorous and may lead to the omission of anomalies. The Generative Model will model the distribution of training samples rather than the training sample itself, and the strong generalization ability enables it to reconstruct some anomaly samples containing similar features with the training samples. Observations of image reconstruction are also shown in Fig. 1 of [23]: model trained with digit 8 can also reconstruct digit 1, 5, 6 and 9, which lead to the low reconstruction error of anomalies. In real life time-series data set, as shown in Fig. 1, some anomaly samples also has similar distribution with normal samples, and they may be well reconstructed. On the other hand, anomaly samples have not been seen by the model before and its reconstruction process is uncertain, so the high reconstruction error of anomaly samples is also not guaranteed.

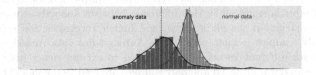

Fig. 1. Distribution of the first dimension in normal samples and anomalies.

Based on the above observation, it is significant to additionally control the reconstruction process of anomaly data when detecting anomalies based on the reconstruction error. In this paper, we proposed a new algorithm named **RAN** for time-series anomaly detection. The target of **RAN** is to ensure higher reconstruction error for anomaly samples, which is achieved by forcing the reconstruction samples of anomaly samples to be similar with normal samples. Firstly, imitated anomaly samples are introduced to provide information of anomalies for model training. Secondly, we specially design the model to control the reconstruction process of anomalies. The Autoencoder constructed by 1D-FCN is utilized to extract richer information from time-series data, and it is also combined with a discriminator to construct the adversary network. Then, we add constraints in both the original data space and latent space of the Autoencoder to control the reconstruction process. In the latent space of Autoencoder, latent vectors of anomaly samples are constrained to be close to these of normal samples. In original data space, the Autoencoder is forced to generate reconstruction samples which obey the distribution of normal samples, when adversarially trained with the discriminator. Then the difference between anomaly samples and the corresponding reconstruction samples is large, and high reconstruction error for anomaly samples is guaranteed.

Extensive experiments on different types of time-series data sets from UCR Repository [7], BIDMC database [2,8] and MIT-BIH datasets [19] show that (i) **RAN** can detect meaningful anomalies and get overall good performance in terms of AUC-ROC. (ii) **RAN** can generate eligible reconstructions and better control the reconstruction process of anomalies. (iii) **RAN** can provide more distinguishable reconstruction errors for anomaly detection.

The remainder of this paper is organized as follows. Related work is briefly introduced in Sect. 2. Then, the details of the proposed anomaly detection algorithm **RAN** is described in Sect. 3. Experimental results and analysis are shown in Sect. 4. Finally, we conclude this paper in Sect. 5.

2   Related Work

2.1   Traditional Anomaly Detection Methods

Traditional machine learning anomaly detection algorithms generally use different data structures to represent data, then calculate distance, density, or other statistic values based on the representation to calculate anomaly scores. Distance-based algorithms [25,27,30] detects samples far away from other samples as anomalies. They represent time series by sequences or symbol sequences with reduced dimensions such as Piecewise Aggregate Approximation (PAA) [11] and Symbolic Aggregate Approximation (SAX) [13]. Extended SAX(ESAX) [16] adds two new points max and min in each time series to generate SAX series for anomaly detection, But the calculation of pair-wise distance between subsequences usually lead to high computational cost. Density-based algorithms detect samples with low density as anomalies such as Local Outlier Factor (LOF) [3] and Relative Density-based Outlier Score (RDOS) [28], but the performance is restricted with the number of neighborhoods. Interval [25] is based on the data interval and each subsequence's boundary probability to calculate the anomaly score, but it may lose the sequential trend information as it only pays attention to the interval information and probability of points falls into data interval. Piecewise Aggregate Pattern Representation (PAPR) [24] add point feature and dispersion feature based on PAA to construct the statistical characteristics matrix for each subsequence and then use Random Walk [20] to calculate the anomaly score. However, PAPR consumes too much time, since it contains the iterative optimization process. Isolation Forest(iForest) [15] constructs isolation trees to represent data and detects samples with short average path lengths as anomalies. But it may loses time-order information when selecting the data attributes randomly. There are also algorithms [20,24] that apply the hidden Markov model to detect samples with low probability as anomalies, but they also consumes lots of time for the iteration process.

2.2 Deep-Learning Anomaly Detection Methods

As the volume and dimension of data grow, deep-learning algorithms are proposed for anomaly detection. Most of these algorithms are based on the generative model and detect samples with high reconstruction error as anomalies. AnoGAN [26] is the first work that applies GAN for image anomaly detection, which uses normal data to train the model and calculate errors from the trained generator and discriminator as anomaly scores. To reduce the test time of AnoGAN, [29] build ALAD upon bi-directional GANs and added an encoder network that maps data samples to latent variables z. Then, ALAD tries to learn the distribution of the normal data so that $p_G(x) = \int p_G(x|z) p_Z(x|z) dz$. Autoencoder (AE) has also been applied in anomaly detection in some researches. [10] first, apply AE for anomaly detection and use reconstruction error to detect the anomaly. Considering that the reduced low-dimension space of AE is unable to preserve essential information, [32] proposed DAGMM by combining AE with a Gaussian Mixture Model (GMM) and adopting the joint training strategy. To mitigate the drawback that AE sometimes can also reconstruct anomalies well, [9] proposed MemAE which equipped the AE with a memory module to strengthen the reconstruction error of anomalies.

There are also anomaly detection algorithms based on LSTM to handle time-series data. LSTM-AD [18] trained the model with normal samples, and the prediction error is used to model a multivariate Gaussian distribution to evaluate anomaly degree. [17] proposed LSTM-ED by constructing the Autoencoder with LSTM units, which combines the advantages of LSTM and AE.

3 Proposed Method: RAN

This section firstly describes the time-series anomaly detection problem and present some symbols used later, then the proposed method **RAN** is introduced in detail.

3.1 Problem Description

Considering that anomalies always have different and uncertain lengths, it is more practical to first detect anomaly subsequences and then take a more detailed examination by experts under most circumstances.

Assuming we have the training data set $X_{nor} = \{X_0, X_1, \ldots, X_{n-1}\}, X_i = \{x_{i,0}, x_{i,1}, \ldots, x_{i,m-1}\}$, which contains n normal subsequences. The test data set is $X_{test} = \{X_0, X_1, \ldots, X_{t-1}\}, X_j = \{x_{j,0}, x_{j,1}, \ldots, x_{j,m-1}\}$, which contains normal subsequences and anomaly subsequences. The task is to output proper anomaly scores for all subsequences in X_{test} and detect these anomaly subsequences.

3.2 Imitate Anomaly Subsequences

According to [5], anomalies can be classified into point anomalies, contextual anomalies, and collective anomalies. It is worth noting that point anomalies can occur in any data set and in most time-series anomaly detection scenarios, anomalies in the anomaly subsequence are usually consisting of small part anomaly points rather than the whole.

Based on the above observation, we imitate the anomaly subsequence based on the normal subsequence by corrupting some normal data points. Firstly, we set the corrupt level and randomly select some column indexes of the subsequence to get the index set R. Then, considering most normalized time series have Gaussian distribution [14], we calculate the corresponding anomaly data value based on the tail of Gaussian distribution to replace the normal data points and obtain the imitated anomaly subsequence. The pseudo-code is shown in Algorithm 1.

Algorithm 1. Imitate anomaly subsequences

Input: X_{nor}: the training data set which contains normal subsequences
Parameter: c: corrupt level, n: number of subsequences in X_{nor}, m: length of the subsequence
Output: $X_{imi} = \{anoX_0, anoX_1, \ldots anoX_n - 1\}$
$anoX_i = \{anox_{i,0}, anox_{i,1}, \ldots, anox_{i,m-1}\}$

1: **for** $i = 0 : n - 1$ **do**
2:    $R =$ randomly select $c * m$ indexes of $[0, 1, \ldots m - 1]$
3:    **for** r in R **do**
4:       $u_r = \frac{1}{n} * \sum_i^n x_{i,r}$ $(x_{i,r} \in X_{nor})$
5:       $\sigma_r = \sqrt{\frac{1}{n} * \sum_i^n (x_{i,r} - u_r)}$ $(x_{i,r} \in X_{nor})$
6:       $anox_{i,r} = u_r + 4 * \sigma_r$ $(anox_{i,r} \in X_{imi})$
7:    **end for**
8:    **for** r not in R **do**
9:       $anox_{i,r} = x_{i,r}$ $(x_{i,r} \in X_{nor}, anox_{i,r} \in X_{imi})$
10:   **end for**
11: **end for**
12: **return** X_{imi}

3.3   Reconstruct Anomalies to Normal

To best utilize the reconstruction error for anomaly detection, we aim to minimize the reconstruction error of the normal samples and maximize this of anomaly samples as possible. The key sight of **RAN** is to ensure the reconstruction samples obey the distribution of normal samples, which means reconstructing normal samples as well as possible and forcing the reconstruction of anomaly samples obey the distribution of normal samples at the same time. In this way, the difference between reconstruction samples and normal samples are small while the difference between reconstruction samples and anomaly samples are large, then higher reconstruction error for anomaly samples is guaranteed.

The structure of our model is shown in Fig. 2. X_{nor} is the normal subsequences we have, and X_{imi} is the imitated anomaly subsequences generated in Sect. 3.2. Z is the latent vector of X_{nor}, and Z_{imi} is the latent vector of X_{imi}

in the latent space. X_{rec} is the reconstruction data generated by the decoder. More details about each component of the model are as follows.

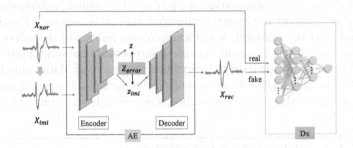

Fig. 2. The structure of the proposed model.

Autoencoder. Autoencoder(AE) is the combination of encoder and decoder, which extracts features of training samples automatically. AE also acts as the generator when combined with the discriminator Dx in the adversarial network.

Encoder. To broaden the vision of the model, we also feed the imitated anomaly subsequences X_{imi} to the encoder. Then we can get the corresponding latent representation Z_{imi}. Latent vector is significant for generating the eligible reconstruction, so we minimize the latent vector error Z_{error} as possible to ensure the latent vector of anomalies consistent with this of normal samples.

Since the encoder is important for generating a good representation in latentspace, we specially design the structure of the encoder to extract better features for time-series data. Considering that data points combined with neighbors can contain more information, we use the 1D-FCN as shown in Fig. 3 to construct the encoder and set different kernel sizes in different layers. The encoder contains four convolutional layers with kernel size of 3, 5, 7, 9.

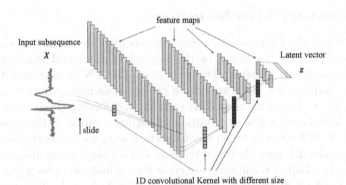

Fig. 3. 1D-FCN to extract the combined information with neighbors.

Decoder. Corresponding to the encoder, we use the 1D deconvolutional neural network to construct it. We use the decoder to generate the reconstruction X_{rec} from the latent representation Z_{imi}. The reasons why not use both Z and Z_{imi} are: 1) we minimize the error Z_{error} between them during the training process; 2) we also force the reconstruction of X_{imi} to have the same distribution with normal samples in the adversarial training, and it will indirectly force Z_{imi} have the same distribution with Z.

Dx. To ensure the reconstruction samples obey the distribution of normal samples, we add the discriminator Dx after AE to construct an adversary network. The decoder contains four deconvolutional layers with kernel size of 9, 7, 5, 3. Dx will output a probability to indicate how real the input sample is. Adversarial learning can force the generator to generate data which obey the distribution of training data. In the adversarial training process, we hope the discriminator to recognize reconstruction samples as fake, the output of $Dx(X_{rec})$ is forced to approach 0; we also hope the discriminator to recognize normal samples as real, so the output of $Dx(X_{nor})$ is forced to approach 1.

Loss Function. The aims of AE are: 1) for normal samples, learning a good representation in the latent space and generating good reconstructions in the original data space; 2) for anomaly samples, learning a representation as normal in the latent space and then generating reconstructions which obey the distribution of normal samples in the original data space. We apply constraints both on latent space and the original data space to achieve these.

The loss function for AE in the training process is as Eq. (1). The weight λ was chosen based on the quality of reconstruction. Z_{error} is the loss between Z and Z_{imi} in the latent space, and gen_{loss} is the loss in the original space.

$$L_{AE} = \lambda * Z_{error} + gen_{loss} \tag{1}$$

$$Z_{error} = Z - Z_{imi} \tag{2}$$

$$gen_{loss} = E_{X_{imi} \sim P_i}[\log(1 - Dx(AE(X_{imi})))] \tag{3}$$

The loss function for Dx in the adversarial training procedure is as Eq. (4). Dx treats normal samples X_{nor} as real and treats the reconstruction samples X_{rec} as fake.

$$L_{Dx} = -(E_{X_{nor} \sim P_X}[\log(Dx(X_{nor}))] + E_{X_{rec} \sim P_{X_r}}[\log(1 - Dx(X_{rec}))]) \tag{4}$$

The pseudo-code of the proposed method RAN is shown in Algorithm 2.

Anomaly Detection. We use Eq. (5) to calculate anomaly scores based on reconstruction errors. Higher anomaly score indicates higher possibility to be anomaly subsequences.

$$Ano\_Score_i = \frac{rec\_errors[i] - Min(rec\_errors)}{Max(rec\_errors) - Min(rec\_errors)} \tag{5}$$

4   Experiments

In this section, we first introduce data sets used in the experiment, then apply our algorithm **RAN** and several baseline anomaly detection algorithms to compare and analyze their performances. We also carried the ablation study to verify the effectiveness of each component in **RAN**.

Algorithm 2. Reconstruct anomalies to normal: **RAN**

Input: X_{nor}: the training set containing normal subsequences, X_{imi} : the imitated anomaly subsequences, X_{test} : the test set
Parameter: N
Output: rec_errors

1: **Training phase:**
2: **for** epoch 1 to N **do**
3:      input X_{nor} and X_{imi} into AE
4:      get the latent vector Z and Z_{imi} , get output X_{rec}
5:      Discriminator Dx update:
6:      $L_{Dx} \leftarrow Dx(X_{rec}, 0) + Dx(X_{nor}, 1)$
7:      Back-propagate L_{Dx} and change Dx
8:      keep Dx fixed
9:      Generator AE update:
10:     $Z_{error} = Z - Z_{imi}$
11:     $gen_{loss} = Dx(X_{rec}, 1)$
12:     $L_{AE} = \lambda * Z_{error} + gen_{loss}$
13:     Back-propagate L_{AE} and change AE.
14: **end for**
15: **Testing phase:**
16: **for** X_i in X_{test} **do**
17:     keep model fixed
18:     $X_{i\_rec} = AE(X_i)$
19:     $rec\_errors[i] = X_{i\_rec} - X_i$
20: **end for**

4.1   Experiments Setup

Data Sets. As shown in Table 1, four different types of time-series data are selected from the UCR Time Series Repository, MIT-BIH data sets, and BIDMC database to test the performance of these algorithms. In ECG data, each subsequence traces the electrical activity recorded during one heartbeat. Anomalies in ECG200 are heart attacks due to prolonged cardiac ischemia. Data in BIDMC_chf07 are collected from a patient who has severe congestive heart failure. Anomalies in MIT-BIH220 are atrial premature beats. Anomalies in MIT-BIH221 are premature ventricular contraction beats. Anomalies in MIT-BIH210 contains four types of abnormal beats (a, V, F, E): atrial premature beats, premature ventricular contraction beats, the fusion of ventricular and normal beats, and ventricular escape beats. Sensor data are collected from different sensors and divided into subsequences. Motion data is obtained according to the center of mass of the action. For image data, the contours of these images are extracted and mapped into a one-dimensional sequence from the center. There are several classes in some data sets, and considering that in real life the types of anomalies are often uncertain, we select one class as normal data and randomly select some samples from the other classes as anomaly data.

Experimental Setup. To verify the effectiveness of **RAN**, we compare it with several baseline methods. For traditional anomaly detection algorithms, we select ESAX, SAX_TD, Interval, RDOS, PAPR, and iForest. We also use some deep-learning anomaly detection algorithms, including AnoGAN, DAGMM, ALAD, MemAE, LSTMAD, and LSTMED. We implemented experiments on the computer server with 10 core CPUs, 3.3 GHz, 64 bits operating system. All codes are built in Python 3.7.

Table 1. The description of time-series data sets

No.	Data sets	Seq_num	Seq_length	Ano_rate	Types
1	ECG200	200	96	33.50%	ECG
2	BIDMC_chf07	5000	140	41.62%	ECG
3	MIT-BIH210	2649	207	8.57%	ECG
4	MIT-BIH220	2047	292	4.59%	ECG
5	MIT-BIH221	2426	191	16.32%	ECG
6	Lighting2	121	637	39.66%	Sensor
7	MoteStrain	1272	84	46.14%	Sensor
8	SonyAIBORobotSurfaceII	980	65	38.36%	Sensor
9	StarLightCurves	427	1024	35.59%	Sensor
10	ToeSegmentation2	166	343	25.30%	Motion
11	GunPointAgeSpan	339	150	32.74%	Motion
12	UWaveGestureLibraryX	950	315	41.16%	Motion
13	DistalPhalanxOutlineCorrect	876	80	38.47%	Image
14	HandOutlines	1370	2709	36.13%	Image
15	DiatomSizeReduction	142	345	30.99%	Image

Performance Evaluation Method. Since most anomaly detection algorithms calculate anomaly scores to detect anomalies, we use the Area Under Receiver Operating Characteristic Curve (AUC-ROC) to have a comprehensive evaluation of these algorithms. In anomaly detection, higher AUC-ROC indicates higher ability for the algorithm to distinguish anomaly data and normal data.

4.2   Comparison with State-of-the-Art Algorithms

Experimental results of the proposed algorithm and other algorithms are recorded in Table 2, and the best AUC-ROC are highlighted in bold font.

From Table 2, we can find that: 1) **RAN** outperform other algorithms in most data sets (8/15), which verifies the ability of **RAN** to detect anomalies for different types of time-series data; 2) MemAE obtains the second-best performance (5/15), which equips autoencoder with a memory module to mitigate the drawback of AE that it sometimes reconstructs the anomalies well. And it also reflects the importance of reconstructing anomalies to normal for reconstruction-based anomaly detection models. 3) Compare to non-deep-learning algorithms, deep-learning algorithms can get overall better performance due to their complex networks to extract more deep features, and they are more appropriate to process complex data.

4.3   Analysis of Performance

Effectiveness to Detect Anomalies. We use the MIT-BIH210 from MIT-BIH Database to show that our algorithm can detect true anomalies. The MIT-BIH210 data set contains five types of heartbeats, of which one type (N) is normal heartbeats and other types (a, V, F, E) are anomaly heartbeats annotated by experts.

Table 2. AUC-ROC of different algorithms

No.	TSAX	SAX_TD	Interval	RDOS	PAPR	iForest	DAGMM	LSTMAD	LSTMED	AnoGAN	ALAD	MemAE	RAN*
1	0.688	0.590	0.549	0.638	0.760	0.854	0.657	0.869	0.873	0.734	0.652	0.864	**0.907**
2	0.638	0.595	0.546	0.507	0.825	0.695	0.963	0.951	0.970	0.891	0.934	0.943	**0.983**
3	0.727	0.602	0.949	0.619	0.945	0.983	0.983	0.975	**0.991**	0.848	0.979	0.986	0.988
4	0.593	0.650	0.509	0.537	0.889	0.999	0.996	**1.000**	0.999	0.999	0.999	**1.000**	**1.000**
5	0.970	0.507	0.518	0.504	0.962	0.911	0.979	0.914	0.976	0.958	0.980	0.988	**0.999**
6	0.745	0.526	0.662	0.608	0.619	0.766	0.603	0.734	0.777	0.641	0.642	**0.858**	0.732
7	0.543	0.580	0.543	0.578	0.659	0.766	0.784	0.759	0.786	0.707	0.821	**0.938**	0.923
8	0.651	0.605	0.525	0.533	0.521	0.794	0.861	0.963	0.965	0.642	0.700	0.874	0.928
9	0.939	0.962	0.557	0.536	0.621	0.740	0.882	0.972	0.972	**1.000**	**1.000**	**1.000**	**1.000**
10	0.549	0.758	0.702	0.766	0.777	**0.784**	0.766	0.586	0.622	0.539	0.510	0.507	0.608
11	0.835	0.784	0.537	0.569	0.695	0.901	0.895	0.825	0.874	0.733	0.866	0.565	**0.934**
12	0.622	0.706	0.534	0.612	0.557	0.908	0.852	0.755	0.852	0.671	0.900	0.904	**0.927**
13	0.517	0.579	0.520	0.747	0.624	0.767	**0.787**	0.755	0.767	0.560	0.613	0.717	0.642
14	0.548	0.538	0.577	0.699	0.728	0.786	0.661	0.903	**0.916**	0.576	0.891	0.845	0.863
15	0.536	0.702	0.824	0.589	0.967	0.940	0.896	**1.000**	**1.000**	**1.000**	**1.000**	**1.000**	**1.000**

A fragment of experiment results is shown in Fig. 4, curve in blue color represents normal subsequence, curve in yellow color represents anomalous subsequences and curve in red color represents the reconstructed subsequences of anomalous subsequences. The first row is test subsequences. The second row is the corresponding reconstructions, and the third row is the corresponding reconstruction errors. From these three subgraphs, we can find that **RAN** reconstruct the normal subsequences well and ensure the reconstruction of anomaly subsequences be similar to normal subsequences. In the third row, reconstruction errors of anomaly subsequences are higher than this of normal subsequences, and anomalies can be detected more easily.

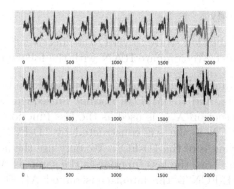

Fig. 4. A fragment of the experiment results from MIT-BIH210.

Ability to Control the Reconstruction Process of Anomalies. To see whether our model can effectively control the reconstruction process of anomalies, we also draw the histogram distribution of original data, reconstruction data, and latent vector.

As shown in Fig. 5, different color represents normal and anomaly. The first row is the distribution of original samples. We can find that distributions of these two data sets are different, and distributions of normal samples and anomaly samples also vary greatly. The second row is the corresponding reconstructions. Reconstructions of anomaly samples are very close to the distribution of normal samples, which prove that the model can ensure the reconstruction of anomaly samples obey the distribution of normal samples. The third row is the distributions of corresponding latent vectors. We can find that distributions of latent vectors of both normal and anomaly samples tend to be similar after the transformation of the encoder, which also proves the effectiveness of latent constraint in our model.

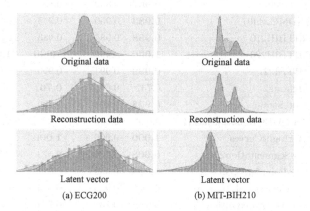

Fig. 5. Histogram distribution of original data, reconstruction data, and latent vector from (a) ECG200 (b) MIT-BIH210. Different color represents normal and anomaly

4.4   Ablation Study

We also carried the ablation study to verify the effectiveness of each component of the proposed model. We compare **RAN** with the following variants.

- **AE**: AE is the standard autoencoder. We only use the normal subsequences for model training, and the MSE of normal subsequences X and the corresponding reconstruction X_{rec} is used as the loss function.
- **AE-FCN**: AE-FCN is the AE constructed by 1D-FCN, and it is used to verify the effectiveness of the 1D-FCN. We only use the normal subsequences for model training, and the loss function is the same as AE.
- **LAE-FCN**: LAE-FCN is the latent-constrained AE-FCN which also constrains the latent vectors of imitated anomaly subsequences and normal subsequences. We introduce the imitated anomaly subsequences in the training phase and add the MSE between Z_{imi} and Z in the loss function of AE-FCN.
- **RAN**: RAN is the proposed method which further constructs the adversarial network in the original data space, and it is used to verify the effectiveness of the original data space constraint component. Except for the loss function of LAE-FCN, we also use the adversarial loss for model training.

The AUC-ROC results of the ablation study are shown in Table 3. AE-FCN outperforms or equals to AE in most data sets (12/15), which verify the effectiveness of the 1D-FCN to extract richer features from time-series data. Reconstruction results of AE and AE-FCN are also shown in Fig. 6, the first row is part of the original time series data from MIT-BIH210. In the second row, AE can not reconstruct two crests well, and the reconstruction marked by the circle

Table 3. AUC-ROC of ablation study

No	Dataset	RAN*	LAE-FCN	AE-FCN	AE
1	ECG200	**0.907**	0.862	0.894	0.833
2	BIDMC_chf07	**0.983**	0.950	0.945	0.979
3	MITBIH210	**0.988**	0.986	0.983	0.984
4	MITBIH220	**1.000**	0.999	**1.000**	**1.000**
5	MITBI221	**0.999**	0.994	0.990	0.991
6	Lighting2	0.732	0.606	**0.761**	0.699
7	MoteStrain	**0.923**	0.903	0.889	0.768
8	SonyAIBORobotSurfaceII	0.928	0.896	0.902	**0.960**
9	StarLightCurves	**1.000**	0.996	**1.000**	0.970
10	ToeSegmentation2	**0.608**	0.508	0.579	0.513
11	GunPointAgeSpan	**0.934**	0.530	0.511	0.784
12	UwaveGestureLibraryX	**0.927**	0.916	0.924	0.881
13	DiatalphalanxOutlineCorrect	0.642	0.730	0.764	**0.795**
14	HandOutlines	0.863	0.877	0.873	**0.907**
15	DiatomSizeReduction	**1.000**	**1.000**	**1.000**	**1.000**

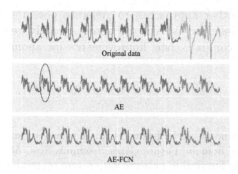

Fig. 6. Original data and the corresponding reconstructions from AE and AE-FCN.

is fuzzy. In the third row, AE-FCN can better reconstruct the first crest, which also verify the effectiveness of 1D-FCN to extract richer shape information. The proposed method **RAN** out performance other variants in almost all datasets and gets overall good performance, which indicates that the imitated anomaly subsequences introduced in the training phase and constraints added in both latent space and original data space greatly improve the model performance.

5   Conclusion

In this paper, a novel anomaly detection algorithm **RAN** is proposed based on the idea of reconstructing anomalies to normal. To mitigate the drawback that some anomaly samples has low reconstruction error and may be miss out, we additionally control the reconstruction process of anomalies to improve their reconstruction errors. Firstly, imitated anomaly samples are feed into the model to provide more information about anomalies. Secondly, the Autoencoder constructed by 1D-FCN is utilized to extract richer temporal information from time-series data, and we constrain both the latent space and original data space of the model to control the reconstruction process. In the latent space, the difference between the latent vector of normal samples and this of the imitated anomaly samples is minimized, which guides the encoder to learn robust features and generate similar latent vectors. In the original space, the discriminator is equipped after the Autoencoder and force the reconstructions to obey the distribution of normal samples through adversarial learning. Finally, the difference between anomaly samples and reconstructions will be large and high reconstruction error for anomaly samples is guaranteed.

Experimental results on diverse types of time-series data sets also show that our algorithm **RAN** can detect meaningful anomalies and generate better anomaly scores to distinguish than other algorithms. In terms of AUC-ROC, **RAN** also outperforms other algorithms on most data sets. The ablation study also shows that each component of **RAN** is meaningful and effective to improve the model performance.

There are also other approaches to generate potential anomalies such as using the density function. We will try more anomaly generation approaches and experiment to compare their improvements for anomaly detection in the future work.

References

1. Ahmed, M., Mahmood, A.N., Islam, M.R.: A survey of anomaly detection techniques in financial domain. Future Gener. Comput. Syst. **55**, 278–288 (2016)
2. Baim, D.S., et al.: Survival of patients with severe congestive heart failure treated with oral milrinone. J. Am. Coll. Cardiol. **7**(3), 661–670 (1986)
3. Breunig, M.M., Kriegel, H.P., Ng, R.T., Sander, J.: LOF: identifying density-based local outliers. In: Proceedings of the 2000 ACM SIGMOD International Conference on Management of Data, pp. 93–104 (2000)
4. Chalapathy, R., Chawla, S.: Deep learning for anomaly detection: a survey. arXiv preprint arXiv:1901.03407 (2019)
5. Chandola, V., Banerjee, A., Kumar, V.: Anomaly detection: a survey. ACM Comput. Surv. (CSUR) **41**(3), 1–58 (2009)
6. Chauhan, S., Vig, L.: Anomaly detection in ECG time signals via deep long short-term memory networks. In: 2015 IEEE International Conference on Data Science and Advanced Analytics (DSAA), pp. 1–7. IEEE (2015)
7. Chen, Y., et al.: The UCR time series classification archive (2015)
8. Goldberger, A.L., et al.: Physiobank, physiotoolkit, and physionet: components of a new research resource for complex physiologic signals. Circulation **101**(23), e215–e220 (2000)
9. Gong, D., et al.: Memorizing normality to detect anomaly: memory-augmented deep autoencoder for unsupervised anomaly detection. In: Proceedings of the IEEE International Conference on Computer Vision, pp. 1705–1714 (2019)
10. Hawkins, S., He, H., Williams, G., Baxter, R.: Outlier detection using replicator neural networks. In: Kambayashi, Y., Winiwarter, W., Arikawa, M. (eds.) DaWaK 2002. LNCS, vol. 2454, pp. 170–180. Springer, Heidelberg (2002). https://doi.org/10.1007/3-540-46145-0_17
11. Keogh, E., Chakrabarti, K., Pazzani, M., Mehrotra, S.: Dimensionality reduction for fast similarity search in large time series databases. Knowl. Inf. Syst. **3**(3), 263–286 (2001)
12. Li, D., Chen, D., Jin, B., Shi, L., Goh, J., Ng, S.K.: MAD-GAN: multivariate anomaly detection for time series data with generative adversarial networks. In: Tetko, I.V., Kůrková, V., Karpov, P., Theis, F. (eds.) ICANN 2019. LNCS, vol. 11730, pp. 703–716. Springer, Cham (2019). https://doi.org/10.1007/978-3-030-30490-4_56
13. Lin, J., Keogh, E., Lonardi, S., Chiu, B.: A symbolic representation of time series, with implications for streaming algorithms. In: Proceedings of the 8th ACM SIGMOD Workshop on Research Issues in Data Mining and Knowledge Discovery, pp. 2–11 (2003)
14. Lin, J., Keogh, E., Wei, L., Lonardi, S.: Experiencing sax: a novel symbolic representation of time series. Data Min. Knowl. Discovery **15**(2), 107–144 (2007)
15. Liu, F.T., Ting, K.M., Zhou, Z.H.: Isolation forest. In: 2008 Eighth IEEE International Conference on Data Mining, pp. 413–422. IEEE (2008)

16. Lkhagva, B., Yu, S., Kawagoe, K.: New time series data representation esax for financial applications. In: International Conference on Data Engineering Workshops, pp. 115–126 (2006)
17. Malhotra, P., Ramakrishnan, A., Anand, G., Vig, L., Agarwal, P., Shroff, G.: LSTM-based encoder-decoder for multi-sensor anomaly detection. arXiv preprint arXiv:1607.00148 (2016)
18. Malhotra, P., Vig, L., Shroff, G., Agarwal, P.: Long short term memory networks for anomaly detection in time series. In: Proceedings, vol. 89, pp. 89–94. Presses universitaires de Louvain (2015)
19. Moody, G.B., Mark, R.G.: The impact of the MIT-BIH arrhythmia database. IEEE Eng. Med. Biol. Mag. **20**(3), 45–50 (2001)
20. Moonesignhe, H., Tan, P.N.: Outlier detection using random walks. In: 2006 18th IEEE International Conference on Tools with Artificial Intelligence (ICTAI 2006), pp. 532–539. IEEE (2006)
21. Nicolau, M., McDermott, J., et al.: Learning neural representations for network anomaly detection. IEEE Trans. Ccybernet. **49**(8), 3074–3087 (2018)
22. Pang, G., Cao, L., Chen, L., Liu, H.: Learning representations of ultrahigh-dimensional data for random distance-based outlier detection. In: Proceedings of the 24th ACM SIGKDD International Conference on Knowledge Discovery & Data Mining, pp. 2041–2050 (2018)
23. Perera, P., Nallapati, R., Xiang, B.: Ocgan: One-class novelty detection using gans with constrained latent representations. In: Proceedings of the IEEE Conference on Computer Vision and Pattern Recognition, pp. 2898–2906 (2019)
24. Ren, H., Liu, M., Li, Z., Pedrycz, W.: A piecewise aggregate pattern representation approach for anomaly detection in time series. Knowl. Based Syst. **135**, 29–39 (2017)
25. Ren, H., Liu, M., Liao, X., Liang, L., Ye, Z., Li, Z.: Anomaly detection in time series based on interval sets. IEEJ Trans. Electr. Electron. Eng. **13**(5), 757–762 (2018)
26. Schlegl, T., Seeböck, P., Waldstein, S.M., Schmidt-Erfurth, U., Langs, G.: Unsupervised anomaly detection with generative adversarial networks to guide marker discovery. In: Niethammer, M., et al. (eds.) IPMI 2017. LNCS, vol. 10265, pp. 146–157. Springer, Cham (2017). https://doi.org/10.1007/978-3-319-59050-9_12
27. Sun, Y., Li, J., Liu, J., Sun, B., Chow, C.: An improvement of symbolic aggregate approximation distance measure for time series. Neurocomputing **138**, 189–198 (2014)
28. Tang, B., He, H.: A local density-based approach for outlier detection. Neurocomputing **241**, 171–180 (2017)
29. Zenati, H., Romain, M., Foo, C.S., Lecouat, B., Chandrasekhar, V.: Adversarially learned anomaly detection. In: 2018 IEEE International Conference on Data Mining (ICDM), pp. 727–736. IEEE (2018)
30. Zhang, C., Chen, Y., Yin, A., Wang, X.: Anomaly detection in ECG based on trend symbolic aggregate approximation. Math. Biosci. Eng. **16**(4), 2154–2167 (2019)
31. Zimek, A., Schubert, E., Kriegel, H.P.: A survey on unsupervised outlier detection in high-dimensional numerical data. Stat. Anal. Data Min. ASA Data Sci. J. **5**(5), 363–387 (2012)
32. Zong, B., et al.: Deep autoencoding gaussian mixture model for unsupervised anomaly detection. In: International Conference on Learning Representations (2018)

Robust Ensembling Network
for Unsupervised Domain Adaptation

Han Sun[1(✉)], Lei Lin[1], Ningzhong Liu[1], and Huiyu Zhou[2]

[1] Nanjing University of Aeronautics and Astronautics, Nanjing, Jiangsu, China
`sunhan@nuaa.edu.cn`
[2] School of Informatics, University of Leicester, Leicester LE1 7RH, UK

Abstract. Recently, in order to address the unsupervised domain adaptation (UDA) problem, extensive studies have been proposed to achieve transferrable models. Among them, the most prevalent method is adversarial domain adaptation, which can shorten the distance between the source domain and the target domain. Although adversarial learning is very effective, it still leads to the instability of the network and the drawbacks of confusing category information. In this paper, we propose a Robust Ensembling Network (REN) for UDA, which applies a robust time ensembling teacher network to learn global information for domain transfer. Specifically, REN mainly includes a teacher network and a student network, which performs standard domain adaptation training and updates weights of the teacher network. In addition, we also propose a dual-network conditional adversarial loss to improve the ability of the discriminator. Finally, for the purpose of improving the basic ability of the student network, we utilize the consistency constraint to balance the error between the student network and the teacher network. Extensive experimental results on several UDA datasets have demonstrated the effectiveness of our model by comparing with other state-of-the-art UDA algorithms.

Keywords: Unsupervised domain adaptation · Adversarial learning · Time ensembling

1 Introduction

In recent years, deep neural networks have played a particularly critical role in the face of many computer vision tasks, such as image classification [12], object detection [22], semantic segmentation [3] and so on. However, training a perfect neural network demands a large amount of data and corresponding data labeling, which is very time-consuming and expensive. When facing a new task or a new dataset, the previously trained model may exhibit poor performance due to the domain shift. We hope to use available network and data to complete the target task through knowledge transfer, where domain adaptation methods are needed. The problem that domain adaptation figures out is how to adapt the model trained in the source domain with rich labels to the target domain with

© Springer Nature Switzerland AG 2021
D. N. Pham et al. (Eds.): PRICAI 2021, LNAI 13032, pp. 530–543, 2021.
https://doi.org/10.1007/978-3-030-89363-7_40

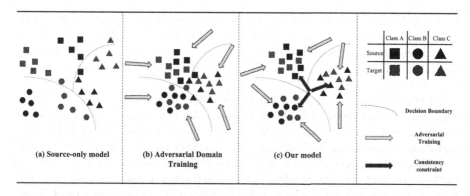

Fig. 1. Comparison between previous adversarial domain training method and ours. **(a):** Before domain adaptation, the data distribution of the source domain and the target domain are quite different. **(b):** The adversarial domain training method aligns the source domain and the target domain by a domain discriminator, and make them as close as possible to each other, which causes the confusion of the category information. **(c):** Our model uses the time ensembling algorithm to obtain a more stable network with the consistency constraint, which effectively avoids the distribution of data samples near the category decision boundary.

sparse labels, and minimize the negative transfer. Besides, UDA means that we only have annotations on the source domain data, without the target domain.

Due to the rapid development of deep learning, many approaches of deep domain adaptation have sprung up [6,16,20]. Among them, many methods try to map the source domain and target domain features into a high-dimensional space, and then perform feature alignment in this space for the reduction of domain shift. The feature alignment method generally uses Maximum Mean Discrepancy (MMD) [2] or its improved versions. Subsequently, as a result of the bloom of Generative Adversarial Networks (GAN) [10], the concept of adversarial learning has also been widely employed to domain adaptation. In this way, the domain bias between the source domain and the target domain can be effectively reduced by adversarial learning.

The previous UDA methods such as feature alignment, adversarial learning, or clustering methods to generate pseudo-labels for the target domain have been relatively mature, whereas most methods rely on the features or the predictions obtained during the network training process with loss constraint. However, it is assumed that the network with the poor generalization ability itself is unstable during the training process due to the insufficient data, which can cause greater errors in the distribution of the source and target domain features extracted by the network, and may eventually result in disappointing performance and poor robustness of the network. Therefore, it is particularly significant to train a more stable network. In addition, the main popular methods often use adversarial learning. Although adversarial learning can effectively shorten the distance between the source domain and the target domain, it can also confuse the category information between the domains. As shown in Fig. 1, the source domain and target domain samples get closer to each other in the process of adversarial learning, but they also become closer to the decision line, resulting in inaccurate classification. Consequently, we propose a more robust network, and decrease misclassification through consistency constraint.

In this paper, we explore a robust ensembling network for UDA, which captures more information-rich global features through a more stable model to achieve domain transfer. Specifically, a basic student network is applied for regular domain adaptation training, and then another ensembling teacher network is applied. The weight of the teacher network is the time series ensembling of the basic student network weights, so that the teacher network not only becames more stable, but also has more global information. The ensembling teacher network is adopted to reversely guide the basic student network to enhance the accuracy of its intra-domain classification. Besides, the instance feature is combined with the prediction of the ensembling teacher network and student network as a new condition for the domain discriminator, thereby adversarially decreasing the difference between domains. The main contribution points of this article are:

- This paper proposes a robust ensembling network for UDA, which can reduce the prediction error caused by network fluctuations during the training process. The features and predictions obtained by network during training will be more stable with more global information, and more conducive to domain transfer.
- We employ the predictions of the ensembling teacher network to reversely constrain the basic student network to raise the stability of the basic student network. Besides, we use the new predictions to constitute dual-network conditional adversarial loss and effectively alleviate the phenomenon of negative transfer.
- The proposed network is better than its baseline CDAN [15], and it presents a competitive result on the various UDA datasets.

2   Related Work

UDA has been widely studied in computer vision mainly for classification and detection tasks. In the era of deep neural networks, the main idea of domain adaptation is to learn domain invariant features between the source and target domain. Among them, several methods exploit MMD [2] and its kernel variants to minimize the difference in feature distribution. With the rise of neural networks, [9] attempts to introduce MMD as a regularization method to minimize the distribution mismatch between the source and target domain in the latent space. In addition to considering the adaptive algorithm of multi-feature representation, [29] also provides an improved conditional maximum mean error.

Recently, adversarial learning-based methods exert a tremendous fascination to bridge the gap between the source domain and the target domain. GAN [10] is motivated by the idea of two-play game in game theory. Adversarial training is the process in which the generator and the discriminator compete against each other. Adversarial learning is firstly applied to domain adaptation in [8]. Its core idea is to adopt the discriminator to learn domain invariant features. A more general framework is proposed by [27] for adversarial domain adaptation. The author of [15] is motivated by [19] and proposes to align category labels by using the joint distribution of features and predictions. Inspired by [1,24] applies the Wasserstein GAN measurement to domain adaptation, and proposes Wasserstein distance guided representation learning.

Semi-supervised learning uses both labeled data and unlabeled data during training. The domain adaptation problem is similar to semi-supervised learning in the strict sense, but the source domain and target domain have domain shift due to various image capture devices, environmental changes, and different styles. Initially, the application of a time series ensembling is proposed by [13], which adopts the average of the current model prediction results and the historical prediction results to calculate the mean square error. Different from historically weighted sum of model predictions in [13,26] uses weighted exponential moving average (EMA) on the weight of the student model. Temporal Ensembling [13] is applied by [7] to the domain adaptation problem, and data augmentation is implemented to increase the generalization ability of the model. The prediction results of time ensembling is utilized as pseudo-labels to cluster and align the feature spaces of the source domain and the target domain in [5].

With the current adversarial domain adaptation methods, the network tends to overlap the source domain and target domain's category distributions during adversarial training, resulting in poor classification results. However, the consistency constraint of semi-supervised learning can just constrain sample distribution and decrease classification errors. In addition, most of the current semi-supervised learning methods in domain adaptation exploit pseudo-label methods, but the wrong pseudo-label may mislead the training of the network. Moreover, most of the previous methods only adopt prediction ensembling methods, and there are few researches on the model ensembling of [26]. Therefore, based on CDAN [15], we propose an UDA method of robust ensembling model.

3   Methodology

This part we mainly provide the specific steps of the method proposed in this article. First we introduce the overall structure of the method in this article; then we dive deep into the loss function of each part; finally we examines the total loss function of the network.

3.1   Overview

In the UDA problem, the labeled source domain is denoted as $\mathbf{D}_s = \{(\mathbf{x}_i^s, y_i^s)\}_{i=0}^{N_s}$, where $\mathbf{N_s}$ represents the number of samples with labels in the

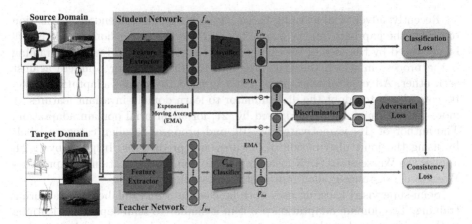

Fig. 2. Overview of the proposed REN model. It principally comprises a student network, a teacher network and a domain discriminator. Both the student network and the teacher network consist of a feature extractor and a classifier. The source and target domain samples are delivered to the student network at the same time to extract features, and the weight of the teacher network is the ensembling of the student network's weights in time series. Then, the predictions of the student and the teacher network are ensembled and multiplied with the features of the student network to form a dual-network conditional adversarial loss. Finally, the classification results of the two models are considered together for consistency loss.

source domain, and the unlabeled target domain is denoted as $\mathbf{D}_t = \left\{ \left(\mathbf{x}_j^t \right) \right\}_{j=0}^{N_t}$, where $\mathbf{N_t}$ represents the number of samples without labels in the target domain [21]. The source domain and target domain samples conform to the joint distribution $P_s \left(X^s, Y^s \right)$ and $Q_t \left(X^t, Y^t \right)$ respectively, and $P \neq Q$. Our goal is to train a deep neural network $\mathcal{F} : X^t \to Y^t$ using source domain data with labels and target domain data, which can accurately predict target domain samples while minimizing domain shift.

As shown in Fig. 2, our model mainly includes two networks, a student network and a teacher network, and a domain discriminator D. Each network has a feature extractor F and a classifier C. Given a picture x, the corresponding feature vector $f = F(x) \in \mathbb{R}^d$ is obtained through the feature extractor F, where d represents the feature dimension, and the corresponding prediction result $p = C(f) \in \mathbb{R}^c$ is obtained through the classifier C, where c represents the total number of classes [8]. According to [8], the adversarial domain adaptation method can be expressed as optimizing the following minimum and maximum problem:

$$\min_{F,C} \max_D \mathcal{L}_c(F, C) - \lambda_d \mathcal{L}_d(F, D), \tag{1}$$

$$\mathcal{L}_c(F, C) = -\mathbb{E}_{(x_s, y_s) \sim (X_s, Y_s)} \sum_{n=1}^{N_s} \left[\mathbf{1}_{[n=y_s]} \log \left[C \left(F \left(x_s \right) \right) \right] \right], \tag{2}$$

$$\mathcal{L}_d(F, D) = -\mathbb{E}_{x_s \sim P_s} \log [D(f_s)] - \mathbb{E}_{x_t \sim Q_t} \log [1 - D(f_t)] \odot, \tag{3}$$

Among them, $\mathcal{L}_c(F, C)$ is the standard supervised classification task, which uses only the cross-entropy loss of labeled source domain data. The domain discriminator D is a two-classifier $D : \mathbb{R}^d \to [0, 1]$, which predicts whether the data comes from the source domain or the target domain.

3.2 Robust Ensembling Network

The previous domain adaptation adversarial methods are limited to some extent due to the problem that the model is unrobust caused by adversarial learning. Although adversarial learning effectively narrows the distribution of the source and target domains, it also confuses category information. The semi-supervised learning method is mainly dedicated to finding the optimal classification decision line. The key of these methods is to enhance the training model with unlabeled data and cluster data points of different labels with perturbations.

We believe that semi-supervised learning and domain adaptation have something in common. Both semi-supervised learning and UDA are limited to the fact that part of the data is not labeled, which makes their solutions intersect. The only difference is that there is a distribution difference between the source domain and the target domain in UDA, so semi-supervised learning methods can be applied to enhance the robustness of the model and raise model prediction accuracy. The main method used in this paper is the mean teacher method, which contains a student network and a teacher network. The student network is trained normally, and the weight update of the teacher network is integrated by the time of the weight of the student network, and the update method is exponential moving average (EMA):

$$\theta'_n = \alpha_\theta \theta'_{n-1} + (1 - \alpha_\theta) \theta_n, \tag{4}$$

Among them, θ_n represents the weight of the student model during the n-th training, θ'_n represents the weight of the teacher model during the n-th training, and α_θ is the smoothing coefficient hyperparameter of the network parameter.

3.3 Dual-Network Conditional Adversarial Learning

The previous adversarial learning is generally limited to the labels without the target domain, so CDAN [15] proposes to jointly consider the feature representation and the prediction result of the classifier in the discriminator part. CDAN believes that the outer product of the feature representation and the prediction result can affect the feature representation, so a discriminator shared by the source domain and the target domain is used to align this conditional feature representation. The general conditional adversarial loss are as follows:

$$\mathcal{L}_d^{con}(F, D) = -\mathbb{E}_{x_s\ P_s} \log [D(f_s, p_s)] - \mathbb{E}_{x_t\ Q_t} \log [1 - D(f_t, p_t)]. \tag{5}$$

This conditional adversarial loss generally utilizes the feature f_s and prediction p_s of the source domain, and also exploits the feature f_t and prediction p_t

of the target domain. However, the features and predictions that this adversarial loss mainly relies on are not stable, and the two may have numerical deviations during the network training process, which will eventually lead to the poor effect of adversarial learning. The dual network proposed in this article can effectively avoid this problem. The student network performs standard domain adaptation adversarial learning, while the update of the teacher network is provided by the student network. The update method is the former time ensembling, so that the teacher network integrates the student network in time series, and the network structure is more stable and robust. In addition to the student's condition adversarial loss, the prediction of the teacher network is also applied as another condition.

$$\mathcal{L}_d^{stu}\left(F_{stu}, D\right) = -\mathbb{E}_{x_s\ P_s} \log\left[D\left(f_s^{stu}, \widehat{p_s^{stu}}\right)\right]$$
$$-\mathbb{E}_{x_t\ Q_t} \log\left[1 - D\left(f_t^{stu}, \widehat{p_t^{stu}}\right)\right], \tag{6}$$

$$\mathcal{L}_d^{tea}\left(F_{stu}, D\right) = -\mathbb{E}_{x_s\ P_s} \log\left[D\left(f_s^{stu}, \widehat{p_s^{tea}}\right)\right]$$
$$-\mathbb{E}_{x_t\ Q_t} \log\left[1 - D\left(f_t^{stu}, \widehat{p_t^{tea}}\right)\right], \tag{7}$$

$$\widehat{p_n} = (1 - \alpha_p)\widehat{p_{n-1}} + \alpha_p p_n, \tag{8}$$

Among them, p_n represents the prediction of the student or teacher model during the n-th training, $\widehat{p_n}$ represents the ensembling prediction during the n-th training and α_p is the smoothing coefficient hyperparameter. The prediction of the student network and the teacher network performs an EMA operation to promote the stability of the prediction. In this way, with global student predictions and global teacher predictions, the network can learn more reliable conditional and transferable information in the process of adversarial learning.

3.4   Consistency Constraint

The student network provides weights for the teacher network, just as student asks the teacher in the classroom, so the teacher needs to answer the student's questions to help the student. Therefore, the teacher network needs to assist the student network, and the method of assistance is to adopt consistency constraint. The core idea of consistency constraint is to perturb high-dimensional data so that it tends to be consistent in the feature space. In other words, we hope that in the process of dimensionality reduction, multiple high-dimensional data can be compressed into a low-dimensional point, so that the feature distribution in the feature space is more compact, which is conducive to the model learning more accurate classification decision lines. We mainly utilize the L2 norm between the student model and the teacher model as the consistency loss.

$$\mathcal{L}_{con} = \|C_{stu}\left(F_{stu}\left(x\right)\right) - C_{tea}\left(F_{tea}\left(x\right)\right)\|_2. \tag{9}$$

3.5 Total Loss Function

In this part, we introduce the total loss function:

$$\mathcal{L}_{all} = \mathcal{L}_c + \lambda_d^{stu} \mathcal{L}_d^{stu} + \lambda_d^{tea} \mathcal{L}_d^{tea} + \gamma \mathcal{L}_{con}, \tag{10}$$

Therefore, the final total loss function is as described above, and it mainly includes four parts: the supervised classification loss $\mathcal{L}_c$ of source domain, a student network adversarial loss $\mathcal{L}_d^{stu}$, a teacher network adversarial loss $\mathcal{L}_d^{tea}$ and finally the consistency loss $\mathcal{L}_{con}$ between the student network and the teacher network. Among them, λ_d^{stu} and λ_d^{stu} are the hyperparameters of student adversarial loss and teacher adversarial loss, and their role is to control the importance of the two in adversarial training. γ is the relative weight that controls the consistency constraint.

4 Experiment

4.1 Experimental Setting

Datasets. *Office-31* [23] contains 31 classes and 4,110 images collected from three different domains: Amazon Website (A) with 2817 images, Web Camera (W) with 498 images and Digital SLR Camera (D) with 795 images. By permuting the three domains, we obtain six transfer tasks: A → W, D → W, W → D, A → D, D → A and W → A. *ImageCLEF-DA* [17] is a dataset created by the ImageCLEF2014 domain adaptation competition. We follow the guidelines of [14] and select 3 sub-domains of Caltech-256 (C), ImageNet ILSVRC 2012 (I) and Pascal VOC 2012 (P), which have 12 common categories. There are six UDA tasks to be evaluated. *Office-Home* [28] is another more challenging dataset for visual domain adaptation. It mainly includes four dissimilar subdomains, namely Artistic images (Ar), ClipArt (Ca), Product images (Pr) and Real-World images (Re). There are 15500 images in 65 different categories. They are all pictures under office and home settings, which constitute a total of 12 domain adaptation tasks.

Comparisons. We compare the REN model with other state-of-the-art methods: (1) ResNet-50 [11]. (2) Domain Adversarial Neural Network(DANN) [8]. (3) Adversarial Discriminative Domain Adaptation (ADDA) [27]. (4) Deep transfer learning with joint adaptation networks (JAN) [17] (5)Conditional Domain Adversarial Network (CDAN) [15]. (6) Cluster Alignment with a Teacher for Unsupervised Domain Adaptation (CAT) [5]. (7) Towards Discriminability and Diversity: Batch Nuclear-norm Maximization under Label Insufficient Situations (BNM) [4].

Implementation Details. The method proposed in this paper is mainly implemented on the Pytorch framework. For a fair comparison, we apply the same network structure in each experiment. We utilize ResNet50 pre-trained on ImageNet without the final fully connected layer as the feature extractor. We adopt all the labeled data in the source domain and all the unlabeled data in the target domain. We apply the SGD optimizer with a momentum of 0.9, the batch size is 32, and the dimension of the bottleneck layer is set to 256. We adopt the learning rate anneal-ing strategy as [8]: the learning rate is adjusted by $\eta_p = \eta_0(1 + \alpha p)^{-\beta}$, where p is the training progress changing from 0 to 1, and $\eta_0 = 0.01$, $\alpha = 10$, $\beta = 0.75$ are optimized by the importance-weighted cross-validation [25]. In the testing phase, we mainly choose the more stable teacher model for testing.

4.2 Results

Table 1 shows the UDA results of the six transfer tasks of the Office-31 dataset. We can observe that the performance of the REN method in this paper is much better than all the previous methods on most tasks. It is worth noting that our method REN is not only on simple transfer tasks, such as $D \rightarrow W$ and $W \rightarrow D$, with superior performance, reaching almost 100% accuracy, but also on tasks that are difficult to transfer due to unbalanced samples, such as $D \rightarrow A$ and $W \rightarrow A$, which have achieved superior results. The main reason for the success of our model is that we have introduced a more robust time ensembling teacher model. The adversarial training of the student model and the teacher model effectively solves the domain offset and enhances the predictive ability of the model.

Table 1. Accuracy (%) on Office-31 for UDA (ResNet-50)

Method	$A \rightarrow W$	$D \rightarrow W$	$W \rightarrow D$	$A \rightarrow D$	$D \rightarrow A$	$W \rightarrow A$	Avg
ResNet-50 [11]	68.4	96.7	99.3	68.9	62.5	60.7	76.1
DANN [8]	82.0	96.9	99.1	79.7	68.2	67.4	82.2
ADDA [27]	86.2	96.2	98.4	77.8	69.5	68.9	82.9
JAN [17]	86.0	96.7	99.7	85.1	69.2	70.7	84.6
CDAN [15]	93.1	98.2	**100.0**	89.8	70.1	68.0	86.6
CDAN+E [15]	94.1	98.6	**100.0**	92.9	71.0	69.3	87.7
CAT [5]	94.4	98.0	**100.0**	90.8	72.2	70.2	87.6
BNM [4]	92.8	98.8	**100.0**	92.9	73.5	73.8	88.6
REN (Ours)	**95.0**	**99.2**	**100.0**	**94.6**	**74.1**	**74.8**	**89.6**

The results of the six transfer tasks of the ImageCLEF-DA dataset are shown in Table 2. Although the number of images in each subdomain in the ImageCLEF-DA dataset is similar, it is still challenging for the transfer task because of the images from various scenarios. Compared to ResNet-50, which only utilizes source domain samples for fine-tuning, the above-mentioned domain adaptation method achieves significant effect. Compared with other methods, the method in this article has achieved significant improvement. The CAT method also adopts the idea of semi-supervised learning, but it only adopts the Pi-model [13] prediction ensembling method, and we utilize model ensembling, which is more effective. This also proves that the student-teacher model of REN can learn more transferable features.

Table 2. Accuracy (%) on ImageCLEF-DA for UDA (ResNet-50)

Method	I→P	P→I	I→C	C→I	C→P	P→C	Avg
ResNet-50 [11]	74.8	83.9	91.5	78.0	65.5	91.2	80.7
DANN [8]	75.0	86.0	96.2	87.0	74.3	91.5	85.0
JAN [17]	76.8	88.0	94.7	89.5	74.2	91.7	85.8
CDAN [15]	76.7	90.6	97.0	90.5	74.5	93.5	87.1
CDAN+E [15]	77.7	90.7	97.7	91.3	74.2	94.3	87.7
CAT [5]	77.2	91.0	95.5	91.3	75.3	93.6	87.3
REN (Ours)	**79.8**	**93.3**	**97.3**	**91.5**	**76.8**	**94.8**	**88.9**

Table 3. Accuracy (%) on Office-Home for UDA (ResNet-50)

Method	Ar ↓ Cl	Ar ↓ Pr	Ar ↓ Rw	Cl ↓ Ar	Cl ↓ Pr	Cl ↓ Rw	Pr ↓ Ar	Pr ↓ Cl	Pr ↓ Rw	Rw ↓ Ar	Rw ↓ Cl	Rw ↓ Pr	Avg
ResNet-50 [11]	34.9	50.0	58.0	37.4	41.9	46.2	38.5	31.2	60.4	53.9	41.2	59.9	46.1
DANN [8]	45.6	59.3	70.1	47.0	58.5	60.9	46.1	43.7	68.5	63.2	51.8	76.8	57.6
JAN [17]	45.9	61.2	68.9	50.4	59.7	61.0	45.8	43.4	70.3	63.9	52.4	76.8	58.3
CDAN [15]	49.0	69.3	74.5	54.4	66.0	68.4	55.6	48.3	75.9	68.4	55.4	80.5	63.8
CDAN+E [15]	50.7	70.6	76.0	57.6	70.0	70.0	57.4	50.9	77.3	70.9	56.7	81.6	65.8
BNM[4]	52.3	**73.9**	**80.0**	**63.3**	**72.9**	**74.9**	**61.7**	49.5	**79.7**	70.5	53.6	82.2	67.9
REN (Ours)	**54.4**	73.6	77.4	61.6	71.1	71.7	61.0	**52.2**	78.8	**73.1**	59.4	**83.5**	**68.2**

Table 3 shows the results of 12 transfer tasks on the Office-Home dataset. Different from the first two datasets, there are more categories in the Office-Home dataset, thus leads to the methods which perform well on the Office-31 dataset may have performance degradation on the Office-Home dataset. Although the method in this paper only has the best effect on 5 transfer tasks, the average accuracy is even better than BNM method. The main reason for this is that the sample size of some categories in Office-Home is extremely unbalanced. For example, the Ruler class in the Art subdomain has only 15 pictures, while the Bottle class has 99 pictures. The main problem that the BNM method solves is this kind of imbalance. Though the method in this paper does not focus on the imbalance of the dataset, due to the stability of the dual network and the ensembling teacher network, the final classification result is not much different from that of BNM. In addition, our method is more effective on difficult tasks such as Ar → Cl, Pr → Cl and Rw → Cl, which are improved by 2.1%, 2.7% and 5.8% respectively than BNM. The above experiments prove the effectiveness of our method.

4.3 Ablation Study and Visualization

Table 4 presents ablation experiments on Office-31 dataset based on CDAN. In this table, we denote performing in mean teacher model ensembling as "M",

Table 4. Accuracy (%) in ablation experiments for REN based on CDAN on Office-31

Method	A → W	D → W	W → D	A → D	D → A	W → A	Avg
CDAN	93.1	98.2	**100.0**	89.8	70.1	68.0	86.6
CDAN+M	93.3	98.9	**100.0**	92.7	71.5	73.0	88.3
CDAN+M+D	94.8	99.0	**100.0**	93.7	72.2	74.5	89.0
CDAN+M+D+C(REN)	**95.0**	**99.2**	**100.0**	**94.6**	**74.1**	**74.8**	**89.6**

dual-network conditional adversarial loss as "D" and consistency constraint as "C". On Office-31, CDAN+M outperforms CDAN by 1.7%. In addition, compared with CDAN, CDAN+M+D and CDAN+M+D+C improve its accuracy by 2.4%, 3%, indicating the effectiveness of our method.

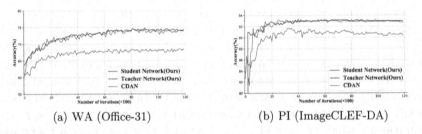

(a) WA (Office-31)   (b) PI (ImageCLEF-DA)

Fig. 3. Comparison of stability of CDAN, student network and teacher network of our model REN. Obviously, the blue line (teacher network) is much smoother and more stable than the red line (student network). (Color figure online)

In order to demonstrate the stability of the method in the training process, we present the results of the classification accuracy of different training processes in Fig. 3. The graph on the left shows the experimental results of task W → A (Office-31), and the right presents the results of task P → I (ImageCLEF-DA). We can find that the accuracy of both the student network and the teacher network in this article is much higher than the result of CDAN. By observing Fig. 3 carefully, we can find that the accuracy curve of the teacher network has less fluctuations than the student network, and the accuracy has also been improved compared with CDAN. In addition, the reason why the accuracy of the student network is also excellent is that the consistency constraint of the teacher network promotes the improvement of the prediction result of the student network. Therefore, according to the curve comparison between CDAN and Teacher Network(Ours), our method has less fluctuation and more stability.

In addition, compared to CDAN, our method is composed of student network and teacher network. It can be seen from Table 5 that the parameters of our method is twice that of CDAN during training, and the training time is relatively longer.

Table 5. Comparison of parameters with CDAN in the training phase on Office-31(12k epoches)

Method	Params	Time
CDAN	24 M	1.3 h
REN (Ours)	48 M	1.8 h

4.4   Ablation Study and Visualization

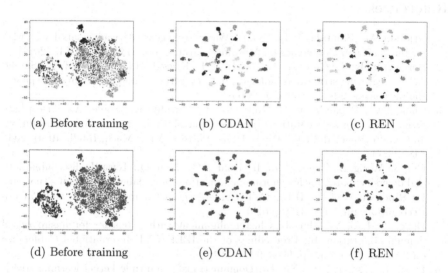

(a) Before training   (b) CDAN   (c) REN

(d) Before training   (e) CDAN   (f) REN

Fig. 4. The t-SNE visualization of A → W(Office-31). (a) (b) (c)represent category information and each color denotes a class. (d) (e) (f) Red circles are the source samples while blue circles are the target samples. (Color figure online)

To present the process of domain adaptation training more intuitively, we utilize the t-distribution Stochastic Neighbour Embedding (t-SNE) [18] method to visualize the low-dimensional changes of features before and after adaptation in Fig. 4. We implement one task, namely A → W (Office-31) to perform these experiments. Obviously, before training, the spatial distribution of the source domain and target domain features is completely different. This indicates that the distribution contains no discernible intrinsic structure. Although after CDAN, most of data has been aggregated, there are still some classes indistinguishable. But after our method, the feature distribution shows a clear clustered structure. The cluster centers of the distribution are closer than before, and the degree of dispersion is more similar. This means that our method greatly improves the distribution in the feature space.

5   Conclusion

We propose a robust ensembling network for UDA based on model time ensembling and consistency constraint. It solves the negative transfer problem of target domain samples, which is close to the edge of the decision line due to adversarial learning. At the same time, the dual-network conditional adversarial loss proposed in this paper effectively decreases the instability in the adversarial learning process, and enables the network to learn more global transferable features. All-round experiments illustrate that our method is superior to the current mainstream methods on various domain adaptation datasets.

References

1. Arjovsky, M., Chintala, S., Bottou, L.: Wasserstein generative adversarial networks. In: International Conference on Machine Learning, pp. 214–223. PMLR (2017)
2. Borgwardt, K.M., Gretton, A., Rasch, M.J., Kriegel, H.P., Schölkopf, B., Smola, A.J.: Integrating structured biological data by kernel maximum mean discrepancy. Bioinformatics **22**(14), e49–e57 (2006)
3. Chen, L.C., Papandreou, G., Kokkinos, I., Murphy, K., Yuille, A.L.: DeepLab: Semantic image segmentation with deep convolutional nets, atrous convolution, and fully connected CRFs. IEEE Trans. Pattern Anal. Mach. Intell. **40**(4), 834–848 (2017)
4. Cui, S., Wang, S., Zhuo, J., Li, L., Huang, Q., Tian, Q.: Towards discriminability and diversity: batch nuclear-norm maximization under label insufficient situations. In: Proceedings of the IEEE/CVF Conference on Computer Vision and Pattern Recognition, pp. 3941–3950 (2020)
5. Deng, Z., Luo, Y., Zhu, J.: Cluster alignment with a teacher for unsupervised domain adaptation. In: Proceedings of the IEEE/CVF International Conference on Computer Vision, pp. 9944–9953 (2019)
6. Duan, L., Tsang, I.W., Xu, D.: Domain transfer multiple kernel learning. IEEE Trans. Pattern Anal. Mach. Intell. **34**(3), 465–479 (2012)
7. French, G., Mackiewicz, M., Fisher, M.: Self-ensembling for visual domain adaptation. In: International Conference on Learning Representations (2018)
8. Ganin, Y., et al.: Domain-adversarial training of neural networks. J. Mach. Learn. Res. **17**(1), 2096–2030 (2016)
9. Ghifary, M., Kleijn, W.B., Zhang, M.: Domain adaptive neural networks for object recognition. In: Pham, D.-N., Park, S.-B. (eds.) PRICAI 2014. LNCS (LNAI), vol. 8862, pp. 898–904. Springer, Cham (2014). https://doi.org/10.1007/978-3-319-13560-1_76
10. Goodfellow, I.J., et al.: Generative adversarial networks. arXiv preprint arXiv:1406.2661 (2014)
11. He, K., Zhang, X., Ren, S., Sun, J.: Deep residual learning for image recognition. In: Proceedings of the IEEE Conference on Computer Vision and Pattern Recognition, pp. 770–778 (2016)
12. Krizhevsky, A., Sutskever, I., Hinton, G.E.: ImageNet classification with deep convolutional neural networks. In: Advances in Neural Information Processing Systems, vol. 25, pp. 1097–1105 (2012)
13. Laine, S., Aila, T.: Temporal ensembling for semi-supervised learning. arXiv preprint arXiv:1610.02242 (2016)

14. Long, M., Cao, Y., Wang, J., Jordan, M.: Learning transferable features with deep adaptation networks. In: International Conference on Machine Learning, pp. 97–105. PMLR (2015)
15. Long, M., CAO, Z., Wang, J., Jordan, M.I.: Conditional adversarial domain adaptation. In: Advances in Neural Information Processing Systems, vol. 31 (2018)
16. Long, M., Wang, J., Ding, G., Sun, J., Yu, P.S.: Transfer joint matching for unsupervised domain adaptation. In: Proceedings of the IEEE Conference on Computer Vision and Pattern Recognition, pp. 1410–1417 (2014)
17. Long, M., Zhu, H., Wang, J., Jordan, M.I.: Deep transfer learning with joint adaptation networks. In: International Conference on Machine Learning, pp. 2208–2217. PMLR (2017)
18. Van der Maaten, L., Hinton, G.: Visualizing data using t-SNE. J. Mach. Learn. Res. **9**(11) (2008)
19. Mirza, M., Osindero, S.: Conditional generative adversarial nets. arXiv preprint arXiv:1411.1784 (2014)
20. Pan, S.J., Tsang, I.W., Kwok, J.T., Yang, Q.: Domain adaptation via transfer component analysis. IEEE Trans. Neural Netw. **22**(2), 199–210 (2010)
21. Pan, S.J., Yang, Q.: A survey on transfer learning. IEEE Trans. Knowl. Data Eng. **22**(10), 1345–1359 (2009)
22. Ren, S., He, K., Girshick, R., Sun, J.: Faster R-CNN: towards real-time object detection with region proposal networks. IEEE Trans. Pattern Anal. Mach. Intell. **39**(6), 1137–1149 (2016)
23. Saenko, K., Kulis, B., Fritz, M., Darrell, T.: Adapting visual category models to new domains. In: Daniilidis, K., Maragos, P., Paragios, N. (eds.) ECCV 2010. LNCS, vol. 6314, pp. 213–226. Springer, Heidelberg (2010). https://doi.org/10.1007/978-3-642-15561-1_16
24. Shen, J., Qu, Y., Zhang, W., Yu, Y.: Wasserstein distance guided representation learning for domain adaptation. In: Proceedings of the AAAI Conference on Artificial Intelligence, vol. 32 (2018)
25. Sugiyama, M., Krauledat, M., Müller, K.R.: Covariate shift adaptation by importance weighted cross validation. J. Mach. Learn. Res. **8**(5) (2007)
26. Tarvainen, A., Valpola, H.: Mean teachers are better role models: Weight-averaged consistency targets improve semi-supervised deep learning results. In: Advances in Neural Information Processing Systems, vol. 30 (2017)
27. Tzeng, E., Hoffman, J., Saenko, K., Darrell, T.: Adversarial discriminative domain adaptation. In: Proceedings of the IEEE Conference on Computer Vision and Pattern Recognition, pp. 7167–7176 (2017)
28. Venkateswara, H., Eusebio, J., Chakraborty, S., Panchanathan, S.: Deep hashing network for unsupervised domain adaptation. In: Proceedings of the IEEE Conference on Computer Vision and Pattern Recognition, pp. 5018–5027 (2017)
29. Zhu, Y., et al.: Multi-representation adaptation network for cross-domain image classification. Neural Netw. **119**, 214–221 (2019)

SPAN: Subgraph Prediction Attention Network for Dynamic Graphs

Yuan Li, Chuanchang Chen, Yubo Tao$^{(\boxtimes)}$, and Hai Lin$^{(\boxtimes)}$

State Key Lab of CAD&CG, ZheJiang University, HangZhou, China
{yuanli,chenchuanchang}@zju.edu.cn, {taoyubo,linhai}@cad.zju.edu.cn

Abstract. This paper proposes a novel model for predicting subgraphs in dynamic graphs, an extension of traditional link prediction. This proposed end-to-end model learns a mapping from the subgraph structures in the current snapshot to the subgraph structures in the next snapshot directly, i.e., edge existence among multiple nodes in the subgraph. A new mechanism named cross-attention with a twin-tower module is designed to integrate node attribute information and topology information collaboratively for learning subgraph evolution. We compare our model with several state-of-the-art methods for subgraph prediction and subgraph pattern prediction in multiple real-world homogeneous and heterogeneous dynamic graphs, respectively. Experimental results demonstrate that our model outperforms other models in these two tasks, with a gain increase from 5.02% to 10.88%.

Keywords: Subgraph prediction · Graph neural networks · Heterogeneous network · Graph attention

1 Introduction

An essential part of network analysis is network evolution analysis [1,4,27], especially subgraph evolution analysis, such as the purchase intention of a group of users in user-product networks. However, previous subgraph research studies [2,5,29] rarely focus on the subgraph prediction problem in subgraph evolution analysis: predicting future connectivity within a subgraph in dynamic graphs.

An intuitive approach for subgraph prediction is a two-stage scheme, including a node embedding method and traditional link prediction. Firstly, a node embedding method [9,18] generates low-dimensional vector representations of nodes. Then, the edge existence of $\frac{k(k-1)}{2}$ edges in a k-node subgraph is independently predictable through traditional link prediction.

However, there are two limitations to this approach. First, traditional link prediction typically requires users to specify or learn a global threshold from data to determine the existence of edges rather than adaptively adjusting the threshold for different local subgraphs. Second, higher-order structures [3,22], such as network function blocks [28], are ignored. Due to higher-order structures, edges in networks are not independent, i.e., an edge's establishment or

© Springer Nature Switzerland AG 2021
D. N. Pham et al. (Eds.): PRICAI 2021, LNAI 13032, pp. 544–558, 2021.
https://doi.org/10.1007/978-3-030-89363-7_41

disappearance may depend on both the similarity between two nodes and their adjacent edges [22]. Subgraph pattern neural networks (SPNN) [15] uses a joint prediction mechanism to solve the edge dependency limitation. However, SPNN focuses on the subgraph pattern prediction problem, which requires both subgraph patterns predefined by humans and subgraphs with a fixed size. Therefore, we design a new method for the subgraph prediction to solve both limitations.

Besides the global threshold and edge dependency limitations, previous research studies on subgraphs predefine [15] or ignore [2,5,29] the collaborative relationship between node attribute information and topology information, e.g., extracting important information from node attributes and topologies separately, and concatenating their representations at last [2]. However, important topology information may also be based on node attribute information, and critical node attribute information may also be related to topology information, which means we cannot deal with them separately. For instance, many topology structures in subgraphs are more important than other topology structures for subgraph evolution due to their specific node attributes, such as meta-path [26] and local structures with high-connection nodes [10]. Similarly, nodes with higher topology centrality in subgraphs are more critical than other nodes in subgraph evolution [13]. Although previous research studies can predefine the collaborative relationship artificially, the real collaborative relationship changes with graphs and only a part of this relationship (e.g., only the relationship between 3-nodes) is covered by the predefined relationship. Therefore, we propose a new method that integrates node attribute information and topology information to extract essential data features for subgraph evolution without human participation.

This paper proposes a novel end-to-end **S**ubgraph **P**rediction **A**ttention **N**etwork (SPAN) model to learn a mapping from subgraph structures in the current snapshot to subgraph structures in the next snapshot. For the global threshold limitation, we introduce an end-to-end learning mechanism to avoid the global threshold. We also use a joint prediction mechanism [3,15] to solve the edge dependency limitation. Furthermore, we develop a twin-tower module with the cross-attention mechanism to extract important data features for subgraph evolution by considering the collaborative relationship between node attribute information and topology information. Our main contributions are summarized as follows:

- We propose a new model, named SPAN, for subgraph prediction and a variant named SPAN-H for subgraph pattern prediction. To the best of our knowledge, SPAN is the first end-to-end model designed to predict the evolution of arbitrary size subgraphs.
- We propose a new mechanism named cross-attention with a twin-tower module for solving the collaborative limitation.
- Experimental results demonstrate that our method is more effective and scalable than state-of-the-art subgraph prediction and subgraph pattern prediction methods.

2 Related Work

Previous methods based on node embeddings and traditional link prediction can be divided into static graph embedding methods and dynamic graph embedding methods. Static graph embedding methods [8,9,12,24,25] are not designed for dynamic graphs, predicting the future connectivity of subgraphs solely based on the current snapshot. In contrast, dynamic graph embedding methods [16,30,31] predict subgraphs' future connectivity based on current and previous snapshots. Recently, with the massive success of the attention mechanism in temporal information extraction, some attention-based dynamic graph embedding methods have been proposed [18,20].

Dynamic subgraph prediction methods focus on the dynamic evolution of subgraphs, which involves higher-order structures with multiple nodes. Previous dynamic subgraph prediction methods are limited, such as edge dependency limitation and global threshold limitation. Higher-order link prediction [3] and SPNN [15] overcome the edge dependency limitation by jointly predicting the connection between multiple nodes. Nevertheless, these methods still have some restrictions, such as human-predefined fixed-sized subgraphs and subgraph evolution patterns. Compared with previous methods, our method overcomes these two limitations and removes these restrictions using a more powerful model and new mechanisms. We also identify a new collaborative limitation that the collaborative relationship between node attribute information and topology information on subgraph evolution, which has been ignored or predefined by humans in previous subgraph research. We address this new limitation using a new mechanism named cross-attention.

3 Proposed Method

Our method is composed of a Bayesian subgraph sampling algorithm and SPAN. Bayesian subgraph sampling is responsible for generating subgraphs, and SPAN model is used for the subgraph prediction of dynamic graphs.

3.1 Bayesian Subgraph Sampling

Given a dynamic graph Γ with T snapshots $\{G_1, ..., G_T\}$, $G_t = (V_t, E_t)$ is a continuous-time graph (i.e., one snapshot), V_t is a node set with node attributes and E_t is an edge set with weights. A subgraph $S_t = (V_t^s, E_t^s)$ is a subset of the snapshot G_t, such that $V_t^s \subseteq V_t$ and $E_t^s = \{(u,v)|u \in V_t^s, v \in V_t^s,$ and $(u,v) \in E_t\}$. Bayesian subgraph sampling aims to sample a series of subgraph evolution pairs $(S_t, S_{t+1}), ...$ from Γ.

First, we randomly choose a snapshot $G_t = (V_t, E_t)$. Second, we sample a node v from G_t randomly, initialize the subgraph $V_t^s = \{v\}$ and determine the number of nodes n sampled from a uniform distribution between 3 and k (the maximum size of subgraphs). Third, we randomly select a node v_i from V_t^s with the probability $1 - \alpha$ for connected subgraphs or randomly select a node v_j in

V_t/V_t^s with the probability α ($\alpha = 0.01$) for disconnected subgraphs. For v_i, we randomly select an adjacent node v_j with the transfer probability $p(v_j|v_i)$ to expand the subgraph. Motivated by the Bayesian network theory, the transfer probability $p(v_j|v_i)$ can be computed as

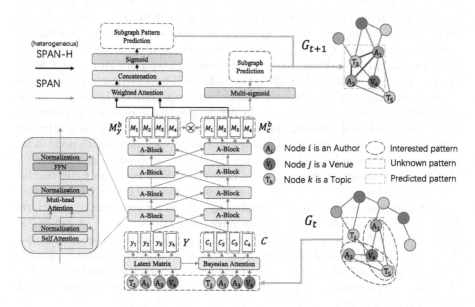

Fig. 1. The architecture of SPAN/SPAH-H with one subgraph as an example.

$$p(v_j|v_i) = \frac{w_{j,i}}{\sum_{(v_k,v_i)\in E_t} w_{k,i}}, \tag{1}$$

where $w_{j,i}$ is the weight of an edge (v_j, v_i) for weighted graphs, and $w_{j,i} = 1$ for unweighted graphs. For v_j, we add this node to the subgraph as a random jump operation. Repeat this node expansion process until the number of nodes in V_t^s reaches n to generate a subgraph. Finally, according to the node set V_t^s, we sample S_t from the current snapshot G_t. S_{t+1} can be constructed via $V_{t+1}^s = V_t^s$ and $E_{t+1}^s = \{(u,v)|u \in V_{t+1}^s, v \in V_{t+1}^s, \text{ and } (u,v) \in E_{t+1}\}$ to compose an evolution pair of subgraphs (S_t, S_{t+1}).

Repeating Bayesian subgraph sampling, we obtain sufficient connected/disconnected subgraph evolution pairs. In addition, the Bayesian network theory minimizes the probability that nodes with many links to the subgraph (i.e., nodes having significant influence over the subgraph) are not included in the subgraph.

3.2 Subgraph Prediction

Given a k-node subgraph $S_t = (V_t^s, E_t^s)$ in the snapshot G_t ($t \in [1, T-1]$), the goal of subgraph prediction is to predict the structure of the subgraph $S_{t+1} =$

(V_{t+1}^s, E_{t+1}^s) in G_{t+1}, where $V_t^s = V_{t+1}^s$. Therefore, we propose an end-to-end subgraph pattern/structure prediction model named SPAN.

As shown in Fig. 1, the architecture of SPAN has two inputs $Y \in R^{k \times D}$ and $C \in R^{k \times D}$, where D is the dimension of the embedding space. For each pair of subgraphs (S_t, S_{t+1}), we consider the structure of S_t and S_{t+1} as the source and target language, respectively. Thus, we flatten the subgraph as a node sequence using the sampling order of nodes during Bayesian subgraph sampling. Each node can be assigned a dense embedding vector to encode its information. All embedding vectors of the entire graph are stored in a latent matrix. The first input Y of SPAN is the nodes' self-information in the subgraph by extracting the corresponding embedding vectors ys from the latent matrix and constructing a set $Y = (y_1, ..., y_k)$. In detail, the latent matrix represents the graph's node attribute information, Y represents the subgraph's node attribute information, and y_i represents the node embedding vector of the ith node in the subgraph, which can be initialized with the degree information of this node in the current snapshot. If the number of nodes n in S_t is less than k, we can use zero padding for y_i, $i \in [n+1, k]$. The second input C of SPAN is the nodes' context information, generated by combining a Bayesian attention layer with the latent matrix to generate inner attention representations $C = (c_1, ..., c_k) = PY$, where $P \in R^{k \times k}$ is the Bayesian attention matrix. Intuitively, the second input represents the topological information of the subgraph. We combine all paths (topology information) from node v_i to node v_j in S_t as a Bayesian network $S_{i,j}$; thus, we can compute the joint probability of $S_{i,j}$ as the attention score of node i to node j as follows:

$$P_{i,j} = \prod_{v_k \in S_{i,j}} p(v_k | parents(v_k)). \tag{2}$$

Based on two inputs Y and C, we design a twin-tower module to synchronously encode the global node attribute information and topology information to generate the intermediate representations M_y^b and $M_c^b \in R^{k \times D}$. Each tower is stacked by b identical attention-based blocks (A-Block). The output of each layer is the input of the next layer. Based on M_y^b and M_c^b, we design different prediction modules for subgraph prediction (SPAN) and subgraph pattern prediction (SPAN-H).

Attention-Based Block. Each attention-based block has three layers: a self-attention layer, a cross-attention layer and a feed-forward layer. A simple self-attention (SA) operation has an input Y representing query, key and value as

$$SA(Y) = softmax(\frac{YY^T}{\sqrt{D}})Y. \tag{3}$$

However, it is difficult for the self-attention mechanism to integrate all dimensional information about queries, keys, and values. Therefore, motivated by the transformer structure [23], we apply the multi-head attention mechanism to our model for integrating all information. Multi-head attention (MA) [23], composed of h linear projection modules with the same structure, enables the model to focus on different representation subspaces at different positions. Also, because of the collaborative relationship between node attribute information and topology information, they cannot be treated separately. Node attribute information can facilitate the extraction of essential topology information, and topology information can help extract essential node attribute information for subgraph prediction. For example, nodes with high-connection attributes (high-degree nodes) play a more important role than nodes with low-connections, i.e., local topology structures with high-connection attributes in subgraphs have faster evolution speed worth more attention [10]. Nodes with similar attributes may have different effects on subgraph evolution due to different subgraph topologies. For instance, nodes with high topology centrality in subgraphs usually have a stronger influence than other nodes on subgraph evolution [13]. If we extract essential topology information only based on topologies for subgraph evolution, data features of some important topology structures (e.g., meta-path, local structures with high-connection nodes) will be unidentified and lost. The same thing happens with existing methods that extract important node attribute information for subgraph evolution only based on node attribute information. Similarly, as the complex collaborative relationship between node attribute and topology information varies with graphs and node number of subgraphs, it could not be predefined fully by humans. For example, according to the collaborative relationship, SPNN [15] defines some important structures artificially and pays more attention to the data features of these structures, but these predefined structures are incomplete, e.g., excluding the local structures with more than four nodes and high-connection nodes. Therefore, we propose a variant of MA named cross-attention to extract important data features based on topology information and node attribute information and include it in A-Block. The formula of the attention block with the cross-attention layer can be described as follows.

First, the formula of MA is

$$MA(Y) = Concat(head_1, ..., head_h)W^o, \qquad (4)$$

$$head_i = Attention(YW_i^Q, YW_i^K, YW_i^V), \qquad (5)$$

where $W^o \in R^{hD \times D}$, $W_i^Q \in R^{D \times D}$, $W_i^K \in R^{D \times D}$ and $W_i^V \in R^{D \times D}$ are the linear projection weight matrices. To approximate a more complex similarity function, each multi-head attention layer is concatenated with a feed-forward layer, which has the same dimension of input and output with the multi-head attention layer as follows:

$$FFN(x) = Max(0, xW_1 + b_1)W_2 + b_2. \qquad (6)$$

Thus, each attention block with the cross-attention layer in the left tower is

$$M_y^{i+1} = FFN(MA(M_c^i, M_c^i, SA(M_y^i))), \qquad (7)$$

where $M_c^i \in R^{k \times D}$ is the i-th output from the other tower, $M_c^0 = C$ and $M_y^0 = Y$. Similarly, each block in the right tower is

$$M_c^{i+1} = FFN(MA(M_y^i, M_y^i, SA(M_c^i))). \qquad (8)$$

To improve convergence, we add normalization and residual sum after each layer in the attention-based block.

SPAN. We use multi-sigmoid as the final activation function to predict existence probabilities of edges in the subgraph as follows:

$$M_f^{S_t} = MultiSigmoid(M_y^b (M_c^b)^T). \tag{9}$$

Since this paper focuses on subgraph prediction of undirected graphs, the prediction matrix, i.e., the adjacency matrix, should be symmetric. We enforce this symmetry by the average of the prediction matrix and its transposition as $M_f = \frac{M_f^{S_t} + M_f^{S_t T}}{2}$. Finally, we employ the cross entropy as the loss function as follows:

$$L = \sum_{S_t \in \hat{S}_t} \sum_{i,j} A_{i,j}^{S_{t+1}} log M_{f_{i,j}}^{S_t} + (1 - A_{i,j}^{S_{t+1}}) log(1 - M_{f_{i,j}}^{S_t}), \tag{10}$$

where $A^{S_{t+1}} \in R^{k \times k}$ is the adjacency matrix of S_{t+1} and $\hat{S}_t$ is the set of sampled subgraphs in the current snapshot.

SPAN-H. We develop SPAN-H for subgraph pattern prediction in heterogeneous networks. Heterogeneous networks have more abundant node attributes, and subgraph pattern prediction is not the same as subgraph prediction. Therefore, we make two modifications for SPAN. First, we increase the dimensions of the original node embedding vectors to encode abundant node attribute information. Second, subgraph pattern prediction requires embedding vectors for subgraphs. Therefore, we employ a weighted attention layer and a concatenation operation to replace the multi-sigmoid layer in SPAN, as shown in Fig. 1. The weighted attention layer can be computed by

$$M_{wy}^{S_t} = \sum_{v \in S_t} \alpha_v M_{y_v}^b, \tag{11}$$

$$M_{wc}^{S_t} = \sum_{v \in S_t} \beta_v M_{c_v}^b, \tag{12}$$

where $M_{y_v}^b$ and $M_{c_v}^b$ are the attention information of node v in the output of the last A-Block, as shown in Fig. 1. The attention score is computed by

$$\alpha_v = \frac{e^{\langle M_{y_v}^b, \sum_{u \in S_t} M_{c_u}^b \rangle}}{\sum_{r \in S_t} e^{\langle M_{y_r}^b, \sum_{u \in S_t} M_{c_u}^b \rangle}}, \tag{13}$$

$$\beta_v = \frac{e^{\langle M_{c_v}^b, \sum_{u \in S_t} M_{y_u}^b \rangle}}{\sum_{r \in S_t} e^{\langle M_{c_r}^b, \sum_{u \in S_t} M_{y_u}^b \rangle}}. \tag{14}$$

Then, the final output is $M_h^{S_t} = Sigmoid([M_{wy}^{S_t} | M_{wc}^{S_t}] W^s)$,

$$L = \sum_{S_t \in \hat{S}_t} B^{S_{t+1}} log M_h^{S_t} + (1 - B^{S_{t+1}}) log(1 - M_h^{S_t}), \tag{15}$$

Table 1. Statistics of dynamic graphs. $|V|$ = number of nodes; $|E|$ = number of temporal edges; $|T|$ = number of days.

Dataset	V	E	T
ia-facebook	46,952	876,993	1,591
soc-epinions	131,828	841,372	944
sx-askubuntu	159,316	964,437	2,047
sx-superuser	194,085	1,443,339	2,426
wiki-talk	1,140,149	7,833,140	2,268

where $W^s \in R^{2D \times 1}$ is the linear projection weight matrix as a classifier, and $M_h \in [0, 1]$ is the probability of the predefined subgraph pattern. Thus, the loss function becomes where $B^{S_{t+1}} \in \{0, 1\}$ is a binary value for indicating whether the subgraph pattern exists in the next snapshot. In summary, we introduce essential mechanisms for the three main limitations in subgraph prediction: twin-tower module with the cross-attention mechanism for the collaborative limitation, joint prediction for the edge dependency limitation, and end-to-end learning for the global threshold limitation.

4 Experiments

We evaluate our models on two tasks: subgraph prediction and subgraph pattern prediction. Subgraph prediction focuses on general subgraphs, whereas subgraph pattern prediction focuses on the evolution of the predefined relationship between nodes in subgraphs. The experiments were conducted on a machine with Intel i7 8700K (CPU) and RTX2070. We use Adam optimizer [11] to train our model, and the initial learning rate is 0.005. In addition, all experiments were repeated ten times, and the average performance of each method is reported.

4.1 Subgraph Prediction

The subgraph prediction task evaluates the ability to capture the evolution of subgraphs in discrete-time dynamic graphs with multiple snapshots. Therefore, multiple snapshots are set as model inputs to predict the next snapshot in this task. As shown in Table 1, we use five public datasets from Network Repository [19] for subgraph prediction. We split the dynamic graph into ten equal parts based on timestamps and construct ten snapshots for each dataset. The first nine snapshots are the training dataset, and the last snapshot is used for testing.

The hyperparameters in our method are set as $D = 128, k = 10$, and $b = 6$, which will be discussed in Sect. 4.4. We select four state-of-the-art dynamic embedding methods as the baseline methods, including EvolveGCN [18], Dyngraph2vec [6], DynamicTriad [30], and DynGEM [7]. For EvolveGCN,

Table 2. AUC scores of subgraph prediction ($D = 128, k = 10, b = 6$).

Dataset	DynamicTriad	DynGEM	Dyngraph2vec	EvolveGCN	SPAN	Gain
ia-facebook	0.833	0.753	0.771	0.785	**0.921**	**10.56%**
soc-epinions	0.778	0.723	0.791	0.804	**0.869**	**8.08%**
sx-askubuntu	0.816	0.811	0.844	0.841	**0.908**	**7.58%**
sx-superuser	0.871	0.856	0.884	0.896	**0.941**	**5.02%**
wiki-talk	OOM	OOM	OOM	OOM	**0.943**	–

Table 3. Parameter statistics of different methods ($D = 128, k = 10, b = 6$).

Dataset	DynamicTriad	DynGEM	Dyngraph2vec	EvolveGCN	SPAN
ia-facebook	15,776,259	500,212,854	72,184,652	**61,527**	4,248,800
soc-epinions	44,294,931	948,889,485	M199,583,528	26,175,567	**9,001,464**
sx-askubuntu	53,530,563	1,067,104,722	240,843,016	18,225,525	**10,540,792**
sx-superuser	65,212,947	1,213,544,964	293,031,285	80,957,922	**12,487,856**
wiki-talk	OOM	OOM	OOM	OOM	**65,467,440** -

EvolveGCN-H is selected for comparison because it uses the GRU mechanism with better convergence. According to the suggestions in [18], we specify the number of GCN layers as two and set the learning rate interval as [0.0001, 0.1]. For Dyngraph2vec, we use the AERNN version because it has higher accuracy than the default version. In addition, we set the look back size as $l = 1, 2, 3$ and other hyperparameters as suggested at [6]. For DynamicTriad [30], we set hyperparameters $\beta1 \in \{0.1, 1, 10\}$ and $\beta2 \in \{0.1, 1, 10\}$ alternatively to achieve the best performance. For DynGEM, we set the initial sizes of autoencoders as [500, 300], $\alpha \in [10^{-6}, 10^{-5}], \beta \in [2, 5], v1 \in [10^{-6}, 10^{-4}], v2 \in [10^{-5}, 10^{-2}]$ as suggested in [7]. We iteratively train SPAN via learning subgraph prediction in adjacent snapshots in chronological order, and other node embedding methods learn node embeddings for each snapshot. In testing, SPAN predicts the subgraphs in G_{10} based on G_9 directly, and other node embedding methods use the node embeddings of G_9 to predict links separately in these sampled subgraphs in G_{10}.

Table 2 lists the AUC scores of the subgraph prediction task. SPAN outperforms other state-of-the-art dynamic methods with an improvement from 5.02% to 10.56%. The method for calculating gain is the same as described in [16]: (the accuracy of our method - the highest accuracy of other methods)/the highest accuracy of other methods. According to Table 2, in our experiment, previous methods fail to predict subgraphs for large dynamic graphs (more than 1 million nodes) due to out-of-memory (OOM) in our experiment environment. As shown in Table 3, the number of parameters in SPAN is lower than other methods and increases linearly with the graph size. The main reason is that SPAN can learn a subgraph with arbitrary size each time and is memory efficient compared to other methods based on the adjacency matrix of all snapshots or graphs.

Table 4. AUC scores of subgraph pattern prediction ($D = 128, b = 6$).

Dataset	SPNN	HAN	HGT	SPAN	SPAN-H	Gain
email-eu	0.872	0.859	0.876	0.885	**0.941**	**7.42%**
DBLP	0.838	0.816	0.834	0.861	**0.889**	**6.09%**
mathoverflow	0.855	0.831	0.840	0.877	**0.915**	**7.01%**

4.2   Subgraph Pattern Prediction

Subgraph pattern prediction predicts that the subgraph would be transformed into a predefined subgraph pattern in a period of time. According to the task definition [15], we select three real-world heterogeneous dynamic graphs for this task. The email network Email-eu [14] is constructed using emails from a large European research institution, comprising 986 staff members, 50,572 emails, and 42 departments. The sampled subgraph has four staff members ($k = 4$), and at least two staff work in different departments in the subgraph. The subgraph pattern is the communication between different departments, i.e., the connectivity between staff members in different departments. DBLP [21] is a scientific paper co-author network with timestamps, including different entity types: 14,376 papers, 14,475 authors, 8,920 topics and 20 venues. We predict the evolution of 3-node subgraphs (author, topic, and venue), i.e., whether an author will publish in a venue and on a topic that the author has not published in the current snapshot. Mathoverflow [17] is a temporal network collected from the same website, including 24,818 users and 506,550 interactions, such as answers to questions, comments to questions, and comments to answers. The subgraph pattern is whether four users will interact more frequently over a period ($k = 4$), i.e., whether there will be more edges of 4-node subgraphs in a period.

The evolution that transforms the subgraph into a predefined subgraph pattern may involve establishing multiple edges at different times, implying that this evolution may include multiple intermediate states in multiple discrete snapshots. However, we cannot ensure the appearance or nonappearance of subgraph patterns based on these intermediate states. Thus, to avoid these intermediate states, we discuss the appearance or nonappearance of subgraph patterns in a continuous-time rather than dividing the time into multiple snapshots. We divide each dynamic graph into two continuous-time graphs. The first continuous-time graph is constructed using the first 70% edges for training, and the second is constructed using the last 30% edges for testing. We sample subgraphs from the first continuous-time graph and train the model by predicting subgraph patterns in the first continuous-time graph. In testing, we predict subgraph patterns in the second continuous-time graph based on subgraphs in the first continuous-time graph.

We compare three state-of-the-art methods, namely, SPNN [15], HAN [25], and HGT [9], with SPAN-H in the subgraph pattern prediction task. SPNN is designed for subgraph pattern prediction based on limited and predefined subgraph patterns. HAN and HGT are based on the attention and graph convolution mechanisms to learn node embeddings for heterogeneous networks. We generate subgraph embeddings for HAN and HGT by averaging node embeddings and predicting subgraph pattern evolution using subgraph embeddings. We also set $D = 128$ and other hyperparameters, as suggested [9,15,25]. Table 4 shows the AUC scores of subgraph pattern prediction on three heterogeneous networks, and that SPAN-H achieves the best performance increasing from 6.09% to 7.42%, compared to other methods. The proposed model can learn the evolution of subgraphs in heterogeneous dynamic graphs more effectively. Compared with previous methods, SPAN-H completely learns the existing subgraph patterns from data and uses a twin-tower module with the cross-attention mechanism to capture the evolution of subgraphs based on diverse information.

4.3 Model Analysis

Our model achieves the best performance on both subgraph prediction and subgraph pattern prediction tasks. We attribute this benefit to some new mechanisms, such as Bayesian attention, the twin-tower module and the cross-attention mechanism. In this section, we discuss how these mechanisms gradually improve our model. As shown in Fig. 2, we design four models for comparative analysis on the subgraph pattern prediction task using the same dataset in Sect. 4.2. As shown in Fig. 2, model 1 only uses node attribute information, model 2 uses context information (the fusion of node attribute information and topology information generated by Bayesian attention), model 3 extends the tower module based on model 2, and model 4 extends model 3 with cross-attention. The reason for choosing this task is that heterogeneous networks have rich subgraph patterns and have numerous practical applications. Figure 3 shows the results of the four models.

As shown in Fig. 3, model 2 outperforms model 1, which means the node attribute information and topology information both play a significant role in subgraph evolution.

In addition, model 3 outperforms model 2 because node attribute information will become fuzzy during the Bayesian attention process in model 2 even though context information can be regarded as the fusion of node attribute information and topology information. Figure 3 also shows that model 4 achieves higher accuracy and faster convergence speed than model 3. The benefit is attributable to the cross-attention mechanism. Important topology information or node attribute information may also be related to each other in subgraph evolution. The cross-attention mechanism integrates topology information and node attribute information to extract important features rather than isolated extraction, enabling our method to avoid feature loss.

4.4 Hyperparameter Analysis

We discuss the significant hyperparameters of subgraph sampling and model learning, respectively. **For subgraph sampling**, the maximum node size of subgraphs is k even though subgraphs can be generated with an arbitrary size

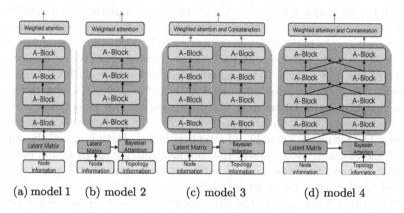

(a) model 1   (b) model 2   (c) model 3   (d) model 4

Fig. 2. Model architectures for comparison: (a) model 1 using only node attribute information, (b) model 2 using only context information, (c) model 3 using both context information and node attribute information, (d) model 4 using a cross-attention mechanism to fuse node and context information in multi-level.

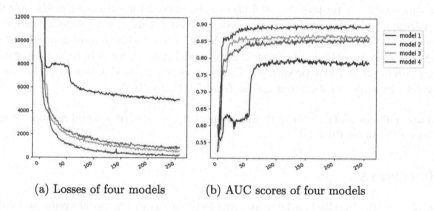

(a) Losses of four models   (b) AUC scores of four models

Fig. 3. The loss curves (a) and AUC score curves (b) of four models over epochs. These curves are averaged across three datasets in subgraph pattern prediction.

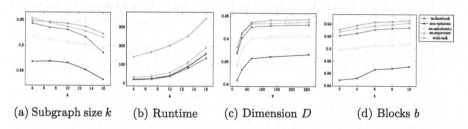

(a) Subgraph size k (b) Runtime   (c) Dimension D (d) Blocks b

Fig. 4. (a), (c), and (d) are the AUC scores of discrete-time subgraph prediction for different settings on hyperparameters k, D and b; (b) is the training time of SPAN with different k (minutes).

($\leq k$) in the subgraph sampling process. Figure 4(a) illustrates that smaller subgraphs can be learned better than larger subgraphs because the evolution pace of bigger subgraphs becomes larger, and effectively predicting these subgraphs is difficult. The number of nodes also affects the training time. We set the hyperparameters ($D = 128$ and $b = 6$) to evaluate the training time of SPAN. Figure 4(b) shows that the training time increases with k and is almost linear with the subgraph size. **For model learning**, the dimension of node embedding vectors in the latent matrix is D, and Fig. 4(c) demonstrates performance changes with different D. Our model's number of attention-based blocks is b, and the stacking of multiple blocks is used to learn the complex function for subgraph evolution. Figure 4(d) shows that the model's performance is generally proportional to b, as fewer blocks would be under-fitted. Since the model's performance increases gradually when $b > 6$, we set the hyperparameter $b = 6$ to reduce the number of parameters and avoid overfitting.

5   Conclusion

In this study, we propose a novel end-to-end model for subgraph prediction in dynamic graphs. We evaluate our model by comparing it with several state-of-the-art methods, including node embedding-based methods and graph neural network-based methods in dynamic graphs with two tasks: subgraph prediction and subgraph pattern prediction. Experimental results demonstrate that our model can achieve substantial gains, from 5.02% to 10.88%.

Acknowledgements. This work was supported by National Natural Science Foundation of China (61972343).

References

1. Albert, R., Barabasi, A.L.: Topology of evolving networks: local events and universality. Phys. Rev. Lett. **85**, 5234–5237 (2001)
2. Alsentzer, E., Finlayson, S., Li, M., Zitnik, M.: Subgraph neural networks. In: Advances in Neural Information Processing Systems, vol. 33, pp. 8017–8029 (2020)
3. Benson, A.R., Abebe, R., Schaub, M.T., Jadbabaie, A., Kleinberg, J.: Simplicial closure and higher-order link prediction. Proc. Nat. Acad. Sci. **115**(48), 11221–11230 (2018)
4. Borgnat, P., Fleury, E., Guillaume, J.L., Magnien, C., Robardet, C., Scherrer, A.: Evolving networks. In: Mining Massive Data Sets for Security, vol. 19, pp. 198–203 (2008)
5. Chiang, W.L., Liu, X., Si, S., Li, Y., Bengio, S., Hsieh, C.J.: Cluster-GCN: an efficient algorithm for training deep and large graph convolutional networks. In: Proceedings of the 25th ACM SIGKDD International Conference on Knowledge Discovery & Data Mining, pp. 257–266 (2019)
6. Goyal, P., Chhetri, S.R., Canedo, A.: dyngraph2vec: capturing network dynamics using dynamic graph representation learning. Knowl. Based Syst. **187**, 104816 (2020)

7. Goyal, P., Kamra, N., He, X., Liu, Y.: DynGEM: deep embedding method for dynamic graphs. In: IJCAI International Workshop on Representation Learning for Graphs (ReLiG) (2017)

8. Hamilton, W., Ying, Z., Leskovec, J.: Inductive representation learning on large graphs. In: Advances in Neural Information Processing Systems, vol. 29, pp. 1024–1034 (2017)

9. Hu, Z., Dong, Y., Wang, K., Sun, Y.: Heterogeneous graph transformer. In: Proceedings of The Web Conference 2020, pp. 2704–2710 (2020)

10. Jeong, H., Néda, Z., Barabási, A.L.: Measuring preferential attachment in evolving networks. EPL (Europhys. Lett.) **61**(4), 567 (2003)

11. Kingma, D.P., Ba, J.: Adam: a method for stochastic optimization. In: International Conference on Learning Representations (2015)

12. Kipf, T.N., Welling, M.: Semi-supervised classification with graph convolutional networks. In: International Conference on Learning Representations, pp. 1120–1134 (2017)

13. König, M.D., Tessone, C.J.: Network evolution based on centrality. Phys. Rev. E **84**(5), 056108 (2011)

14. Leskovec, J., Kleinberg, J., Faloutsos, C.: Graph evolution: densification and shrinking diameters. ACM Trans. Knowl. Discovery from Data (TKDD) **1**(1), 2-es (2007)

15. Meng, C., Mouli, S.C., Ribeiro, B., Neville, J.: Subgraph pattern neural networks for high-order graph evolution prediction. In: Proceedings of the AAAI Conference on Artificial Intelligence, vol. 32 (2018)

16. Nguyen, G.H., Lee, J.B., Rossi, R.A., Ahmed, N.K., Koh, E., Kim, S.: Continuous-time dynamic network embeddings. In: 3rd International Workshop on Learning Representations for Big Networks, pp. 969–976 (2018)

17. Paranjape, A., Benson, A.R., Leskovec, J.: Motifs in temporal networks. In: Proceedings of the Tenth ACM International Conference on Web Search and Data Mining, pp. 601–610. ACM (2017)

18. Pareja, A., et al.: EvolveGCN: evolving graph convolutional networks for dynamic graphs. In: Proceedings of the AAAI Conference on Artificial Intelligence, vol. 34, pp. 5363–5370 (2020)

19. Rossi, R., Ahmed, N.: The network data repository with interactive graph analytics and visualization. In: Proceedings of the AAAI Conference on Artificial Intelligence, vol. 29 (2015)

20. Sankar, A., Wu, Y., Gou, L., Zhang, W., Yang, H.: DySAT: deep neural representation learning on dynamic graphs via self-attention networks. In: Proceedings of the 13th International Conference on Web Search and Data Mining, pp. 519–527 (2020)

21. Sun, Y., Han, J., Yan, X., Yu, P.S., Wu, T.: PathSim: meta path-based top-k similarity search in heterogeneous information networks. Proc. VLDB Endowment **4**(11), 992–1003 (2011)

22. Tang, J., Lou, T., Kleinberg, J.: Inferring social ties across heterogenous networks. In: Proceedings of the fifth ACM International Conference on Web Search and Data Mining, pp. 743–752 (2012)

23. Vaswani, A., et al.: Attention is all you need. In: Advances in Neural Information Processing Systems, vol. 29, pp. 5998–6008 (2017)

24. Veličković, P., Cucurull, G., Casanova, A., Romero, A., Lio, P., Bengio, Y.: Graph attention networks. In: International Conference on Learning Representations, pp. 1710–1721 (2018)

25. Wang, X., et al.: Heterogeneous graph attention network. In: The World Wide Web Conference, pp. 2022–2032 (2019)
26. Wang, X., Lu, Y., Shi, C., Wang, R., Cui, P., Mou, S.: Dynamic heterogeneous information network embedding with meta-path based proximity. IEEE Trans. Knowl. Data Eng. (2020)
27. Watts, D.J., Strogatz, S.H.: Collective dynamics of 'small-world' networks. Nature **393**(6684), 440–442 (1998)
28. Yang, C., Liu, M., Zheng, V.W., Han, J.: Node, motif and subgraph: leveraging network functional blocks through structural convolution. In: 2018 IEEE/ACM International Conference on Advances in Social Networks Analysis and Mining (ASONAM), pp. 47–52 (2018)
29. Zeng, H., Zhou, H., Srivastava, A., Kannan, R., Prasanna, V.: GraphSAINT: graph sampling based inductive learning method. In: International Conference on Learning Representations (2020)
30. Zhou, L., Yang, Y., Ren, X., Wu, F., Zhuang, Y.: Dynamic network embedding by modeling triadic closure process. In: Proceedings of the AAAI Conference on Artificial Intelligence, vol. 32, pp. 571–578 (2018)
31. Zhu, L., Guo, D., Yin, J., Ver Steeg, G., Galstyan, A.: Scalable temporal latent space inference for link prediction in dynamic social networks. IEEE Trans. Knowl. Data Eng. **28**(10), 2765–2777 (2016)

WINVC: One-Shot Voice Conversion with Weight Adaptive Instance Normalization

Shengjie Huang[1,2], Mingjie Chen[3], Yanyan Xu[1,2(✉)], Dengfeng Ke[4(✉)], and Thomas Hain[3]

[1] School of Information Science and Technology,
Beijing Forestry University, Beijing, China
{huangshengjie,xuyanyan}@bjfu.edu.cn
[2] Engineering Research Center for Forestry-Oriented Intelligent Information
Processing of National Forestry and Grassland Administration, Beijing, China
[3] Computer Science Department, University of Sheffield, Sheffield, UK
{mchen33,t.hain}@sheffield.ac.uk
[4] School of Information Science, Beijing Language and Culture University,
Beijing, China
dengfeng.ke@blcu.edu.cn

Abstract. This paper proposes a one-shot voice conversion (VC) solution. In many one-shot voice conversion solutions (e.g., Auto-encoder-based VC methods), performances have dramatically been improved due to instance normalization and adaptive instance normalization. However, one-shot voice conversion fluency is still lacking, and the similarity is not good enough. This paper introduces the weight adaptive instance normalization strategy to improve the naturalness and similarity of one-shot voice conversion. Experimental results prove that under the VCTK data set, the MOS score of our proposed model, weight adaptive instance normalization voice conversion (WINVC), reaches 3.97 with five scales, and the SMOS reaches 3.31 with four scales. Besides, WINVC can achieve a MOS score of 3.44 and a SMOS score of 3.11 respectively for one-shot voice conversion under a small data set of 80 speakers with 5 pieces of utterances per person.

Keywords: One-shot voice conversion · Generative adversarial networks (GANs) · Weight adaptive instance normalization

1 Introduction

Voice conversion aims to preserve the source voice content information while replacing the non-content information in the voice with the target speaker. It has attracted many researchers for its potential applications in security [1], medicine [2], entertainment [3] and education [4].

There are two types of VC, parallel and non-parallel. Due to the difficulty and expensiveness of parallel data collection, several methods based on parallel data, such as the gaussian mixture model (GMM) [5], dynamic time warping (DTW) [6], and deep neural network (DNN) [7], are not particularly effective solutions. In

© Springer Nature Switzerland AG 2021
D. N. Pham et al. (Eds.): PRICAI 2021, LNAI 13032, pp. 559–573, 2021.
https://doi.org/10.1007/978-3-030-89363-7_42

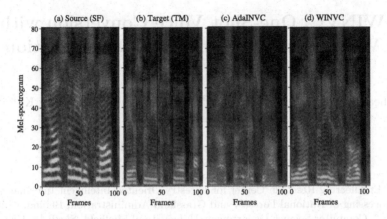

Fig. 1. Comparison of source, target, and converted mel-spectrograms.

order to overcome this limitation, the phonetic posteriorgrams(PPG) based models [8], generative adversarial network (StarGAN) based models [9,10], and variational auto-encoder (VAE) based models [11] are adopted to solve the problem of non-parallel VC. These methods get rid of the dependence on parallel data. However, when dealing with unseen speakers, a long time adaptation process or a large amount of data is required.

One-shot voice conversion [12–14] and zero-shot voice conversion [15,16] solve the unseen speaker problem. They convert the source voice to an unseen speaker's voice by referring to only a few target utterances. Moreover, neither the source nor the target utterances appear in the training set during the training phase. They require the model to have a solid ability to separate content information from non-content information in the voice.

Due to the development of the normalization strategy, the performance of the one-shot voice conversion task has been improved. There are two mainstream frameworks for better one-shot VC in recent years, including the auto-encoder based one [12,15] and the vector quantization (VQ) based one [13,14]. [15] uses the batch normalization (BN) [17] strategy to implement the one-shot voice conversion successfully. In [13,14], the instance normalization (IN) [18] strategy is adopted. Compared with the BN strategy used in [15], IN normalizes each input object separately to improve one-shot voice conversion quality. Moreover, AdaINVC [12] innovatively adopts the adaptive instance normalization (AdaIN) [19] strategy. The AdaIN strategy significantly improves the one-shot voice conversion and achieves an improved similarity. Nevertheless, it is challenging to disentangle speaker information and content information through an unsupervised learning method. Moreover, researchers are helpless if the similarity of converted speech is unsatisfying.

In this paper, we propose a weight adaptive instance normalization (WIN) voice conversion system for one-shot VC. The model framework bases on StarGAN-VC2 [10] because it has good effectiveness and convenience, and the model structure is improved. We use the speaker encoder jointly trained with the generator to extract the non-linguistic information of the target speaker. Under the VCTK [20] data set, we compare the WINVC with AdaINVC. The mel-spectrograms (Fig. 1) show that WINVC performs better in content intelligibility and retention, and subjective evaluations show that WINVC achieves better results than AdaINVC on the one-shot voice conversion task. Furthermore, WINVC achieves a competitive one-shot voice conversion performance under the extreme training conditions of using only 80 speakers with 5 utterances per person. In addition, we apply the WIN [21] strategy to AdaINVC, and experimental results show that AdaINVC's one-shot performance has been improved.

To summarize, we list the core contributions of this paper as follows:

1. We design a new model WINVC based on the WIN strategy and StarGAN-VC2. It outperforms the state-of-the-art (SOTA) model AdaINVC naturally and similarly on one-shot voice conversion tasks under non-parallel data.
2. Furthermore, WINVC can perform competitive one-shot voice conversion results even with small amount of data.
3. We also apply the WIN strategy to the previous SOTA model AdaINVC and significantly improves its performance.
4. We use the jointly trained speaker encoder as the non-linguistic information extractor and employ the speaker embedding cycle loss to help the model perform the one-shot VC task better.

2 StarGAN-VC/VC2

This section reviews two previous StarGAN-based voice conversion models: StarGAN-VC [9] and StarGAN-VC2 [10]. As shown in Fig. 2, StarGAN-VC uses the StarGAN [22] model for voice conversion, which includes three modules: a generator (G), a discriminator (D) and a domain classifier (C). G takes an acoustic feature sequence $x \in \mathbb{R}$ with an arbitrary attribute and a target attribute label c as the inputs, and generates an acoustic feature sequence,

$$\hat{y} = G(x, c) \tag{1}$$

D is designed to produce a probability $D(y, c)$ that an input y is a real speech feature whereas C is designed to produce class probabilities $p_C(c \mid y)$ of y.

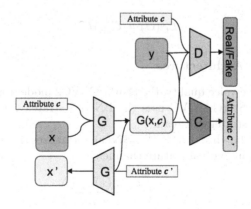

Fig. 2. The architecture of StarGAN-VC.

2.1   Training Objectives

StarGAN-VC/VC2 includes adversarial loss [23], cycle consistency loss [24], and identity mapping loss [25]. StarGAN-VC2 deletes classification loss [26] and updates the BN strategy to the CIN strategy. These loss functions are as follows.

Adversarial loss is

$$\mathcal{L}_{\text{adv}}^{D}(D) = -\mathbb{E}_{c\sim p(c),\mathbf{y}\sim p(\mathbf{y}|c)}[\log D(\mathbf{y},c)] \\ -\mathbb{E}_{\mathbf{x}\sim p(\mathbf{x}),c\sim p(c)}[\log(1-D(G(\mathbf{x},c),c))], \tag{2}$$

$$\mathcal{L}_{\text{adv}}^{G}(G) = -\mathbb{E}_{\mathbf{x}\sim p(\mathbf{x}),c\sim p(c)}[\log D(G(\mathbf{x},c),c)]. \tag{3}$$

Cycle-consistency loss is to preserve the composition in conversion, which is presented as follows:

$$\mathcal{L}_{\text{cyc}}(G) = \mathbb{E}_{c'\sim p(c),\mathbf{x}\sim p(\mathbf{x}|c'),c\sim p(c)}[\|G(G(\mathbf{x},c),c') - \mathbf{x}\|]. \tag{4}$$

Identity-mapping loss is to facilitate input preservation, which is presented as follows:

$$\mathcal{L}_{\text{id}}(G) = \mathbb{E}_{c'\sim p(c),\mathbf{x}\sim p(\mathbf{x}|c')}[\|G(\mathbf{x},c') - \mathbf{x}\|]. \tag{5}$$

Classification loss is to force the generated data to be similar to the target speaker's, which has been abandoned in StarGAN-VC2:

$$\mathcal{L}_{\text{cls}}^{C}(C) = -\mathbb{E}_{c\sim p(c),\mathbf{y}\sim p(\mathbf{y}|c)}[\log p_{C}(c\mid\mathbf{y})], \tag{6}$$

$$\mathcal{L}_{\text{cls}}^{G}(G) = -\mathbb{E}_{\mathbf{x}\sim p(\mathbf{x}),c\sim p(c)}[\log p_{C}(c\mid G(\mathbf{x},c))]. \tag{7}$$

To summarize, the full objectives of StarGAN-VC to be minimized with respect to G, D and C are given as:

$$\mathcal{L}_{G}(G) = \mathcal{L}_{\text{adv}}^{G}(G) + \lambda_{\text{cls}}\mathcal{L}_{\text{cls}}^{G}(G) + \lambda_{\text{cyc}}\mathcal{L}_{\text{cyc}}(G) + \lambda_{\text{id}}\mathcal{L}_{\text{id}}(G), \tag{8}$$

$$\mathcal{L}_{D}(D) = \mathcal{L}_{\text{adv}}^{D}(D), \tag{9}$$

$$\mathcal{L}_{C}(C) = \mathcal{L}_{\text{adv}}^{C}(C). \tag{10}$$

2.2   Generator Architectures

In order to improve voice quality, the StarGAN-VC2 model removes the domain classifier module. StarGAN-VC uses the BN [17] strategy, and StarGAN-VC2 uses the CIN [27] strategy instead.

Given an input batch $x \in R^{BCHW}$, $\text{BN}(x)$ normalizes the mean and standard deviations for the individual feature channel:

$$\text{BN}(x) = \gamma_{single}\left(\frac{x - \mu(x)_{batch}}{\sigma(x)_{batch}}\right) + \beta_{single}, \tag{11}$$

where $\gamma, \beta \in R^C$ are affine parameters learned from data. $\mu(x)$, $\sigma(x) \in R^C$ are the mean and standard deviations, computed across batch size and spatial dimensions independently for each feature channel.

[13] and [14] employ the IN [18] strategy of image style conversion to achieve a better one-shot voice conversion performance.

$$\text{IN}(x) = \gamma_{single} \left(\frac{x - \mu(x)_{sample}}{\sigma(x)_{sample}} \right) + \beta_{single}, \tag{12}$$

where x is the input feature. γ and β form a single set of affine parameters learned from data. μ and σ are computed across spatial dimensions independently for each channel and each sample.

StarGAN-VC2 [10] uses the conditional instance normalization (CIN) [27] strategy, as shown in Eq. (13), where $\gamma(e_{xy})$ and $\beta(e_{xy})$ are domain-specific scales and bias parameters that allow transforming the modulation in a domain-specific manner. e_{xy} is selected depending on both the source domain code e_x and the target domain code e_y.

$$CIN(x, e_{xy}) = \gamma_{styles}(e_{xy}) \left(\frac{x - \mu(x)_{sample}}{\sigma(x)_{sample}} \right) + \beta_{styles}(e_{xy}), \tag{13}$$

$$e_{xy} = \text{concat}([e_x, e_y]). \tag{14}$$

3 The Proposed Model

3.1 Workflow

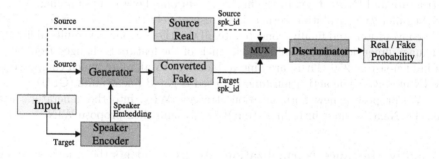

Fig. 3. The workflow diagram of the proposed model

This section introduces the various modules and implementation details of our proposed model[1]. The entire workflow is shown in Fig. 3, consisting of a Generator, a Discriminator, and a Speaker Encoder, where **MUX** means randomly sending source real data or converted fake data to Discriminator.

---

[1] Further details may be found in our implementation code:
https://github.com/One-Shot-Voice-Conversion-with-WIN/WINVC.

3.2　The Generator with Weight Adaptive Instance Norm

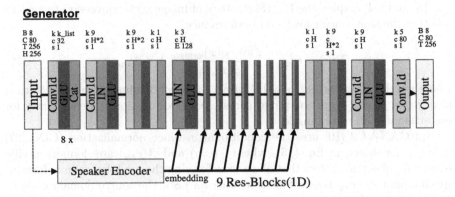

Fig. 4. The module details of G. In input, output, and res-block layers, B, C, T, H and E represent batch, channel, the number of frames, the hidden size and the embedding size of speaker embedding respectively. In each convolution layer, k, c, and s denote the kernel size, the number of channels and stride, respectively. IN, GLU, Cat and WIN indicate instance normalization, gated linear unit, concatenating and the proposed weight adaptive instance normalization.

As shown in Fig. 4, the generator is composed of 1D-convolution, which includes three parts: up-sampling, bottleneck resblocks, and down-sampling. Unlike StarGAN-VC2, our upsampling and downsampling both use the 1D-convolution structure and IN strategy. In the first convolutional layer of upsampling, we use eight different convolution kernel sizes (respectively [1, 1, 3, 3, 5, 5, 7, 7]) with 1D-convolution, and finally, concatenate all the 1D-convolution results along the channel dimension. The number of channels of the feature is changed from 80 to a hidden-size of 256. There are nine resblocks in total, all of which composed of WIN modules. The activation function used is gated linear units (GLU).

We propose a new normalization strategy, WIN, into the generator's resblocks. Next, we first introduce AdaIN briefly, and then propose WIN.

Adaptive Instance Normalization. AdaINVC adopts the AdaIN strategy, a particular case of instance normalization, which makes a simple extension to CIN. AdaINVC uses a speaker encoder to extract the speaker embedding $e_y = E(y)$, making it possible to exploit rich information in speaker embedding. The speaker embedding controls the scaling and bias variables of AdaIN. Unlike BN, IN, or CIN, AdaIN has no learnable affine parameters. Instead, it adaptively computes the affine parameters from the style input e_y.

$$\text{AdaIN}(x, e_y) = \sigma(e_y) \left(\frac{x - \mu(x)_{sample}}{\sigma(x)_{sample}} \right) + \mu(e_y). \tag{15}$$

In Eq. (15), x is a content input to the operator, and e_y is the speaker embedding. $\mu(x)$ and $\sigma(x)$ are the mean and the standard deviations of the feature x across time. $\sigma(e_y)$ and $\mu(e_y)$ are adaptive linear functions. AdaIN (Eq. 15) performs standard modulation on feature x first, and then uses the adaptive scaling and bias variables, obtained according to the speaker embedding, to perform standard normalization on the features, and finally achieves the integration of feature x and speaker embedding.

Weight Adaptive Instance Normalization. To improve the data efficiency of one-shot voice conversion task, we propose the WIN [21] strategy in the bottleneck blocks of the generator, which was initially proposed for image style transfer tasks. Figure 5 illustrates the architectur of WIN [21] module:

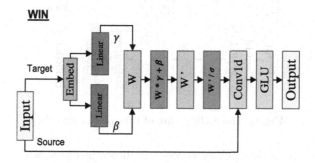

Fig. 5. The architecture of the WIN module.

$$w'_{ijk}(w_{ijk}, e_y) = \gamma_i(e_y) * w_{ijk} + \beta_i(e_y) \tag{16}$$

$$\sigma_j = \sqrt{\sum_{i,k} w'_{ijk}{}^2} \tag{17}$$

$$WIN(w_{ijk}, e_y) = w'_{ijk} / \sqrt{\sum_{i,k} w'_{ijk}{}^2 + \epsilon} \tag{18}$$

In Eq. (16), w and w' are the original and modulated weights, i denotes the ith input feature map, and j and k enumerate the output feature maps and spatial footprint of the convolution, respectively. e_y is target speaker embedding. In Eq. (17), σ_j is the standard deviation of modulated weights. In Eq. (18), ϵ is a small constant to avoid numerical issues.

Different from AdaIN, the demodulation strategy of WIN (Eq. 18) is related to weight normalization [28]. The modulation (Eq. 16) and demodulation (Eq. 18) strategies perform as a part of reparameterizing the weight tensor w. In Eq. (16), $\gamma_i(e_y)$ and $\beta_i(e_y)$ are two affine transformations applied to speaker embedding e_y corresponding to the ith input feature map, which generate style-dependent scaling and the bias variables. Then they are applied to normalize the convolution weight w_{ijk}, and finally get the intermediate variables w'_{ijk}. In Eq. (18), we demodulate it again into the convolution weights, which is now embedding related.

The WIN strategy in our proposed WINVC model shows a better one-shot voice conversion performance than the state-of-the-art model AdaINVC. Also, we replace AdaIN with WIN in the baseline AdaINVC. The subjective evaluation shows that WIN enables AdaINVC to achieve a better MOS score and SMOS score, indicating better voice quality and better similarity. Furthermore, the objective evaluation shows that WIN helps AdaINVC get higher speaker verification accuracy.

3.3   The Speaker Encoder and the Discriminator

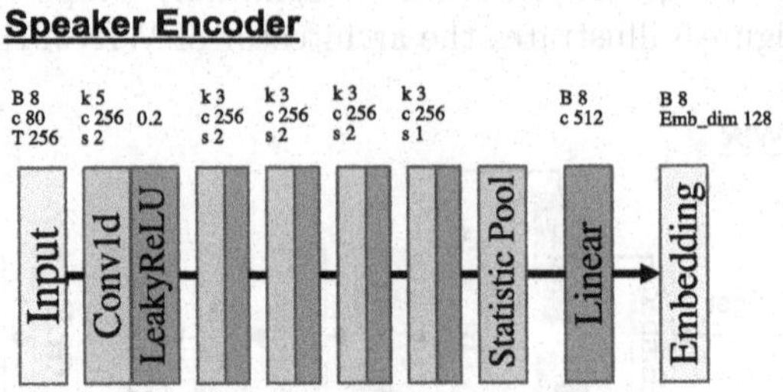

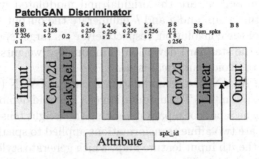

Fig. 6. The architecture of the speaker encoder.

The architecture of the speaker encoder is shown in Fig. 6, which adopts a full 1D-convolution form and uses the LeakyRelu activation function after each convolution layer. And it uses a statistic pooling layer as in the xvector [29]. We pass the pool results through a linear function to generate a speaker embedding. Further more, we use a speaker embedding cycle loss (Eq. 19) to help model get better similarity:

$$\mathcal{L}_{spkcyc} = \cos\left(E\left(x_t\right), E\left(G\left(x_s, E\left(x_t\right)\right)\right)\right), \tag{19}$$

where E is the speaker encoder, x_s and x_t denote the source feature and target feature.

Fig. 7. The module details of D. LeakyRelu indicate LeakyRelu activation. spk_id and Num_spks denote the speaker attribute label and the number of speakers used.

The discriminator structure is shown in Fig. 7, which introduces Patch-GAN [30] which uses convolution in each layer to reduce parameters and stabilize GAN training. After the last 2D-convolution, the data size obtained is [Batch, num_speakers]. Finally, by specifying the target speaker attribute, the evaluation result of real or fake probability is obtained.

3.4   Training Objectives

We use the speaker encoder to extract the non-linguistic information of the target speaker, which is jointly trained with the generator G. And then send the extracted speaker embedding to the generator. G generates the voice conversion result, which is then judged by the discriminator D. In the one-shot stage, AdaINVC, together with most unsupervised models, is helpless if the converted speech's similarity is not satisfactory. However, our model can further improve the similarity of the existing results.

In our proposed model, there are four training objectives: adversarial loss (Eq. 2, 3), cycle consistency loss (Eq. 4), identity loss (Eq. 5), and speaker embedding cycle loss (Eq. 19). The adversarial loss, cycle consistency loss and identity loss are consistent with the corresponding formulas in StarGAN-VC2. The speaker embedding cycle loss is used to calculate the cosine similarity between the converted voice and the ground truth target voice.

Full objective: The full objective is written as

$$\mathcal{L}_D = -\mathcal{L}_{t-adv}, \tag{20}$$

$$\mathcal{L}_G = \lambda_{adv}\mathcal{L}_{t-adv} + \lambda_{spkcyc}\mathcal{L}_{spkcyc} + \lambda_{cyc}\mathcal{L}_{cyc} + \lambda_{id}\mathcal{L}_{id}. \tag{21}$$

where D and G are optimized by minimizing $\mathcal{L}_D$ and $\mathcal{L}_G$ respectively.

4   Experiments

4.1   Datasets

Our experiments are conducted on the VCTK English data set. All selected training utterances are longer than 256 frames. And we use third-party pre-trained Parallel WaveGAN [31][2] as vocoder for all comparison models. For the one-shot voice conversion experiment, we use a training dataset of 80 speakers with all utterances, another dataset of 10 unseen speakers, including 5 men and 5 women for unseen-to-unseen one-shot voice conversion. In addition, to further improve the similarity on the existing results, we take an adaption stage, with only one utterance each is used to adapt the pretrained model quickly, and the objective evaluation (Fig. 11) show that the similarity can quickly upgrade within 5,000 iterations. For a fair comparison, we make the training set of AdaINVC also contain the 10 unseen speakers with one utterance each. In the end, among the 10 one-shot speakers, we use their other voice data to complete the unseen-to-unseen one-shot voice conversion experiments.

---

[2] https://github.com/kan-bayashi/ParallelWaveGAN.

4.2   Training Details

The learning rates of G and D are 2e-4 and 1e-4, respectively. The batch size is 8, and the minimum length of the training data is 256 frames. The values of λ_{id}, λ_{cyc}, λ_{adv} and λ_{spkcyc} are 2, 4, 1 and 5. The WIN convolution kernel size is 3. The number of training iterations is 100k, with the training converging in 10 h on a single 1080ti. The further adaption stage can be converged within half hour with 5k iterations.

4.3   Subjective Evaluations

We analyze the performance[3] differences among the ground truth VCTK utterances (***Target***), our proposed model trained with (80 speakers × all utterances) and adapted with another (10 speakers × 1 utterance) (***WINVC***), the proposed model trained with (80 speakers × 5 utterances) and adapted with another (10 speakers × 1 utterance) (***WINVC5***), the baseline model trained with (80 speakers × all utterances + 10 speakers × 1 utterance) (***AdaINVC***), and the baseline model replaces AdaIN strategy with WIN strategy and is also trained with (80 speakers × all + 10 speakers × 1 utterance) (***AdaINVC_W***).

We conduct mean opinion score (MOS) tests, similarity mean opinion score (SMOS) tests, and ABX tests. The target ground truth utterances (Target) are used as anchor samples. Evaluation utterances are selected based on gender combination for each model. Each gender combination includes 2 pairs of speakers. Each pair of speakers have 20 utterances. Each model is evaluated with $4 \times 2 \times 20 = 160$ utterances. Each utterance is evaluated once. All subjective tests are evaluated with 13 participants.

MOS. As shown in Fig. 8, "F" means "female", "M" means "male". For example, "F-M" denotes that female source voice is converted into male target voice, and so on. "Target" means the ground truth voice of corresponding target speaker. In the subjective naturalness test (MOS), WINVC achieves the highest MOS scores. WINVC5 trained with few data can also achieve a competitive results. In addition, the MOS score of AdaINVC_W is higher than AdaINVC, which indicates that the WIN strategy can indeed make AdaINVC achieve more natural results.

SMOS. Figure 9 shows the similarity SMOS. WINVC achieves the highest SMOS scores, WINVC5 can also achieve competitive results. The scores of WINVC and WINVC5 are very close, and all outperform AdaINVC, which denotes that WINVC5 with low resource of training data can also achieve nice similarity. And AdaINVC_W also performs better than AdaINVC, this indicates that the WIN strategy can indeed make AdaINVC achieve better similarity results.

---

[3] For more details, please refer to the website:
https://one-shot-voice-conversion-with-win.github.io.

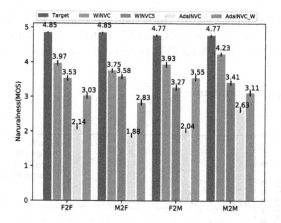

Fig. 8. Naturalness results for baseline model and our proposed WINVC model with 95% confidence intervals.

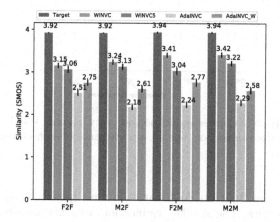

Fig. 9. Naturalness results for baseline model and our proposed WINVC model with 95% confidence intervals.

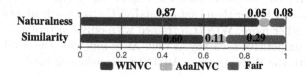

Fig. 10. The ABX test between WINVC and AdaINVC from the aspects of naturalness and similarity.

The ABX Test. As shown in Fig. 10, in the ABX tests, participants need to choose better voice conversion results for the samples of WINVC and AdaINVC from two aspects: similarity and naturalness. From the results, we can conclude that WINVC achieves significant results compared to AdaINVC. Together with the results of MOS and SMOS, which indicate that WIN strategy can indeed enhance the performance AdaINVC, and WINVC can perform better one-shot voice conversion task than AdaINVC from both naturalness and similarity.

4.4   Objective Evaluations

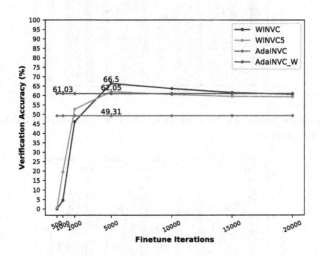

Fig. 11. Comparison of speaker verification accuracy between WINVC and AdaINVC. For better similarity comparison, one unseen utterance of each unseen speaker is used for quick adaption.

The Speaker Verification Accuracy. We use speaker verification accuracy as objective metrics. The speaker verification accuracy measures whether the transferred voice belongs to the target speaker. For fair comparison, we used a xvector [29] pretrained with all data of VCTK to verify the speaker identity from the converted voices. As shown in Fig. 11, the verification accuracy of our model is obviously higher than that of AdaINVC after quick adaption with 5,000 iterations. Further more, WINVC5 trained with only 5 utterances each speaker, and achieve competitive accuracy as well. After replacing the AdaIN strategy in AdaINVC with the WIN strategy, AdaINVC_W achieved better similarity than AdaINVC.

Disentanglement Discussion. In addition to the speaker verification accuracy comparison with AdaINVC, we conduct a t-SNE [32] visualization of the latent spaces of the WINVC model. As shown in Fig. 12, speaker embeddings from the same speaker are well clustered, and speaker embeddings from different speakers separate in a clean manner. The clear pattern indicates our speaker encoder can verify the speakers' identity from the voice samples.

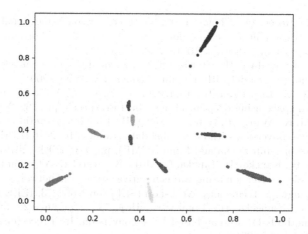

Fig. 12. t-SNE visualization for speaker embeddings of WINVC. The embeddings are extracted from the voice samples of 10 different one-shot speakers. 3,000 embeddings for each person.

5   Conclusions

In this paper, we proposed a novel WIN strategy. In addition, we proposed a WINVC model to perform one-shot voice conversion under the condition of multi-speaker non-parallel data, which achieved significant results. Furthermore, even with a smaller amount of training data, it has achieved a better performance from subjective and objective evaluations than the baseline model, which trained with a larger amount of training data. Besides, with the help of the WIN strategy, the baseline model also performed better. Based on this work, the cross-lingual one-shot voice conversion can be further studied in the future.

Acknowledgement. This work was supported by the Fundamental Research Funds for the Central Universities (grant number 2021ZY87).

References

1. Sisman, B., Zhang, M., Sakti, S., Li, H., Nakamura, S.: Adaptive wavenet vocoder for residual compensation in GAN-based voice conversion. In: 2018 IEEE Spoken Language Technology Workshop (SLT), pp. 282–289. IEEE (2018)
2. Nakamura, K., Toda, T., Saruwatari, H., Shikano, K.: Speaking aid system for total laryngectomees using voice conversion of body transmitted artificial speech. In: Proceedings of Interspeech, September 2006
3. Villavicencio, F., Bonada, J.: Applying voice conversion to concatenative singing-voice synthesis. In: Eleventh Annual Conference of the International Speech Communication Association (2010)
4. Mohammadi, S.H., Kain, A.: An overview of voice conversion systems. Speech Commun. **88**, 65–82 (2017)

5. Godoy, E., Rosec, O., Chonavel, T.: Voice conversion using dynamic frequency warping with amplitude scaling, for parallel or nonparallel corpora. IEEE Trans. Audio Speech Lang. Process. **20**(4), 1313–1323 (2011)
6. Toda, T., Saruwatari, H., Shikano, K.: High quality voice conversion based on gaussian mixture model with dynamic frequency warping (2001)
7. Nakashika, T., Takashima, R., Takiguchi, T., Ariki, Y.: Voice conversion in high-order eigen space using deep belief nets. In: Interspeech, pp. 369–372 (2013)
8. Sun, L., Li, K., Wang, H., Kang, S., Meng, H.: Phonetic posteriorgrams for many-to-one voice conversion without parallel data training. In: 2016 IEEE International Conference on Multimedia and Expo (ICME), pp. 1–6. IEEE (2016)
9. Kameoka, H., Kaneko, T., Tanaka, K., Hojo, N.: StarGAN-VC: non-parallel many-to-many voice conversion using star generative adversarial networks. In: 2018 IEEE Spoken Language Technology Workshop (SLT), pp. 266–273. IEEE (2018)
10. Kaneko, T., Kameoka, H., Tanaka, K., Hojo, N.: Stargan-vc2: Rethinking conditional methods for stargan-based voice conversion. In: Proceedings Interspeech 2019, pp. 679–683 (2019)
11. Kameoka, H., Kaneko, T., Tanaka, K., Hojo, N.: ACVAE-VC: non-parallel many-to-many voice conversion with auxiliary classifier variational autoencoder. arXiv preprint arXiv:1808.05092 (2018)
12. Chou, J.c., Lee, H.Y.: One-shot voice conversion by separating speaker and content representations with instance normalization. In: Proceedings Interspeech 2019, pp. 664–668 (2019)
13. Wu, D.Y., Lee, H.Y.: One-shot voice conversion by vector quantization. In: ICASSP 2020–2020 IEEE International Conference on Acoustics, Speech and Signal Processing (ICASSP), pp. 7734–7738. IEEE (2020)
14. Wu, D.Y., Chen, Y.H., Lee, H.y.: Vqvc+: One-shot voice conversion by vector quantization and u-net architecture. In: Proceedings Interspeech 2020, pp. 4691–4695 (2020)
15. Qian, K., Zhang, Y., Chang, S., Yang, X., Hasegawa-Johnson, M.: AutoVC: zero-shot voice style transfer with only autoencoder loss. In: ICML (2019)
16. Zhang, Z., He, B., Zhang, Z.: Gazev: Gan-based zero-shot voice conversion over non-parallel speech corpus. In: Proceedings Interspeech 2020, pp. 791–795 (2020)
17. Ioffe, S., Szegedy, C.: Batch normalization: accelerating deep network training by reducing internal covariate shift. In: International Conference on Machine Learning, pp. 448–456. PMLR (2015)
18. Ulyanov, D., Vedaldi, A., Lempitsky, V.: Improved texture networks: maximizing quality and diversity in feed-forward stylization and texture synthesis. In: Proceedings of the IEEE Conference on Computer Vision and Pattern Recognition, pp. 6924–6932 (2017)
19. Huang, X., Belongie, S.: Arbitrary style transfer in real-time with adaptive instance normalization. In: Proceedings of the IEEE International Conference on Computer Vision, pp. 1501–1510 (2017)
20. Veaux, C., Yamagishi, J., MacDonald, K., et al.: Superseded-CSTR VCTK corpus: English multi-speaker corpus for CSTR voice cloning toolkit (2016)
21. Karras, T., Laine, S., Aittala, M., Hellsten, J., Lehtinen, J., Aila, T.: Analyzing and improving the image quality of styleGAN. In: Proceedings of the IEEE/CVF Conference on Computer Vision and Pattern Recognition, pp. 8110–8119 (2020)
22. Choi, Y., Choi, M., Kim, M., Ha, J.W., Kim, S., Choo, J.: StarGAN: unified generative adversarial networks for multi-domain image-to-image translation. In: Proceedings of the IEEE Conference on Computer Vision and Pattern Recognition, pp. 8789–8797 (2018)

23. Goodfellow, I.J., et al.: Generative adversarial nets. In: NIPS (2014)
24. Zhou, T., Krahenbuhl, P., Aubry, M., Huang, Q., Efros, A.A.: Learning dense correspondence via 3D-guided cycle consistency. In: Proceedings of the IEEE Conference on Computer Vision and Pattern Recognition, pp. 117–126 (2016)
25. Taigman, Y., Polyak, A., Wolf, L.: Unsupervised cross-domain image generation. arXiv preprint arXiv:1611.02200 (2016)
26. Odena, A., Olah, C., Shlens, J.: Conditional image synthesis with auxiliary classifier GANs. In: International Conference on Machine Learning, pp. 2642–2651. PMLR (2017)
27. Dumoulin, V., Shlens, J., Kudlur, M.: A learned representation for artistic style. arXiv preprint arXiv:1610.07629 (2016)
28. Salimans, T., Kingma, D.P.: Weight normalization: a simple reparameterization to accelerate training of deep neural networks. In: NIPS (2016)
29. Snyder, D., Garcia-Romero, D., Sell, G., Povey, D., Khudanpur, S.: X-vectors: robust DNN embeddings for speaker recognition. In: 2018 IEEE International Conference on Acoustics, Speech and Signal Processing (ICASSP), pp. 5329–5333. IEEE (2018)
30. Li, C., Wand, M.: Precomputed real-time texture synthesis with Markovian generative adversarial networks. In: Leibe, B., Matas, J., Sebe, N., Welling, M. (eds.) ECCV 2016. LNCS, vol. 9907, pp. 702–716. Springer, Cham (2016). https://doi.org/10.1007/978-3-319-46487-9_43
31. Yamamoto, R., Song, E., Kim, J.M.: Parallel waveGAN: a fast waveform generation model based on generative adversarial networks with multi-resolution spectrogram. In: ICASSP 2020–2020 IEEE International Conference on Acoustics, Speech and Signal Processing (ICASSP), pp. 6199–6203. IEEE (2020)
32. Van der Maaten, L., Hinton, G.: Visualizing data using t-SNE. J. Mach. Learn. Res. 9(11) (2008)

Fusion Graph Convolutional Collaborative Filtering

Zeqi Zhang[1]([✉])(iD), Ying Liu[2], and Fengli Sun[1]

[1] China Aerospace Academy of Systems Science and Engineering, Beijing, China
yangxingge3568@ruc.edu.cn
[2] Beijing Institute of Aerospace Control Devices, Beijing, China

Abstract. Recently, Graph Neural Network (GNN) has been proved to be an efficient technique to solve the problem of graph-structured data, and many graph-based methods of recommendation have shown noticeably good performances. However, many approaches use pure GNN layers as the encoder of the nodes, which we think may limit the performance of the model. In this paper, we propose Fusion Graph Convolutional Collaborative Filtering (FGC-CF) which uses DeepWalk and graph convolutional layers to be the encoder of nodes to enhance the capability of the node encoder. For better modeling the similarity of user and item, we involve the local inference of the ESIM [3] to obtain the user representations by considering the interacted items, and the item representations by considering the interacted users. We conduct experiments on four datasets and the results not only show the remarkable performance of FGC-CF but also prove the necessity of using DeepWalk and ESIM local inference technologies.

Keywords: Collaborative filtering · Graph convolutional network · DeepWalk · Convolutional network · Local inference

1 Introduction

Traditional collaborative filtering algorithms assume that nodes are independent of each other or try to calculate similar nodes for each node through a certain similarity measure, and regard nodes with higher similarity as neighbors. The first method ignores the similarity between the features of neighboring nodes, while the second method considers similar nodes but has high complexity and the reasonableness of the similarity measure has become an important determinant of algorithm performance. The graph neural network uses the adjacency matrix to represent the graph and uses the spectral domain or spatial domain method to aggregate the neighborhood of the nodes, by treating the graph as a signal based on the graph theory. It reduces the complexity of the algorithm on the one hand, and on the other hand, it enhances The rationality of the features of neighboring nodes.

Therefore, a mainstream approach is to treat users and items as graph nodes, and their interactions are constructed as graph signals, and graph neural network

© Springer Nature Switzerland AG 2021
D. N. Pham et al. (Eds.): PRICAI 2021, LNAI 13032, pp. 574–584, 2021.
https://doi.org/10.1007/978-3-030-89363-7_43

algorithms are used to aggregate adjacent nodes, thereby introducing adjacent node features in the learning process. [13] used multi-layer GNN to aggregate the high-order neighbor node features of nodes, and trained the embedded vector representations of users and items respectively, and achieved good results on multiple data sets. [1] proposed GC-MC, a graph auto-encoder framework based on distinguishable messages transmitted on two-way interactive graphs. This method treats the interaction between users and items as two-way bipartite graphs. The graph convolutional layer constructs an auto-encoder to separately encode the features of the users and the items and then combines the probabilities of different score levels to predict the user's score for a specific item through a weighted summation. [4] analyzed the relationship and characteristics of the two types of graphs in the recommendation system-homogeneous graphs and heterogeneous graphs, and considered the problem that researchers usually use only a single type of the graphs to solve their problems, and proposed GCN4RS that combines the interaction of the vertices of the homogeneous graph and the heterogeneous graph.

However, most researches based on graph neural network algorithms only focus on the performance of models with a single structure of neural networks after graph layers, which ignores the factor of similarity between user and item. Additionally, we think combining the network embedding approaches and GCN layers as the encoder of nodes can further improve the performance of the model.

In this paper, we propose a Fusion Graph Convolutional Collaborative Filtering (FGC-CF) framework. After trying to train the node vector representations through DeepWalk and GCN layers, we use one-dimensional convolutional neural network and the ESIM local inference module to extract the interactive features between the vectors, thereby improving the recommendation performance.

We make the following contributions in this paper:

- We propose a new collaborative filtering framework FGC-CF which uses DeepWalk and GCN to obtain the embedded representations and then combines CNN and ESIM local inference modules to get the rating prediction.
- We conduct experiments on the four datasets, which show the state-of-the-art performance of FGC-CF on three of them.
- We conduct extensive experiments to prove the necessity of the DeepWalk embedding and ESIM local inference.

The rest of this paper is organized as follows. The background, including the problem description and related works, are given in Sect. 2. The proposed FGC-CF approach is depicted in Sect. 3. Section 4 presents the experiment design, results, and analysis. The paper is concluded in Sect. 5.

2   Related Works

Our work lies in the intersection between the network embedding and the graph-based collaborative filtering. Therefore, we mainly review the most related works in the two areas in this section.

2.1 Network Embedding

Network embedding aims to learn latent representations of nodes in the network. [10] proposed the first network embedding method called DeepWalk, which uses the word embedding model like Skip-gram. [12] developed LINE, which constrains the neighborhood to be nodes 1 to 2 hops away from the center. [5] extended DeepWalk with the BFS and DFS strategies in the process of random walk.

2.2 Graph-Based Collaborative Filtering

The recommend problem can be formulated as a link prediction problem. The users and items can be regarded as nodes in a bipartite graph, in which the edges denote the interactions between the users and items. [1] proposed a framework that encodes the nodes by a graph convolutional encoder and uses bilinear decoder to reconstruct the rating matrix. [14] developed a new approach that extracts the latent components of the graph which denote the latent purchasing motivation. [13] uses multiple embedding propagation layers to model the high-order connectivity in the user-item graph. [2] used GCN layers and RNNs to model the dynamics of user's preference which gives the model powerful capability to learn the time-dependent factors. Many approaches reviewed in this section use a single type of network after the graph-based layers. In this work, we attempt to combine the node embedding algorithm, CNN, and ESIM local inference techniques with the aim of learning the similarity between user and item embeddings.

3 The Proposed Method

3.1 Overview

Figure 1 shows the overall structure of the FGC-CF model. We can see that the model takes the user-item interaction bipartite graph as input. First, learning to initialize the embedded representation of users and items through DeepWalk embedded representation, and then we use GCN layers as the node aggregation part. Specifically, the embedded representations of users are aggregated with the embedded representation of items that have been interacted, and the embedded representations of items are aggregated with the users who interact with them. After the L-layer graph convolution, they respectively enter the convolution module and the ESIM local inference module to extract the interactive features, and finally, we concatenate the outputs of the two modules to obtain the final prediction score through the linear output layer.

3.2 Graph Encoder

User-Item Interactive Bipartite Graph. When considering the recommendation problem from the perspective of a graph, the most important question

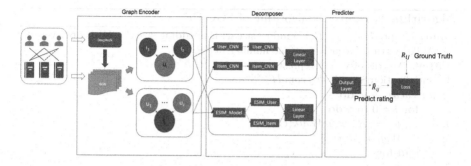

Fig. 1. The structure of the Fusion Graph Convolutional Collaborative Filtering(FGC-CF), which consists of the Graph Encoder, Decomposer, and Predicter.

is how to represent the interaction between the users and the items. In this paper, we treat the interaction between users and items as edges in an undirected weighted graph, and ignore the heterogeneity between users and items, and treat them as the same type of nodes. We define the bipartite graph as

$$\mathcal{G} = \{V, \varepsilon, R\} \tag{1}$$

where V represents the user and item nodes, and R contains the rating level $\{1,\ldots, R\}$. For this graph, we use an adjacency matrix A to denote it, which is defined as follows

$$A[u, i] = \begin{cases} 1 & rating[u, i] \geq threshold \\ -1 & rating[u, i] < threshold \end{cases} \tag{2}$$

The $rating\,[u, i]$ represents the rating of user u on item i. When the rating is greater than the threshold, we think that u likes item i, so the nodes tend to be adjacent, otherwise, u hates item i, and the two tend to deviate. The nodes in the graph have a feature matrix $M = [m_1, m_2, \ldots, m_N]^T \in R^{N \times d_m}$, where N represents the number of nodes and d_m represents the dimension of the node feature.

DeepWalk Algorithm. Before sending the bipartite graph to the model for training, we consider initializing the embedded representation of each node through the DeepWalk algorithm. We still assume that users and items in the graph belong to the same type of node. $SkipGram$ is the classic Skip-Gram algorithm [8], which will not be explained here, and the specific parameter settings will be explained in the experiment part. According to the Skip-Gram algorithm, for each path $w_{v_i} \in W$ established by a random walk, each node $v_i \in w_{v_i}$ has an optimized objective function as follows:

$$\min_{\Phi} - \log Pr(\{v_{i-\omega}, \ldots, v_i, \ldots, v_{i+\omega}\}|\Phi(v_i)\}) \tag{3}$$

Algorithm 1. DeepWalk algorithm of FGC-CF

Input: Graph $\mathcal{G} = \{V, \varepsilon, R\}$; Window size ω; Embedding size d_m; Walks per vertex γ;
   Walk length t; Negative sample number $negative$
Output: Matrix of vertex representations $\Phi \in R^{N \times d_m}$
 1: Initialization:Sample Φ $from$ $\mathcal{U}^{N \times d_m}$
 2: **for** $each v_i \in V$ **do**
 3:     **for** $i = 0$ to γ **do**
 4:         $w_{v_i} = RandomWalk(G, v_i, t)$
 5:         $W.append(w_{v_i})$
 6:     **end for**
 7: **end for**
 8: $SkipGram(\Phi, W, \omega, negative)$

Graph Convolutional Layer. After obtaining Φ, we hope to further aggregate and extract the features of the node and its neighborhood through the GCN layer. We define the Laplacian matrix of the graph as

$$\mathcal{L} = D^{-0.5}(A + I)D^{-0.5} \in R^{N \times N} \tag{4}$$

where $D \in R^{N \times N}$ is the degree matrix of the adjacency matrix A, and $I \in R^{N \times N}$ is the identity matrix. Next, we focus on the transformation of the embedded representations of user u and item i in the GCN layer.

In the above-defined graph, it can be found that those that directly interact with user nodes are all item nodes, and those who directly interact with item nodes are all user nodes. Therefore, the aggregation process can be expressed as follows:

$$\Phi_{agg(u)} = Aggregate(\{u, i_1, \ldots, i_n | \forall i_n \in V \& (u, i_n) \in \varepsilon\}) \tag{5}$$

$$\Phi_{agg(i)} = Aggregate(\{i, u_1, \ldots, u_n | \forall u_n \in V \& (u_n, i) \in \varepsilon\}) \tag{6}$$

Assuming that the number of GCN layers is L_g, although in the previous article we assumed that users and items belong to the same type of nodes, in actual situations, the features of users and items are very different. Therefore, for each layer l, we use different shared weights for users and items. The embedded representations of u and i can be expressed as:

$$Emb_u^{(l)} = \sigma_u^{(l)}\left(\Phi_{agg(u)}W_u^{(l)} + b_u^{(l)}\right) \tag{7}$$

$$Emb_i^{(l)} = \sigma_i^{(l)}\left(\Phi_{agg(i)}W_i^{(l)} + b_i^{(l)}\right) \tag{8}$$

where σ represents the nonlinear activation function, W represents the weight of the transformation, and b represents the bias. Then for the L_g layer GCN, the complete embedded representations of u and i are finally obtained as

$$Emb_u = [\Phi_u || Emb_u^{(1)} || \ldots || Emb_u^{(L_g)}] \tag{9}$$

$$Emb_i = [\Phi_i || Emb_i^{(1)} || \ldots || Emb_i^{(L_g)}] \tag{10}$$

3.3   Decomposer

Convolutional Neural Network. We use a convolutional neural network to further extract the features of the encoded users and items. Since the encoded features are all one-dimensional sequences, we use one-dimensional convolutions for feature extraction respectively. Since the handlings of users and items are symmetrical, we only use the feature of user u as an example for derivation. Assuming that the feature of user u is Emb_u, the feature obtained after convolution is expressed as:

$$Conv_u = AvgPool\left(Conv1D_{2,u}\left(AvgPool\left(Conv1D_{1,u}\left(Emb_u\right)\right)\right)\right) \tag{11}$$

After obtaining the convolution features, we expand and concatenate the features of u and i.

$$Conv_{u,i} = [Flatten\left(Conv_u\right) \| Flatten\left(Conv_i\right)] \tag{12}$$

After that, the interaction between the two features is modeled through a linear layer, and the output of the module is calculated as follows:

$$Convdense_{u,i} = \sigma\left(Conv_{u,i}W_{Convdense} + b_{Convdense}\right) \tag{13}$$

ESIM Local Inference. The design of this module is inspired by the ESIM model in [3], and the local inference mechanism is introduced to model the interaction between u and i. For Emb_u and Emb_i, we use the vector inner product method to construct the transformation matrix $e \in R^{d_m \times d_m}$, where

$$e_{mn} = Emb_{u,m} \times Emb_{i,n} \tag{14}$$

$Emb_{u,m}$ represents the m-th element on the vector Emb_u. Based on the matrix e, we can select the part of Emb_u that is relevant to the user and use it to represent the user, and vice versa. But before that, we need to normalize the transformation matrix. Using the softmax function here, we can get the corresponding representation of u and i.

$$\widetilde{Emb}_{u,m} = \sum_{n=1}^{d_m} \frac{\exp\left(e_{mn}\right)}{\sum_{n=1}^{d_m} \exp\left(e_{mn}\right)} Emb_{i,n}^T \tag{15}$$

$$\widetilde{Emb}_{i,n} = \sum_{m=1}^{d_m} \frac{\exp\left(e_{mn}\right)}{\sum_{m=1}^{d_m} \exp\left(e_{mn}\right)} Emb_{u,m}^T \tag{16}$$

Through the formulas above, the correlation between the users and items can be expressed. This idea coincides with the method of aggregating item nodes' features to represent user's features in the GCN layers we mentioned earlier. Next, we construct another feature based on the representation we just obtained by subtracting Emb_u and $\widetilde{Emb}_u$ element by element. Based on all the features constructed above, we respectively perform concatenate operations on user u and item i as follows:

$$Esim_u = \left[Emb_u||\widetilde{Emb}_u||Emb_u - \widetilde{Emb}_u\right] \tag{17}$$

$$Esim_i = \left[Emb_i||\widetilde{Emb}_i||Emb_i - \widetilde{Emb}_i\right] \tag{18}$$

Then we get the output of this module through linear layers:

$$Esim_{u,i} = \sigma\left(Dropout\left(\sigma\left((Esim_u||Esim_i)\,W_1 + b_1\right)\right)W_2 + b_2\right) \tag{19}$$

3.4 Predictor

After getting the final output of each module (like, $Convdense_{u,i}$, $Esim_{u,i}$), we concatenate them and get the final rating prediction $\hat{r}_{u,i}$ through the linear layer. We use the Mean Square Error(MSE) as the objective function.

$$Feature_{Conv\_Esim} = [Convdense_{u,i}||Esim_{u,i}] \tag{20}$$

$$\hat{r}_{u,i} = \sigma\left(Feature_{Conv\_Esim}W_{predict} + b_{predict}\right) \tag{21}$$

4 Experiments

We conduct experiments on four real datasets, and evaluate our proposed model. We answer the following questions:

- **Q1**: How does FGC-CF perform compared with the state-of-the-art collaborative filtering algorithms?
- **Q2**: Does the DeepWalk embedding method we use have better representation capabilities than the simple embedding method?
- **Q3**: How do the ESIM local inference module and the 1D-Convolutional module affect FGC-CF?.

4.1 Experimental Settings

Datasets. We conduct experiments on four public data sets:

- **Movielen-100K(ml-100k)**: A widely used dataset to measure the performance of recommendation models. It contains a total of 100,000 rating records for 943 users and 1682 movies.
- **Movielen-1M(ml-1m)**: An extension of the ml-100k dataset, with more users, movies, and rating records, including a total of 1,000,000 rating records for 6,040 users and 3,883 movies.
- **Amazon**: A widely used dataset with 65,170 rating records for 1000 users and 1000 items.
- **Yelp2018**: A dataset contains 30, 838 ratings from 1, 286 users to 2,614 business.

For ml-100k, Amazon, and Yelp2018, we randomly select 80% of the dataset as the training set and the remaining 20% as the test set. For the ml-1m dataset, we randomly select 90% as the training set and 10% as the test set.

Baselines. We compare FGC-CF with some state-of-the-art methods, which can be divided into three categories, namely matrix factorization, self-encoding-based models, and graph convolution-based collaborative filtering models. The matrix factorization models include: PMF [9], BiasSVD [6], LLORMA [7]. Auto-encoding models include: AUTOREC [11], CF-NADE [15]. Collaborative filtering models based on graph convolution include: GC-MC [1], MCCF [14]. In addition, it should be noted that for the AUTOREC model, we select the experimental scores obtained by its item-based variant I-AUTOREC as a representative, because the scores obtained by I-AUTOREC are better than the item-based variant U-AUTOREC.

Implementation. In the DeepWalk part, we consider changing the number of walks γ of each node in the range of {10,20,40,60}, the length of random walk path t in the range of {10,20,30,40}. We change the size of window ω changes within the range of {2,4,6,15}, the negative sample number changes within the range of {5,10,20,30}. We vary the dimension of the embeddings d_m within the range of {16,32,64,128}. In the neural network part, we consider that all the dense layers use the LeakyRelu activation function, while the one-dimensional convolutional layer uses the Relu activation function. We change the slope k of LeakyRelu within the range of {0.3,0.1,0.05,0.01}, and the ratio of dropout layer dr changes in the range of {0.1, 0.3, 0.5, 0.7}. We randomly initialize the weights and bias with a uniform distribution. For model training, we consider changing batch size in the range of {64,128,256,512,1024}, and varying the learning rate r in range{0.005,0.001,0.0005,0.0001}. We set *threshold* as 3. We use Adam as the optimizer, and the commonly used root mean square error (RMSE) is used as the evaluation metric for models' performance. We adapt a five-fold cross-validation method and finally use the average result.

4.2   Performance Comparison(Q1)

We compare the performance of the models in each data set. Table 1 shows the performance of all models on different data sets.

Table 1. Performance comparison of rating prediction, RMSE is the evaluation matric.

Baselines	PMF	BiasSVD	LLORMA	AUTOREC	CF-NADE	GC-MC	MCCF	FGC-CF
Yelp2018	0.3967	0.3902	0.3890	0.3817	0.3857	0.3850	0.3806	**0.3307**
Amazon	0.9339	0.9028	0.9019	0.9213	0.8987	0.8946	0.8876	**0.8844**
ml-100k	0.9638	0.9257	0.9313	0.9435	0.9229	0.9145	0.9070	**0.8932**
ml-1m	0.883	0.845	0.833	0.831	**0.829**	0.832	–	0.832

*The performances of the baselines on Yelp2018, Amazon and ml-100k are taken from [14]. The performances on ml-1m are taken from [1].

We have the following observations: (1) The FGC-CF model we propose outperforms all the baselines on Yelp, Amazon, and ml-100k datasets, and the performance of FGC-CF on the ml-1m dataset is comparable to GC-MC. (2) Our model's performance on the Yelp dataset has a great improvement compared to the baselines. The reason may be that the Yelp dataset is quite sparse, and most of the ratings are 1 or 2. In our proposed model, the relationships between nodes with ratings less than 3 have unique representations in the adjacency matrix, which enables the model to learn more effectively about whether a user likes an item. (3)It shows that the graph neural network models on many datasets have better performance than other models, especially when the scales of the datasets are not very large. But for large datasets, the self-encoding models seem to have very powerful performances, but this type of model requires a lot of hardware resources to support when it is running. The larger the dataset, the greater the space consumption required. And it may take a long time. In comparison, the graph neural network models can obtain performances close to the self-encoding models with less time and hardware consumption.

4.3   Effect of DeepWalk(Q2)

The Effect on Performance. In terms of model parameters, we set d_m to 64, the slope k of LeakyRelu to 0.1, and dr to 0.5. For DeepWalk, we set the window size ω to 6, the walking path length t to 20, and the number of walks γ to 20, The negative sample number $negative$ is 10, the learning rate is set to 0.0001, and the batch size is set to 512. The performance of the model before and after DeepWalk is calculated as follows:

Table 2. Performance comparison of FGC-CF with or without DeepWalk

Datasets	FGC-CF(without DeepWalk)	FGC-CF(full)
ml-100k	0.9198	0.8932
Amazon	0.8914	0.8844

It can be seen that the DeepWalk approach has greatly improved the performance of the model. We think that the main reason for the improvement is that the DeepWalk algorithm learns the correlation between nodes in advance, and the learned representation makes the nodes with strong connections closer in space.

Visualization of DeepWalk Embeddings. To confirm our conjecture, we selected the Embedding representation obtained by DeepWalk training on the ml-100k dataset and performed a two-dimensional visualization. Take the user numbered 846 (u_{846}) as an example. After 0, 5, 15, 20 rounds of training, the node spatial position relationship is shown in Fig. 2. It can be seen that after multiple epochs of training, the nodes associated with u_{846} Have a closer spatial relationship.

4.4   Effects of ESIM Local Inference

ESIM local inference module is also an important part of FGC-CF. We conduct experiments on ml-100k and amazon datasets to evaluate how it affects the performance of the model, with the same parameter settings as 3.3. In Table 3, we find that FGC-CF has a good performance without the ESIM module, but it becomes better with ESIM, which shows that ESIM local inference is helpful.

Table 3. Performance comparison of FGC-CF with or without ESIM local inference

Datasets	FGC-CF(without ESIM)	FGC-CF(full)
ml-100k	0.9056	0.8932
Amazon	0.8866	0.8844

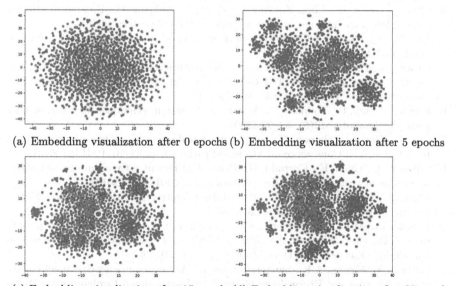

(a) Embedding visualization after 0 epochs (b) Embedding visualization after 5 epochs

(c) Embedding visualization after 15 epochs (d) Embedding visualization after 20 epochs

Fig. 2. Embedding visualizations after different epochs, the green dot denotes u_{846}, the blue dots denote the items that are not interacted by u_{846}, and the orange ones are those that u_{846} interacts with. (Color figure online)

5   Conclusions and Future Works

We propose a novel collaborative filtering model called Fusion Graph Convolutional Collaborative Filtering(FGC-CF). The idea of FGC-CF is to encode the features of users and items by DeepWalk and GCN layers, then the edges are decomposed by the combination of one-dimensional convolutional module and ESIM local reference module. The experiments we conducted show that our method outperforms the baselines on 3 datasets. It can be seen that we just involve the classic network embedding method DeepWalk into the graph encoder. In the future, we will try to explore more effective approaches based on FGC-CF.

Acknowledgments. We thank the anonymous reviewers for their contribution to the publication of this paper.

References

1. Berg, R.V.D., Kipf, T.N., Welling, M.: Graph convolutional matrix completion. arXiv preprint arXiv:1706.02263 (2017)
2. Bonet, E.R., Nguyen, D.M., Deligiannis, N.: Temporal collaborative filtering with graph convolutional neural networks. In: 2020 25th International Conference on Pattern Recognition (ICPR), pp. 4736–4742. IEEE (2021)
3. Chen, Q., Zhu, X., Ling, Z., Wei, S., Jiang, H., Inkpen, D.: Enhanced lstm for natural language inference. arXiv preprint arXiv:1609.06038 (2016)
4. Yao, G., Songchan, C.: Graph convolutional network for recommender systems. J. Softw. **031**(004), 1101–1112 (2020)
5. Grover, A., Leskovec, J.: node2vec: scalable feature learning for networks. In: Proceedings of the 22nd ACM SIGKDD International Conference on Knowledge Discovery and Data Mining, pp. 855–864 (2016)
6. Koren, Y., Bell, R., Volinsky, C.: Matrix factorization techniques for recommender systems. Computer **42**(8), 30–37 (2009)
7. Lee, J., Kim, S., Lebanon, G., Singer, Y.: Local low-rank matrix approximation. In: International Conference on Machine Learning, pp. 82–90. PMLR (2013)
8. Mikolov, T., Chen, K., Corrado, G., Dean, J.: Efficient estimation of word representations in vector space. arXiv preprint arXiv:1301.3781 (2013)
9. Mnih, A., Salakhutdinov, R.R.: Probabilistic matrix factorization. Adv. Neural Inform. Process. Syst. **20**, 1257–1264 (2007)
10. Perozzi, B., Al-Rfou, R., Skiena, S.: Deepwalk: online learning of social representations. In: Proceedings of the 20th ACM SIGKDD International Conference on Knowledge Discovery and Data Mining, pp. 701–710 (2014)
11. Sedhain, S., Menon, A.K., Sanner, S., Xie, L.: Autorec: autoencoders meet collaborative filtering. In: Proceedings of the 24th International Conference on World Wide Web, pp. 111–112 (2015)
12. Tang, J., Qu, M., Wang, M., Zhang, M., Yan, J., Mei, Q.: Line: large-scale information network embedding. In: Proceedings of the 24th International Conference on World Wide Web, pp. 1067–1077 (2015)
13. Wang, X., He, X., Wang, M., Feng, F., Chua, T.S.: Neural graph collaborative filtering. In: Proceedings of the 42nd International ACM SIGIR Conference on Research and Development in Information Retrieval, pp. 165–174 (2019)
14. Wang, X., Wang, R., Shi, C., Song, G., Li, Q.: Multi-component graph convolutional collaborative filtering. In: Proceedings of the AAAI Conference on Artificial Intelligence, vol. 34, pp. 6267–6274 (2020)
15. Zheng, Y., Tang, B., Ding, W., Zhou, H.: A neural autoregressive approach to collaborative filtering. In: International Conference on Machine Learning, pp. 764–773. PMLR (2016)

Multi-label Learning by Exploiting Imbalanced Label Correlations

Shiqiao Gu, Liu Yang[✉], Yaning Li, and Hui Li

College of Intelligence and Computing, Tianjin University, Tianjin, China
{gushiqiao,yangliuyl,lyn2018216114,li_hui1998}@tju.edu.cn

Abstract. Multi-label classification refers to the supervised learning problem where an instance may be associated with multiple labels. It is well known that exploiting label correlations is important for multi-label learning. Existing approaches typically assume that the distribution of classes is balanced. In many real-world applications, multi-label datasets with imbalanced class distributions occur frequently, which may make various multi-label learning methods ineffective. Since the existing multi-label learning algorithms pay less attention to the problem of correlation with imbalanced label sets, this paper proposed a Multi-Label learning model by exploiting Imbalanced Label Correlations (ML-ILC). ML-ILC uses graph convolution neural network to learn the correlation between labels. At the same time, we suggest that the regularization of minority classes is stronger than that of frequent classes, which can improve the generalization error of minority classes. To investigate the performance of the proposed multi-label learning model, we considered two benchmark datasets including VOC2007 and COCO. The proposed method successfully achieved better classification performance compared to the state-of-the-art compression methods.

Keywords: Multi-label learning · Imbalanced class distributions · Label correlation

1 Introduction

Nowadays, the explosive growth of online content such as images and videos has made developing classification system a very challenging problem. Such a new classification system is usually required to assign multiple labels to one single instance [30]. Multi-label classification has many application scenarios such as computer vision [9,33], text classification [9], bioinformatics [21], network mining [1], information retrieval [15], label recommendation [27] and medical diagnosis [21]. For example, for the image classification task, the goal of multi-label learning is to assign many semantic labels to one image based on its content. In recent years, some large-scale hand-labeled datasets have been established, such as MS-COCO [13] and PASCAL VOC [6]. Compared with single-label classification task, multi-label learning methods [18,20,24] are more complex due to the combinatorial nature of the output space, but more practical in real-world applications.

© Springer Nature Switzerland AG 2021
D. N. Pham et al. (Eds.): PRICAI 2021, LNAI 13032, pp. 585–596, 2021.
https://doi.org/10.1007/978-3-030-89363-7_44

In multi-label learning, with the increase of the number of label categories, the number of possible label sets predicted by the instance will increase exponentially. For example, in multi-label learning, if the label space has 20 label categories, the possible set of instances of labels will exceed 1 million (that is, 2^{20}). In order to solve this problem, existing algorithms mainly study the relationship between labels [19]. The original multi-label models are essentially limited by ignoring the complex topology structure between objects. This makes many researchers realize the importance of label relevance research. Order-free Recurrent Neural Network (RNN) [4] is proposed for image multi-label classification which uniquely integrated and learned of visual attention and long short term memory layers. The Spatial Regularization Network (SRN) [32] can learn the attention maps of all labels, and mine the potential relationship between labels through the learnable convolution. It combined the regularization classification results and the ResNet-101 network [8] classification results. The RNN-Attention model [23] recorded the image and extracted the response image of the last-layer feature and the spatial transformation layer located in the "attention region" in each cycle. The Regional Latent Semantic Dependencies (RLSD) model [29] can effectively capture the latent semantic dependencies at the regional level. However, these methods are essentially limited by ignoring the complex topology structure between objects. This makes many experts and scholars realize the importance of label relevance research.

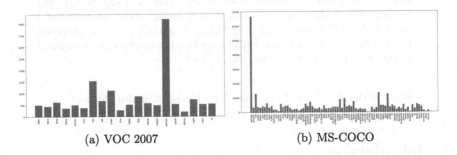

(a) VOC 2007   (b) MS-COCO

Fig. 1. The imbalanced distribution of categories in multi-label datasets.

ML-GCN models [5,22] are proposed to use GCN to propagate information among multiple labels to learn the interdependence of each image label. Since the number of some categories may be far more than that of other categories. As shown in Fig. 1, the distribution of classes is imbalanced in VOC 2007 and MS-COCO datasets, which may lead to the deterioration of the performance of most classification methods [7].

Class imbalance has been regarded as a fundamental threat to the performance of multi-label learning algorithms. In order to deal with class imbalance in the context of multi-label data, the first approach is to use resampling technique [3], which is applied to the preprocessing step and is independent of the specific multi-label learning algorithm that is subsequently applied to the data. Another group of methods focuses on multi-label learning methods to deal directly with category imbalance [11,14,25,28,31]. They are mainly used to solve the problem of class imbalance, and they are suitable for datasets with extracted features, such as Birds, CAL500. While they are not designed for the multiple labels with the original images and do not consider the imbalanced label correlations.

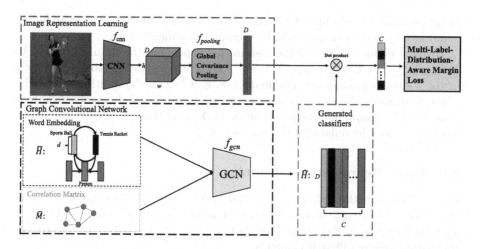

Fig. 2. Overall framework of our ML-ILC model for multi-label image recognition.

Based on the problems in the above multi-label learning, we proposed a learning Multi-Label model that explores the Imbalanced Label Correlations (ML-ILC). The overall framework of our approach is shown in Fig. 2, which is composed of three main modules, i.e., image representation learning, GCN based classifier learning and multi-label distribution aware margin learning. Specifically, we represent each node of the graph as word embeddings of the label, and use GCN to directly map these label embeddings into a set of interdependent classifiers, which can be directly applied to an image feature for classification. And we suggest that the weights of minority classes and frequent classes are different, so we propose to use multi-label distribution aware margin loss to solve the problem of class imbalance.

The main contributions of this work can be summarized as follows:

– ML-ILC explicitly describes the correlation between labels based on a re-weighted scheme to create an effective label correlation matrix to guide information propagation among the nodes in GCN.
– ML-ILC introduces the multi-label distribution aware margin loss functions to solve the problem of class imbalance in the multi-label problem.

– Experiments have been conducted on two benchmark multi-label image recognition datasets by comparing ML-ILC with existing methods. The numerical results demonstrate the effectiveness and efficiency of ML-ILC.

2 Approach

In this section, we will introduce the details of model that considers the imbalanced label correlations for multi-label image classification.

We first define the goal of the task in this paper. Let the training dataset be $\{(\boldsymbol{x}_i, \boldsymbol{y}_i)\}_{i=1}^N = \{\boldsymbol{X}, \boldsymbol{Y}\}$, where $\boldsymbol{X} \in \mathbb{R}^{N \times \mu}$ indicates a set of N labeled instances in the μ-dimensional space. The matrix $\boldsymbol{Y} \in \mathbb{R}^{N \times C}$ is the multi-label matrix, where C denotes the numbers of categories. The multi-label classification task aims to find a mapping function from $\boldsymbol{X}$ to $\boldsymbol{Y}$, and then we predict the multi-label vector for the unlabeled test dataset $\dot{\boldsymbol{X}}$.

2.1 Image Representation Learning

For each image $\boldsymbol{x}$, through the $f_{cnn}(\cdot)$ function we can obtain feature representation with the last convolution. Then, we employ the second-order pooling with $f_{pooling}(\cdot)$ to obtain the visual-level feature $\hat{\boldsymbol{x}} \in \mathbb{R}^D$ for better exploiting the correlation among different channels:

$$\hat{\boldsymbol{x}} = f_{pooling}(f_{cnn}(\boldsymbol{x}; \theta_{cnn}), \theta_{pooling}) \tag{1}$$

where θ_{cnn} and $\theta_{pooling}$ indicate the parameters in the convolution and the pooling process respectively.

We can use any CNN basis model to learn the features of the image, but the difference is that the pooling layer uses global covariance pooling $f_{pooling}(\cdot)$. Li et al. [12] proposed to replace the first-order global average pooling with a second-order or even high-order statistical method. The practice of global covariance pooling is to select the value that can represent the data distribution of the feature map by calculating the covariance matrix (second-order information) of the feature map. Compared with global average pooling, second-order pooling takes more account of the relationship between channels and has stronger representation capability.

2.2 Graph Convolutional Network

Traditional CNN-based multi-label methods do not consider the correlation between the labels. We build the graph structure based on two parts. One is the word embedding $\bar{\boldsymbol{H}}$ to represent C labels with d-dimensional word vector. The other part represent the relationship between different labels with $C \times C$ adjacency matrices $\hat{\boldsymbol{M}}$. We use stacked GCNs where each GCN layer takes the node representations from previous layer as inputs and outputs new node representations. For the last layer of GCN, the output is $\hat{\boldsymbol{H}} \in \mathbb{R}^{C \times D}$ with D denoting the dimensionality of the image representation. Then we can learn inter-dependent object classifiers, $i.e.$, $\hat{H} = \{h_i\}_{i=1}^{C}$, from label representations via a GCN based mapping function. By applying the learned classifiers to image representations, we can obtain the predicted scores as

$$\hat{y} = \hat{H}\hat{x} \tag{2}$$

The basic idea of graph convolution is to update the node representation by propagating information between nodes. Unlike standard convolutions that operate on local Euclidean structures in an image, the goal of GCN [10] is to learn a function $f_{gcn}(\cdot, \cdot)$ on a graph G, which takes feature descriptions $H^l \in \mathbb{R}^{C \times d}$ for $(l = 0, \cdots, P)$ and the corresponding correlation matrix $\hat{M} \in \mathbb{R}^{C \times C}$ as inputs (where C denotes the number of nodes and d indicates the dimensionality of node features), and updates the node features as $H^{l+1} \in \mathbb{R}^{C \times d'}$. Every GCN layer can be written as a non-linear function by

$$H^{l+1} = f_{gcn}(H^l, \hat{M}) \tag{3}$$

After employing the convolutional operation, $f_{gcn}(\cdot, \cdot)$ can be represented as

$$H^{l+1} = o_{gcn}(\hat{M}_{nor} H^l W^l) \tag{4}$$

where $W^l \in \mathbb{R}^{d \times d'}$ is a to be learned transformation matrix and $\hat{M}_{nor} \in \mathbb{R}^{C \times C}$ is the normalized version of correlation matrix $\hat{M}$, and $o_{gcn}(\cdot)$ denotes a non-linear operation, which is acted by LeakyReLU in our experiments. In our model, for the first layer, the input is the $H^0 = \bar{H} \in \mathbb{R}^{C \times d}$ matrix, where d is the dimensionality of the label-level word embedding which are already pre-trained. Then the relationship between each node will learn form $\hat{M}$. For the last layer, the output is $H^P = \hat{H} \in \mathbb{R}^{C \times D}$ with D denoting the dimensionality of the image representation. Thus, we can learn and model the complex inter-relationships of the nodes by stacking multiple GCN layers.

Inspired by [5], we construct the correlation matrix $\hat{M}$ in a data-driven way.

$$\hat{M}_{ij} = \begin{cases} p/\sum_{\substack{j=1 \\ i \neq j}}^{C} \bar{M}_{ij}, & \text{if } i \neq j \\ 1 - p, & \text{if } i = j \end{cases} \tag{5}$$

where $\hat{M}$ is the re-weighted correlation matrix, $\bar{M}$ is the binary correlation matrix, and p determines the weights assigned to a node itself and other correlated nodes.

2.3   Multi-label Distribution Aware Margin Loss

We assume that the ground truth label of an image is $y_i \in \mathbb{R}^C$, where $y_i^{(c)} = \{0, 1\}$ denotes whether label c appears in the image or not. Let (x_i, y_i) be an example and $\hat{y}_i$ be the output of the model f. For simplicity, we use $z_i^{(c)} = \hat{y}_i^{(c)}$ to denote the c-th output of the model for the c-th class.

Similar to previous work [2], we define the training margin for class c as:

$$\gamma_c = \min_{i \in S_c} \gamma\left(\boldsymbol{x}_i, \boldsymbol{y}_i\right) = \min_{i \in S_c}(z_i^{(c)} - \max_{j \neq c} z_i^{(j)}) \tag{6}$$

where $S_c = \left\{i : y_i^{(c)} = 1\right\}$ represent the sample index corresponding to class c. We hope to improve the generalization error of minority classes by encouraging the minority classes to have larger margins. For multiple classification, as derived in [2], the optimal trade-off is $\gamma_c \propto n_c^{-1/4}$ where n_c is the sample size of the c-th class. Therefore, we also enforce a class-dependent margin for multiple classes of the form

$$\gamma_c = \frac{T}{n_c^{1/4}} \tag{7}$$

Here T is a hyper-parameter to be tuned. Therefore, by extending the traditional multi-label loss function, ML-ILC adopts the following Multi-Label Distribution Aware Margin loss function to better solve the problem of class imbalance.

$$L((\boldsymbol{x}_i, \boldsymbol{y}_i); f) = -\sum_{c=1}^{C} [y_i^{(c)} log(\frac{e^{z_i^{(c)} - \Delta_c}}{e^{z_i^{(c)} - \Delta_c} + \sum_{j \neq c} e^{z_i^{(j)}}})$$

$$+ (1 - y_i^{(c)}) log(1 - \frac{e^{z_i^{(c)} - \Delta_c}}{e^{z_i^{(c)} - \Delta_c} + \sum_{j \neq c} e^{z_i^{(j)}}})] \tag{8}$$

$$where \ \Delta_c = \frac{T}{n_c^{1/4}} \ for \ c \in \{1, ..., C\} \tag{9}$$

This loss replaces the traditional multi-label classification loss during training and can regularize the minority classes more strongly than the frequent classes. Therefore we can improve the generalization error of minority classes without sacrificing the model's ability to fit the frequent classes.

3   Experiments

In this section, we first introduce some algorithms for comparison and evaluation metrics. Then we describe the implementation details. And finally we introduce two benchmark multi-label image recognition datasets, i.e., MS-COCO [13] and VOC 2007 [6] and show the empirical results on these two datasets.

3.1   Algorithms for Comparison and Evaluation Metrics

In this part, we will firstly introduce some algorithms for comparison, and then we show the evaluation metrics.

DataSets. PASCAL Visual Object Classes Challenge (VOC 2007) [6] is a popular dataset for multi-label recognition. It contains 9,963 images from 20 object categories, which is divided into train, val and test sets. Following [23], we use the *trainval* set to train our model, and evaluate the recognition performance on the test set. Microsoft COCO [13] is a widely used benchmark for multi-label image recognition. It contains 81,636 images as the training set and 39,946 images as the test set. The objects are categorized into 80 classes with about 2.9 object labels per image.

To comprehensively evaluate the performance of ML-ILC, a total of two benchmark multi-label datasets have been collected for experimental studies. For each multi-label data set X, N and C represent the number of examples and classes. In addition, several multi-label statistics [17] are further used to characterize properties of X. $LCard(X)$ is the label cardinality which measures the average number of relevant labels per example. $LDen(X)$ is the label density which normalizes label cardinality by the total number of class labels. $DL(X)$ is the distinct label sets which measures the number of distinct relevant label set. $PDL(X)$ is the proportion of distinct label sets which normalizes distinct label sets by the number of examples. The level of class-imbalance on X can be characterized by the average imbalance ratio ImR_{mean}, the minimum imbalance ratio ImR_{min}, and the maximum imbalance ratio ImR_{max} across the label space. Table 1 summarizes characteristics of the experimental datasets.

Table 1. Characteristics of the benchmark multi-label datasets.

Dataset	N	C	$LCard$	$LDen$	DL	PDL	ImR_{min}	ImR_{max}	ImR_{mean}
VOC 2007	9,963	20	1.437	0.072	251	0.025	1.377	50.092	18.558
MS-COCO	121,582	80	2.899	0.036	24,336	0.200	1.219	11051.9	343.38

Compared Algorithms. We compare our method with the standard training and several state-of-the-art techniques that have been widely adopted on multi-label datasets.

- ResNet-101 [8] is used to be the feature extraction backbone, which is pre-trained on ImageNet.
- VeryDeep [18] has smaller convolution kernels, smaller pooling kernels, deeper layers and full connection convolution.
- HCP [24] is a flexible deep CNN infrastructure based on Hypotheses-CNN-Pooling, which combines the results of different CNNs into one final result.
- Order-free RNN [4] integrates attention and LSTM models, which jointly learns the labels of interest and their co-occurrences.
- SRN [32] is Spatial Regularization Network, which generates attention maps for all labels and captures the underlying relations between them via learnable convolutions.

- RNN-Attention [23] obtains attention regions corresponding to multiple semantic annotations, and obtains the global context dependence of these regions.
- RLSD [29] includes a fully convolutional localization architecture to localize the regions that may contain multiple highly-dependent labels.
- ML-GCN [5] uses GCN to map the label representation to an interdependent object classifier.
- CNN-RNN [20] is mainly divided into two parts: CNN for extracting semantic information, and RNN for establishing label relationship and label dependency.

Evaluation Metrics. A comprehensive study of evaluation metrics for multi-label classification is presented in [26], and also following conventional settings [20,32], we employ macro/micro precision, macro/micro recall, macro/micro F1-measure, and Mean Average Precision (mAP) for performance comparison. For precision/recall/F1-measure, if the estimated label confidences for any label are greater than 0.5, the labels are predicted as positive. Macro precision (denoted as "CP") is evaluated by averaging per-class precisions, while micro precision (denoted as "OP") is an overall measure which counts true predictions for all images over all classes. Similarly, we can also evaluate macro/micro recall ("CR"/"OR") and macro/micro F1-measure ("CF1"/"OF1"). For fair comparisons, we also report the results of top-3 labels. In addition, loss value is also one of our evaluation indicators.

3.2   Implementation Details

The ML-ILC network consists of two GCN layers with output dimensionality of 512 and 1024, respectively. For label representations, we adopt 300-dimensional GloVe [16] trained on the Wikipedia dataset. For the categories whose names contain multiple words, we obtain the label representation as average of embedding for all words. Following [5], we set τ to be 0.4 and p to be 0.2. In the image representation learning branch, we adopt LeakyReLU with the negatives lope of 0.2 as the non-linear activation function, which leads to faster convergence in experiments. We adopt ResNet-101 [8] as the feature extraction backbone, which is pre-trained on ImageNet.

3.3   Comparisons with State-of-the Art Methods

Results on VOC 2007 Dataset. The results of VOC 2007 are presented in Table 2. In order to compare with other state-of-the-art methods, we report the results of average precision (AP) and mean average precision (mAP) in Table 2. Concretely, the proposed ML-ILC obtains 94.2% mAP, which outperforms state-of-the-art by 1%.

As can be seen from the Table 2, it is about 0.6% higher than the current best algorithm in the category of "aero", 1.6% higher than the current best algorithm in the category of "bottle", and 1.7% higher than the current best algorithm in the category of "table". In terms of accuracy of most minority classes, the ML-ILC is superior to other methods. Obviously, especially for minority classes, the proposed ML-ILC gives better results. More details of minority classes are shown in Fig. 3.

Table 2. Comparisons of AP and mAP (%) on VOC 2007 dataset.

Methods	Aero	Bike	Bird	Boat	Bottle	Bus	Car	Cat	Chair	Cow	Table
CNN-RNN	96.7	83.1	94.2	92.8	61.2	82.1	89.1	94.2	64.2	83.6	70.0
RLSD	96.4	92.7	93.8	94.1	71.2	92.5	94.2	95.7	74.3	90.0	74.2
VeryDeep	98.9	95.0	96.8	95.4	69.7	90.4	93.5	96.0	74.2	86.6	87.8
HCP	98.6	97.1	98.0	95.6	75.3	**94.7**	95.8	97.3	73.1	90.2	80.0
RNN-Attention	98.6	**97.4**	96.3	96.2	75.2	92.4	**96.5**	97.1	76.5	92.0	87.7
ML-GCN	98.6	94.6	97.7	**97.1**	84.9	89.5	96.0	96.8	86.1	**95.4**	87.9
ML-ILC(Ours)	**99.2**	95.3	**98.0**	96.9	**86.5**	93.7	96.4	**97.7**	**88.5**	94.9	**90.9**
Methods	Dog	Horse	Motor	Person	Plant	Sheep	Sofa	Train	Tv	mAP↑	
CNN-RNN	92.4	91.7	84.2	93.7	59.8	93.2	75.3	99.7	78.6	84.0	
RLSD	95.4	96.2	92.1	97.9	66.9	93.5	73.7	97.5	87.6	88.5	
VeryDeep	96.0	96.3	93.1	97.2	70.0	92.1	80.3	98.1	87.0	89.7	
HCP	97.3	96.1	94.9	96.3	78.3	**94.7**	76.2	97.9	91.5	90.9	
RNN-Attention	96.8	97.5	93.8	98.5	81.6	93.7	82.8	98.6	89.3	91.9	
ML-GCN	**97.3**	**98.2**	94.0	98.3	86.2	91.9	87.6	**97.6**	89.9	93.2	
ML-ILC(Ours)	93.6	97.6	**97.1**	**99.1**	**87.8**	93.9	**90.3**	95.5	**92.1**	**94.2**	

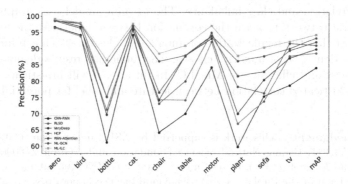

Fig. 3. Performance on minority classes on the VOC 2007 dataset.

Results on MS-COCO Dataset. Table 3 shows the experimental results on MS-COCO. The performance of ML-ILC is almost the best because the MS-COCO dataset has 80 classes, while Voc2007 has only 20 classes. The data sample points of MS-COCO are also more than Voc2007, and the data imbalance is more obvious, so using the Multi-Label Distribution Aware Margin Loss to solve the class imbalance can provide a more significant performance improvement.

ML-ILC improved mAP by 83.5% and reduced the loss to 0.0756. The experimental results show that it is effective to use the GCN to obtain the label correlation and to improve the traditional loss function into the Multi-Label Distribution Aware Margin Loss function on the MS-COCO dataset.

Table 3. Comparisons of state-of-the art methods on MS-COCO dataset.

Methods	All		Top-3					
	loss↓	mAP↑	CP↑	CR↑	CF1↑	OP↑	OR↑	OF1↑
ResNet-101	–	77.3	84.1	59.4	69.7	89.1	62.8	73.6
CNN-RNN	–	61.2	66.0	55.6	60.4	69.2	66.4	67.8
RNN-Attention	–	–	79.1	58.7	67.4	84.0	63.0	72.0
Order-Free RNN	–	–	71.6	54.8	62.1	74.2	62.2	67.7
SRN	–	77.1	85.5	58.8	67.4	87.4	62.5	75.2
ML-GCN	0.0812	82.1	**87.5**	64.2	73.4	83.1	60.7	69.5
ML-ILC(Ours)	**0.0756**	**83.5**	83.2	**71.3**	**76.8**	**86.2**	**77.1**	**81.4**

4   Conclusion

In this paper, we made an attempt to take full consideration of correlation information lying in the label space and class imbalance for effective multi-label image recognition. To this end, we propose a learning multi-label model that considers both correlation and class imbalance. The learning model uses graph convolution neural network to learn the correlation between labels. At the same time, we suggest that the regularization of imbalanced classes, which can improve the generalization error of minority classes. The numerical results demonstrate the effectiveness and efficiency of ML-ILC. In future, we will investigate to model more sophisticated correlation between feature and label for potential improvement.

Acknowledgments. This work is supported by NSFC under Grant 62076179, and Grant 61732011, Beijing Natural Science Foundation under Grant Z180006, Tianjin Science and Technology Plan Project under Grant 19ZXZNGX00050, Funded by Open Research Fund of the Public Security Behavioral Science Laboratory, People's Public Security University of China under Grant 2021SYS02.

References

1. Agrawal, R., Gupta, A., Prabhu, Y., Varma, M.: Multi-label learning with millions of labels: Recommending advertiser bid phrases for web pages, pp. 13–23 (2013)

2. Cao, K., Wei, C., Gaidon, A., Arechiga, N., Ma, T.: Learning imbalanced datasets with label-distribution-aware margin loss (2019)
3. Charte, F., Rivera, A., del Jesus, M.J., Herrera, F.: A first approach to deal with imbalance in multi-label datasets. In: Pan, J.-S., Polycarpou, M.M., Woźniak, M., de Carvalho, A.C.P.L.F., Quintián, H., Corchado, E. (eds.) HAIS 2013. LNCS (LNAI), vol. 8073, pp. 150–160. Springer, Heidelberg (2013). https://doi.org/10.1007/978-3-642-40846-5_16
4. Chen, S., Chen, Y., Yeh, C., Wang, Y.F.: Order-free rnn with visual attention for multi-label classification. In: AAAI Conference on Artificial Intelligence, pp. 6714–6721 (2018)
5. Chen, Z., Wei, X., Wang, P., Guo, Y.: Multi-label image recognition with graph convolutional networks. In: Conference on Computer Vision and Pattern Recognition, pp. 5172–5181 (2019)
6. Everingham, M., Van Gool, L., Williams, C., Winn, J., Zisserman, A.: The pascal visual object classes (voc) challenge. Int. J. Comput. Vis. **88**(2), 303–338 (2010)
7. He, H., Garcia, E.A.: Learning from imbalanced data. IEEE Trans. Knowl. Data Eng. **21**(9), 1263–1284 (2009)
8. He, K., Zhang, X., Ren, S., Sun, J.: Deep residual learning for image recognition. In: IEEE Conference on Computer Vision and Pattern Recognition, pp. 770–778 (2016)
9. Kao, T.: Advanced parametric mixture model for multi-label text categorization (2006)
10. Kipf, T.N., Welling, M.: Semi-supervised classification with graph convolutional networks. In: International Conference on Learning Representations, pp. 1–7 (2017)
11. Li, L., Wang, H.: Towards label imbalance in multi-label classification with many labels. arXiv (2016)
12. Li, P., Xie, J., Wang, Q., Gao, Z.: Towards faster training of global covariance pooling networks by iterative matrix square root normalization. In: Proceedings of the IEEE Conference on Computer Vision and Pattern Recognition, pp. 947–955 (2018)
13. Lin, T., et al.: Microsoft coco: common objects in context. In: European Conference on Computer Vision, pp. 740–755 (2014)
14. Liu, B., Tsoumakas, G.: Making classifier chains resilient to class imbalance. In: Asian Conference on Machine Learning, pp. 280–295. PMLR (2018)
15. Ma, H., Chen, E., Xu, L., Xiong, H.: Capturing correlations of multiple labels: a generative probabilistic model for multi-label learning. Neurocomputing **92**, 116–123 (2012)
16. Pennington, J., Socher, R., Manning, C.D.: Glove: global vectors for word representation. In: Conference on Empirical Methods in Natural Language Processing, pp. 1532–1543 (2014)
17. Read, J., Pfahringer, B., Holmes, G., Frank, E.: Classifier chains for multi-label classification. Mach. Learn. **85**(3), 333 (2011)
18. Simonyan, K., Zisserman, A.: Very deep convolutional networks for large-scale image recognition. In: International Conference on Learning Representations, pp. 1–8 (2015)
19. Tsoumakas, G., Zhang, M.: Learning from multi-label data (2009)
20. Wang, J., Yang, Y., Mao, J., Huang, Z., Huang, C., Xu, W.: Cnn-rnn: a unified framework for multi-label image classification. In: IEEE Computer Society Conference on Computer Vision and Pattern Recognition, pp. 2285–2294 (2016)

21. Wang, X., Li, G.Z., Zhang, Q., Huang, D.: Multip-schlo: multi-label protein sub-chloroplast localization prediction. In: 2014 IEEE International Conference on Bioinformatics and Biomedicine (BIBM), pp. 86–89. IEEE (2014)
22. Wang, Y., Xie, Y., Liu, Y., Zhou, K., Li, X.: Fast graph convolution network based multi-label image recognition via cross-modal fusion. In: Proceedings of the 29th ACM International Conference on Information & Knowledge Management, pp. 1575–1584 (2020)
23. Wang, Z., Chen, T., Li, G., Xu, R., Lin, L.: Multi-label image recognition by recurrently discovering attentional regions. In: IEEE International Conference on Computer Vision, pp. 464–472 (2017)
24. Wei, Y., et al.: Hcp: a flexible cnn framework for multi-label image classification. IEEE Trans. Pattern Anal. Mach. Intell. **38**(9), 1901–1907 (2016)
25. Wu, B., Lyu, S., Ghanem, B.: Constrained submodular minimization for missing labels and class imbalance in multi-label learning. In: The Thirtieth AAAI Conference on Artificial Intelligence (AAAI) (2016)
26. Wu, X.Z., Zhou, Z.H.: A unified view of multi-label performance measures. In: International Conference on Machine Learning, pp. 3780–3788. PMLR (2017)
27. Wu, Y., Wu, W., Zhang, X., Li, Z., Zhou, M.: Improving recommendation of tail tags for questions in community question answering, pp. 3066–3072 (2016)
28. Zeng, W., Chen, X., Cheng, H.: Pseudo labels for imbalanced multi-label learning. In: 2014 International Conference on Data Science and Advanced Analytics (DSAA), pp. 25–31. IEEE (2014)
29. Zhang, J., Wu, Q., Shen, C., Zhang, J., Lu, J.: Multi-label image classification with regional latent semantic dependencies. IEEE Trans. Multimedia **20**(10), 2801–2813 (2016)
30. Zhang, M., Zhou, Z.: A review on multi-label learning algorithms. IEEE Trans. Knowl. Data Eng. **26**(8), 1819–1837 (2014)
31. Zhang, M.L., Li, Y.K., Yang, H., Liu, X.Y.: Towards class-imbalance aware multi-label learning. IEEE Trans. Cybern. **99**, 1–13 (2020)
32. Zhu, F., Li, H., Ouyang, W., Yu, N., Wang, X.: Learning spatial regularization with image-level supervisions for multi-label image classification. In: IEEE Conference on Computer Vision and Pattern Recognition, pp. 2027–2036 (2017)
33. Zhu, Z., Chen, H., Hu, Y., Li, J.: Age estimation algorithm of facial images based on multi-label sorting. EURASIP J. Image Video Process. **2018**(1), 1–10 (2018). https://doi.org/10.1186/s13640-018-0353-z

Random Sparsity Defense Against Adversarial Attack

Nianyan Hu, Ting Lu$^{(\boxtimes)}$, Wenjing Guo, Qiubo Huang, Guohua Liu, Shan Chang, Jiafei Song, and Yiyang Luo

Donghua University, Shanghai, China
luting@dhu.edu.cn

Abstract. More recently, with the development of deep learning and the expansion of its applications, deep learning became the targets of attackers. Researchers found that adversarial perturbations have excellent efficiency for attacking deep neural network. The adversarial examples that are crafted by adding tiny and imperceptible perturbations to modify pixels can make the classifier output wrong results with high confidence. This demonstrates the vulnerability of deep neural network. In this paper, we proposes a method to defend the adversarial attack, reducing output distortion owing to the attack. The proposed method, called random sparsity defense, is a combination of whitening and random sparsity. The method increases randomness in sparsity-based defense and weakens the adverse effects of randomness through whitening. Experimental results on MNIST dataset show that the proposed random sparsity defense can resist attack well and has a good ability to correct classification results.

Keywords: Adversarial attack · Sparse representation · Random · Whitening

1 Introduction

As the development of deep learning, it is widely used in various fields such as medical treatment [1], military [2] and multimedia [3] et.al. However, the vulnerability of deep learning algorithm under attack brings many security risks, common attack methods include data poisoning [4], model inversion attack [5], membership inference attack [6] and adversarial attack [13–15]. These attack algorithms not only expose the vulnerability of deep learning model, but also threaten the security and reliability of deep learning model in practical application. Especially, recent developments of adversarial attack attracted much attention, which brings great challenges to the security of deep learning model. Adversarial attack is to design the attack algorithm which could cause a certain disturbance to input sample, then makes the classification network produce predict errors on input sample.

Since Szegedy and Goodfellow et al. [7] discovered the vulnerability of deep learning networks to small adversarial disturbances in 2012, adversarial attacks and defenses have developed by leaps and bounds. The classical defense methods include adversarial training [8], defensive distillation [9] and pixel deflecting [10]. Adversarial training

© Springer Nature Switzerland AG 2021
D. N. Pham et al. (Eds.): PRICAI 2021, LNAI 13032, pp. 597–607, 2021.
https://doi.org/10.1007/978-3-030-89363-7_45

uses clean examples and adversarial examples to train the network, then strengthen the robustness of network. Adversarial training needs to produce adversarial examples in every iteration of training. Thus, it causes the problems of high computing costs and long training time. Defensive distillation trains the initial deep neural network according to the original sample X and the label Y, and obtains probability distribution. Then, the output of the first part is taken as the label of original sample X, sample X trains a distillation network with the same structure and the same distillation temperature to obtain the new probability distribution. Finally, the whole network is used to classify or predict, which is an effective defense against adversarial attack. For pixel deflecting, PixelCN is an input conversion defense method that reconstructs adversarial examples to fit the distribution of training images.

In this paper, we proposed the random sparsity defense to improve the performance of original sparsity-based defense. Sparsity-based defense has been proved that it is a provable defense method and has enough reliability and verifiability [12]. It can be applied to various classifier network architecture and has good generalization ability. Sparsity-based defense represents the input samples exactly with less eigenvectors, so as to reduce redundant information. In addition, as we all know that randomization is a wonderful way to defend adversarial attack. In order to enhance the ability of deep neural network and weaken adversarial effect into random effect, we add randomness on the basis of sparsity-based defense, which makes the ability of defending attack better.

We organize this paper as follows. Section 2 states the classical attack algorithm, used to evaluate the proposed method. Section 3 presents the proposed preprocessing method of whitening and random sparsity. The performance of the proposed method is evaluated in Sect. 4, Sect. 5 summarizes the paper.

2 Adversarial Threat

In this section, we introduce the adversarial attack algorithms which is used in experiment. All of these algorithms proceed from image gradient and produce image perturb to affect the classification results.

Fast Gradient Sign Method (FGSM) and Iteration Fast Gradient Sign Method (I-FGSM). Goodfellow et.al proposed FGSM attack in [8]. The algorithm along with the direction of gradient sign executes gradient update once. The gradient perturb can be represented as,

$$\rho = \epsilon \ sign(\nabla_x J((\theta, x, y))) \tag{1}$$

where ϵ is the step size, $\nabla_x J(\cdot)$ calculates the gradient operator of cost function around the current values of model parameters θ, x and y, θ represents the network parameters, x is the input image, y is the truth label of x, $sign(\cdot)$ denotes sign function.

The I-FGSM attack is derived from FGSM with multiple iterations. The image after I-FGSM [13] attack can be represented as

$$X_0^{adv} = X, \tag{2}$$

$$X_{N+1}^{adv} = Clip_{X \in} \left\{ X_N^{adv} + \alpha sign\left(\nabla_X J\left(X_N^{adv}, y_{true} \right) \right) \right\} \tag{3}$$

where X_0^{adv} denotes the initial input image, X_{N+1}^{adv} is the adversarial sample generated after $N + 1$ iteration, y_{true} denotes the truth lable, the function $Clip_{X \in}\{\cdot\}$ performs per-pixel clipping of the image, this function replaces the overflow value with boundary value in calculation, and the changed value of each pixel in each step is α. Usually, $\alpha = 1$. The function $J\left(X_N^{adv}, y_{true} \right)$ is used to calculate the cross entropy cost of neural network between X_N^{adv} and y_{true}.

Locally Linear Attack and Iterative Locally Linear Attack. Locally linear attack was proposed to test defense effect by Soorya et.al in [11, 12]. Iterative locally linear attack is the iterative version of locally linear attack. Locally linear attack takes advantage of the weakness of linear network and enlarges image disturbance in linear part of network, thus increasing the success probability of attack. The adversary can turn off the nonlinear of softmax layer, since its goal is simply to the output value of the t-th neuron greater than the target output value (except $i = t$, t represents the category value of input image). Therefore, the adversary can consider L-1 binary classification problems, and solve for disturbance which try to maximize $y_i \neq y_t$ for each $i \neq t$. We apply locally linear attack and its iterative version to the test of our proposed defense method. After figuring out the distortion of each pairs, the following formula describes how adversary applied the attack budgets to the largest distortion pairs,

$$\max_{i,e} y_i(x + e) - y_t(x + e), \quad s.t. \ ||e||_\infty \leq \epsilon, \cdot \tag{4}$$

where y_i denotes the output value of the i-th neuron, y_t denotes the output value of the t-th neuron, x is input image, e means adversarial disturbance.

Momentum Iterative Fast Gradient Sign Method (MI-FGSM). The MI-FGSM attack proposed by Dong et al. [14] is similar to I-FGSM with the application of momentum method. Momentum method is an algorithm to accelerate gradient descent by accumulating velocity vector along the gradient direction of loss function during iteration. MI-FGSM integrates momentum with I-FGSM to update stably and avoid generating the local value of difference. MI-FGSM is defined as follows,

$$g_{m+1} = g_m + \frac{\nabla L(x_m, y_c; \theta)}{||\nabla L(x_m, y_c; \theta)||_1}, \tag{5}$$

$$x_{m+1} = clip_\epsilon(x_m + \alpha.sign(g_{m+1})) \tag{6}$$

where g_{m+1} is the gradient of the $(m + 1)$-th iteration, x_m is the adversarial image after m iteration attack, y_c denotes the label of clean image, $\nabla L(x_m, y_c; \theta)$ calculates the gradient operator of loss function around the values of network parameters θ, x_m and y_c, $clip_\epsilon(\cdot)$ is clipping function, $sign(\cdot)$ is sign function.

Projected Gradient Decent (PGD). The PGD attack [15] is an iterative attack that applies FGSM for m iterations with small step size α. It controls adversarial examples through clipping the disturbance within specified range, so that the new adversarial sample can still stay in the $\in$ neighborhood of x. PGD is the strongest first-order attack algorithm, it can be described as

$$x'_{t+1} = \prod_{x+S} \left(x'_t - \alpha \cdot sign(\nabla(loss_t(x))) \right) \tag{7}$$

where x'_t denotes the image of the clean example after iterative attacking with t times. $\prod_{x+S}(\cdot)$ presents projection to S, the allowable disturbance is in the sphere with x as the center and l_∞ as the radius, and $\nabla(loss_t(x))$ is the gradient of misclassification loss of input image x.

3 Proposed Method

3.1 Random Sparsity

Sparse representations uses less linear combination of basis signal to represent most of original signal or all of it [16, 17]. Assume that we use a $M \times N$ matrix to express dataset X, each row indicates an example and each column represents an attribute. Generally speaking, the matrix is dense in which most elements are not zero. The meaning of sparse representations is to find a coefficient matrix $A(k \times n)$ and a dictionary matrix B $(m \times k)$, so that $B \times A$ can restore the dataset X as much as possible and A is as sparse as possible. In this hypothesis, A is the sparse representations of X. The most important two steps of sparse representations are obtaining dictionary and sparse coding of samples. There are two ways to obtain dictionary. One is using predefined dictionary, for example wavelet dictionary, DCT dictionary and curvelet dictionary etc. Another one is dictionary learning which is obtained by training and learning a large number of data similar to the target data. The methods of dictionary learning include MOD algorithm [18], generalized PCA [19] algorithm and K-SVD algorithm [20]. K-SVD is widely used among them. In this paper, we use a predefined over-complete dictionary. Over-complete dictionary consists of vectors that can form the original image, and its dimension is greater than the original image dimension. The second step of sparse coding aimed to find the most suitable sparse coefficient in the obtained dictionary to make sample as close as possible to original sample. Sparse representations makes it easier to obtain the information contained in image and makes further efforts to process the image.

In this paper, we aim to improve the robustness of the network by taking advantage of the randomization method [22] which has been proven to be effective against adversarial attack. The proposed method maps the feature vector of image to wavelet basis Ψ. Then, it selects K values randomly in the wavelet with low frequency domain of input samples and sets them to zero, instead of selecting K values lower than the threshold value as zero. The selection of K value is related to the signal-to-noise ratio, and the specific formula analysis is described in detail in [12]. The purpose of randomization is to make the range of sparse values wider and retain the K coefficients largest in magnitude, so as to eliminate the adversarial disturbance better. At the same time, the application of randomization can convert the confrontation effect generated by adversarial attack on input sample into random effect to a certain extent, which is conducive to the implementation of defense strategy. The random sparsity algorithm is described as follows:

Algorithm 1: Random Sparsity

1: **Input:** A batch of image Set X, the sparsity level rho, the attack disturbance psi, the dimentional of inputs dim

2: Map the feature vector of image to wavelet domain as orthonormal basis Ψ

- Compute sparsity K: $K = rho * dim$
- Obtain random seed r
- Choose a paragraph with length K behind index r and set the value of this segment to zero

3: Map the vector on wavelet domain to natural domain

4: **Output:** The image set X' after process

Figure 1 shows the work procedure of our defense model. The proposed defense model consists of random sparsity-based preprocessing and a classifier model. In Fig. 1, $H_K(\cdot)$ is the processing function of random sparse representation, Ψ^T denotes the results of mapping image to wavelet basis, Ψ denotes orthonormal basis where X can be random K-sparse represented.

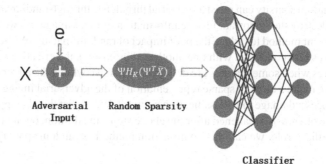

Fig. 1. The diagram of the proposed method. It consists of two sections. One is random sparsity defense, another one is classifier.

3.2 Whitening

Whitening [21] is to centralize data by removing mean value. According to convex optimization theory and related knowledge of data distribution, whitening conforms to the data distribution law, and it is easier to obtain the generalization effect after training. Therefore, whitening becomes one of the common data preprocessing methods. In this paper, we use whitening to obtain the constant information contained in image which is not affected by outside world. The purpose of whitening is to remove the redundant information of input data. Whitening can make different features have the same scale.

In this way, it reduces the correlation among image features when learning parameters with the gradient descent method, so that different features have different influence on parameter.

Whitening includes two steps: 1) project the dataset onto the eigenvectors. This is equivalent to rotate dataset so that the correlation between features has been affected. 2) normalize the eigenvectors to make the variance of whole dataset be one. This is done by dividing each component with the square root of its eigenvalue. The way of whitening is to change the average pixel value to zero and change the variance of image to one. We need calculate the average value W and variance of original image, then transform each pixel value of the original image, the formulation can be written as

$$W = \frac{x - \mu}{stddev}, \tag{8}$$

$$stddev = max\left(\sigma, \frac{1.0}{\sqrt{N}}\right), \tag{9}$$

where x denotes image matrix, μ is the average value, $stddev$ is the variance of input data x, σ denotes the variance of all image pixel, N is the number of image samples.

3.3 Combination of Random Sparsity and Whitening

Although random sparsity can resist adversarial turbulence through random mechanisms, it also may destroy the important feature information of input image. So we use whitening pretreatment method to reduce the poor impact of random sparsity. Whitening makes image features less correlated with one another, thus ensures the effectiveness of whole image features when some features are destroyed. First, we whiten the adversarial example. Then, we make a random sparse representation of the adversarial image. Finally, we input the processed image into classification network. We expect that the opposability of image can be obviously weakened after the above steps. In addition, owing to whitening plays an auxiliary role, we call this combination method as random sparsity defense in this paper.

 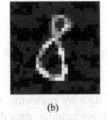 

(a)   (b)   (c)

Fig. 2. (a) is clean image, (b) is adversarial image under FGSM attack, (c) is image with random sparsity defense under FGSM attack.

Figure 2 shows the image effect without attack and under FGSM attack. (a) is clean image, (b) is adversarial image under FGSM attack, and (c) is image with random sparsity defense under FGSM attack. Through the comparison between Fig. 2 (a) and (b), we find that the image disturbance increases greatly after FGSM attack. We can see from Fig. 2 that the last two images with random sparsity defense reduces the disturbance in adversarial image and makes it close to the clean image.

4 Experiments

4.1 Steup

We use two kinds of CNN on the MNIST dataset to evaluate the effectiveness of our proposed method. In experiment, we test binary-classification via a two-layer CNN and test multi-classification via a four-layer CNN. For random sparsity representation, we use Cohen-Debauchies-Feauveau 9/7 wavelet [23] and Generalized Coiflets wavelet [24] as dictionary. We mainly evaluate the proposed approach with six attacks, i.e., FGSM, locally linear attack, iterative locally linear attack, I-FGSM, MI-FGSM, PGD, respectively. We also compare the proposed random sparsity defense with existing sparse defense method.

4.2 Comparison

Table 1 reports on binary classification accuracies for two-layer CNN where the attacks use $\varepsilon = 0.2$ and $\rho = 3\%$ that is same as the setting in [12]. As shown in Table 1, we can see that the proposed random sparsity defense greatly improve classification precision, and the classification precision of random sparsity defense is about 4% higher than that of sparsity-based defense method. It demonstrated the robustness of the proposed method. In addition, we can see that the efficiency of iterative attack (iterative locally linear attack) is higher than that of one-step attack (locally linear attack). Meanwhile, we found that the proposed method not only maintains the robustness of network, but also further improves the classification accuracy on clean image.

Table 1. Binary classification accuracies for two-layer CNN, with $\in= 0.2$ for attacks and $\rho = 0.03$ for defense.

Attack	Defence		
	No defense	Sparsity-based defense	**Proposed method**
No attack	99.36	99.28	**99.31**
Locally linear attack	29.91	92.07	**95.69**
Iterative locally linear attack	23.28	91.16	**95.42**

For binary-classification, we use Peak Signal-to-Noise Ratio (PSNR) index to measure the quality of images in quantitative analysis. Figure 3 shows comparison results of sparsity-based defense and random sparsity defense. In Fig. 3, the top right corner indicates better PSNR and prediction accuracy. As shown in Fig. 3, we can see that the proposed random sparsity defense achieves the highest PSNR and better classification accuracy under locally linear attack and iterative locally linear attack.

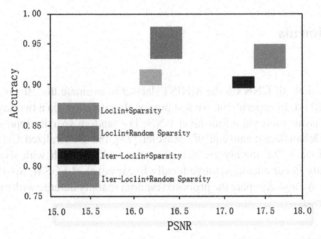

Fig. 3. The PSNR of locally linear ($\epsilon= 0.2$) and iterative locally linear ($\epsilon= 0.2$) attack after sparsity-based defense and random sparsity defense, respectively. The closer to the upper right corner the better.

Table 2. Multiclass classification accuracies for 4-layer CNN, with $\epsilon= 0.2$ for attacks and $\rho = 3.5\%$ for defense.

Attack	Defense		
	No defense	Sparsity-based defense	**Proposed Method**
FGSM	28.43	85.35	**89.72**
Locally linear attack	42.01	82.03	**94.44**
Iterative locally linear attack	7.36	76.04	**93.70**
I-FGSM	6.34	74.85	**94.07**
MI-FGSM	6.99	74.67	**93.94**
PGD	5.12	64.5	**93.64**

In order to carry out the comparative experiment, we set the parameters of attack as $\epsilon= 0.2$ and $\rho = 3.5\%$, which are the same as the experimental in [6]. Table 2 reports on multiclass classification accuracies for 4-layer CNN. Through the horizontal comparison of table data, we can see that the proposed random sparsity defense greatly improves the classification accuracy of adversarial examples in neural network, and the overall defense effect of the proposed random sparsity defense method is better than sparsity-based defense method. The proposed random sparsity defense achieves the best effect in local linear attack, and improves the classification accuracy to 94.44%. From results in Table 2, we also can see that random sparsity defense increases accuracy from 5.12% without defense to 93.64% in the worst-case scenario.

In Fig. 4, we choose the first one of each digit label images to illustrates the effect of input image after various processing. Figure 4 (a) is clean images without attack and (b) is adversarial images on FGSM attack with $\epsilon = 0.2$. Figure 4 (c) is the heatmap images of adversarial inputs which blue signs perturbation and pink signs original clean pixel. We use Fig. 4 (d) to show the images that random sparsity defense effectively purified, and (e) is the heatmap of purified images. From the comparison of Fig. 4 (a) and (b), we can see that there are extremely apparent image perturbations in Fig. 4 (b). Comparing the two heatmaps (Fig. 4 (c) and Fig. 4 (e)) before and after defensive treatment, we find our defense remove most of disturbance and has bad defense effect in few images due to the randomness.

(a)

(b)

(c)

(d)

(e)

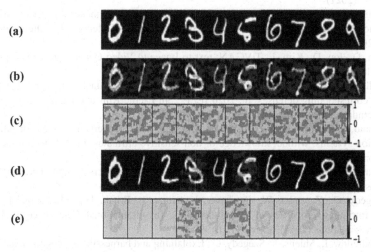

Fig. 4. Qualitative comparison of input transformations on FGSM attack.

5 Conclusion

This paper proposes a random sparsity defense method that is the combination of whitening and random sparsity. As shown through our experiments on MNIST dataset, the random sparsity defense not only reduces the adverse impact of defense on natural images, but also reduces the effectiveness of adversarial disturbance when adversary attempting to fool the model. In contrast to the sparse-based frontend defense, experiment results demonstrate that the proposed random sparsity mechanism can be more effective to resist adversarial attacks. We show that the primary reason that the random sparsity defense can further improve the accuracy of classification networks against disturbances is due to randomization somewhat helps in decreasing the transferability of the adversarial attacks.

We consider that there are a great deal of work for further research. Developing more sparse generation models to expand the application of our method, and there is still room for improvement in the sparse dictionary we use. It is crucial to develop more universally and reliable defense models for practical applications.

Acknowledgments. This work is supported by Shanghai Municipal Natural Science Foundation (Grant No. 21ZR1401200, Grant No.18ZR1401200), Special Fund for Innovation and Development of Shanghai Industrial Internet (Grant No. XX-GYHL-01–19-2527).

References

1. Chae, J., Hong, K.Y., Kim, J.: A pressure ulcer care system for remote medical assistance: residual U-Net with an attention model based for wound area segmentation. arXiv:2101. 09433 (2021)
2. Adhikari, A., Hollander, R.D., Tolios, I., Bekkum, M.V., Raaijmakers, S.: Adversarial patch camouflage against aerial detection. In: SPIE Security + Defence 2020 Digital Forum 21 (2020)
3. Kim, D., Joo, D., Kim, J.: TiVGAN: text to Image to Video Generation with Step-by-Step Evolutionary Generator. In: IEEE Access PP (2020)
4. Müller, N., Kowatsch, D., Böttinger, K.: Data poisoning attacks on regression learning and corresponding defenses. In: 2020 IEEE 25th Pacific Rim International Symposium on Dependable Computing (PRDC), pp. 80–89 (2020)
5. Hidano, S., Murakami, T., Katsumata, S., et al.: Model inversion attacks for online prediction systems: without knowledge of non-sensitive attributes. In: IEICE Transactions on Information and Systems, pp. 2665–2676 (2018)
6. Hidano, S., Kawamoto, Y., Murakami, T.: TransMIA: membership inference attacks using transfer shadow training. arXiv:2011.14661 (2020)
7. Szegedy, C., Zaremba, W., Sutskever, I., Bruna, J., Erhan, D., Goodfellow, I., Fergus, R.: Intriguing properties of neural networks. In: International Conference on Learning Representations (2014). arxiv:1312.6199
8. Goodfellow, I., Shlens, J., Szegedy, C.: Explaining and harnessing adversarial examples. In: International Conference on Learning Representations (2015). arxiv:1412.6572
9. Papernot, N., McDaniel, P., Wu, X., Jha, S., Swami, A.: Distillation as a defense to adversarial perturbations against deep neural networks. In: 2016 IEEE Symposium on Security and Privacy (SP), pp. 582–597 (2016)
10. Song, Y., Kim, T., Nowozin, S., Ermon, S., Kushman, N.: PixelDefend: leveraging generative models to understand and defend against adversarial examples. In: International Conference on Learning Representations (2018). arxiv:1710.10766
11. Marzi, Z., Gopalakrishnan, S., Madhow, U., Pedarsani, R.: Sparsity-based defense against adversarial attacks on linear classifiers. In: IEEE International Symposium on Information Theory (ISIT) (2018). arxiv:1801.04695
12. Gopalakrishnan, S., Marzi, Z., Madhow, U.: Robust adversarial learning via sparsifying front ends. In: IEEE International Symposium on Information Theory (ISIT) (2018). arxiv:1810. 10625
13. Kurakin, A., Goodfellow, I., Bengio, S.: Adversarial examples in the physical world. arXiv: 1607.02533 (2016)
14. Dong, Y., et al.: Boosting adversarial attacks with momentum. In: Proceedings of the IEEE Conference on Computer Vision and Pattern Recognition (2018). https://ieeexplore.ieee.org/document/8579055

15. Madry, A., Makelov, A., Schmidt, L., Tsipras, D., Vladu, A.: Towards deep learning models resistant to adversarial attacks. In: International Conference on Learning Representations (2018). https://openreview.net/forum?id=rJzIBfZAb
16. Bruckstein, A.M., Donoho, D.L., Elad, M.: From sparse solutions of systems of equations to sparse modeling of signals and images. In: SIAM Review, vol. 51, pp. 34–81 (2009)
17. Chen, S.S., Donoho, D.L., Saunders, M.A.: Atomic decomposition by basis pursuit. In: SIAM Reviews, vol. 43, pp. 129–159 (2001)
18. Engan, K., Aase, S.O., Husoy, J.H.: Method of optimal directions for frame design. In: Proceedings IEEE International Conference on Acoust Speech Signal Process (ICASSP), vol. 5, pp. 2443–2446 (1999)
19. Abdi, H., Williams, L.J.: Principal component analysis. In: Wiley Interdisciplinary Reviews Computational Statistics, pp. 433–459 (2010)
20. Aharon, M., Elad, M., Bruckstein, A.M.: The K-SVD: an algorithm for designing of overcomplete dictionaries for sparse representation. In: IEEE Trans. Signal Process. **54**, 4311–4322 (2006)
21. Bhagoji, A.N., Cullina, D., Sitawarin, C., Mittal, P.: Enhancing robustness of machine learning systems via data transformations. In: Conference on Information Sciences and Systems (CISS) (2018). https://ieeexplore.ieee.org/document/8362326
22. Xie, C., Wang, J., Zhang, Z., Ren, Z., Yuille, A.: Mitigating adversarial effects through randomization. arXiv:1711.01991 (2017)
23. Daubechies, I.: Ten lectures on wavelets. Philadelphia. In: PA:SIAM Books (1992)
24. Cohen, A., Daubechies, I., Feauveau, J.C.: Biorthogonal bases of compactly supported wavelets. In: Commun. Pure Appl. Math. **45**(5), 485–560 (1992)

Author Index